THE PROPHETIC
FAITH OF OUR FATHERS
VOLUME III

HARRY ANDERSON. ARTIST

FROM HEAD OF GOLD TO FEET OF IRON AND CLAY

The Course of History Traced by Colonial American Writers Against the Luminous Background of Prophecy. Interpreting Was the Common Order of the Day Among Civic as Well as Religious Leaders. The Nineteenth Century Revival of Interpretation Centered on the Feet and Toes

The
PROPHETIC FAITH
OF OUR FATHERS

The Historical Development
of Prophetic Interpretation

by

LE ROY EDWIN FROOM

VOLUME III

PART I Colonial and Early
National American Exposition

PART II Old World Nineteenth
Century Advent Awakening

REVIEW AND HERALD
WASHINGTON, D.C.

To ALL Students of Prophecy Who Seek a Clearer Understanding of the Past That They May Better Discern the Significance of the Present, and More Readily Recognize the Full Meaning of the Impending Future, This Volume Is Sincerely Dedicated

Contents

Illustrations and Charts

Introduction to Volume III

ONE may easily become confused by the complex history of the centuries with their conflicting crosscurrents and eddies of prophetic interpretation. We must therefore keep the grand outline sharply before us. And we must occasionally take a comprehensive preview of that new portion of the path we are about to traverse. We must periodically lift our eyes from the microscopic examination of the immediate surroundings, to survey the centuries with telescopic sweep. Thus we may clearly envision the relation of part to part in the divine plan of the ages.

Each major epoch or event involves, not an isolated voice or two, but an impressive cluster of witnesses to recognized fulfillments of prophecy, an inescapable chorus of voices speaking for the time. This cumulative evidence gives to the history of the advent hope and the progressive development of prophetic interpretation their full force and significance. Let us, then, at the beginning of Volume 3, take such a preview and retrospect.

I. A Preview of Things to Come

With the passing of the French Revolution, and the ending of the 1260 years in the episodes of 1798, as set forth in the closing chapters of Volume 2 of *The Prophetic Faith of Our Fathers,* we enter upon a new epoch in prophecy, with a new center of prophetic interest and study. As evidenced by Volumes 1 and 2, whenever a major epoch or event of prophecy is reached, always there are reverent students whose minds are led by the Spirit of God to special study and recognition of the fulfillment. This is ever contemporaneous with the event. God never leaves the great fulfillments of prophecy to be acclaimed by only one or two witnesses. Rather, a whole cluster of witnesses, usually in different lands and employing different languages, announce to the world the fact that another major milepost of prophetic fulfillment has been, is being, or is about to be passed.

Note the process through the centuries. Observe the major epochs thus far traversed. When Rome, the fourth prophetic world power, ruled the world, men knew it and left the explicit record, not merely in one language but in five or six.[1] Then when Rome was in the process of division, another cluster of men attested it as a major fulfillment of prophecy actually taking place before their eyes—Rome's breakdown, the mingling of the predicted clay and iron of division—as they awaited with deep concern the appearance of the prophesied but as yet unidentified Antichrist.

Next, when the variously specified but nevertheless identical Antichrist—Beast, Babylon, Harlot, or Little Horn—had developed its full powers to the point of identification, another great chorus of voices broke out in pre-Reformation and Reformation times declaring that the Papacy had been and then was fulfilling this startling prophecy.

Finally, in the century preceding the French Revolution and culminating in the captivity of Pope Pius VI in 1798, a score or more of men on both sides of the Atlantic pointed the finger to France as the coming instrument—the predicted "tenth part" of the ecclesiastical "city," Babylon—and to the approaching close of the allotted 1260-year era of the Little Horn. And at last, when the pope was taken captive and the symbolic Beast received his deadly wound, still another group of voices, in the Old World and the New, proclaimed the ending of the period and the entry upon the final epoch in mankind's prophesied history.

Note particularly that following the French Revolution and the ending of the 1260 years, the greatest shift in the center of prophetic interest and emphasis recorded in history is to be found. This was from Daniel 7—with the fourth empire, the

---

[1] This progressive development here outlined is fully presented and thoroughly documented, with precise citations translated into English, in Volumes 1 and 2 of *The Prophetic Faith of Our Fathers*, already written but not yet published.

subsequent divisions, the emergence of the Little Horn, and now the ending of that allotted period—over to Daniel 8:14, with the ending of the 2300 year-days and the cleansing of the "sanctuary" about 1843, 1844, or 1847. And with it came to be coupled the warning of the great judgment hour impending. Nothing like it had ever been proclaimed before. Simultaneously, in England, Scotland, Ireland, Germany, France, Switzerland, Scandinavia, America, India, Northern Africa, and the Near East, a growing chorus of voices were heard, springing up independently but proclaiming the same message and prophetic time period. It bore all the earmarks of a true advance in contemporary recognition of a currently fulfilling epoch in the grand prophetic outline.

II. A Retrospect of Past Developments

The new center of interest involved a prophetic time period which had not been emphasized through the centuries—the 2300 years of Daniel 8:14. To this, the longest of all Daniel's prophetic time periods, the year-day principle of prophetic calculation was now applied. First, however, let us take a retrospective glance over the centuries to see the relationship of the new emphasis to the slowly growing recognition of the year-day principle of prophetic calculation.

First, the seventy weeks "of years" (Alexandrian Septuagint) was discerned by the Jews, at least by the third century B.C.E.[2] It was the one and only time period of Daniel which had contemporary application and concern to the Old Testament church of the time. The seventy weeks were cut off for the Jews, and led to the cutting off of the Messiah in the seventieth week, or end-week, of years. This principle of a day for a year was tenaciously held by the Jews in the succeeding centuries, and came to be well-nigh universally accepted by Christian expositors.

Then, after the great persecuting apostasy had come to full

---

2 "Before the Common, or Christian, Era," the Jewish designation for B.C.

fruition, and the year A.D. 1260 was approaching, Joachim of Floris, just before the close of the twelfth century, was led to apply the year-day principle to the 1260 days (or forty-two months, or three and a half times) of both Daniel and the Apocalypse.[3] This became an accepted principle among both Catholics and the opponents of Catholics. It was held as a cardinal principle in the Protestant Reformation, until it was challenged by Cardinal Bellarmine in the seventeenth century. Meantime a score of conspicuous Jewish expositors applied this year-day principle to all the time periods of Daniel.

Among the Christians it was applied beyond the seventy weeks and 1260 years, to the 1290 and 1335 years, and finally under Nicholas (Krebs) of Cusa, in the fifteenth century, to the 2300 days—dating their beginning from the time of the vision. Two centuries then passed before John Tillinghast projected the new principle that the seventy weeks are a lesser epoch within the larger one of the 2300 years, but he did not yet understand the precise relationship. Finally, shortly before the French Revolution, two men—Petri of Germany and Wood of Ireland —declared the seventy weeks to be the first part of the 2300 years, but did not date them with full accuracy.[4]

But beginning about 1810, just after the French Revolution and the close of the 1260 years in 1798, in the new era of "running to and fro" in the prophecies, predicted and taking place in the time of the end, a simultaneous study of the 2300 years and the impending judgment hour broke out in the various countries of Christendom. On both sides of the Atlantic, and in different lands, men were led independently to similar conclusions. Not one or two voices, but a swelling chorus of men on three continents and in different countries, as well as in the British Isles, proclaimed the approaching terminus of the 2300 years as the message of prophecy for the hour. It was as unique, emphatic, and clear as any contemporary emphasis in the advancing epochs of the past. It was obviously the message and the

---

[3] These features are each discussed and documented in detail in Volumes 1 and 2.
[4] All to be found in Volume 2.

emphasis then due, calling for the most urgent inquiry and proclamation.

III. Scope and Purpose of Volume 3

This volume comprises the third of the series tracing the prophetic faith of our fathers. The set covers the entire Christian Era, as well as certain antecedent Jewish interpretations of prophecy carried over into the Christian church. The precise field of discussion for Volume 3, its limits and its relationships, may be seen at a glance from the accompanying diagram.

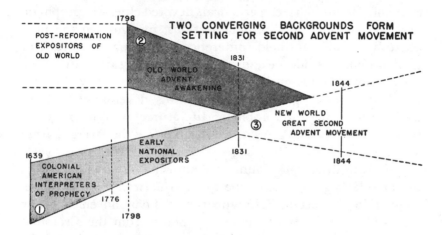

Two independent but vitally significant lines of prophetic exposition converge to form the background and setting of the nineteenth-century great Second Advent Movement of the New World. The first part (No. 1) presents the little-known colonial American and early national interpreters, who were independent of, but nevertheless closely paralleled, the Old World expositors. They begin with John Cotton in 1639, and continue with increasing clarity, fullness, and accuracy for nearly two centuries. They, with their contemporary Old World expositors of the seventeenth and eighteenth centuries, form the ancestral line from which William Miller and his associates of the early nineteenth century drew most of their leading positions on the prophetic symbols and time prophecies.

The second line (No. 2) that converges to form the immediate background of the American Advent Movement is the Old World Advent Awakening of the early decades of the nineteenth century. These prophetic expositors were scattered over Great Britain and the Continent of Europe, and definitely touched Asia and Africa. Their work slightly antedates and partly parallels the rising Advent Movement of the New World.

This great galaxy of Old World witnesses, two hundred strong, produced hundreds of separate books and pamphlets, and issued some fourteen periodicals devoted chiefly to prophetic discussion. They formed organizations, inaugurated the plan of study groups, and held conferences on prophecy. Much of their prophetic evidence and argument set the early pattern for their fellow heralds of the advent in America. They also provided the initial publications, pending development of an indigenous American prophetic literature. On most points they were in virtual agreement, but on a few they were sharply at variance.

Only as these backgrounds are known and understood does the broader significance of the great American Advent Movement (No. 3) become fully apparent. That movement drew most of its leading positions on prophecy from these colonial American and Old World post-Reformation expositors, and the revived Reformation expositions of the British and Continental European students of the early nineteenth century.

In this way we are enabled to see the larger import as well as that greater scope and deeper rooting of the last-day Advent Movement. The world character of this great modern revival of prophetic study and proclamation assumes a place and a significance otherwise impossible. The immediate purpose is therefore to develop and portray this twofold background. The goal of all our quest—the unfolding story of the great nineteenth-century Advent Movement of America—must be reserved for the final volume.

To this unique task we shall address ourselves, summoning the witnesses, noting their names, the leading facts in their lives, their competence to testify, and the amazingly explicit witness of their writings on prophecy.

IV. Scope, Limitations, and Procedures

This investigation follows the orderly sequence of the major outline and time prophecies of the books of Daniel and the Revelation, usually in combination. The quest compasses the essential features of Daniel 2, 7, 8, 9, 11-12. And in the Revelation we trace the understanding of the seven churches, the seven seals, the seven trumpts, the two witnesses, the earth-quake and tenth part of the city, the great dragon and the woman in white of chapter 12, the two beasts of Revelation 13, the angelic messengers of chapter 14, the seven vials of Revelation 16, Babylon, the beast, and the woman in scarlet of Revelation 17, the thousand years of chapter 20, and the new earth of Revelation 21, 22.

Because of these clearly defined limitations, little note will be taken of agitation over the restoration of the Jews that permeates many of the writings of the centuries traversed. We shall not go into these for the simple reason that such views are based chiefly upon scriptures outside the two books of prophecy we are tracing. Failure to include this other line is not due, therefore, to lack of acquaintance with these paralleling views, or a desire to avoid them, but to the allotted scope of this work. Our field of research is thus clear and consistent.

Throughout the chapters to follow, a succession of statements from the numerous witnesses cited will appear. That the reader may have assurance of having before him the thought, intent, and phrasing of the author quoted, these verified extracts are reproduced *verbatim et literatim*. The ofttimes quaint spelling, capitalization, punctuation, and italic and full-capital emphasis have been preserved—and even the obvious typographical errors of the original printing. Obvious corrections are occasionally inserted in brackets.

Through this procedure the reader can be assured of the precise thought of the various expositors whose testimony is constantly introduced. Extracts translated from languages other than English lean to the literal rather than the literary rendering. These have been made by competent linguists, whose names appear in the acknowledgment on pages 753-755.

The date of publication, if known, will usually be placed in parentheses following the first mention of a book title. And if the volume title is in some language other than English, the English equivalent will likewise appear in parentheses, or at least in the footnote credit.

A summarizing table appears at the close of Part I, covering the leading Colonial American and Early National Expositors of the seventeenth and eighteenth centuries, with a similar table at the end of Part II on the Old World Nineteenth-Century Advent Awakening. These epitomize the basic interpretations of the principal writers examined throughout the two sections of this volume. Thus is brought before the investigator at a glance the over-all picture of the similarities and dissimilarities of exposition, as well as the cumulative evidence of the period surveyed. The convenient page citation provides easy reference to the complete presentation in the body of the text. The usefulness of these tables will be at once apparent.

PART I

COLONIAL AMERICAN AND
EARLY NATIONAL WRITERS
ON PROPHECY

ROGER WILLIAMS PREMISED HIS PLEA ON PROPHECY

The Monument of This Apostle of Religious Liberty, and Founder of Rhode Island, Stands in Providence. His Impressive *Bloudy Tenent*, Published in 1644, Dedicated to the British Parliament, Was Based on the Bible Prophecies

CHAPTER ONE

Prophecy's Key Place
in Colonial American Thought

Having traversed the centuries up to the French Revolution in Volumes 1 and 2, in tracing the history of prophetic interpretation in the Old World, we now turn to the New. Volume 2 closed with the recognized and proclaimed ending of the 1260-year era of the Little Horn, accomplished through the instrumentality of the French, as the outgrowth of the French Revolution. In Volume 3 we first retrace our steps for three centuries —back to colonial American times—thus to pick up the paralleling American thread of prophetic exposition, which matches and supplements that of England and the Continent.

I. Historical Setting for the Great Colonial Venture

Let us now note the historical setting for the great colonial venture. In 1602 a group of earnest church people in England entered into a covenant to worship God "without humane Inventions and Additions." For this they accepted banishment to the Netherlands. The exiled Pilgrim Fathers, fleeing from England, under the reign of James I (1603-1625), settled in Leyden, Holland, in 1608. Seeking civil and religious liberty for themselves, holding the Calvinist faith, and desiring to establish congregational churches, they found conditions so unfavorable at Leyden that about a hundred men, women, and children resolved and arranged to emigrate to New England.[1]

---

[1] Cotton Mather, *Magnalia Christi Americana: or The Ecclesiastical History of New-England* (1702), book 1, chap. 2, pp. 5-10.

The Pilgrim Fathers were determined to follow the increasing light that God had for them. This is clearly expressed in the parting counsels of their pastor, JOHN ROBINSON (*ca.* 1575-1625),[2] in 1620, just before they started on their long journey to the New World. Referring to the solemnity of the parting, and admonishing them to follow him "no further than he followed Christ," Robinson declared himself "very confident the Lord had more truth and light yet to break forth out of His holy Word." And after deploring the condition of the Reformed churches that "would goe no further then the instruments of their Reformation," he illustrated his point thus:

"As for example, the Lutherans they could not be drawne to goe beyond what Luther saw, for whatever part of Gods will he had further imparted and revealed to Calvin, they will rather die then embrace it. And so also, saith he, you see the Calvinists, they stick where he left them: A misery much to bee lamented; For though they were precious shining lights in their times, yet God had not revealed his whole will to them: And were they now living, saith hee, they would bee as ready and willing to embrace further light, as that they had received. Here also he put us in mind of our Church-Covenant (at least that part of it) whereby wee promise and covenant with God and one another, to receive whatsoever light or truth shall be made known to us from his written Word: but withall exhorted us to take heed what we received for truth, and well to examine and compare, and weigh it with other Scriptures of truth before we received it; For saith he, *It is not possible the Christian world should come so lately out of such thick Antichristian darknesse, and that full perfection of knowledge should break forth at once.*"[3]

True to that vision of increasing light, the colonial leaders of those rigorous early decades laid much stress on prophecy. Moreover, this interest was not limited to the clergy. As the years lengthened, prominent laymen—college presidents, teachers, physicians, historians, soldiers, governors, judges, and officials in other public offices—wrote in the intriguing field of prophecy with a clarity often surpassing that of the Reformers.

----

[2] Robinson ministered to a church near Norwich until he was suspended for his Puritan tendencies. In 1604 he ministered to a church of dissenters at Scrooby. In 1608 he and his flock escaped to Amsterdam. Later in the year he went to Leyden, and there in 1611 established a church. In 1620, after his memorable sermon, he saw them set sail for America.

[3] Edward Winslow, *Hypocrisie Unmasked* (1646), pp. 97, 98. See also "Winslow's Brief Narration," in Alexander Young's *Chronicles of the Pilgrim Fathers of the Colony of Plymouth from 1602 to 1625* (1841), p. 397.

Indeed, the symbols and phrases of prophecy, and their related time periods, were common in the thinking and writing of the early American church.

During the early years of the reign of Charles I (1625-1649), thousands of Puritans emigrated to New England, having secured charters from the king. In 1628 a second Massachusetts colony—of nonconformist Puritans—settled at Salem, and a larger colony established itself on Massachusetts Bay in 1630, equipped with capable civil leaders and well-educated ministers. The Massachusetts Bay colonists professed loyalty to the Church of England, but they were pronounced in opposition to the forms and ceremonies of the English Church. They proceeded to establish a theocracy with citizenship dependent upon fellowship in a church.

Similar colonies, strongly Presbyterian in sentiment, were formed in Connecticut by Puritans from Massachusetts Bay, and in New Haven by London Puritans, under the leadership of John Davenport.[4] Then came the founding of Providence in 1636 by the Separatist Roger Williams, whose opposition to theocratic government so irritated the Massachusetts authorities that his banishment was decreed. This was followed by the founding of the Rhode Island colony and the establishing of the first American Baptist church. In 1638 another company, likewise forced to leave Massachusetts, settled in Rhode Island, and later joined Williams in setting up a constitution providing for democracy and liberty of conscience.[5]

The Puritans of England had fled from persecution to the virgin soil of the New World, where they might worship God more freely. But they no sooner found an asylum for themselves than they began to persecute those differing from them.

[4] "The first settlers of New Haven were Millenarians, i.e., they were believers that the second coming of Christ will precede the millennium, and that there will be a literal resurrection of the saints who will reign with Christ on earth a thousand years. This appears to have been the prevalent belief in New England."—EDWARD R. LAMBERT, History of the Colony of New Haven (1838), p. 50.

[5] The various trading companies played their part in the picture. The London Company, chartered in 1606, led the way in Virginia. The Massachusetts Bay Company, incorporated in 1629, saved the Plymouth fellowship from destruction and started New England on its course. Then the Dutch West India Company, established in 1621, laid in the New Netherlands the basis upon which England in 1664 erected the province of New York. See Charles A. and Mary R. Beard, The Rise of American Civilization (rev. ed., 1936), vol. 1, p. 36.

Despite the fact that as dissenters they themselves had been driven to seek refuge from oppressive rules of the state church, they tried to establish a Puritan theocracy in New England, with their civil code based on the Bible and the enjoyment of civil rights dependent upon profession of the accepted religion. But in the struggle for independence and civil liberty, the guarantee of freedom of worship according to the dictates of conscience came in for due consideration, especially in Rhode Island, as will be noted later.

Such is the historical setting for the American exposition of prophecy. The scores of illustrious men—strong, independent thinkers who had fled the tyranny of the Old World —to whose testimony we shall listen, were scattered throughout all these colonies, holding to different forms of doctrinal faith, yet having remarkable unity on the basic principles of prophetic interpretation. Again we shall see the determining influence that both the true and the false understanding of prophecy exerted in colonial America, as had been the case in the Old World through the centuries.

II. Colonial Consciousness of the Prophetic Scheme

The Puritans were the chief theologians of seventeenth-century colonial days. The dominant questions for discussion centered, for the most part, on ecclesiastical order, the sovereignty of God, the supremacy of the Scriptures, baptism, the Lord's supper, salvation through Christ. And along with these went the prophecies. Such were the great religious themes brought over by the Pilgrims and Puritans as they crossed the Atlantic from Holland and England to the shores of Massachusetts. Their early concepts on the prophecies were drawn, of course, from the earlier English Reformation writings and from the intimate contacts with the more recent Continental Reformers during their periods of exile from Britain. There were literally hundreds of volumes on prophecy printed in Germany, Switzerland, Holland, England, and France, with which they were acquainted. From these their initial views were obtained.

These New World men "were the peers in learning and ability of any in the Puritan wing of the Church of England." [6] In Virginia, where the Episcopal Church of England held sway, there was little interest in theological discussion. But not so in New England. Both Puritans and Separatists were keenly interested in prophecy and were fruitful in the production of thoughtful exposition.

The painstaking examination of hundreds of these writings of colonial America's religious and civil leaders brings out this impressive fact, which stands forth with indelible force and conclusiveness: Prophecy, with prophetic study and interpretation, was inextricably woven into the very warp and woof of colonial thinking and expression. It molded the motives and objectives of these men, and controlled their conduct. It runs back and forth like a golden thread through their sermons and their secular literature, and gives warmth, richness, and color to the writings of the great preachers and teachers of the time. Indeed, it highlights the whole colonial background, as we shall see.

Moreover, despite creedal differences on other matters among Presbyterian, Congregationalist, Baptist, Seventh Day Baptist, Episcopalian, and later the Methodist writers, there was remarkable unity in basic prophetic interpretation—the four world empires of prophecy, the divisions of Rome, the Antichrist, the year-day principle, and the approaching judgment and second advent.

The emphasis sometimes centered upon the premillennial second advent as the grand consummation of all prophecy, rather than upon detailed exposition of the outline prophecies and the prophetic periods of Daniel and the Apocalypse. There were many others, however, who ventured into this fuller field. And these New World expositors, forming a perfect parallel to the Old World writers, were less affected by the spreading

---

[6] Williston Walker, *A History of the Congregational Churches in the United States*, p. 98.

Jesuit Preterist and Futurist counterinterpretations that were permeating Europe.[7] Many of the most distinguished colonial fathers were decided and outspoken premillennialists. The Augustinian theory of the 1,000 years of the medieval reign of the church had been rejected by virtually all, and the blight of Whitby's postmillennial concept had not yet touched the church in either the Old World or the New.

These men were consciously dealing with the prophesied "Beast." They knew its historical identity, and were conscious of its perverting and coercive power. They also believed that its power would be broken, and that the allotted 1260 years would end erelong. They believed that it would be destroyed at the second advent. For this transcendent event they prayed. They were intelligently discussing the revealed plan of the ages, and their own part, place, and time therein. Some were seeking to separate Protestantism from the coercive spirit of the Beast, which was still manifested by many of the stern Puritans. For this they likewise pleaded. Thus their lives were lived, their books were written, and their sermons were preached under the vivid consciousness of the prophetic scheme.

But along with this historic characteristic must be placed an astonishing modern corollary that should never be forgotten: Not only has such a concept largely passed from the thinking and expression of popular churchmen and educational and civic leaders of today, but the entire field of prophecy has lost interest for the church or secular historian to the extent that he is now virtually silent as regards the almost universal historical emphasis on prophecy, the judgment, and the advent by men whose names are otherwise familiar to every student of American history.

Little attention has been paid by writers on New England

---

[7] Fully discussed in Volume 2. One reason for this was the isolation of the colonies. Three thousand miles of water lay between the colonies and Europe. While up to eight weeks was required to make the voyage to England, one might wait months before finding a ship bound for his destination. Trading merchantmen usually made but one round trip a year, so six months was commonly required to reach America. Correspondence was equally difficult. If a dispatch was too late to go by one ship, it might not reach its destination under a year. See Thomas J. Wertenbaker, *The First Americans, 1607-1690*, pp. 2-5.

theology—such as Walker, Parrington, Chitwood, Miller, Sweet, Foster, Murdock, and Rutgers—to this wealth of prophetic interpretation, and the related second advent, as held and taught by the American theologians of the seventeenth and eighteenth centuries.[8] This notable silence is one of the serious omissions of the chroniclers of the period. Whether thoughtless or designed, it stands as a serious indictment and constitutes a significant trend of the times, for, whatever the reason, the picture has been seriously blurred and is incomplete, with one of the primary colors omitted. This we shall seek to correct.

III. The New England Writers and Their Writings

While relatively few of these New England Fathers wrote entire books on prophecy, we are not left without adequate information as to the views of the rest. They injected them into their sermons, a goodly portion of which have been preserved. They expressed them in illuminating introductions to expositions by other writers.[9] In other instances their words and sentiments are recorded by their contemporaries or near contemporaries, as by Cotton Mather in his colonial church history, *Magnalia Christi Americana.*[10]

The intellectual caliber and competence of these men can be judged by observing their education, training, and recognized accomplishments. These factors will be noted in the biographical sketches that accompany each expositor. This is not emphasized to laud scholastic degrees or achievements, but as evidence that these men had trained minds, were schooled in logical reasoning, and possessed broad language and history backgrounds, apart from their theological proclivities. It will

[8] Wilbur M. Smith, "Prophetic Literature of Colonial America," *Bibliotheca Sacra,* January-March, 1943 (vol. 100), p. 69.

[9] Such as John Davenport's preface to Increase Mather's *The Mystery of Israel's Salvation* (1669), and William Hooke's preface to Davenport's *The Saints Anchor-Hold* (1661).

[10] For purposes of our early quest, Cotton Mather's *Magnalia Christi Americana: or The Ecclesiastical History of New-England* is of unique value, dealing as it does with the lives of sixty of the leading New England ministers of the seventeenth century, the lives of governors and magistrates, the history of Harvard and its graduates, and the Statements of Faith of the seventeenth century.

be increasingly apparent that they were the intellectual leaders
of their respective generations.

IV. Archbishop Laud Enforces Papal Rituals on England

Before entering upon the examination of the various
colonial expositors, it is desirable to have before us a brief
picture of Archbishop Laud and the events of his creating.
These had a marked bearing upon the lives and convictions of
many of the early colonial clergy who left England because
of the coercive pressure he was able to exert.

WILLIAM LAUD (1573-1645), born at Reading, England,
became imbued with High Church principles while at Oxford.
Ordained in 1601, he rose by preferment to bishop of London
(1628), chancellor of Oxford in 1629, and finally Archbishop
of Canterbury and primate of all England (1633), thus becoming almost absolute in ecclesiastical power. He introduced
extreme ritualism, a semi-Catholic altar, a sacrificial supper,
and stressed the divine right of bishops and kings. His theological teaching was strongly Romanist, and he declared his
essential agreement with Rome. Charles I, who was a Romanist
at heart, Strafford (Charles' chief civil adviser), and Bishop
Laud formed a triumvirate seeking absolutism in church and
state, in opposition to Puritanism and democratic tendencies.

They believed in the use of force to achieve these ends.
The Star Chamber and an ecclesiastical court, the Court of
High Commissions, became a veritable Inquisition, and Calvinistic preaching was prohibited. In Scotland, Laud's attempt
to Anglicize the Scottish church (1635-1637) gave birth to the
riot of St. Giles, Edinburgh, which produced the National
Covenant, resulting in the "Bishop's Wars." Eventually the
Long Parliament, on December 18, 1640, impeached Archbishop Laud for treason. Ten weeks later it sent him to the
Tower. In 1644 he was voted guilty of endeavoring to subvert
the laws, to overthrow the Protestant religion, and to act as
an enemy to Parliament. He was beheaded on Tower Hill in

January, 1645. This was followed by the Grand Remonstrance, calling for the co-operation of the Scotch Presbyterians, the acceptance of the Covenant,[11] and finally the Westminster Assembly of 1643, with its Confession of Faith of 1648 and the Larger and Shorter Catechisms.[12]

V. The Clash of Puritanism and Separatism

It will be desirable to bear in mind throughout these early chapters that the Massachusetts Bay immigrants were Puritan Anglicans who, while deploring her ritualism and Romeward trends, nevertheless professed love for the mother Church of England and were unfriendly to the principles of Separatism.[13] Calvinistic in view, the Puritans came to America to establish the Genevan discipline in the New World. On the contrary, the *Mayflower* leaders, landing at Plymouth, were Separatists. And the "two consorted ill together." [14] In their prior stay on the European Continent, under the guidance of Pastor Robinson, the Pilgrims had been disciplined in Congregationalism. Thus the democratic principle was brought to America. Such, then, was the sharp differentiation between the two concepts.[15]

The Puritans regarded themselves as the particular repositories of righteousness. Their goal was a close-knit church-state. Centralization of power was natural and inevitable under this scheme. Dissenters must be held in subjection. Theocracy was inevitable.[16] Jehovah was the Lawgiver; the

---

[11] "The National Covenant, or The Confession of Faith of the Kirk of Scotland," was subscribed successively in 1580, 1590, 1638, and 1639. It specifically states: "We abhore and detest all contrary Religion, and Doctrine: But chiefly, all kind of Papistry, in general and particular Heads, even as they are now damned and confuted by the *Word of God*, and Kirk of Scotland: But in special we detest and refute the usurped Authority of that *Roman Antichrist.*" —Page 2.

[12] On October 22, 1647, Parliament authorized the printing of six hundred copies of *The Humble Advice of the Assembly of Divines . . . at Westminster Concerning a Larger Catechisme*. In this are the words: Christ "shall come again at the last day in great power, and in the full manifestation of his own glory, and of his Fathers, with all his holy angels, with a shout, with the voice of the Archangel, and with the trump of God, to judge the world in righteousness."—Page 13.

[13] Separatism was a comprehensive term including the radical Anabaptists, Diggers, and Fifth-Monarchy men, the mystic Quakers, the Seekers (who were influential individuals rather than a sect), and the Congregationalists. These aroused the antagonism of both the Presbyterians and the Anglicans. See Vernon L. Parrington, *The Colonial Mind* (1620-1800), pp. 9, 10.

[14] Parrington, *op cit.*, pp. 16, 17.

[15] *Ibid.*, p. 17.

[16] *Ibid.*, p. 19.

Bible, the statute book; and the minister, the interpreter of the law.[17] But sanctuaries were close at hand for the dissenters from theocracy—Connecticut for Congregationalists, Rhode Island for the Separatists, and Maine for the rebellious individualists.[18]

VI. Molded by a Highly Trained Ministry

While the first English settlers came to New England in 1620, accessions at first were slow. But between 1630 and 1640 they thronged every ship that pointed its prow toward the New England shores. They had come to find in the New World what was denied them in the Old. Then immigration stopped, with twelve independent groups of colonists—fifty towns, having a total population of some 21,000.[19] Yet from these progenitors descended the majority of New Englanders. By 1660 they numbered 60,000, and 200,000 by 1689.[20]

The contrast between the Pilgrims and the Puritans was pronounced. The Pilgrims, as Separatists, had collided with the Church of England and fled across the North Sea to Holland, where they worked long hours and learned remunerative trades. They were poor and relatively few when they came to the American shores.[21] On the contrary, the Puritans to the north, who had settled first at Massachusetts Bay, wanted moderated reforms in the Church of England, but nothing revolutionary. Among them were men of wealth, and representatives of the various professions, including scholars of light and learning. And they had a formal charter from the king.[22]

The proportion of learned men among these early immigrants was extraordinary. There were as many Cambridge and Oxford graduates as could be found in any similar popu-

---

17 *Ibid.*, p. 21.
18 *Ibid.*, p. 26.
19 Moses C. Tyler, *A History of American Literature During the Colonial Time*, vol. 1 (1607-1676), p. 94; Francis A. Walker, "Growth and Distribution of Population," in Theodore D. Woolsey, F.A.P. Barnard, and others, *The First Century of the Republic*, p. 215.
20 Evarts B. Greene and Virginia D. Harrington, *American Population Before the Federal Census of 1790*, p. 3; Warren S. Thompson and P. K. Whelpton, *Population Trends in the United States*, p. 1.
21 Beard, *op. cit.*, pp. 48, 49.
22 *Ibid.*, p. 52.

lation in the mother country—every two hundred and fiftieth person being a son of Cambridge.[23] The proportion of scholarly clergymen[24] was marked, including such names as Cotton, Davenport, Mather, Eliot, Norton, Williams, Bulkley, Shepard, and Chauncy. Of these Tyler asserts: "Probably no other community of pioneers ever so honored study, so reverenced the symbols and instruments of learning." [25]

Universal education seemed to them a universal necessity, and was promptly provided, with public instruction compulsory in every colony except Rhode Island. Six years after Winthrop's arrival in Salem harbor, plans were under way to found a university. Religion was accounted the chief thing. They largely abolished the secular and retained the sacred. The state became part of the church, politics a department of theology, and citizenship the privilege of the church member. They believed intensely in Providence and in prayer and in a kind of asceticism. There were even laws against the sinfulness of tobacco. So, with it all, among the Puritans came intolerance and the militant spirit of the persecutor.[26]

VII. Influence of Racial and Religious Factors

Numerous non-English stocks—the Swedes on the Delaware, the Dutch on the Hudson, the Welsh Quakers in Pennsylvania, and the German Pietists at Germantown—were interspersed among the English. Then, following the revocation of the Edict of Nantes in France, in 1685, hundreds of Huguenots found their way to the American colonies. These settled in Massachusetts, Rhode Island, New York, Virginia, and South Carolina. In addition there were Negroes, and of course the Indians—the latter, one of the familiar sights.[27]

The heterodox religious complexion is equally important. In New Hampshire, Massachusetts, and Connecticut the Con-

---

[23] Tyler, *op. cit.*, vol. 1, p. 98.
[24] In the Norman tongue the word *clergie* means "literature." In the seventeenth century, when learning was largely the monopoly of the clergy, they held almost the whole power of church and state. See John W. Thornton, *The Pulpit of the American Revolution*, p. x.
[25] Tyler, *op. cit.*, vol. 1, p. 99.
[26] *Ibid.*, pp. 99-109.
[27] James T. Adams, *Provincial Society, 1690-1763*, pp. 4-9.

gregational Dissenter had legal eccleciastical establishment, to
which the taxpayers were compelled to contribute support—
whether members or not.   In Rhode Island there was no
establishment.   In New York the Dutch Reformed establishment had fallen at the time of the English conquest.   Then
the Church of England sought to pass an act of establishment,
but did not succeed.   In New Jersey there was no establishment, nor in Pennsylvania and Delaware.

In Virginia, in Maryland from 1692, and in the Carolinas,
the Church of England was the state church, but with many
Dissenters in Virginia and Catholics in Maryland.   Such was
the extreme religious diversity.   Meantime, forces were at
work "tending to disintegrate the belief in the necessity or
desirability of a union between church and state." [28]

VIII. The Power of the Colonial Clergy

In the planting of the New England colonies and the
founding of its towns, the building of the meetinghouse and
parsonage and the choosing of a minister usually had precedence.[29]   For about sixty years, New England was a theocracy,
with the Bible sanctions reproduced as the civil code.[30]   The
ministers were actually the chief advisers of state.   Marked
deference was paid to them, and they usually conducted themselves in a manner worthy of this prestige.   The pulpits of the
churches were high and remote from the congregations, typifying the elevation of the sacred office.[31]

Sunday was a solemn day, meet only for preaching, praying,
and Bible study.[32]   The sermon challenged undivided attention
—and well it might, for attendance thereto was required.
Absentees were subject to fine, and persistent indifference led
to public exposure in the stocks or wooden cage.[33]   Moreover,
the sermons not infrequently lasted from three to five hours,
actually measured by the hourglass on the pulpit.   The entire

[28] *Ibid.*, pp. 17, 18, 150, 151.
[29] Tyler, *op. cit.*, vol. 1, p. 187.
[30] Beard, *op. cit.*, pp. 139, 146.
[31] Tyler, *op. cit.*, vol. 1, p. 188.
[32] Beard, *op. cit.*, p. 139.
[33] Tyler, *op. cit.*, vol. 1, p. 189.

community was present, for there were no newspapers, radios, theaters, lectures, or musical entertainments to disturb or compete. These diversified sermons are therefore among the most representative records of the times extant.[34] This was particularly true of the "election" sermons. About 1633 the governor and his assistants began to appoint someone to preach on the day of election. This was the beginning of the annual "election" sermons, which continued for several generations.[35]

The matter of early official and clerical censorship also had a bearing. Not only was means of production limited, but the few printing plants—only five in Boston by 1715, one in Philadelphia, one in New York, and one in New London—were all under censorship. In this the controlling clergy exercised a rigid though unofficial control. Bradford's imprisonment in Philadelphia in 1692 was for printing matter displeasing to the Quaker cause, and led to his removal to New York and the establishment of his press there.[36]

The first newspaper, *Publick Occurrences,* was ended after a single issue, in 1690, by "censorial infanticide . . . murdered in its first issue."[37] In 1695 a Salem Quaker was proceeded against for circulating a book he had had printed in New York, but escaped in the general reaction following the witchcraft excitement.[38] In 1700 Colman of Massachusetts had to send his answer to Cotton Mather to New York to be published, because of control of the clerical clique.[39] And William Brattle had to send his book against Mather to London for printing, and when it was returned it was publicly burned in Harvard College churchyard.[40]

Poor postal facilities and high costs presented yet further difficulties. The population of the colonies was scattered, and there was only slight communication between Massachusetts

---

[34] *Ibid.,* pp. 191, 192.
[35] Thornton, *op. cit.,* pp. xxiii, xxiv, xxvi.
[36] Isaiah Thomas, *The History of Printing in America,* vol. 2, pp. 7-24, 91; see also James T. Adams, *op. cit.,* p. 128.
[37] James T. Adams, *op. cit.,* pp. 128, 129.
[38] Clyde A. Duniway, *The Development of Freedom of the Press in Massachusetts,* pp. 68, 69, 70-73.
[39] James T. Adams, *op. cit.,* p. 129.
[40] *Ibid.*

and the New England colonies, and Maryland and Virginia.
In 1711 the cost of sending a letter between New York and
Philadelphia was 9 pence, and between New York and Boston,
1 shilling.[41]

IX. Transition From British-born to American-born

Prior to 1676 the new civilization of America was largely
in the hands of Americans born in England. After 1676 it
was principally in the hands of Americans born in New England. The writings of the first period were therefore largely
by immigrant Americans. The literature of the second period
was largely by the children of those immigrants, and represented their reactions to life in the New World.

During this second period the American colonies underwent a portentous change—the struggle for independence.[42]
In 1643 half of the eighty ministers in New England were
graduates of Cambridge or Oxford. Fifty years later seventy-
six out of eighty-seven in Massachusetts and thirty-one out of
thirty-six in Connecticut were graduates of Harvard.[43] So from
the beginning of the eighteenth century we deal with the rise
of distinctly colonial culture.[44]

And now follow the American expositors of the early
colonial period, in the form employed in Volumes 1 and 2—
first a biographical sketch and then the prophetic positions of
the writer. This notable group is first visualized on the over-
all chart which appears on pages 44 and 45.

---

[41] Wesley E. Rich, *The History of the United States Post Office to the Year 1829*,
pp. 23-25.
[42] Tyler, *op. cit.*, vol. 2, pp. 5-9.
[43] James T. Adams, *op. cit.*, p. 113.
[44] *Ibid.*, p. 114.

EARLY COLONIAL STALWARTS EXPOUND PROPHECIES

Left to Right (Upper): John Cotton, Puritan Theocrat; John Eliot, Apostle to Indians; John Davenport, Puritan Pastor. (Center): William Burnet, Governor of New York and Massachusetts; John Clarke, Baptist Preacher-Physician; William Stoughton, Massachusetts Jurist. (Lower): Increase Mather, Harvard President; Cotton Mather, Congregational Theologian

CHAPTER TWO

Earliest Colonial Writings
Include Prophecy

We now turn to the testimony of the earliest colonial stalwarts who wrote on prophecy—the stern Puritan John Cotton of Massachusetts, the Calvinist theologian Thomas Shepard of Cambridge, and the liberty-loving Baptist Roger Williams of Rhode Island. As the picture unfolds with its progression of names in succeeding chapters, the extent of the fields covered, the range of principles enunciated, and the essential unity of exposition on the part of these men of differing church affiliation, especially in regard to the Antichrist of prophecy in relation to the grand prophetic outline, will become increasingly impressive. Added to this is the diversity of life interests and professions of these expositors as men prominent in secular pursuits, as well as leading clergy, give themselves to the intensive study of prophecy.

I. John Cotton—First Puritan Expounder of New World

America's first prophetic expositor was JOHN COTTON (1584-1652), learned Puritan minister of Plymouth and Boston, often called the "Patriarch of New England," and noted as an antagonist of Roger Williams. He was born at Derby, England. His father was a lawyer, and his mother was exceptionally pious. His intellectual powers were so unusual that he was admitted to Trinity College, Cambridge, at only thirteen. Upon the invitation of Emmanuel College, likewise of Cam-

3

bridge, he transferred there, becoming an expert in classical languages, particularly Hebrew.[1]   He became a tutor, then head lecturer, dean, and catechist of the college.   He later received his B.D. degree from Cambridge.

Cotton became New England's most authoritative representative of priestly stewardship.   He dreamed of a Utopia of the saints, and sought to make it real.   He doubtless left a greater impress upon seventeenth-century New England than any other minister.[2]   (Portrait on opposite page.)

Cotton's funeral oration upon Dr. Some brought him into prominence in a new light.   Through this typical "university sermon," he was invited to preach while still unconverted.   But his sermons were so filled with the "Florid Strains" of "pompous Eloquence," he states, that he later destroyed the notes.   He experienced a spiritual awakening, however, and in 1612 became vicar of the church at Boston in Lincolnshire, England. Here he was soon cited to appear before the Bishops' courts for his Puritan views, and was silenced for a time.   In the twenty years he served at Boston (England), Cotton on Sundays conducted a catechetical class in the afternoon, preached expository sermons in the morning from the great chapters and books of the Bible, and also delivered daily lectures.

After a period of illness and renewed persecution by Archbishop Laud, Cotton emigrated to Massachusetts in 1633, finally becoming the preacher at Boston.   He endeavored to establish a theocracy with the Mosaic law substituted for the common law, the sufficiency of the Scripture for all needs being considered axiomatic.   At the request of the General Court he drew up an abstract from the law of Moses entitled *Moses His Judicials* (1636).   This code was not accepted, but for many years was erroneously considered to be an abstract of the Massachusetts code of laws.[3]   He defended the whipping of Quakers and was the bitter antagonist of Roger Williams,

---

[1] Cotton Mather, *Magnalia*, book 3, The First Part, chap. 1, sec. 4, p. 15.
[2] Vernon L. Parrington, *The Colonial Mind (1620-1800)*, p. 27.
[3] John Cotton, *An Abstract of the Lawes of New England as they are Now Established*. See also F. C. Gray, "Remarks on the Early Laws of Massachusetts," in *Collections of the Massachusetts Historical Society*, 3d Series, vol. 8, pp. 192-194; Parrington, *op. cit.*, pp. 32, 33.

writing *The Bloudy Tenent, Washed, And made white in the bloud of the Lambe* (1647) in answer to Williams' *Bloudy Tenent* (1644). He is said to have introduced into America the practice of keeping "Sabbath" from Saturday evening to Sunday evening.[4]

"The Sabbath he [Cotton] began the Evening before: For which keeping of the *Sabbath, from evening to evening,* he wrote Arguments before his coming to New England: And I suppose, 'twas from his Reason and Practice, that the Christians of New England have generally done so too." [5]

Cotton was author of several works, including three on prophecy—*An Exposition upon the Thirteenth Chapter of the Revelation* (1655); *The Powring Ovt of the Seven Vials: or an Exposition, of the 16. Chapter of the Revelation* (1642); and *The Churches Resurrection, or the Opening of the Fift and sixt verses of the 20th Chap. of the Revelation* (1642). *His Spiritual Milk for Boston Babes in either England* (1656)[6] was very popular. As an expositor Cotton reasons with singular clarity. Through these three works on prophecy we have Cotton's exposition of Revelation 13, 16, and 20.

Cotton reached a commanding pinnacle attained by no other pioneer clergyman. He was a powerful preacher, his reasoned eloquence swaying his congregations trained to argumentative discourse.[7] In sheer acquisition of knowledge, probably no man of his time outdid him. His was the heroic pattern of the seventeenth century—a four-hour sandglass turned three times marking his day's work.[8] Here are Cotton's positions on prophecy.

1. FIRST BEAST IS ROMAN CATHOLIC CHURCH.—According to Thomas Allen's preface, the *Exposition upon the Thirteenth Chapter of Revelation* was comprised of sermons from Cotton's weekly lectures on prophecy at Boston, in the winter of 1639-40,

---

[4] *Century Cyclopedia of Names* (1906), p. 284.
[5] Cotton Mather, *Magnalia,* book 3, The First Part, chap. 1, sec. 30, p. 27.
[6] Very few of the early American books were published in New England until we reach the fifties and sixties.
[7] Parrington, *op cit.,* p. 28.
[8] Moses C. Tyler, *A History of American Literature During the Colonial Time,* vol. 1, pp. 212-214.

"where he went over the other chapters of Revelation, as he did this thirteenth."[9]   This in itself is remarkable—a weekly lecture on the prophecies by the most prominent colonial minister of the time soon after the establishment of the colony!   How we wish the entire series had been preserved!   Cotton begins with the basic premise that the dragon of Revelation 12 is Satan, ruling through pagan Rome.[10]   Then, coming to chapter 13, he says clearly, "I conceive to be the first beast, the Roman Catholick visible Church," with the Pope as head.[11]   The seven heads he identifies from Revelation 17.   He says:

> "The seven heads are seven Mountaines on which the Woman sitteth, which are the mountaines of the City of Rome, it is built upon seven hills, and the seven heads are also seven Kings, that is, seven Kingly governments, sovereign governments: The first were Kings, then Consuls, then Decemvins, then Dictators, then Tribunes, and then the Caesars: Five were fallen, that is, were past in John's time, the sixth were then extant, and they were Caesars; the Pope he makes the seventh: Now the Pope then is the seventh of these Heads, but the seventh head and the beast are two distinct things, though he be one that rules the beast, and hath a great influence in the guiding of it." [12]

2. Seventh Head—Popes; Ten Horns—Ten Kingdoms. —The ten horns, he continues, are "so many kings," or kingdoms, "broken off from the Roman Empire," giving their dominion to the papal Beast.[13]   And the names of blasphemy are the papal assumptions—Pontifex Maximus, Pardoner of sins, Judge of Scriptures, etc.   The animal characteristics of the Beast refer to Daniel 7, where the four beasts are Babylon, Persia, Grecia, and Rome.[14]   The "seate" given by the dragon is Rome—so that civil emperors thereafter dwelt at Ravenna.[15]

3. Justinian Banishes Goths; Establishes Papal Primacy.—The wound, Cotton thought, was "given by Goths and Vandalls," [16] Huns and others.   And the wound was healed, he surmised, by Justinian's destroying the Goths out of Italy and establishing the Justinian Code, constituting the Bishop

---

[9] John Cotton, *An Exposition upon the Thirteenth Chapter of the Revelation*, "To the Reader," preceding p. 1.   (Title page reproduced on p. 56.)
[10] *Ibid.*, p. 1.
[11] *Ibid.*, p. 7; see also pp. 22, 47, 228.
[12] *Ibid.*, p. 9; see also p. 22.
[13] *Ibid.*, p. 10; also p. 22.
[14] *Ibid.*, pp. 10-12.
[15] *Ibid.*, p. 23.
[16] *Ibid.*, pp. 34, 35.

of Rome "to be the first (or to have the Primacy) of all Priests," [17] as he was made "inspector over all the rest," with the conferring of powers and estates. [18] It is the power also called the "great whore" in Revelation 17.

"Remember the Beast is the Roman Catholick visible Church, whereof Rome was the mother City, and mother Church, accounted of all the Churches in the world, and the Pope is the visible head of this Church, in this Chapter called the seventh head." [19]

4. 1260 Days Involve 1260 Years.—The Beast's allotted period—forty-two months—is the time of consent to the Beast from the "tenne Horns," enabling the Beast "to make Warre" for that period. [20] And Cotton stoutly contends that the forty-two months of the Beast, the 1260 days of the witnesses in sackcloth, and the three and a half times of the woman in the wilderness (Waldenses) are all one and the same: "All these are manifest to be contemporary, (as they call it) to begin together in the same period of time, and to end together." [21] Cotton flatly rejects the idea of three and a half literal years for a Jewish Antichrist, just before the great judgment day. [22] But, "taking a day for a year," [23] he seeks the beginning year as possibly when the pope assumed the title Pontifex Maximus, about 395, [24] according to Brightman. Prophetic interpretation thus starts in America with the clear recognition of the year-day principle. This should ever be remembered.

5. Period Suggested From 395 to 1655.—As to the chronological timing of the 1260 years, Cotton says:

"If you reckon from 395 years, and adde to that 1260. years, putting these two together, they will expire in the yeare, that shall be according to the Roman account 1655. I will not be two confident, because I am not a Prophet, nor the Son of a Prophet to foretell things to come, but so far as God helps by Scripture light, about the time 1655. there will then be such a blow given to this beast, and to the head of this beast, which is Pontifex maximus, as that we shall see a further gradual accomplishment and fulfilling of this Prophecy here." [25]

---

[17] *Ibid.*, p. 35.   [18] *Ibid.*, p. 42.   [19] *Ibid.*, p. 47.
[20] *Ibid.*, pp. 81, 82.
[21] *Ibid.*, p. 83; see also his *Bloudy Tenent, Washed*, pp. 68, 69.
[22] *Ibid.*, p. 84.   [23] *Ibid.*, p. 85.   [24] *Ibid.*, p. 88.
[25] *Ibid.*, p. 93.

This is as clear as any Old World suggestion of the time. And France is brought into the picture as the "tenth part" of the city to fall away.[26]   And the warring against the saints definitely included the Waldenses and Albigenses.[27]

6. SECOND BEAST SYMBOLIZES POPE HIMSELF.—Cotton thought that the second beast, having "supream power in Spritualls," "is no other but the Pope of Rome; The heads of the Roman Catholique visible Church, from one succession to another." [28]   This, too, was a common contemporary view in Europe.

7. 666 IS STILL UNFATHOMED.—Discussing the various attempts to decipher the 666, Cotton rejects the suggestion that it is the "number of his years." [29]   Nor is it attached to A.D. 666, though some cite Boniface's claim of the title of "Chief Bishop" in 606—but "606 is not 666." Nor does he feel that *Latinus* or *Ecclesia Catholica* provides the name,[30] and frankly concludes, "But yet wee are not at the bottome." [31]

8. MILLENNIUM FOLLOWS ANTICHRIST'S DESTRUCTION.—In Cotton's exposition of the millennium, written in 1642, he first of all places himself clearly on record that the thousand years begin *after* the destruction of Antichrist and Rome.[32] Denying the Augustinian theory of the millennium in the Middle Ages,[33] Cotton avers it could not have begun with Constantine or Theodosius, for neither had the keys to the bottomless pit, but only Christ.   And further:

> "This casting of Satan into the bottomlesse pit, was to this end, that he should not deceive the Nations any more; But a thousand yeares after Constantine he deceived the world with more corrupt and Superstitious Religions then before; and even with Pagan Religion also: The Holy Ghost puts no difference between Popish Pagancie and Heathenish Pagancie." "These thousand yeares therefore doe most properly begin from the destruction of Rome." [34]

9. STILL HOLDS TO SPIRITUAL FIRST RESURRECTION.—But Cotton still clings, inconsistently, to the Augustinian concept

---

[26] *Ibid.*
[27] *Ibid.*, p. 99.
[32] John Cotton, *The Churches Resurrection*, p. 5.
[33] Fully covered in Volume 1 of *Prophetic Faith*.
[34] *Ibid.*, p. 5.
[28] *Ibid.*, p. 225.
[29] *Ibid.*, p. 250.
[30] *Ibid.*, pp. 250, 251.
[31] *Ibid.*, p. 253.

of the first resurrection as "the rising of men from spirituall death to spirituall life." [35] They rise to experience and accomplish a reformation. [36] He warns against formalism and mere church membership, [37] and appeals to New England not to follow in the steps of the Reformation churches in Europe. But he insists that the devil's binding *follows* the "destruction of antichrist and the ruine of Rome." [38] This, too, was in harmony with the clearest exposition of the Old World.

10. SEVEN VIALS FOR WORSHIPERS OF BEAST.—Cotton's *The Powring out of the Seven Vials* (1642) was an exposition of Revelation 16, "with an Application of it to our Times." Declaring this work to be "fit and necessary for this Present Age," the preface ends pointedly:

"Now the Father of lights, and God of all grace, fill our hearts with the life and power of faith and zeale, to pray for, long for, speed, and waite for the most desired ruine, and speedy begunne-downefall of that most cursed Kingdome of Antichrist, according to the scope and drift of that Prophesie, expressed in the powring out of these Seven Vials." [39]

Asserting the seven angels to be God's messengers of wrath, Cotton defines those who receive the mark of the beast, or Papacy, as those who receive their orders from that Church of Rome. [40] He further asserts that the seven vials are the "judgments of God vpon the Roman Antichristian state." [41] These judgments are progressive, [42] encompassing all. The Romish church is built upon tradition and perversion, with the hierarchy as the Pope's "invention and appointment." [43]

11. THE SEAT OF THE BEAST IS ROME.—Discoursing voluminously on each vial, Cotton declares the "seat of the beast," or Babylon, of the fifth vial, to be the city of Rome, which the Dragon, or pagan Rome, gave over to the Beast, or papal Rome. [44]

12. EUPHRATES: STREAMS OF SUPPORTERS OF BABYLON.— The river Euphrates, Cotton interestingly construes not as the

[35] *Ibid.*, p. 9.   [36] *Ibid.*, p. 10.   [37] *Ibid.*, p. 20.   [38] *Ibid.*, p. 12.
[39] John Cotton, *The Powring out of the Seven Vials: or an Exposition, of the 16. Chapter of the Revelation*, Preface.
[40] *Ibid.*, "The First Viall," p. 4.   [41] *Ibid.*, p. 10.
[42] *Ibid.*, "The Second Viall," p. 19.   [43] *Ibid.*, p. 29.   [44] *Ibid.*, "Fift Viall," p. 2.

literal river in Chaldea but as pertaining to Rome rather than to Turkey.[45] This he applies to the streams of papal supporters for papal, or modern, Babylon, with the drying up as the taking away of his "maintenance." The general agreement of expositors to the "foure families of the Turkes," [46] or Turkish dominion, is noted, however, with the kings of the East as the Jews. But from such an interpretation Cotton dissents.[47]

The hating of the whore in Revelation 17, by the ten Christian states, is duly noted.[48] Then he remarks:

"For after the Lord hath beene pleased to scome the Churches from their Hierarchicall monarchy, then the next newes you shall heare of, will be, that Christian Princes begin to see the lewdnesse that is found in their worship, the wickednesse of their Murders, Sorceries, Fornications, and Thefts, whereby they robbed their soules, as well as their bodies, then will they dry up these streames, and so Euphrates (that did wash this Rome, and the Turkish Empire also) will be dryed up." [49]

As the river Euphrates cannot mean the literal river that watered old Babylon, but that which "waters the throne of the Beast; that waters the seat of antichrist," so will the "drying up of this Euprates dry up the force, and strength of the new Babylon," [50] according to Cotton. This concept appeared periodically in the writings of others in later years.

13. TEN-HORNED BEAST IS ANTICHRIST OF ROME.—Cotton contends that the sixth trumpet involves the Turks,[51] and that the Beast with the seven heads, or "seven hills," and the ten horns, or "ten governments," is "antichristian Rome" and the false prophet "the Bishop (or Antichrist) of Rome." [52] And out of this gathering of forces will come Armageddon.[53] Note it:

"When the streames of Rome begin to decay: the streames that doe water and refresh Rome. Then looke for Warres, and Tumults of Warres, great Warres, mustering up of Popish Princes, and their Armies, and pagan Princes, and their Armies, there will be no backwardnesse in these earthly spirits, in this case, to the captivating of all (if it were possible) to the maintenance and supportance of Rome." [54]

---

[45] Ibid., "Sixth Viall," p. 17.
[46] Ibid., pp. 17, 18.
[51] Ibid., pp. 29-33.
[52] Ibid., p. 32.
[49] Ibid., p. 23.
[47] Ibid., p. 18.
[50] Ibid., "The Second Part of the Sixth Viall," p. 29.
[53] Ibid., p. 93 (correctly p. 36).
[54] Ibid., p. 41.
[48] Ibid., p. 22

Cotton ends by speaking again of the "wasting and drying
up of the corruptions of Religion which shall waste Rome," [55]
and declares:

"It shall not be a great day to the Papists, not a great day to the Dragon,
nor to the Romish Catholique Church except it be a great day of their
destruction, and that it will be indeed, as yee shall see when this battell is
to be fought in the nineteenth Chapter, and they shall never trouble the
World more that will be the issue of it." [56]

14. SECOND ADVENT THE CLIMAX.—This all leads up to
the climax of Christ's second advent.[57] And Armageddon will
be fought at Megiddo,[58] the "last battell, which Christian Princes
shall fight against Antichrist and his Adherents." [59]

15. TURKS SENT AGAINST APOSTATE CHRISTENDOM.—In his
Bloudy Tenent Washed, Cotton declares that, according to the
sixth trumpet of Revelation 9:14, 20, the Turks were sent
against apostate Christendom as a punishment.[60] And he insists in his chapter 27 that praying for the coming of Christ's
kingdom involves praying "for the comming downe of all
opposite Kingdomes," and particularly for "vengeance on the
Roman Antichrists." [61]

II. Shepard—Kingdom to Be Established by Second Advent

The second New World interpreter of prophecy was
THOMAS SHEPARD, or Shepheard (1604-1649), Calvinist pastor
at Cambridge, Massachusetts. He was born in Towcester,
England. Possessed of a precocious mind, he entered Emmanuel
College, Cambridge, when only fifteen. He received his B.A.
and M.A. degrees in 1623 and 1627 respectively. In the latter
year he was ordained and became a lecturer at Earles-Colne
for three years, and for the same period at his native Towcester,
with many conversions resulting. But he, too, was silenced
and unfrocked by Bishop Laud of London, for his nonconform-

---

[55] Ibid.   [56] Ibid., p. 42.
[57] Ibid., "Third Sermon on Sixth Viall," pp. 2, 3.
[58] Ibid., "Fourth Part Upon the Sixt Viall," pp. 2-5.
[59] Ibid., p. 7.
[60] John Cotton, The Bloudy Tenent, Washed, And made white in the bloud of the
Lambe, p. 13.
[61] Ibid., pp. 52, 53.

ity, and was forbidden to "preach, read, marry, bury," or to exercise any ministerial function.[62] Things could not continue on indefinitely in this fashion.

Shepard studied the ceremonies of the Established Church, but disliked them increasingly. Going to remote Yorkshire and then to Northumberland, where the bishops also oppressed him because of Laud's attitude, he determined to leave England. The departure of John Cotton and others for America led him to take shipping for New England. Shepard reached Boston in 1635, and later moved to Cambridge. He was again ordained in 1637 and became pastor at Newtown (Cambridge). Admirer and friend of John Harvard, he had to do with the selection of Cambridge for the location of Harvard College, which became a reality in 1638.

Shepard was famed as a pulpit orator, though unprepossessing in appearance and frail in body. A tireless worker and preacher, Shepard was active in the controversies of his day, especially with Catholicism, and also in opposing the Antinomians. In 1644 he asked the commissioners of the united colonies to found scholarships for needy students. He wrote sixteen works, such as *The Sincere Convert* (1640), some passing through many editions. In 1647 he was responsible for the publication of the Cambridge Confession of Faith, which was legally recognized by the General Court as the Platform of the Congregational Church of Massachusetts. Deeply interested in the Indians, he wrote *The Clear Sun-shine of the Gospel Breaking Forth upon the Indians in New-England* (1648).[63] A profound thinker and vigorous writer, he made his most important contribution from the viewpoint of prophetic exposition in *The Parable of Ten Virgins Opened & Applied* (1660). He taught expressly that the wheat and the tares would grow together until the end, the separation not coming

---

[62] New England is under obligation to Archbishop Laud for sending to the colonies their ablest and noblest men. It was his intense hatred of nonconformity, and the persistence and cruelty with which he scoured all England to hunt out the ministers who were committing the unpardonable sin of dissent, that accomplished this result. See Tyler, *op. cit.,* vol. 1, p. 204.

[63] Published posthumously from transcripts of sermons. See Cotton Mather, *Magnalia,* book 3, The Second Part, chap. 5, sec. 16, p. 90.

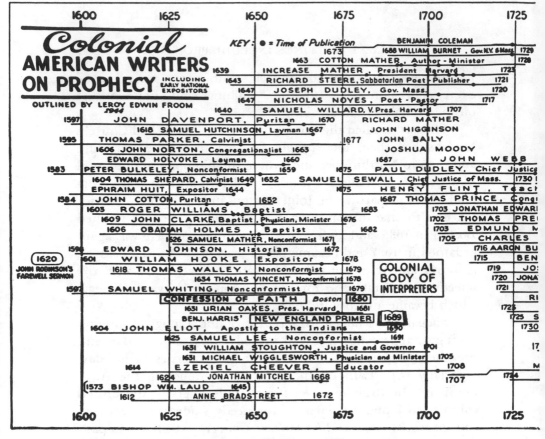

This Imposing Body of Colonial American Writers on Prophecy (up to 1776), and the Early National Expositors Following, Are Here Shown in Panoramic Survey. The Life Span Is Indicated, as Well as the Religious Affiliation and the Dates of Their Individual Expositions. The Wide Range of Professions—Ministers, Teachers, Publishers, College Presidents, Physicians, Judges, Governors, Legislators, Librarians, Editors, and Other Public Officials—Is Noteworthy. At the

till the judgment. After fifteen years' witness Shepard died at the early age of forty-four.

1. PROGRESSIVE EVENTS OF LAST DAY PORTRAYED.—Shepard held that at the sound of the last trump the "dead arise," and the living are translated.[64] He also strongly stressed Christ's personal, literal, glorious advent in the flaming heavens.[65] "First Antichrist must be consumed," and then "Christ shall breake out of the third heaven and bee seene in the aire, before any dead arise and this shall be with an admirable shout,

---

[64] Thomas Shepard, *The Sincere Convert*, p. 82 (G3v). (Pages wrongly numbered; hence the folio designations as guide.)
[65] *Ibid.*, p. 83 (G3r).

44

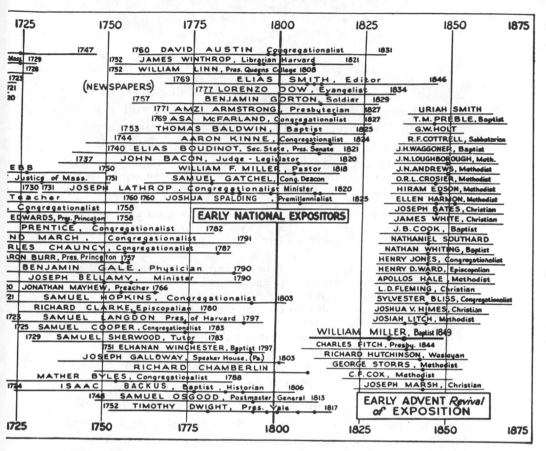

Extreme Right, the Leading Early Interpreters in the Nineteenth-Century Advent Movement Are Tabulated, With Their Writings, to Show Their Chronological Relationship to the 200-Year Colonial Background; Such Is the Over-all Picture of American Expositors Up to the Nineteenth Century. The Slight Repetition of Those Portions of the Chart Nearest the Separating Space Between the Pages Is to Facilitate the Complete Reading of Each Page

as when a King commeth to triumph over his subjects and enemies." Then Christ, with the "voyce of the arch-angell," appears in the clouds of heaven. Next, "the bodies of them that have dyed in the Lord shall rise first, then the others that live, shall like *Enoch,* be translated and changed, 1. Cor. 15."[66] Finally, the elements shall melt, and the sinners will cry for the rocks to hide them.[67]

2. DAYS OF NOAH REPEATED BEFORE ADVENT.—Writing on the "state of the times," "about the days of his [Christ's] coming," Shepard declared they will be sensual and degenerate,

---

[66] *Ibid.,* p. 82 (G3v).   [67] *Ibid.,* p. 83 (G4r).

as in the days of Noah.[68] These days Christ singled out as signs
of the times. Christ will then come in power and glory to
inherit the kingdom.[69] Shepard warns against carnal security
and drowsiness.[70]

> "For the blessed appearing, and glorious coming of Christ Jesus at his
> first coming, 1 Pet. 1. 10, 11, 12. they searched after, and waited for his
> coming, and rejoyced to see that day; so should we now for his second." [71]

3. Tribulations of Antichrist's Reign Precede Advent.
—The cutting off of Antichrist by or before the advent is
clearly stressed:

> "With some things which shall be before His coming, viz. subtill and
> strong delusions, mixt with sore tribulations and oppressions, especially in
> the time of Antichrist's raigne, as also great confusions, in all hearts and
> Churches, if not throughout all the world after the tribulation of those
> daies; And then (saith he) verse 30. shall appear the sign of the Son of man,
> and he shall be seen coming in power and great glory." [72]

III. Williams—Prophecies Motivate Quest for Soul Freedom

The third prophetic expositor to appear was none other
than Roger Williams (ca. 1603-1683), founder of Rhode Island
and pastor of the first Baptist church in America, worthy antagonist of John Cotton, and Apostle of Religious Liberty. He
was born in Wales, and was educated at Cambridge, with a B.A.
in 1627. He early became skilled in shorthand, and was also
proficient in several ancient languages. After taking orders in
the Church of England, in 1629, he turned nonconformist, considering Puritanism a reforming force within the church, and
demanding simplification of ritual, a Calvinistic theology, and
a modification of the episcopal form of government. It offered
a freer, more individualistic life. And he stood for the sovereignty of Parliament as against the divine right of kings.[73] He
was the incarnation of Protestant individualism.[74] (Williams'
monument appears on page 18.)

---

[68] Thomas Shepard, The Parable of the Ten Virgins Opened & Applied [part 1], chap. 1,
sec. 1, p. 2.
[69] Ibid., chap. 3, sec. 1, p. 9.
[70] Ibid., part 2, chap. 1, sec. 2, p. 2.
[71] Ibid., chap. 19, p. 202.
[72] Ibid. [part 1], chap. 1, sec. 1, p. 2.
[73] L. C. Wroth, Roger Williams, pp. 3-8.
[74] Parrington, op. cit., p. 65.

Williams pleaded in vain, however, for recognition of the sanctity of the human conscience. He believed in a God of love in a world of material things. So, in search of some freedom and to escape the persecution of Bishop Laud,[75] he emigrated to New England in 1631. Becoming assistant pastor at Salem, Massachusetts, he was soon dismissed because of his opposition to the New England theocracy and his denial of the right of the state to punish Sabbathbreaking and heresy, that is, breaches of the "First Table."[76] He proved to be the most provocative figure that had come to the American shores.

Williams' theory of life was disturbing to Massachusetts. He found he could not join the church at Boston, because it compromised on the question of the English church as part of the "abomination of antichrist." "You are not a separated people," he declared. So he became assistant pastor at Plymouth from 1631 to 1633, spending much time among the Indians, acquiring their language, promoting their welfare, and antedating the efforts of John Eliot. His *Key into the Language of America* (1643) in parallel Indian and English columns taught clearly the literal creation week of Genesis 1 and 2, some six thousand years ago.[77] Returning to Salem, Williams was pastor in 1634-1635. But once more he became involved in controversy with the Puritan Massachusetts administrators over theocratic government and disregard of conscience. He rebelled against the synodical government in the Congregational churches. This he continued to protest.

Summoned, in 1636, before a general council swayed by his bitter antagonist, John Cotton, he was sentenced to banishment for his assaults upon the oath and the holding of land by patent from the king without payment to the Indians, and the nonseparateness of the church, for his maintenance of the rights of free speech, and his denial of the right of the magis-

---

[75] William Laud, who became bishop of London in 1628, did not become Archbishop of Canterbury until 1633.
[76] John Winthrop, *Journal, 1640-1649*, vol. 1, pp. 61, 62 (vol. 18 of *Original Narratives of American History*).
[77] Roger Williams, *A Key into the Language of America*, pp. 124-126.
[78] Wroth, *op. cit.*, pp. 9, 10.

trate to act in matters that lie between man and his God, which principles became the obsession of his life. Williams escaped custody by flight into the "wilderness" in midwinter. He made his way to Narragansett Bay amid peril and bitter hardship, where he was joined by sympathizers, and founded the colony that developed into Rhode Island—on the basis of absolute liberty of conscience—the land being purchased from the aborigines.[79] In June, 1636, Williams and a few like-minded friends founded a safe retreat in this wilderness, fittingly calling it "Providence," an asylum for the oppressed of all creeds or none, a "shelter to persons distressed for conscience." [80] Thus he sought to escape the "monstrous paradox" of "God's children" persecuting "God's children." [81]

Believing that the "apostasy of Antichrist" had corrupted the churches, and convinced that infant baptism was unscriptural, he and others formed the first Baptist church in America in 1638, and introduced immersion anew. In the absence of any Scripturally baptized person in the New World, one of their number, Ezekiel Holliman, was deputed to baptize Roger Williams. Then he, in turn, baptized Mr. Holliman and "some ten more." In 1643 the four settlements in the growing colony sent him to England to obtain a charter for Rhode Island, with guarantees of protection from the aggressive Puritans of the Massachusetts Bay Colony. This he secured. Later, in 1647, the General Assembly adopted a code of laws guaranteeing full religious liberty—not partial toleration, as in Maryland.

It was during his year in England that Williams published first his *Mr. Cotton's Letter Examined* (1644)—a reply to Cotton's justification of Williams' banishment—and *Queries of Highest Consideration* (1644), and then his immortal book on soul liberty, *The Bloudy Tenent, of Persecution, for Cause of Concience, discussed in a Conference betweene Truth and Peace* (1644).[82] It was an answer to the thesis of Cotton and

---

[79] James Ernst, *Roger Williams, New England Firebrand*, pp. 161, 167.
[80] Thomas Armitage, *A History of the Baptists*, p. 643.
[81] Ernst, *op. cit.*, p. 156.
[82] Published anonymously, February 5 and 9 and July 15 respectively. See Joseph Sabin, *A Dictionary of Books Relating to America*, vol. 28, pp. 442, 443, 438.

of Calvin, and was addressed to both Houses of Parliament, for the question of toleration was the topic of the day. It was a dispute with Cotton over two schools of political thought— autocracy and democracy. Williams' main contention was that civil states are "civil, and therefore not judges, governors, nor defenders of the spiritual." [83] His books consequently belong to the Old World as well as the New. While in England Williams made the acquaintance of Cromwell and Milton, and advocated the cause of liberty in Westminster.[84] Still another self-explanatory title was *Christenings Make Not Christians* (1645).[85] Later he wrote *The Hireling Ministry None of Christs* (1652). Holding this as an article of faith, he turned for his own living to farming and the Indian trade.

1. "BLOUDY TENENT" PREMISED ON PROPHECY.—At the very outset of his *Bloudy Tenent,* in the dedication to Parliament, Williams appeals directly and significantly to the symbols of prophecy:

"Your Honours know the Babylonian Monarch hath the Lyon, the Persian the Beare, the Grecian the Leopard, the Romane a compound of the former three most strange and dreadfull, Dan. 7." [86]

Williams held that the spirit of persecution was the spirit of the Beast. And in employing persecution against Dissenters, Protestants were likewise exhibiting the spirit of the Beast. A perusal of Williams' writings shows the prophecies, which he frequently cites, to have been a motivating factor in his struggle for the principles of soul freedom. It was prophecy that formed the basis of his immortal appeal for full religious liberty in the eloquent reasoning which called for a break with the coercive spirit of the papal Antichrist. Williams had studied history in the light of prophecy, and his memorable book is permeated with the terms, symbols, and applications of prophecy. His logic is sound, and his application remarkably accurate. At least fifty times such references appear.

---

[83] Roger Williams, *The Bloudy Tenent, of Persecution,* Fifth Introductory Proposition.
[84] Herbert L. Osgood, *The American Colonies in the Seventeenth Century,* vol. 3, pp. 109, 110.
[85] Sabin, *op. cit.,* p. 439.
[86] Roger Williams, *The Bloudy Tenent, of Persecution,* dedication, first page.

Under the influence of the Presbyterians, Parliament ordered the "public burning" of the book by the hangman. Thus it joined the immortal company of good books so sentenced.[87] John Cotton replied in 1647 with *The Bloudy Tenent, Washed, And made white in the bloud of the Lambe,* and in 1652 Williams, in England on a second trip, published a vindication called *The Bloody Tenent Yet More Bloody.* Returning to America in 1654, Williams was elected "president" of Rhode Island. During his administration all groups, including the Quakers, were granted religious freedom.

The first Sabbatarian church in America was founded in Rhode Island in 1671, and its establishment created quite a stir. The report reached England that Rhode Island colony did not keep "the Sabbath." Roger Williams denied the report but called attention to the fact that there was no Scripture for "abolishing the 7th day," adding, "You know yourselves doe not keep the Sabbath, that is the 7th day." [88]

2. WILLIAMS WARNS THE TEN HORNS.—After touching upon the cries of the persecuted "soules under the Altar (Rev. 6)," [89] and the "spirituall Virgins, who abhorre the spirituall defilements of false worship," [90] together with the persecutions of the beast of Revelation 13,[91] Williams utters this solemn warning in his *Bloudy Tenent:*

"Be wise therefore O ye Kings (especially those ten hornes, Rev. 17) who under pretence of fighting for Christ Jesus give their power to the Beast against Him, and be ye warned ye Judges of the earth." [92]

3. ANTICHRIST DESTROYED WHEN SINS ARE RIPE.—Insisting that the tares will grow with the wheat until the "harvest or end of the world," and to the "world's end," Williams asserts that "when the world is ripe in sinne, in the sinnes of Antichristianisme," [93] then—

"The Angels, with their sharpe and cutting sickles of eternall

[87] Wroth, *op. cit.,* p. 17.
[88] "A Letter . . . Roger Williams to Major Mason," June, 1670, in *Collections of the Massachusetts Historical Society, 1792-1801* [1st Series], vol. 1, p. 381.
[89] *The Bloudy Tenent, of Persecution,* p. 18.
[90] *Ibid.*   [91] *Ibid.,* p. 62.   [92] *Ibid.,* p. 73.
[93] *Ibid.,* p. 88 (correctly p. 48).

vengeance, shall downe with them, and bundle them up for the everlasting burnings.

"Then shall that Man of Sin, 2 Thess. 2. be consumed by the breath of the mouth of the Lord Jesus, and all that worship the Beast and his picture, and receive his mark into their forehead or their hands, shall drink of the Wine of the wrath of God which is poured out without mixture into the Cup of his indignation." [94]

4. ANTICHRIST'S SUCCESS IS FOR TIME APPOINTED.—Williams refers to conditions obtaining in the Pergamos and Thyatira churches, declaring:

"All may see how since the Apostacie of Antichrist, the Christian World (so called) hath swallowed up Christianity, how the Church and civill State, that is the Church and the World are now become one flocke of Jesus Christ." [95]

Then comes this impressive exposition:

"It is most true what Daniel in his 8. and 11. and 12. Chapters, and John in his Revel. 11. 12. and 13. Chapters write of the great successe of Antichrist against Christ Jesus for a time appointed." [96]

5. DEVIL TO BE IMPRISONED; BEAST ENGULFED IN FIRE.—Then follows a reference to wars of extirpation against the Waldenses, and a reference to the Dragon of Revelation 12 as the "Devill in the Romane Emperours," [97] with a later reference to the "prison for the Devill himselfe a thousand yeares, Rev. 20. And a Lake of eternall fire and brimstone, into which the Beast and False Prophet" shall be cast. [98]

6. WOMAN CARED FOR IN PAPAL PERIOD.—Referring to the papal church as mystical Babylon, he continues:

"In the wildernesse (Rev. 12.) God provideth for the sustentation of the woman, Rev. 12. by which provision even in the most Popish times and places, yea and by most false and Popish callings." [99]

"Antichrist (by the helpe of Civill Powers) hath his prisons, to keep Christ Jesus and his members fast: such prisons may well be called Bishops prisons, the Popes, the Devils prisons: These inquisition houses have ever been more terrible then the Magistrates." [100]

7. HARLOT CLAIMS LANDS OF CHRISTENDOM.—Williams parallels Nebuchadnezzar's decree of the worthies and the fiery

---

94 *Ibid.*, p. 49.   96 *Ibid.*, p. 98.   99 *Ibid.*, p. 166.
95 *Ibid.*, p. 89.   97 *Ibid.*, p. 99.   100 *Ibid.*, p. 153.
                         98 *Ibid.*, p. 153.

furnace with this second compulsion—the killing of all that receive not the mark of the Beast in Revelation 13[101]—and says:

"It is true that Antichrist hath christned all those Countries whereon the Whore sitteth, Rev. 17. with the Title of Christ's land, or Christian land." [102]

8. TEN KINGDOMS GIVE POWER TO THE BEAST.—In commenting on the call of God to separation from Babylon, Williams laments that many Protestants are still clinging to the spirit of popery, and refers to the coming "destruction of the Beast and the Whore." [103] But one of his clearest statements concerning the papal Antichrist and her cup of abominations, in relation to Rome's divisions, is this:

"We finde in the tyrannicall usurpations of the Romish Antichrist, the 10 hornes (which some of good note conceive to be the 10 Kingdomes, into which the Romane Empire was quartred and divided) are expresly said Revel. 17.13. to have one minde to give their power and strength unto the Beast, yea (ver. 17.) their Kingdome unto the Beast, untill the Words of God shall be fulfilled." [104]

9. PRETENDED VICAR PRESIDES OVER GOD'S TEMPLE.—Of papal claims, and the prophetic depictions of Daniel, Paul, and John, Williams has this to say:

"The pretended Vicar of Christ on Earth, who sits as God over the Temple of God, exalting himselfe not only above all that is called God, but over the soules and consciences of all his vassals, yea over the Spirit of Christ, over the holy Scriptures, yea and God himselfe, Dan. 8 & 11 chap. and Rev. 15. together with 2 Thes. 2." [105]

"Yet doth he upon the point challenge the Monarchicall or absolute power also, being full of selfe exalting and blaspheming, Dan. 7.25. & 11.36. Rev. 13.6. speaking blasphemies against the God of Heaven, thinking to change times and Lawes: but he is the sonne of perdition arising out of the bottomlesse pit, and comes to destruction, Revel. 17. for so hath the Lord Jesus decreed to consume him by the breath of his mouth, 2 Thes. 2." [106]

10. TEN KINGDOMS BOWED TO POPE'S YOKE.—Again, he refers to "the whole Pagan World under the Roman emperours, and the whole Antichristian World under the Roman Popes, Rev. 12 & 13." [107] Note this:

---

[101] Ibid., p. 170.
[102] Ibid., p. 182.
[103] Ibid., p. 185.
[104] Ibid., p. 191.
[105] Ibid., p. 199.
[106] Ibid., p. 200.
[107] Ibid., p. 207.

"Those 10 Hornes signifie those many Kings, Kingdoms, and Governments, who have bowed down to the Pope's yoake, and have committed fornication with that great Whore the Church of Rome." [108]

Williams' closing paragraphs on the final desolation of the church of Rome (Revelation 17 and 18) by "her great lovers," and the perplexity of many as to just how this will be accomplished, are interesting.[109] The great Harlot had robbed kings and nations of their power and strength. Their love shall turn into hatred and make her desolate.[110] Thus the prophetic strand is woven into the very warp and woof of this famous book.

11. WITNESSES SLAIN AT END OF 1260 YEARS.—In response to Cotton's answer of 1647—*The Bloudy Tenent Washed, And made white in the bloud of the Lambe*—Williams published *The Bloody Tenent Yet More Bloody*. This treatise reiterates his former statements in even stronger language and greater specificness, and involves the year-day principle, thus:

"If the fourty-two moneths of the Beasts reign, and the two hundred and threescore dayes of the prophesie of the Witnesses of Jesus in Sackcloth be expired: yet I fear the three dayes and a halfe of the greatest slaughter of the Witnesses is not over." [111]

Then he declares that God will subdue all His enemies, particularly the two mighty opposers, "the Turkish and Popish Empires," and reiterates the "42 moneths of the reign of this mighty and dreadfull Beast"—with the slaughter of the witnesses "not long before his own eternall dounfall." [112]

12. CATHOLIC CHRISTENDOM IS PROPHESIED BEAST.—Throughout Williams' *Christenings Make Not Christians* runs the same strain of Catholic Christendom as the Beast, and the people worshiping the Beast[113]—The Roman power being "transferred from the Roman Emperour to the Roman Popes and the Popish kingdomes, branches of that Roman-Root." [114]

---

[108] *Ibid.*, p. 245.   [109] *Ibid.*, p. 246.   [110] *Ibid.*
[111] Roger Williams, *The Bloody Tenent Yet More Bloody*, "To the Reader," unpaged.
[112] *Ibid.*   [113] Roger Williams, *Christenings Make Not Christians*, pp. 4-6.
[114] *Ibid.*, p. 6.

Further on he remarks:

"For the Catholicks conversion, although I believe I may safely hope that God hath his in Rome, in Spaine, yet if Antichrist be their false head (as most true it is) the body, faith, baptisme, hope (opposite to the true, Ephes. 4.) are all false also." [115]

13. SLAUGHTER OF WITNESSES NEARLY ACCOMPLISHED.—In *The Hireling Ministry None of Christs*, Williams contends that "the greatest soul oppression in this nation" comes through national churches and their "Hireling Ministrie" and subservient universities, and declares, "It is the absolute duty of the civil state to set free the souls of all men from that so long oppressing yoake of such ministries," and all persons should be permitted to "make free choice of what worship . . . they please." Then follows a characteristic statement:

"Ever since the beast Antichrist rose, the Lord hath stirred up the ministrie of Prophesie, who must continue their witness, and prophesie until their witness be finished, and slaughters probably neer approching accomplished." [116]

14. FULLNESS OF GENTILES FOLLOWS PAPAL FALL.—Castigating Protestant attempts to plead apostolic succession by running "into the Tents of Antichrist," [117] and for the aping of popish titles, ceremonies, and holy Gowns, cassocks, caps, scarfs, rings, and boots, [118] Williams declares the "fullnesse of the Gentiles is not yet come, and probably shall not, untill the downefall of the Papacy." [119]

15. PROPHESYING OF WITNESSES PARALLELS BEAST'S REIGN.—The witness against the "falshoods of Antichrist" must continue among the saints, he declares, adding:

"The Ministry of Service of Prophets, and Witnesses, mourning and Prophecying in Sack-cloath, God hath immediately stirred up and continued all along the reigne of the Beast, and Antichrist of Rome.

"This Witnesse is (probably) neer finished, and the bloudy storme of the slaughter of the Witnesses, is yet to be expected and prepared for." [120]

---

[115] *Ibid.*, p. 10.
[116] Roger Williams, *The Hireling Ministry None of Christs*, summary preceding dedication page, secs. 1-5, 6, 8.
[117] *Ibid.*, p. 6.
[118] *Ibid.*, p. 15.
[119] *Ibid.*, pp. 20, 21.
[120] *Ibid.*, p. 21.

Such are the earliest American expositors of prophecy. Utterly opposite in church polity, they were nevertheless impressively united in the main prophetic outline—with Rome the fourth prophetic empire, the Papacy as the subsequent Antichrist, the year-day principle, and the second advent as the sublime climax of all.

At the close of the prophetic expositors of the seventeenth century, a summary will be given, bringing together and crystallizing the otherwise scattered evidence on the basic features of interpretation covered in this survey. Only as the cumulative force of the aggregate witness is brought together does the full significance of the individual testimony appear. The same plan of summarization will be followed at the close of the eighteenth-century witness.

IV. First American Poet Employs Prophetic Symbolism

It is significant, as well as interesting, to find America's first woman poet employing the prophetic symbolism of Daniel 2, 7, and 8, and Revelation 17, just as the preachers, educators, statesmen, judges, and physicians about her were doing. Such common usage implies common knowledge and understanding.

ANNE BRADSTREET (1612-1672), earliest professional poet of her sex in New England, was born in Northampton, England. Her father was Governor Thomas Dudley, a stern Puritan with military background. Strictly and religiously upreared, and possessed of a brilliant mind, Anne was married at sixteen to Simon Bradstreet, a Cambridge M.A. graduate, son of a nonconformist minister, and future governor of Massachusetts. A few years later, in 1630, they came to New England, where her husband was advanced from colonial secretary to judge, legislator, governor, ambassador, and royal councilor.

Anne had a scholar's thirst for knowledge. With her husband she had settled at Ipswich, but they removed to North Andover about 1644.[121] She became the champion of her sex,

---

[121] Helen Campbell, *Anne Bradstreet and Her Time*, p. 175; *Dictionary of American Biography*, vol. 2, pp. 577, 578; comprehensive sketch by J. H. Ellis, in "Introduction" to *The Works of Anne Bradstreet*.

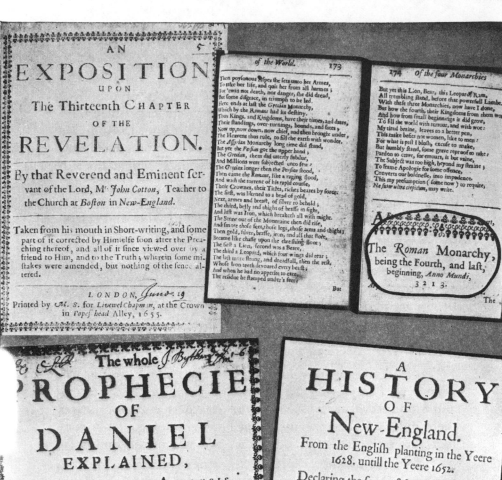

PIONEERS IN FOUR FIELDS EMPHASIZE PROPHECY

First Colonial Exposition, Made by John Cotton (Upper Left); First Colonial Poems, by Anne Bradstreet, Employ Prophetic Symbols (Upper Right); First Complete Commentary on Daniel, Composed by Ephraim Huit (Lower Left); and First New England History, by Edward Johnson, Uses Graphic Prophetic Terms (Lower Right, With Inset)

protesting the traditional disparagement of womankind, and glorying in the career of Queen Elizabeth. Though the mother of eight children, she found time to write more than 7,000 lines of verse.[122] In fact, she produced the first book of poems[123] by an English woman in America. Though sometimes crude in technique and form, they were the best of the time, and were rather remarkable when time, place, and circumstance are considered. She was a faithful student of history. And the longest of her poems, written about 1642, is significantly called "The Foure Monarchies," [124] patterned after Sir Walter Raleigh's *History of the World* (1614). Into this general structure she wrought the prophetic element in an impressive way.

1. THE TRUMPETRIE OF FALLEN ROME.—On the ecclesiastical side of politics, Anne was strongly anti-Romanist and anti-ritualistic, as the invective of the ringing lines that follow attest. And the terse prophetic symbolism employed is to be noted, running as it does with consistent pattern through much of the literature of the time. Penned in 1642, "A Dialogue between Old England and New," concerns contrasting conditions and attitudes. Her strong phrases are characteristic of the time. Exclaiming—

> "Blest be thy Preachers, who do chear thee on,
> O cry: the sword of God, and Gideon"—

she then declares:

> "These are the dayes, the Churches foes to crush,
> To root out Prelates, head, tail, branch, and rush.
> Let's bring Baals vestments out to make a fire,
> Their Myters, Surplices, and all their tire,
> Copes, Rochets, Crossiers, and such trash,
> And let their names consume, but let the flash
> Light Christendome, and all the world to see
> We hate Romes Whore with all her trumperie." [125]

---

[122] John Woodbridge, pastor at Andover in 1645, nephew of Thomas Parker, the prophetic expositor of Newbury, returned to England in 1647, taking her poems to London with him, having them published in 1650.

[123] Anne Bradstreet *The Tenth Muse . . . by a Gentlewoman* (1650). (Author's name on p. 2.)

[124] *Ibid.*, pp. 65-179. See Ellis, *op. cit.*, pp. xli, xliii; Thomas J. Wertenbaker, *The First Americans, 1607-1690*, p. 243; Tyler, *op. cit.*, vol. I, pp. 278-288.

[125] *The Tenth Muse*, p. 188; also in *The Works of Anne Bradstreet*, pp. 340-341.

She closes with the note of triumph addressed to the church:

"For sure the day of your redemption's nigh." [126]

2. THE KINGDOMS OF THE METALLIC MAN.—But the ready pen of the expositor thrusts the prophetic symbols of Daniel 2 and 7 into the heart of her major poem, "The Foure Monarchies of the VVorld." [127] The first of four parts is the "Assyrian," including the later Babylonian, which she identifies explicitly. "This was of monarchies that head of gold." [128] Then comes "The Second Monarchy, being the Persian," [129] followed by the Grecian, third, with its four telltale divisions—

"Seleuchus, Ptolomy, Cassander joynes,
Lysimachus to make a fourth combines." [130]

Soon appear these truly remarkable lines of prophetic exposition in the familiar pattern:

"Here ends at last the Grecian Monarchy,
Which by the Romans had its destiny.
Thus Kings, and Kingdoms, have their times, and dates,
Their standings, over-turnings, bounds, and fates;
Now up, now down, now chief, and then brought under,
The Heavens thus rule, to fill the earth with wonder.
The Assyrian Monarchy long time did stand,
But yet the Persian got the upper hand;
The Grecian, them did utterly subdue,
And Millions were subjected unto few:
The Grecian longer then the Persian stood,
Then came the Romane, like a raging flood,
And with the torrent of his rapid course,
Their Crownes, their Titles, riches beares by force.
The first, was likened to a head of gold,
Next, armes and breast, of silver to behold;
The third, belly and thighs of brasse in sight,
And last was Iron, which breaketh all with might.
The Stone out of the Mountaine then did rise,
And smote those feet, those legs, those arms and thighs;
Then gold, silver, brasse, iron, and all that store
Became like chaffe upon the threshing-floor." [131]

---

[126] *The Tenth Muse*, p. 190.
[127] Running title in original edition of 1650, *The Tenth Muse*, pp. 65-179.
[128] *Ibid.*, p. 80.
[129] *Ibid.*, p. 87.
[130] *Ibid.*, p. 163.
[131] *Ibid.*, p. 173. (Reproduction of page appears on p. 56.)

3. Prophetic Beasts Are Paralleling Symbols.—Turning immediately to the symbolism of Daniel 7, she rehearses the standard view:

> "The first a Lion, second was a Beare,
> The third a Leopard, which four wings did rear;
> The last more strong, and dreadfull, then the rest,
> Whose iron teeth devoured every beast;
> And when he had no appetite to eate,
> The residue he stamped under's feet:
> But yet this Lion, Bear, this Leopard, Ram,
> All trembling stand, before that powerfull Lambe.
> With these three Monarchies, now have I done,
> But how the fourth, their Kingdoms from them won;
> And how from small beginnings it did grow,
> To fill the world with terrour, and with woe." [132]

The boldness of her attempt seems to overwhelm her, and she adds, apologetically:

> "My tired braine, leaves to a better pen,
> This taske befits not women, like to men:
>
> .   .   .   .
>
> The Subject was too high, beyond my straine." [133]

The final part of the discussion, that of "the Roman Monarchy," the fourth and last, is incomplete. When she later attempted to finish it, her manuscript was unfortunately destroyed by fire when her home was burned, and it was never rewritten.[134] Such is Anne Bradstreet's early contribution to our quest in 1642.

---

[132] *Ibid.*, pp. 173, 174.
[133] *Ibid.*, p. 174.
[134] *Ibid.*, pp. 175-179. See "An Apology" in the Ellis reprint (from the second edition), also pp. lxi, 40, 328, 329.

CHAPTER THREE

First Two Systematic Commentaries Appear

We now come to the earliest of the systematic commentaries on the prophecies of Daniel and the Apocalypse, issued in colonial times—Huit in 1644 and Parker in 1646. Of these, the Parker exposition is the more comprehensive. These will launch us into the heart of our quest for the over-all interpretation of Daniel 2, 7, 8, 9, 11, and 12, and their time periods; and the seals, trumpets, witnesses, beasts, and vials, the overthrow of Babylon, and the millennium of the Apocalypse. Comparison can then be made between the American and paralleling Old World interpreters of the same period, presented in Volume 2.

I. Huit—First Colonial Exposition of Daniel

The first systematic exposition of Daniel to appear in the colonies was by EPHRAIM HUIT, Huet [Hewit or Hewett] (d. 1644), pastor at Windsor, Connecticut. He, too, was born in England and educated at St. John's, Cambridge. Later curate in Warwickshire and then preacher in Wroxall, Huit was persecuted for his nonconformity, the intention being to reform or punish him. Similarly silenced by Archbishop Laud in 1638, and driven from Old England "by the tyranny of the prelatical party," to use his own words, he was one of the group following Roger Williams to Connecticut in quest of soul freedom, as he fled from Massachusetts Bay in 1639.[1] Huit's arrival in Windsor

---

[1] "Aug. 1639. Mr. Ephraim Hewit and divers others came up from the Bay to Windsor to settle here."—Daniel Howard, *Glimpses of Ancient Windsor From 1633 to 1933*, p. 23; see also Windsor, Connecticut, *Some Early Records and Documents of and Relating to the Town of Windsor, Connecticut, 1639-1703*, pp. 9, 79.

brought an epoch to the town, his piety, character, and talents endearing him to his flock.

He is tersely catalogued by Cotton Mather, in his *Ecclesiastical History of New England (Magnalia)*, as among the seventy-seven good men who had been ministers first in England and then were "instruments of bringing the Gospel into this Wilderness," thus: "28. Mr. Ephraim Huet, of Windsor [Connecticut]." [2] The slab of red sandstone which serves as his monument, indicates the respect in which he was held:

"Heere Lyeth Ephraim Hvit, sometime Teacher to ye chvrch of Windsor, who dyed September 4th, 1644.

"Who when hee Lived Wee drew ovr vital Breath,
Who when Hee Dyed his dying was ovr death,
Who was ye Stay of State, ye Chvrches Staff,
Alas the times Forbid an *Epitaph*." [3]

Huit wrote the first complete commentary on prophecy by a colonial minister; it was, significantly enough, on the book of Daniel. He had previously written *Anatomy of Conscience* (1626), while still in England. Nathaniel Homes, his contemporary British premillennialist, in his *Resurrection Revealed* (1653),[4] calls him "the learned and godly Mr. E. Huet," and says that he advances "many very considerable things which are strong for our position." [5] His views of the millennium were, however, rather mixed, and he made much of the conversion of the Jews. But the fifth kingdom was held to be visible and actual, and not a mere spiritual reign.

This earliest American prophetic commentary on the entire book of Daniel was rather lengthily titled *The Whole Prophecie of Daniel Explained, by a Paraphrase, Analysis and briefe Comment: wherein the severall Visions shewed to the Prophet are clearly Interpreted, and the Application thereof vindicated against dissenting Opinions* (1644).[6] While this initial Ameri-

---

[2] Cotton Mather, *Magnalia*, Introduction to book 3, pp. 2, 3.
[3] H. R. Stiles, *History . . . of Ancient Windsor*, vol. 1, p. 79; also "Decease of the Fathers of New England," *The New England Historical and Genealogical Register*, January, 1847 (vol. 1, no. 1), p. 74.
[4] [Joshua W. Brooks], *A Dictionary of Writers on the Prophecies*, p. xli.
[5] *Ibid.*, p. xliii.
[6] Both Brooks, *op. cit.*, and William Crowe, *An Exact . . . Catalogue of Our English Writers on the Old and New Testament*, p. 110, mention a 1643 edition.

can exposition is less clear and satisfactory than those that followed, because of its historical importance we sketch its content more fully than would otherwise be warranted. Let us note the particulars as they appear in quaint spelling and phrasing.

1. ANTICHRIST'S REIGN PLACED FROM 600 ONWARD.—Huit declares, "The latter dayes according to the phrase of the Prophets, signifieth the declining ages of the world." [7] And in discussing the Christian Era he locates the reign of Antichrist, and in colonial English, differentiates it from the Turk. His expressions are not always clear:

"Sometime for the middle time thereof, which the Apostle designes to the apostacie of Antichrist, 1 Tim. 4:1, 2, 3. The speciall degrees whereof, are eminent in the world, from the first 600 yeares, and have pestred the church this 1000:yeares. . . . Now if we apply this, either to Antichrist, or to the Turke, to both of whom it doth fully agree, the Time when either of them shall be so revealed." [8]

2. DANIEL 2—STANDARD EXPOSITION OF FOUR EMPIRES.—The standard Old World historical scheme of exposition of the four kingdoms of Daniel 2 is employed, and the empires named and described as Babylon, Persia, Grecia, and Rome—with the stone as the kingdom of Christ (applied, however, to the literal Jews). [9]

3. ADMIXTURE OF CLAY MIXING OF CHURCH AND STATE.—The admixture of clay and iron in the feet is the mixture of the church of Rome with the temporal states of Europe—"the Popes of Rome mixed themselves with the Emperials," "by intermedling into the affaires of States." But this was without success, as "the Emperours and Popes had continuall warres." [10]

4. DANIEL 7: SAME FOUR EMPIRES OF PROPHECY.—The same standard exposition of the same four world powers of Daniel 7 is next given, declaring:

"This vision is the same with that of the Image and foure metalls, and yet is to be repeated, for first, their scope is different, that of the Image intends (according to the Kings thoughts) the succession of Tyrants over the church, this the Churches succession into their Kingdomes." [11]

---

[7] Ephraim Huit, *The Whole Prophecie of Daniel Explained*, p. 40. (Title page reproduced on p. 56.)
[8] *Ibid.*, p. 41.
[9] *Ibid.*, pp. 46-63.
[10] *Ibid.*, pp. 56-62.
[11] *Ibid.*, p. 173.

The four heads of the Grecian leopard are "Cassander head of Macedonia, Antigonus of Asia, Seleucus of Siria, and Ptolomie of Egypt, all possessing Imperiall dignity at once." [12] The strength and tyranny of Rome is then stressed, with its "ten hornes, or tyrannicall states." [13]

5. THE TEN DIVISIONS OF ROME ENUMERATED.—As to these divisions, Huit comments that "there were ten distinct divisions of the Romane Empire, both interpreters and Histories consent." These are named and numbered as follows: "1. Brittaine, 2. France, 3. Germany, 4. Spayne, 5. Italy, 6. Affrica, 7. Asia, 8. Graecia, 9. Syria, 10. Egypt." [14]

6. LITTLE HORN APPLIED TO TURKISH POWER.—Confused as to the Little Horn, as were some of the Old World expositors, Huit nevertheless gives explicit reasons why it cannot be Antiochus Epiphanes—for the Little Horn, after the blasphemies and persecutions, is cast into the burning flame, while the kingdom of Antiochus continued on after his "villanies." Moreover, the kingdom is to be taken by the saints upon the fall of the Little Horn, whereas Antiochus' kingdom was taken over by the Romans.[15] But Huit says, "This little horne [of Daniel 7] intends the Turkish state," which subdued Asia, Grecia, and Syria.[16] However, the Papacy is reckoned the Antichrist. Then, after the Little Horn, comes the "coming of the Son of Man in the clouds." [17]

7. THREE AND A HALF TIMES MADE CENTURIES (1300-1650).—Curiously enough, in this time period only, the three and a half "times" are taken by Huit to be three and a half centuries of the rule of the Turk over the Jews, "to be at the yeare 1300. the addition of 350. years doth terminate their service of him in the yeare 1650." Huit recognizes the uncertainty of this reasoning, and adds, "If this exposition holds true." [18] Evidently the expression "times" made him uncertain. This 350

[12] *Ibid.*, p. 177.
[13] *Ibid.*, pp. 180-182.
[14] *Ibid.*, p. 184.
[15] *Ibid.*, p. 187.
[16] *Ibid.*
[17] *Ibid.*, p. 196.
[18] *Ibid.*, pp. 211, 212.

years of domination of the Turk over the Jews, from 1300 to 1650, is repeated in his exposition of Daniel 12:7.[19]

8. MEDO-PERSIAN RAM, GRECIAN GOAT, AND ALEXANDER.— The ram and he-goat are given the standard application to Medo-Persia and Grecia, with Alexander as the notable horn. But again, this Little Horn which grew exceeding great is mistakenly explained as Antiochus Epiphanes.[20] The "daily" is expounded as the daily worship of God in the church,[21] and the 2300 days are taken as but literal time—six years, three months, and 20 days.[22]

9. SEVENTY WEEKS OF YEARS DATED FROM ARTAXERXES.— The seventy weeks are expounded as seventy "weekes of yeares,"[23] with subdivisions as follows:

"The former sums of 490. yeares is here distributed into 7. weeks or 49. years, into 62. weeks or 434. years, into one week or seven years. The events of the 49. years are handled in 25. The events of the 434. are mentioned in 26. and the events of the seven years in the 27. The seven weeks restore and re-edifie Jerusalem: The 62. weeks bring in the Messiah, and stretch toward the end of his private life; and the last weeke finishes the sacrifice of the Lord, and begins both the calling of the Gentiles and the rejection of the Jewes."[24]

While the precise dating of the period is not given, Huit takes note of the reign of Artaxerxes Longimanus, which he takes to be "agreeable to this Prophecie."[25] At the close of the first half of the seventieth week, "the Lord in three years and halfe of His ministry hath disannulled the Jewish ceremonies. Matt. 27:50, 51."[26] This is the closest application made.

10. DANIEL 11: PARALLELS EARLIER VISIONS; PAPACY IN VERSE 36.—Huit treats Daniel 11 in the standard historical fashion, expounding it as the literal parallel to the preceding lines of prophecy in chapters 2, 7, and 8, from Medo-Persia on through Grecia and Rome. In verse 30, instead of "ships of Kittim," he plainly paraphrases them as "the Navie of the

---

[19] *Ibid.*, pp. 346-348 (correctly pp. 356-358).
[20] *Ibid.*, p. 223.
[21] *Ibid.*, p. 228.
[22] *Ibid.*, p. 230.

[23] *Ibid.*, p. 42.
[24] *Ibid.*, p. 265.
[25] *Ibid.*, p. 266.
[26] *Ibid.*, p. 268.

Romans." [27]   The blasphemous king of verse 36 he expounds thus:

"The holy Apostle citing these words of *Exalting himselfe above all that is called God,* applies it to the Romane Antichrist; such is the authority of that Spirit, by which he speaks." [28]

11. BEAST'S EIGHTH HEAD IS PAPACY.—While the Little Horn of Daniel 7 had been expounded as the Turks, the Papacy is here made the eighth head of the Roman Beast along with the Turkish horn. Note it:

"The prosperity of the Romane Tyrant, under some of the heads or hornes, is here foretold to continue long, even to the end of the affliction of the Jewes; true it is that many of her heads are fallen long since, yet we may see the Papacy, the eighth head & the Turkish State the little horne, do yet domineer in the Church." [29]

The "notes" of the Papacy are then tabulated—"outward shew," "establishing another propitiary sacrifice, daily to be offred, and . . . the coining in of new Advocates and Intercessors," "new Articles of faith," "despising of honest marriage," "Idolatrie," and "Potency and prosperity." [30]

12. TURKEY NAMED AS KING OF THE NORTH.—In verse 40 the sallies of Turks, as the king of the north, are discussed.[31] The year 1300 is taken by Huit as the beginning of the Ottoman Turks,[32] and Revelation 16 is connected with the picture. Daniel 11:45 pertains to "the overthrow of the Turkish State," followed by the "Turkish utter overthrow," [33] though "the Turke is now the Terrour of the World." [34]   The calling of the Jews is again brought in, and a spiritual resurrection stressed.[35]

13. 1290 AND 1335 YEARS END IN 1650 AND 1695.—In Huit's exposition of Daniel 12, while the three and a half "times" are rendered 350 years, from 1300 to 1650, the 1290 and 1335 days are explicitly expounded as years, on the year-day principle. The 1290 years are dated by Huit from 360, when the Jewish

[27] *Ibid.,* p. 310.
[28] *Ibid.,* p. 321; see also pp. 319, 320.
[29] *Ibid.,* p. 325.
[30] *Ibid.,* pp. 326-331.

[31] *Ibid.,* pp. 331-333.
[32] *Ibid.,* pp. 334, 340.
[33] *Ibid.,* p. 342.
[34] *Ibid.,* p. 343.

[35] *Ibid.,* p. 350.

sacrifices were removed by Julian, to 1650,[36] which he believed
would end the Jews' dispersion. And the 1335 years, likewise
beginning in 360 and extending forty-five years beyond the
terminus of the 1290 years (in 1650), are set to end in 1695,[37]
four decades beyond Huit's own time.

14. REVELATION 9: TURKISH PERIOD FROM 1300-1695.—
Huit then brings in the "395 years" (365 + 30) of Revelation
9:15, likewise applying it to the Turks—extending from A.D.
1300 to 1695, according to the "Propheticall manner to use a
day for a year, Eze. 4:6." Here is his declaration:

> "The which time is the same for end with Rev. 9:15. limiting his
> Tyranny to an hower, a day, a moneth and a year, amounting to 395. years,
> each day being put for a year, both which adde 45. to the time, times and
> half, in 7. Now that these dayes are to be understood of the Propheticall
> dayes, each being put for a year." [38]

Such is the first recorded colonial exposition of the book of
Daniel in the New World—though printed in London, for
printing facilities were not yet available here in America. It is
not so clear as others, but it is the first.

II. Bulkeley—Kingdom Established at Seventh Trump

PETER BULKELEY, or Bulkley (1583-1659), founder and minister of Concord, New Hampshire, in 1636, was born in Bedford-
shire, England. His father was also a minister, and author of
the supplement to Foxe's *Book of Martyrs*. Peter was educated
at St. John's College, Cambridge, receiving his M.A. in 1608.
He was soon after admitted to the Anglican priesthood, and was
university preacher in 1610, and rector of Odell, 1620-1635.
Though a nonconformist, he was not molested by the Bishop of
Lincoln during this long pastorate. Then he was accused by
Archbishop Laud, and fled to America in 1635. Settling for a
short time at Cambridge, he went out into the "wilderness"
and founded Concord, New Hampshire, in 1636. Here he
gathered a church about him and became its pastor until 1659.

---

[36] *Ibid.*, pp. 352, 355, 356 (correctly pp. 362, 365, 366).
[37] *Ibid.*, p. 366.
[38] *Ibid.*, p. 356 (correctly p. 366); compare p. 358.

A distinguished scholar, especially in Latin, he contributed part of his personal library to serve as a nucleus in establishing the library of Harvard College. He was known for his extreme Puritanism, his austere looks, and his brevity of hair. His ponderous *Gospel-Covenant; or the Covenant of Grace Opened,* with Introduction by Thomas Shepard, was published in London in 1646, and passed through several editions. It exemplified the intellectual robustness of the age.[39] In this he states that only at the sounding of the seventh trumpet shall Christ's kingdom be established and Jerusalem become the throne of glory.

Bulkeley refers to the stone kingdom that is to fill the earth (Dan. 2:35), and speaks of Rome as the stumbling block to that fulfillment. Upon its removal "then shall that be fulfilled, that *all the kingdomes of the earth shall be the kingdomes of the Lord Christ,* Apoc. 11:15." [40] Such is the essence of his teaching.

III. Parker—Stone Kingdom to Be Established at Advent

Of great importance is the testimony of THOMAS PARKER (1595-1677), of Newberry, Massachusetts, another pioneer American minister likewise listed by Mather,[41] who was born at Wilts, England. His father, Robert, was a prominent nonconformist divine, driven from England for opposing Romish ceremonies, and forced to take refuge in the Netherlands in 1607. Thomas was educated at Magdalen College, Oxford, and at Trinity College, Dublin, under Bishop Usher, who was also deeply interested in Bible prophecy. Young Parker was an indefatigable student, and in 1614 went to the Netherlands, to the University of Leyden, where he studied theology, and later to the University of Franeker, receiving the master's degree.

Parker was "learned in the tongues as well as the arts," especially in Greek, and by 1617 was assistant master of a grammar school. In 1634 he emigrated with friends and relatives to

---

[39] Moses C. Tyler, *History of American Literature During Colonial Time,* vol. 1, pp. 217, 218.
[40] Peter Bulkeley, *The Gospel-Covenant; or the Covenant of Grace Opened,* pp. 18, 19.
[41] Cotton Mather, *Magnalia,* Introduction to book 3, p. 3; John J. Currier, *History of Newbury, Mass.,* pp. 323, 325.

Massachusetts, finally becoming minister at Newberry. In doctrine he was an orthodox Calvinist; in church polity, a Congregationalist—with some friction over the polity. In addition to
his preaching, he conducted a school to prepare boys for Harvard. Later in life Parker became blind. But so familiar was
he with Latin, Greek, and Hebrew, that he could still teach them
with perfect ease.[42]

Then "in the latter part of his Life, he bent himself unto the
study of Scripture-Prophecies," [43] devoting the remainder of his
days thereto, often with fasting and prayer. He wrote several
volumes in this field, the greater part of them in Latin. Only
one was published, a comprehensive work on Daniel in English,[44]
titled *The Visions and Prophecies of Daniel Expounded:
Wherein the Mistakes of Former Interpreters are modestly discovered* (1646). The Introduction by Thomas Bayly describes
Parker as "a man of singular parts, eminent in Learning, super-
eminent in Grace, strangely mortified to the World, wholly
addicted to the service [of] God and the church." [45]

In addition to giving Parker's own exposition, this work
embraces a careful and logical analysis and rebuttal of certain
popular expository fallacies that had arisen in England, such
as the fourth kingdom being the Seleucidae, with Antiochus or
Mohammed as the Little Horn. Parker shows by a series of
clear arguments that such positions contravene the demands of
prophecy. He shows why Rome is the fourth kingdom, and the
Papacy must be the Little Horn. He frequently cites leading
Old World expositors—Napier, Brightman, Perkins, Alstead,
Pareus, and Morland (on the Waldenses).

Parker contends for the consecutiveness and literality of the
four monarchies of Daniel 2 and 7, and the establishment of the
fifth kingdom at and by the second advent, until which time the
church will be trodden underfoot. He holds that the fourth

---

[42] W. B. Sprague, *Annals of the American Pulpit*, vol. 1, p. 41.
[43] Cotton Mather, *Magnalia*, book 3, chap. 25, sec. 9, p. 144.
[44] *Ibid.; Dictionary of American Biography*, vol. 14, pp. 241, 242.
[45] Thomas Bayly, Introduction (dated Jan. 7, 1646) to Thomas Parker, *The Visions and
Prophecies of Daniel Expounded: Wherein the Mistakes of Former Interpreters are modest':
discovered.*

beast of Daniel 7 will extend to the coming of Christ in the clouds of heaven—this to be followed by the heavenly kingdom and the New Jerusalem state, which will fill the whole earth. He extends the fourth beast until the great judgment by fire. Still holding to the fallacy of the thousand years as in the past— as did many in the Old World at this time—Parker looked for the end of all things about 1859 on the basis of the prophetic periods.[46] Because Parker is among the earliest and most complete of the colonial expositors, we also note his positions in some detail.

1. RELATIONSHIP OF PROPHETIC TIME PERIODS.—The prophetic time periods were of first concern to Parker, the initial sentence in his preface stating:

"The interpretation of a great part of Prophecies, dependeth on a just and due accomodation of the number of the yeers. But the numbers are various, the 1290, 1260, 490, 1000, 2300. To set the beginning and end to one of those without relation to the rest, and so run at large, is easie." [47]

Parker projects two alternative time schemes—one ending the "reign of Antichrist and beginning the glory of the New Jerusalem, about the yeer 1650: the other way, about the yeer 1860, that is above 200 yeers hence." [48] He adds that two or three more years of study would probably settle the perplexing question.

2. OVERTHROWS FALLACIES OF SELEUCIDAE AND STONE KINGDOM.—Each of Parker's expositions is divided into two parts: (1) The controversial phase, disproving the fallacious assumptions of others, and (2) what he himself believed to be the true exposition. Thus, with Daniel 2 he states the "main controversie" in this vision is "about the Iron feet and legs, and the stone that smote them." First, there is contention of some that the feet "signifie the Successors of Alexander in the Grecian kingdom, and especially the Seleucidae," and "the stone cut out of the mountain, Christ at his first coming, and his spiritual Kingdom following." Parker's terse rejoinder is: "This cannot

---

[46] Daniel T. Taylor, *The Reign of Christ on Earth*, p. 302.
[47] Parker, *The Visions and Prophecies of Daniel Expounded*, "To the Reader," dated Nov. 20, 1645.
[48] *Ibid.*

stand, first, because every metal signifieth a distinct Kingdom, and the fullnesse and complement thereof." [49]

He argues, clearly and incisively, that the golden head signified the "whole Babylonian kingdom," the silver the "whole Persian," the brazen belly and thighs the "whole Grecian, including the *Seleucidae* and other successors in the same kingdom." [50] Secondly he declares that the vision reaches "unto the last days, . . . which could not be, if the leggs and feet, the extreme and utmost part of the Image, should end in the Seleucidae." [51] Thirdly, the "leggs . . . of Iron" were to be stronger than the brass, but the Seleucidae were weaker than Alexander, and fourthly, the kingdom of God was to be set up during the feet-and-toes portion, but the kingdom of the Seleucidae was "utterly dissolved before the birth of Christ." [52] The argument is sound and conclusive.

3. STONE KINGDOM NOT ESTABLISHED TILL ANTICHRIST'S DOWNFALL.—Then, as to the stone's not being Christ at His first coming, Parker logically argues, first, that the stone was to break in pieces all the kingdoms, whereas the Seleucidae had disappeared before the birth of Christ. Secondly, "his Kingdom that was and is between His first and second Coming, was not appointed for the breaking down of all earthly kingdoms," but covered the period "for the Church to be troden under foot." [53] Thirdly, the other kingdoms are to become extinct, and the stone kingdom "alone doth stand in place of them," and this cannot be until the fall of Antichrist. [54]

4. IRON LEGS ARE ROME, UNITED AND DIVIDED.—Parker affirms, further, "the leggs and feet of iron do signifie the Romane kingdom," [55] for they were a distinct monarchy coming after the Grecian, stronger than the preceding, the ten toes corresponding to the ten horns, or kingdoms, of Daniel 7 and Revelation 12, 13, and 17, continuing under Antichrist to the "end of time."

---

[49] *Ibid.*, p. 1.
[50] *Ibid.*

[51] *Ibid.*, p. 2.
[52] *Ibid.*, pp. 2, 3.
[53] *Ibid.*, p. 3.

[54] *Ibid.*
[55] *Ibid.*, p. 4.

5. Antichrist's Fall Precedes Setting Up of Kingdom.—
The stone is the kingdom of the saints to be set up at the fall of
Antichrist, destroying all "adverse kingdoms in the world," [56]
without human hands or help, rising about the time of the
seventh trumpet, which corresponds to the fall of Antichrist.
"Then, and not before, it shall fill all the earth." [57]

6. Ten Divisions Named; Reunitings Futile.—Parker
presents the standard Protestant Historical School of exposition
of the four kingdoms, with such interesting details as the two
arms signifying Media and Persia, and the "ancles," the "joynt"
dividing between the "leggs and feet," denoting the "intercision
of the Empire by the Northern Barbarians," by which the
Roman Empire was "dissolved and broken into ten kingdoms."
This took place after Valentinian. The "ten parts" are named
as: Britons, Saxons, Franks, Burgundians, Wisigothes, Sueves
and Alans, Vandals, Alemans, Ostrogoths, Greeks—some "weak
and transient," some "strong and permanent." The Goths and
Vandals were brittle and quickly dissolved, while the iron
strength appears in the Franks. The mingling is endeavoring
"again by Marriages to unite the divisions," but the division
persists. [58] The "stone, or kingdom of the Saints," is to be set
up in the days of "Antichrist and the ten horns signified by the
feet and ten toes," and after the destruction of Antichrist is to
fill the whole earth. [59]

7. Little Horn Neither Antiochus nor Mohammed.—
Coming to Daniel 7, in the controversial part Parker again
denies the theory of the Seleucidae as the fourth empire and Antiochus Epiphanes as the Little Horn, for he says, "The kingdom
of the Seleucidae belongeth to the third Beast, and is one of the
four parts into which the Grecian kingdom was divided after
Alexander's death, expressly represented in his four wings and
four heads." This is further proved by Daniel 11. [60] Moreover,
the fourth beast was to subdue the world, but Alexander had
done that, and the Seleucidae simply succeeded to what he had

---

56 *Ibid.*, p. 4.
57 *Ibid.*, pp. 4, 5.
58 *Ibid.*, pp. 5-7.
59 *Ibid.*, pp. 7, 8.
60 *Ibid.*, pp. 8, 19.

conquered. But the fourth was to be greater and stronger than
the third. This was not true of the Seleucidae, which was weaker
than Alexander. Further, the fourth was to be different from
its predecessors, but the Seleucidae were like them.[61] These
arguments, it may be added, are equally pertinent today.

As to the Little Horn, it was to exist at the same time with the
ten divisions, but was to grow increasingly greater than the
others, whereas Antiochus was not so great as his father, and no
three kingdoms fell before him.[62] Nor does the prophetic time
period of three and a half times agree with Antiochus, who profaned the temple but three years and ten days.[63] Neither did
the kingdom of Antiochus extend to the last judgment, the final
fires and the second advent, when all kingdoms become those of
our Lord—and not true of the Seleucidae.[64] On the contrary,
Parker affirms each of these specifications to be true of the
Roman kingdom, and the Little Horn "as to Antichrist of the
Romane kingdom." [65] And Parker dismisses the idea of Mohamet, because he arose outside the territory of the Roman
beast.[66]

8. ROME FULFILLS FOURTH BEAST REQUIREMENTS.—Contending for the Little Horn as the Papacy, because it was "con-
joyned with the ten horns," exhibited the character attributed
to it, and existed at the time allotted to it,[67] Parker, in the
"explication," expounds the four beasts, showing each require-
ment of the fourth beast fulfilled by Rome, with the seven
heads as "Kings, Consuls, Tribunes, Decemviri, Dictators,
Romane Emperours, Popes, with the ten Kings." [68] And the
ten horns were listed as the Britons, Saxons, Franks, Burgundians, Wisigothes, Sueves and Alanes, Vandals, Alemans, East-
gothes, and Greeks.[69] The wars against the Waldenses are then
detailed, with the crusades, first used against the Turk, and then
turned against the Waldenses.[70]

---

[61] *Ibid.*, pp. 9, 10.
[62] *Ibid.*, p. 11.
[63] *Ibid.*, p. 12.

[64] *Ibid.*
[65] *Ibid.*, pp. 12, 13.
[66] *Ibid.*, p. 14.
[67] *Ibid.*, p. 15.

[68] *Ibid.*, pp. 20, 21.
[69] *Ibid.*, p. 21.
[70] *Ibid.*, pp. 22-26.

9. PAPAL HORN ENTHRONED AMONG ROME'S DIVISIONS.—
Parker next outlines the chronological sequence of papal emergence among Rome's divisions, the open enthronement in 606,[71]
and its ecclesiastical significance. Then he parallels the two
great horns of Daniel 7 and 8.[72] And he declares the Papacy
changes laws "by removing the daily sacrifice, or true Worship,"
and ordaining holydays.[72] And it continues till the second
advent and the resurrection.[74]

10. PERSIAN RAM, GRECIAN GOAT, AND ROMAN HORN.—
The Medo-Persian ram and the Grecian goat, and the Alexandrian great horn and subsequent four divisions, are next
detailed.[75] Then the wars of the Papacy toward the north, the
east, and Judea are sketched, and its attack upon the true worship.[76] But the 2300 evenings and mornings Parker thinks to be
"just half so many compleat days, to wit, 1150," which he suggests as from 367 to about 1517.[77] European writers in this
period were likewise less clear over the 2300 days than over any
other time prophecy. The time had not yet come for understanding this period.

11. STRANGE PLACEMENT OF THE SEVENTY WEEKS.—Holding that the seventy weeks of Daniel 9 are 490 years, Parker
strangely places the first period of forty-nine years from 1160 to
1209,[78] with the sixty-two weeks ending in 1642,[79] and the midst
of the seventieth week falling in 1646,[80] the entire period ending
in 1649,[81] at the same time as the 1260 years, which he dates
from 390. Parker presents an alternative for the 490 years—
from Wycliffe in 1370 to 1860, which terminus would agree
with the 1260 years as from A.D. 600.[82] This curious allocation
as to time is about the least consistent of all Parker's expositions.

12. DANIEL 11 EMBRACES THE POPE (VERSE 36 FF.)—The
great literal prophecy outline of Daniel 11, traversing the history
of Persia, Grecia, and Rome, is then expounded.[83] Verse 21

---

[71] *Ibid.*, pp. 27, 28. [73] *Ibid.*, p. 31. [75] *Ibid.*, pp. 35-42.
[72] *Ibid.*, pp. 28, 29. [74] *Ibid.*, p. 34. [76] *Ibid.*, pp. 43-47.
[77] *Ibid.*, p. 49. Parker also suggests another alternative, 360-1510.
[78] *Ibid.*, p. 58. [80] *Ibid.*, p. 64. [82] *Ibid.*
[79] *Ibid.*, p. 60. [81] *Ibid.* [83] *Ibid.*, pp. 71-98.

Parker applies to the pope,[84] and the verses following to his wars against the Turks, Saracens, and Waldenses.[85] Parker makes the Kittim of verse 30 to be Italy.[86] He again denies that Antiochus is intended from verse 36 onward. He identifies the willful king with Antichrist.[87]

Verses 36-40, Parker applies to Antichrist's exploits—his exaltation, prosperity, disregard of the God of his fathers, and the desire of women,[88] and his wars as well,[89] involving Turk and Christian. Coming to verse 40, Parker says:

"Now by those expeditions, and especially by the last against the Turks and Sarasins in the East, the King of the North, that is, Antichrist, rushed against the Mahometans like a whirlewind, with Charets and Horses, and with great fleets or with many ships, and overflowed and passed thorow. At length he came into the Holy-land (as they call) or into Judea, called the pleasant land, many Countries falling under him. He came into the Holy-land, at the last term of his inundation." [90]

Parker believed that the tidings from the East involved the Turks and Saracens.[91] Of verse 45 he says:

"And he shall plant the Tabernacles of his palace between the seas in the glorious and holy mountain. Not between two seas, but seas: because in the Countries bordering on the Mediterranean and Ocean seas, where the Church was seated, signified by the glorious and holy mountain, he erected his Kingdom, oppressing the Waldenses, Verse 31, 32. But shortly he shall come to his end, the yeers 1260 being expired." [92]

Then comes the sixth seal, the seventh trump, and the seventh vial, and the ending of the 1335 years (1290 + 45), and the last plague on Antichrist.[93]

13. ALL TIME PERIODS ON YEAR-DAY BASIS.—The time periods of Daniel 12 and related prophecies (Daniel 7, and Revelation 11, 12, 13) are then discussed with the events that mark them out[94]—the witnesses in sackcloth, the treading down of the Holy City, the achievements of the Little Horn, the relation of the Dragon and the Beast, and the woman in the wilderness. Parker seeks the beginning of all the periods on the basis of the

---

[84] *Ibid.*, p. 98.
[85] *Ibid.*, pp. 99-106.
[86] *Ibid.*, p. 106.
[87] *Ibid.*, pp. 111-115, citing Gratserus and Brightman.
[88] *Ibid.*, pp. 118-121.
[89] *Ibid.*, pp. 122, 124.
[90] *Ibid.*, pp. 122, 123.
[91] *Ibid.*, p. 124.
[92] *Ibid.*
[93] *Ibid.*, pp. 124, 125.
[94] *Ibid.*, p. 125 ff.

year-day principle.[95] The 1260 years of Antichrist, the 1290 years from the setting up of the abomination, and the glorious state of the new Jerusalem at the end of the 1335 years, are all set forth.[96]

14. ALTERNATIVE DATES SUGGESTED FOR PERIODS.—Not certain of their precise beginning, he suggests two—one with the beginning of the Papacy "before the year 400," and the other "the more evident, open and perfect state thereof, about the year 600." [97] He first gives the arguments for 360 and 390, and offers this diagram:

"According to this way, thus we may settle the terms of the years.

1290			360		
1260	⎫		390	⎫	do end to-
490	⎬ Beginning	1160	⎬ gether in
575		at the year	1075		the year
390	⎭		1260	⎭	1 6 4 9" [98]

15. THE 390 YEARS OF TURKISH WOE.—The 390 years are explained of the Turk on the early time schedule in this way, with the anticipated ending:

"The years 390 according to the round number, or at large 391. and an hour, Ap. 9. 14. do appertain unto the solution of the Turks; which, by the dissentions of the Latines, and movings of the Tartars, began to be loosed from about the year 1260. and two years before in some degree: so that the hour may be in 1258. the day, the year following, and the 390 from 1260. See Brov. annal. Thus the Turks will cease to be loosed in the year 1649. and the next year following may they begin to fall together with the Pope, if this former way of Accommodation doth hold." [99]

16. LATER ALTERNATIVE BEGINS PAPACY ABOUT 600.—The second method of placing the years would begin the periods from the more "open state" of the Papacy—after the barbarian incursions and the time of Justinian, when the glory of Antichrist's kingdom was established, which Parker denominates "reasonable and satisfactory."

---

[95] *Ibid.*, pp. 125-132.
[96] *Ibid.*, pp. 132, 133.
[97] *Ibid.*, p. 134; see also pp. 141, 143.
[98] *Ibid.*, p. 138. (The 490 years are the curiously placed seventy weeks, and the 575 are the 2300 ÷ 4, which number "may onely comprehend the times of the most perfect raign of Antichrist."—Page 138.
[99] *Ibid.*, p. 139.

"According to this second way, we may set beginnings thus unto the years.

1290 ⎫		⎧ 570 ⎫	
1260 ⎬ From		600 ⎬ end in the year 1859." [100]
1150 ⎪		710 ⎪
490 ⎭		⎩ 1370 ⎭

Parker says, "The 1260 yeers may fitly begin in the yeer 600, according to the round number." [101] Concerning the Turkish period, in this second enumeration, and bringing in the 150 years, Parker remarks:

"The solution of the Turks, notwithstanding this second way may begin in the foresaid yeer 1260. and continuing 390 yeers may end immediately before 1650: or else beginning from about 1300 may possibly run out 40 yeers after. Or happily beginning in remisse degrees from about 1169 may be extended to 1559. and so the end of the strength of the Turkish Kingdom may be determined by these yeers, proportionably to the five moneths of the Kingdom of the Sarasins, and not the absolute and perfect end thereof." [102]

17. STILL PLACES THOUSAND YEARS IN PAST.—Parker still clings to a Protestant accommodation of the Augustinian theory of the thousand years, dating them from Constantine's overthrow of paganism, with the devil's power retarded till the end of the 1,000 years. [103] He begins them with the seven vials, and again offers two alternatives—from 620 or from 840. [104] Parker believed that the fifth vial began in 1370, with Wycliffe, when that vial began to be poured out on the throne and kingdom of the Beast; and the sixth began with Luther. [105]

18. VIALS END BY 1860; NEW JERUSALEM FOLLOWS.—Parker then concludes that if those vials began from 620, then accordingly the sixth "will end and therewithall the 1000 yeers in 1620." [106] But if they "begin from 840, then accordingly the sixth vial will end, and therewith all the 1000 years, the space of about 20 years before 1860." [107] After this will follow the glorious time of the New Jerusalem, and the downfall of Antichrist, the gen-

100 *Ibid.*, pp. 139-141.   101 *Ibid.*, p. 141, citing Alstead and Perkins.
102 *Ibid.*, pp. 142, 143.
103 *Ibid.*, pp. 143-147. This was likewise characteristic of European expositors, it will be remembered. See Volumes 1 and 2 of the present work.
104 *Ibid.*, pp. 152, 153.   106 *Ibid.*, p. 153.
105 *Ibid.*, p. 153.   107 *Ibid.*, pp. 153, 154.

eral resurrection, and the last judgment.[108]   Such are Parker's tentative attempts as to the placement of the time of the millennium.   He then closes with the generous words:

"If any of my Reverend Brethren, otherwise minded, can shew unto me better light, I shall count my self and the Church of God beholding unto them for it, and willing receive it at their hands.   In the meantime this is my judgment." [109]

---

[108] *Ibid.*, p. 154.
[109] *Ibid.*, p. 156.

CHAPTER FOUR

Physicians, Legislators, and Historians Contribute

The predominantly Protestant aspect of the American colonies, and their vast distance from Europe, in the light of travel time then required, saved them from the penetrations of the Roman Catholic counterinterpretations of prophecy which soon began to be noticeable among the compromisers in Old World Protestantism. New England Catholicism was so much in the minority that it was virtually silent, fearing to speak, and exerting little influence. While there was ample acquaintance with the expositional literature of the Old World, America's religious views were independently formed and were fully as advanced as any to be found in England or Continental Europe, whether compared for the seventeenth, eighteenth, or early nineteenth century.

I. Clarke—Persecution Brings Confession of Prophetic Faith

Of somewhat different character is the testimony of JOHN CLARKE (1609-1676), learned minister, physician, and writer, one of the founders of Rhode Island and of the American Baptists. He emigrated from England to Boston in 1637, where his Baptist principles soon brought him into conflict with the Massachusetts General Court. Later he was driven out of Massachusetts, but was received by Roger Williams and settled in Aquidneck, Rhode Island. In 1639 he assisted in founding the Baptist church at Newport—the next oldest after the Williams church of 1638.   Clarke likewise accompanied Williams to England as an agent for the colony.   Between 1664 and 1669 Clarke was a member of the Rhode Island General Assembly, and from 1669-1671 was deputy governor and codified the Rhode Island laws.   In 1663 he obtained a second charter from Charles II for Rhode Island, which secured the liberty of the colony in matters of religion.   Then he resumed the care of the Newport Baptist church, keeping his pulpit strongly premillennial until his death.   (Portrait appears on page 34.)

In 1651 Clarke, in company with Obadiah Holmes, was arrested, fined, and imprisoned for holding a religious meeting, preaching the gospel, and celebrating the ordinances on Sunday, at meeting time, in a private house for the benefit of William Witter, an aged blind member of Clarke's church, residing just over the provincial line from Rhode Island at Lin (Lynn), Massachusetts.[1]   This arrest was carried out under the old Massachusetts law of 1644 against Anabaptists, and concerning "Heresie" and "Disturbing of Churches."[2]   Fortunately, Clarke's full story of the graphic episode has been preserved in his *Ill Newes From New-England* (1652), in the very preface of which Clarke refers to the second advent and the prophecies.

Here Clarke speaks of Antichrist, "which mystery being brought to this height, then shall Christ Jesus consume him with the spirit of his mouth, and shall destroy him with the brightness of his coming."[3]   He refers to the papal "Beast" of prophecy, and cites the call to come out and be separate, and refers to the tribulation before the second glorious advent.   Then he gives a faithful recital of the persecution of Obadiah Holmes and himself, "meerly for conscience towards God."[4]   The little meeting mentioned (with only about a dozen present) was in progress when two constables interrupted and broke it up, forcing Clarke and his companions to attend the orthodox

---

[1] John Clarke, *Ill Newes From New-England: or A Narrative of New-Englands Persecution;* Isaac Backus, *A History of New England. With Particular Reference to . . . Baptists,* vol. 1, p. 178; J. D. Knowles, *Memoir of Roger Williams,* pp. 238-245.
[2] Clarke, *op. cit.,* pp. 35, 38.
[3] *Ibid.,* "To the Reader," unpaged.
[4] *Ibid.,* p. 1.

Congregational meeting on their way to the common prison at Boston.[5]

A few days later they were tried before the court, which was somewhat embarrassed by Clarke's able defense.[6] He was sentenced to pay a fine of £20, or be well whipped.[7] And this "without producing either accuser, witness, jury, law of God, or man." [8] This he refused to pay, as that would be an acknowledgment of guilt. So he was sent back to prison. Here Clarke thrice sent out a petition to meet the local clergy in public discussion. The proposal was first accepted and a day fixed.[9] But on second thought, the clergy deemed it inexpedient to debate with so worthy an antagonist. Clarke's fine was paid without his knowledge and consent, and he was released, escaping the lash.[10] But not so with Holmes, as will be noted in the next sketch.

Clarke quotes the "Laws of Massachusetts" under which he was prosecuted,[11] with the section on "Blasphemy," as well as the "Lawes Ecclesiastical" against gathering for worship without civil approbation or failure to attend the established preaching of the Word, and also for "Heresie" and "Disturbing of Churches"—with punishment in fines or banishment for violation.[12] That these are a true copy of the original statutes in *The Book of the General Lauues and Libertyes Concerning the Inhabitants of the Massachusets* (1648) is evident from a comparison. The statute against "Heresie" significantly involves, be it noted, those who deny the lawful authority of the Magistracy to "punish the outward breaches of the first Table." [13]

Roger Williams wrote to Governor Winthrop concerning the matter.[14] And Sir Richard Saltonstall, one of the Massachusetts magistrates, likewise wrote a letter of protest about such tyranny and persecution, imprisoning and whipping men for

[5] *Ibid.*, pp. 2-4; Knowles, *op. cit.*, p. 240.
[6] Knowles, *op. cit.*, p. 241.
[7] See sentence in full in Clarke, *op. cit.*, pp. 5, 6.
[8] *Ibid.*, p. 5.
[9] *Ibid.*, pp. 7, 13; Knowles, *op. cit.*, p. 241.
[10] Knowles, *op. cit.*, p. 241.
[11] *Ibid.*, p. 35.   [12] *Ibid.*, pp. 35-39.
[13] *The Book of the General Lauues and Libertyes Concerning the Inhabitants of the Massachusetts* (1648 ed.), p. 21 (1660 ed.), p. 34.
[14] Probably August, 1651. See *Letters of Roger Williams*, edited by John R. Bartlett, in *Publications of the Narragansett Club*, First Series, vol. 6, pp. 210-212.

their consciences.   To this Cotton replied lamely but with asperity, being "chafed" by the rebuke.[15]

1. ANTICHRIST REIGNS PRIOR TO SECOND ADVENT.—It was while in prison and seeking a public discussion of his faith that Clarke wrote out his notable "Testimony," or Confession of Faith.   Following his name were the words "a prisoner of Iesus Christ at Boston," waiting "in hope of that glorious Kingdom which shall ere long appear." [16]   The first proposition pertains to Jesus Christ, His resurrection and ascension—not only as Saviour, but as Prophet, Priest, and returning King.   The part of the Antichrist in relation to this sequence is clearly stated in his later explanation:

"And as he [Christ] was the Prophet, opening his Fathers Bosome, and shewing the things that were past and present, so the things also that were to come; he tells them how many things he must suffer of the Elders, and Chief Priests, and Scribes, and be killed, and raised again the third day, and therein foresheweth his Office of Priesthood; he also foretells how after he is risen as a Lord, he will set his House in order, and so depart to his Father to receive his Kingdom, and to return, and what shall befall his Servants in the time of his absence, by the reign and rage of the Beast, and the Spirit of Antichrist, and what will be each ones portion at his return, as appears in the book of the Revelation, which is surrounded with blessings to him that readeth, Chapter 1.3. and curses to him that addeth to it, or taketh from it, Chapt. last 18.19." [17]

2. ETERNAL KINGDOM FOLLOWS THE FOUR MONARCHIES.— The second part of the same proposition pertained to "The Annointed King, who is gone unto his Father for his glorious Kingdom, and shall ere long return again." [18]   Declaring (in his explanation) "he shall appear indeed in the form of a King with thousands of his Saints, and ten thousand times ten thousand of the heavenly Hosts," [19] Clarke refers to His coming kingly office as fulfilling the prophecy of Daniel, with the coming kingdom approaching.

"As the dream of Nebuchadnezzer hath been found certain, and the interpretation of Daniel sure, concerning those four Monarchies or King-

---

[15] Knowles, op. cit., pp. 244, 245.
[16] Clarke, op. cit., pp. 9, 10; see also Backus, op. cit., pp. 182-184.
[17] Clarke, op. cit., p. 46.
[18] Ibid., pp. 9, 47; see also Backus, op. cit., p. 222.
[19] Clarke, op. cit., p. 47.

doms of men which should come to pass in the Earth, so certain and sure it is, that the day is aproaching that the God of Heaven will set up his King- dom by that despised yet Corner-stone that was cut out without hands, Dan. 2.44, 45." [20]

Then follows an earnest declaration of freedom to worship God without a commanding or ordering power, and free from "the inventions and commandements of men," not by "carnall commandments seconded with carnall weapons." [21]

II. Holmes—Prophetic Faith Sealed With Stripes at Boston

The companion of Clarke was OBADIAH HOLMES (1606- 1682), also a Baptist minister, who came over from Manchester, England, in 1639. First becoming a member of Clarke's church at Newport, Rhode Island, he was ordained by the First Baptist church of Newport, Rhode Island, in 1652. He also served as commissioner from 1656 to 1658.[22] Not yet ordained in 1651, he accompanied Clarke over the line from Rhode Island into Lynn, Massachusetts, to visit the aged member of the Newport, Rhode Island, church residing there, as just noted. And he helped to celebrate the ordinances. He was accordingly con- demned by the General Court to be fined or whipped. Bravely choosing the latter, he was kept in prison from July until the Court met in September. He was cruelly scourged at Boston, in 1651, with thirty lashes from a three-corded whip.[23] So merciless was this lashing that for a considerable period he could find no ease except on his elbows and knees.[24] Later, in 1675, for the information of friends in England, he wrote out his confession of faith. He had previously concurred in Clarke's declaration:

"33. I believe the promise of the Father concerning the return of Israel and Judah, and the coming of the Lord to raise up the dead in Christ, and to change them that are alive, that they may reign with him a thousand years, according to the scripture. 34. I believe the resurrection of the wicked to receive their just judgment, go ye cursed to the devil and his angels forever. 35. I believe as eternal judgment to the wicked, so I believe

---

[20] *Ibid.*, pp. 47, 48.   [21] *Ibid.*, pp. 48, 49.
[22] F. L. Weis, *The Colonial Clergy and the Colonial Churches of New England*, p. 108.
[23] Clarke, *op. cit.*, pp. 16-22; Backus, *op. cit.*, vol. 1, p. 192.
[24] *Letters of Roger Williams*, p. 211n; Knowles, *op. cit.*, p. 243.

the glorious declaration of the Lord saying, come ye blessed of my Father, enter into the joy of your Lord, which joy, eye hath not seen, ear hath not heard, neither can it enter into the heart of man to conceive the glory that God hath prepared for them that love and wait for his appearance; wherefore come Lord Jesus, come quickly." [25]

His declaration closes with the words, "For this faith and profession I stand, and have sealed the same with my blood in Boston, in New-England, and hope through the strength of my Lord, shall be enabled to witness the same to death." [26] The testimonies and confessions of Clarke and Holmes, wrought by persecution, are strikingly similar to the great Baptist "Confession or Declaration of Faith" presented to Charles II in March, 1660. This was signed by forty-one names, and "owned and approved by more than 20,000." [27] The Baptists in the Old World and the New were strong premillennialists, awaiting the return of their Lord. Here are the classic Articles XXI, XXII:

"XXI. That there shall bee after the Resurrection from the graves of the Earth, An eternall judgement, at the appearing of Christ, and his Kingdom, 2 Tim. 4.1. Heb. 9.27. at which time of judgement, which is unalterable, and irrevocable, every man shall receive according to the things done in his body, 2 Cor. 5:10.

"XXII. That the same Lord Jesus, who showed himself alive after his passion, by many infallible proofs, Act, 1.3. which was taken up from the Disciples, and carryed up into Heaven, Luk. 24.51. Shall so come in like manner as hee was seen go into Heaven, Act. 1.9, 10, 11. *And when Christ who is our life shall appear, wee shall also appear with him in glory,* Col. 3.4. *For then shall hee bee King of Kings, and Lord of Lords,* Rev. 19.16. for the Kingdom is his, and hee is the Governour among the Nations, Psal. 22.28. and King over all the Earth, Zech. 14.9. *And wee shall reign (with him) on the Earth,* Rev. 5.10 the Kingdoms of this world (which men so mightily strive after here to enjoy) shall become the Kingdoms of our Lord, and his Christ, Rev. 11.15. for All Is Yours. (O yee that overcome this world) *for yee are Christs, and Christ is Gods,* 1 Cor. 3.22, 23. *For unto the Saints shall bee given the Kingdome, and the greatness of the Kingdom,* under (mark that) *the whole Heaven,* Dan. 7, 27. Though (alasse) now many men bee scarce content that the Saints should have so much as a being among them; But when Christ shall appear, then shall bee their day, then shall bee given unto them power over the Nations, to rule them with a Rod of Iron, Rev. 2.26, 27. then shall they receive a Crown of life, which no man shall take from them, nor they by any means turned, or overturned

[25] Backus, *op. cit.*, pp. 208, 209.   [26] *Ibid.*, p. 260.
[27] *Baptist Confession or Declaration of Faith*, at close of signatures in broadside form.

from it, for the oppressor shall bee broken in peeces, Psal. 72.4 and their now vain rejoycings turned into mourning, and bitter Lamentations, as it it written Job 20. 5, 6, 7. *The triumphing of the wicked is short, and the joy of the Hypocrite but for a moment; though his Excellency mount up to the Heavens, and his head reach unto the clouds, yet shall hee perish for ever, like his own dung; they which have seen him, shall say, where is hee?"* [28]

III. Eliot—Second Advent the Burden of All Discourses

Interest attaches to JOHN ELIOT (1604-1690), "apostle to the Indians," and pastor of Roxbury, who was born in Herts, England. He was graduated from Cambridge in 1622, and was early converted by Thomas Hooker, who also influenced him to become a nonconformist. Eliot first became a schoolman, assisting Hooker, but felt called to the gospel ministry. Bishop Laud was working strenuously to bring England into modified Catholicism, multiplying unwarranted ceremonies. Hundreds were coming to America to establish congregational churches, and in 1631 Eliot came to Boston. In 1632 he settled as "teacher" of the church at Roxbury, and was ordained shortly thereafter, preaching in the neighboring towns. (Portrait appears on page 34.)

Burdened for the heathen Indians, he was moved to evangelize these worshipers of the sun and moon gods, and believed them to be the dispersed tribes of Israel.[29] He learned their language and reduced it to a grammar, afterward publishing it. By 1642 he preached without an interpreter before the Indians at Nonantum (now Newton), Massachusetts. Thereafter he devoted much time to evangelizing the Indians, raising up six churches in New England [30] and training native pastors—sending some through college and establishing Indian schools.[31]

In 1649 Eliot founded in London the Society for Propaga-

---

[28] *Ibid.*, tractate form, pp. 9, 10.
[29] Cotton Mather, *Magnalia*, book 3, The Third Part, part 3 ("Eliot as an Evangelist"), p. 193.
[30] *Ibid.*, p. 194 ff.
[31] Eliot paused in the midst of his missionary labors to write *The Christian Commonwealth* (1659), based upon the theocratic Mosaic example. It rejected the Separatist theory of natural rights. Since the law had been declared once and for all, there was no need for the legislative branch of government. And since Christ is sole Ruler and King, there is no place for a profane head of state. All that was needed was a competent magisterial system to hear causes and adjudicate differences. See Vernon L. Parrington, *The Colonial Mind, 1620-1800*, p. 83.

tion of the Gospel Among the Indians, and in 1651 settled in Natick, raising up the first Protestant Indian church in America. In 1653 he produced a *Catechism*, the earliest book printed in the Massachusetts Indian language. Then Eliot translated the Bible into the Indian tongue—the New Testament in 1661 and the Old Testament in 1663—which was the first Bible ever printed in America. The Indian grammar followed in 1666, and an Indian primer in 1669.[32]

Eliot held views on prophecy similar to those of Huit. He writes of "the great kingdom of Christ, which we wait for, when all kingdoms and nations shall become His." Mather records that his discourses ran largely upon "the coming of our Lord Jesus Christ," whatever his subject.[33] Of this he talked and prayed and longed. And prophecy held a key place, as will be noted.

1. To OVERTHROW ANTICHRIST AND ACCOMPLISH PROPHE-CIES.—Eliot's impressive *Tears of Repentance: or A further Narrative of the Progress of the Gospel Amongst the Indians in New-England* (1653) was published by the Corporation for Propagating the Gospel. With its dedication addressed to Oliver Cromwell, it opens with the significant statement that God had raised Cromwell up "to overthrow Antichrist, and to accomplish, in part, the Prophesies and Promises of the Churches Deliverance from that Bondage."[34]

2. EARTHLY KINGDOMS BEING BROKEN.—On the same page Eliot repeats this double design—"First, To overthrow Antichrist by the Wars of the Lamb; and Secondly, To raise up His own Kingdom in the room of all Early Powers which He doth cast down, and to bring all the World subject to be ruled in all things by the Word of His mouth." The salutation "To the Reader" likewise speaks of "such actings of Faith as accord with the accomplishment of those Prophesies, when the time of their

---

[32] James C. Pilling, *Bibliography of the Algonquian Languages*, art. "Eliot." (82 title-page facsimiles are reproduced.)
[33] Cotton Mather, *Magnalia*, book 3, part 3, p. 207.
[34] John Eliot, *Tears of Repentance: or A further Narrative of the Progress of the Gospel Amongst the Indians in New-England*, fol. A2r.

accomplishment is come." And he adds, "In these times the Prophesies of Antichrist his down fall are accomplishing." [85]

A further statement asserts all "contrary Kingdoms and Powers" are being "broken in pieces and destroyed," and cites Daniel 2:35, 44, 45, and 7:26, 27. [36] Then follow confessions of Christ by various Indians. So the prophetic element was the motivating principle in this earliest work in America for the Indians.

IV. Davenport—Advent Truth Buried Under Papal Darkness

Another important witness is JOHN DAVENPORT (1597-1670), Puritan pastor at Boston, born in Coventry, England, his father being mayor. Educated at Brazen-Nose College, Oxford, he received both the M.A. and the B.D. degrees in 1625. At nineteen he was an assistant preacher in London, visiting each family during the dread plague. In 1631 he came into conflict with Bishop Laud because of his nonconformist views, John Cotton having already fallen under the bishop's displeasure and fled. In 1633 Davenport withdrew from the Established Church and retired to Holland, where he was invited to be the colleague of an aged pastor. In 1635 we find him protesting the promiscuous baptizing of children. (Portrait appears on page 34.)

In 1637 he responded to Cotton's invitation to come to New England, where he co-operated with Theophilus Eaton in founding the colony of New Haven. [37] In 1665 Davenport accepted the pastorship of the First Church of Boston. A diligent student and a powerful preacher, he was author of a number of works, chief among which were *The Saints Anchor-Hold in all Storms and Tempests* (1701), [38] *The Knowledge of Christ* (1653), and *Another Essay for the Investigation of Truth* (1663). Prophecy also had a prominent place in his preaching and writing.

---

[35] *Ibid.*, sig. B₁ r.
[36] *Ibid.*, "To the Christian Reader."
[37] Cotton Mather, *Magnalia*, book 3, The First Part, chap. 4, secs. 1-8, pp. 51-54; *Dictionary of American Biography*, vol. 5, art. "John Davenport."
[38] Signed "J.D." Identified as Davenport in Joseph Sabin, *A Dictionary of Books Relating to America*, vol. 5, p. 238.

1. ANTICHRIST IN LAST HALF OF ALLOTTED PERIOD.—Davenport stressed the personal, premillennial second advent, and the rising and reigning of the saints with Christ for the 1,000 years. He stood stanchly with Mede, Goodwin, and Gill against a spiritual resurrection. His sermon on Matthew 24 (*The Knowledge of Christ*) is cited by Hutchinson, Mather, Cheever, and others. He tells how the truth of the Lord's advent lay buried under papal darkness until the day dawn. Now it is shining gloriously again "since the Antichrist entered into the last half Time of the Period allotted for him." [39]

2. LITERAL RESURRECTION AT BEGINNING OF MILLENNIUM.— A supporting introduction to Increase Mather's *The Mystery of Israel's Salvation, Explained and Applyed*[40] was written by John Davenport (1667), as later noted. In the Introduction, Davenport makes the keynote the second advent, as foretold in Daniel 2 and 7, and in Revelation 19. The first resurrection is literal, at the beginning of one thousand years, with the general, or executive, judgment at the end of the thousand years. Davenport utterly rejected the Augustinian theory of the thousand years as in the past. The influence of this stand was far reaching.

3. OUTLINE PROPHECY OF DANIEL 7.—In his *Knowledge of Christ* (1653), comprising "demonstrative proofs" from the prophecies that Christ was the true Messiah, Davenport leads up to the feature of Christ as the prophesied Stone. He sets forth the gold, silver, and brass of Daniel 2 as corresponding with the lion, bear, and leopard of Daniel 7, with the parallel symbols referring to Babylon, Persia, and Grecia with its four divisions.[41] But, like Broughton of England, whom he cites, Davenport at this time (1653) looked upon the fourth phase as another aspect of the Hellenistic power. In this he stood largely apart from the other American expositors, and here turned from the majority view of the Reformation writers on prophecy.

4. DIVISIONS OF SEVENTY WEEKS CHAINED LINK TO LINK.— On the time feature of the seventy weeks, or "seventy sevens of

---

[39] Cotton Mather, *Magnalia*, book 3, The First Part, chap. 4, sec. 14, pp. 56, 57.
[40] See p. 127.   [41] John Davenport, *The Knowledge of Christ*, p. 38.

years," Davenport stresses the exactness and literality of the fulfillment. Discussing the three divisions of the seventy weeks, he
says, "Thus the time is chained linke unto link, by the Angel's
speech." [42] In this way the certainty of prophetic time is established, as he adds, "And that this text is meant of the Messiah,
Jesus Christ to come, is granted by the best interpreters." [43]

V. Aspinwall—Echoes Fifth Monarchy Dream

WILLIAM ASPINWALL (fl. 1630-1662), who came over with
Winthrop, was an eminent man in the colony, a deacon in the
Boston church, and a member of the General Court. In 1637 he
was disfranchised and expelled from the Court for his anti-
nomianism, whereupon he went to Providence with Ann Hutchinson's party; but in 1642 he returned, and his submission was
accepted by both church and government.[44] Slight echoes of the
"Fifth Kingdome" emphasis in Britain reached the colonial
shores in his tractate, *A Brief Description of the Fifth Monarchy,
or Kingdome that shortly is to come into the World* (1653). The
four monarchies of Daniel 2 and 7, he holds, soon will be superseded by the everlasting and universal fifth monarchy of God.[45]
It is also the stone cut out of the mountain without hands, with
Christ as the Sovereign.[46] This will bring to an end "that
mother of harlots (which is the very stump of the fourth Monarchy)." [47] And this will be followed by the thousand-year reign
and rule of Christ, during this fifth monarchy.[48]

Attempting to give a "hint of the time," Aspinwall suggested it should not be later than 1673, by which time the "ten
horns, or kings, which are the strength of the beast," should be
broken. But "as for the precise yeare, I dare not determine." [49]
It is brief, but indicates the common interest in prophecy.

---

[42] *Ibid.*, p. 42.
[43] *Ibid.*
[44] F. C. Gray, "Remarks on the Early Laws of Massachusetts Bay," *Collections of the Massachusetts Historical Society*, 3d series, vol. 8, pp. 193, 194.
[45] William Aspinwall, *A Brief Description of the Fifth Monarchy, or Kingdome that shortly is to come into the World*, p. 2.
[46] *Ibid.*
[47] *Ibid.*, p. 3, citing Revelation 17 and 19.
[48] *Ibid.*, p. 4.
[49] *Ibid.*, p. 14.

VI. Wigglesworth—Day of Deliverance Drawing Nigh

A unique witness with a poetic bent now appears—MICHAEL WIGGLESWORTH (1631-1705), minister, physician, and poet of Malden, Massachusetts. Born in Yorkshire, England, he came to Massachusetts Bay with his Puritan parents when only seven, settling in New Haven, Connecticut. He went to school to Ezekiel Cheever, who will be noted a little later, and completed his education at Harvard, where he was soundly converted. Tutoring from 1652 to 1654, he began preaching in 1653, without ordination. He was ordained in 1656 and preached at Malden. He also studied and practiced medicine. He was offered the presidency of Harvard in 1684, but declined it because of ill-health.

Called by Tyler the "rhymer of the Five Points of Calvinism," he phrased in verse the faith of Puritan New England. His poems stress the prevalent concept of total depravity—the most of men doomed in advance to "an endless existence of ineffable torment." Such was the general theme. One poem was called "God's Controversy with New England." Wigglesworth is rated as the most representative poet of New England.[50]

In 1653 Wigglesworth dreamed of the "dreadful day of judgment," and so wrote the noted book-poem, *The Day of Doom* (1662). Called "an epic of New England Puritanism in dramatic form," it had an immediate sale of 1,800. As in all of New England there were then only 36,000 settlers, it can be rightly named a best seller—one to every twenty persons. It ran through sixteen editions and was much read in the latter part of the seventeenth century. The bibliographer Evans declares that for a century it was more popular than any other book save the Bible and exercised an influence secondary only to the Bible and Shorter Catechism.[51] It pictured death, the resurrection, and the advent in dramatic form. Ardently religious, Wigglesworth wrote only to "serve God."

---

[50] Moses C. Tyler, *History of American Literature*, vol. 2, pp. 23-25; Thomas J. Wertenbaker, *The First Americans*, p. 243.
[51] Charles Evans, *American Bibliography*, vol. 1, p. 15.

The opening lines read:

> "Still was the Night, serene and bright,
>   When all Men Sleeping lay,
> Calm was the Season and carnal Reason,
>   Thought it would last for ay:
> Soul take thine Ease, let Sorrow cease,
>   Much good thou hast in store;
> This was their Song, their Cups among,
>   The Evening before."

Then comes the great surprise.

> "For at Midnight, brake forth a Light,
>   Which turn'd the Night to Day,
> And speedily an hidous cry
>   Did all the World dismay.
> Sinners awake, their Hearts do ake,
>   Trembling, their Loins surprizeth,
> Amaz'd with Fear with what they hear
>   Each one of them ariseth.
>
> "They rush from Beds with giddy Heads,
>   And to their Windows run,
> Viewing this Light which shone more bright
>   Then doth the Noon-Day Sun;
> Streightway appears (they see't with Tears)
>   The Son of God most dread,
> Who with His Train comes on amain,
>   To Judge both Quick and Dead.
>
> "Before his Face the Heavens give place,
>   And Skies are Rent Asunder,
> With mighty Voice and hidous Noise
>   More terrible than Thunder
> His Brightness damps Heaven's glorious Lamps,
>   And makes them hide their Heads
> As if afraid and quite dismay'd,
>   They quit their wonted steads.
>
> "Ye Sons of Men that durst contemn
>   The Threatenings of God's Word,
> How chear you now? your Hearts (I trow)
>   Are thrill'd as with a Sword,
> Now Atheists blind, whose Brutish Mind
>   A God could never see:
> Dost thou perceive, dost thou believe,
>   That Christ thy Judge shall be?" [52]

[52] Michael Wigglesworth, *The Day of Doom* (1711 ed.), pp. 1, 2.

The moving lines depict the consternation of earth's potentates, captains, and men of might, the lamentation, the hiding in rocks and caves, the cry to insensate boulders for shelter, the coming of the Judge, the smoking mountains, the supernal glory, the sounding trump, the rising of the dead to judgment.

> "The Judge draws nigh, exalted high,
>   Upon a lofty Throne,
> Amidst the Throng of Angels strong,
>   like Israel's holy one.
> The excellence of whose Presence,
>   and awful Majesty,
> Amazeth Nature, and every Creature,
>   doth more than terrifie.

> "The Mountains Smoak, the Hills are shook,
>   The Earth is rent and torn,
> As if she should be clean disolv'd,
>   or from her Centre born.
> The Sea doth Roar, forsake the shoar,
>   and shrinks away for fear;
> The Wild Beasts flee into the Sea,
>   as soon as he draws near;

> "Whose glory bright, whose wondrous might,
>   Whose Power Imperial,
> So far surpass, whatever was
>   in Realms Terrestrial,
> That Tongues of Men (nor Angels Pen)
>   cannot the same express,
> And therefore I must pass it by,
>   least speaking should transgress." [53]

Such were the scenes made vivid and fresh to all in this remarkable poem. Finally, in a Postscript to the Reader, the advent note rings out:

> "The Day of your Deliverance draweth near.
> Lift up your Heads, ye upright ones in Heart,
> **Who in Christ's Purchase** have obtained a part,
> Behold he Rides upon a Shining Cloud,
> With Angels Voice, and Trumpet sounding loud.
> He comes to save his Folk from all their Foes,
> And plague the Men that Holiness oppose.
> So, Come Lord Jesus, quickly come away.
> We pray thee come, hast our Redemption Day." [54]

---

[53] *Ibid.*, p. 4.   [54] *Ibid.*, p. 67.

VII. Historian Johnson—Rome the "Seat and Center" of Beast

Historians add their bit as will be seen of EDWARD JOHNSON (1598-1672), early colonial chronicler, who was born in Herne Hill, Kent, England. In 1630 he emigrated from Kent to Massachusetts Bay Colony, bringing the dominant religious conceptions of England with him. In 1636 he settled in Charlestown, Massachusetts, during the midst of the antinomian controversies. Getting his theological bearings from Thomas Shepard, he found his perplexities over this issue vanishing. A man of property, in 1643 he became one of the founders of Woburn, and for thirty-two years identified himself with its public activities. He was entrusted with every office within the gift of his fellow townsmen—proprietor, clerk, selectman, captain of militia, deputy to the General Court, and inspector. He kept his head in the witchcraft excitement.[55] Johnson's fame rests on the reliability of his realistic *History of New-England (1628-52),* begun in 1650, and commonly called *Wonder-working Providence of Sions Saviour.* It was a defense of New England and of God's planting of His church here. This was his simple objective. But into this also were wrought his views of prophecy.

1. LONGING FOR OVERTHROW OF MAN OF SIN.—Historian Johnson looked upon Anglican ritualism as harking back to paganism. To deliver from this, he maintained that God had raised up a New England that the people might engage in "the service of the King of Kings."[56] He discusses the "time of Antichrists fall," refers to Antichrist as "Babylon," stresses the call to come out of her,[57] and tells how she is to be burnt up root and branch.[58] He states as a commonplace that "it hath been the longing expectation of many, to see that notable and wonderfull worke of the Lord Christ, in casting down that man of sin who hath held the whole world (of those that profess any Christ) under his Lordly power."[59]

---

[55] Tyler, *op. cit.,* vol. 1, p. 138.
[56] *Ibid.,* p. 139.
[57] Edward Johnson, *A History of New-England (1628-52),* p. 231; (Anonymous; identified in Samuel Halkett and John Laing, *Dictionary of Anonymous and Pseudonymous English Literature,* vol. 3, p. 72.) (Title page reproduced on p. 56.)
[58] *Ibid.,* p. 123.   [59] *Ibid.,* p. 230.

2. ITALY THE SEAT AND CENTER OF BEAST.—Early in his history Johnson utters these remarkable words: "Listen a while, hear what his herauld proclaimes, *Babylon* is fallen, is fallen, both her Doctrine & Lordly rabble of Popes, Cardinalls, Lordly-Bishops." [60] Then to Italy he exclaims pointedly, "Oh Italy! the Seat and Center of the Beast, Christ will pick out a People from among you for himself." And to Spain he says, "Oh! Yee Spaniards and Portugalls, Christ will shew you all abominations of that beastly Whore, who hath made your Nations drunke with the Wine of her Fornication." [61] Such is the ideology of prophecy and its very terms, employed by Historian Johnson. Whatever the vocation or religious persuasion, the language of prophecy was understood by all.

VIII. Norton—Looked for Speedy Second Advent at Resurrection

JOHN NORTON (1606-1663), Congregationalist Puritan pastor at New Ipswich, Massachusetts, and Cotton's successor, was born in Herfordshire, England, and graduated from Cambridge University with a B.A. in 1627. He soon became curate at Stortford, where he was spiritually reborn, and subsequently was chaplain to Sir William Masham. Proficient in the "tongues and arts," he gave himself to the study of divinity. He disliked rites and ceremonies, and, because of his growing Puritanism, declined several advances involving compromise. This drove him away from England, and in 1634 he sailed with Thomas Shepard for America. They had a narrow escape from shipwreck, Shepard gathering the sailors above deck, and Norton between decks, for earnest prayer. Turned back by the storm, they sailed again and reached Plymouth harbor.

Norton settled in Massachusetts Bay, became "teacher" in the church of Ipswich, and was ordained in 1638. In 1645 he wrote the first book to be composed in Latin in this country,[62] on church government. And in 1647 he was one of those appointed

---

[60] *Ibid.*, p. 24. [61] *Ibid.*, p. 33.
[62] Cotton Mather, *Magnalia*, book 3, The First Part, chap. 2, sec. 14, p. 34. (It was entitled *Responsio ad totam quaestionum syllogen a clarissimo viro.* London: Crook, 1648.)

to draw up revisions for the proposed *Platform of Church Discipline*,[63] accepted by the famous 1648 Synod at Cambridge, in which he had a leading part. He succeeded to John Cotton's pastorate in Boston in 1652, upon the latter's suggestion, and in 1654 was instated as overseer of Harvard. In 1662 he accompanied Bradstreet as an agent of the colonies to petition Charles II to continue civil and religious liberties, with pure Scripture worship and a good conscience, and without conformity.

He was bigoted and tyrannical in certain matters and had a prominent part in the persecution of the Quakers. A real scholar and grammarian, he was both an able speaker and a forceful writer. He was also an ardent student of the prophecies and held views similar to those of Shepard. Such are the inconsistencies of frail humanity. He was author of numerous works, the most important being *The Orthodox Evangelist* (1654), dealing with God, Christ, justification, and the future estate of the saints. He, too, looked to the near, premillennial coming of Christ, and the resurrection of the body at that time.[64]

IX. Layman Holyoke—Prophecies Concerning the Papacy

Laymen as well as ministers delved into prophecy and made substantial contribution. EDWARD HOLYOKE (d. 1660), Congregationalist layman of Lynn, Massachusetts, and great-grandfather of Edward Holyoke, president of Harvard, was from Tamworth, Warwickshire. Early in life his mind was directed to sacred things, and in 1612, just before his marriage, he wrote a remarkable letter to his fiancée, declaring he was resolved to "follow the Eternal," and to "cleave unto Him" all his days. Listing many particulars, and pledging his love and life, he stressed in it all preparation for eternal union "with Christ Jesus in the last day." [65] Coming to America, he settled in Lynn, where he became a farmer and landowner of 500 acres, a man of note in the colony and honored in its councils. He was a

---

[63] *Ibid.*, pp. 34, 35.
[64] John Norton, *The Orthodox Evangelist*, pp. 354, 355.
[65] Alonzo Lewis and J. R. Newhall, *History of Lynn, Essex County, Massachusetts (1629-1864)*, pp. 121-124.

member of the Essex court, and represented Lynn in the Massachusetts Legislature for many years, between 1639 and 1648.[66]

Holyoke wrote a unique book on prophecy titled *The Doctrine of Life, or of Mans Redemtion* (1658), in question-and-answer form. He held to a calling of the Jews, but not to restoration to their former land, declaring that idea to be fraught with absurdities. But the day of the Lord's coming was the insistent note of his book and his life. In his will Holyoke bequeathed to each of his sons-in-law—of course with other things—a copy of his book.

" (Being instructed chiefly by an understanding of the Scriptures) I doubt not my booke will giue him A hart of all sound doctrine." [67]

1. THRONE OF PROPHESIED BEAST IN ROME.—The heading of chapter 15, in his *Doctrine of Life* (1658), is devoted to "proving that Rome in Gods just judgement, is the place that he hath given unto the power of Satan for the setting up the mystery of iniquity." [68] Answering the specific question as to "what place," Holyoke says succinctly, "Rome in Italy," and adds:

"Satan used all signes, and lying wonders to advance there the Throne of the Beast, the man of sin, or the Pontificalitie: And when the Pontificalitie was set up by the decree of God, then nations from East to West; obeyed and Worship the Pope, and the image of the Imperial State as of old time they did the profane Emperours." [69]

The Beast's imperial state was thus re-erected in the pontificality.[70]

2. BEAST OF DANIEL 7 AND OF REVELATION 13 IDENTICAL.— Discussing the prophetic symbols of the Roman Empire, Holyoke says, under Question 6:

"The Empire is described by one Beast coming out of the Sea, who hath seven heads and ten horns: yea also in this Beast is comprized the Pontificality, being the Reviver of the wounded Head. This beast hath his arms, from the four Beasts in Daniel chap. 7. For Rome having subdued all those Countries that those Beasts ruled, and being like them for idolatry

---

[66] James Savage, *A Genealogical Dictionary of First Settlers of New England*, vol. 2, p. 456.
[67] Lewis and Newhall, *op. cit.*, p. 122.
[68] Edward Holyoke, *The Doctrine of Life, or of Mans Redemtion*, p. 215.
[69] *Ibid.*   [70] *Ibid.*, p. 236.

and cruelty in afflicting the holy city descending from heaven, is a monster compounded of all four: Being a Beaste of seven heads and ten horns, mouthed like a Lion, footed like a Bear, and spotted like a Leopard." [71]

It is also the embodiment of the power prophesied in 2 Thessalonians 2,[72] and is likewise the two-horned Beast.[73]

3. SIXTH HEAD, CAESARS; SEVENTH, POPES.—Interpreting the seven heads, Holyoke says that these are first the seven hills on which Rome was built, and secondly seven kinds of government—"1. Kings, 2. Consulls, 3. Decemviri, 4. Dictators, 5. Triumviri, 6. Caesars, 7. Pope." [74]

4. TEN HORNS ARE ROME'S DIVISIONS.—The ten horns are the kingdom-divisions of Rome that gave power to the Beast.[75]

"The four Beasts are termed four Kings, that is four Kingdomes, Daniel chap. 7. So the ten horns of the Roman Beast are ten Kings that is Kingdomes that gave their power to the Beast." [76]

5. HISTORICAL GROWTH OF MYSTERY OF INIQUITY.—Chapter 15 contends that the Mystery of Iniquity began the struggle for supremacy from Constantine's time:

"From Constantines time, Ecclesiasticall Teachers were never quiet, but still aspired after Supremacy, and drew Princes to their factions till 600 years after Christ, then about that time, Boniface the third Pope of Rome, obtained by the help of the murderer Phocas, to be called universall Bishop. And this universall Supremacy did so increase untill the tenth Century." [77]

It reached its height, Holyoke asserted, in the thirteenth, fourteenth, and fifteenth centuries.[78]

6. MARK OF THE BEAST IS YIELDING TO POPE'S LAW.—Declaring the mark of the Beast to be the mark of his "Politie," he says:

"The Popes Canon-Law telleth that none may live under the Empire, but by yielding to the Popes Lawes, in his subscribing to his Imperial and Ecclesiasticall Supremacy, and oath of fidelity as a mark on the hand, and some open token of communion with him, and profession of his decrees as a mark in the forehead." [79]

---

[71] *Ibid.*, p. 218.
[72] *Ibid.*, pp. 220, 222.
[73] *Ibid.*, pp. 219, 236.
[74] *Ibid.*, p. 226; see also pp. 216, 219, 220.
[75] *Ibid.*, p. 220.
[76] *Ibid.*, p. 222.
[77] *Ibid.*, p. 229.
[78] *Ibid.*, p. 230. (They are listed on page 226.)
[79] *Ibid.*, p. 236.

Holyoke held that the papal power began decreasing from Protestant Reformation times onward,[80] then stressed the call to come out of Mystical Babylon, for her everlasting destruction was near at hand.[81]

7. TURKS ARE THE SIXTH TRUMPET.—Declaring that the Turks were raised up to be a scourge to the "Apostasie of the Greek Churches," [82] Holyoke thought the locusts of the fifth trumpet to be the papal clergy and the monks.[83]   And some in the Old World had thought the same.

---

[80] *Ibid.*, p. 237.
[81] *Ibid.*, p. 240.

[82] *Ibid.*, pp. 261, 267.
[83] *Ibid.*, pp. 216, 217.

CHAPTER FIVE

Laymen, Governors, and Educators Expound

Variety of vocation characterizes the witnesses who testify to their understanding of the prophecies. They are noticeably men of learning, promise, and leadership in their respective communities. Their testimony carries weight. But they wrote as individuals, not as members of a group organized or meeting for the study of prophecy. The exposition of prophecy was, however, a common interest among men in all walks of life, and the terms and symbols of prophecy were familiar to all and had the same general connotation. In this chapter we summon five more ministers, a layman, a catechist, a governor, and another Harvard president. In addition, we hear the concerted testimony of the *Confession of Faith* of the New England churches concerning Antichrist—the only instance of its kind in the colonial period. We shall now hear their witness.

I. Layman Hutchinson—2300 Years Not Yet Run Out

SAMUEL HUTCHINSON (1618-1667), bachelor, layman, scholar, and author of one of the early avowedly premillennial volumes treating on the prophecies to be written in America, was "of Boston in New England," as the title page of his treatise puts it. Biographical data is meager, but his life is summed up in this terse sentence:

"Samuel Hutchinson, the brother of William, lived in Boston, unmarried, until his death, 1667, and was accounted a scholar in his time, and published a work on the Millennium." [1]

His book, in the form of a "Letter sent to a Friend," [2] in England, was published by the "Friend," who signed himself "T.T.," and whose advent hymns adorn the work. [3] Hutchinson was well read, and buttresses his positions with numerous citations from the early and Reformation churches.   He also quotes freely from such seventeenth-century Old World writers as Mede, Archer, Caryl, Sterry, Alstead, Tillinghast, Holmes, Goodwin, Mercer, and the colonial John Davenport of New Haven.   Hutchinson, however, has Christ and the saints on earth during the millennium, and at the close ascending to heaven to reign.   Hutchinson rightly calls the details "tedious," but the uniqueness and the importance of this treatise amply justify a survey of its laborious discussions. [4]   Here is an over-all concept of the last things.

1. CHANGES ATTENDANT UPON THE ADVENT.—In the introduction "T.T." tabulates in verse the "fifteen changes" believed to mark the second "Personal Appearance" of King Jesus, when the seventh angel sounds:

"1. The Saints deceased ....Royal Jesus brings:
  2. The rest released, ...Mount on Angels Wings.
  3. To Israel's Mourning, ...Sounds a glorious Call:
  4. To Babels Burning, ...An eternal Fall.
  5. The World combined, ...Hath a fatal Blow;
  6. Satan confined ....To his Den below.
  7. The whole Creation ....Findes a full Release;
  8. And every Nation ....Flourisheth with Peace.
  9. The Mount asunder ....Cleaves t' enlarge the plain.
    (That Vale of Wonder ....Where the Lord must reign)
 10. The glorious City ....From Gods Throne doth glide:
 11. The Nuptial Ditty ....Ushers in the Bride.
 12. Thus Saints regaining ....An immortal state,

---

[1] "Memoir of Governor Hutchinson," *The New England Historical and Genealogical Register*, October, 1847 (vol. 1, no. 4), p. 299. See also W. H. Whitmore, "A Brief Genealogy of the Hutchinson Family," *Ibid.*, January, 1865 (vol. 19, no. 1), pp. 14, 15.
[2] Samuel Hutchinson, *A Declaration of a Future Glorious Estate of a Church to be here upon Earth, at Christs Personal Appearance for the Restitution of all things, a Thousand Years before the Ultimate day of the General Judgement*, p. 3.
[3] *Ibid.*, pp. 3, 18, 19.
[4] *Ibid.*, pp. 4, 8.

13. In glory reigning _____While the Sun bears date.
14. The Nations bending, _____Virgin Voices raise;
15. All Duties ending _____In Joy, Love, and Praise." [5]

Number 9 is to be noted especially.

2. MILLENNIUM BOUNDED BY TWO RESURRECTIONS.—At the very outset Hutchinson expressly declares, "I do not approve of such Fifth-Monarchy-Men as taking up Arms against Commonwealths and Governments." He supported only the true "Fifth-Monarchy-Men that Daniel prophesied of, Dan. 2. 44, 45. and 7.13,14. which will not be till Christ appear in the Clouds, for the Restitution of all things, according to Act. 3:20." [6] The treatise proper begins with "A Letter sent to a Friend in Old England," in answer to a letter written in 1659. Noting opposite opinions held by good men, Hutchinson rightly places the two resurrections a thousand years apart, but with the ascension of the saints into the clouds to be forever in heaven at the end of the thousand years. The annihilation of all things is at the "ultimate Day of Judgment," which he places at the millennium's close.[7] The wicked dead are not raised till then,[8] and this will be followed by the eternal state.[9]

3. TAKES KINGLY OFFICE AT SECOND ADVENT.—Referring to Christ's prophetical and priestly offices, contingent upon His first advent, Hutchinson observes, "But his Kingly Office personally he would not then take, because that he reserved till his second coming." [10] He looked for the conversion of the Jews during the thousand years.[11] This thought he frequently weaves into his treatise.

4. STONE NOT YET CUT OUT OF MOUNTAIN.—In the body of the work Hutchinson declares that the saints must reign with Christ on earth during the thousand years, as was held generally in primitive times. Approving the position in the catechism in the days of Edward VI, that they "saw not yet the little Stone cut out of the Mountain without hands, that should break to

---

5 *Ibid.*, p. 3.
6 *Ibid.*, p. 3.
7 *Ibid.*, pp. 4, 5.
8 *Ibid.*, p. 5; compare p. 8 and title.
9 *Ibid.*, p. 8.
10 *Ibid.*, p. 6.
11 *Ibid.*, pp. 6, 7.

pieces all the Kingdomes of the Earth," [12] he declares the Davidic promise of a visible kingdom wherein the righteous dwell, will be fulfilled in the new earth and the New Jerusalem,[13] during the thousand years. Then enmity shall cease and the Little Horn's persecutions end forever. Though his phrasings are a bit tedious, it is highly desirable to follow his own words:

"For before this *New Jerusalem come,* there must be such troubles as never was upon the face of the Earth, for it is said in Dan. 7.21. That *the Little Horn made War with the Saints, and prevailed against them;* and if ye ask how long? he tells you in Vers. 22. *Until the Ancient of Days came, and Judgement was given to the Saints of the most High; and the time came that the Saints possessed the Kingdom;* and then, as in Vers. 26. *The Judgement shall sit, and they shall take away his Dominion to consume and destroy it to the end.* God shall then so destroy this little Horn, that it shall never rise again. And then, as in Vers. 27. *The Kingdom and Dominion, and the greatness of the Kingdom under the whole Heaven, shall be given to the People of the Saints of the most High, whose Kingdom is an everlasting Kingdom, and all Dominions shall serve and obey him."* [14]

5. ANTICHRIST CONTINUES UNTIL SECOND ADVENT.—Not till the second advent will Antichrist be destroyed. Note Hutchinson's exact phrasing:

"Now before this great Restitution of all things, we must expect Christ's second coming, before which Antichrist will never utterly be destroyed, according to that in *2 Thess. 2.8.* where it is said, *He will destroy him with the brightness of his coming,* that is, by his Personal Appearing, according that in *Dan. 7.21.* where it is said, *The Little Horn made War with the Saints, and prevailed against them;* then if you demand how long, he tells you in the next verse, *till the Ancient of Days came, and Judgement was given to the Saints of the most High; and the time came that the Saints possessed the Kingdom."* [15]

All this involves the great battle of Armageddon.[16]

6. WICKED DESTROYED AT THE ADVENT.—Again, citing Tillinghast, Hutchinson stresses the approaching advent of Christ when He comes as a flaming fire to destroy the wicked.[17] So long as the church is in the world she shall have trouble. Only by the advent will she be delivered. The Little Horn is clearly identified:

---

[12] *Ibid.,* pp. 8, 9.   [14] *Ibid.,* p. 13.   [15] *Ibid.,* p. 15.
[13] *Ibid.,* pp. 9, 13; see also p. 36.   [16] *Ibid.,* p. 17.
[17] *Ibid.,* pp. 15, 16. Tillinghast is discussed in Volume 2 of *Prophetic Faith.*

"Thus we see, as in Dan. 7. 21, 22. *The Little Horn,* which is the Papal Power, *made war with the Saints, and prevailed against them,* till Christ appeared for the delivering of them: But when they made war with the Lamb, as in Rev. 17.14. *The Lamb overcame them, for He is Lord of Lords, and King of Kings; and they that are with him are Called, Chosen, and Faithful.* Thus we see the Church that shall never be delivered from all her troubles, till Christ appear in the Clouds for the Restitution of all things." [18]

7. EXECUTIVE JUDGMENT AT MILLENNIUM'S CLOSE.—What many look for as heaven, Hutchinson holds, will be "a Heaven upon earth," because "they shall have no Devil to tempt them all that Thousand Years." At the close of this period he will have power to tempt all for that "little season." Hutchinson places the judgment during the thousand years. Then comes the "ultimate day of judgment." [19] After a roll call of the "received opinion" of the advocates of Christ's personal reign on earth, recorded in the early centuries—Justin Martyr, Irenaeus, Tertullian, Cyprian, Methodius, and others, Hutchinson cites Holmes and Alstead and others to sustain the position that the wicked are raised at the close of the thousand years. [20] He expressly states, concerning the thousand years, "I do not conceive that He [Christ] will be all that while upon the Earth." [21] He and the saints "may ascend from Earth to Heaven, and descend from Heaven to earth." The position of the Papacy over Europe is then discussed, and the assertion is made that the ruin of Rome will come when she is in her "full strength," and seemingly "most secure." [22] He appeals for a greater study of the doctrine of the kingdom. [23]

8. "PROGNOSTICKS" OF APPROACHING GLORIOUS ESTATE.— The various "Prognosticks" of the approach of the glorious estate are alluded to—the state of the Turk and the Papacy, the earth filled with wickedness, and the strange celestial signs of Matthew 24, with war and tribulations. [24] The seals, trumpets, and vials he thinks are well fulfilled, [25] and the raising of the witnesses awaited. As to the time of the advent, Hutchinson

[18] *Ibid.,* p. 17.
[19] *Ibid.,* p. 17; cf. p. 24.
[20] *Ibid.,* pp. 20-22.
[21] *Ibid.,* p. 23.
[22] *Ibid.,* p. 24.
[23] *Ibid.,* p. 25.
[24] *Ibid.,* p. 25.
[25] *Ibid.*

says that from Daniel 12 "We may know the very year of Christ's coming to judgment for the Restitution of all things," a thousand years "before the ultimate day of the general Judgment by the Scriptures alone." The prophetic day stands for a year, and the 1290 and 1335 are years. Thus he says, in the heavy style that characterizes his entire treatise:

> "The Church, we know, was to remain in the Wilderness 1290 days, as appears in Dan. 12.11. that is, as Interpreters expound it, 1290 years: Now the Witnesses being once raised, it shews the expiration of those years in the which the Church was to remain in the Wilderness; and that 45 years after, Christ should appear in the Clouds, as you may see, Vers. 12. compared with 13. and therefore in Vers. 12. he saith, *Blessed is he that waiteth, and cometh to the 1335 days;* that is years: And why blessed? Because then, as you may see in Vers. 13. *Daniel* must be raised again from the dead, and stand in the end of his Lot; this is the time that *Christ* will appear with all his Saints and Angels, for the judging those that are upon the Earth, for the Conversion of the Jews, and for the bringing in or the fulness of the Gentiles, a thousand years before the ultimate day of the general Judgement: So that though the day and hour of *Christ's* coming is kept secret, yet the year is made manifest, beyond which it cannot be, according to *Daniel's* accompt: Sooner it may be, because our Saviour tells us, in *Mat.* 24. *That for the Elects sake, those days shall be shortened;* to teach us all to watch and pray, and wait continually for the appearing of Jesus *Christ,* lest that day come upon us unawares." [26]

Citing Tillam, Hutchinson asserts that the last events of Daniel 11 and Revelation 16, involving the Turk and the drying up of the Euphrates, will be followed by the standing up of Michael and the deliverance of His ancient people by His glorious second advent. Then will occur the destruction of the Man of Sin.[27] The New Jerusalem as a literal city is to descend to the spacious plain created for it by the cleaving of the Mount of Olives.[28]

9. 2300 YEARS NOT YET RUN OUT.—Hutchinson then discusses the relationship of the 2300 years to the 1290 and 1335 years, citing Mercer, and leaving this significant record:

> "But in the number of years I do acknowledge that I cannot bring them to a just sum; for so much as the 2300 is not double as much as 1290: But this thing I shall leave to the all-seeing Providence, as all other things are

---

[26] *Ibid.,* p. 26.   [27] *Ibid.,* pp. 27, 28.   [28] *Ibid.,* p. 30.

to be left to him. But this, I conceive, is certain, that if we take that Idol of Desolation set up by Antiochus in the Temple, to be it, then the 2300 years are not yet out; and if we take the Desolation of Jerusalem by Titus, to be it, then the 1290 days, are much past; and if we take the polluting of the Ordinances to be it, then it is not yet fulfilled: However, I must leave it as a secret, touching the time, waiting when the Lord will deliver His People." [29]

Stressing the special work given to each generation, Hutchinson quotes Tillinghast approvingly as saying, *"To disobey then the visible Call of a Dispensation . . . is to disobey the command of God."* [30] He then quotes Holmes to the effect that the work of this generation is to stand for Christ's coming kingdom, which impends. [31] Such will have a hiding place from the coming storm.

In a bit of verse Hutchinson leads us to the gates of eternity and the "everlasting Day," and closes his discussion:

> "The Heavens and the Earth must fly away,
>   But that must be at the ultimate Day,
>   When Christ, his Saints and Angels all, shall be
>   In highest Heavens to Eternity.
>   Thus Christ delivers all up to his Father,
>   That God may be all in all, when together
>   All Saints and Angels are mounted on high.
>   To live with God and Christ Eternally.
>   To sing Hallelujah's forever and aye,
>   And this is that great everlasting Day. S.H." [32]

So spoke this interesting layman.

II. Catechist Vincent—Papal Church Seat of Antichrist

THOMAS VINCENT (1634-1678), English nonconformist, was born in Herford, England, and graduated from Christ's Church, Oxford, with an M.A. in 1654. He was chosen a catechist in the same year, but left Oxford to become a chaplain. In 1656 he connected with Cambridge and became rector of St. Mary Magdalene's Church, London. But in 1662 he was ejected by the Act of Uniformity. He retired to Hoxton, where he preached

---

[29] *Ibid.*, p. 31.
[30] *Ibid.*, p. 32.
[31] *Ibid.*
[32] *Ibid.*, p. 34.

privately, assisting in a school at Bunhill Fields. In 1667 he wrote a graphic account of the Great Plague and the Great Fire in London—*God's Terrible Voice in the City* (1667). He developed a large congregation at Hoxton and suffered persecution for his nonconformity. He was the author of numerous writings, his *Explicatory Catechism* of 1673 being frequently reprinted up to 1848, the Northampton 1805 edition being extensively circulated in America.

The temper and testimony of this "Explanation of the Assembly's Shorter Catechism" is evidenced by the rejection of the position of the Catholic Church concerning the Scriptures and tradition, for these reasons:

1. "Because the church, on whose testimony they say, the scriptures do depend, is an apostate and corrupt church, and the seat of Antichrist. 2. Because the true church of Christ doth depend in its being on the scriptures; and therefore the scriptures cannot depend upon the church for its authority." [33]

III. Hooke—End of Papal 1260 Years Approaching

WILLIAM HOOKE (1601-1678), pastor at New Haven, Massachusetts, and colleague of John Davenport, was born in Southampton, England, and educated at Trinity College, Oxford. Coming to New England, he first went to Taunton, where he was ordained, and then settled in New Haven. He later returned to England, where he served as chaplain to Oliver Cromwell. Through Davenport, he became a premillennialist, and was joint author of a preface to Davenport's *The Saints Anchor-Hold in all Storms and Tempests*.[34] In this, Hooke writes of the "last days, in which God is shaking Heaven, Earth, and Sea" before the "appearing of the Desire of all Nations." [35]

Hooke "loved the study of prophecy" and the second advent, and wrote eight treatises thereon between 1640 and 1681. His best-known work was *The Priviledge of the Saints on Earth*

---

[33] Thomas Vincent, *Explicatory Catechism* (1805 reprint), p. 16.
[34] The preface is signed by "W.H." and "J.C.," identified in the British Museum catalogue as W. Hooke and J. Caryl.
[35] William Hooke, "Preface to the Christian Reader," A₂ v., in John Davenport, *The Saints Anchor-Hold in all Storms and Tempests*.

Beyond Those in Heaven to which is added, A Short Discourse of the Nature and Extent of the Gospel-day (1673). He endorsed Increase Mather's strong position on the premillennial advent and literal resurrection, writing an extended preface to Mather's *The Mystery of Israel's Salvation Explained and Applied* (1669). In this, Hooke declares, quoting the words of Scripture:

> "*As the lightning cometh out of the East and shineth even to the West, so shall the coming of the Son of man be,* who shall come as a thief in the night, under the sixth vial, when he shall appear at the setting up of his Kingdom." [36]

1. ANTICHRIST AND TURK PERISH BEFORE ADVENT.—Antichrist, Hooke insists, must be finished and destroyed under the seventh trumpet, and the power of the Turk dried up under the sixth vial, with the destruction of Rome coming about the same time—the second coming of Christ being after the sixth vial. [37]

2. SIXTH TRUMPET, OR OTTOMAN POWER, BEGAN 1300.—Hooke places the beginning of the papal apostasy period in the sixth century, adding, "As the Centuries increased, so did the Darkness," [38] through increasing errors and heresies. As John began to show "things to come," he revealed them through the seals and trumpets and vials. [39] The first four trumpets were judgments, the fifth was the papal "smoak" from the bottomless pit, [40] while of the sixth trumpet Hooke says, "The Sixth Trumpet, which began to sound about the Year 1300. when the Ottoman Power arose, which yet continueth to this day." [41]

3. ONLY GOD KNOWS EXACT EPOCH OF BEAST.—The greatest height of the papal Antichrist was shortly before the Reformation, Hooke believed. Some suppose its rise was in the fourth or fifth centuries. The experience of the Two Witnesses must

---

[36] William Hooke, "To the Reader," b₄ v, in Increase Mather, *The Mystery of Israel's Salvation Explained and Applied* (preface signed "W. H."; identified in Thomas J. Holmes, *Increase Mather*, vol. 2, p. 354).
[37] *Ibid.*
[38] William Hooke, *A Short Discourse of the Nature and Extent of the Gospel-Day*, p. 131 of *The Priviledge of the Saints on Earth . . . to which is added a Short Discourse of the . . . Gospel-Day.*
[39] *Ibid.*, p. 132.   [41] *Ibid.*, p. 134.
[40] *Ibid.*, pp. 131, 133.

parallel it, and continue 1260 days, "a day put for a year." [42]
Only the Lord knows the precise "epocha of the reign of the
Beast, and his Number, 666." [43]   But Antichrist shall be "greatly
consumed with the breath of Christs mouth." [44]   Then the Pope
and the Turk shall be destroyed.[45]   Hooke declares that darkness
grew in proportion to the exaltation of the Man of Sin, but the
night is far spent and the day is at hand.[46]

4. BABYLON'S FALL COMES AT ADVENT.—Babylon's fall, and
the establishment of the kingdom, come at the second advent.
Agreeing with Davenport's views, Hooke adds his longings for
the accomplishment of the great things of those last days.   He
fervently declares:

> "We should love the Kingdom of Christ above all the Kingdoms in
> the World. . . . Let the Kingdom of the Lord Jesus come, whatever become
> of any Kingdom, or of all the Kingdoms under Heaven." [47]

IV. Governor Stoughton—Antichrist to Be Destroyed at Advent

WILLIAM STOUGHTON (1632-1701), Massachusetts justice
and colonial governor, was born in England, but was brought to
America in infancy.   Graduating from Harvard with an M.A. in
1650, he went to Oxford to study theology. He preached a while,
but returned to New England in 1662, becoming a noted
preacher but declining a settled charge.   His wealth, talent,
learning, dignity, and public spirit won him a large measure
of public confidence.[48]   He held all the great offices of the commonwealth.   He became a member of the Council, then a justice
of the Superior Court of Massachusetts.   In 1692 he was made
chief justice of the Special Tribunal for the fatal witchcraft
trials.   Departing from his usual cool judgment, he "became
a protagonist among the persecutors." [49]   In the same year he
was appointed lieutenant governor (1692-1701), which post he
held till death; and was acting governor for a time.[50]   He was

---

[42] *Ibid.*, p. 135.   [43] *Ibid.*, p. 140.   [44] *Ibid.*, p. 142.
[45] *Ibid.*, p. 146.   [46] *Ibid.*, "To the Reader" [118, 119].
[47] William Hooke, *The Priviledge of the Saints on Earth*, pp. 36, 37.
[48] Moses C. Tyler, *A History of American Literature During the Colonial Time*,
vol. 2, p. 161.   [49] *Ibid.*, p. 162.
[50] *Dictionary of American Biography*, vol. 18, art. "William Stoughton"; Frederick L.
Weis, *The Colonial Clergy and the Colonial Churches of New England*, p. 196.

a friend of Governor Joseph Dudley, likewise interested in prophecy. (Stoughton's portrait appears on page 34.)

Stoughton once said, "God sifted a whole nation that He [might] send His choice grain over into this wilderness." [51] Though not in the regular ministry, in 1668 he preached a remarkable election sermon,[52] *New-Englands True Interest; Not to Lie,* from which we quote:

> "It is not long before the Lord will *finish his great works* in the world: *Antichrist* shall be destroyed, *Israel* shall be saved, *Zion shall be redeemed with judgement, and her converts with righteousness;* though the Lord bear long with his Elect, yet he will avenge them speedily. That he *bears long,* hath been already fulfilled; what remains therefore to be accomplished, but only that now he *avenge them speedily?* . . . *Yet a little while and he that shall come will come, and will not tarry.* Blessed are they that *wait* for, and can abide the day of his coming. Shall we lose our *share* in those *times* of refreshment which are so near to come?" [53]

V. Samuel Mather—Antichrist's 1260-Year Reign Among the Ten Kingdoms

SAMUEL MATHER (1626-1671), minister at Rawley and Boston (1649), and older brother of Increase Mather, was born in Lancashire, England. Coming to New England in 1635, he was graduated from Harvard with an M.A., but returned to England in 1650, where the Lord Mayor of London noted his abilities and made him chaplain. Thus he became acquainted with the most prominent ministers of the kingdom. He was preacher at Gravesend and Oxford, and chaplain of Magdalen College, Oxford. Then he preached in Scotland for two years. But in 1655 he was back in England.

The "Romanizing faction in the church of England" was gaining, and a storm of persecution arose. Mather was chosen to preach against the "revival of those dead superstitions." So he preached two sermons in a great auditorium, contending

---

[51] William Stoughton, *New-Englands True Interest,* p. 19.
[52] Election sermons, it should be noted, were established by appointment of the governor and his assistants. By Charter of 1691 the last Wednesday of May was specified as annual election day, with a sermon before the legislative body as the order of the day. These sermons had wide circulation and frequently contained prophetic exposition or allusion. The first provincial Congress of 1774 gratefully acknowledged obligation to these preachers as friends of civil and religious liberty. See Justin Winsor, editor, *The Memorial History of Boston,* vol. 2, p. 247.
[53] Stoughton, *op. cit.,* pp. 32, 33.

that the compromising ceremonies were the old leaven of popish corruption, the ceremonies of Antichrist.[54] In 1662 Mather was one of 2,000 ministers expelled from all public places. He became increasingly interested in prophecy, and wrote to his younger brother, Increase Mather, later president of Harvard:

"I must needs tell you, how much I do rejoyce, that it hath pleased God to stir up your Spirit to search into the Prophetical Parts of the Scrip-tures; of which I have often thought and still do, That it is a great pity they are so little minded and seen into, by many, both ministers and others, who do deprive themselves of much satisfaction, which they might receive thereby." [55]

1. TEN KINGDOMS MAKE UP PAPAL KINGDOM.—Cotton Mather records him as a premillennialist and a thorough student of the prophetic numbers and times. He held that the ten king-doms were the ten horns of the papal kingdom wherein Anti-christ reigns, and that erelong the 1260 years would expire and God's kingdom come. Mather wrote *A Defence of the Protes-tant Christian Religion against Popery, wherein the manifold Apostasies, Heresies, and Schisms of the Church of Rome . . . are briefly laid open* (1672).[56]

2. SEVENTH TRUMP FOLLOWS THE 1260 YEARS.—Mather made special note of the fulfillments of prophecy already accom-plished, from "thence to make Computation of the Times, that were yet before us, and of the Things to be done in those Times." He makes this significant statement:

" 'That whenever God sets up in any of the ten Kingdoms, which made the ten Horns of the Papal Empire, such an Establishment, Sovereign and Independent, wherein antichrist shall Have . . . neither Power of Laws, nor Force of Arms, to defend him and his Corruptions; Doubtless, then, the Witnesses of our Lord, are not more trodden down, to prophecy in sack-cloth, any longer. Then therefore expires the 1260 Years, and since that such a Kingdom well may be called The Lord's, then will the seventh Trumpet begin to sound. Which, that it is Near, even, at the Door, I may say, through Grace, I doubt not.' " [57]

---

[54] Cotton Mather, *Magnalia*, book 4, part 2, chap. 2, sec. 10, pp. 147-150.
[55] *Ibid.*, sec. 14, p. 152.
[56] "By an English Protestant," but signed "S. M.," and identified in British Museum Catalogue as Samuel Mather.
[57] Cotton Mather, *Magnalia*, book 4, part 2, chap. 2, sec. 14, p. 152.

VI. Harvard President Oakes—Longs for Iron-Age to Expire

URIAN OAKES, or Oaks (c. 1631-1681), colonial poet, Congregational clergyman, and president of Harvard, was born in England. While yet a child he came to New England with his father, in 1634. He was graduated from Harvard in 1649, staying until he received his second degree and became a recognized Greek and Latin scholar. He preached his first sermon in Roxbury and tutored Harvard students from 1650 to 1652. Returning to England in 1653, he served as chaplain and pastor of Tichfield. But he was soon persecuted for his nonconformity and silenced by the Act of Uniformity. In 1662 he was headmaster of a grammar school, and when persecution of Dissenters abated, formed the Congregational church of Tichfield.

In 1671 Oakes was called to the Cambridge, Massachusetts, church in New England. With Increase Mather he was appointed censor of the Massachusetts press. A shining light, he twice declined the offer of the presidency of Harvard, but served as acting president, and finally was president from 1679 to 1681. He was a notable orator and writer, and he published several books of sermons and wrote the preface to Increase Mather's *Day of Trouble Is Near.*

President Oakes' faith was fixed on that "Glorious Day, when your Warfare shall be ended." [58] He urged all "Christian Souldiers" to "love and long for the Glorious Appearance of Christ." He admonished them to "Look upwards, and Sigh to Heaven," with the victory and triumph to be brought about "at the Appearing of the Lord Jesus Christ." [59] He was strongly premillennial in his beliefs.

Longing for "an End of the warres and bloud-sheds" that fill the world, he exclaims—reverting to the symbolism of Daniel 2 —"Oh when will this Iron-Age expire, and that glorious Morn appear." [60]

---

[58] Urian Oakes, *The Unconquerable, All-Conquering . . . Souldier* (1674), p. 36.
[59] *Ibid.,* p. 37.   [60] *Ibid.*

VII. United Testimony of Churches on Antichrist in 1680

Various individual catechisms had been published by Cotton, Norton, Mather, Davenport, Noyes, Eliot, and others.[61] Then the group statement of the Cambridge Synod, of August-September, 1648, appeared. This large body, representing the New England churches, after deliberation, framed, agreed upon, and published *A Platform of Church Discipline Gathered Out of the Word of God: and Agreed Upon by the Elders: And Messengers of the Churches Assembled at the Synod of Cambridge in New England* (1649), in which it concurred with the doctrinal part of the *Westminster Confession.* And now by formal vote, the Massachusetts churches on May 12, 1680, with Increase Mather as moderator, owned and consented to *A Confession of Faith* (1680), a modification of the *Savoy Confession,* which was based on the *Westminster Confession of Faith.* This most representative declaration of the Cambridge Synod goes on record concerning the pope as the prophesied Antichrist:

"There is no other Head of the Church but the Lord Jesus Christ, nor can the Pope of Rome in any sense be Head thereof, but is that Antichrist, that man of sin, and son of perdition, that exalted himself in the Church against Christ, and all that is called God, whom the Lord shall destroy with the brightness of his coming." [62]

And Antichrist, they declared, is to be destroyed in the latter days:

"According to his promise, we expect that in the latter dayes, Antichrist being destroyed, the Jews called, and the adversaryes of the kingdome of his dear Son broken." [63]

Such was the general seventeenth-century American position on Antichrist. Nothing could be more explicit; nothing more representative and general. The full significance of this group statement must not be lost on us. We repeat: *This was the commonly accepted colonial American position.*

---

[61] Cotton Mather, *Magnalia,* book 5, The First Part ("The Faith Professed"), p. 3.
[62] *Confession of Faith* (1680), chap. 26, art. 4, p. 55. Compare the *Westminster Confession,* chap. 25 ("Of the Church"), art. 6; and the *Savoy Confession,* chap. 26, art. 4. See Williston Walker, *The Creeds and Platforms of Congregationalism,* pp. 183-185, 396, 420-422.
[63] *Confession of Faith* (1680), chap. 26, art. 4, p. 55. (Title page appears on p. 152.)

VIII. Lee—Believed Living Near Beginning of "Happy Time"

SAMUEL LEE (1625-1691), the learned minister of New
Bristol, Rhode Island, was born in London and educated at
Oxford, receiving an M.A. in 1648. He became proctor of the
University of Oxford in 1656. In 1677 he was serving as minister to the nonconformist congregation at Holborn, and subsequently in two other churches. By 1686 he had emigrated to
New England, settling in Bristol, Rhode Island, where he was
ordained. Lee was one of the most learned men of his day, there
being scarcely any department of knowledge into which he had
not penetrated.

He wrote much on future events and the last day. He held
the thousand years and the new-earth state were still future. He
constantly cited Justin Martyr, and computed the prophetic
periods, fixing on 1811 or 1812 for the probable beginning of
the "Happy Time." He was author of several books, including
a sermon in 1687, *A Summons or Warning to the Great Day of
Judgment* (1692),[64] with an introduction by Cotton Mather.
His earlier *Contemplation of Mortality* (1669)[65] also pertained
to the glories of the resurrection and the second advent.

In his *Antichristi Excidium* (The Cutting Off of Antichrist), Lee maintains that the Roman Pontiff is the Antichrist
of prophecy, and the time of his tyranny 1260 year-days, or forty-
two months.[66]

"*Convenit inter omnes Ecclesiae Evangelicae fautores Pontificem
Romanum esse Antichristum, ejusque tyrannidem in 1260 dies propheticos
(id est annos).* [It is agreed among all maintainers of the Evangelical
Church that the Roman Pontiff is Antichrist, and his tyranny in 1260
prophetic days (that is, years).]"[67]

There is a lengthy discussion of the ten kingdoms rising out
of the fourth, or Roman, empire,[68] and the Little Horn in their
midst. Lee lists the ten kingdoms as the Alamanni, Ostrogoths,

---

[64] Also given as *The Great Day of Judgment.*
[65] See also *Joy of Faith* (1687), and *Israel Redux* (1697).
[66] Samuel Lee, *Antichristi Excidium,* pp. 1, 2, 8.
[67] *Ibid.,* p. 1.
[68] *Ibid.,* pp. 5-8.

Visigoths, Huns, Britons, and Saxons, Suevi, Alans, Vandals, Burgundians, and Franks.[69]

Lee then discusses the various calculations of the 1260 years current in his day, such as dating them 259-1519 or 410-1670.[70] But he seems to prefer 476-1736.[71] He places the destruction of Antichrist at the close of the 1260 years, with the interval between that event and "that most blessed millennium of the septenary age" (*Beatissimum illud septeni saeculi millennium*) as perhaps embracing the destruction of the Turkish Empire, the conversion of the Jews, and the fullness of the Gentiles. He expects that if the golden age of the church comes before the end of the sixth thousand years, then at the end of the seventh thousand years will come the war of Magog, followed later by the last universal day of judgment.[72]

Lee determined to return to England, but was captured by French privateers, who detained him in France. Like Wycliffe, who was made a martyr after his death, he died and was buried outside the city as a heretic.[73] Lee's library of 1,100 titles—voluminous for those days—was offered for sale at his death.[74] Largely in Latin, it includes many works on prophecy, and many on history and chronology. The expositions on prophecy are from such authors as Fox, Goodwin, Brightman, Jewell, Durham, Mede, Napier, Broughton, and Cotton, his viewpoints largely concurring with theirs.

1. MIDNIGHT CRY AND WORLD'S END.—Discoursing on the parable of the midnight cry, and "the Suddenness of our Lord's Advent, and the S[t]upidity and Security of the World with reference thereto," [75] Lee asserts:

"Midnight, is the End of the World, before the morning of the Resurrection. The Cry is an Angelical Voice: as soon as the clock strikes Twelve, then the Angel sets his Trumpet to his mouth, and proclameth so." [76]

---

[69] *Ibid.*, pp. 12-172.
[70] *Ibid.*, pp. 183, 186.
[71] *Ibid.*, pp. 184-187, 190.
[72] *Ibid.*, pp. 185, 186.
[73] Cotton Mather, *Magnalia*, book 3, The Fourth Part, chap. 6, art. 4, pp. 223, 224.
[74] *The Library of the Late Reverend and Learned Mr. Samuel Lee* (Catalogue).
[75] Samuel Lee, *A Summons or Warning to the Great Day of Judgment*, p. 49.
[76] *Ibid.*, p. 51.

8

2. RESURRECTED SAINTS ENTER NEW JERUSALEM.—Then, at the resurrection, earth and sea "shall yield their Dead." Next, the "Saints are then led unto the Nuptuals in the New Jerusalem." [77] Lee closes with an appeal not to follow the fatal indifference and slumber of the time of the Flood.

---

[77] *Ibid.*

CHAPTER SIX

Prophetic Terms
Permeate Secular Literature

The molding influence of the standard writings of colonial New England had a definite bearing on the common, or popular, concept of the Papacy. *The New England Primer*[1] (168?) for example, which will be noted in detail, was doubtless the most important of its class, serving for six generations as the principal text of the Dissenters in New England, and spreading into the West and South. Used for a century and a half, unnumbered thousands of copies, through many editions, were sold. Sometimes called the "Little Bible of New England," it exercised a profound influence over the thinking of the populace. Its circulation in the one hundred and fifty years is said to have totaled literally millions of copies.[2] Its significance will become apparent.

I. Publisher Harris—Uses Prophetic Idioms in New England Primer

Unusual importance attaches to BENJAMIN HARRIS (fl. 1673-1716), Anabaptist bookseller, publisher, and author, and publisher of the first American newspaper. Born in England, he began his publishing career by printing a religious work, *War with the Devil* (1673). This he produced at his bookshop in London, which served as a center for the dissemination of his

---

[1] Charles F. Adams, *Three Episodes of Massachusetts History*, vol. 2, pp. 778, 779.
[2] Paul Leicester Ford, *The New-England Primer; a History of Its Origin and Development*, p. 19; Clement Ferguson, "The New England Primer, 1690," in *Magazine of American History*, August, 1888 (vol. 20), pp. 148, 149.

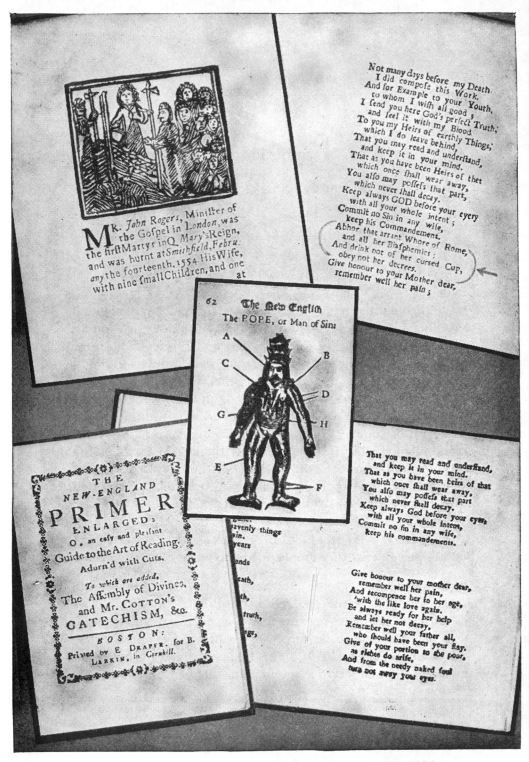

Mr. *John Rogers*, Minister of the Gospel in London, was the first Martyr in Q. Mary's Reign, and was burnt at *Smithfield*, February the fourteenth, 1554. His Wife, with nine small Children, and one at

Not many days before my Death,
I did compose this Work,
And for Example to your Youth,
to whom I wish all good;
I send you here God's perfect Truth,
and seal it with my Blood
To you my Heirs of earthly Things,
which I do leave behind,
That you may read and understand,
and keep it in your mind,
That as you have been Heirs of that
which once shall wear away,
You also may possess that part,
which never shall decay,
Keep always GOD before your eyes,
with all your whole intent;
Commit no Sin in any wise,
keep his Commandment.
Abhor that arrant Whore of *Rome*,
and all her Blasphemies;
And drink not of her cursed Cup,
obey not her decrees.
Give honour to your Mother dear,
remember well her pain;

62   The New English
The POPE, or Man of Sin.

A
C
G
E
B
D
H
F

THE
NEW-ENGLAND
PRIMER
ENLARGED:
O, an easy and pleasant
Guide to the Art of Reading.
Adorn'd with Cuts.

To which are added,
The Assembly of Divines,
and Mr. COTTON'S
CATECHISM, &c.

BOSTON:
Printed by E. DRAPER, for B.
LARKIN, in *Cornhill*.

eavenly things
sin.
years
ands
eath,
th,
truth,
g,

That you may read and understand,
and keep it in your mind,
That as you have been heirs of that
which once shall wear away,
You also may possess that part
which never shall decay.
Keep always God before your eyes,
with all your whole intent,
Commit no sin in any wise,
keep his commandments.

Give honour to your mother dear,
remember well her pain,
And recompence her to her age,
with the like love again,
Be always ready for her help
and let her not decay,
Remember well your father all,
who should have been your stay.
Give of your portion to the poor,
as riches do arise,
And from the needy naked soul
turn not away your eyes.

FAMOUS NEW ENGLAND PRIMER INTERPRETS SYMBOLS

Passing Through Unnumbered Editions, the Harris Reader Included Prophetic Terms in Smithfield Martyr Rogers' Poem (Upper), With Lines Omitted in Modern Reproduction (Lower).
Man of Sin Pictured in Early Editions (Center)

views. From 1676 to 1686 Harris published much, including books, broadsides, ballads, and tracts, against the perversities of the Jesuits and the pope.[3] Prominent among these was *The Protestant Tutor* (1679),[4] the preface of which was addressed to "All Protestant Parents, School-Masters and School-Mistresses of Children." These publications brought him into sharp conflict with the civil authorities. He engaged in denouncing the "Popish Plots" and published the journal *Domestick Intelligence,* which name was soon changed to *Protestant (Domestick) Intelligence.*[5] In 1681, because of pressure and differences over publishing policies, it ceased publication. But while it was being issued under the latter name this advertisement appeared:

"There is lately Published by Benjamin Harris, a Book Intituled, *The Protestant Tutor,* Instructing Children to Spell and Read English, and Grounding them in the True Protestant Religion, and Discovering the Errors and Deceits of the Papists."[6]

In 1686 Harris left for Boston with a stock of books and opened a bookshop in the center of the town, establishing himself on a firm basis. Competition was keen, but he was successful in launching *An Almanack for the Year of Our Lord MDCLXXXVII,* by John Tulley.[7] This he continued to publish. The 1694 issue contains a bit of prophetic interpretation following the Almanack proper. In 1687 Harris went back to London to procure more books, returning to Boston in 1688. In 1690 he started *Publick Occurences, Both Forreign and Domestick,*[8] the first "genuine newspaper" to be published in America.

---

[3] George E. Littlefield, *Early Boston Booksellers, 1642-1711,* p. 147.

[4] 2d edition, 1680; an American reprint, 1685. See also Littlefield, *op. cit.,* pp. 109, 148, 157.

[5] *Domestick Intelligence* (No. 1) was dated July 9 [7], 1679. It was published frequently but irregularly up to No. 114, dated April 15, 1681. The name was changed with No. 56, Jan. 16, 1679, i.e., 1680 New Style. (It was not until 1752 that English countries adopted the Gregorian calendar by dropping eleven days and beginning the year in January instead of in March; hence the issues of this periodical continue to bear the date 1679 until that of March 26 changes to 1680. This is shown by the sequence of the numbers and verified from the Old Style calendar by the days of the week. See Henry Fitch, *The Perfect Calendar for Every Year in the Christian Era,* pp. 28, 29, and tables.) Throughout the series there is constant reference to papal activities and dangers, and notice of books on the Papacy. (See file in Harvard College Library, or Columbia University Law Library.)

[6] *Protestant (Domestick) Intelligence,* Feb. 27, 1679, i.e., 1680 n.s.

[7] Littlefield, *op. cit.,* pp. 148, 149.

[8] The only issue, along with the order suppressing it, is reproduced in S. Abbott Green, *Ten Fac-Simile Reproductions Relating to Old Boston and Neighborhood,* following page 4. See also Littlefield, *op. cit.,* p. 152; Clarence S. Brigham, "Bibliography of American Newspapers 1690-1820," *Proceedings of the American Antiquarian Society,* New Series, vol. 25, part 1 (April, 1915), p. 279.

But the word "Publick" was construed as constituting an official document sustained by the government. The colonial authorities were therefore compelled to suppress it.[9] So the first American newspaper was short-lived.

But Harris' best claim to fame was the publication of *The New England Primer*. As previously noted, before coming to New England, Harris had brought out *The Protestant Tutor*, containing a Protestant catechism and a "Little Book of Martyrs," designed to teach children spelling and "the true Protestant religion," as well as the errors and iniquities of the "Papists." Much of the *Tutor* seems to have been incorporated into *The New England Primer*,[10] which, as a textbook for children, became "probably the most remarkable book that was ever published in this country." In this enterprise, Harris was apparently aided by Cotton Mather, Samuel Willard, and Judge Sewall. This *New England Primer* had a "mighty influence in moulding the mind, forming the habit, and coloring the creed of our ancestors." It is a mirror of the Puritanism of the time, even including leading points in prophetic interpretation. By it millions were taught to read, that they might read the Bible. From it numberless individuals drew their first instruction in religious principle. With it they were drilled and catechized.[11]

The New England Primer is aptly described thus:

"In prose as bare of beauty as the whitewash of their churches, in poetry as rough and stern as their storm-torn coast, in pictures as crude and unfinished as their own glacial-smoothed boulders, between stiff oak covers, which symbolized the contents, the children were led . . . to God."[12]

Ginn and Company's "Foreword," accompanying a modern (1937) facsimile reproduction, declares:

"*The New England Primer* was one of the greatest books ever published. It went through innumerable editions; it reflected in a marvellous way the spirit of the age that produced it, and contributed, perhaps more

---

[9] A clear statement of this first attempt by Harris to start a newspaper, and its suppression by Chief Justice Sewall, because it was printed without first obtaining authorization and license, is found in Lyman H. Weeks, *An Historical Digest of the Provincial Press*, pp. 24-33; see also Littlefield, *op. cit.*, p. 154; Green, *op. cit.*, pp. 1-4.
[10] Ford, *op. cit.*, pp. 15, 16.
[11] Littlefield, *op. cit.*, pp. 154, 155; Ford, *op. cit.*, p. 4.
[12] Ford, *op. cit.*, p. 1.

than any other book except the Bible to the moulding of those sturdy generations that gave to America its liberty and its institutions."

The second edition, advertised in Newman's *News from the Stars*,[13] in 1690, indicates that its success was immediate. Wherever there was a local press it was reprinted—though changed until no two editions were exactly alike.[14] Prior to 1800 alone there were more than forty known editions. The New England presses could not supply the demand, and many were printed in Old England and imported; its total sales were literally "numbered by millions." [15]   Charles F. Heartman gives doubtless the most elaborate bibliographical check list extant—tabulating publishers and printers in more than seventy different cities. He puts the number issued between 1680 and 1830 as six to eight million.[16] In England the *Primer* was popular in an edition, presumably the same in text, entitled *The New English Tutor*,[17] but it was more popular under its own name.

In 1690 Harris produced more than ten publications, and in 1692 he became the official printer to the governor. But in 1695, after only eight years in Boston, he returned to London, having become the leading publisher and bookseller of the seventeenth century in America.[18] Of the fifty-five book titles in a list of early American imprints between 1692 and 1694, thirty-two were printed by Harris.[19]

1. PROPHETIC TERMINOLOGY IN "TUTOR" AND "PRIMER."— Harris' *Protestant Tutor,* upon which draft was made for his *New England Primer* and *New English Tutor,* dwelt upon the "Cruelties, Treasons, and Massacres" of "Papists" beginning under Bloody Mary—such as the Spanish Armada of 1588, the Gunpowder Plot of 1605, the "Massacre of Ireland" of 1642, and the massacre of the French Protestants (1572), Waldenses and others (1655-56).[20] It also was permeated with the prophetic terms and applications characteristic of the time. One standard feature in all three works was the alleged last message of John

[13] *Ibid.,* p. 17.   [17] Ford, *op. cit.,* pp. 17, 18.   [19] *Ibid.,* p. 160.
[14] Littlefield, *op. cit.,* p. 158.   [18] Littlefield, *op. cit.,* p. 161.
[15] *Ibid.,* p. 155.   [20] *The Protestant Tutor* (1679 ed.), pp. 53-77.
[16] Charles F. Heartman, *The New-England Primer Issued Prior to 1830,* p. xxii.

Rogers, minister of St. Sepulcher's Church in London, and first martyr at Smithfield under Queen Mary, in 1554. Along with other admonitions in verse, Rogers, as illustrated by a woodcut of the victim at the stake, is quoted as saying to his children:

"Abhor that arrant Whore of Rome,
    And all her Blasphemies;
And drink not of her cursed Cup,
    obey not her Decrees." [21]

2. CATECHISM'S ANSWERS FROM THE PROPHECIES.—Another feature replete with prophetic citations and admonitions was the "Catechism" for children, which was part of Harris' *Protestant Tutor*. Questions 19 and 20 deal with the explicit terms and texts of prophetic exposition, and read:

"19. Q. Is the Pope rightly termed his Holiness?
      A. No. 2 Thes. 2.3. THAT man of SIN.
"20. Q. Is the Pope's Power from God or from Satan?
      A. Satan. Rev. 13.2. The Dragon gave him his Power, and his
         Seat and great Authority." [22]

The concluding questions in the series are even more pointed:

"42. Q. Is Rome stiled Babylon in the Revelation?
      A. Yes. Rev. 17.3, 5, 9, 18. I saw a Woman sit upon a Scarlet-
         coloured Beast, full of names of Blasphemy? having seven
         Heads: and upon her Fore-head was a Name written *Mystery,*
         Babylon the great, the Mother of Harlots and Abomination
         of the Earth. The seven Heads are seven Mountains, on
         which the Woman sitteth: and the Woman which thou sawest,
         is that great City which reigneth over the Kings of the Earth.
"43. Q. May we joyn with Rome?
      A. No. Rev. 18. 4, 5. I heard a Voice from Heaven, saying, Come
         out of her my People, that ye be not partakers of her Sins,
         and that ye receive not of her Plagues. For her sins have
         reached unto Heaven, and God hath remembred her iniqui-
         ties." [23]

3. PROPHETIC TERMINOLOGY IN "LITTLE MARTYRS."—In Harris' *Protestant Tutor* the "Little Book of Martyrs" depicts

---

[21] *Ibid.*, p. 45; *The New English Tutor Inlarged*, pp. 29, 31; see also Ford, *op. cit.*, pp. 89, 90, 167, 169.
[22] *The Protestant Tutor*, p. 121.
[23] *Ibid.*, p. 130 (correctly p. 131).

the papal persecutions in England for several hundred years. Starting with John Wycliffe, we quote these lines:

> "And now John Wickliff boldly did begin
> To preach 'gainst Antichrist, that Man of Sin:
> Who many Troubles stoutly did abide,
> Yet spight o'th Pope, he naturally dy'd:
> And being dead, from out the grave was turn'd;
> And had his martyr'd Bones to Ashes burn'd.
> Which Ashes they did cast into a Brook,
> Because he had the Romish Faith forsook." [24]

Then comes the roster of such names as Sawtrey, Badly, Thorp, Cobham, Brown, Beverley. Later come these lines:

> "After which Thomas Bilney did begin
> To teach and preach against the Man of Sin,
> And in St. Georges Church in Ipswich Town,
> The Papists from the Pulpit pluckt him down." [25]

Now follows the recital of the fires of Smithfield, Oxford, and other places under Bloody Mary, with the martyr names of John Rogers, Laurence Saunders, John Bradford, Bishop Hooper, Latimer, Ridley, and Cranmer—800 slaughtered and 12,700 persecuted under Henry and Mary.[26]

4. CUT OF TRIPLE-CROWNED MAN OF SIN.—Most striking of all, and doubtless the most offensive to Catholics, was a cut, or print, of a man with a triple crown, bearing the caption, "The Pope, or Man of Sin." This appeared in Harris' *New English Tutor,* and in various editions of *The New England Primer,*[27] appearing as late as the 1770 Boston printing.[28]

It was obviously based on the familiar figure of a man used to illustrate the signs of the zodiac in the almanac, with lines from different members of the body radiating out to the letters A B C, etc.—only with the superimposed papal tiara. The key read:

> "Child, behold that Man of Sin, the *Pope,* worthy
> of thy utmost hatred.

---

[24] *Ibid.,* pp. 102, 103 (correctly pp. 136, 137).
[25] *Ibid.,* p. 109 (correctly p. 143).
[26] *Ibid.,* pp. 111-113 (correctly pp. 145-147).
[27] Heartman, *op. cit.,* p. xvii.
[28] An original copy in American Antiquarian Society, Worcester, Massachusetts.

'Thou shalt find in his head, (A) *Heresy.*
In his Shoulders, (B) *The Supporters of Disorder.*
In his Heart, (C) *Malice, Murder, and Treachery.*
In his Arms, (D) *Cruelty.*
In his Knees, (E) *False Worship and Idolatry.*
In his Feet, (F) *Swiftness to shed Blood.*
In his Stomach, (G) *Insatiable Covetousness.*
In his Loyns, (H) The worst of Lusts." [29]

In the 1737 edition of the *Primer* the cut was reproduced, but the key[30] was omitted. Later altered editions all omit the figure. (Reproduction of cut appears on page 116.)

5. ALTERATIONS OF THE TEXT.—Wherever there was a local press it was reprinted, and variations in the text reflected political changes, religious trends, or the publishers' taste or business interests, but there were certain characteristics which preserved the identity of the *Primer*—the alphabet, syllabarium, Scripture quotations, Lord's prayer, Apostles' Creed, catechism (either Cotton's *Milk for Babes* or the Westminster *Shorter Catechism* or both), the famous alphabetical rhymes beginning—

"In Adam's Fall
We sinned All"—

and the even more famous poem and picture of the martyr John Rogers.[31]

This last affords a glaring example of modern tampering—irrespective of the motive—as it affects the constantly used and commonly understood idioms of prophetic interpretation in the seventeenth century. Virtually all the early editions had a cut of the martyred John Rogers, with the accompanying admonition to his children, which contained the lines before mentioned:

"Abhor that arrant Whore of Rome,
And all her Blasphemies;
And drink not of her cursed Cup,
obey not her decrees." [32]

---

[29] *The New English Tutor Inlarged,* pp. 61, 62; facsimile in Ford, *op. cit.,* pp. 247, 248, and plate xix; Sister Mary Augustina (Ray), *American Opinion of Roman Catholicism in the Eighteenth Century,* p. 121.
[30] Ford, *op. cit.,* p. 50.
[31] *Ibid.,* pp. 23-32, 37, 38; Heartman, *op. cit.,* pp. xix-xxii.
[32] We have personally examined some sixty-five editions of the *Primer.* Fully two thirds of these varied editions by different publishers contain the Rogers poem entire. Some abbreviated editions leave out the entire text of the poem, a few retaining the cut but completely

But in the "Twentieth Century Reprint," previously noted, these four lines only of the poem have been expunged from the facsimile plate, simply leaving a blank space, while the rest of the poem is retained intact.   This indicates a motive behind the change today from the emphasis and attitude of those earlier generations in colonial America when this Historical School of Protestant interpretation of prophecy was wrought into the very fabric of the basic literature of the time.

---

omitting the poem.   In no other instance, however, where the poem is used, and such generally is the case, are the four lines in question omitted.   Furthermore, the original copy from which the "Twentieth Century" facsimile reproduction was made is now in deposit in the Plimpton Library at Columbia University, and contains the four lines in question, which were simply deleted from the reproduction plate.

CHAPTER SEVEN

High-Water Mark
in Colonial Exposition

I. The Mather Dynasty of New England

RICHARD MATHER (1596-1669), founder of the "Mather dynasty," was persecuted by the Archbishop of York in 1635 for not wearing a surplice, which the Puritans regarded as "the rags of Antichrist." [1] Therefore he left England for Boston. Of extensive learning in the classics and Scriptures, he quickly became minister at Dorchester. He was a constant student and a prolific writer, and a leader in church and state.

Of his six sons, four became famous, the most prominent being INCREASE MATHER (1639-1723), who entered Harvard at twelve, graduated at seventeen, and was preaching by nineteen. Increase returned to Trinity College, Dublin, for further training, and at twenty-six he was back in America as pastor of North Church in Boston. Books flowed from his pen in a constant stream.[2] Because of his learning, logic, eloquence, and energy, he became the most powerful figure in New England. He was a pronounced theocrat. When he died, the spirit of the old Presbyterianism passed in Harvard. Later it was superseded by Unitarianism.[3]

Increase's son, COTTON MATHER (1663-1728), the third generation, became the most famous of all. A veritable prodigy, he surpassed in influence all pre-Revolution Americans, with the

---

[1] William W. Sweet, *Religion in Colonial America*, p. 19.
[2] Vernon L. Parrington, *The Colonial Mind (1620-1800)*, p. 105.
[3] *Ibid.*, p. 106.

124

exception of Jonathan Edwards and Benjamin Franklin.[4] He was called the "literary behemoth" of colonial New England because of his enormous literary output. In him, however, the inquisitorial pettiness of the Genevan system was "revealed so disagreeably."[5] He lived in a transition hour. He belonged to the past, the "cold granite" of Puritan formalism, that was rapidly passing. In his later life the shadows of disappointment fell across his pathway, for the world had moved on from the positions of the previous generation that constituted his very life.[6] Of Increase and Cotton much will be noted.

II. President Mather—Most Comprehensive Expounder

Unquestionably the most notable witness of the seventeenth century was INCREASE MATHER (1639-1723),[7] Congregationalist pastor and author of Boston and president of Harvard. He was born in Dorchester, Massachusetts, and graduated from Harvard in 1656. He visited England, and in 1658 secured an M.A. from Trinity College, Dublin. He first preached in England at Great Torrington and Guernsey, but refused to comply with the Act of Conformity. So he returned to Boston in 1661, where several churches sought his services. Mather became minister of the North Church of Boston in 1664, holding this office, along with his other responsibilities, for fifty-nine years, or until his death in 1723. Of strictly Calvinistic mold, and "austerely forbidding," and with strong theocratic convictions, he was tolerant only of "views that were not error."[8] He presided at the Synod of Boston in 1680, already noted, which adopted a *Confession* based on the *Savoy Confession,* which concurred *in* the *Westminster Confession of Faith.* (Portrait appears on page 34.)

In 1685 Mather was chosen president of Harvard,[9] in which

---

[4] Moses C. Tyler, *A History of American Literature During the Colonial Time*, vol. 2, pp. 74 ff.
[5] Parrington, *op. cit.*, p. 107.   [6] *Ibid.*, pp. 114-117.
[7] His name, Increase, was given in gratitude to God for the providential increase and prosperity of the colony. See Chandler Robbins, *A History of the Second Church in Boston*, p. 15.   [8] Parrington, *op. cit.*, pp. 101, 102.
[9] JOHN HARVARD (1607-1638), Puritan clergyman, born in England and educated at Cambridge University, was the principal founder of Harvard College. Settling in Massachusetts

position he served for about fifteen years.   In 1687 he was
selected by the New England ministers to convey their vote of
thanks to James II for the latter's declaration of liberty for all
faiths.   This vote of thanks Mather conveyed to the king when
he went to England in 1688 to negotiate a new charter for Massachusetts.   In 1701 he retired from the presidency of Harvard but
retained his pastorate until his death.   He was the first Doctor
of Divinity in British America.

It was Mather's habit to spend sixteen hours daily in study.
None exercised a more potent and prolonged influence upon
early American Congregationalism.[10]   By the time he was
forty-five Mather had produced twenty-five volumes, and in all
between 102 and 158 different books and pamphlets—the number depending on whether smaller works are included.[11]   Ten of
these[12] bear more or less upon prophecy.   In one of his earliest
books he tells of his slow acceptance of premillennialism:

"I was exceeding backward to entertain such a notion, and did long
oppose it, as conceiving it might be at best an innocent errour of some that
wished well to the kingdom of Christ: But blessed be the Lord God who
gave me an heart at that very time to search (according to my poor
measure) the Scriptures and other Books which might be helpful in this
case, both such as argued for, and such as argued against the Chiliad; and
to look up to Him that is in heaven and heareth on earth, that I might see
and embrace the truth, and only the truth.   And methinks, I would desire
no more, if I could but persuade all serious and gracious men to go that
way to work in this matter." [13]

Shortly after returning to America Mather became fully

Bay, he died soon after his arrival.   But he left his library of 300 volumes and £779, to which
the General Court of the colony added an appropriation.   The college was founded in 1638 and
incorporated in 1679.   Its purpose was to educate "English and Indian youth in knowledge
and godliness," with a view to educating future Puritan ministers.   See William S. Perry, ed.,
Historical Collections Relating to the American Colonial Church, vol. 3, pp. 67-71; John Eliot,
New England's First Fruits, p. 12 (anonymous; identified in Samuel Halkett and John Laing,
Dictionary of Anonymous and Pseudonymous English Literature).
   [10] Williston Walker, "The Services of the Mathers in New England Religious Development," *Papers of the American Society of Church History*, vol. 5 [1st series] (1893), p. 69.
   [11] Increase Mather's literary output was enormous—102 whole works, excluding prefatory
and fragmentary items.   (Thomas J. Holmes, *Increase Mather: A Bibliography of His Works*,
vol. 1, p. xxvi; vol. 2, pp. 353-357.)   It requires nearly five pages just to list them (pp. xxviii-
xxxii).   Holmes' exhaustive two-volume work requires 711 pages to compass them, with the
leading title pages reproduced in facsimile.   See also Stanley J. Kunitz and Howard Haycraft,
American Authors, p. 517; Frederick L. Weis, *The Colonial Clergy and the Colonial Churches
of New England [1620-1776]*, p. 136; *The Cambridge History of American Literature*, vol. 1,
pp. 398-406.
   [12] Increase Mather's most complete and learned prophetic exegesis is still in manuscript
at the American Antiquarian Society at Worcester, Massachusetts, titled *Triparadisus*.   But
virtually all positions are set forth in his various works, which we shall cite.
   [13] Increase Mather, *The Mystery of Israel's Salvation, Explained and Applyed* (1669),
"Author's Preface to the Reader," c₄ v., c₅ r.

persuaded that the millennium would begin and the kingdom of God would be established by the second advent at the close of the fourth empire—after the long tribulation allotted under Antichrist and after Antichrist's destruction by the advent. Then would occur the resurrection of the dead and the beginning of the Happy State and the restitution of all things. This, he came to find, was the belief of the early church before the Bishop of Rome sought to supplant the true concept of the kingdom of Christ by the false kingdom of Antichrist. This view he wrote out in 1668 in *Diatriba de Signo Filii Hominis, et de Secundo Messiae Adventu,*[14] later published at Amsterdam in 1682.[15] Mather constantly sought God for direction and assistance in the composing of his book.[16]

With Increase Mather we reach the high-water mark in seventeenth-century prophetic interpretation. In fact, Mather is the connecting link binding the seventeenth and eighteenth centuries together, as his prophetic writings span a period of three or four decades. We now note Mather's leading positions as unfolded in the chronological progression of his published books on prophecy.

1. TURKISH POWER SIGNIFIED BY EUPHRATES.—In *The Mystery of Israel's Salvation, Explained* (1669)—with introductions by John Davenport and William Hooke—while the conversion of the Jews is the main theme,[17] Mather held that the thousand years are not past but future, and that the coming of Christ to judgment is near.[18] Asserting that "one of the greatest sins of many that truly fear God" is that they are "so slow and negligent in searching into the things spoken by the prophets," [19] Mather deals succinctly with the "Saracenical locusts" and the

---

[14] Cotton Mather, *Parentator, Memoirs of Remarkables in the Life and Death of . . . Increase Mather,* pp. 63, 64. (Anonymous; identified in *Dictionary of American Biography,* vol. 12, p. 394.)
[15] Increase Mather, *A Dissertation Wherein The Strange Doctrine . . . is Examined and Confuted,* Appendix, p. 103; see also Holmes, *op. cit.,* vol. 2, pp. 150, 151.
[16] Cotton Mather, *Parentator,* p. 65.
[17] It should be stated at this point that various colonial writers on prophecy were ardent believers in the literal return of the Jews. Omission of their arguments in support of this view is due neither to unawareness of their positions nor to any desire to ignore or minimize their contentions. They are passed by solely because this volume is fundamentally a tracement of the exposition of the outline prophecies of Daniel and the Revelation, whereas their views on the Jews were based largely on other premises not germane to our field of inquiry.
[18] Increase Mather, *The Mystery of Israel's Salvation,* pp. 160, 161.
[19] *Ibid.,* p. 74.

Turks of Revelation 9, which he believed must be destroyed—as well as papal Rome, the Antichrist—before the conversion of Israel.[20] The Turks and Jews are both thought by him to be involved in Daniel 11:44, 45, the Roman Antichrist having been introduced in verse 36 as the "willful king."[21] Then come the "fearful devastations, which the Ottomanical family hath made upon the Roman Empire." Mather plainly calls the "King of the North" the "Turkish Ottomanical family."[22] Of this same power in Revelation 9 he says:

> "The Turkish power is signified by Euphrates, Rev. 9.13, 14. *I heard a voice saying, loose the four Angels which are bound in the great River Euphrates.* The meaning of the place may be, That the Turks which lay on both sides of the River Euphrates, and were divided into four Sultanies or Kingdoms should be let loose, partly by composing their civil dissentions, and partly by being united under one Ottomanical head, to make a dreadful irruption upon the Roman Empire."[23]

This treatise was greatly admired by John Caryl, prophetic student in England, and extensively circulated and read in Europe. Mather at this time refused to have anything to do with time setting and the "great variety of computations."[24]

2. ROMAN BIRDS OF PREY EYING AMERICA.—*Heaven's Alarm to the World* (1680), on great signs in Heaven as "the Presages of Great Calamities at Hand," deals with the "thickening" wars, earthquakes, and commotions of Luke 21 that would constitute signs of Christ's coming to judge the world,[25] the literal resurrection of the saints taking place thereafter. Uttering a warning of danger to colonial America, he writes, "The Roman Eagles, those birds of prey, are hastening upon you," and he closes with the suggestive appeal: "O New England! New England! dost thou not know that the birds of prey are designing to devour thee?"[26] (Title page reproduced on page 206.)

3. SAINTS CAUGHT UP AT SECOND ADVENT.—Mather's "Discourse About the Day of Judgement" (1686)[27] pictures that

---

[20] *Ibid.*, pp. 24, 25. [22] *Ibid.*, p. 28. [24] *Ibid.*, pp. 140, 141.
[21] *Ibid.*, p. 26. [23] *Ibid.*, p. 33.
[25] Increase Mather, *Heaven's Alarm to the World*, pp. 2-12. [26] *Ibid.*, p. 38.
[27] Increase Mather, *The Greatest Sinners Exhorted . . . to come to Christ*, pp. 64-75.

great day which will mark the glorious appearance of the returning Christ. All the angels of heaven will attend Him, and innumerable thousands minister unto Him. Then the saints of
earth shall be caught up to meet Him. And then shall the everlasting reign and dominion of the Messiah take place. [28]

4. CHURCH OF ROME "MOTHER OF HARLOTS."—In his
*Ichabod or . . . the Glory of the Lord, is Departing from New-
England* (1702), Mather portrays the various inroads of the
great papal apostasy in Africa and Europe:

> "Look into Africa. Time was when there were Thousands of Glorious
> Churches there: & many Famous Ministers, some of whose writings are still
> of use to the Church of God; such as Tertullian, Cipran, Austin. But now
> the Glory is wholly removed out of that vast Continent. Look into Europe,
> and we shall see many places there from whence the Glory is gone. There
> was once in Rome it self, an holy Church. A People beloved of God, called
> to be Saints, whose Faith was spoken of throughout the whole world. Rom.
> 1.7, 8. But what is that Church come to? Her Name is now, THE
> MOTHER OF HARLOTS, AND ABOMINATIONS OF THE EARTH.
> Rev. 17.5." [29]

5. SEAT OF THE BEAST IN EUROPE.—Discussing Europe as
the seat of the Beast and the location of the ten kings, Mather
declares:

> "Our Lord will have a Church somewhere or other in Europe until
> his Second coming. The witnesses must there Prophesy in Sackcloth; there
> be Slain, there Rise again. The Ten Kings which give their Power to the
> Beast are in Europe: That part of the world was to be principally the Seat
> of the Church of Christ during the Reign of Antichrist, who must continue
> until Christ Himself shall destroy him with the Brightness of His coming." [30]

Mather was concerned that God had not seemed to indicate
a special work or achievement for the Americas—with most of
the inhabitants pagan or Antichristian. He refers to the aborted
attempt from Geneva to settle the Protestant religion in South
America. [31]

6. INCREASE IN EARTHQUAKES INDICATES ADVENT NEAR.—
Mather's *Discourse Concerning Earthquakes* (1706) stresses the

---

[28] *Ibid.*, pp. 82-85.
[29] Increase Mather, *Ichabod or . . . the Glory of the Lord, is Departing from New-
England*, p. 61.
[30] *Ibid.*, p. 64.   [31] *Ibid.*, pp. 64, 65.

9

increased number of earthquakes as a predicted sign of Christ's coming, which growing fulfillment indicates that the second advent is nearing.[32] Examples are cited in Asia, Europe, and America.

7. TURKISH PLAGUE IS THE SECOND WOE.—Mather's *Dissertation* [on] . . . *Strange Doctrine* (1708), with an appendix showing that "within a very few years there will be a Glorious Reformation," is devoted to a study of how long the reign of Antichrist would continue, till his allotted end—whether three hundred years, as one "late writer" places it.[33] He cites Mede, Whiston, Beverley, Jurieu, and others as having varied views. Mather held that it would be within a relatively "few years." [34] In presenting his reasons for the near approach of the "Happy Time," he again stresses the fulfillment of the Turkish, or second, woe, citing Brightman:

"It is generally agreed among Interpreters, that by the Second Wo, the Turkish Empire is intended, which has for many Ages been a Woful Plague to the Third Part of men, by which Europe, a Third part of the formerly known World may be meant. It is said of the Turkish Empire, That it is prepared for an Hour, and a Day, and a Month, and a Year; Which according to the Prophetical account, is Three Hundred Ninety Six Years [365 + 30 + 1], Rev. 9.15 (a) Mr. Brightman, above an Hundred Years ago, did from thence conclude, that the Turk, who began his Reign Anno Domini 1300 would cease to be a Wo to the Apostate Christian World, in the Year 1696." [35]

8. TURKISH PERIOD, MAY 19, 1300, TO SEPT. 1, 1697.— Alluding to his own published statement, made twenty-six years previous, Mather notes how William Whiston, professor of mathematics at Cambridge, emphasizes the period down to a day, with "an accuracy not elsewhere to be observed in the Prophetical Writings." [36] Taking the 365-day common year instead of the 360-day prophetic year, here are the specifications:

"An Hour, in the Prophetical Style, is Fifteen Days: A Day, is a Year: A Month, is Thirty Years: A Prophetical Year, is Three Hundred Sixty Five Years. The Total is, Three Hundred Ninety Six Years, and a Hun-

---

[32] Increase Mather, *Discourse Concerning Earthquakes*, pp. 17-27.
[33] Increase Mather, *Dissertation* [on] . . . *Strange Doctrine*, Preface, A₄ v.
[34] *Ibid., Appendix*, p. 91.   [35] *Ibid.*, p. 93.   [36] *Ibid.*, p. 94.

dred and Six Days. This author, by a diligent search into Histories and Chronologies, finds that the Beginning of the Turkish Empire, is to be Dated from May, 19. Anno Dom. 1301. To which add, 396 Years, and 106 Days, and we shall come to September the first, Anno Dom. 1697. On which very Day, by a famous Victory over the Turk, it seems as if an End was put to the Second Wo; and immediately followed the peace at Carlowitz; which no Temptations have prevailed with the Turk to Violate." [37]

9. ANTICHRIST'S 1260 YEARS FROM 456 TO 1716.—Turning next to the end of the 1260 years (forty-two months, or three and a half times) of Antichrist's evil reign, which will be followed by Christ's glorious reign, Mather says, "If we can find when there were Ten Distinct Kingdoms in the Roman Empire, we are to reckon the Beasts reign from that very Hour." [38] To this end he cites Mede, Lee, Jurieu, and Allix—how they did not rise all at once. Then he lists the ten kingdoms, which were established within the old Roman Empire by 456, he thinks, and adds:

"Consequently from that Year, we are to Date the Commencement of Anti-Christs Reign: which is to continue from First to Last, but 1260. years, which added to 456 brings us to the Year, 1716." [39]

Others, he observes, date the period from 476 or from 606. [40]

10. 2300 YEARS LIKEWISE END IN 1716.—Mather also notes, without comment, Whiston's allocation of the 2300 years, on the year-day principle, from the third year of Belshazzar to 1716. [41] But this prophecy did not particularly attract his attention, nor did he attempt an application.

11. 666 YEARS: FROM 1050 TO 1716.—Identifying the "Pope of Rome" as the Man of Sin, the False Prophet, the two-horned Second Beast, and the Little Horn of Daniel, Mather cites Pastor Samuel Petto, of Sudbury, Suffolk, as dating the 666, as years, from 1050—likewise leading to 1716. [42] These are given as the suggestions of others which "may not be so understood."

12. FRANCE TENTH PART OF GREAT CITY.—Irrespective of differing details, "things are now hastning to their centre." The tyranny of the Little Horn was soon to end, as was the 1260 years of the Witnesses' sackcloth. Moreover, the principal king-

[37] Ibid.
[38] Ibid., p. 95.
[39] Ibid., pp. 95, 96.
[40] Ibid., pp. 99, 109.
[41] Ibid., pp. 97, 98.
[42] Ibid., p. 99.

dom of the ten supporting the Beast—a tenth part of "Babylon the Great City"—was to undergo a revolution. Citing Goodwin's conjectures that it would be France, Mather adds, "Several things may incline us to be of that Opinion." [43]

13. CUSA'S REMARKABLE PREDICTION NOTED.—Tabulating men like Wycliffe, Huss, Jerome, Luther, and Zwingli, who looked forward to the great era of the last days, Mather comments on the remarkable declaration of Nicholas Krebs of Cusa (Cusanus),[44] as pointing to the same general conclusion:

"It is a little surprizing, that a Cardinal, who lived 250 Years since, should be aware of this. Yet so it was: For Cusanus so long ago, building his Opinion on Daniels Numbers, concluded that soon after the Year 1700, Anti-christ will be Destroyed, and the Church have a Glorious Resurrection." [45]

Mather was remarkably familiar with contemporary and prior Old World interpretation.

14. FATAL BLOW TO ANTICHRIST'S KINGDOM IMPENDING.— Then Mather concludes, "That the Time for the fulfilling of Glorious Prophecies is near, we have Scripture ground to Hope." [46] Again citing eleven Old World expositors with whom he found himself largely in agreement, he declared that the "Un-sealing of these Mysteries, is a sign that the Time of the End is at hand," [47] and adds:

"For my own part, I do not expect to Live to the accomplishment of these things, which I have now mentioned as not far off. Nor can I desire to continue so long in this Sinful World. Nevertheless, I am comforted in seeing the Day is approaching, when the Kingdom of Anti-christ will receive an happy fatal blow, & the Holy Kingdom of our Lord Jesus Christ will prevail, & break in pieces all that shall stand in opposition thereunto." [48]

15. FOURTH MONARCHY ON "LAST LEGS."—In introducing Mather's *Discourse Concerning Faith and Fervency in Prayer* (1710), respecting the kingdom of God, which he expected soon to compass the earth, and "the Time wherein our Lot is cast,"

---

[43] *Ibid.*, pp. 100-102.
[44] We present Cusa in detail in Volume 2.
[45] *Ibid.*, p. 109.
[46] *Ibid.*, p. 109.
[47] *Ibid.*, p. 110.
[48] *Ibid.*

Joseph Jacob,[49] in the London edition (1713), employs these significant words in his comprehensive dedication:

"It is Now indeed the Last Time, for the Last of all the four Monarchies is upon its Last Legs, or rather on its Stinking Toes of Iron and Clay (Its Political, and Ecclesiastical Contrivances) which as they could never well cement, are now about to be quite broken to pieces, to make way for That Kingdom which shall fill the Whole Earth; Now are the three Less Numbers and Last Epocha's drawing to an End, which Daniel mentions in his Last Chapter, and which terminate his Large Number of 2300 Mornings and Evenings; for Now is hastening to be sounded the first of the three last [*vae-euge tubae*] Wo-Joy Trumpets, which with the same Breath sound Wo to Antichrist, but Joy to the Saints of the Most High; The Reign of the Locusts (People or Priests of any Sort, with Mens Faces and Womens Hair) is Now well nigh at an End; The Fall of the tenth Part of the great City hastens apace; with the pouring out of the Vial on the Seat of the Beast, which shall be attended with the rising of the Witnesses, or the Call of the Jews, and a large Accession of Gentiles." [50]

16. STONE NOT YET WORLD-FILLING MOUNTAIN.—Mather registers agreement with numerous authors in Old and New England—Mede, Goodwin, Davenport, and others—that the "Millenary Reign will begin after the Death of Antichrist." [51] This is to be so because the "sure word of Prophesy has foretold, that it would be so." [52] Mather maintains that the stone has not yet become the mountain filling the whole earth, citing numerous supporting texts.[53]

17. FOUR MONARCHIES AND DIVISIONS SPECIFIED.—The four kingdoms of prophecy are expounded thus:

"It was reveal'd to the Prophet Daniel, that there should be Four great Monarchys on the Earth successively; First, the Babylonish, after that the Persian, then the Grecian, and lastly the Roman: And that this should be divided into Ten Kingdoms; and that among them there should spring up an Horn (a King) which should be diverse from the other Kings, viz. Antichrist: All this has been fulfilled. But then 'tis foretold that this Horn should make War with the Saints and prevail over them, and continue for a Time, and Times, and the dividing of Time, and after that be destroyed,

---

49 JOSEPH JACOB (1667-1722), Congregational minister, preached in Parish Street Meeting House, Southwark. He introduced the then-novel practice of standing for congregational singing. He held to a strict code of life—wigs were not allowed and the mustache was obligatory.
50 Increase Mather, *Discourse Concerning Faith and Fervency in Prayer*, "An Epistle Dedicatory," pp. xi, xii.
51 *Ibid.*, Preface, pp. iii, iv.
52 *Ibid.*, p. ix.
53 *Ibid.*, p. x.

and then shall be given to CHRIST, Dominion, and Glory, and a Kingdom, (Dan. 7.14) that ALL People, Nations and Languages should fear Him." [54]

18. PRAY FOR ANTICHRIST'S DOWNFALL.—Mather declares that "the Seventh Trumpet will sound e'er long," when the kingdoms of the world will become the kingdoms of Christ.[55] Then he writes concerning Antichrist:

"Antichrist's Kingdom is contrary to CHRIST'S: For a Scepter of Righteousness is a Scepter of CHRIST'S Kingdom. But Antichrist is made up of Unrighteousness. Hence he is call'd, The Man of Sin. There is a World of Iniquity in his Kingdom, in respect of Corruption both in Doctrine, and in Manners. It consists in idolatrous Superstition; and subsists by Persecution. We should pray for the Downfal of that Kingdom: And that therefore the Kings of the Earth, who have given their Power to the Beast, may have their Eyes opened to see how they have been deluded, and that they may hate and destroy that Great Whore, of which Antichrist is the Head. For this also there is a sure Word of Prophecy, that it shall be done; and therefore we should pray for the Fulfillment of it; and this the rather because the Time draws on." [56]

19. ANTICHRIST'S YEARS ARE ALMOST FINISHED.—And as to the approaching end of the 1260 years Mather says:

"Let us consider what Scriptures are now Fulfilling. We know that when Antichrist's Kingdom is destroyed, CHRIST will have a glorious Kingdom over ALL the Earth. Antichrist has in all but Twelve Hundred and Sixty Years allowed him to reign in. If we consult Historians and Chronologies, (as Daniel understood by Books) and we shall find that those Years are almost finished." [57]

That is the explicit testimony of the clearest and most comprehensive of the colonial expositors—Harvard's illustrious president.

III. Justice Sewall—First Resurrected Ones Not Touched by Fire

SAMUEL SEWALL (1652-1730), colonial jurist and learned layman, is the last witness of the seventeenth century we shall note. He was born at Bishopstoke, England, but was brought to New England when only nine. Educated at Harvard, from which he received his M.A., he tutored for a while and studied divinity, "was Keeper of the College Library," and preached

---

[54] *Ibid.*, p. 19.   [55] *Ibid.*, pp. 18, 19.   [56] *Ibid.*, pp. 33, 34.
[57] *Ibid.*, p. 47.

occasionally. Then Increase Mather and Samuel Willard, both writers on prophecy, offered him the management of the only licensed press at Boston.

This press Sewall carried from 1681 to 1684.[58] Then he embarked on a political career. From 1692 to 1728 he was judge of the Superior Court of Massachusetts, and also served as one of the judges at the Salem witchcraft trials in 1692.[59] Later, convinced of the innocence of the victims, he had the courage to make a public confession before the Old South Church, in Boston, of his error and sorrow.[60] He was chief justice for Massachusetts from 1718 to 1728. (Portrait on page 144.)

Sewall was one of the first Americans to renounce and denounce the crime of Negro slavery as practiced in New England, and wrote the earliest work against slavery printed in Massachusetts,[61] *The Selling of Joseph—a Memorial* (1700).[62] In the form of a lawyer's brief, fortified by Scripture and illuminated by high ethical principles, it was a statement followed by a series of four objections and their answers.

In religious faith Sewall was a lifetime student of prophecy[63] and a strong premillennialist. In 1649 he became a commissioner of the "Society for the Propagation of the Gospel." In his *Phaenomena quaedam Apocalyptica . . . A Description of the New Heaven* (1697),[64] he maintains that those who have part in the first resurrection will not be hurt by the lake of fire,[65]

---

[58] George E. Littlefield, *Early Boston Booksellers*, pp. 111-113; also his *Early Massachusetts Press, 1638-1711*, vol. 2, art. "Sewall."

[59] Persecutions for witchcraft in colonial America occurred in Massachusetts, Connecticut, and elsewhere. The most violent outbreak was near Salem, Massachusetts, fostered by the extravagant opinions of Cotton Mather. (See Montague Summers, *History of Witchcraft and Demonology;* George L. Kittredge, *Witchcraft in Old and New England.*)

[60] Tyler, *op. cit.*, vol. 2, p. 100.

[61] *Ibid.* Because of the scarcity of labor, the colonies in time had turned to Negro slavery—no scruples being noted in the writings of that period against enslavement of fellow men. Between 1713 and 1780, 20,000 slaves annually were brought over the sea, herded like cattle in the fetid air of windowless ships. (Charles A. and Mary R. Beard, *The Rise of American Civilization*, vol. 1, pp. 105-107.) Though Sewall wrote his tract to disparage the importation of Negroes, it was without effect. Prior to that, George Keith, of Philadelphia, in 1693, and before that the Mennonites of Germantown, in 1688, had been outspoken. But soon powerful advocates of antislavery appeared in Pennsylvania, New Jersey, and New York, rather than in New England, where trade in slaves was already established. And popular sentiment was against educating them or allowing them to meet in the churches for religious services. (James Truslow Adams, *Provincial Society, 1690-1763*, pp. 164, 165.)

[62] See Charles Evans, *American Bibliography*, vol. 1, p. 146 (no. 951); Samuel Sewall, "Commonplace Book," in *Sewall Papers*, vol. 2, *Collections of Massachusetts Historical Society*, Fifth Series, vol. 6, pp. 16-20.

[63] Parrington, *op. cit.*, p. 93; Tyler, *op. cit.*, vol. 2, p. 101.

[64] Dedicated to Lieutenant Governor William Stoughton.

which is prepared for those raised in the second resurrection. He also wrote *Proposals Touching the Accomplishment of Prophesies Humbly Offered* (1713). This work shows a remarkable familiarity with Old and New World writers on prophecy, citing them and giving exact documentation, though on some matters Sewall is more hazy than other writers.

1. PLAGUES BEING POURED OUT; SIXTH AFFECTS PAPACY.—Sewall cites many writers on prophecy and declares the probability that five of the vials had already been poured out, as noted in "Rome's gradual Decay." [66] He further suggests that the pouring out of the sixth vial will dry up "the Antichristian Interests in the New World" as well. He questions Brightman's coupling of Revelation 16:16 with Daniel 11:45, and suggests: "For Euphrates must needs be parcel of the waters upon which the Whore sits at the time when this great river comes to be dried up." [67] Sewall's concept had evidently been derived from Cotton, whose weekly lectures on the Revelation, formerly given at Boston, are approvingly mentioned. [68] He had no sympathy with "Alcasar's dream" of Preterist interpretation, which had been adopted by some Protestants in Europe. [69]

2. TEN KINGS TO EXECUTE VENGEANCE ON ROME.—Alluding to the fifth seal and the "Invasions of Antichrist," Sewall specifies the "dreadfull Massacres and Murthers of the Waldenses in Piedmont." [70] Of the retribution to come upon Rome, he adds, "When the Seventh Vial's Turn comes, the Ten Kings will do it perfectly, and with a Vengeance. For Rome will be reserved untill then." [71]

3. ANTICHRIST'S END AFTER TYRANNIZING NEW WORLD.—In his second work Sewall admonishes looking for the second advent as "very seasonable." [72] Holding the Papacy to be the power of the latter part of Daniel 11 to come to its end, he says:

---

[65] Samuel Sewall, *Phaenomena quaedam Apocalyptica . . . A Description of the New Heaven As It makes to those who stand upon the New Earth*, p. 42.
[66] *Ibid.*, p. 24. [69] Fully discussed in Volume 2 of *Prophetic Faith*.
[67] *Ibid.*, p. 25. [70] *Ibid.*, Dedication, pp. [2, 3].
[68] *Ibid.*, p. 29. [71] *Ibid.*, p. 24.
[72] Samuel Sewall, *Proposals Touching the Accomplishment of Prophecies*, p. 1.

"When Antichrist should clamber up to the top of his imperial Tyranny, by extending it over the New World also; then he was to come to his End." [73]

4. WITNESSES SLAIN WITHIN BEAST'S JURISDICTION.—Citing Goodwin, Phillipot, and Jurieu, Sewall agrees with them that the "Two Witnesses" are to be slain in the French part of the great Babylonian "City"—in its "street." [74]   In any event, it "must be within the compass of the Beast's Jurisdiction." [75]

---

[73] *Ibid.*, p. 2.
[74] *Ibid.*, p. 10.
[75] *Ibid.*

CHAPTER EIGHT

Seventeenth-Century
Positions and Transitions

I. Summary of Predominant Seventeenth-Century Exposition

After listening to the detailed witness of the colonial expositors of the seventeenth century, let us pause to recapitulate their prophetic faith before passing over the line into the eighteenth century. Leading voices, eminently representing the different religious groups in America—secular leaders of life and thought as well as clerics—all joined in enunciating certain basic beliefs. This unity of witness upon essentials constitutes the dominant prophetic faith of our colonial American forefathers.

Of the twenty-five prominent writers on prophecy between 1639 and the close of the seventeenth century, virtually every one is premillennialist in belief. And every one who referred to Antichrist applied the dread epithet to the Papacy, as well as the various prophetic symbols of Little Horn, Beast, Man of Sin, Babylon, and Harlot. Half of these writers referred to one or more of the various prophetic time periods, and explicitly applied the year-day principle to them. The remainder did not attempt to discuss the time feature. Conscious of living in the divided-kingdom state that followed the fourth, or Roman, empire, they awaited the everlasting, world-filling kingdom of God, represented by the stone as the climax of the prophetic outlines and of all human history.

Daniel's seventy weeks of years was recognized as applying to the Jews and as leading directly to the first advent of the Messiah. And John's Turkish power in Revelation 9, with its special time period of 391 year-days, was referred to by several. Even the tenth part of the papal "city," that was to fall away from Babylon, or Catholic Christendom, is likewise mentioned. And the Witnesses, in sackcloth for the 1260 years, were understood to parallel the Beast's persecution of the church. Even their death for the three and a half year-days, at the close of the long period, is noted.

The dragon of Revelation 12 is applied to pagan Rome, identified as the "let" or hindrance, and the woman in white is recognized as the true church under persecution. The Beast of Revelation 13 is universally acclaimed the Papacy, and even the 666, as either the name or years of the papal power, is mentioned by two or three. The seven vials of Revelation 16 are believed to involve the Papacy and the Turk under the symbols of the "seat of the Beast" and the Euphrates. The Babylon and harlot of Revelation 17 are likewise applied to the Papacy, and separation therefrom is called for. The seven heads of the Beast, involving the seven hills of Rome, were applied to the Roman power, with the emperors as the "sixth" head and the popes as the "seventh." And the ten horns were declared to be the generally designated divisions of Rome.

With the exception of two early adherents to the Augustinian position, which placed the millennium back in the Middle Ages, all colonial writers who touched upon the millennium held it to be introduced by the second personal advent of Christ and the literal resurrection of the righteous. With this they united the destruction of the Papacy and the Turk. And the second resurrection they placed at its close, with the reign of the righteous commonly understood as following.

Such is the composite, panoramic picture of the prophetic belief of the seventeenth century in America. Postmillennialism was as yet unknown, for Whitbyanism had not yet been loosed upon England and the world. And Futurism had not yet made any headway outside of papal circles, for it was not until the third decade of the nineteenth century that this papal counter-interpretation was first adopted by any Protestant. And to the

individual writers is to be added the representative group statement of 1680 on the Papacy as the Antichrist of prophecy. Nothing could be clearer or more universal as a belief. The simple
Historical School of interpretation of the Reformers was still intact and thriving in the New World.

With this over-all background of the seventeenth century
before us, we are now prepared to note the slow but steady en-
croachment of profound changes in the beliefs of the church
after we enter the eighteenth century. These involve a revolutionary concept of the millennium. This will unfold before us
as we progress. But before we cross the century line let us note
a few general features in retrospect.

II. The Changing Religious Outlook

During the seventeenth century Virginia was the only English colony on the American continent in which the majority of
the people adhered to the faith of the Established Church of
the mother country. In Maryland the church was set up by law
in 1692. For a generation after the founding of South Carolina
the door was open to all sorts of Dissenters. When at last, in
1704, a conformity bill was passed, the Anglicans comprised but
a third of the population. Elsewhere the Church of England
had but few adherents, and lived only by sufferance. So increasing changes were inevitable.[1]

We have observed that the seventeenth-century New Englanders were prolific writers. The energies of the most vigorous
minds of the period, clerical and lay, were expended chiefly in
theological discussion,[2] including a goodly number of prophetic
expositions. The ministry especially devoted their time to expounding their beliefs and answering their opponents. Thus
of the one hundred three works published in Boston from 1682
to 1689, fifty-six were sermons and thirty-nine others were religious in character.[3] And while the clergy encouraged education, they had taken the pains to control and direct it. The

---

[1] Thomas J. Wertenbaker, *The First Americans, 1607-1690*, p. 115.
[2] *Ibid.*, pp. 237, 238.   [3] *Ibid.*, pp. 241, 242.

textbooks were chosen with a view to inculcating the precepts of the church, and the schools were supported from church funds.[4] The interests of all were thus bound together.

We have also noted that two conflicting tendencies were at work by the close of the seventeenth century—toward greater toleration on the one hand, and, on the other, toward established churches and persecution for dissenters.[5] The former was more noticeable farther north. But in 1691 the new charter of Massachusetts did away with the Congregational test for the franchise. An alteration in the control of the school system resulted. Similarly, the towns had become too large to be served by a single church, and there were divisions to suit the needs of the neighborhoods. So by 1700 there were a number of Baptist churches in New England, and the sectarian spirit began to melt away. Mutual toleration was growing.

III. The Groundwork of Religious Liberty

On the right were partisans of the Established Church, clinging to lawful order. On the left were the Independents, or Separatists, who proposed to abandon, if not to abolish, Establishment. The Puritans merely wished to purify the Anglican system. But ultimately the advocates of uniformity and suppression failed. In the process of time, out of the clash of the sects, the ferment of opinion, and the growth of doubt, came religious toleration.[6]

Thus the gates of the American colonies were gradually opened to every religious faith that was stirring the Old World —Catholics, Separatists, Puritans, Quakers, Presbyterians, and Baptists from the British Isles, and Lutherans, Dunkards, Moravians, Mennonites, Huguenots, and Salzburgers from the Continent. All found sanctuary in the New World.[7] The tra-

---

[4] *Ibid.*, p. 245.
[5] There was persecution for Roman Catholics in Maryland. Becoming a royal province in 1691, with the Church of England established, all citizens were taxed for its support. Laws were passed aimed directly at Catholics, forbidding them to hold public office, taking away their franchise, and denying the right of holding public religious services. Priests were forbidden to preach, hear confession, or to administer the sacraments. (Sanford H. Cobb, *The Rise of Religious Liberty in America*, pp. 397, 398; James Truslow Adams, *Provincial Society, 1690-1763*, p. 155.)
[6] Charles A. and Mary R. Beard, *The Rise of American Civilization*, vol. 1, p. 29.
[7] *Ibid.*, p. 30.

ditional solidarity of church and state ultimately disintegrated by the incoming of a revolutionary philosophy of individual rights which freed the individual from subjection to a fixed group status.[8] The transition to the rationalism of the eighteenth century in the other colonies was gradual. But in New England it was marked by a spiritual crisis. The reaction from the witch trials was one factor. The rising tide of belief in separation of church and state, rather than in a theocracy, was another.[9]

IV. Witchcraft Trials Mar the Century

The colonists had brought with them from Europe a vivid consciousness of the supernatural. The seventeenth century, in both the Old World and the New, was an age of magic and witchcraft. Comets and similar phenomena were often regarded as supernatural manifestations, purported to mark some event of special importance. Thus the "blazing comet" of 1680 was the occasion of Increase Mather's *Heaven's Alarm to the World.*[10]

The seventeenth century marked the height of the witchcraft prosecutions, and the Mosaic injunction was invoked, "Thou shalt not suffer a witch to live." [11] In the previous century in Europe hundreds had been burned for witchcraft.[12] The scenes were far flung, including Italy, Spain, France, Switzerland, Germany, and even England. In Scotland this prosecution of witches reached even greater heights of horror. And it was during the period of seventeenth-century Puritan ascendancy that the witchcraft inquest reached its zenith in the American colonies.[13]

While there were some witchcraft charges in Virginia and Maryland, it was in New England that it reached its greatest excesses.[14] There were two well-defined epidemics of these witch burnings—one from 1647 to 1663, the other from 1688 to 1693.[15] Trials and executions followed with "monotonous

---

[8] Vernon L. Parrington, *The Colonial Mind 1620-1800*, p. 5.
[9] Adams, *op. cit.*, pp. 120-122.   [11] Ex. 22:18.
[10] Wertenbaker, *op. cit.*, p. 139.   [12] Wertenbaker, *op. cit.*, p. 143.
[13] *Ibid.*, pp. 143, 144; also Wallace Notestein, *A History of Witchcraft in New England From 1558 to 1718*, pp. 97-101.   [14] *Ibid.*, pp. 145-150.   [15] *Ibid.*, p. 151-155.

regularity" in Connecticut and Massachusetts. The climax was reached at Salem. This continued until the terrible epidemic wore itself out through its own excesses.[16] It came at last to be recognized that most of the persons executed had been innocent, and this proved a fatal boomerang against the clergy.

The witchcraft debacle had occurred in the stifling atmosphere of a theocracy-glutted generation. Then the stark terror of witchcraft was followed by reactionism. The Salem outbreak was the logical outcome of the long policy of repression that hanged Quakers and destroyed independent thought. The witchcraft madness was the dramatic aftermath.[17] Thus power finally slipped from the hands of the oligarchy. The old order was breaking.

V. The Collapse of the Theocratic Experiment

The closing years of the seventeenth century witnessed a profound change in Massachusetts. The experiment of a theocratic Bible commonwealth had failed. The influence of the clergy in civil government, though not eliminated, was greatly restricted, and their hold upon the people definitely weakened. During the half century of its supremacy it had been subjected to a succession of shocks—the struggle for representative government, the stand of Roger Williams, the Quaker invasion, the annulling of the old charter, and reaction from the witchcraft prosecutions. Each had played its part in the overthrow.[18]

But more powerful than all these was perhaps the gradual trend toward rationalism, the development of liberalism, and the widening of human sympathies. The old school churchmen remained rigid and unyielding, and sought to perpetuate the pattern of the Puritan founders in the great American venture. In this they failed. Wertenbaker phrases it well:

"In the last analysis the New England theocracy failed because it tried to crystalize the Puritan spirit of the seventeenth century, while the tide of a new civilization swept over and past them." [19]

---

[16] *Ibid.*, p. 161.
[17] Lucien Price, "Witchcraft, Then and Now," in *The Nation*, (Oct. 4, 1922), vol. 115, no. 2987, pp. 331-333; Parrington, *op. cit.*, p. 86.
[18] Wertenbaker, *op. cit.*, p. 113.   [19] *Ibid.*, pp. 113, 114.

EIGHTEENTH-CENTURY LEADERS CONTINUE PROPHETIC INTERPRETATION

Left to Right (Upper): Thomas Prince, Congregational Clergyman; Jonathan Mayhew, Dudleian Lecturer; Aaron Burr, Presbyterian President of Princeton. (Center): Charles Chauncy, Congregational Minister; Samuel Sewall, Massachusetts Jurist; Jonathan Edwards, Revivalist and Princeton President. (Lower): Isaac Backus, Baptist Historian; Timothy Dwight, President of Yale; William Linn, President of Queen's College

CHAPTER NINE

Theologians, Schoolmasters, and Poets Join

I. Characteristic Features of Eighteenth Century

The intellectual leadership of the clergy remained undiminished in the eighteenth century, and that among a laity that was both strong and literate. This was due not alone to the high authority of the clerical office but to the personal greatness of the men who filled that office. In the field of literature their tireless activity, learning, and sheer force of character kept them in the forefront through their theological exposition, and this included prophetic exposition. Thus the sons maintained the strong traits of their pioneering forefathers.

With Cotton Mather we enter a period marked by the disruptive rise and spread of the Whitbyan postmillennial theory, with its figurative view of the first resurrection, as already noted in Volume II. Starting in England, it not only penetrated Continental Europe but began to take root in America. With its acceptance came the breakdown in the solidarity of the preceding century. JOSEPH BELLAMY, in his sermon on "The Millennium" (1758), JONATHAN EDWARDS, in his *History of . . . Redemption* (1774), SAMUEL HOPKINS, in his *Treatise on the Millennium* (1793), and others, now begin to teach this new view, repudiating the premillennial advent hope cherished in the preceding century.

However, in fairness it should be stated that, in contrast to Old World postmillennialists, even some of these men believed that the millennial kingdom would be introduced by a crisis—a terrific outpouring of God's judgments on evil world powers and Antichrist—and not by quiet transition. On the other hand such stalwarts as Cotton Mather, Thomas Prince, Benjamin Dale, and perhaps the majority of the other prophetic expositors, were still decided premillennialists. There is no material change in emphasis upon the fundamentals of interpretation— only gradual clarifications and advances. Thus, as in the Old World, two groups now stand opposed on the millennial issue.

In this century we also pass from the colonial into the early national era, from 1776 onward. The American Declaration of Independence, followed by the Constitution with its Bill of Rights, marks one of the great advances in the progress of liberty, crowning the new era inaugurated by the Reformation. It was in this country that for the first time the separation of church and state was realized in the interest of true religion, as protected in the Bill of Rights found in the first ten amendments to the Constitution.

Moreover, many premillennial works from the pens of European expositors were republished in America in the latter part of the eighteenth century. JOHN GILL's *Three Sermons on the Present and Future State of the Church,* at Boston (1756) and Northampton (1797); DAVID IMRIE's *Letter,* in Boston (1756); JAMES PURVES' *Dissertation on the seals, the trumpets, and the Vials,* in New York (1788), and on the *Apocalypse* (1787); THOMAS NEWTON's volume on prophecy, in New York (1787) and Northampton (1796); JOSEPH PRIESTLY, in Philadelphia (1794); and JAMES BICHENO, at Providence, Rhode Island (1795), and in West Springfield, Massachusetts (1796). These, and others, were scattered everywhere and did much to mold American opinion.

The writers on prophecy in this century were even more varied in personal background, profession, and achievement. Earlier inaccuracies were corrected and distinct advances were made. Despite the serious division that had now arisen over the exposition of the millennium, the idioms and general understandings of prophecy were common, and the Historical School of exposition was still prevalent. Not only were the great epochs and time periods clearly held on the year-day principle, but particular events, such as the Lisbon earthquake of 1755 and the great dark day of 1780, were recognized as prophesied harbingers of the approaching climax of the ages. We proceed now with the examination of the witnesses of the eighteenth century.

II. Cotton Mather—All Prophecies Indicate End Nearing

As the first major witness we summon COTTON MATHER (1663-1728), Congregational theologian, scholar, and author, who was born in Boston. The eldest son of Increase Mather, he became the most distinguished clergyman of his day, and one of the most remarkable men of his age. Markedly precocious as a child, he was the youngest student ever to enter Harvard— being admitted when only twelve. He was graduated in 1678 and began to preach, assisting his father in ministry at the Second Church at Boston. Obtaining his M.A. in 1681, and receiving ordination in 1685, he continued to fill the pulpit of the Second Church till his death. He was also overseer at Harvard. And in 1701, when his father gave up the presidency of Harvard, Cotton mourned the passing of the institution into hands less orthodox, and came to look upon Yale as the hope of Congregational education. Celebrated for his own learning, he was offered its presidency, but declined. (Portrait on page 34.)

When, back in 1692, the Royal Charter for Massachusetts was secured, the new governor appointed a court to try those suspected of witchcraft, which phenomenon had just appeared in Salem. Mather plunged into the controversy, and to convince the world, wrote his *Wonders of the Invisible World* (1693).[1] He was deeply involved in these witchcraft prosecutions of 1692, and believed obsession could be cured by fasting and prayer. Intensely emotional, high strung, and overwrought, he was involved in a constant succession of quarrels.[2]

---

[1] Barrett Wendell, *Cotton Mather, The Puritan Priest*, chap. 6; Abijah P. Marvin, *The Life and Times of Cotton Mather*, p. 152.
[2] Vernon L. Parrington, *The Colonial Mind 1620-1800*, pp. 107, 108.

With almost incredible industry, Cotton Mather amassed a prodigious amount of knowledge[3] and left nearly four hundred fifty published treatises.[4] Twenty volumes pertained to eschatology, and prophetic exposition characterized a number of the leading titles. His most celebrated work, *Magnalia Christi Americana; or The Ecclesiastical History of New-England* (1702), is a veritable mine of information on the noted seventeenth-century colonial leaders—preachers, governors, judges, and educators—the church synods and Confessions of Faith, and the story of Harvard. Intimate glimpses are given of their prophetic faith, invaluable in our quest. An epitome of Mather's interpretations of prophecy is given by his son Samuel (not to be confused with Cotton Mather's uncle of the same name, who has been discussed earlier, on page 108).[5]

1. ANTICHRIST'S KINGDOM ENDED BY SECOND ADVENT.—Discoursing on the coming kingdom of God in *Things to be Look'd For* (1691), on the "Speedy Approaches of that State Which is Reserved for the Church of God in the Latter Dayes," Mather stresses the second phase of the stone kingdom of Daniel 2, which is to follow the "four monarchies," as it becomes a mountain filling the whole earth.[6] He observes succinctly that "the World is a little while hence to have a *New Face* upon it; and in that New World, the Lord Jesus Christ shall have as much Influence in the Hearts and Lives of men as now the Divel has."[7] But the papal Antichrist will continue until the 1260 years are finished, and must be destroyed before the saints possess the kingdom. The "Antichrist afterwards accepted the profer of the Divel" of the kingdom offer rejected by Christ, and so becomes his vicar.[8] The breakup of Rome, and the ten barbarous kingdoms succeeding, he believes, throw the rise of Anti-

[3]Charles A. and Mary R. Beard, *The Rise of American Civilization*, vol. 1, p. 147.
[4] The sheer physical output of Cotton Mather's principal printed works, exclusive of all prefaces, postscripts, and newspaper contributions, is tremendous—444 in all! See T. J. Holmes, *Cotton Mather: A Bibliography of His Works*, vol. 1, p. ix. The actual listing takes thirteen pages of small type. This classic three-volume Holmes bibliography of 1,395 pages reproduces in facsimile the title pages of the leading works, with notes on each item, thus affording the most complete and accurate data extant. However, very little in the field of our quest is brought to the surface in the Index. See also *Dictionary of American Biography*, vol. 12, p. 388.
[5] Samuel Mather, *The Life of . . . Cotton Mather*, pp. 140-145.
[6] Cotton Mather, *Things to be Look'd For*, p. 11. (Title page reproduced on p. 152.)
[7] *Ibid.*, p. 10.   [8] *Ibid.*, p. 11.

christ around 456.[9] This 1260-year period should therefore
end soon, he thought, though he would not set the year.

2. BEGINS TURKISH WOE PERIOD IN 1300.—Applying the
second woe trumpet to the Turks, with their prophesied period
of time, beginning about 1300, he says:

"You cannot but allow me, with all sensible Interpreters, that the
second Wo Trumpet is the Turkish Empire; which begun to play its Reaks
upon the Roman Empire in the Tenth and Eleventh Century, and at last
between the years Fourteen and Fifteen hundred, siez'd Constantinople
it self into its hands. All those Execrable Plunderers whom we call, Con-
querors, from the beginning of the World, have hardly shed such Rivers
of Blood, as these woful Turks have done. But how long must this game
hold? There seems to be a Term allotted for them, in Rev. 9.41, 15. Loose
the Four Angels, which are bound in the great River Euphrates; and the
four Angels were loosed, which were prepared for an Hour, and a Day, and
a Month, and a Year, to slay the Third part of men.

"There were four Sultanies, or Kingdoms of Turks, hovering about
the River Euphrates; until they all united in the one Ottoman family, under
which, by the Year Thirteen hundred, they were making themselves a
formidable Wo to the Roman Empire. Now cast up, an Hour, a little space
for preparation; a Day, that is one year; a Month, which is Thirty years;
and a Year, which comes to Three hundred and Sixty five [or perhaps, but
Sixty] years; according to the Prophetical Cypher of Dayes for Years; and
one would Suspect, that within less than Seven Years from this Time, the
Turk should be under such Humiliations, as might Obstruct his ever
giving Europe Trouble any more. If we should shortly hear of a general
Peace or Truce with him, it would add unto our Probabilities." [10]

3. APPROACHING END OF PROPHETIC TIMES.—The first four
trumpets he applies to the barbarian incursions upon the Western Empire—such as by Alaric and Genseric [11]—with the seventh
seal of the seventh trumpet to come soon. The fifth-trumpet
first woe was thought to be the Saracens.[12] Maintaining that
these phases were already accomplished, Mather stressed the
approaching end of the remaining prophetic times.[13] Such supporting names as Jurieu are cited.

4. FLATLY REJECTS THE GROTIAN ANTICHRIST.—Mather
sharply rejects Grotius' Preterist idea of an early pagan Roman
Antichrist, saying pointedly, "The Day Light is now a little too

---

[9] *Ibid.*, pp. 28-31.   [11] *Ibid.*, pp. 38, 39.   [13] *Ibid.*, p. 47.
[10] *Ibid.*, pp. 31, 32.   [12] *Ibid.*, p. 40.

broad for us, to take the Sorry Puppet of the Grotian Antichrist, for the Man of Sin." [14] In contrast, Mather contends explicitly that it must be an empire, with a false religion, whose chief city must be seated on seven mountains, ruling over the kingdoms of the earth. It must be a continuation of the fourth monarchy, sitting in the temple of God with ten kings as supporters.[15] Then he appeals to men not to pay homage to this Babylon, but to come out from her.[16]

5. CITES COUNCIL OF RHEIMS, AND EBERHARDT.—Mather closes this remarkable treatise by referring to the declaration of Antichrist's identity at the Council of Rheims, in 991, and the identification of the Antichrist by Archbishop Eberhardt of Salzburg in 1240, as the historical Papacy,[17] as fully noted in *Prophetic Faith,* Volume 2. Among his last admonitions is this: "Tis not possible for a man to Do a more Dangerous thing, than to Continue in the Romish Communion, at such a Time as this." [18]

6. 2300 YEARS TO BABYLON'S FALL.—In 1692, in connection with the "Tryals of Several VVitches," Mather preached a discourse on *The Wonders of the Invisible World* (1693), declaring that the book of Revelation is a commentary on Daniel.[19] He stresses the fourth, or Roman, monarchy, with the fifth as the coming kingdom of God. He refers approvingly to Beverley's *Line of Time* concerning the "Two Thousand and Three Hundred Years, unto that New Jerusalem, whereto the Church is to be advanced, when the Mystical Babylon shall be fallen. At the Resurrection of our Lord, there were seventeen or eighteen Hundred of those Years, yet upon the Line, to run unto, The Rest that remains for the People of God." [20]

7. TRUMPETS BRING DOWNFALL OF PAGANISM AND PAPACY. —Mather then summarizes the prophecies of the Apocalypse, especially the seals and trumpets which involve the downfall of paganism and the Papacy.[21] The 1260 years of Antichrist are

---

[14] *Ibid.*, p. 65.
[15] *Ibid.*
[16] *Ibid.*, p. 66.
[17] *Ibid.*, pp. 66-69.
[18] *Ibid.*, p. 69.
[19] Cotton Mather, *The Wonders of the Invisible World*, p. 3.
[20] *Ibid.*
[21] *Ibid.*

next pictured,[22] with his continual oppression of the people of God.   Referring to the first four or five hundred years of the Christian Era, he adds that it "shows us the Face of the Church, first in Rome Heathenish, and then in Rome Converted, before the Man of Sin was yet come to Mans Estate." [23]

8. SEVEN-HEADED BEAST ON SEVEN-HILLED CITY.—Leading from this, Mather affirms that the devil and fallen spirits vex mankind,[24] and from this premise enters into the discussion of witches.   Toward the end of Satan's time, as it grows short, the devil descends with wrath upon mankind.[25]   Mather next calls the papal power Satan's "Antichristian Vicar, the seven-headed Beast on the seven-hilled city," who will go down to the bottomless pit when he shall have spent his "determined years." [26]   This will produce the perilous times of the last days.[27]

Later he writes:

"The views both of Daniel and of John, do assure us that whatever Monarch, shall while the Papacy continues go to swallow up the Ten Kings which received their power upon the Fall of the Western Empire, he must miscarry in the attempt." [28]

9. CENTRAL PLACE GIVEN ADVENT HOPE.—The central place given the advent hope and expectancy by Cotton Mather is clearly expressed:

"I am verily perswaded, *The Judge is at the Door;* I do without any hesitation venture to say, *The Great Day of the Lord is Near, it is Near, and it hastens Greatly.*   O That our Minds May be as deeply Engaged in Thinking on the Second coming of our Lord, as the Saints of old were in thinking on His First." [29]

10. END OF 1260 YEARS MAY BE KNOWN.—In *Things for a Distress'd People to Think Upon,* in the 1696 election sermon of the General Assembly, Mather cites Daniel's understanding by books of the approaching end of the Jewish captivity.   He declares past mistakes should aid in reaching more accurate conclusions.

---

[22] *Ibid.*, p. 4.
[23] *Ibid.*
[24] *Ibid.*, pp. 4, 5.
[25] *Ibid.*, p. 13.
[26] *Ibid.*
[27] *Ibid.*, p. 14.
[28] *Ibid.*, p. 40.
[29] "Preparatory Meditations," p. 36, in Samuel Lee, *A Summons or Warning to the Great Day of Judgment.*

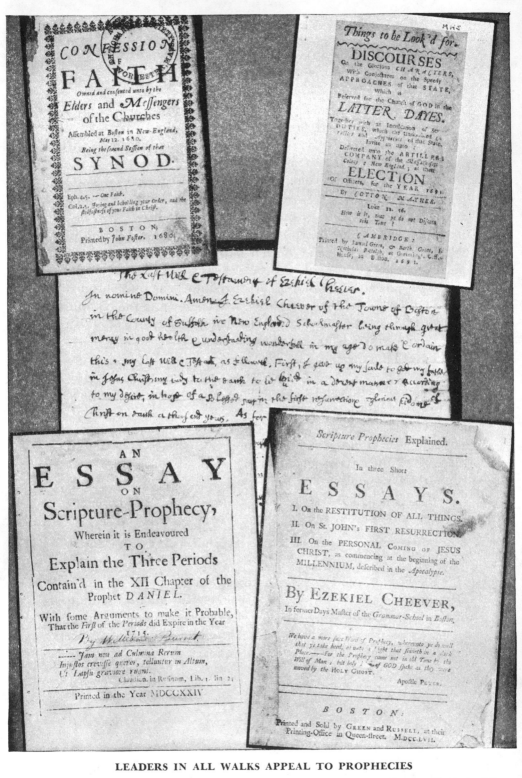

LEADERS IN ALL WALKS APPEAL TO PROPHECIES

Group Statement of Faith, of 1680, Identifies Papal Antichrist (Upper Left); Noted Clerics Like Cotton Mather Write Book Upon Book on Prophecy (Upper Right); Governor Burnet Expounds Prophetic Time Periods (Lower Left); and Famous New England Schoolmaster Cheever Explains Scripture Prophecies (Lower Right), Even Injecting His Prophetic Faith Into His Will (Center)

"When the Twelve Hundred & Sixty years assigned unto the Reign of the Antichristian Apostasy, draw towards their Period, this Period also may be Known, as well as any of the former. The Mistakes that have been in the Guesses of some Learned men, about this Happy Period, are far from Inferring a Necessity of Wrong Reckonings to the Worlds end; No, they rather make it more easy now to Reckon Right." [30]

Declaring that he appears with a message from heaven of a "Revolution and a Reformation" to be at hand, Mather insists that the "Abominable City" is to experience an earthquake, and the Turk would cease to be a "wo to Christendome." [31]

11. LAST SANDS OF HOURGLASS RUNNING.—Asserting that Christ's kingdom will succeed upon the kingdom of the "Vicar at Rome," he makes this declaration:

"Tis very certain, That there will be no more than Twelve Hundred & Sixty years allow'd unto that Papal Kingdom: Tis very certain, That when Ten Soveraign Kings arise, in the broken Roman Empire, the Twelve Hundred & Sixty years of the Papal Kingdom, are Commenced: And It is very certain, That by the middle of the Fifth century, Ten several Distinct Kingdomes, took advantage from the Distractions then upon the Roman Empire, to set up for themselves. By this Calculation, we have nothing less than a Demonstration, that the Papal Kingdom, has the last Sands, of its last Hour-glass, now running for it." [32]

12. WILL GIFTS BE RESTORED BEFORE ADVENT?—Mather deplores those schemes that put off this most "Happy Period, unto further and further ages." [33] He closes by suggesting that the gifts of the Spirit, particularly of healing, which continued in the early church until the growth of the great apostasy, might be restored under the "Mighty Shower" of the Spirit when the allotted period of the apostasy should be over. [34]

13. CATECHISM IDENTIFIES ANTICHRIST; URGES SEPARATION. —Concerning his *Fall of Babylon* (1707), [35] Mather explains that Maryland contains many papists. Therefore he "printed some hundreds of the catechism by itself, to be dispersed in Maryland.

---

[30] Cotton Mather, *Things for a Distress'd People to Think Upon*, p. 33.
[31] *Ibid.*, pp. 33, 34.   [33] *Ibid.*   [34] *Ibid.*, p. 36.
[32] *Ibid.*, p. 35.
[35] First published separately in 1707. Second edition appeared in 1708 as Essay 1 in *The Man of God Furnished*. A later edition of this larger work was published in 1721 under the title *The Way of Truth laid out. A Catechism . . . In Seven Essays.*

I considered also, that it was a Blessedness, to do a part in the work of this Day, ye pulling down of ye *Romish Babylon*. Accordingly, I entitled the little peece of work, The Fall of Babylon." [36]   Dealing first with the distinction between canonical and apocryphal writings, the treatise leads on to the sole mediatorship of Christ, and the sacrilege of employing images in the worship of God.[37]   Further on we find these two searching questions and answers:

"Q. Is the Pope of Rome, to be look'd upon as, The Antichrist, whose coming and Reigning was foretold in the ancient Oracles?
"A. The Oracles of God, foretold, Rising of an ANTICHRIST in the Christian Church; and in the POPE of Rome, all the Characters of that Antichrist, are so marvellously answered, that if any who read the Scriptures do not see it, there is a Marvellous Blindness upon them.
"It is Written, [2 Thes. 2.2, 8, 9, 10.] *Then shall that wicked one be Revealed, whom the Lord shall consume with the Spirit of His mouth, & shall Destroy with the Brightness of His coming; Even him, whose coming is after the working of Satan, with all Deceivableness of Unrighteousness in them that perish; because they receive not the Love of the Truth that they might be Saved.* [Dan. 7.20, 21.]
"Q. Is the Church of Rome that Babylon, from which the Churches of the Reformation have done well to make a Separation?
"A. The Church of Rome, has, in its PLACE, and its Idolatry and Cruelty and Filthiness, the Unquestionable Marks of the MYSTICAL BABYLON. And all that would be Saved, ought to Separate from the Communion of it." [38]

14. COMPREHENSIVE SUMMARY OF PROPHETIC VIEWS.— There is extant a Cotton Mather unpublished manuscript dated Boston, December 25, 1703, and titled "An Essay Concerning the Happy State Expected for the Church Upon Earth; Endeavoring to Demonstrate that the Second Coming of the Lord Jesus Christ Will be at the Beginning of that Happy State. With Some Thoughts Upon the Characters and Approaches of it." [39] Its scope is so comprehensive and illuminating that a terse summary is here given, with pages indicated:

---

[36] Charles Evans, *American Bibliography*, vol. 1, p. 190 (no. 1309). Thomas J. Holmes, *Cotton Mather, A Bibliography*, vol. 1, p. 368 (no. 126).
[37] Cotton Mather, *Fall of Babylon*, in *The Way of Truth Laid Out*, pp. 1-6.
[38] *Ibid.*, pp. 18, 19 (brackets his).
[39] In manuscript group titled *Problema Theologicum*, by Cotton Mather, at American Antiquarian Society, Worcester, Massachusetts.

1. The second advent comes at the beginning of the Happy Estate. (P. 4.)

2. The thousand years are not yet begun—striking at Augustine's false theory. (P. 17.)

3. Satan has never yet been bound for a thousand years from deceiving the nations. (P. 19.)

4. After the tribulation the stars will fall literally—then comes the advent. (P. 27.)

5. In Daniel 7 and Revelation 13 the ten horns are ten divisions of Rome. (P. 37.)

6. Of the Little Horn he says: "Behold, the Bishop of Rome, and his Kingdome, in most lively colours." He has all under his sway. (P. 41.)

7. The fourth beast was understood to be Rome by Jewish rabbis for nine hundred years after the giving of the prophecy. (P. 43.)

8. The first resurrection (of the just) is at the second advent. (Pp. 44, 58, 59.)

9. The destruction of Antichrist is at the beginning of the thousand years. (P. 48.)

10. It will come soon after the destruction of the Turk. (Pp. 52, 53.)

11. The first woe was the Saracens. (Pp. 54, 55.)

12. The second, or Turkish, woe is 1300 to 1697. (Pp. 56, 57.)

13. The 1260 years and 1290 and 1335 began about A.D. 440 or 450. (Pp. 88, 89.)

III. President Willard—Advent Hope Illuminates Last Days

The second expositor of the eighteenth century is SAMUEL WILLARD (1640-1707), vice-president of Harvard and minister at Boston. Born at Concord, Massachusetts, and educated at Harvard, with an M.A. in 1659, he was ordained in 1664. He served as pastor of the church at Groton, then became co-pastor of the Old South Church, Boston (1678-1707), and vice-president and acting president of Harvard from 1701 to 1707. Though he was the author of numerous books between 1674 and 1707, his most noted were *The Fountain Opened* (1700) and *A Compleat Body of Divinity* (1726).

1. NEW-EARTH STATE IS IMMINENT.—In the former work Willard holds to the national restoration of the Jews but describes the triumphant state of the church, yet to come, in this way:

"The whole Creation groans for this day, and we ought to live upon the Hope of it, Rom. 8:19-23. . . . It will not be long before these days

Commence. Although we cannot tell the day, or month, or year; . . . yet we are fully assured that it is hastning." [40]

This he believed comes after the Gospel-Church has been in its "prefixed time" in the wilderness—1260 days.[41]

2. ANTICHRIST'S DESTRUCTION AND THE CALL OUT OF BABYLON.—Referring to the "things foretold" in the prophecies yet to be "brought to pass," and particularly to the destruction of Antichrist, he adds:

"God will doubtless prepare the way to the destruction of the Man of Sin, who stands in the way, by giving an enlarged Commission for the Preaching of the Everlasting Gospel, which shall Call His out of Babylon, and convince the Great Ones of their egregious folly." [42]

3. SECOND ADVENT NOT FAR OFF.—In the latter work Willard looked for the premillennial advent, declaring, "This is the day that I love, that I wait for," [43] and stating, "It will not be long before that day shall come; these are the last days, and the winding up of the time that we live in." [44] The titles of three other works reveal the burden of his heart and show the central place held by the advent hope in his thinking: *Checkered State of the Gospel Church* (1701), *Rules for the Discerning of the Present Times* (1693), and *Peril of the Time Displayed* (1700).

IV. Noyes—Prophecies Basis of Election Sermon

NICHOLAS NOYES (1647-1717), poet and pastor at Haddam, Connecticut, for thirteen years, and then pastor at Salem, Massachusetts, was born at Newbury, Massachusetts. He was a Harvard graduate—an M.A. of 1667—and was ordained in 1683. He ultimately adopted the advent view of the Mathers. In 1698 he preached the annual election sermon, in which he maintained that the thousand years were yet future. In 1702 he wrote *Last Conflagration Will Not Annihilate but Purify the Earth, Bringing Times of Restitution*. With Cotton Mather and others he had promoted the Salem witchcraft trials of 1692, for all of

---

[40] Samuel Willard, *The Fountain Opened* (1722 ed.), p. 22.
[41] *Ibid.*, p. 16.
[42] *Ibid.*, p. 17.
[43] Samuel Willard, *A Compleat Body of Divinity*, p. 424.
[44] *Ibid.*, p. 421.

which he afterward publicly confessed his error.   In 1703 Cotton Mather discussed the millennial times with Noyes, who was still a bit hazy.   Then Mather's ninety-one-page letter-essay "Concerning the Happy Estate" [45] apparently drew him over to a full acceptance.

1. PROPHECIES THE BASIS OF OUR FAITH.—Noyes preached the election sermon in 1698, published as *New-Englands Duty and Interest, to be an Habitation of Justice, and Mountain of Holiness,* concerning the reformations promised for the last days. In a supporting introduction John Higginson, pastor at Salem, laid down the principle that "we are not to expect full understanding of the prophecies until they be fulfilled"; nevertheless, the prophecies are the "ground of our Faith, Hope and Prayer, relating to their Accomplishment." [46]

2. 1260-YEAR PERIOD OF ANTICHRIST'S REIGN.—After referring to the promised "Resurrection of the Witnesses," from "Romish Idolatry and Tyranny," Noyes says:

"The Lord Jesus held some kind of possession of the West Empire during the 1260 years of Antichrist's Reign, by his Witnesses that Prophesied all that time, though in Sackcloth.   He hath held possession likewise in the East Empire, notwithstanding the fury and cruelty of the Arabian and Saracen or Mahometan Harpyes." [47]

3. ANTICHRIST'S DAY OF RETRIBUTION COMING.—He then refers to the known and expected destruction of Antichrist:

"What if Antichrist Exalteth himself above all that is called God, or that is worshipped, and sitteth in the Temple of God, and hath done so above a thousand years; is not that Man of Sin, a Son of perdition?   Doth not God see; yea and his people too, that his day is coming?   2 Thes. 2. 3, 4, 8." [48]

4. METALLIC IMAGE STANDING ON "LAST LEGGS."—As the basis of his belief in that imminence, he cites the prophecy of the great image of Daniel 2, as well as the state of the Turk:

---

[45] In *Problema Theologicum.*   See note 39, p. 153.   See also Holmes, *op. cit.,* vol. 2, pp. 854, 855.
[46] John Higginson, "Epistle Dedicatory," A₄ v., in Nichols Noyes, *New Englands Duty and Interest.*
[47] Nicholas Noyes, *New-Englands Duty and Interest, to be an Habitation of Justice, and Mountain of Holiness,* pp. 32, 33.
[48] *Ibid.,* p. 67.

"Nebuchadnezzars Image standing upon his last Leggs, and it seemeth as if both of them had received a blow from the Stone cut out of the mountain without hands, that maketh them stagger. It is probable, Delay will not be much longer. The Great Turk, the Oppressor of the Jews & Eastern Christians, seemeth to be at his last prayers, and they likelier to reconcile him to Hell, than to Heaven. And considering what is said of the Kings of the East, Rev. 16.12. and of the Western Kings, Rev. 17.16. We ought to expect and pray for the coming of the time, when the Kingdoms of this World shall become the Kingdoms of our Lord and of his Christ. Rev. 11.15." [49]

Noyes believed that the American continent would "partake of the goodness of God in the latter days." [50]

V. Governor Dudley—Premillennialist Student of Prophecy

JOSEPH DUDLEY (1647-1720), chief justice of New York and second governor of Massachusetts, was born in Roxbury, Massachusetts. In 1665 he graduated from Harvard with the intention of becoming a minister, but soon turned to politics. He was, however, a Christian scholar and philosopher. In 1673 he was made a member of the Massachusetts General Court, representing Roxbury. And in 1682 he was sent to England with John Richards to prevent the threatened repeal of the Massachusetts charter. He also served as censor of the press.

Dudley was appointed president of the territory of New England—Massachusetts, Maine, New Hampshire, Rhode Island—for a few months in 1686, and was then named judge of the Superior Court in 1687, and in 1691-92 was chief justice of New York. Next for eight years he served as lieutenant governor of the Isle of Wight, and was finally appointed governor of Massachusetts, from 1702 to 1715. While pursuing his official career, Dudley began the investigation of the millennium and the approaching end of the age, his interest being aroused by Ezekiel Cheever, the schoolmaster. Cotton Mather dedicated to his friend Governor Dudley the manuscript written in 1703 to Nicholas Noyes. Mather says:

---

[49] *Ibid.*, p. 68.   [50] *Ibid.*, p. 69.

"May it please your Excellency. It gave me an uncommon satisfaction, when I was informed, That a person of so much Erudition & Sagacity, & such superiour Sentiments, as your Excellency, has upon the Encouragement of One of the Greatest Literators in the Age, applied his mind unto the study of those Divine Prophecies, which concern the Kingdome of God, that is to arrive, when His Will is to be done on Earth, as it is in Heaven. . . . I have had the Honour of Engaging Two Governours, that were men of Learning, to subscribe unto my sentiments." [51]

The winning of two governors to the premillennial view is indeed a significant achievement for Cotton Mather.

VI. Schoolmaster Cheever—Implants Premillennial Faith in Others

The educational aim of the early settlers was to instruct children and youth so that they might search the Scriptures. Indeed, as noted, Harvard was founded principally as a training school for the clergy.[52] Civil and ecclesiastical functions blended in those early times. But under the Massachusetts Charter of 1691, control of the church over the state was abolished. Consequently, school administration became a secular matter. So, with the passing of the religious sanctions for education there came a decline in educational emphasis for a time. Then the district school began to be developed, and Ezekiel Cheever's Boston Latin School, from 1670 to 1708, was one of the best. A struggle to liberalize Harvard developed,[53] and the Connecticut church leaders seized the opportunity to found the collegiate school to be known as Yale.[54]

EZEKIEL CHEEVER (1614-1708), American classicist, educator, and one of the founders of New Haven, Connecticut, was born in London and educated at the University of Cambridge, England. Inspired to seek a home in the New World, he came to Boston in 1638, at twenty-four, and to New Haven in 1639. Here he sought to assist in founding a new community that

---

[51] Cotton Mather, "An Essay Concerning the Happy State Expected for the Church upon Earth," pp. i, ii.
[52] Wertenbaker, *The First Americans, 1607-1690*, p. 248.
[53] *Ibid.*, p. 249. During the last quarter of the century, Harvard became the battleground of the conservative and liberal groups in Massachusets, and suffered in consequence.
[54] James Truslow Adams, *Provincial Society, 1690-1763*, pp. 134, 135.

would be a guide and beacon to the nations. Appointed master of the public school, and teaching there until 1650, he was a man of prestige, representing the town from 1646 to 1650 in the General Court. He was also one of the pillars of the local church, serving as a deacon, and occasionally officiating as a preacher.

From 1650 to 1661, Cheever taught at Ipswich. At Charleston (1661-69) he established a free school endowed by annual taxes. Then at Boston he was master of the Boston Latin School for thirty-eight years (1670-1708). Famous as a skillful teacher, he had governors, judges, ministers, and magistrates in their teens as pupils, and left an indelible mark upon New England.

While teaching in Boston, Cheever wrote his famous *Short Introduction to the Latin Tongue,* which for a century was the handbook of Latin students. By 1785 it had run through twenty editions. His leading religious work—published after his death—was *Scripture Prophecies Explained, in Three Short Essays* (1757), on the restitution of all things, the first resurrection, and the second advent at the beginning of the millennium. A clear premillennialist, Cheever held to the second literal advent and a literal resurrection, and shaped the views of future leaders to this end. (Title page reproduced on page 152.)

1. ADVENT HOPE WRITTEN IN LAST WILL.—In common with the church of the early centuries he held to the personal reign of Christ in the grand millennial day—a day of judgment, the terrible day of the Lord. The new earth is a restoration to its state before the fall.[55] Cheever's last will, on record in, and secured from, the probate court in Boston, plainly declares that he dies—

"In hope of a blessed part in the first resurrection, and glorious kingdom of Christ on earth a thousand years." [56]

2. RESTORATION TO EDENIC STATE.—In Essay I, Cheever held that the restitution was not a new creation but a restoration to the Edenic state that was before the fall, which time of renova-

---

[55] Ezekiel Cheever, *Scripture Prophecies Explained,* p. 6.
[56] Last will and testament, Probate Court records (Boston), Liber 16, p. 466 (no. 3119). (Reproduced on p. 174.)

tion will coincide with the first judgment, foretold by the prophets.[57]

3. THOUSAND YEARS BETWEEN TWO RESURRECTIONS.—In Essay II he held that the first resurrection of the saints is "a thousand years before the resurrection of the wicked at the last general judgment." [58]

4. SECOND ADVENT INTRODUCES MILLENNIUM.—Maintaining, in Essay III, that the second personal advent would mark the beginning of the thousand years,[59] Cheever states that this all comes after the great period of the church's heavy tribulation (Matt. 24:30), from "Antichrist and his party, whom Christ comes to destroy" [60]—and all before the thousand years. And with the signs of that great day this interpretation "doth fitly agree."

5. COMES AT END OF FOURTH MONARCHY.—This present world will perish just as did the antediluvian world.[61] Christ receives His kingdom from the Ancient of days (Daniel 7) at the second advent.

"This coming is a personal coming, the time of it after the destruction of antichrist's kingdom, and the end of the four monarchies, as appears from Dan. ii. and Rev. xxi. which places shew that it is an outward visible kingdom, which Christ, together with his saints, shall have in this world." [62]

And this is all while Antichrist is still alive, whom Christ destroys with the brightness of His coming.[63]

VII. Sabbatarian Poet Steere Writes of Babylon's Doom

RICHARD STEERE (1643-1721), colonial poet, man of means, and diligent student, was born in England. Coming to New England, he probably settled in Providence, Rhode Island, and was led to accept the religious opinions of John Rogers, at that time of New London. Back in 1638 certain citizens of Boston had been banished on account of their religious faith, fleeing to Rhode Island. In 1674 John Rogers joined the Seventh Day

---

[57] Cheever, *Scripture Prophecies Explained*, pp. 1, 6.
[58] *Ibid.*, p. 7.   [60] *Ibid.*, p. 22.   [62] *Ibid.*, p. 26.
[59] *Ibid.*, p. 21.   [61] *Ibid.*, p. 23.   [63] *Ibid.*, p. 27.

Baptists of Newport, Rhode Island. In 1675, because of certain differences, Rogers and others separated from the Newport group and formed the New London church, becoming known as Rogerenes—distinctly nonresistant, and the first to make a stand against ecclesiastical legislation in Connecticut. And Steere had presumably become a member of this New London church that followed Rogers.

One of the earlier tenets of the Rogerene faith was, of course, that the seventh day of the week is the Sabbath, and should be observed instead of the first. In 1694 Rogers was warned to desist from working on the first day. Refusing, he was arrested and imprisoned. While he was in prison, a printed attack was made on the government and colony of Connecticut, signed by Richard Steere, Samuel Beebe, and Jonathan and James Rogers. It accused the colony of persecuting dissenters, of exhibiting narrow principles, domineering, and compelling people to pay for a Presbyterian preacher—which was against the laws of England—of robbery and oppression. Special court was held to consider the libelous paper, and its subscribers were then fined £5 each. Appeal was made to the higher court, which only confirmed the decision.[64]

Such was the Steere who, in 1713, published a small volume of poems titled after the leading one, *The Daniel Catcher. The Life of the Prophet Daniel*.[65] Along with it appeared some remarkable verse with the extended title "Antichrist Display'd in a brief Character of the Sordid Ignorance, and Implacable Cruelty of the Church of Rome, called in Scripture Mistery Babylon the Great. With the Certainty of her Total Fall, Final Destruction and Desolation, which produceth matter for Sions Ejaculation and Consolation."[66]   (Title page reproduced on page 232.)

1. Babylon Astride the Seven-headed Beast.—Steere employed strong language, characteristic of the times, saturated

---

[64] George E. Littlefield, *The Early Massachusetts Press*, vol. 1, pp. 3-9.
[65] Signed "R.S."; for identification as Richard Steere and a discussion of the publication of the book, along with a full facsimile reproduction, see Littlefield, *op. cit.*, vol. 1, p. 5, and vol. 2, pp. 61, 62, and facsimile.
[66] Richard Steere, *The Daniel Catcher*, p. 73.

with the phrasings of the prophets.   The opening lines read:

> "I Need no Heathen Deity Implore,
> To Charactrise this Babylonish whore;
> She is Display'd Beyond the Art of men,
> (As in Prophetick writings may be seen)
> And might have spar'd the Labour of my Pen.
> Yet as an Abstract of her Scarlet Sins,
> My Muse her bloody Character begins;
> Litt'ral Babel which in Chaldea stood,
> Did Tipify this Curst Confused Brood;
> That was, so this is in Confusion Hurl'd:
> For Myst'ry Babel hath Amus'd the World;
> As mounted on the seven headed Beast,
> Her Antichristian Tricks make Manifest.
> First view her Legend, so much doted on,
> Each Cheat is counted Revelation." [67]

Tracing her beginning from near the beginning of the gospel days, "till the Black night of Ignorance, Eclips'd the Churches Light," Steere declares:

> "And like a Strumpet did Debauch her life,
> Yet would be call'd the true and Lawful wife." [68]

2. SEPARATE BEFORE HER COMING FALL.—"Sitting on many waters," reigning over empires and kingdoms, she made them "slaves and vassals," defiling her hands with blood.[69]   Then citing Ireland, Piedmont, France, and the days of Mary in Britain, Steere continues:

> " 'Tis this Insatiate and Bloodthirsty whore,
> Whose Scarlet Robe is dy'd in Christian Gore,
> To whom the Pathmos Revelator, John,
> Ascribes this title, Myst'ry Babylon.
> O view her Cruelty in these Latter Times." [70]

Then the call for separation is sounded, with the declaration of her coming doom.

> "As Divine Prophesies foretold it shou'd.
> And shall this Drunken whore forever Reign?
> Drunk with the Blood of Martyrs, she hath slain?
> Shall the Kingdoms of the Earth Subdue?
> And Glory over those she Overthrew?

---

[67] Ibid., pp. 73, 74.
[68] Ibid., p. 75.

[70] Ibid., pp. 77, 78.
[69] Ibid.

"Shall her Tyranick Monarchy Endure?
Shall Romes Foundations always stand secure?
No, no, Come out of her ye People all,
For God hath said Great Babylon shall fall;
Partake not of her Sins, least you should be
At last confounded in her Misery;
Take Courage Sion, for the Pow'rs above
Have made a Resolution, to Remove
This Over-Ruling, Bold, Audacious Whore:
Down, She shall down: And she shall rise no more,
But as a Mill-stone cast into the Main,
So shall she sink, never to rise again." [71]

Thus the Sabbatarian poet's views on prophecy were in accord with those of differing religious persuasions. Here is a unity that cannot be brushed aside as accidental or incidental. Prophetic truth on the identity of Antichrist had a universality that is inescapable.

VIII. The "Great Awakening" Moves the Masses

Religion was at low ebb in the opening decades of the eighteenth century. A survey of the various election sermons of the period indicates that nearly all were denunciatory of the deplorable religious conditions of the times. The original Puritan fervor had passed. The encroachments of Arminianism, deism, and rationalism were making a marked impress, drawing men away from the old positions. There was a growing secularism, a fatal coldness and formalism in religious life.

The hour was ripe for a new kind of religious emphasis and leadership. Then began an extended revival movement, climaxing in the Great Awakening of 1740. Before the coming of George Whitefield[72] there were stirrings, here and there, among the Lutherans and Reformed. Around 1720 Theodore Freling-

---

[71] *Ibid.*, pp. 78, 79.

[72] GEORGE WHITEFIELD (1714-1770), English evangelist and revivalist and founder of Calvinistic Methodists, was born in Gloucester. At Oxford he met the Wesleys, and with them founded the Holy Club. Ordained a deacon in 1736, he went to London. In 1738 he followed the Wesleys to the Georgia plantations, returning to England to receive his orders. He paid seven visits to America, preaching in Georgia, Pennsylvania, and New England. His association with Dissenters and his unconventional ways of preaching and conducting services brought strained relations between him and the Established Church. And doctrinal differences separated him from Wesley. Preaching more than 18,000 sermons, he augmented his great pulpit power by his manner of delivery.

huysen, of New Jersey, began to proclaim the imperative necessity of conversion, and to denounce outward formalism. Gilbert Tennent, an eloquent Presbyterian divine, with his "Log College" evangelists, did a conspicuous work in Pennsylvania. Then came Jonathan Edwards, perhaps the greatest figure of his generation, but preaching an extreme predestination, setting God forth as a being of wrath, and man as "utterly helpless in his moral strivings." [73]

The chief criticism was that the preaching of some of the revivalists terrified the people, resulting in "fainting, cries, and bodily agitations." Yet Princeton's first five presidents were all revivalists—including Aaron Burr and Jonathan Edwards.[74]

Edwards has been called the "Father of the Revivalist Type of Protestantism in America." His revival work, which began in 1734 by sermons on justification by faith,[75] proceeded from the necessity of finding a new method of bringing religion to the great masses of the religiously indifferent. It was rooted in Pietism, not in Calvinism. And Congregationalism became revivalistic when it began to center its interest in the redemption of the individual.[76]

Prior to the visit of Whitefield, Edwards had always preached from notes. He saw thousands assembled to hear the impassioned preaching of Whitefield, whose marvelous voice and dramatic utterances were a welcome relief, as he substituted human features for prosaic logic.[77] He caught the ear and gripped the heart of the masses. Taking advantage of the rising tide of religious concern, Edwards began *extempore* preaching on "awakening" themes.

Charles Chauncy of Boston was the principal critic of the revival. Cold and prosaic, he was utterly out of sympathy with all emotionalism. But for multiplied thousands religion was made vital. And humanitarianism was an inseparable part of

[73] James T. Adams, *op. cit.*, pp. 282, 283.
[74] William W. Sweet, *Religion in Colonial America*, pp. 278-281.
[75] Joseph Tracy, *The Great Awakening*, p. 1.
[76] Sweet, *op. cit.*, p. 282.
[77] *Ibid.*, pp. 283-287; see also Ola E. Winslow, *Jonathan Edwards 1703-1758*, pp. 136, 137, 180-183.

Whitefield's message—such as orphan homes and conversion of
the slaves and Indians.[78]

Trumbull puts the number of members added at 30,000
to 40,000.[79] Tracy states that some 150 new Congregational
churches were formed between 1740 and 1760, besides in-
creases among Presbyterians, Separatists, and Baptists.[80] While
there were unfortunate excesses,[81] it was, nevertheless, the most
extensive religious revival America had ever had.[82]

While primarily affecting Congregationalism in New England, the Great Awakening affected the Southern colonies as
well. And it touched the Presbyterians, Baptists, and Methodists alike—emotional revivalism being most marked among
those of little education. In fact, Sweet holds that the rise of
Methodism in America was part of the Great Awakening.[83]

Previous to the Great Awakening there had been but three
colleges in America—Harvard (1636), William and Mary
(1693), and Yale (1701). But under the impulse of the Great
Awakening others came into being, such as Hampden-Sydney,
and Washington and Lee. Then came the College of Philadelphia (later the University of Pennsylvania). Whitefield played
a prominent part in the establishment of both the College of
New Jersey (Princeton) and Wheelock's Indian School (later
Dartmouth), in 1754. King's College (later Columbia), in
1754, and Rhode Island College (afterward Brown), in 1764,
were direct results of the revival.[84]

A renewal of interest in Indian missions was another by-
product. David Brainerd, a convert of the revival expelled from
Yale because of his insistent revivalism, transferred his membership to the Presbyterians and devoted the remainder of his life

[78] Sweet, *op. cit.*, p. 290; Adams, *op. cit.*, pp. 282-284; Tracy, *op. cit.*, chaps. ix-xiii.
[79] Benjamin Trumbull, *A Complete History of Connecticut, Civil and Ecclesiastical* (1630-1764), vol. 2, p. 263.
[80] Tracy, *op. cit.*, pp. 389, 390.
[81] The greatest excesses took place under Tennent's "hell-fire and damnation" preaching, and that of James Davenport, a Yale graduate, who in Boston was so violent in his condemnation of the clergy that he was imprisoned by the authorities and sent home. (Sweet, *op. cit.*, pp. 287-289.)
[82] Trumbull, *op. cit.*, vol. 2, p. 263; Sweet, *op. cit.*, p. 291.
[83] Sweet, *op. cit.*, pp. 291-311, where numerous authorities are cited.
[84] *Ibid.*, pp. 313-316; Adams, *op. cit.*, pp. 309, 310. (Some authorities place the founding of Harvard in 1638.)

to work among the New Jersey and Pennsylvania Indians.   Furthermore, Samuel Hopkins' insistence that Christ died for all—Indians, Negroes, and the underprivileged—laid the foundation for the first antislavery impulses, and Hopkins was a student of Jonathan Edwards.   Such was the impact of the Great Awakening on the American outlook.[85]

---

[85] Sweet, *op. cit.*, p. 317.

CHAPTER TEN

Harvard Lectures
on Romanism Inaugurated

The roll call of witnesses continues—a teacher, a governor, several clergymen. Emphasis on earthquakes enters the picture. Then a chief justice founds a notable lectureship at Harvard on religion, including the subject of Romanism. Catholic complaints of colonial Protestant applications are next noted. And finally the expositions of a great revivalist and Princeton president complete the chapter. Meantime, the Whitbyan postmillennial view begins to take its toll among American expositors. Thus the panorama continues to unfold.

I. Teacher Flint—Last Judgment Follows Antichrist's Fall

HENRY FLINT, or Flynt (1675-1760), tutor at Harvard for more than half a century, son of the minister at Dorchester, Massachusetts, was graduated with an M.A. from Harvard in 1693. He preached at Norwich, Connecticut, beginning in 1696, and taught at Harvard from 1699 to 1754—fifty-five years.[1] He was also secretary of the Board of Overseers. In addition to a volume of sermons, he wrote *The Doctrine of the Last Judgment, Asserted and Explained* (1714), with a preface by Increase Mather.

1. JUDGMENT PRECEDES END AND ADVENT.—In this Flint declared that the impending judgment day would come "in the End of the World, when the Prophecies are all fulfilled, and the

---

[1] Clifford K. Shipton, *Biographical Sketches of Those Who Attended Harvard College in the Classes of 1690-1700*, pp. 162-167.

wickedness of men is come to the heighth." [2]   Then will Christ
come the second time, in power and glory, and the dead in Christ
will be raised, and the righteous living be translated.[3]

2. SAINTS ASSIST IN JUDGING MANKIND.—Then the judgment scenes will occur, involving the participation of the saints.

"They will set down with Christ as Auditors, Spectators & Assessors
in Judging the rest of the World: The Books will be opened; the Book of
Scripture, the Book of Providence, and the Book of Gods Remembrance:
The cases of all Men will be fairly heard and justly determined, according
to the things Written in the Books; their Consciences also bearing witness,
and giving Sentence agreeable to the Judgment of God." [4]

3. ONLY ANTICHRIST'S DOWNFALL DELAYS.—Nothing hinders its coming but the downfall of Antichrist and the calling of
Israel, he thought, though no man knows the exact day or hour.[5]

II. Governor Burnet—Makes Terminus of Periods Imminent

WILLIAM BURNET (1688-1729), scholarly governor of New
York and New Jersey, and later of Massachusetts, was born at
The Hague during the temporary residence there of his father,
Gilbert Burnet, bishop of Salisbury, England.   He was educated
at Trinity College, Cambridge, was an astronomer, and had wide
acquaintance with prominent men.   Possessor of unusual abilities, he was appointed governor of New York and New Jersey
by King William and Queen Mary in 1720, and promptly sailed
for the New World.   In this office he made an honorable record
and helped resolve the Indian question.   His successor was appointed in 1728, and he was then made governor of Massachusetts.   (Portrait appears on page 34.)

1. DATES 1260-YEAR PAPAL PERIOD 455-1715.—Though a
layman, like Sir Isaac Newton, Burnet was also an earnest student of prophecy.   And in 1724, while pressed with the bur-
dens of high official position, he set forth suggested dates of the
three time periods of Daniel 12 in relation to the papal Antichrist, in *An Essay on Scripture-Prophecy*.   In this he says:

---

[2] Henry Flint, *The Doctrine of the Last Judgment, Asserted and Explained*, p. 2.
[3] *Ibid.*, pp. 2, 3.   [4] *Ibid.*, p. 3.   [5] *Ibid.*

"All these passages compared with one another give so full and plain an account of the popes of Rome, from first to last, that a very moderate knowledge of history serves to satisfy us that they are meant of them, and cannot be applied to any other time." [6]

The 1260 years (time, times, and half a time), he thought, must on the year-day principle be from 455 to 1715—beginning when the Western Empire ended under Valentinian III.[7] The "daily," he held, pertains to the tabernacle of Christ our High Priest.[8] The papists, he taught, have polluted the sanctuary by setting up a man to be worshiped, to be vicar of God, and to dispense with God's laws. (Dan. 11:37 ff.; 2 Thessalonians 2, etc.)[9] The 1290 years are also dated from 455 and expire in 1745. And the 2300 years ending at the same time would begin in 555 B.C. The 1335 years would extend to 1790, when he believed the first resurrection should occur.[10] Thus he concluded that the kingdom of God was indeed nigh at hand.[11]

2. APPLIES YEAR-DAY PRINCIPLE TO PERIODS.—In the Introduction, Burnet appeals to the prophecies as the distinguishing proof of the true God, who inspired them.[12] He bemoans the indifference so apparent on the part of many, and urges St. John's advice to hear and heed the prophecy.[13] Dealing with the three prophetic periods—the 1260, 1290, and 1335 years—he holds that the 1260 days are the same as the forty-two months and three and a half times, and that all stand for years, on the basis of Numbers 14 and Ezekiel 4.[14] All Catholics, as well as Protestants, recognize the seventy weeks as 490 years.[15] And the fourth beast of Daniel 7 is to be compared with the Beasts of Revelation 13 and 17.[16]

3. STANDARD INTERPRETATION FOR DANIEL 2 AND 7.—The standard application is given to Daniel 2 and 7,[17] with the feet and toes as the divided Europe of Western Rome, and the Stone as the coming kingdom of Christ.[18] The Little Horn is the papal Man of Sin, the Babylonian element of the Beast of Revelation

---

[6] William Burnet, *An Essay on Scripture-Prophecy*, p. 27. (Title page reproduced on p. 152.)
[7] *Ibid.*, pp. 105-109.
[8] *Ibid.*, p. 129.
[9] *Ibid.*, p. 142.
[10] *Ibid.*, pp. 154-158.
[11] *Ibid.*, p. 166.
[12] *Ibid.*, p. 2.
[13] *Ibid.*, p. 9.
[14] *Ibid.*, pp. 27-29.
[15] *Ibid.*, p. 32.
[16] *Ibid.*, p. 38.
[17] *Ibid.*, pp. 48-50.
[18] *Ibid.*, p. 52.

13.[19] Burnet also follows the usual interpretation of the ram and he-goat.[20]

He interprets the seven heads as forms of government and names the ten horns—Visigoths, Vandals, Francks, Burgundians, Hunns, Alans, Sueves, Herules, Ostrogoths, and Lombards.[21] The three horns plucked up were the Herules, Ostrogoths, and Lombards.[22]

Such were the scholarly governor's concepts of prophecy.

III. Webb—Falling of Stars Precursor of Advent

Brief mention should be made of JOHN WEBB (1687-1750), educated at Harvard and pastor at Boston. He was occasionally preacher of election sermons. In his *Practical Discourses* (1726) he lays stress on the harbingers of the coming day of judgment, with a call to solemn preparation of heart therefor. (Matt. 24:42.) After specifying the "Fore-runners and the Evidences of its near approach," Webb cites the prophesied falling of the stars, recorded in Matthew 24, Mark 13, and Luke 21, that will precede it.[23] The judgment will come as the climax in the prophetic line portrayed in Daniel 7.[24] And the second advent with inconceivable glory and power will be attended by the resurrection of the dead. This is the great prophesied end.[25]

IV. Prince—Prophecy the Favorite Study of Life

THOMAS PRINCE (1687-1758), Congregationalist clergyman and historian, was born in Sandwich, Massachusetts. In 1709 he was graduated from Harvard, receiving his M.A. degree in 1710, and then for several years studied and traveled in Europe. His learning was widely recognized, and he took courses in law, medicine, and theology. He preached occasionally for a time in England, principally in Suffolk. In 1717 he returned to Boston, was ordained in 1718, and became pastor of the Old South Church in Boston. Prince conceived the plan of a New England

---

[19] *Ibid.*, pp. 61, 92.
[20] *Ibid.*, pp. 67, 68.
[21] *Ibid.*, pp. 85, 86.
[22] *Ibid.*, pp. 87, 88.
[23] John Webb, *Practical Discourses*, pp. 92, 93.
[24] *Ibid.*, p. 109.
[25] *Ibid.*, pp. 112, 113.

Library, and starting in 1703, amassed one of the finest private libraries of colonial times—books and manuscripts on the history of New England and its divines. His collection was partly destroyed and otherwise dispersed at the occupation of Boston by the British (1755-56), but the remainder (1,899 volumes) is now in the Boston Public Library.[26] (Portrait appears on page 144.)

He was the author of several printed sermons. His *Earthquakes the Works of God & Tokens of His Just Displeasure* (1727) supplanted an earlier volume. Prince was an ardent champion of Whitefield's evangelism, and made prophecy the favorite study of his life.[27] In his preface to the *Life of Cotton Mather* he speaks forth his interest in prophecy, and his anxiety that other ministers, like Mather, should aid in preparing the world for the glorious second advent.[28]

In his *Six Sermons* (1785), on the basis of Matthew 24:14, Prince tells of the gospel light to illuminate the earth in the last days, and then the conflagration and the glorious eternal state with no longer a devil to tempt after the resurrection of the saints.[29] He looked upon Gog and Magog as the wicked raised at the close of the thousand years, whom the devils will inflame to rage against the saints a little season.[30]

V. Increasing Earthquakes Seen Fulfilling Prophecy

A good many sermons by scholarly men were preached on the increasing earthquakes, particularly the quake of October 29, 1727. For example, there was a book by NATHANIEL GOOKIN (M.A.), pastor in Hampton, New York, on *The Day of Trouble Near, The Tokens of it, and a Due Preparation for It* (1728). There was another by JOHN BARNARD (M.A.), pastor of the Marblehead church, on *Earthquakes Under the Divine Govern-*

---

[26] Carl L. Cannon, *American Book Collectors and Collecting From Colonial Times to the Present*, pp. 1-12. Examination of the titles in the 159-page Prince Library Catalog of the Boston Public Library discloses many works on prophecy, a dozen on earthquakes, numerous items on the second advent of Christ, and some on ancient history. Such familiar names as Goodwin, Brightman, Mede, More, and Whitby appear.
[27] See Joshua Spalding, *Sentiments, Concerning the Coming and Kingdom of Christ*, Appendix, p. 260.
[28] Thomas Prince, Preface, p. 6, Samuel Mather, *The Life of Cotton Mather*.
[29] *Ibid., Six Sermons*, p. 28.
[30] Joshua Spalding, *op. cit.*, p. 260. In this he declared his agreement with the contemporary English John Gill (1697-1771).

ment (1727), and one by SAMUEL WIGGLESWORTH (M.A.), of Ipswich, on *A Religious Fear of God's Tokens, Explained and Urged* (1728), who stressed the prophetic aspect—based on Matthew 24 and Luke 21. There was also BENJAMIN COLMAN, of Boston, on *The Judgments of Providence in the Hand of Christ; His Voice to us in the Terrible Earthquake* (1728). In this latter presentation, there is in addition a vigorous presentation of the four world empires of prophecy.

VI. Justice Dudley—Founds Harvard Lectures on Romanism

PAUL DUDLEY (1675-1751), Puritan jurist, was born in Roxbury, Massachusetts. Both his father and grandfather had been governors of Massachusetts. Paul was graduated from Harvard with an M.A. in 1693 and then studied law at Middle Temple, London, being admitted to the bar in 1700. Returning to America, he was appointed attorney general of the province of Massachusetts and elected a member of the legislature. He introduced several judicial reforms. By 1718 he was promoted to the superior court bench, and was made chief justice of Massachusetts in 1745, which position he held until his death. In all these positions Dudley served with distinction. He was also an accomplished naturalist and a fellow of the Royal Society of London—a rarity in colonial America in those days. A pronounced Puritan in religious matters, he wrote several theological tracts.

In his will he left a bequest to Harvard College providing for certain annual lectures.[31] These were initiated largely because of certain profound conclusions he had reached on perils confronting America—perils which would come because of a failure to see the prophetic significance of the Papacy. Long before he inaugurated the Dudleian Lectures, he had written an anonymous pamphlet entitled *An Essay on the Merchandize of Slaves & Souls of Men, Revel. XVIII.13. with an Application thereof to the Church of Rome* (1731).[32] It is noteworthy that

---

[31] *Dictionary of American Biography*, vol. 5, p. 483.
[32] *Ibid.*; signed "By a Gentleman." (Identified in *Dictionary of American Biography*.)

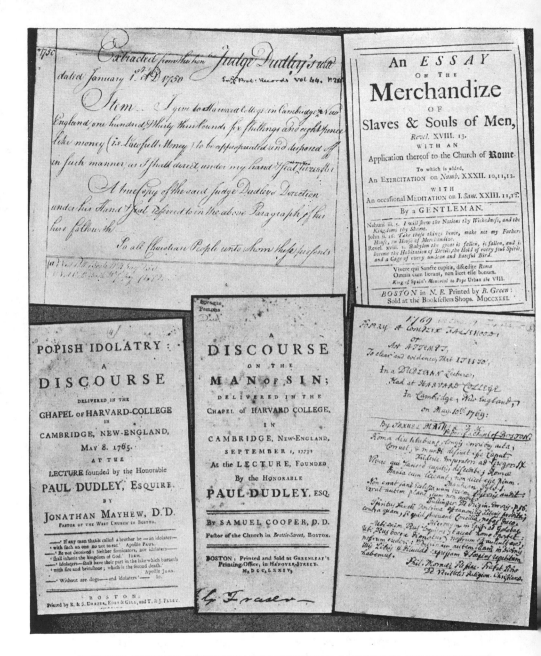

JUSTICE DUDLEY INAUGURATES HARVARD LECTURES ON PROPHECY

Judge Paul Dudley's Exposition of Revelation 18 (Upper Right); Portion of Will Founding Lectureship on Prophecies of Antichrist for Harvard (Upper Left); Jonathan Mayhew's and Samuel Cooper's Printed Lectures in the Field Specified, and Manuscript Copy of Samuel Mather's Sermon of 1769, Typical of Other Printed and Manuscript Sermons in the Series

various authors and cataloguers in citing this title give only the first part of the full title—*An Essay on the Merchandize of Slaves and Souls of Men*—and omit the final portion which reveals its prophetic aspect; namely, *Revel. XVIII.13. with an Application thereof to the Church of Rome.* It is characteristic of a definite softening and tempering to remove the historical strictures against Rome. (Title page appears on page 174.)

In its earlier years forty per cent of Harvard's entire enrollment entered the ministry.[33] Many became important figures in church and state. The ministers of New England were supplied by her graduates. The college was controlled by a Congregational clergy of Calvinistic affiliations. The bequest, left to Harvard [34] by Dudley in his will of January 1, 1750, was for a continuing lectureship. Its purpose, as later fully defined, was to provide for an annual discourse on various aspects of religion—the third in each four-year cycle, to deal with the doctrines and practices of the church of Rome.[35] Its specific scope is stated in the Dudley will:

> "The third Lecture to be, for the detecting, and convicting and exposing the Idolatry of the Romish Church, their Tyranny, Usurpations, damnable heresies, fatal Errors, abominable superstitions, and other crying wickednesses in their high places, and finally that the Church of Rome is that mystical Babylon, that Man of Sin, That Apostate Church spoken of in the New Testament." [36]

The Dudleian speakers formed a distinguished list, the full series being inaugurated by Harvard's President Edward Holyoke in 1755. The lecturers, all able men, included Joseph Willard, a later president of Harvard, for the lecture in 1785. Thus the institution itself was tied vitally into the plan. The five special lectures between 1757 and 1773 on the "Errors of the Church of Rome" were as follows:

1. "Infallibility," by Edward Wigglesworth (1757).

---

[33] Samuel E. Morrison, *The Founding of Harvard College*, p. 247 n.
[34] Probate Court records, vol. 44, p. 476 (no. 9697). Boston Court House.
[35] Copy of Judge Dudley's bequest, in *Donations Book*, Harvard University, pp. 194-196. Also prefixed by President Quincy of Harvard to first manuscript volume of series *Dudleian Lectures, 1755-1770* in Harvard University Library. Compare *Harvard College Records*, Part 2, College Book IV, pp. 336-334 [*sic*], in *Publications of the Colonial Society of Massachusetts*, vol. 16, pp. 854-857.
[36] *Donations Book*, p. 196.

2. "The Supremacy of the Bishop of Rome," by Thomas Foxcraft (1761).

3. "Popish Idolatry," by Jonathan Mayhew (1765).

4. "Popery a Complexity of Falsehoods," by Samuel Mather (1769).

5. "The Church of Rome the Man of Sin," by Samuel Cooper (1773).

Personal scrutiny of the actual text of the Dudleian Lectures from 1755 onward discloses the following facts: There were some twenty-three individual speakers in this special graduated series on Romanism, between 1755 and 1853 inclusive. Five of the lectures were printed, while the rest remain on file in manuscript at Harvard.[37] The earlier presentations frequently applied the symbols of prophecy to the Papacy. But a definite change in tone and treatment marks the transition of the years, the intent of the founder being increasingly forgotten. These earlier lectures carried great weight and exerted a molding influence. A frank Catholic appraisal of these lectures and their content is also available.[38]

The sequel of the story is significant: The lectures continue up till 1857, when a break occurs. A memorandum for "1857-1887," states, "The lectures were discontinued after 1857 in order that the fund might be increased." [39] Then appears an interesting entry for 1890-91, listing John J. Keene as lecturer on "Revealed Religion, delivered in Harvard University Chapel"—this being none other than the Roman Catholic bishop of the Catholic University of America, the "Rt. Rev. J. J. Keene." [40] Then in May, 1891, fifty-eight members of the Harvard faculty of arts and sciences, law, and divinity petitioned the University Corporation to suppress the third Dudleian lecture of the cycle, or to abolish the whole series if necessary. This, however, brought the following action:

---

[37] Listed in *Contents Book*, vol. 6, pp. 543-555, at Harvard College Library, with the original manuscripts in the Archives Division. The printed lectures are in the Houghton Rare Book Library.

[38] Sister Mary Augustina (Ray), *American Opinion of Roman Catholicism in the Eighteenth Century*, pp. 126-138, 379, 380.

[39] O. H. Gates, *List and Dates of Dudleian Lectures, 1755-1918*. Archives Division, Harvard University Library. The next lecture, on the validity of nonepiscopal ordination, was delivered in 1888. See Harvard University Library, *Bibliographical Contributions*, edited by Justin Winsor, no. 38, p. 9.

[40] A clipping in the Harvard files from the *Register* comments on the liberalizing of the policy. See also *Bibliographical Contributions*, no. 44, p. 12.

"The Corporation cannot concur in this conclusion and is of opinion that the suppression of one of the four lectures provided for under this bequest would be a breach of trust which might amount to a renunciation of the whole trust. . . .

"The Corporation must decline therefore to take the steps proposed in the remonstrance either in whole or in part." [41]

However, in 1910 the president and Fellows of Harvard, with the concurrence of the trustees, decided that the third lecture should be omitted and the other three continued.[42] The entire series was brought to an end in 1928, the presentations of the last twenty-five years not being on the topic.

And now a few extracts, first from Dudley and then from but two special Dudleian lecturers in the years following, in the very chapel of Harvard College itself, will show its unique place and influence.

1. MAN OF SIN'S DESOLATIONS ENDED BY ADVENT.—In the Introduction to his *Essay on the Merchandize of Slaves & Souls of Men, Rev. XVIII.13. with an Application thereof to the Church of Rome,* Dudley frankly avows it to be an indictment of the Man of Sin. Writing in 1731, twenty-four years before his notable lectureship was inaugurated, he surveys the ruin that came to the churches of Bohemia, Hungary, Piedmont, and France, and exclaims concerning the "Romish Church," "Oh! thou Enemy! What Desolations hast thou wrought." [43] Then he declares that the "Man of Sin" will be "destroyed by the Brightness of His [Christ's] coming," observing further that before the "final Ruine of Antichrist," there will be a short time of "Distress of Nations, and of Tribulation to the Church of God, as the Ages past never saw." [44] But Dudley insisted that the exact hour and order could not be determined "before the accomplishment." [45]

2. IDENTIFIED SO AS TO BE SHUNNED.—In his opening sentence Dudley asserts it to be of "mighty Consequence" to dis-

[41] *Harvard University Bulletin*, vol. 6, no. 51, 1890-1892, pp. 342, 343. ("Official. From the Records of the Corporation.")
[42] Ray, *op. cit.*, p. 380 n, concerning letter from secretary of President Lowell, dated May 24, 1933.
[43] Paul Dudley, *Essay on the Merchandize of Slaves & Souls of Men, Rev. XVIII.13. with an Application thereof to the Church of Rome,* p. ii.
[44] *Ibid.*, p iii.   [45] *Ibid.*

cover Antichrist's identity, so as to be able to separate from it. Then he proceeds to identify it as the scarlet-colored Mystical Babylon, the Mother of Harlots, sitting as a queen, drunken with blood, on seven-hilled Rome, reigning over the kings of the earth,[46] her merchandise being the slaves and the "Bodies and bones of men"—the relics of canonized saints. This traffic is denominated dishonest, and the buyers "cheated & abused." [47]

3. STIRRED BY PROPOSED UNION WITH ROME.—The occasion of Dudley's concern was the fact that certain leading Protestants had proposed an unthinkable union with papists. Concerning this Dudley cites the dread warning of Revelation 14:9 against worshiping the Beast and receiving his mark.[48] The then-present plight and trend was declared to exist because the preaching of the angelic messages of Revelation 14 had not resulted in the people's coming out of Babylon. While Britain, Holland, parts of Germany, Switzerland, and Scandinavia responded, France, Spain, Italy, and the greater part of Germany were still "perishing in Antichristian darkness." [49]

4. MATHER EXPOUNDS PAPAL LITTLE HORN (1769).—SAMUEL MATHER,[50] Dudleian prophetical lecturer at Harvard chapel for 1769, chose as his topic, "Popery a Complexity of Falsehoods." [51] This remarkable discourse was based on 2 Thessalonians 2, the key sentence being, "The prophecy had its accomplishment in the Bishops of Rome and their adherents." [52] Mather located the apex of early usurpation under Boniface III, and the climax about 1300. The closing sentences exemplify his exposition of Daniel 7:

"After the Division of the Romish Empire, mentioned in the foregoing lecture, the 10 horns then began to emerge, concerning which we read in Rev. XVII.12; or such a number of kingdoms or nations, by means whereof the Power of the Empire was greatly broken and shattered. . . .

---

46 *Ibid.*, pp. 1, 2. 48 *Ibid.*, pp. 36, 37.
47 *Ibid.*, pp. 21-36. 49 *Ibid.*, pp. 38, 39.
50 SAMUEL MATHER (1706-1785), of Boston, was the son of Cotton Mather. A graduate of Harvard, he received honorary degrees in America and Europe, and held prominent pastorates. He was the preacher of important election and convention sermons, as well as this Dudleian lecture.
51 Thirty-one pages, in manuscript volume of *Dudleian Lectures*, Harvard University Library, Archives Division.
52 Samuel Mather, *Popery a Complexity of Falsehoods*, p. 3. (Title page reproduced on p. 174.)

"Now amidst the Disturbances and Confusion in the Western Empire, are that Little Horn concerning which the prophet Daniel predicted and prophecys in Dan. VII.24, i.e. the Power of the Romish Bishops." [53]

VII. Cooper—Identifies Papacy as Prophesied Man of Sin

SAMUEL COOPER (1725-1783), Congregational Boston pastor, was born in Boston and graduated from Harvard in 1743. In the same year he was elected to the pastorate of Brattle Square Church (4th Puritan), in Boston, which became the scene of his lifework. Ordained in 1746, he was an able and eloquent preacher, but wrote little. In 1767 he was given a D.D. by the University of Edinburgh. Intimate with Adams and Franklin, he was active in the cause of American freedom. In 1774 he declined the presidency of Harvard, but was a member of the Corporation for many years.[54]

A typical clergyman of the period—with wig, gown, and bands—he was the patron of mission work among the Indians. Polished in manner and elegant in diction, he was made vice-president of the Academy of Arts and Sciences in 1780. Cooper preached the rather remarkable *Discourse on The Man of Sin*. This was delivered in 1773 in the Chapel of Harvard College, as one of the Dudleian lecture series. As previously noted, the purpose of these lectures was frankly "to prove that the church of Rome is that mystical Babylon, that MAN OF SIN, that apostate church, spoken of in the New-Testament." [55] (See cut on p. 174.)

1. LOCATES ANTICHRIST IN CHAIR OF ST. PETER.—At the very outset Cooper takes cognizance of the insistent Catholic contention that Antichrist is a single person—not a combination or succession—whose "continuance upon earth will be very short," [56] three and a half literal years. Cooper then makes the flat declaration, "If Antichrist is not to be found in the chair of St. Peter, he is no where to be found." [57] Contending that "there is a portion of obscurity intermingled with the light of

---

[53] *Ibid.*, p. 28.
[54] *Dictionary of American Biography*, vol. 4, pp. 410, 411.
[55] Samuel Cooper, *A Discourse on The Man of Sin*, p. 12.
[56] *Ibid.*, p. 22.
[57] *Ibid.*, p. 24.

Scripture prophecies, before their accomplishment," [58] and "time illustrates what was dark, and explains what was mysterious in the prophecies," [59] Cooper then avers that Paul's statement (in 2 Thessalonians 2) involved a long period of time, far beyond the destruction of Jerusalem. [60]

2. INTENT OF TERM "MAN OF SIN."—Commenting on the term "Man of Sin," Cooper declares explicitly:

"By this Man, in the singular number, the absolute monarchy in the church of Rome is well described; though we do not suppose any particular Pope is intended, but the Bishops of Rome in succession. It gives us a general character of that order of men, and of those who have had the principal share in their ecclesiastical administration; the chief promoters and defenders of the Romish apostacy." [61]

3. HISTORICAL FULFILLMENT OF PROPHESIED CHARACTERISTICS.—Then is rehearsed its prophesied "opposition" to Christ, its "arrogance," and its "cruel and oppressive power," as predicted by Daniel and by John, and as attested by the persecutions under Mary, the massacres of Paris, and the slaughter of the Waldenses. [62] Next the symbol of the mystical woman that was drunk with the blood of saints and martyrs was similarly applied. [63]

4. DESTRUCTION AT ADVENT THE CLIMAX.—The climax of the sequel, declares Cooper, will be the destruction of Antichrist at the second advent of Christ, when Antichrist will be consumed. [64]

Other Dudleian lectures will be noted later.

VIII. Catholic Complaint of Colonial Protestant Application

There is very little from Roman Catholics in this period, as they feared to express their views because of persecution from Protestants. Indeed, the first book to be printed by a Catholic did not appear until 1773. But a Roman Catholic writer, who has made very careful investigation, complains that the English

---

[58] *Ibid.*
[59] *Ibid.*, p. 25.
[60] *Ibid.*, p. 39.
[61] *Ibid.*, p. 40.
[64] *Ibid.*, p. 60.
[62] *Ibid.*, pp. 42, 43.
[63] *Ibid.*, p. 43.

emigrants brought with them the common concept that the pope was Antichrist. Here are three typical excerpts from Sister Mary Augustina (Ray) attesting the prevalent colonial attitude toward her church, as she has found it, and the prophetic terms commonly applied to the Catholic Church:

"She [the Roman church] was the 'Beast,' the 'Scarlet Woman' of the Apocalypse, who, usurping the throne of the Almighty, had demanded for herself the homage due to Him alone." [65]

"That tradition which identified the Papacy with 'that highest distinction of the Puritan vocabulary'—Antichrist." [66]

"Small wonder that with such tutoring English emigrants should have brought with them to the New World the conviction that the Pope was indeed Antichrist." [67]

IX. Revivalist Edwards—Prophecy Unfolds History of Redemption

JONATHAN EDWARDS (1703-1758), noted Congregational revivalist, champion of Calvinism, theologian, and third president of Princeton for a brief time,[68] was born at East Windsor, Connecticut, of Congregational ancestry. A precocious child, he became pre-eminently a thinker, and laid the foundations for a new system of religious thought.[69] He began the study of Latin at six, and had a good knowledge of it before he entered college. He also had deep religious impressions as a child, and was soundly converted at seventeen—the whole universe appearing changed to him. When only thirteen he entered Yale, graduating with honors in 1720. Then he continued two years more, studying divinity. At nineteen he became preacher to the Presbyterian congregation in New York. His sun was rising as Cotton Mather's sank on the western horizon.[70]

In 1733 he received his M.A. and became tutor at Yale. By 1727 he was ordained and became pastor of the Congregational

[65] Ray, op. cit., p. 15.
[66] Ibid., p. 22 (citing W. H. Frere, History of the English Church in the Reigns of Elizabeth and James I, 1558-1625, p. 311).   [67] Ibid., p. 34.
[68] Princeton came into being as the College of New Jersey by the action of the Synod of Philadelphia in 1739. First located at Elizabethtown, it was removed to Princeton in 1756. Its growth was slow during the Revolutionary period.
[69] Ola E. Winslow, Jonathan Edwards, 1703-1758, p. 325.
[70] Charles A. and Mary R. Beard, The Rise of American Civilization, vol. 1, p. 148; Moses C. Tyler, A History of American Literature During the Colonial Time, vol. 2, pp. 177-192.

church at Northampton, being strongly Calvinistic in conviction. Conspicuously conscientious, learned, and independent, he served this church until 1750. In 1734 Edwards led out in a great revival. He had a passionate evangelistic temperament and preached the gospel with violence. In 1740 Whitefield visited Northampton, and the far-reaching revival, known as the Great Awakening, swept over the country, resulting in the conversion of some 50,000. (Portrait appears on page 144.)

Edwards, last of the Puritan mystics, opposed the prevailing laxity of communion for the still unregenerate, and was "driven forth" or dismissed from his pastorate in 1751 without position or support. So he became a missionary to the Indians at Stockbridge, Massachusetts, from 1751 onward. One of his daughters had married Aaron Burr, president of Yale, and after Burr's death Edwards was called to the presidency of the College of New Jersey (Princeton), in 1757, dying of smallpox soon after.

Edwards wrote much between 1746 and 1758, his most important works being those produced while he was a missionary to the Indians. Although emaciated by constant application to study, he prepared his essay on the *Freedom of Will* (1754) during this ministry to the Indians. It is difficult to understand his earlier contemplations of hell, as set forth in *Sinners in the Hands of an Angry God* (1741), and his belief that we are saved only by the arbitrary will of a wrathful God. He was the fountainhead of the rigid Puritanism of his time, shaking all New England over the roaring flames of hell.[71] His Calvinism was postulated on a God of wrath.[72]

Edwards' *History of the Work of Redemption*[73] exemplifies the sublime and comprehensive character of his mind. To him, all history, with its changes and revolutions, was one great divine work carried forward ceaselessly, from age to age, for the redemption and recovery of mankind. The Bible was the book of redemption, and its histories and prophecies were the his-

---

[71] Beard, *op. cit.*, p. 145.
[72] Vernon L. Parrington, *The Colonial Mind, 1620-1800*, p. 148.
[73] Preached in Northampton in 1739 and edited and published posthumously in Edinburgh, 1774. See Franklin B. Dexter, *Biographical Sketches of the Graduates of Yale College*, p. 225.

tories and prophecies of that redemption. The Apocalypse had
the place of pre-eminence. What Daniel, Paul, and John predicted, history sealed with seventeen centuries of unerring testimony. The prophecies afforded an unanswerable argument for
the inspiration of the Scriptures, doubly needed in days of
threatened unbelief.

Edwards, however, fell a prey to the new Whitbyan view,
adopting a figurative resurrection and a temporal millennium,
introduced by divine judgments. But rationalism was in the
air. The issue was dogma versus rationalism. There was a
growing dissatisfaction with Calvinism.[74]

1. 1260 YEARS DATED FROM 456.—In his *Humble Attempt To promote Explicit Agreement* (1747), Edwards takes
strong exception to Lowman's unusual dating of the 1260 years,
as from 756 and ending about A.D. 2000—250 years from his
time. This dating was obtained by starting with the temporal
dominion under Pepin of France in 756.[75] Instead, Edwards
suggests 456, after Genseric had taken the city of Rome, upon
completion of the division of the empire.[76] The variously designated but identical periods—of the woman in the wilderness,
the witnesses in sackcloth, the court trodden underfoot, the scattering of the power of the holy people, and the period of the
wearing out of the saints—are all indicated as one and the
same,[77] and Antichrist's destruction in two stages comes at the
close.[78]

2. MOHAMMEDAN TURKS EMERGE ABOUT 1300.—In his *History of the Work of Redemption*, Edwards identifies the "Pope
and his clergy" as the power prophesied in 2 Thessalonians 2,
Daniel 7, and Revelation 13 and 17,[79] and as the first of the two
great antagonists of the kingdom of Christ. The second antagonist was Mohammedanism, operating first through the Saracens
and then the Turks, in Revelation 9.[80] Of the Turks he
declares:

---

[74] Parrington, *op. cit.*, p. 150.   [76] *Ibid.*, p. 139.
[75] Jonathan Edwards, *An Humble Attempt To promote Explicit Agreement*, pp. 126,
127, 133.   [77] *Ibid.*, p. 142.   [78] *Ibid.*, p. 149.
[79] Jonathan Edwards, *A History of the Work of Redemption*, p. 20.
[80] *Ibid.*, pp. 20, 21, 215, 216.

"They began their empire about the year of Christ 1296, and began
to invade Europe about 1300, and took Constantinople, and so became
Masters of all the Eastern empire in 1453." [81]

The prophesied period of the Turk is implied, but not
expressly stated.

3. TEN HORNS EMERGE UNDER FOUR TRUMPETS.—The
greater portion of Revelation pertains, he believed, to the overthrow of Pagan Rome, on through papal Antichrist's reign till
his overthrow, and Christ's coming to judgment.[82]   First, the
invasions of Goths, Vandals, and other heathen nations divided
the empire—

"into ten kingdoms, with which began the ten horns of the beast; for we are
told, that the ten horns are ten kings, who should rise in the latter part
of the Roman empire: these are also represented by the ten toes of Nebuchadnezzar's image.   The invasion and conquests of these Heathen nations
are supposed to be foretold in the 8th chapter of Revelation, in what came
to pass under the sounding of the four first trumpets." [83]

4. 1260 YEARS BEGIN POSSIBLY IN 606.—Contending the
papal Antichrist to be "the masterpiece of all the contrivances
of the devil," [84] Edwards holds that the 1260-year "continuance
of Antichrist's reign did not commence before the year of Christ
479; because if they did, they would have ended, and Antichrist
would have fallen before now." [85]   The reason for the date 479
is obvious: This was first given in sermon form in 1739; and
1739 minus 1260 equals 479.   So Edwards now suggests 606 as
the time when the civil power of the emperor confirmed the
universal bishopric of the pope.

5. PROPHECY STRONG ARGUMENT FOR INSPIRATION.—Edwards believed that the vials of Revelation 16 were poured out
on the throne of the beast during the Reformation, and thus
the pope's power and the extent of his dominion were diminished.   This persecuting Little Horn of Daniel 7 is declared
in summation to be the same as the Beast of Revelation 17, the
Woman of Revelation 17, drunk with the blood of martyrs,

---

[81] *Ibid.*, p. 21.   [83] *Ibid.*, p. 213.   [85] *Ibid.*, p. 217.
[82] *Ibid.*, p. 211.   [84] *Ibid.*, p. 216.

reigning over multitudes and kingdoms, and changing the ordinances of God, rising through craft and policy, the Man of Sin— all of which "is exactly fulfilled in the Church of Rome." [86] He then concludes, "How strong an argument is this, that the Scriptures are the Word of God?" [87]

---

[86] *Ibid.*, p. 223.　　　　　[87] *Ibid.*, p. 245.

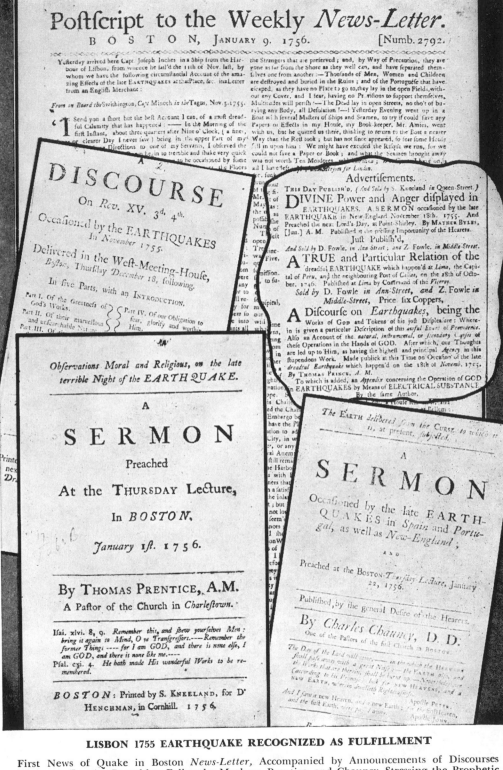

LISBON 1755 EARTHQUAKE RECOGNIZED AS FULFILLMENT

First News of Quake in Boston *News-Letter*, Accompanied by Announcements of Discourses Thereon (Inset). Pamphlets Follow by Mayhew, Prentice, and Chauncy, Stressing the Prophetic Significance of the Earthquake

CHAPTER ELEVEN

Lisbon Earthquake
and the Celestial Signs

I. Significance of Lisbon Earthquake Recognized

When the vivid descriptions of the terrors and havoc of the Lisbon earthquake of November, 1755, reached America, a number of treatises appeared immediately stressing the prophetic aspect, similar to those before noted of England.[1] Thus the *Boston Weekly News-Letter* for January 9, 1756 (no. 2792), in folio size, issued an extra "Postscript" page giving the comprehensive eyewitness account of Captain Joseph Inches. Significantly enough, on the back side of the sheet appear advertisements of four Biblical treatises on the earthquake by American clergymen. Even a poem, "The God of Tempest and Earthquakes," was listed along with them. These were indicative of the familiarity of New England with the phenomenon, and of the pointed expositions of prophecy current.

Detailed descriptions appeared in *The London Magazine* for November and December, 1755, with even a drawing of the city. The extent of the area affected was noted, and the centering of the disaster in Portugal and Spain, with Lisbon, once the richest city in the world, as the "particular mark of divine displeasure."[2] The time of the catastrophe was stressed, as it was at the very time appointed for the celebration of the auto-da-fé, when the "convicts of the inquisition go in procession thro' the

---

[1] See Volume 2 of *Prophetic Faith*.
[2] *The London Magazine*, December, 1755, p. 586.

city, and frequently Protestants and others are burnt by the sentence of that infernal tribunal." [3]

The February, 1756, issue prints a communication from "S.T." with the appeal:

"Tremble then ye nations, ye inhabitants of a fallen world, repent, and turn unto the Lord your God, in sackcloth dust, and ashes, that ye may be saved, saved from the wrath to come." [4]

Appealing to Protestant England, he continues:

"O London, art not thou pained for the report? And wilt thou sing as an harlot, and take the harp to make sweet melody, sing many songs, and turn to thy hire (without either feeling or repenting) and commit fornication with all the kingdoms of the world? Why will you, amidst all this general calamity, ruin, and distress, put on a face of wanton gaiety, and smiling affluence, and live too, even without God in the world? Are not these the signs of sad approaching desolation, ruin, what not? Not signs only, but the very causes too?" [5]

We now note three American contemporary writers on the significance of the Lisbon earthquake.

II. Prentice—Lisbon Earthquake Forerunner of End

THOMAS PRENTICE (1702-1782), Congregational clergyman, was born in Cambridge, and graduated from Harvard in 1726. Ordained in 1728, he settled in Arundel, Maine. Then the Indian War of 1737 dispersed the church, and Prentice returned to Cambridge. In 1739 he was installed as associate pastor in Charlestown, becoming sole pastor in 1774.[6] It was during this time that the Great Awakening took place—Whitefield arriving in Boston about 1740. Then, following the great Lisbon earthquake of 1755, Prentice gave emphasis to it as a sign of the times. In 1775 Charlestown was reduced to ashes and its people scattered. Prentice retired to Cambridge, Massachusetts, where he was overseer of Harvard College.

1. EARTHQUAKE HERALD OF APPROACHING END.—Prentice published a sermon of January 1, 1756, *Observations . . . On*

---

the Late Terrible Night of the Earthquake, based on the premise of earthquakes as a token of the approaching end of the age, the climax being when God ariseth to shake terribly the heavens and the earth. Treating specifically of the Lisbon quake, he says:

"Go now, in your Meditations, unto Cadiz! Go unto the vast City of Lisbon, and see what God did to them, but this Day two Months past; a little before the Earthquake reach'd us; to the latter of them especially. You have heard, how the Lord then did it; and how he hath by repeated Shocks, and the Flames of devouring Fire, bro't it since to pass; to lay waste, one of the largest, the most wealthy and flourishing Cities, in the World; and turn it into a ruinous Heap." [7]

2. PRECURSORS OF THE SECOND ADVENT.—First, citing Revelation 18, Prentice says, "May we not look on this dreadful Event, as pointed at in that Prophecy, and a notable Beginning of its Fulfilment." [8] Then, referring to Matthew 24:27, he remarks:

"We should regard terrible Earthquakes, as some of the last Judgments, God brings on a wicked People, and which he will bring upon a wicked World; and as fearful Presages, of their nearly approaching Ruin. Our Lord mentions these as Forerunners, both of the Destruction of Jerusalem, and of the World, in general, and his appearing to the Judgment of the last Day, Matth. 24.27." [9]

3. SIGNS OF THE LAST TIMES.—These earthquake judgments of the latter days, when the world is getting ready for destruction, Prentice insists, are "Signs of the last Times," [10] visited upon "Popish kingdoms and cities." This will reach its climax when God ariseth to shake terribly "not only the earth, but the Powers of Heaven." [19] (Title page appears on page 186.)

4. SIXTH SEAL EARTH'S CLIMAX.—Finally, Prentice urges, "We should carry our Observations from the terrible Night of the [Lisbon] Earthquake, unto the End of the World, and the Coming of the Son of Man to Judgment." [12] This leads to the climax of his argument—the events of the sixth seal as a harbinger of the end:

---

[7] Thomas Prentice, *Observations . . . On the Late Terrible Night of the Earthquake,* p. 8.   [9] *Ibid.,* p. 10.   [11] *Ibid.,* p. 22.
[8] *Ibid.,* p. 9 n.   [10] *Ibid.,* p. 11.   [12] *Ibid.,* pp. 21, 22.

"Terrible Earthquakes mentioned by our Lord Himself, as Forerunners of that great and notable Day, should bring it, with all it's Terrors to the Wicked, and Joys to the Righteous, into our Minds: When, not only the Earth, but the Powers of Heaven, shall be shaken: The last Groans of dying Nature; the Wreck of Matter, the Crush of mingling Worlds, be everywhere heard, and seen, and felt! When the most dismal Consternation! the blackest Horror, shall universally seize the Ungodly! And that notable Passage, have it's fullest Accomplishment." [13]

Following the quoting of Revelation 6:12-17 and 20:11-15, Prentice closes with the admonition:

"Let all previous Shakings carry our Minds forward, as they were designed to do, unto that last, that universal Shaking and Dissolution, to that irreversible Judgment of Quick & Dead: *When the Lord Jesus shall be revealed from Heaven, with his mighty Angels, in flaming Fire, taking Vengeance on them that know not God, and that obey not the Gospel of our Lord Jesus Christ: Who shall be punished with everlasting Destruction, from the Presence of the Lord, and from the Glory of his Power: When he shall come to be glorified in his Saints, and to be admired in all them that believe. 2 Thes. 1.7,—.*" [14]

III. Chauncy—Lisbon Earthquake Harbinger of Coming Dissolution

CHARLES CHAUNCY (1705-1787), Congregational minister, and grandson of the second president of Harvard, was born in Boston. Prepared for college at the Boston Latin School, he graduated from Harvard with an M.A. in 1724, was ordained in 1727, and became minister of the First Church at Boston— first as the associate pastor of Thomas Foxcraft, and then continuing there as pastor for sixty years. He was considered the most influential clergyman in New England, with the exception of Jonathan Edwards, and was the acknowledged leader of the liberals of his generation. He received an S.T.D. from Edinburgh in 1742. He was author of numerous works. Coldly intellectual and despising all emotionalism, he was noted for his opposition to the popular revivalism of Whitefield and others, which grew out of the Great Awakening, of which Edwards was the defender and Whitefield the leading preacher.[15] He stood

---

[13] *Ibid.*   [14] *Ibid.*, p. 23.
[15] Charles Chauncy, *The Late Religious Commotions in New-England Considered.* (40 pp.)

for that intellectualism that later culminated in Unitarianism.[16]
He had profound faith in the divine management of the universe. (Portrait appears on page 144.)

On the border line between the colonial age and that of
the Revolution, Chauncy belonged to both. He represented
the vast influence which the clergy still exerted in this period.
His words and his writings molded deeply the thought of his
time. His intellectual genuineness and his utter scorn of hypocrisy drove him to endless study to understand the current prob-
lems. He was unwilling to take anything secondhand. On the
Episcopacy he bestowed four years of hard study, and did likewise with other themes.[17]

Chauncy engaged in a bitter controversy over Episcopalian-
ism, protesting against the proposed introduction of Anglican
bishops into America. He was among the pulpit champions of
the American Revolution.[18]

1. WARNING OF PROPHESIED RUIN.—Following the 1755
Lisbon earthquake, Chauncy preached *A Sermon Occasioned by
the late Earthquakes in Spain and Portugal* (1756), in which he
asserted the earth's destiny to be dissolution, reconstruction, and
regeneration, with a new earth springing from its ashes. Many
ministers preached similarly on that anniversary occasion. Contending that such earthquakes are "instruments of Providence,"
he details the ruin at Cadiz, with the inundation of the sea, and
destruction at Lisbon, where the city was "intirely ruined in one
fatal minute." He compares the loss of European and American
trade to the condition prophesied in Revelation 18, and cites it
as a warning to repent, or experience similar judgments in the
future.[19] (Title page appears on page 186.)

2. OPPOSES WHITBY'S POSTMILLENNIAL POSITIONS.—His
Mystery Hid from Ages (1784)[20] stressed the literal first resur-

---

[16] Moses C. Tyler, *A History of American Literature During the Colonial Period*, vol.
2, p. 200.   [17] *Ibid.*
[18] Moses C. Tyler, *The Literary History of the American Revolution*, p. 280; William B.
Sprague, *Annals of the American Pulpit*, vol. 8, pp. 9, 10.
[19] Charles Chauncy, *A Sermon Occasioned by the late Earthquakes in Spain and
Portugal*, pp. 21, 22.
[20] Anonymous, identified by Joseph H. Allen and Richard Eddy, *Universalism in
America*, pp. 382, 383.

rection, and the eternal kingdom of Christ with the redeemed to follow. But the earth will be filled with wickedness prior to the advent.[21] He takes decided issue with the Whitby and Lowman theory of a figurative resurrection.[22]

IV. Mayhew—Dudleian Lecturer Notes Lisbon Earthquake

JONATHAN MAYHEW (1720-1766), Dudleian lecturer at Harvard for 1765, was born at Martha's Vineyard. Graduating with honors from Harvard in 1744, he was called to the pastorate of West Church, Boston, in 1747, was ordained the same year, and remained there until death. He was the author of a dozen works, his volume of sermons in 1749 being recognized with the degree of D.D. from Aberdeen in 1757. He stalwartly championed the right of private judgment, taking his stand against every form of arbitrary authority in church and state, and was a stanch upholder of civil and religious liberty, early breaking with New England ecclesiasticism. He defended disobedience when a civil command is in contravention to God's laws. The weight of his influence was on the side of the Revolution. A true Puritan, he detested prelatical institutions, Roman and Anglican, and likewise censured the scheme of introducing an American episcopate.[23] (Portrait appears on page 144.)

1. HARBINGERS OF LAST GREAT EARTHQUAKE.—Mayhew's *Discourse . . . Occasioned by the Earthquakes in November 1755* was delivered in the Boston West-Meeting-House on December 18, within a few days of the arrival of the news from Europe.[24] Denominating them "uncommon and alarming occurrences of divine providence," he declared they were harbingers of the coming "final destruction" foretold of that "antichristian power which is emblematically described by 'a woman arrayed in purple, and scarlet' . . . Babylon the Great, the Mother

---

[21] Charles Chauncy, *The Mystery Hid from Ages,* Appendix, pp. 381-384.
[22] *Ibid.,* pp. 381, 383.
[23] Moses C. Tyler, *The Literary History of the American Revolution,* vol. 1, pp. 122-132; Sprague, *op. cit.,* vol. 8, pp. 22-26; John Wingate Thornton, *The Pulpit of the American Revolution,* p. 45.
[24] Jonathan Mayhew, *A Discourse . . . Occasioned by the Earthquakes in November 1755,* p. 52. (Title page reproduced on p. 186.)

of Harlots, and Abominations of the earth." [25] These catastrophes were to be successive and cumulative, until the final
calamity of the last great earthquake of Revelation 18.[26] Thus
with great violence would Babylon be thrown down in her
final overthrow and destruction.

Mayhew defined Babylon as she that sitteth on the seven
hills, that reigneth over the kings of the earth, and that is stained
with "the blood of prophets, and of saints." [27] These judgments
are "judicial acts of God" in the course of His providence, as
He is the "moral Governor of the world." [28] Mayhew then
appeals to his hearers to refrain from all conformity to the
corruptions of Babylon, adhering to the Holy Scriptures in doctrine, discipline, worship, and practice, and repudiating her
decrees and councils. Thus we may avoid being cast with the
Beast into the fire.[29] And the Lisbon earthquake, he concludes,
is a harbinger of the woes and plagues culminating in the great
last earthquake soon to be visited upon Babylon.[30]

2. CALLS FOR SEPARATION FROM BABYLON.—Ten years later
Mayhew delivered the Dudleian lecture at Harvard for 1765,
titled *Popish Idolatry*. Defining Babylon and her idolatry, he
cites Revelation 18 as "sufficient warrant to come out of a
church, whether Rome or any other, to which the characters of
Babylon actually agree." [31] Mede, More, and Newton are noted.
Mayhew deprecates the strides being made by popery in England, and the agents of Rome who compass land and sea to
make proselytes. But the Man of Sin will be destroyed by the
brightness of the coming of the Lord.[32] (Title page reproduced
on page 174.)

V. Imrie Reprint—Looks for Great Events About 1794

Prominent among the American reprints of books on prophecy was the *Letter* of DAVID IMRIE, minister of St. Mungo,
Annandale, Scotland, on *The Speedy Accomplishment of the*

---

[25] *Ibid.*, pp. 7, 8, 52 n.   [27] *Ibid.*, pp. 8, 9.   [29] *Ibid.*, pp. 46, 47.
[26] *Ibid.*   [28] *Ibid.*, p. 35.   [30] *Ibid.*, p. 52 n.
[31] Jonathan Mayhew, *Popish Idolatry*, p. 47.   [32] *Ibid.*, pp. 50-52.

great, awful and glorious Events which the Scriptures say are to be brought to pass in the Latter Times (1756).[33] This treatise declares that "the answer of many prayers is at hand," the "stone" is soon to become the "great mountain," and the kingdom of God established.[34] Threading his way through the "labyrinth of scripture prophecies relating to the latter times," Imrie sets forth the "destruction of the Romish Antichrist" as one of the events to be accomplished.[35]

Dreadful days will come before the "blessed period" commences, though the precise year cannot be determined.[36] The numbers of both Daniel and the Revelation declare it.[37] Imrie agrees with Fleming, Newton, and Mede, whom he cites, and looks for the "great day" somewhere about the year 1794,[38] placing the 2300 years from the first of Medo-Persia, or 538 B.C. He appeals to others to pray for their speedy accomplishment.[39] The 1756 American reprint, in an "N.B.," at the close cites Imrie as mentioning the recent earthquakes as "preludes of more prodigious ones," and believing that the French will be involved in accomplishing the predicted judgments.[40]

Another English pamphlet, by ISAAC AMBROSE (1604-1664), entitled *Christ in the Clouds Coming to Judgment,*[41] frequently reprinted in America—between 1729 and 1814—was a further reflection of the times. It deals with the approaching day of doom, Christ coming to judgment, and the signs that precede. The second advent is held to be personal, visible, and accompanied by the literal resurrection of the dead.[42]

VI. Secular Literature Uses Prophetic Idioms

A definitely antipapal strain also runs through the secular works of the eighteenth century, such as the almanacs of the time, Franklin's *Poor Richard's Almanac* being an example.

---

[33] Reprint from Edinburgh, 1755 ed.
[34] David Imrie, *A Letter . . . Predicting the Speedy Accomplishment of the great, awful and glorious Events which the Scriptures say are to be brought to pass in the Latter Times,* p. 5.
[35] *Ibid.*, pp. 5, 6.   [37] *Ibid.*, p. 10.   [39] *Ibid.*, p. 15.
[36] *Ibid.*, pp. 6, 7.   [38] *Ibid.*, p. 12.   [40] *Ibid.*, p. 17.
[41] Sometimes wrongly credited to William Bates.
[42] Isaac Ambrose, *Christ in the Clouds Coming to Judgment,* pp. 8, 9.

These almanacs were as common as the Bible in the homes of the people, and had extensive circulations—up to 10,000 copies a year for twenty-five years.[43] The information contained within their covers gave them an honored place. In these almanacs there was frequent allusion to popery. The Catholic Sister Mary Augustina (Ray), before cited, has assembled numerous examples.[44] The same emphasis was true of many of the broadsides and the religious pamphlets.[45]

The newspapers of the time likewise carried frequent advertisements of books, and contained articles and letters warning against the influence of popery and applying to it the commonly used prophetic terms "beast" and "whore of Babylon." [46] A letter to the publishers from "A Puritan" in the *Boston Gazette* warns of the danger lest—

"this enlightened continent should become the *worshippers of the Beast.* . . . There is a variety of ways in which Popery, the idolatry of christians, may be introduced into America; which at present I shall not so much as hint at. . . . Yet, my dear countrymen—suffer me at this time . . . to warn you all, as you value your precious civil Liberty, and everything you can call dear to you, to be upon your guard against Popery. . . .

"Bless me! could our ancestors look out of their graves and see so many of their own sons, deck'd with the worst of *foreign Superfluities,* the ornaments of the *whore of Babylon,* how it would break their sacred Repose!" [47]

Magazines, too—*The American Magazine, The American Museum, The Universal Asylum*—though often short lived, frequently contained the same sentiments. Strong, gripping poems also appeared, like *The Last Day* (1786), by Edward Young.

VII. Bellamy—Millennium Begins After Papacy Falls

JOSEPH BELLAMY (1719-1790), minister at Bethlehem, Connecticut, was born in Connecticut. Graduating from Yale in 1735, he then studied for the ministry, partly under Jonathan Edwards, for two years. He served as supply for the pulpit at

---

[43] James Parton, *Life and Times of Benjamin Franklin*, vol. 1, p. 227.
[44] Sister Mary Augustina (Ray), *American Opinion of Roman Catholicism in the Eighteenth Century*, pp. 165-171.
[45] *Ibid.*, pp. 172-182.   [46] *Ibid.*, pp. 182-190.
[47] *Boston Gazette and Country Journal*, April 4, 1768. See *Gazette* of April 11, 1768, for second letter.

Bethlehem from 1738 onward, and was ordained in 1740. He was then given full charge of the Bethlehem congregation, which post he held for fifty years, until his death. He also traveled considerably as an itinerant missionary. At Bethlehem he opened a theological school.

Bellamy was full of enthusiasm over the Great Awakening inaugurated by Edwards, and helped found the system of theology associated with Jonathan Edwards. He received a D.D. from Aberdeen in 1768, and wrote several books. In 1750 his *True Religion delineated,* dealing with the great revival, was published, with Preface by Edwards, as a result of careful research and wide reading. Then, in 1758, there appeared his *Sermons Upon the following Subjects, viz. The Divinity of Jesus Christ, The Millennium, The Wisdom of God, in the Permission of Sin.* With Edwards and Hopkins he held to the new Whitbyan view of a temporal millennium and repudiated the premillennial advent. But he was crystal clear on the identity of Antichrist, and its period of 1260 year-days.

1. MILLENNIUM HAS NOT YET BEGUN.—Holding to the millennium as a time when Satan shall be bound, when Christ shall reign, and the church " 'enjoy Purity of Religion in Peace,' " Bellamy contends first that it is not in the past,[48] as Catholics assert.

"They were not accomplished in the Days of Constantine the Great: for, it is since then that the Man of Sin has been revealed. Nor are they accomplished to this Day: for, Satan is still walking to and fro thro' the Earth, and going up and down therein." [49]

2. CANNOT BEGIN TILL PAPAL PERIOD ENDS.—Answering the question, "When shall they be accomplished?" Bellamy gives this answer:

"Not till 'the Woman has been in the Wilderness a Time and Times and half a Time.' (Rev. XII.14.) Now a Time and Times and half a Time, i.e. three Years and a half, is equal to forty two Months; which is equal to one Thousand two Hundred and sixty Days; which doubtless means 1260 Years, a Day for a Year." [50]

---

[48] Joseph Bellamy, *Sermons Upon the following Subjects, viz. The Divinity of Jesus Christ, The Millennium, The Wisdom of God, in the Permission of Sin,* pp. 52, 53.
[49] *Ibid.,* p. 53.   [50] *Ibid.* See also p. 64.

3. UNIVERSAL BISHOPRIC RECOGNIZED IN 606.—Insisting that the seventy weeks of years, or 490 years, prove the year-day principle, Bellamy tells of the steady rise of the Roman Bishop to power, reaching the place of recognition of his claimed universal popeship in 606. But as his temporal powers came not till later (756), so hundreds of years were consumed in reaching the height of his power. In like manner, since the Reformation it has been falling, and will continue to do so till "Babylon sinks as a millstone into the sea." [51]

VIII. President Burr—Panorama of Prophecy Nearing Climax

AARON BURR[52] (1716-1757), Presbyterian minister and president of Princeton, was born at Fairfield, Connecticut. Graduating with honors from Yale at nineteen, and having specialized in Latin and Greek, he did graduate work in the classics. During this period he underwent a marked religious experience, which turned him to theological study. In 1735 he was licensed to preach, becoming pastor of the First Church of Newark, New Jersey. He became interested in the extensive religious revivals of the Great Awakening and began his career as an educator—gathering eight or ten pupils in English and the classics.

Burr soon became identified with a movement to establish a college in the middle colonies to rank with Harvard and Yale in New England, and the William and Mary of Virginia. He was one of seven original trustees of the College of New Jersey (later Princeton), which opened in 1747 under President Dickinson, who died in less than six months. Burr was elected the second president in 1748, and the college moved to Newark. He drew up the entrance requirements, the first courses of study, the code of rules, and supervised the construction of the first building, which was completed in 1756. Consequently he may be said to be its real founder. Several small works were written by him. (Portrait appears on page 144.)

In common with fellow college presidents like Increase

---

[51] *Ibid.*, p. 54.
[52] Not to be confused with his son of like name (1756-1836), who was Vice-President under Jefferson, and later cleared of the charge of treason to the United States.

Mather of Harvard, and Timothy Dwight of Yale, as well as his own successor, Jonathan Edwards, at Princeton, Burr was an earnest and discerning student of prophecy. Small wonder that ministers and professional men were interested in prophecy and familiar with its terms and expectations, when the outstanding educators of their own colleges were ardent students and expositors of inspired prediction.

The contrasting evaluation and summary of Burr's sermons during the period as seen through Roman Catholic eyes, is couched in these words:

"The second, Aaron Burr, held the presidency [of Princeton] from 1748 to 1757. His sermons delivered during that period are of the politico-religious type which begins with the Roman Empire and the barbarian invasions, traces the triumphant career of Antichrist to the Reformation, which dispelled the 'dark and dismal Night' brought on by 'Popery and Mohamet,' reviews the 'slaying of the Witnesses' (i.e., the Protestants) in the religious wars which followed, and concludes with a summary of the political situation in Europe and America." [53]

Burr preached one of these truly typical yet remarkable sermons at Newark, in 1756, before the Synod of New York. It was titled *The Watchman's Answer to the Question, What of the Night* (1757).[54] Its significance will become more impressive as this epitome unfolds—the prophetic outline of the Christian Era, the allotted periods of the two great antagonists of the church, and the approaching day of deliverance.

1. APOSTOLIC LIGHT OBSCURED BY DARKNESS.—Applying the "watchmen" to the ministry on the walls of God's Jerusalem, he refers first to Israel's time, when they might have seen that the scepter was about to depart from Judah and "Daniel's 70 weeks or 490 years, were near expiring." [55] The dawn then began to break under John the Baptist, just before Christ, the Sun of Righteousness, appeared. This same light and beauty enshrouded the early church—clothed with the sun, the moon under her feet, and the crown of twelve stars on her head.[56] But

---

[53] Ray, *op. cit.*, p. 145.
[54] The original edition was titled *A Sermon Preached before the Synod of New-York at Newark, . . . September 30, 1756.* "Published by the Desire of the Synod."
[55] Aaron Burr, *The Watchman's Answer to the Question, What of the Night,* pp. 5, 12.
[56] *Ibid.*, p. 13. (Frontispiece reproduced on p. 206.)

the light was soon obscured, as darkness and superstition crept in. Honor, position, and riches corrupted the clergy.[57]

2. PAPAL APOSTASY AND MOHAMMEDAN IMPOSTURE.—Then the barbarian incursions swept over the empire, and ignorance engulfed the Christian world.[58] This gave opportunity for the Bishop of Rome to reach his ambitious height of head of all the churches.[59] But even this darkness was heightened by the rise of Mohammedanism, symbolized by smoke and locusts from the bottomless pit of Revelation 9, the Turks succeeding the Saracens.[60] Thus the night of the church was deepened, until day again began to dawn under Wycliffe, the Waldenses, Huss, and Luther.

3. BEAST IN POWER; CHURCH IN WILDERNESS.—The duration of the papal Beast's power is 1260 years (or forty-two months, or three and a half times), the Roman state being the prophesied "Let." Burr applies the year-day principle thus:

"These several Numbers in prophetic Stile, taking a Day for a Year, make the same Period 1260 Years. So long the persecuting Power of the Beast will continue; and while it does, the Church will be in a Wilderness State, and the faithful Ministers of Christ will Prophesy in Sackcloth." [61]

This oppressed state of the church will be followed by Satan's confinement in the bottomless pit.[62]

4. NEITHER PAPAL NOR TURKISH PERIODS ENDED.—The time of the Little Horn dates, then, from Rome's division into ten kingdoms. Therefore the destruction of Antichrist and the end of this "Night of Popish Darkness" are near at hand.[63] Yet the darkest part—the three and a half days, or years, for the slaying of the Two Witnesses—will come first, and is near at hand.[64] The second woe, or sixth trumpet, is not yet ended. Burr adds:

" 'Tis evident, this woe bro't by the Mahometan Imposture, is not yet passed away, great Part of the World still groaning under it; and it is probable, this Woe is to End with the total Destruction and Abolition of the Turkish Empire." [65]

---

[57] *Ibid.*, pp. 16, 17.
[58] *Ibid.*, p. 16.
[59] *Ibid.*, p. 17.
[60] *Ibid.*, pp. 18, 20.
[61] *Ibid.*, p. 21.
[62] *Ibid.*
[63] *Ibid.*, p. 22.
[64] *Ibid.*, pp. 22, 23, 27.
[65] *Ibid.*, pp. 25, 26.

Neither has the tenth part of the Antichristian city fallen, as represented by the earthquake.[66]

5. DESTRUCTION OF ANTICHRIST AT ADVENT.—During the brief triumph of the "Whore of Babylon or mystical Rome," when she shall say, "I sit a queen," then—

"happy shall they then be, who have come out from her, and are not Partakers of her Sin, that they may not receive of her Plagues. The Destruction of Antichrist, will not be at once; yet on the Resurrection and Exaltation of the Witnesses, he shall receive a deadly Wound, of which he shall never be healed, but consume away by the Breath of Christ's Mouth, and Brightness of his Coming. Such sudden and awful Judgments will then be brought upon him, as shall affrighten the Rest of the World, and cause them to give Glory to God." [67]

This time of receiving the deadly wound indicated a new view, of which more will be heard later.

6. ETERNAL DAY SOON TO BREAK.—The third woe and the sounding of the seventh trump "will issue in the final and complete Destruction of Antichrist." Burr continues:

"Then shall be heard great Voices in Heaven, and the joyful Sound will spread far and wide on the Earth, saying, *The Kingdoms of this World are become the Kingdoms of our Lord, and his Christ, and he shall reign for ever and ever.* Then, My Brethren, tho' we may be entering on the darkest, and the most gloomy Part of the Night, which has continued so long, we may lift up our Heads with Joy, our Salvation draws near. The *Night is far spent, and the Day is at Hand.*" [68]

This will be followed by the millennial period—the thousand years—some holding that Christ will reign on earth after the resurrection of the saints.[69]

7. WATCHMEN RESPONSIBLE FOR WARNING.—Appealing to his ministerial brethren to sound the warning of approaching judgment, Burr asserts:

"This may especially be expected of us, who are appointed as Watchmen, to give warning to others. Tho' we can't pretend to penetrate into the Council of Heaven, as to future Events, yet he that runs, may read the present threatening Aspect of divine Providence; the loud Calls God is giving to the World, and to his Churches, to prepare to meet him." [70]

---

[66] *Ibid.*, p. 26.
[67] *Ibid.*, p. 32.
[68] *Ibid.*
[69] *Ibid.*, p. 33.
[70] *Ibid.*, p. 37.

IX. Episcopalian Clarke—Ends Periods in Our Day

RICHARD CLARKE (died *c.* 1780), rector of St. Phillip's Episcopal Church, Charleston, South Carolina, was better known outside of the community than any other resident of South Carolina. Born in England, he was ordained to the Episcopal ministry in 1753, and was sent to South Carolina in the same year by the Society for the Propagation of the Gospel in Foreign Lands. He was interested in a Negro school, which by 1757 was filled with children. He resigned his rectorship in 1759, and returned to England as a lecturer at Stoke Newington of St. James', London. Several of the inhabitants of Charleston sent their children over to England to place them in his school. He was author of several works between 1759 and 1770. Popular as a preacher to crowded churches, he also gave weekly lectures on the Bible.[71]

His best-known work was a twenty-four-page pamphlet, *The Prophetic Numbers of Daniel and John Calculated; In order to shew the Time, when the Day of Judgment . . . is to be expected* (1759). Less sharp and clear than the expository discourses of some of his New England contemporaries, Clarke's is the only Southern exposition of his generation we have found. Like various others, he falls into the fallacy of seeking to end the periods in his own day.

1. WHORE OF BABYLON IS CHURCH OF ROME.—Like his fellow ministers in the Northeast, Clarke declares that "the whore of Babylon, and the great city, signify the corrupt church of Rome only," [72] which has brought in "one confusion and false lip of interpretation after another." [73]

2. ENDS PROPHETIC PERIODS IN OWN DAY.—Without giving a sound basis for his conclusions, Clarke terminates the 1335 days, or years, in 1763 or 1765.[74] The 1260 years of the Witnesses in sackcloth he ends in 1758 or 1759,[75] while the 2300 days

---

[71] W. B. Sprague, *Annals of the American Pulpit*, vol. 5, pp. 146-148; David Ramsay, *The History of South-Carolina*, vol. 2, pp. 452-454.
[72] Richard Clarke, *The Prophetic Numbers of Daniel and John Calculated; In order to shew the Time, when the Day of Judgment . . . is to be expected* (Boston ed.), p. 5.
[73] *Ibid.*, p. 6.   [74] *Ibid.*, pp. 7, 24.   [75] *Ibid.*, pp. 8, 24.

when the truth would be trodden down and false religion supported, would be from 538 B.C., ending in 1762.[76] This would
in some way lead to the "midnight," when Babylon will fall.[77]
Clarke closes his pamphlet with these words: "May the Christ
of God anoint our eyes, that we may see and be wise to understand the signs of the times." [78]

X. March—Celestial Signs to Precede Advent

EDMUND MARCH (1703-1791), concerning whom there is
little biographical data, was a native of Newbury, Massachusetts,
and a graduate of Harvard in 1722 with B.A. and M.A. degrees.
He was ordained to the Congregational ministry in Amesbury
in 1722, where he settled as pastor from 1728 to 1743.[79] That
he wrote the anonymous *Divine Providence . . . Visibly Engaged
in Fulfilling Scripture-Prophecies* (1762) is clearly established.[80]
It was originally sent to "an association of ministers" in 1762.[81]

Merely alluding to the papal apostasy, which Man of Sin
will be destroyed by Christ's coming, March refers to the slaying
of the Witnesses and the darkening of the sun and moon as
among the predicted signs of the coming of the Son of man,
and the subsequent establishment of the kingdom of God.[82]
But the special signs recorded by Matthew, Mark, and Luke
appear to be of the greatest concern, for after their appearance
our redemption will draw nigh. These include celestial signs,
distress of nations on earth, marine violence, and human fear
for the future.[83] Then follows this paragraph:

"If we could find the Signs in the Sun, and in the Moon, and in the
Stars; particularly the Sun dark[e]ned, the Moon witholding her Light, and
the Stars of Heaven fallen, we should be ready perhaps to think the Coming of the Son of Man just at Hand: For upon the Earth is Distress of
Nations, with Perplexity, the Sea and the Waves roaring; and doubtless
in many Places, Men's Hearts failing them for Fear, and for looking after
those Things that are coming upon the Earth." [84]

---

[76] *Ibid.*, pp. 11, 12, 24.   [77] *Ibid.*, p. 13.   [78] *Ibid.*, p. 24.
[79] W. B. Sprague, *op. cit.*, vol. 1 (Congregational), p. 292; F. L. Weis, *Colonial Clergy
and Colonial Churches of New England*, p. 133.
[80] Charles Evans, *American Bibliography* (no. 9167), vol. 3, p. 321.
[81] Edmund March, *Divine Providence . . . Visibly Engaged in Fulfilling Scripture-
Prophecies*, p. 35.
[82] *Ibid.*, pp. 8, 17, 28, 34, 39.   [83] *Ibid.*, pp. 30, 32.   [84] *Ibid.*, p. 32.

Of this we shall soon hear more from other sources. March observes that the day may be at hand when the light of the moon shall be as the sun, and the sun seven times brighter—the glories of the eternal world.

XI. Sherwood—America "Place" of Refuge From Papal Persecution

SAMUEL SHERWOOD (1730-1783) was born at Fairfield, Connecticut, and graduated from Yale in 1749. He tutored for several years at the College of New Jersey (Princeton), of which his uncle was president, and with whom he completed his theological studies. Receiving a license to preach in 1751, he resigned his tutoring in 1752 and began preaching at Bridgeport, and later at Berlin, Connecticut. In 1757 he accepted a call to Weston, continuing there until his death. He was an ardent patriot in the Revolution.

Sherwood's *The Church's Flight into the Wilderness: An Address on the Times,* delivered on a "public occasion" in 1776, contains a number of "important observations on Scripture prophecies." Holding that Daniel, Paul, and John all depict the papal power under various terms,[85] Sherwood enlarges upon her dreadful persecutions, as of the Waldenses, which were all foretold.[86] The flight of the church into the "remote wilderness" is noted, and he expresses the belief that "her place" of refuge, reserved by Providence, is this "American wilderness."[87] The period of persecution is referred to, but the American refuge from papal tyranny is the point emphasized.[88]

XII. Ultimate Triumph of Religious Liberty

During the first three hundred years of the Christian Era the Christian church had no legal status with the state. But in 313 Constantine placed the Christian religion on the same legal footing as the worship of the Roman gods.[89] This changed the

---

[85] Samuel Sherwood, *The Church's Flight into the Wilderness: An Address on the Times,* pp. 10, 11.
[86] *Ibid.,* pp. 14, 15.   [87] *Ibid.,* pp. 19-25.   [88] *Ibid.,* pp. 26-38.
[89] M. Searle Bates, *Religious Liberty: An Enquiry,* pp. 133, 134.

whole status of the church. From Constantine onward, it was increasingly dependent upon the state. But as the state began to disintegrate, the church sought to free itself from state control. And by the time of Gregory VII, the revolutionary concept of the right of the church to control the state was asserted.

Anomalously enough, the rise of Protestantism was accompanied by an outburst of intolerance and cruelty on her part. To the Protestant the Papacy was plainly the Antichrist of prophecy.[90] But the national Protestant churches were not only hostile to the Romanists, they were intolerant of the smaller Protestant sects arising about them.[91] However, Protestant intolerance was wholly outmatched by the fearful Catholic persecution of Protestants, as in the Massacre of St. Bartholomew and the Spanish Inquisition.

Nevertheless, out of the Reformation came a large number of despised and humble groups advocating primitive Christianity and contending for separation of church and state.[92] It was always the minority groups that advocated religious liberty, never powerful state churches. But in America the minority attitude toward toleration finally came to be the prevailing one. For the first time in history there had come into being a group of civil states in which there was no majority religion.

The Quakers, Baptists, Mennonites, and Dunkards were all advocates of religious liberty in principle. And the Anglicans, Catholics, Presbyterians, Lutherans, and Reformed churches, while not opposed to a state church, were on the side of religious liberty where they were not in the privileged situation.[93] Thus it came to pass for the first time in the centuries, that complete separation of church and state, and liberty of conscience, became facts in the Rhode Island colony.[94] It was not only a bold experiment but a successful one.

There was yet another element. By the end of the colonial period there was an astonishing number of unchurched liberals

---

[90] William W. Sweet, *Religion in Colonial America*, p. 320.
[91] *Ibid.*, p. 321; Bates, *op. cit.*, pp. 154-179.
[92] Sweet, *op. cit.*, p. 321; Bates, *op. cit.*, pp. 179-186.
[93] Sweet, *op. cit.*, pp. 322, 323.
[94] *Ibid.*, p. 326.

in America. Membership was not easily achieved, even where there were state churches. In New England, where Congregationalism was the state church, church membership had actually been for the few, not for the masses. By 1760, Sweet states, only one person in five was a church member,[95] and in the middle colonies the percentage was still lower. So by the opening of the Revolutionary War there was an extraordinarily large body of the religiously indifferent. Jefferson, Madison, and Franklin were noted examples among the prominent.[96] They were not unfriendly to Christianity, but were not church members.

The English philosopher John Locke[97] made a marked impress upon many. And Voltaire's views on religion also found wide acceptance among the American liberals. Thus it was that the political and religious liberalism of eighteenth-century England and France was impressed upon the American colonies by a group of prominent unchurched leaders.[98]

With the coming of the American Revolution, the long struggle for religious freedom and separation of church and state was virtually won. When independence was declared, it was necessary that new instruments of government be formed. In every instance, except in Massachusetts, Connecticut, and New Hampshire—where Congregationalism had long constituted the majority in religion—separation of church and state, with the peerless principle of freedom of conscience, was written into the new State constitutions, and ultimately into the Federal Constitution itself.[99]

---

[95] *Ibid.*, pp. 334, 335; cf. Ezra Stiles, *Extracts from the Itineraries and other Miscellanies of Ezra Stiles*, pp. 92-94.

[96] Sweet, *op. cit.*, p. 336.

[97] JOHN LOCKE (1632-1704), English philosopher and Oxford graduate, advocated a rationalized religion. He affirmed the sovereign right of human reason to determine the reality and meaning of revelation. He promoted rationalism though he professed Christianity, and wrote *The Reasonableness of Christianity* (1695). See H. R. Fox Bourne, *The Life of John Locke*.

[98] Sweet, *op. cit.*, pp. 338, 339.

[99] *Ibid.*, p. 339; Bates, *op. cit.*, pp. 210-215.

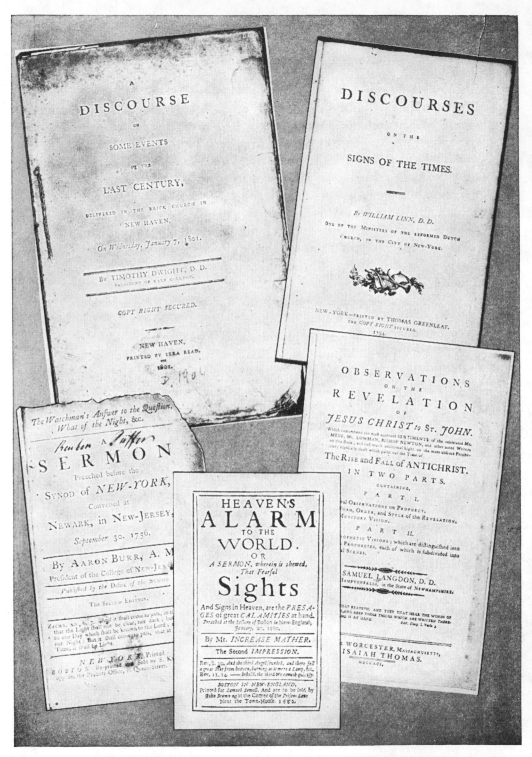

CONSPICUOUS COLLEGE PRESIDENTS EXPOUND PROPHECY

Increase Mather and Samuel Langdon, Presidents of Harvard, Aaron Burr of Princeton, Timothy Dwight of Yale, and William Linn of Queen's College, All Impress Prophecy on Their Students, Thus Popularizing the Interest in and Understanding of Prophecy

CHAPTER TWELVE

Emphasis Upon Turkish Woe Trumpet

I. Colonial Isolationism Replaced by Nationalism

With the year 1776 we enter the Early National period. Prior to 1774—the assembling of the first Continental Congress —there had been no united American people, but rather several local centers of English civilization spread over Massachusetts, Rhode Island, New York, Connecticut, Pennsylvania, Maryland, Virginia, Georgia, and the Carolinas, differing widely in their characteristics, their spirit, and their custom.   No cohesive principle prevailed.   And each had a separate literary emphasis. Thus the literature of the Established churchman of Virginia differed from the literature of the colonists of New England, and contained practically no prophetic exposition.   And between the two extremes came the Dutch Presbyterians of Pennsylvania and New York and the Quakers of Pennsylvania.[1]

But a change came through the rise of journalism and the founding of new colleges.   The aborted Boston *Public Occurences,* of 1690, was followed by *The Boston News-Letter* of 1704 —the first paper to live.   Then in 1719 came *The Boston Gazette,* and in the same year the Philadelphia *American Weekly Mercury.*   The first newspaper in New York appeared in 1721, the first in Maryland in 1727, and the first in Rhode Island and South Carolina in 1732.   By 1765 forty-three newspapers had been established.[2]

---

[1] Moses C. Tyler, *A History of American Literature During the Colonial Time,* vol. 2, pp. 299-301.
[2] Isaiah Thomas, *The History of Printing in America,* vol. 2, pp. 1-174; Clyde A. Duniway, *The Development of Freedom of the Press in Massachusetts,* pp. 68-79; Tyler, *op. cit.,* vol. 2, pp. 303, 304.

These little papers began to lift the eyes of the people beyond their own borders, and led toward colonial union. Then the magazines made their appearance—Benjamin Franklin's Philadelphia *General Magazine and Historical Chronicle* in 1741, and in 1743 the Boston *American Magazine and Historical Chronicle.*[3] Interchange of thought was in operation.

Another material factor was the founding of seven colleges prior to 1765—Harvard (1636); William and Mary (1693); Yale (1700); New Jersey, now Princeton (1746); King's, now Columbia (1754); Philadelphia, now University of Pennsylvania (1755); and Rhode Island, now Brown University (1764). The study of the classics prevailed in all. Each gathered students from the other colonies, and among them there developed a sense of fraternity. Thus colonial isolationism ended by 1765, as the minds of all were swept into the same great current of absorbing thought. Henceforth there is one united people.[4]

In the field of prophecy the emphasis still continues on the year-day principle, as applied to the papal 1260-year period, and the Turkish sixth woe epoch. Definite cognizance is taken of the dark day of 1780. A minister, a deacon, a doctor, a historian, a postmaster, and a noted theologian each contribute to the picture. And again postmillennialism's growing strides are to be seen.

II. President Langdon—Expounds Papal Period on Year-Day Principle

SAMUEL LANGDON (1723-1797), Congregational clergyman of Portsmouth, New Hampshire, and president of Harvard, was born in Boston. Conspicuous for his intellect and of high scholarship, he was graduated from Harvard in 1740. After conducting a grammar school at Portsmouth, New Hampshire, he studied theology and was licensed to preach. He first served as chaplain of the local regiment; then he became pastor of North Church, Portsmouth, and was ordained in 1747. In 1762 he obtained an S.T.D. from the University of Aberdeen. In 1774,

---

[3] Tyler, *op. cit.*, vol. 2, pp. 305, 306.   [4] *Ibid.*, pp. 307, 317, 318.

because of his high character, he was called to the presidency of Harvard. From this he resigned in 1780 on account of war conditions, to become pastor of the Congregational church at Hampton-Falls, New Jersey. In 1788 he was made a member of the New Hampshire convention for ratifying the Constitution.[5] He was president of the American Academy of Arts and Sciences, and gave the Dudleian Lecture at Harvard in 1775.

Being deeply interested in the study of prophecy, he wrote *A Rational Explication of St. John's Vision of the Two Beasts, in the XIIIth Chapter of the Revelation* (1774), and seventeen years later, *Observations on the Revelation of Jesus Christ to St. John . . . the Rise and Fall of Antichrist* (1791). One was therefore produced before and the other after his presidency of Harvard. Little wonder, it may be repeated, that the prophetic torch was kept aflame when university presidents were reverent students and expositors of prophecy!

1. THE BEAST THE SYMBOL OF POPERY.—In his work on Revelation 13, Langdon maintained, according to the title page, "that the Beginning, Power, and Duration of Popery are plainly predicted in that Vision, and that these Predictions have hitherto been punctually verified." Of its extended time period, he writes:

"It is expressed by forty and two months; which reduced to days makes 1260, and according to the prophetic way of reckoning, each day is to be taken for a year. So that from the time of the revival of the Beast, and his receiving Power to exercise this high tyranny, he will continue 1260 years." [6]

2. FIVEFOLD RECORD OF HIS 1260 YEARS.—In a lengthy footnote Langdon expands his exposition of the papal time period, affecting both church and world:

"This same Period is mentioned no less than five times within the compass of three chapters, viz, the 11, 12, and 13th.—The outer court of the Temple is given to the Gentiles to be trodden under foot 42 months. The two Witnesses prophecy in sackcloth 1260 days. The support of the Woman, i. e. the Church, in the Wilderness is limited by two distinct

---

[5] F. B. Sanborn, *President Langdon: Biographical Tribute.*
[6] Samuel Langdon, *A Rational Explication of St. John's Vision of the Two Beasts, in the XIIIth Chapter of the Revelation*, p. 12. (Title page reproduced on p. 206.)

14

accounts of time; first it is said to be 1260 days; and then, a time, times, and and [sic] half, i.e. in plain language, one year, two years, and a half a year, which taken together make the same number of 1260 days. And so the Beast after his revival is to continue, or practise according to his will 42 months. All these numbers contain the same space of time, and relate to the same series of events in different views." [7]

Contending it could not mean a literal three and a half years, as it would be impossible for so many "surprising incidents" to take place in such a "small space," he contends for the year-day principle, climaxing his argument with Daniel's seventy weeks:

"As we find in the old Testament several examples in which days are answerable to years, it is sufficient to justify the same way of reckoning in the prophecies of this Book. Thus Num. 14, 34, it is said, 'After the number of the days in which ye searched the land, even 40 days, each day for a year, shall ye bear your iniquities, even forty years.' And in Ezek. iv, 4, 5, 6, a day for a year is appointed the Prophet to bear the iniquities of Israel and Judah. But Daniel's prophecy of the time of the Messiah's coming makes this prophetic way of reckoning quite clear. The time is there fixed to 70 Weeks, and the accomplishment is a sufficient proof to christians that these weeks are to be reduced to days, and each day taken for a year, making 490 years." [8]

3. TRUMPETS EMBRACE BARBARIANS, MOHAMMEDANS, TURKS.—In his *Observations on the Revelation of Jesus Christ to St. John,* after declaring substantial agreement with Mede, Bishop Newton, and others, and after discussing the seven churches and seals, Langdon declares the first four trumpets to be the incursions of the "barbarous nations from the north," upon the Western Roman Empire, by which its power was "totally abolished." [9] The fifth trumpet, or first woe, is interpreted as "Mahomet, and the armies of Saracens," and the sixth trumpet, or second woe, is applied to the "power of the Turkish armies." [10]

4. TWO WOMEN SYMBOLIZE THE TWO CHURCHES.—Chapter 11 is declared to be a "view of the profanation of the church under the reign of Antichrist, and the afflicted state of the true

---
[7] *Ibid.*   [8] *Ibid.*
[9] Samuel Langdon, *Observations on the Revelation of Jesus Christ to St. John,* contents summary of chap. 8.
[10] *Ibid.,* chap. 9.

worshipers of God through a long period of twelve hundred and 60 years." Then, after the slaying and resurrection of the Witnesses, Langdon asserts that the seventh trumpet will introduce Christ's universal kingdom and destroy the empire of Antichrist.[11] The woman in the wilderness is the church in its "purest state," while the beast of Revelation 13 portrays the Roman Empire under seven forms of government, and the "rise of Antichrist."[12]

5. JUDGMENTS UPON HARLOT ACCOMPLISH FALL.—Chapters 15 to 19, Langdon avers, depict the particular judgments brought upon the "empire of Antichrist," the great Harlot being an emblem signifying "Antichristian Rome, called by the mystical Name of Babylon," and disclosing her ultimate fall.[13] Thus again we have the clear testimony of a former Harvard College president.

III. Deacon Gatchel—Dark Day Sign of Times

SAMUEL GATCHEL,[14] deacon of the Second Congregational Church in Marblehead, wrote a curious tract titled *The Signs of the Times: or Some Expositions and Remarks on Sundry Texts of Scripture, relative to the remarkable Phenomenon, or Dark-Day, which appeared in New-England on the Nineteenth of May, 1780* (1781). Contending that this event was a fulfillment of Joel 3:15, concerning the darkening of the sun and moon, for which no adequate human or "second cause" was known, he sees the time of its occurrence to be related to the 2300 years of Daniel 8:14 and the 1335 years of Daniel 12:12.[15] And it occurred in New England where the woman, or church, had fled into the wilderness from the Antichrist for 1260 years.[16] (Title page reproduced on page 232.)

---

[11] *Ibid.*, chap. 11.   [12] *Ibid.*, chaps. 12, 13.   [13] *Ibid.*, chaps. 15-19.
[14] Biographical data lacking, except that Gatchel was held in high esteem in the community, and was a lieutenant in a Massachusetts regiment of General Washington's army. (Samuel Roads, *The History and Traditions of Marblehead*, pp. 13, 14, 26, 157; John H. Sheppard, "Commodore Samuel Tucker," *The New-England Historical and Genealogical Register*, April, 1872, vol. 26, no. 2, p. 106.)
[15] Samuel Gatchel, *The Signs of the Times: or Some Expositions and Remarks on Sundry Texts of Scripture, relative to the remarkable Phenomenon, or Dark-Day, which appeared in New-England on the Nineteenth of May, 1780*, p. 4.
[16] *Ibid.*, pp. 6, 7.

Without soundness of general reasoning, it appears about the first contemporary comment on the 1780 darkening of the sun and moon as a fulfillment of prophecy. The history of Marblehead notes the famous dark day of May 19, 1780, at Marblehead, with the necessity of artificial lights, and birds and beasts retiring to their places of rest.[17] Mention is also made of the fact that "by some it was thought to be a warning that the end of the world was drawing near" [18]—Gatchel obviously being one of the "some."

In noting differences in interpretation that had developed between Dr. Nathaniel Whitaker and John Wise, Deacon Gatchel indicates his belief that while "the Pope is Anti-Christ," in the primary application, he felt that the term Antichrist included certain Protestant likenesses to the great apostasy. The one, he contended, "doth not exclude" the other.[19] Gatchel likewise discusses the Messiahship of Christ from the Old Testament prophecies, and His manifestation in the time of the Roman Empire in harmony with the prediction of Daniel the prophet.[20]

IV. Historian Backus—Makes Second Beast Protestant

ISAAC BACKUS (1724-1806), distinguished Baptist historian and champion of religious liberty,[21] was born in Norwich, Connecticut. Without formal college graduation he received an honorary M.A. from Rhode Island College (Brown University) in 1797. In 1741, under the Great Awakening, he was soundly converted. He heard Whitefield preach in 1745, and, in 1746, feeling called to preach, he started out on a preaching tour. In 1748 he was ordained pastor of the Congregational church of Middlesboro, Massachusetts. In 1749 a number of his members accepted the doctrine of immersion. He at length joined in their beliefs, and in 1751 was immersed with them.

---

[17] Roads, *op. cit.*, p. 132.
[18] *Ibid.*
[19] Samuel Gatchel, *A Contrast to the Reverend Nathaniel Whitaker, D.D., His Confutation of the Reverend John Wise, A.M.* (1778), p. 18.
[20] *Ibid.*, p. 19.
[21] Tyler, *op. cit.*, vol. 2, p. 391.

In 1756 they organized a Baptist church and installed him as their pastor, which position he held for fifty years. To his efforts the Baptists of America owe much of their success. He was a strong protagonist of religious liberty—protesting against civil control of religion. He was a member of the Continental Congress in 1774, and of the Massachusetts convention for the ratification of the Federal Constitution at Boston, in 1778.[22] His life was filled with controversies and voluminous literary activities, chiefest among which was *A History of New-England, with particular Reference to the Denomination of Christians Called Baptists* (1777-1796). (Portrait appears on page 144.)

1. CHURCH OF ROME MOTHER OF HARLOTS.—In a discourse first published in 1767[23] under the title *The Infinite Importance of the Obedience of Faith, and of Separation from the World,* Backus, in stressing the principle of "separation of the church of Christ from the world"—not being unequally yoked together with unbelievers—declares:

"She ["the church of Rome"] is the mother of harlots, and all churches who go after any lovers but Christ, for a temporal living, are guilty of playing the harlot." [24]

Her beginnings are put in the second and third centuries, when her teachers, carried away with vain philosophy, set themselves up as priests, and some of these above others as bishops. This fact was capitalized by Constantine, who used "secular force to support Christian ministers."

"By removing the seat of the empire to Constantinople, and dividing it among his three sons, Constantine made way for the bishop of Rome to exalt himself above all men upon earth, and above the God of Heaven, who can never violate his promise or oath, or entice any into sin. 2 Thess. ii. 3-12." [25]

2. OPPRESSION BY SECOND (PROTESTANT) BEAST.—Of exceptional interest is the new application by Backus of the second

---

[22] A quickening of the intellectual and emotional energies marked the times of Revolutionary excitement. It was the classic period of the pamphlet, the immediate ancestor of the newspaper. (Tyler, *A Literary History of the American Revolution*, vol. 1, pp. 6, 17 ff.)
[23] Charles Evans, *American Bibliography*, vol. 8, p. 117 (no. 23140).
[24] Isaac Backus, *The Infinite Importance of the Obedience of Faith, and of Separation from the World*, p. 16.
[25] *Ibid.*, p. 26.

beast of Revelation 13:11-18: "For the Protestant Beast hath
carried blood and slavery round the world, in galleys and
gallant ships, as far as the first beast ever did." [26]   Then he adds
that "spiritual tyranny" had penetrated into "several of the
United States of America," [27] as illustrated by forcible public
support of "public protestant teachers of piety, religion and
morality" in Massachusetts. [28]

3. WITNESSES SLAIN BY PROPHESIED PAPACY.—Backus introduces his *Testimony of the Two Witnesses, Explained and Improved* (1786), by asserting that "the most important events,
from the apostolic age to the end of time, are exactly described
in this book [Revelation]." [29]   And the Two Witnesses of Revelation 11 prophesy in sackcloth, when the holy city is trodden
underfoot the forty-two months, at the close of which the beast
from the pit slays them for three and a half days. [30]   This beast
of Revelation 13 is as "spotted as a leopard, as cruel as a bear,
and as terrible as a lion." [31]   This beast is Rome, and its seven
heads are different forms of government—kings, consuls, dictators, decemvirs, tribunes, emperors, and popes. [32]   Then the
"little horn, the bishop of Rome, assumed the command over
all the churches, to whom the ten horns gave their power." [33]

4. TWO HORNS—CHURCH CENSURES AND TEMPORAL PUN-
ISHMENTS.—No sooner had America been discovered than the
head of the Church of Rome—which "arose out of the raging
confusions of the Roman empire, by a mystical confounding of
Jewish ceremonies with Christian worship" [34]—"presumed to
dispose of it" by formal deed, under the assumed "power of
dividing all the world among its votaries."   And "when temporal princes were set up as heads of the church, they exercised
the same power"—the two horns being "church censures and
corporal punishments." [35]   The "American charters were given
from that power; and from thence came our late most cruel

---

26 *Ibid.*   Of this principle we shall see more in the nineteenth century.
27 *Ibid.*   28 *Ibid.*, pp. 26, 27.
29 Isaac Backus, *The Testimony of the Two Witnesses, Explained and Improved*, p. 1.
30 *Ibid.*, p. 10.   32 *Ibid.*, pp. 11, 12 n.   34 *Ibid.*, p. 12.
31 *Ibid.*, p. 11.   33 *Ibid.*, p. 12 n.   35 *Ibid.*, pp. 12, 13.

[Revolutionary] war." [36] But God has promised to destroy the Man of Sin by the brightness of His appearing (2 Thess. 2:3-12),[37] and from the sorceries of the whore of Babylon. That is the testimony of the Baptist historian.

V. Doctor Gale—Student of Prophecy Awaited Near Advent

BENJAMIN GALE (1715-1790), Connecticut physician and writer, was born in Jamaica, Long Island, and graduated from Yale with an M.A. in 1733. He then studied medicine and surgery. Settling in Killingsworth, he took over his father-in-law's practice. He also developed a wide reputation as an advocate, and had extensive correspondence with English and Continental scientists. From 1747 to 1767 Dr. Gale was a representative in the General Assembly. An ardent Bible student, he wrote *A Brief Essay, or, An Attempt to Prove, from the Prophetick Writings of the Old and New Testament, What Period of Prophecy the Church of God is now under* (1788). His tombstone at Killingsworth, Connecticut, bears abiding testimony to his interest in prophecy:

"In memory of Doct. Benjamin Gale, who, after a life of usefulness in his profession, and a laborious study of the Prophesies, fell asleep May 6th, A. D. 1790, AEt. 75, fully expecting to rise again under the Messiah, and to reign with him on earth." [38]

The writer who preserved this choice epitaph comments thus upon it:

"It appears by this inscription, that Dr. Gale was a believer in the ancient doctrine of *Millenarians*, a name given to those who believe that the second coming of Christ will precede the Millennium, and that there will be a literal resurrection of the saints, who will reign with Christ on earth a thousand years. This appears to have been the belief of pious persons at the time of the first settlement of New England: even as late as the great earthquake [1755], many Christians were looking for, and expecting the second coming of Christ." [39]

1. ANTICHRIST'S DESTRUCTION COINCIDENT WITH ADVENT.—According to Gale, the destruction of Antichrist and the anti-

---

[36] *Ibid.*, p. 13.   [37] *Ibid.*, pp. 14, 15.
[38] John W. Barber, *Connecticut Historical Collections*, p. 531.
[39] *Ibid.*

christian world, the second coming of Christ, and the restitution of all things, will be "synchronical and instantaneously executed." [40] This proposition is put clearly, unequivocally, and repeatedly.

2. DESTRUCTION OF BABYLON TERMINATES PROPHETIC LINES.—The seals are placed by Gale in the early centuries, followed by the trumpets, which he begins about the time of the death of Constantine. The seventh seal, seventh trumpet, and seventh vial, he believed, all "terminate at one and the same period of time, viz., with the destruction of *mystical Babylon*." [41]

3. MOUNTAIN FILLS EARTH AT DESTRUCTION OF IMAGE.— The stone smites the image of the kingdoms of Daniel 2, upon the feet of iron and clay, which is the last form of Roman tyranny "in which civil and ecclesiastical powers are united and blended together." [42] The four parts of the image, which represent the four great monarchies, "receive a most compleat destruction at one and the same period of time. Then the mountain fills the earth." [43]

4. STILL UNDER PERIOD OF SIXTH TRUMPET.—Gale holds the fifth trumpet to be the "irruptions" of the Mohammedan Saracens, and the sixth trumpet, the period of Turkish tyranny which had not yet ended, though its decay was under way. [44]

"The Euphratean horsemen are yet in being, and the Turkish tyranny and imposture still continue, and not come to a final end; I think there can be no doubt but we are still under the period of the sixth trumpet." [45]

5. THE BEAST REPRESENTS THE PAPACY.—The Roman "Beast" and "Whore," he stoutly contends, represent the Papacy, [46] which will ultimately be stripped by denying her to be the head of the churches. Both the first and second beasts of Revelation 13 were, he maintained, aspects of the Papacy— the two horns of the second beast representing her civil and ecclesiastical tyranny. [47]

---

[40] Benjamin Gale, *A Brief Essay, or, An Attempt to Prove, from the Prophetick Writings of the Old and New Testament, What Period of Prophecy the Church of God is now under*, p. 8.
[41] *Ibid.*, pp. 9, 10.　　[42] *Ibid.*　　[43] *Ibid.*
[44] *Ibid.*, pp. 9, 11, 15.　　[46] *Ibid.*, pp. 11, 12.
[45] *Ibid.*, p. 10; see also p. 19.　　[47] *Ibid.*, p. 18.

6. LITTLE HORN LIKEWISE THE PAPACY.—The Little Horn of Daniel 7 he believed is likewise a symbol of the Papacy. And the three horns plucked up were the Dukedom of Rome, the Exarchate of Ravenna, and the kingdom of the Lombards.[48]

7. YEAR-DAY PRINCIPLE APPLIED TO 1260.—The 1260 days, which Gale interprets as years, he applied to both the Papacy and Mohammedanism, the destruction of the two being coincident.[49] Moreover, the numbers of Revelation harmonize with those of Daniel,[50] the 1290 and 1335 days likewise signifying years.

8. SECOND ADVENT PRECEDES THE MILLENNIUM.—Dr. Gale is similarly clear on the personal second advent as preceding the millennium. [51]

VI. Theologian Hopkins—Places Millennium Before Advent

SAMUEL HOPKINS (1721-1803), Congregationalist theologian, was born at Waterbury, Connecticut. After graduating from Yale in 1741, he studied theology with Jonathan Edwards. In 1743 he was ordained pastor at Great Barrington. Since he was severe in preaching and dull in delivery, his congregation dismissed him in 1769 because of the decreasing membership. In 1770 he became pastor of the First Congregational Church at Newport, Rhode Island.

In 1776 the British took possession of Newport, and Hopkins was compelled to seek refuge in Great Barrington. From 1777 onward he preached in several places. In 1780 he returned, after the evacuation of the British, to find his church in ruins and his congregation in poverty. An indefatigable student, he put in fourteen hours a day in study, living abstemiously and taking no exercise. In 1790 Brown University bestowed upon him the degree of Doctor of Divinity. He was afflicted with paralysis, however, from 1799 until his death.

Hopkins was one of the first Congregationalist ministers

---

[48] Ibid.   [49] Ibid., pp. 15, 48.   [50] Ibid., pp. 47, 49.
[51] Ibid., p. 21.

to denounce slavery. In his *Dialogue Concerning the Slavery of the Africans* (1776) he pointed out that the slaves were sunk down in a state of heathenism, with very little being done to help them to be civilized. He urged universal liberty for both whites and blacks, contending that to continue holding men in slavery might bring down the wrath of God upon us.[52] This called for exceptional heroism, since Newport was then the center of the slaveholding interests. He raised money to free slaves, and in 1773 joined in an appeal for raising money for the training of colored missionaries for Africa.

Hopkins profoundly influenced New England theology. Pupil and friend of Jonathan Edwards, he carried Edwards' principles to their ultimate conclusions. He was the first to form the principles into a closely articulated system, and was a strong postmillennialist, being influenced by the British Lowman, disciple of Whitby. He wrote voluminously, but his most famous work was *The System of Doctrines Contained in Divine Revelation* (1793), with which was published his *Treatise on the Millennium* (1793). This he anticipated as beginning some two hundred years distant, after a gradual fall of the Papacy and recovery of the purity of the church—with the advent at its close. Postmillennialism was now firmly entrenched in the Protestant church, though still held by the minority.

1. TYPE AND TIME OF THE MILLENNIUM.—Hopkins holds to the seventh thousand years as the millennium but insists that "the particular years of the beginning or end of this time cannot be known before it actually takes place," as "it will be introduced gradually." [53] He stresses seven as a "sacred number," and the seventh month in each year under the Mosaic ritual the supreme "festival and sacred month" of the year, with its Feast of Trumpets, Day of Atonement, and Feast of Tabernacles—the latter typifying the "happy, joyful millennium." [54] Likewise in the prophecies of Daniel, the rise and 1260-year continuance of the Little Horn (the same as the Beast of Revela-

---

[52] Samuel Hopkins, *A Dialogue Concerning the Slavery of the Africans*, pp. iii, iv, 53.
[53] Samuel Hopkins, *A Treatise on the Millennium*, p. 84.   [54] *Ibid.*, pp. 85, 86.

tion), and the affliction of the church during that time, will lead to the seventh thousand years of the millennium.[55] The forty-two months of the Beast of Revelation, and the three and a half times, are the same as the **Little Horn's 1260 years.** Then, says Hopkins:

"So long the beast, the idolatrous persecuting power, exercised by the Bishop of Rome, the Pope, is to continue; during which time, the church of Christ is to be oppressed, afflicted and opposed, represented by the holy city being trodden under foot by the Gentiles; the two witnesses prophecying in sackcloth; and a woman persecuted and flying into the wilderness, to hide herself from her enemies, where she is fed and protected during the reign of the beast, which is to continue a thousand two hundred and sixty years, a prophetical day being a year." [56]

This will be followed by the destruction of the Church of Rome and the kingdom of the devil in the world—and then will come the millennium not long thereafter.[57]

2. MILLENNIAL TRIUMPHS FOLLOW LITTLE HORN'S REIGN. —The question then arises, When did the 1260 years begin? Hopkins believes this to have been in 606, which by adding 1260 years would lead to the year 1866.[58] But as the Pope did not acquire temporal power till 756, it is more probable that this delays the terminus until 1260 years from that date.[59] Hopkins holds that Rome was the fourth empire of prophecy, that the ten horns arose historically, and the Little Horn is indeed the Pope of Rome.[60] The kingdom of God will succeed in the "universal prevalence and reign of his church and people." [61]

3. MILLENNIAL REIGN BEGINS AS 2300 YEARS END.—The exceeding great horn of Daniel 8, coming out of one of the Greek divisions, is also Rome standing up against the Prince of princes, and persecuting the saints under both paganism and the power of Antichrist in the Church of Rome.[62] After its destruction the kingdom of Christ will prevail.[63] The time prophecy of this chapter—the treading of the sanctuary under-foot—is 2300 years, "a day being put for a year." The sole

---

[55] *Ibid.*, p. 86.
[56] *Ibid.*, p. 87.
[57] *Ibid.*

[58] *Ibid.*
[59] *Ibid.*, p. 88
[60] *Ibid.*, pp. 88, 89.

[61] *Ibid.*, p. 89.
[62] *Ibid.*, pp. 89, 90.
[63] *Ibid.*, p. 89.

difficulty in "fixing on the time of the end of these days, lies in determining at what time the reckoning begins." [64] Concerning this, Hopkins is in uncertainty. He rehearses the developments in Grecia and Rome, suggesting that the period might be from the time when the western horn, or Rome, began (at the partitioning of Greece) about 300 years before Christ. [65] In any event, when the reign of Antichrist ends, the millennial reign of Christ begins.

4. MILLENNIAL RECOVERY WITHIN 200 YEARS.—In Daniel 12 the 1260 years are repeated. [66] Then the 1290 and 1335 years are brought in. Hopkins is not clear as to the beginning of these two periods, but he thinks they possibly start with the 1260 years, and therefore end after their close, [67] for their closing events are not the same but reach to the recovery of the church of Christ. This will take time after the Church of Rome is destroyed, and the restoration of the pure state is beyond that, Hopkins holds. The first resurrection symbolizes this recovery. [68]

5. PAPAL FALL GRADUAL LIKE ITS RISE.—As the Papacy was gradual in its rise, till its height in 756, so its fall will doubtless be gradual, Hopkins declares. [69] Then will come the casting out and binding of Satan. The fall of the Papacy has been going on since Reformation times. Religious liberty has advanced. [70] So Hopkins looks for the millennium to "begin about 200 years from the end of the present century." [71]

6. FIFTH VIAL POURED DURING REFORMATION.—The judgments of the seven vials Hopkins begins centuries previous, the fifth being poured out on the seat of the Beast in Reformation times. [72] He believes the sixth vial had been running for perhaps a century. Babylon is the type of the Church of Rome. [73] The seventh will follow with the great battle of the day of the Lord. [74]

---

[64] *Ibid.*, p. 91.
[65] *Ibid.*, p. 92.
[66] *Ibid.*, p. 93.
[67] *Ibid.*, p. 94.

[68] *Ibid.*, pp. 94, 95.
[69] *Ibid.*, pp. 96, 97.
[70] *Ibid.*, p. 97.
[71] *Ibid.*, p. 98.

[72] *Ibid.*, pp. 99, 100.
[73] *Ibid.*, p. 101.
[74] *Ibid.*, pp. 105, 106.

7. CHRIST COMES AT END OF MILLENNIUM.—Christ will at last come in flaming fire at the end of the thousand years, Hopkins insists, taking vengeance on those who have obeyed not the gospel.[75] Such is the intriguing millennial theory of postmillennialist Hopkins.

VII. Postmaster Osgood—Commences Sixth Trumpet in 1299

SAMUEL OSGOOD (1748-1813), soldier and legislator, was born at Andover and educated at Harvard, graduating in 1770. He planned on the ministry, but because of ill-health joined his brother in business in 1770. In the Revolutionary War he entered the army as a captain of minutemen at Lexington (1775), subsequently attaining the rank of colonel. A member of the Essex Convention in 1774, the Constitutional Convention in 1779, the State senate in 1780, he served in the Continental Congress from 1781 to 1784, where he was on important committees. He was one of three commissioners of the United States Treasury, 1785-89. In 1789 to 1791 he was Postmaster General; 1801-1803, speaker in the New York Assembly; and from 1803 to 1813 was naval officer for the port of New York.

Osgood's rather bulky and detailed *Remarks on the Book of Daniel and on the Revelations* (1794), was sent forth anonymously, but its authorship is clearly identified in the Library of Congress files.[76] It was apparently written between his postmaster-generalship and his speakership of the New York Assembly. In the introduction he notes that Porphyry was the first who sought to prove that the book of Daniel was "not authentic." And he cites Newton and others frequently, showing familiarity with preceding writers on prophecy in Europe and America, agreeing with some and differing from others.

1. PERIOD OF THE FEET FAST EXPIRING.—He clearly delineates the four empires of prophecy, naming and describing the metallic parts of the great image. The last phase he depicts thus:

---

[75] *Ibid.*, p. 156.
[76] Also in Evans, *op. cit.*, vol. 9, p. 230 (no. 26663).

"The feet and toes may now be considered as the last political head of the image, the duration of which cannot be much longer according to the course of nature." [77]

2. STONE REPRESENTS THE SECOND ADVENT.—Osgood declares the stone to be the "kingdom of Christ," not the "invisible kingdom which operates only on the hearts of individuals from Christ's first to His second advent. This stone represents the second advent." [78]

3. MOHAMMEDANISM TIED TO DANIEL 7.—On Daniel 7, Osgood was in confusion, believing the second beast to represent the Mohammedan power. But he held that the great judgment scene of verses 10 and 26 described the millennium, which succeeds the period of the worldly nations. [79]

4. SUPPOSES LITTLE HORN TO DESIGNATE POPE.—In another place, however, Osgood says, "Out of the ten, or after the ten horns, another horn arises, which we suppose designates the pope as a single head." [80]

5. 2300 YEARS DATED FROM END OF PERSIA.—The 2300 days of Daniel 8 are reckoned so many years, with this chronological placement:

"It is most probable that the 2300 days commence with the end of the Persian and the beginning of Alexander's empire, and shall end when the image shall be broken and scattered as chaff by the wind." [81]

This he believed might end in 1970. [82]

6. SEVENTY WEEKS TO CROSS DATED FROM ARTAXERXES.— The seventy weeks, or 490 years, of Daniel 9 are terminated with the death of Christ,[83] and are dated from the seventh year of Artaxerxes.[84] The 1260, 1290, and 1335 periods are all recognized as based on the year-day principle.[85]

7. OTTOMAN POWER STRESSED IN DANIEL 11.—Many pages are devoted to the exposition of Daniel 11 as a literal, consecutive prophecy, in the central portion of which the Mohamme-

---

[77] Samuel Osgood, *Remarks on the Book of Daniel and on the Revelations*, p. 36. See also pp. 235, 236.

[78] *Ibid.*, pp. 44, 45.
[79] *Ibid.*, pp. 57, 58, 257, 259, 260.
[80] *Ibid.*, pp. 234, 475.
[81] *Ibid.*, p. 63.
[82] *Ibid.*, pp. 64, 253, 434.
[83] *Ibid.*, pp. 68, 460.
[84] *Ibid.*, pp. 70, 466, 470.
[85] *Ibid.*, p. 45.

dans are voluminously traced. The Ottoman power is stressed in the latter part (verse 40 ff.) as the power that will go forth furiously, but come to its end at the second advent.[86]

8. 1260 YEARS LINKED TO MOHAMMEDANISM (630-1860).— The prophetic "time" in Daniel is a year of 360 days,[87] and the 1260 years are linked to the Mohammedan power,[88] possibly from the years 630 to 1890.[89]

9. 150 YEARS OF FIFTH TRUMPET (622-772).—Passing to the Apocalypse, Mohammed is the "star falling from Heaven" of Revelation 9,[90] with A.D. 622 as the key date[91]—the "five months" of the fifth trumpet extending from 622 to 772,[92] exactly 150 years.

10. 391 YEARS OF SIXTH TRUMPET (DATED FROM 1299).— The sixth trumpet, applied to the Turks, is repeatedly keyed to July 27, 1299,[93] with "the unusual exactness of the prophetic period, which is 391 years and 15 days allotted to them." [94] In one place Osgood suggestively places this from 997 to 1388, but with the observation that the Turks were in "full operation" in 1388, and it would therefore carry beyond that date, with 1403 mentioned as a possible terminal date.[95] But in the appendix he says:

"They are manifestly designed as scourge to wicked Christians, and seem apparently to commence with or about the time of Othman, A.D. 1299." [96]

11. 1260 YEARS TO WEST AS WELL AS EAST.—The ten horns are designated as Germany, France, Spain, England, Scotland, Sweden, Denmark, Poland, Hungary, and Bohemia;[97] and the two-horned Beast is the same as Paul's "mystery of iniquity" of 2 Thessalonians 2.[98] The 1260 years of Mohammedanism are paralleled by the Western Empire and its 1260 years allocated from 392 to 1652.[99] The woman in the wilderness is placed from

---

[86] *Ibid.*, pp. 250, 251.
[87] *Ibid.*, p. 239. (360 year-days, p. 340.)
[88] *Ibid.*, pp. 253, 323.
[89] *Ibid.*, pp. 266, 268, 323, 470.
[90] *Ibid.*, p. 308.
[91] *Ibid.*, p. 309.
[92] *Ibid.*, pp. 340, 471, 496.

[93] *Ibid.*, pp. 309-311, 317.
[94] *Ibid.*, pp. 310, 311.
[95] *Ibid.*, pp. 471, 474, 497.
[96] *Ibid.*, p. 498. (The pouring out of the vials.)
[97] *Ibid.*, p. 359.
[98] *Ibid.*, p. 372.
[99] *Ibid.*, pp. 464, 465.

630 to 1890, while Rome is taken to be the seat of the Beast.[100] The seven churches are spread over the Christian Era, Osgood connecting Thyatira with the papal period.[101]

This is the testimony of the Postmaster General.

VIII. Winchester—Second Advent Follows End of Turkish Woe

ELHANAN WINCHESTER (1751-1797), Baptist clergyman, but later an exponent of universalism, was born in Brookline, Massachusetts. Despite limited schooling, he had an unusual mind and became competent in Hebrew, French, and German. Converted in 1769, he joined the local Baptist church and soon began to preach, drawing large audiences. He was ordained in 1771. Because of conflicting views on open communion, he withdrew from the Baptist faith. Following several pastorates in Welch Neck and Philadelphia, he accepted the theory of universal restorationism, or universalism.[102] This disrupted his church in Philadelphia. So he withdrew and held separate services in the Assembly Hall of the University of Pennsylvania.

In 1787 Winchester went to England to preach, even preaching in Parliament Court. He had the warm friendship of Joseph Priestly and John Wesley. His best-known work is a *Course of Lectures on the Prophecies that Remain to Be Fulfilled* (1789), written in England. Returning to America in 1794, he wrote *Ten Letters Addressed to Mr. Paine* (1794).

1. FIRST WOE FULFILLED BY SARACENS.—While still in London in 1793, Winchester gave two addresses on *The Three Woe Trumpets*. In this exposition he contends that the fallen star of the fifth trumpet, or the first woe, is Mohammed, and remarks on the common consent of "most expositors" that the tormenting locusts "represent the armies of the Saracens," [103] with 150 years as their allotted period.

2. 391-YEAR PERIOD OF TURKISH WOE (1281-1672).—The four angels of the sixth trumpet are the four sultanies of the

---

[100] *Ibid.*, pp. 465, 474, 475, 477.   [101] *Ibid.*, pp. 471, 472.
[102] See William Vidler, *A Sketch of the Life of Elhanan Winchester*; John E. Hoar, "Elhanan Winchester, Preacher and Traveler," in Brookline [Mass.] Historical Society, *Publications*, 1903, pp. 7-12.
[103] Elhanan Winchester, *The Three Woe Trumpets* (1794), pp. 4-7.

Turks, or Othman horsemen.[104]   Discussing various key dates—
including Othman's accession in 1299, their first passage into
Europe in 1357, the capture of Constantinople in 1453, and the
last of their conquests—Winchester places the 391 years thus:

"Now it is wonderfully remarkable, that the first conquest of the
Othmans over the Christians, was in the year of the Hegira, 680, and in
the year of Christ 1281.   For Ortogrul, in that year, (according to the
accurate historian Saadi) crowned his victories with the conquest of the
famous city Kutahi, from the Greeks:—Compute three hundred and ninety-
one years from that time, and they will terminate in the year 1672; and,
in that year Mahomet the fourth took Cameniac from the Poles; and forty-
eight towns and villages in the territory of Cameniac were delivered up to
the Sultan, upon the treaty of Peace.   Whereupon Prince Cantemir hath
made this memorable reflection, 'This was the last victory by which any
advantage accrued to the Othman state, or any city or province was an-
nexed to the ancient bounds of the empire.' " [105]

3. LACK OF INFORMATION AFFECTS FIFTEEN DAYS.—Concerning the specific fifteen days, Winchester says:

"Here then the prophecy and the event agree exactly in the period
of three hundred and ninety-one years; and if we had more accurate and
authentic histories of the Othmans, and knew the very day on which
Kutahi was taken, as certainly as we may know that wherein Cameniac
was taken, the like exactness would doubtless be found in the fifteen
days." [106]

4. FRANCE THE "TENTH PART OF THE CITY."—Turning to
Revelation 11:13—the earthquake, the tenth part of the city
falling, and the slaying of 7,000 names—Winchester contends
that the earthquake signified a "great political shaking of some
nation, whereby the government shall be overthrown"—and this
"to happen in one of the ten kingdoms, constituting the great
hierarchy of Rome . . . the great city." [107]   This one kingdom will
"fall off from Rome, and will no longer support the papal government." [108]   His exposition is explicit:

"France is certainly a tenth part of the city or hierarchy of Rome, it
is one of the ten horns of the beast, one of the ten kingdoms that gave its
power and authority to the beast, which it has done in a most remarkable
manner, from the days of Pepin, and his son Charlemagne, or Charles the
Great, until the late Revolution.   These kings of France, were the very
persons who first made the Pope of Rome a temporal prince, by conquer-

---

[104] *Ibid.*, p. 19.   [106] *Ibid.*, p. 24.   [108] *Ibid.*, p. 33.
[105] *Ibid.*, pp. 23, 24.   [107] *Ibid.*, pp. 32, 33.

ing Italy, subjecting the same to the Bishop of Rome, and laying the keys
at his feet. And France has all along been a steady and constant supporter
of the papal religion, power and dignity; but it is now fallen, from that
connection, to rise no more." [109]

5. SLAUGHTER OF NAMES IS FINAL PROOF.—The slaughter
of the names is given as added proof:

"But it is to be observed, that in the earthquake or total Revolution
that hath taken place in France, that there has been an entire slaughter
of the *names of men,* that is of all *titles* of every kind. This is an event,
however trifling in itself, that marks this period with the utmost precision
and exactness. This has never taken place in any one of the kingdoms
before that has fallen off from its connection with Rome; and consequently
proves the Revolution in France to be intended." [110]

6. JURIEU AND FLEMING PREDICTED IT.—Commenting that
"now the event having taken place, it is easy to see the exact
correspondence between the prediction and its accomplishment," he points out that Jurieu, a hundred years before, not
only specified France but set the time in the decade 1780 to
1790. [111] And Fleming in 1701 likewise pointed to France and
cited the year 1794. [112] However, Winchester believes that this
was not by any of the seven vials, which he believed were all
still future. [113]

7. FRENCH REVOLUTION CLOSES EPOCH; OPENS ANOTHER.—
Regarding the second woe as past, or completed, Winchester
makes this impressive statement:

"I regard the late events in France, therefore, as Signs of the Times,
and they mark the close of the preceding period with great exactness; and
in this light their consequence is very great: they shew us whereabouts we
are, and tend to confirm the authority of the Scriptures, and especially the
book of the Revelation of St. John." [114]

8. SEVENTH TRUMP USHERS IN SECOND ADVENT.—He then
declares that the next period is about to begin—the sounding
of the seventh trumpet—and this will continue until the seven
vials of wrath are poured out, and Christ's second personal
appearance takes place, and the kingdoms of this world become
the kingdoms of our God and of His Christ. [115]

---

[109] *Ibid.,* pp. 33, 34.   [110] *Ibid.,* p. 34.   [111] *Ibid.,* p. 35.
[112] *Ibid.,* pp. 35, 36. Both Fleming and Jurieu are fully dealt with in Volume 2 of
Prophetic Faith.
[113] *Ibid.,* p. 36, 50-61.   [114] *Ibid.,* p. 38.   [115] *Ibid.,* pp. 38, 61.

CHAPTER THIRTEEN

Daystar of Premillennial Hope Reappears

The eighteenth century roll of prophetic witnesses is closed with the testimony of a college president, a college librarian, several preachers, and lastly the president of Yale whose tenure spanned the latter years of the French Revolution and the close of the 1260 years. The continuity of evidence is remarkable, and the luminous Daystar of the returning premillennial advent hope reappears in the midst of the heavy pall of postmillennialism that had spread over the New World as well as the Old.

I. President Linn—French Revolution Fulfilling Prophecy

WILLIAM LINN (1752-1808), Presbyterian clergyman, educator, and president pro tempore of Queen's College (Rutgers), was born near Shippensburg, Pennsylvania, and graduated from the College of New Jersey (Princeton) in 1772. Ordained to the Donegal presbytery in 1775, he first served as chaplain in the Continental Army in 1776. Then in 1777 he was called to the pastorate of the Presbyterian church at Big Spring, where he served until 1784. He next took charge of an academy in Somerset, Maryland, but soon returned to a pastorate in Elizabethtown, New Jersey. During 1786-1805 he preached in the Dutch Reformed Collegiate Church in New York City. He was a pulpit orator of power, rising to great heights in grandeur of expression. His sermons were written and then committed to memory. (Portrait appears on page 144.)

Part of this time (1791-1794) Linn acted as president of Queen's College, of which he had been a trustee since 1787. For twenty-one years prior to his death he was one of the regents for the University of New York. He was also the first chaplain in the U. S. House of Representatives. In 1789 Princeton conferred upon him the degree of D.D. In the same year he was chosen president of Union College, Schenectady, New York.

1. TENTH OF PAPAL CITY IS FALLING.—In April, 1793, during the midst of the French Revolution, Linn began a series of *Discourses on the Signs of the Times* (1794). In the preface he declares prophecy to be in the very process of fulfilling, preparatory to the general spread of the gospel.[1] Prophecy is averred to be the strong proof of divine revelation. And Linn adds that the nearer the fulfillment, the more its perception is unfolded. Specific reference is made to France as the tenth part of the Babylonian city, and to the Beast as Rome, with citation to many prophetic writers holding the same view.[2]

2. ADVENT DELIVERS FROM ANTICHRIST'S TYRANNY.—Reviewing the Bishop of Rome's clinid to power from Constantine's day onward, resulting in spiritual tyranny, Linn follows with the declaration that the Papacy is the Antichrist, the Beast, the Man of Sin,[3] and the great Whore.[4] Then he points to the second advent as the time of glorious coming deliverance.[5]

3. 1260 YEARS FROM 553 TO 1813.—In his discourse on Daniel 7:25, Linn refers to the general agreement of expositors that Daniel's Little Horn, Paul's Man of Sin, and John's Beast are the same, and are all fulfilled in popery. The Latin *Vicarius Filii Dei* is cited for his name, along with the customary tabulations—the Greek *Lateinos,* the Hebrew *Romiith.*[6] The 1260 years are noted as in both Daniel and the Apocalypse, with several possible beginning and terminal points—one of which is 553-1813.[7] The destruction of Antichrist will precede the millennium. Such is the exposition of yet another college president.

---

[1] William Linn, *Discourses on the Signs of the Times,* pp. iii, iv. (Title page reproduced on p. 206.)
[2] *Ibid.,* pp. 25, 26.   [4] *Ibid.,* p. 59.   [6] *Ibid.,* pp. 150, 151.
[3] *Ibid.,* pp. 49-51.   [5] *Ibid.,* pp. 114, 115.   [7] *Ibid.,* pp. 156-159.

II. Librarian Winthrop—Terminates 1260 Years With French Revolution

JAMES WINTHROP (1752-1821), librarian and jurist, was graduated from Harvard in 1769. In 1770 he took over the work of librarian at Harvard and was formally appointed in 1772. Of broad learning, he spoke the leading languages of Europe. He was also postmaster at Cambridge, and in 1791 became judge of Common Pleas in Middlesex. He was founder of the Massachusetts Historical Society and promoter of the Cape Middlesex Canal. He finally became overseer of Allegany College and bequeathed his extensive library to it.

Though a layman, Winthrop's chief literary efforts were in the field of prophecy. His earliest work was *An Attempt to Translate the Prophetic Part of the Apocalypse of Saint John* (1794). His leading treatise was *A Systematic Arrangement of Several Scripture Prophecies Relating to Antichrist; With their Application to the Course of History* (1795). His *An Appendix to the New Testament* (1809) was a combination of three of his previous works. Winthrop's chief interest lay in the location of the time periods of Daniel and of Revelation.

1. 1260-YEAR PERIOD OF ANTICHRIST'S PROSPERITY.—Discussing the time period of Antichrist's dominance, Winthrop contends that the "two equal periods of twelve hundred and sixty years" in Revelation 12 and 13 are identical and are "assigned for the prosperity of that power." [8] He also places with them the similar period of the oppression of the Two Witnesses.[9]

2. OTHER PERIODS LEAD TO JUDGMENT AND MILLENNIUM. —He then alludes to the 1290 years as leading up to the judgment, with the 1335 years reaching to the millennium—the 2300 years also probably terminating about the same time.[10] Twice mentioning the 391 years, Winthrop terminates them in 1775.[11] The precise basis for this timing is not explicitly given.

---

[8] James Winthrop, *A Systematic Arrangement of Several Scripture Prophecies Relating to Antichrist, With Their Application to the Course of History*, p. 21.
[9] *Ibid.*, p. 23.   [10] *Ibid.*, pp. 21-23.   [11] *Ibid.*, pp. 23, 32.

3. Ten Horns Contemporary With Seventh Head.—
The seven heads and ten horns of Revelation 12 and 13 are said
to be "seven successive governments, and the horns to be ten
contemporary states," the last head having his power along with
the ten horns.[12]

4. 1260 Years Dated From 532-1791.—Winthrop dates the
rise of Antichrist about 532, when "the first horn received its
power by the union of the French Monarchy." [13]   He dates the
close of "popish prosperity" about 1791, when France declared
herself "independent of Rome." [14]   He likewise begins the 1290
years in 532, allowing thirty years to complete the judgment of
Antichrist.[15]   The joint beginning of the two was to become
common a little later.

III. Spalding—Daystar of Returning Premillennial Hope

Joshua Spalding   (1760-1825), ardent premillennialist,
later lauded by the Millerites, was born at Killingsly, Connecticut.   He studied under Ebenezer Bradford, and was likewise a
student of theology under Jonathan Edwards and Samuel Hopkins, both outstanding postmillennialists.   Set on becoming a
minister, Spalding practiced preaching in an old abandoned
church at Killingsly.   At twenty-two he was licensed to preach,
and in 1785 he "settled over" the Tabernacle Church at Salem
as pastor.[16]   This church was a continuation of the First Church,
founded in 1629.   It was built by the Reverend Nathaniel
Whitaker and was greatly improved during Spalding's tenure.[17]
The Tabernacle Church was the cradle of the Massachusetts Missionary Society and of the American Board of Commissioners for
Foreign Missions.   Spalding received his M.A. degree from Dartmouth in 1786.   Significantly enough, differences with the
church board led to his dismissal in 1802.   But dissatisfaction
over his dismissal led to the formation of the branch church by a

---

[12] *Ibid.*, pp. 26, 27.
[13] *Ibid.*, p. 27.
[14] *Ibid.*, pp. 32, 33.
[15] *Ibid.*, pp. 21, 22, 27.
[16] Samuel M. Worcester, *A Memorial of the Old and New Tabernacle, Salem, Mass.*, p. 9.
[17] Charles S. Osgood and Henry M. Batchelder, *Historical Sketch of Salem*, p. 90.

large group, of which he became pastor. From this he later resigned, removing to Newbury, New York, where he died.[18]

Earnest and godly and fond of study, he was a "great reasoner." Revivals were frequent wherever he preached, particularly around 1808. He brought out *The Lord's Songs* (1805), hymns "used in the late Glorious revivals." He also introduced the practice of holding religious meetings in private homes, and of getting crowds of people to study the Bible. Spalding's notable book *Sentiments, Concerning the Coming and Kingdom of Christ, Collected from the Bible, and from the Writings of Many Antient, and Some Modern, Believers* (1796) had a far-reaching influence. Stanchly premillennial, it was later reprinted and widely circulated by J. V. Himes in the early part of the Millerite movement. Himes designated it "the day-star of returning light to the American churches on the subject of the near coming and kingdom of our Lord Jesus Christ." [19] The preface of the J. V. Himes 1841 reprint declares, "The church will yet honor the memory of the man who, in the midst of obliquy and reproach, stood boldly forth as the messenger of God to a sleeping church." [20] (Title page reproduced on page 232.)

1. EVENTS SURROUNDING THE SECOND ADVENT.—The titles of the nine lectures comprising Spalding's volume reveal its scope and viewpoint in sharp contrast to his teacher, Samuel Hopkins. These were "The Coming of Christ," "The Last Trump," "The First Resurrection," "The Battle of that great Day of God Almighty," "The Kingdom of Christ," "The Restitution of All Things," "The New Heavens and New Earth," "The New Jerusalem," and "Gog and Magog." This was the new note, or rather the revival of the old note. The destruction of Antichrist is directly connected with the advent by Spalding, who cites Cotton Mather in support.[21] And neither the restitution, the new heavens and earth, nor the millennium, said he, will occur until the glorious advent of Christ.[22] It will be pre-

---

[18] Charles W. Spalding, *The Spalding Memorial*, p. 203.
[19] Joshua Spalding, *Sentiments, Concerning the Coming and Kingdom of Christ*, 1841, Preface to second edition by Himes and Litch, p. iii.
[20] *Ibid.*, p. iv.   [21] *Ibid.* (1st ed., 1796), p. 5.   [22] *Ibid.*, p. 14.

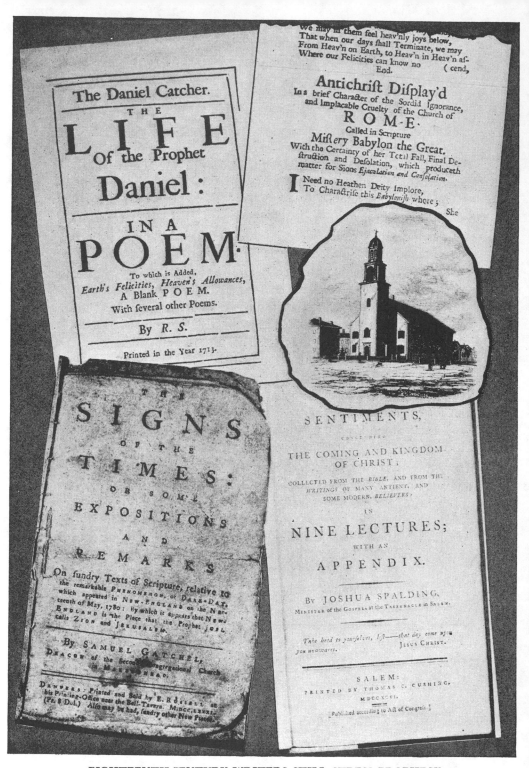

EIGHTEENTH-CENTURY WRITERS STILL STRESS PROPHECY

Sabbatarian Poet Steere Weaves Terms Into Verse (Upper Pair); Deacon Gatchel Notes Dark Day
of May, 1780 (Lower Left); Daystar of Returning Premillennial Hope, Joshua Spalding, and
His Salem Tabernacle (Inset)

ceded by a period of great tribulation, and will bring the redemption of God's people on the one hand and the destruction of the wicked on the other.[23]

2. BABYLON'S DESTRUCTION FOLLOWS BRIEF TRIUMPH.— The overthrow of Great Babylon's queenship, her plagues, and her destruction will come suddenly and unexpectedly. Daniel 11:44, 45, is applied by Spalding to Antichrist going forth "with great fury to destroy and utterly to make away many," and then coming to his end with none to help.[24]

3. CELESTIAL SIGNS BEING FULFILLED.—The signs in nature, and particularly the celestial signs of Joel, Matthew, Mark, and Luke, are next mentioned. Not only is reference made to strange sights, such as the Northern Lights, visible both in America and in Europe, but the remarkable destructiveness of the elements is noted. Of the celestial signs, Spalding says, "We have seen wonderful and alarming phenomena of darkness of the sun and moon," [25] obviously that of May, 1780. The glorious advent, he asserted, therefore may soon take place.

4. SEVENTH-MONTH TRUMPETS BETOKEN LAST TRUMP.— Spalding prefaces his remarks on the seventh, or last, trump by an allusion to the use of the trumpets in the Mosaic dispensation. These were particularly employed for the day of blowing, on the first day of the seventh month, which heralded the great Day of Atonement, the Feast of Tabernacles, and the great Jubilee.[26] These, he held, were symbolic of the final restitution of all things when the kingdoms of the world become the kingdoms of our Lord, and the saints are gathered unto Him at the sound of the last trump, which will close all "probationary dispensations, and times." [27] Israel of old assembled, marched, celebrated their feasts, and joined battle, all by the sound of the trumpet. Hence its import. This feature is destined to become increasingly prominent in the nineteenth-century records.

5. END OF SIXTH TRUMPET NEARING.—The day of God's wrath, with the destruction of Antichrist and the world's con-

[23] *Ibid.*, pp. 14, 15, 18, 19.   [25] *Ibid.*, pp. 19-21.   [27] *Ibid.*, pp. 29, 36, 37.
[24] *Ibid.*, pp. 18, 19.   [26] *Ibid.*, pp. 27, 28.

flagration, precedes the great millennial kingdom, and that day is near.[28] Then comes Spalding's courageous declaration, "If I am alone, I must believe that the great day of God's wrath which shall consume all the wicked, and drive them out from the face of the earth, will precede the millennial kingdom of Christ and the saints under the seventh trumpet."[29] "The sixth trumpet, and also the sixth vial, are now passing over us, as the events of Providence do plainly show, and are drawing towards the close; and the seventh trumpet may daily be expected to begin to sound."[30]

6. FRANCE TENTH PART OF CITY.—Spalding cites Jurieu and Mede, who more than a century previously had declared that France is the prophesied "tenth part" of the great papal city, with its ten supporting kingdoms, this one falling away from the Papacy under the influence of a "great earthquake"— and the upheaval was even then taking place in France, in 1796.[31] Spalding then adds that the current wars of France "greatly support" these early interpretations.[32]

7. ARMAGEDDON WILL PRECEDE MILLENNIUM.—Armageddon, or the great battle of Megiddo, as it is called, will "precede and open the millennium." Many texts support this—the time of trouble (Daniel 12), the deliverance of the church, the harvest, the judgment.[33] And God Himself will fight this battle.[34] The angelic proclamations of Revelation 14 precede it. And the spirit of expectancy will be abroad in the world, despite the fact that postmillennialists are mistakenly looking for peace and prosperity and world conversion, and the deists to an age of reason. But tragic disappointment impends for all such.[35]

8. FOUR EMPIRES OF DANIEL 2 AND 7.—Spalding holds to the standard four empires of Daniel 2 and 7—Babylon, Medo-Persia, Grecia, and Rome—followed by the Papal Little Horn[36] with its allotted 1260 days, "that is years."[37] Then, at the time

[28] Ibid., p. 50.
[29] Ibid., pp. 50, 51.
[30] Ibid., pp. 51, 52.
[31] Ibid., pp. 51-53 n.
[32] Ibid., p. 53 n.
[33] Ibid., pp. 86, 104, 110, 111.
[37] Ibid., p. 127.
[34] Ibid., p. 110.
[35] Ibid., pp. 111-113.
[36] Ibid., pp. 126, 127.

appointed, the stone will smite the image, the beast will be slain, and the Son of man will take the kingdom. This is at the last trump. But this cannot be until Antichrist is destroyed. Spalding asserts that it is we "upon whom the ends of the world are come."[38] The millennium cannot come until after the Beast is destroyed, for Antichrist and Christ cannot reign together.[39]

9. NEW JERUSALEM TO BE ON EARTH.—Following the destruction of the old world comes the new earth[40] and the New Jerusalem. In this New Jerusalem there will be no weakness, no error, no sin. It will be "heaven upon earth," as the seat of the New Jerusalem will be in this new earth to come, coming down from God out of heaven.[41] But the world will be so asleep to its danger that the warning voice will be drowned by the cry of peace and safety. But God's elect will hear His voice.[42]

10. 1335 YEARS LEAD TO FIRST RESURRECTION.—No day or year was set by Spalding. But the 1290- and 1335-year periods of Daniel 12 are cited, as leading to the first resurrection and the New Jerusalem.[43] The growing opposition and perversion under universalism is duly noted, and the almost prophetic words are used, "We expect opposition."[44] The saints live with Christ in His appointed kingdom a thousand years.[45] Christ will come the second time, at the time appointed, and will be announced by the midnight cry.[46] Meantime Christ serves as Advocate before the Father for us.[47] Such was the remarkably clear and ringing premillennial testimony of this daystar of the nineteenth-century advent revival, just as the eighteenth century was closing.

IV. Lathrop—French Revolution Fulfills Prophesied Earthquake

The dramatic impact of the French Revolution upon the American colonies was profound, giving birth to extraordinary hopes and fears. It gave impetus to the movement to democratize American life and institutions. The English declaration of

---

[38] *Ibid.*, pp. 127, 128.
[39] *Ibid.*, pp. 127, 161.
[40] *Ibid.*, pp. 174, 175.
[41] *Ibid.*, pp. 204, 205.
[42] *Ibid.*, p. 240.
[43] *Ibid.*, p. 241 n.
[47] *Ibid.*, p. 271.
[44] *Ibid.*, p. 241.
[45] *Ibid.*, Appendix, p. 270.
[46] *Ibid.*, pp. 270, 271.

war on France produced a crisis in America. At the beginning
of the struggle the sympathy of America as a whole went to
France. The mere adherence of Lafayette justified the cause.
On the other hand, the Federalist group denounced the "infidel
French mobocracy," [48] and many protested against the infidelic
trends. Yet these found their way into such a stronghold of
orthodoxy as Harvard College.

JOSEPH LATHROP (1731-1820), Congregationalist pastor,
was born in Norwich, Connecticut. After graduating from Yale
in 1754, he taught at Springfield, Massachusetts, while studying
theology. In 1756 he was ordained pastor of the Congregational
church of West Springfield, continuing to serve that one congregation for sixty-two years. Yale conferred the degree of D.D.
upon him in 1791, and Harvard the same in 1811. In 1793 he
declined the professorship of divinity at Harvard. Lathrop was
author of several works, [49] among which were *God's Challenge to
Infidelity* (1797), *Christ's Warning to the Churches* (1789), *The
Prophecy of Daniel, Relating to the Time of the End* (1811),
and *The Angel Preaching the Everlasting Gospel* (1812).

These books clearly reveal the course of his thinking. The
last-named title was a sermon preached at Springfield, April 21,
1812, "at the institution of a Society for the Encouragement of
Foreign Missions" and published for the society. Based on Revelation 14:6, 7, it mentioned attempts to apply the angel messages
to the Reformation period, but he connected it with the fall of
Babylon [50] and the world missionary movement now under way.
The gospel is everlasting or changeless because in contradistinc-
tion to the corruptions of the age. It flies with winged speed to
every nation. It pertains to the time of "liberty" to follow the
"1260 years," when the tyrannical power of the Papacy is cast
down. [51] In the copy examined, the sermon was followed by the
constitution of the society, signed by the officers, with Lathrop
as president.

---

[48] Vernon L. Parrington, *The Colonial Mind, 1620-1800*, pp. 321-324.
[49] Franklin B. Dexter, *Biographical Sketches of the Graduates of Yale*, vol. 2, pp. 333-343.
[50] Joseph Lathrop, *The Angel Preaching the Everlasting Gospel*, pp. 3, 4.
[51] *Ibid.*, pp. 5-7.

1. Believed Last Plagues Had Begun.—But it is in his *Sermon on the Dangers of the Times* (1798), that Lathrop is most explicit on the prophecies. Delivering the sermon soon after word of the great papal crisis had reached America, he solemnly asserted:

"The period in which we live, is, in my own belief, marked out in prophecy as a part of that which is included within the effusion of the seven vials. The fifth of these I consider as unquestionably poured out at the Reformation. According to this scheme, we are now under the sixth, or the seventh." [52]

3. Earthquake Is French Revolutionary Upheaval.——Asserting that the "seat of the beast" of the fifth vial is his throne and his power, Lathrop applies the fulfillment to the effects of the Reformation, and the resultant darkness to the Papacy.[53] And of the sixth vial and the Euphrates, he contends that as the literal Euphrates was the source of the wealth, strength, and safety of ancient literal Babylon, so—

"the symbolical Babylon, or the Babylon of the Apocalypse, is the Romish spiritual Empire. The symbolical Euphrates, here mentioned is a source of wealth, strength, and safety, to that empire. To dry up this Euphrates, is to diminish, or destroy, that source of wealth, strength, and safety." [54]

3. Earthquake Is French Revolutionary Upheaval.—The "earthquake" in the tenth part of the "great city," is the revolutionary convulsion, or upheaval, in France, with all the horrors of the Reign of Terror and the blotting out of the Word and worship of God—the unclean spirits seeking "the destruction of Christianity, and the subjugation of mankind." [55] Lathrop expresses great concern over alliance to an infidelic power, and appeals to men to "return to God." [56] "Turn your eyes to Europe," he appeals. "The day, in which our lot is fallen, is a day of wrath, a day of trouble and distress." [57]

4. 1260-Year Era of Papal Apostasy.—On April 11, 1811, on the occasion of a public fast, Dr. Lathrop delivered two addresses on *The Prophecy of Daniel Relating to the Time of the*

---

[52] Joseph Lathrop, *A Sermon on the Dangers of the Times*, p. 8.
[53] *Ibid.*, p. 9. [55] *Ibid.*, pp. 16, 17, 26-31. [57] *Ibid.*, p. 53.
[54] *Ibid.*, p. 11. [56] *Ibid.*, pp. 52, 53.

End, dealing with "the prophetic Scriptures relating to their own times." Beginning with the "general apostasy in the Christian church, which would be accompanied with great oppression and persecution, and would continue 1260 years," [58] he refers to the supposition by some that these date from 606.

"If we compute from that time according to our present calendar, the end of this period will be in the year 1866. If we compute, as perhaps we ought, according to the calendar in use in the times of the prophets, popery will come to its end in 1842." [59]

5. ATHEISTIC OUTBURST MARKS PERIOD'S END.—Discussing the conditions of the time of the end, Lathrop quotes the prophets as saying:

"When the papacy is fast declining to its end, there will be a daring and awful eruption of atheism and infidelity, and that this will be accompanied with an unusual corruption of morals, and with horrible wars among the nations of the earth." [60]

6. FRENCH REVOLUTION AT "TIME OF END."—On this "time of the end," Lathrop cites Faber, an English writer on the prophecies:

"The French revolution coincides with the time marked in the prophecy, 'the time of the end;' the time when we were to expect, and when many did expect some great change in the political state of Europe." [61]

The sacrilegious acts of the atheistic French republic are recited—denying the existence of God and the religious liberty of man, shutting the churches, altering the calendar, and so forth. [62]

7. DESTRUCTION OF ANTICHRIST IMMINENT.—Speaking next of the impending advent, when the Man of Sin will be destroyed by the brightness of Christ's coming, Lathrop says that, on the basis of Daniel's prediction, "this event cannot be very remote. It may be within about 30 years, or it may be at a distance of half a century." [63]

8. RUNNING TO AND FRO WITH GOSPEL.—Speaking finally of the running to and fro and increase of knowledge, Lathrop

---

[58] Joseph Lathrop, *The Prophecy of Daniel Relating to the Time of the End,* p. 4.
[59] *Ibid.,* pp. 4, 5.   [61] *Ibid.,* p. 8.   [63] *Ibid.,* p. 14.
[60] *Ibid.,* p. 5.   [62] *Ibid.,* pp. 8-10.

stresses the discussion of the gospel in the "last days." Missionaries and Bible and tract societies, spreading throughout Africa, Asia, India, China, Turkey, and Arabia, have brought the new era.

"The missionary spirit of the present day bears a striking resemblance to the tenor of prophecy. Such a zeal for the spread of the gospel, as now appears, has never been known since the apostolic age. This is a new era in the Christian church." [64]

9. ANGEL OF REVELATION 14 FLYING.—The next year, in 1812, came Lathrop's sermon at the institution of the Foreign Missionary Society of Springfield, entitled *The Angel Preaching the Everlasting Gospel*. This message of the angel in the time of the latter-day world corruption, introductory to the glorious day, was to be followed by "some great judgment on the papal church, usually in this book called Babylon." [65] This is to go to every nation, with the message of the Creator.

10. PAPAL PERIOD IS NEARLY ENDED.—Touching the prophetic side, Lathrop dwells on the great apostasy from the truth foretold, involving "spiritual tyranny and cruel persecution," which would continue "1260 years," to be cast down at its end by the power of God, and the way opened for the final spread of pure religion. [66] Therefore a great reformation is to be expected in these last days.

"The papacy, with its superstitions and cruelties, has continued for more than 1200 years; and there can be no doubt, but the time of its end is approaching." [67]

V. Austin—Papal Mother Has Protestant Daughters

DAVID AUSTIN (1760-1831), widely known to his contemporaries because of his extreme views on the millennium, was born in New Haven, Connecticut. Graduating from Yale in 1779, he studied theology under Joseph Bellamy. He was licensed to preach by the New Haven Association of Congregational Ministers in 1780. The following year he went to Europe for travel

---

[64] *Ibid.*, pp. 16, 17.
[65] Joseph Lathrop, *The Angel Preaching the Everlasting Gospel*, pp. 4-6.
[66] *Ibid.*, p. 7.   [67] *Ibid.*, p. 8.

and study. Upon his return he supplied several churches. In 1788 he was ordained and installed as pastor of the Presbyterian Church in Elizabethtown, New Jersey. Here, in 1789, he edited a religious magazine, *The Christian's, Scholar's, and Farmer's Magazine;* also *The American Preacher.*

A man of great energy, he was regarded as brilliant but eccentric. In 1791 he became interested in the study of prophecy and became convinced that the millennium was near at hand. Little in life mattered thereafter but the second advent. He believed, on none too sound a basis, that it would begin about 1796. He broke with Presbyterianism, and built houses for the Jews, whom he believed would assemble on their way to the Holy Land to await the returning Messiah. He preached for the Baptists and then for the Congregationalists. His published works were numerous. In his *The Millennium, or Thousand Years of Prosperity, Promised to the Church of God* (1794), the first two parts are based upon dissertations by Bellamy and Jonathan Edwards.

1. LOCATING TIME ON ALMANAC OF PROPHECY.—Austin's high esteem for the "Almanac of Prophecy" and his belief in the propriety of ascertaining the time in the prophetic night are forcefully expressed in his Preface to *The Millennium:*

"If the prophetic parts of the oracles of God form what may be stiled 'a sacred Calendar,' or, 'an Almanac of Prophecy,' it is with the greatest propriety that the Watchmen of Zion are disposed, now and then, to consult this sacred calendar, in view of determining the watch of the night, and, of consequence, how long before the arrival of the long-wished-for promised day. From premises which the sacred Scriptures afford, calculations may, with a good degree of precision, be made, respecting the time of the accomplishment of the prophecies which relate to the future prosperity of the Zion of God." [66]

2. PAPAL BABYLON'S FALL FOLLOWED BY MILLENNIUM.— Identifying Babylon as the Papacy, Austin longed for the church's deliverance from her long bondage, and saw in the developing French Revolution the divine judgments falling

---

[66] David Austin, *The Millennium*, Preface.

and the millennial day near, according to the sacred calendar of prophecy:

"The redemption of the church of God from the bondage of Papal Babylon, as well as from the general dominion of the Powers of Darkness, is a glorious and animating subject of prophecy. The Lord hath spoken, and the decree shall be fulfiled.—If, in ancient time, the people of God believed what the Lord had spoken respecting the redemption of His people; if, from the sacred calendar they discovered the time of the promised redemption—prayed for, and actually saw the fulfilment of the object of their hopes, in Temporal and in spiritual deliverances; what forbids that, in this day of general captivity, the prophets of the Lord should look with the same faith and prayer for the fulfilment of those promises which respect the spiritual deliverance of the Christian Church, both from the bondage of Babylon, and from the thraldom of Satan?—And more especially, as we evidently see marks of the divine progress in this work, in His present judgments among the nations of the earth, and particularly on mystical Babylon; which all allow, are but a little to precede the glorious redemption and prosperity of the Church in the Millennial-day." [69]

3. WITNESSES' DEATH IN FRANCE AT END OF 1260 YEARS.— In his *Downfall of Mystical Babylon; or A Key to the Providence of God, in the Political Operations of 1793-4* (1798),[70] Austin puts the death of the Witnesses in France at the end of their prophesying in the scheduled 1260 years.[71] He holds that the Little Horn of Daniel, the Man of Sin of Paul, and the Beast of John are the same, and refer to the Papacy.[72]

4. 1260 YEARS BEGAN BETWEEN 500-553.—His allotted period of 1260 years must begin sometime between A.D. 500 and 553. If the former date is accepted, it will terminate in 1760.[73] In any event, the end of the great era is approaching. The night is far spent; the day is at hand.[74]

5. CLAY AND IRON STATE AND CHURCH POWER.—The intermingled iron and clay of the image, according to Austin, may represent the civil and ecclesiastical power of Rome. If the civil and ecclesiastical power of Rome forms the iron and the clay, well may its destruction be predicted by the rolling of the stone.[75]

---

[69] *Ibid.*   [70] Charles Evans, *American Bibliography*, vol. 12 (no. 33340).
[71] David Austin, *The Downfall of Mystical Babylon*, pp. 346, 347.
[72] *Ibid.*, pp. 361, 362, 419.
[73] *Ibid.*, pp. 366, 367.   [74] *Ibid.*, p. 425.   [75] *Ibid.*, p. 388.

6. PROTESTANT DAUGHTERS OF PAPAL MOTHER.—In his *Prophetic Leaf* (1798), Austin draws a pointed parallel between Rome Papal and Rome Protestant, calling the latter "the ecclesiastical establishments under the dominion and controul of the civil powers." [76] These establishments were the "daughters of Mystical Babylon," and "bear the image of their papal mother." And as the "connexion between the civil and ecclesiastical powers of papal Rome formed the papal cup," so "the same connexion between the protestant civil and ecclesiastical powers formed the protestant mystical cup." [77]

7. TWO NAMES FOR 666 SUGGESTED.—In answer to a question as to the number of the Beast, or Rome Papal, Austin suggests *Ludovicus* and *Vicarius Filii Dei,* "the Chief Vicar of the Court of Rome." [78] This latter title was frequently alluded to in Europe during and following the French Revolution. [79]

VI. President Dwight—Stresses Historical View of Antichrist

TIMOTHY DWIGHT (1752-1817), Congregational clergyman, president of Yale, and stalwart defender of the earlier faith, was born at Northampton, Massachusetts, his mother being the daughter of Jonathan Edwards. With a remarkably acquisitive mind, he is said to have read the Bible through at four. [80] At six, in grammar school, he learned Latin from the books of older boys while they were out at play. Beginning at the age of eight he read Josephus, Prideax, Rollin, Hooke, and other historians. At thirteen he entered Yale, [81] and at seventeen, in 1769, was graduated with honors. In 1771 he returned as tutor for six years and assisted in administrative lines, receiving his M.A. in 1772. He was an intensive student, putting in fourteen hours a day in study, and eating frugal and hurried meals.

During the Revolutionary War, Dwight served as chaplain in the Army, resigning in 1779, and served two terms in the

---

[76] David Austin, *A Prophetic Leaf*, p. 3.   [78] *Ibid.*, p. 20.
[77] *Ibid.*   [79] See Volume 2 of *Prophetic Faith.*
[80] Moses C. Tyler, *Three Men of Letters,* pp. 72-127.
[81] Yale College was founded in 1701 at Saybrook, in Connecticut, as the collegiate school for the colony, and removed to New Haven in 1718. Its charter was granted in 1745, and a chair of divinity added in 1755. Later, schools of medicine, theology, and law were established.

legislature. He was ordained in 1783, and from 1783 to 1795 served as pastor of the Congregational church at Greenfield Hill, Connecticut. At the same time he established and was principal of a boys' school. In 1795 he was elected president of Yale and professor of divinity, in which position he remained for twenty-one years, or until his death. Of commanding presence, he was perhaps the most conspicuous figure in New England at the time. He was a great preacher and theologian, a distinguished administrator and natural leader.[82] The maturity of his life spanned the period of the French Revolution, the prophetic significance of which profoundly impressed him. His literary life also spans the closing decades of the eighteenth century and the early years of the nineteenth. He is therefore the last witness cited for the eighteenth century. (Portrait on page 144.)

When Dwight took charge of Yale, the blatant infidelity of French philosophy was rampant. Student membership at church was nearly extinct. He took up the cudgels with Hume and Voltaire. Dwight's vigorous challenge to infidelity in his *Discourse, on the Genuineness and Authenticity of the New-Testament* (1794), and his 1797 baccalaureate sermon, *Nature, and Danger, of Infidel Philosophy* (1798), sounded his call to meet the issue.[83] Fresh from its own fight for freedom, America first felt that the French were aiming at the same objectives. This gave further receptivity and emphasis to infidelity in this country.[84] The vastness of the French convulsion and the splendor of its victories overawed the students of the American commonwealth. In 1796 there was only one freshman in Yale professing Christianity.[85]

Infidelity claimed Christianity could only be assumed by authority, not established by evidence and argument. Dwight's "Lectures on the Evidences of Divine Revelation"[86] forced the enemy to take the defensive. He showed the fallacy of such

---

[82] Parrington, *op. cit.*, pp. 359, 360.
[83] Charles E. Cuningham, *Timothy Dwight, A Biography*, p. 294.
[84] *Ibid.*, pp. 296, 297. [85] *Ibid.*, p. 302.
[86] Anonymous, in *The Panoplist, and Missionary Magazine United* (Boston), vols. 6, 7, 9, New Series, vols. 3, 4, 6. These articles appeared over a period of three years (1810-1813).

reasoning. He deluged them with arguments, ridiculing origin by chance and expounding the law of cause and effect. He taught the Genesis view of creation, the fall, the Flood, and the origin of races.[87] In 1802 a momentous revival broke forth, and one third of Yale's students were converted. More than thirty of these became interested in the ministry, and the college church now embraced from one fourth to one half the student body.[88]

1. PROPHETIC PORTRAYAL OF THE PERIOD.—Back in 1781, in *A Sermon Preached at Northampton,* occasioned by the capture of the British under Cornwallis, Dwight dealt with the precursors of Christ's glorious kingdom in the latter days, and with the apostasy of 2 Thessalonians, Timothy, and 2 Peter, and the general wickedness prevalent—a "deceit reduced to system, and wrought into maxims, or established rules of practice." [89] He stresses the coincidence of these prophecies with current conditions as fulfillments among the nations, declaring:

"A slight survey of the affairs of Europe, the principal part of the globe, for two centuries past, will convince us, that the prophets above mentioned saw with intrutive [intuitive] certainty the general state of events among the Christian nations, during that period." [90]

2. PAPAL ANTICHRIST SEATED IN CHURCH.—Discoursing on the "character of antichrist" as "unfolded to us by St. Paul" in 2 Thessalonians 2, Dwight observes:

"This discription, the clergy, especially the Popes, of the Romish church, have, for many ages, literally verified. They have seated themselves in the church, or temple of God, and shewed that they were God, by assuming powers, which belong only to God: The powers, for instance, of making laws to bind the consciences of men; of pardoning sin; of forming religious establishments; of introducing new laws for the conduct and government of the church; or, in one word, the mighty powers, denoted by that comprehensive title; The supreme Head of the Church; which belongs only to the Lord Jesus Christ. They have even gone farther, and claimed a power, to which God himself never pretended, the power of

---

[87] Cuningham, *op. cit.*, pp. 306-310.
[88] *Ibid.*, pp. 303, 304, 393; Timothy Dwight, "Brief Account of the Revival of Religion Now Prevailing in Yale College," *Connecticut Evangelical Magazine*, vol. 3 (July, 1802), pp. 30-32.
[89] Timothy Dwight, *A Sermon Preached at Northampton*, p. 3.
[90] *Ibid.*, p. 5.

indulging in sin. Thus have they exalted themselves above all that is called God, or is worshipped." [91]

3. Antichrist's Ruin at Second Advent.—Dwight denominates this the "most fatal opposition ever made to the kingdom of Christ," and adds that Providence calls for an "entire separation between civil and ecclesiastical things." [92] He then stresses the climax of Paul's prophecy—the second, literal coming of Christ to "accomplish the ruin of the enemy." [93]

4. The Jesuits, France, and the Deadly Wound.—Alluding to the loss of the supporting power of the Jesuits, and the abolition of persecution, Dwight felt in 1781, that these contemporary events might be that "most fatal wound." [94] And France's part was duly noted. Dwight's climax concerns America's part, and her revolution to bring about for the first time civil and religious liberty. Here "constitutions of civil government have, for the first time, been formed, without invasion of God's prerogatives to govern his church." [95]

5. Millennium Begins With Antichrist's Destruction.—Despite his close relationship to Jonathan Edwards, the postmillennialist, Dwight is strictly a premillennialist, and makes this clear observation on the still future thousand years:

"The great period of a thousand years, in which the church shall enjoy unexampled peace and felicity, is yet to begin. Its commencement is expected by the most judicious commentators, at a time, near the year 2000. It begins, in the Revelation of St. John, with the destruction of Antichrist, under the seventh vial." [96]

6. American Revivals Follow French Infidelity.—In another *Discourse on Some Events of the Last Century,* preached January 7, 1801, when president of Yale, Dwight alludes first to the great American revival in New England, and bears witness to its freedom from fanaticism:

"Of the last of these revivals of religion, that which still extensively exists, it ought to be observed, that it has absolutely, or at least very nearly, been free from every extravagance." [97]

---

91 *Ibid.,* pp. 27, 28.   93 *Ibid.*   95 *Ibid.,* p. 33.
92 *Ibid.,* p. 28.   94 *Ibid.,* p. 30.   96 *Ibid.,* p. 27.
97 Timothy Dwight, *A Discourse on Some Events of the Last Century,* p. 18. (Title page reproduced on p. 206.)

7. Present Time Marked Out by Prophecy.—Dwight reviews the "change in the religious character of the people of this country" for the worse, beginning about 1755. Next, the American war "increased these evils." And then "infidelity began to obtain in this country." [98] With the searching question, "What shall the end of these things be?" Dwight makes this impressive statement:

"The present time is, at least in my view, distinctly marked out in prophecy, as a time of singular deception, sin, and hostility against religion and against its author. In exact accordance with Revelation, spirits of singular falshood, foulness, pertinacity, and impudence, have issued from the mouth of the Dragon, or secular persecuting power, of the Beast, or ecclesiastical persecuting power, . . . That these two persecuting powers are in the view of the scriptures wholly united, and that they entirely co-operate, cannot, I think, be reasonably questioned. Both of them are described as having seven heads, and ten horns. From the angel interpreter we know, that the seven heads are the seven mountains of Rome, the great city which at that time reigned with undivided empire over the kingdoms of the earth; and that the ten horns are the ten kingdoms, into which that empire was finally divided. Those spirits, therefore, that is, the false teachers designated by them, were to spring, as they have sprung, from Antichristian ground." [99]

8. Various Prophetic Names for Antichrist.—Discussing the prophesied Antichrist, Dwight gives this illuminating exposition of its comprehensive scope:

"The Romish Hierarchy, or ecclesiastical persecuting power already mentioned, is exhibited in the scriptures under various names; as the Beast, the Man of Sin, the Son of perdition, and the Wicked, or rather the Lawless One. Each of these names is intended to denote some particular characteristic of this power. Thus the Beast directly exhibits its ferocious, sanguinary, or persecuting character; the Man of sin its pre-eminent wickedness; the Son of perdition its certain destination to singular perdition; and the Lawless One its distinguished refusal of being restrained by the laws of either God, or man." [100]

9. Its Overthrow Is Under Way.—Climaxing with the prophesied destruction of the Wicked One, Dwight expresses the belief that the process is under way—though he adds, "Yet some time must doubtless elapse before this abomination of desolation shall be finished."

---

[98] *Ibid.*, pp. 18, 19.   [99] *Ibid.*, p. 35.   [100] *Ibid.*, p. 36.

"The kings, or states, into which the secular persecuting power was divided, have begun to hate the Whore, to eat her flesh, and to burn her with fire. The ecclesiastical persecuting power is in a fair way to be soon destroyed. The secular persecuting power is rapidly wasting itself, and that not the less because of the present splendour of one of its constituent parts. The reign of the spirits of deceit is exhibited in prophecy, as short, and the coming of Christ to destroy them, as sudden, unexpected, and dreadful." [101]

10. PAGAN DRAGON PERSECUTES WOMAN-CHURCH.—In *A Discourse in Two Parts,* delivered in the chapel of Yale College on July 23, 1812, on the occasion of a sobering "Public Fast," Dwight based his sermon on Revelation 12-16. He began by showing how through death Christ triumphed over principalities and powers, and by His resurrection He led captivity captive.[102] The devil's sense of shortened time and futility excited his wrath and activity to greater persecution in the early church period of Pergamos, where Satan dwelt.[103] Imprisonment, slavery, exile, and massacre by pagan Rome reached their climax just before Constantine.[104] Dwight depicts the woman clothed with the sun and crowned with stars as the Christian church, and the dragon ready to devour her progeny. He continues:

"This dragon is afterward called the serpent, the devil and satan, who, by the agency of the pagan Roman empire, carried on a violent persecution against the church. Hence the dragon is said to have 'seven heads and seven crowns,' in allusion to the seven hills on which Rome was built, and to the seven forms of government, which successively took place in the empire:—and he is said to have 'ten horns,' typifying the ten kingdoms into which the empire was afterward divided. Thus the scenery is explained to John by an angel." [105]

11. PAGAN ROME SUCCEEDED BY PAGANIZED CHRISTIANITY. —With his power still further curtailed by the Christianization of the Roman Emperor Constantine, Satan's "mortification and disappointment" led him to inject heresy, party strife, and ecclesiastical ambition, and to bring in the floods of northern bar-

---

[101] *Ibid.,* p. 39.
[102] Timothy Dwight, *A Discourse in Two Parts,* p. 8.
[103] *Ibid.,* pp. 8, 9.
[104] *Ibid.,* p. 10.   [105] *Ibid.,* p. 9.

barians. But these victorious pagans embraced the Christian faith.[106] Then Satan introduced popery.

"When idolatry was abolished by the powers of government, the devil introduced, under the mask of christianity, a new and refined species of idolatry, which has continued for more than a thousand years. As light has been increasing, the papal idolatry has declined."[107]

12. FRANCE PREDICTED AGENT OF OVERTHROW.—But the papal power was not to continue on indefinitely, as God had put metes and bounds to it. So Dwight observes:

"And at this period, when popery seemed near its exit, the devil has adopted, in its stead, this new artifice to undermine the credit, and defeat the influence of the gospel. The same light which has chafed away the clouds of papal superstition, he is perverting into the means of spreading infidelity under the specious names of liberty, reason, and philosophy."[108]

"The scripture has foretold this very circumstance, as what will accompany the great events of the present period.

"It announces the downfall of the papal power; and this, if not fully accomplished, is probably near its accomplishment.

"It has predicted, that the destruction of this power will be effected by some of those very kingdoms, which were once its principal supporters. France has been one of its chief defenders; and France is now the great agent in its overthrow."[109]

13. FIFTH VIAL INVOLVED IN FRENCH REVOLUTION.—Dwight then turns to the fifth vial, poured out on the throne of the Beast, and the resultant blasphemy of men. These, he felt, implied licentious morals and atheistical principles, pre-eminently characteristic of the French Revolution. That the devil's time is short "the word of prophecy imports." The Revolution had produced great horrors on the continent of Europe, wasting immense treasure and taking millions of lives. "It has overturned states, and changed times and seasons."[110]

14. IF NOT ALREADY ACTIVE, SIXTH VIAL DUE.—Dwight's final point concerns the sixth vial and the dragon—the "infernal combination" of the unclean spirits of the dragon, the beast, and the false prophet.[111] Of the final fulfillment he says:

"Whether we are now under this particular vial, I pretend not to determine. Be this as it may; there are multitudes of this noxious breed of frogs, (more pestiferous than those which plagued old Egypt) now scattered over the earth, croaking and spawning in every lake and fen, vexing the air with their noise, and poisoning the waters with their slime. These spirits of devils are gone into all the world, corrupting the religious principles, and breaking the political peace of the nations, and directly instigating or indirectly constraining the kings and powers of the earth to gather themselves to the battle." [112]

"If this is not the time intended in the prophecy, there is reason to fear, a time is coming, when the prophetic description will be more fully realized." [113]

VII. Nineteenth-Century American Expositors Deferred

Discussion of the remaining American expositors of prophecy, scattered over the first two decades of the nineteenth century—as tabulated in chapter 1, on the Colonial and Early American Writers on Prophecy chart—is reserved for the final volume in this series. The expositors will appear in their proper sequence in relation to the later American aspect of the world-wide Advent Awakening of the nineteenth century. We shall now turn for a brief, retrospective glance at the French Revolution, and the attendant wounding of the papal power in 1798, [114] at the terminus of the 1260 years. This, as previously noted, was clearly recognized and proclaimed at the time by various students of prophecy, both in Europe and in America. Following this, we shall trace in detail the world-wide prophetic and advent awakening that first compassed the Old World and then shifted to the New. This will be visualized by a new chart. [115]

The completion of the highly important investigation outlined will bring us back again to the American scene at the beginning of the nineteenth century. A preliminary review of the historical setting and background of the great Millerite movement in this country will then lay the foundation for the American phase of the world-touching Advent Movement, which reached its consummation in North America.

---

[112] *Ibid.*, p. 20.   [113] *Ibid.*   [115] See p. 252.
[114] Discussed and fully documented at the close of Volume 2 of *Prophetic Faith*.

CHAPTER FOURTEEN

Summing Up the Witness
for North America

I. Last of the Eighteenth-Century Witnesses

Such was the last of the eighteenth-century American prophetic witnesses whose testimony is surveyed in this volume.
TIMOTHY DWIGHT, educator and prophetic expositor, stood
as the stalwart champion of the Historical School of interpretation. Following upon the heels of Joshua Spalding, he was
about the last to raise a protest against the rising tide of change
and repudiation steadily creeping over the religious world.
Strong, clear, and consistent, Dwight's message stands out above
the increasing confusion and abandonment all about him.

It seems fitting that this final voice be that of another
college president. The change from advocacy of the Historical
School of Protestant interpretation, first to silence and then to
hostility, on the part of the great colleges and universities of the
land, typified the change in the attitude of the ministry and the
populace at large. The waning interest in prophecy, the repudiation of the prophetic faith of our colonial fathers, and the
espousal of the fascinating fallacy of a thousand years of world
betterment before the appearance of Christ among men were
now increasingly ascendant.

That was the condition of affairs in America when the
great second advent message began to be sounded in the early
decades of the nineteenth century. The ministry was divided
and apathetic. The schools were largely indifferent or antago-

nistic. And a growing percentage of the religiously inclined were persuaded of a millennium of world betterment and peace gradually getting under way—a millennium without an antecedent second advent, without a literal resurrection of the dead, or a catastrophic end of the age. That is the historical setting. And that is the basic issue confronting, as we pause with our witnesses here at the threshold of this vibrant period, which in its later American phase must be reserved for the final volume in this series.

II. Resume of Eighteenth-Century Prophetic Exposition

Thirty-four late colonial and early national expositors of prophecy who have left written works in the eighteenth century have been examined. Among them all we find continuance of the same undeviating position on the Papacy—that it is indeed the prophesied Antichrist, disclosed under various symbols. The Preterist concept of Antichrist, introduced in the eighteenth century by Grotius among certain Protestants in Europe, was flatly rejected in America during this century.

A second prevailing belief was the year-day principle for all time prophecy. This was constantly invoked for the 1260 years of the Little Horn, along with an increasing effort to determine their true chronological placement. The 2300 days were also assuredly years, but the timing was still hazy—though a Persian dating for the beginning is noted by several. That the seventy weeks reach to the cross is axiomatic. The 150 years of the Saracen and the 391 years of the Turkish woe are periodically mentioned.

For many, the advent hope loomed larger and nearer than ever, with the new-earth state imminent. Babylon's fall and the Turk's destruction were awaited, along with the ending of the prophetic outlines of Daniel 2 and 7. The symbolic stone was soon to fill the earth. France was stressed as the "tenth part" of the "city" and the approaching end of the papal period. The prophesied signs of the times—first the Lisbon earthquake, and then the 1780 darkening of the sun and moon—now for the

No.	Name	Page	Date	Dan. 2	Clay-Iron	Stone	Dan. 7	10 Horns	Little Horn	1260 Days	Dan. 8	2300 Days	70 Wks.	Dan. 11	1290 Days
1	Cotton, Jno.	33	1639				B-P-G-R	Mentioned	Papacy	395-1655		(Year-Day)		(Latter Part)	
2	Williams, Rog.	46	1644				Standard	Mentioned	Papacy	Years	Horn-Rome			Last-Rome	
3	Bradstreet, A.	55	1642	B-P-G-R	Church-State	Future	Standard								
4	Huit, Eph.	60	1644	Standard	Intermarriage	Christ's Kgdm.	Standard	Named	Turk-Popes	3½ Cent.	P-G	Literal	490 Yrs.	Turk	360-1650
5	Parker, Thos.	67	1646	Standard		Kgdm.-Saints	Standard	Named	Papacy	600-1859	P-G-R	367-1517	490 Yrs.	Papacy	570-1859
6	Davenport, J.	86	1653	Standard		Christ	B-P-G-G			Years			Yrs. to Chr.		
7	Johnson, Ed.	92	1652												
8	Holyoke, Ed.	94	1658				Standard	Mentioned		600-				Turk	Years
9	Hutchinson, S.	98	1667	Standard		2d Advent	Standard		Papacy						
10	Hooke, Wm.	105	1669							Fr. 5th Cent.		Not Yet Out			
11	Mather, S.	108	1672				Standard	Mentioned		Years					
12	Confession-Faith	111	1680			(Pope of Rome Is Antichrist—Destroyed at 2d Advent)									
13	Harris, Benj.	115	168?			(Pope—Triple-crowned Man of Sin)								Papacy-Turk	
14	Mather, In.	125	1669	Standard		Not Yet	Standard	Named	Papacy	456-1716				Papacy	
15	Sewall, Sam.	134	1697									Yrs. to 1716			
16	Mather, C.	147	1702	Standard		God's Kgdm.	Standard	Mentioned	Papacy	456-					450-
17	Noyes, Nich.	156	1698	Standard		God's Kgdm.	Standard		Papacy	Years		Yrs. to Fall			
18	Cheever, Eze.	159	1757	Standard		Christ's Kgdm.	Standard		Papacy						
19	Stoere, Rich.	161	1719												
20	Burnet, Wm.	169	1724		Div. Europe	Christ's Kgdm.	Standard	Named	Papacy	455-1715	P-G	B.C. 555-1745	490 Yrs.	Papacy	455-1745
21	Dudley, Paul	173	1731	Standard											
22	Cooper, Sam.	179	1773							Years					
23	Edwards, Jon.	181	1739	Standard	10 Kgdms.		Standard	Mentioned	Papacy	456 or 606					
24	Prentice, Thos.	188	1756												
25	Mayhew, Jon.	192	1756												
26	Imri (Reprint)	193	1756	Standard			Standard			Years		B.C. 538-1794	490 Yrs.		Years
27	Bellamy, Jos.	195	1758							606-			490 Yrs.		
28	Burr, Aaron	197	1757				Standard	Mentioned	Papacy	Years					
29	Clarke, Rich.	201	1759							-1759		B.C. 538-1762			
30	March, Ed.	202	1762												
31	Langdon, Sam.	208	1774				[Standard]			Years			490 Yrs.		
32	Catchel, Sam.	211	1781	[Standard]			[Standard]					Years	490 Yrs.		
33	Backus, Is.	212	1767					Mentioned	Bp.-Rome						Years
34	Cole, Benj.	215	1788	Standard	Church-State	God's Kgdm.	Standard	Mentioned	Papacy	Years					Years
35	Hopkins, Sam.	217	1793			God's Kgdm.	Standard		Papacy	606-1866	P-G-R	Yrs. (Ending)			
36	Osgood, Sam.	221	1794	Standard	Present	2d Advent	Confused	Named	Pope	630-1890		Yrs. Fr. Persia	490 (Art.)	Turk	Years
37	Winchester, El.	224	1793												
38	Linn, Wm.	227	1794				Standard	Mentioned	Papacy	553-1813					
39	Winthrop, Jas.	229	1794				Standard			532-1791		Yrs. to Mill.			532-Jdgt.
40	Spalding, Jos.	230	1796	Standard		Christ's Kgdm.	Standard		Papacy	Years				Papacy	To Res.
41	Lathrop, Jos.	235	1789				Standard			606-1866					
42	Austin, Dav.	239	1794	Standard	Church-State	Soon	Standard		Papacy	500-1760					
43	Dwight, Tim.	242	1781					Mentioned							

This comprehensive chart presents at a glance the key positions held by America's leading prophetic expositors of the seventeenth and eighteenth centuries. The names are arranged in chronological sequence in the vertical column at the left, and their expositions follow logically and progressively, from left to right. Each expositor is followed by the *page,* in Volume 3 of *Prophetic Faith,* on which the detailed record of this individual's exposition begins. Next appears the principal *date* of the preaching or publishing of his interpretation. Then come the essential features of each major prophecy interpreted, from Daniel 2 to Daniel 12. A similar procedure follows, after the separating column for 2 Thessalonians 2, for the leading prophecies in the book of Revelation from the seven seals on through to the millennium.

Both the outline prophecies and the time features are noted. The frequency and the similarity or dissimilarity of exposition on a given feature can easily be ascertained by scanning the vertical columns. And thus the preponderant testimony on a given line or major point can easily be deduced. On the other hand, the over-all position of any given expositor on these prophecies is likewise easily obtained by following progressively through the horizontal lines, which cover all the leading features of the prophecies. Thus we have at once a simplified and co-ordinated visual index of essentials.

The abbreviations are simple and easily understood. "B-P-G-R" means Babylon, Persia, Grecia, and Rome; "Standard," in the same column, means that these four accepted or standard kingdoms are taught; "Kgdm." stands for *kingdom;* "Yrs." for *years;* "Jdgt." for *judgment;* "Fr. Rev." for *French Revolution;* "Pagan R." for *Pagan Rome;* "Pre-M." for *premillennialist;* and "Post-M." for *postmillennialist.* Certain fundamental positions, that scarcely follow the usual progression, are placed in parentheses, stretching across several columns, such as " (1755 Lisbon Earthquake—Harbinger)," or ("Dark Day—May 19, 1780—Fulfilled)."

WRITERS ON PROPHECY (17th and 18th Centuries)

1335 Days	2 Thess.	7 Seals	4 Trumpets	5th Trump.	6th Trump.	2 Witnesses	1/10 of City	Rev. 12	Rev. 13 (1st)	Rev. 13 (2d)	Rev. 14	Rev. 16	Rev. 17	10 Horns	7 Heads	Rev. 20
	Papacy				Turks	1260 Yrs. Slain at End	France	Pagan R.	Cath. Ch.	Pope		In Progress	Papacy	Cath. Kgdms.	7th Popes	Pre-M
								Pagan R.	Papacy				Papacy	10 Kgdms.		Pre-M
360-1695 Years	Papacy			150 Yrs.	1300-1695							6th-Turk	Papacy		8th Rome	
					1169-1559							In Progress	Papacy		7 Listed	Augustinian
	Papacy			Clergy (Fulfilling)	Turks				Papacy Pontificate	Papacy	Obedience		Papacy		7th Popes	Pre-M
Years	Papacy	Fulfilling			1300-	1260 Yrs.		True Ch.				6th-Turk	Papacy	10 Kgdms.		Pre-M
	Papacy			Papacy								6th-Turk	Papacy			Pre-M
	Papacy				(7th-Near)	In Sackcloth							Papacy			Pre-M
	Papacy			Saracens	1300-1696	In Sackcloth (Slain in France)	France	Pagan R.	Papal R.				Papacy	10 Kgdms.		Pre-M
	Papacy	5th Papacy							Papacy			5 Are Past	Papacy	10 Kgdms.		Pre-M
450-	Papacy	In Progress	Barbarians	Saracens	1300-1697	In Sackcloth		Pagan R.	Papacy				Papacy	10 Kgdms.	Papacy	Pre-M
	Papacy			Saracens	Turks				Papacy			6th-Turk	Papacy	10 Kgdms.		Pre-M
	Papacy								Papacy				Papacy		Mentioned	Pre-M
455-1790	Papacy								Papacy				Papacy	10 Kgdms.	7 Govts.	Pre-M
	Papacy								Papacy		Papacy		Papacy		Mentioned	Pre-M
	Papacy								Papacy				Papacy			Pre-M
	Papacy		Barbarians	Saracens	1296-1453			Pagan R.	Papacy			During Ref.	Papacy			Post-M
	Papacy	(1755 Lisbon Earthquake—Harbinger)											Papacy			Pre-M
	Papacy	(1755 Lisbon Earthquake—Harbinger)				France		True Ch.					Papacy			Post-M
Years	Papacy	(1755 Lisbon Earthquake—Harbinger)						Pagan R.	Papacy				Papacy			Pre-M
-1765	Papacy	(Sun—Moon to Be Darkened)		Saracens	Turks	Sackcloth -1759 To Be Slain	1/10 Europe	Papacy					Papacy			Pre-M
	Papacy	(Dark Day—May 19, 1780—Fulfilled)	Barbarians	Saracens	Turks	In Sackcloth		1260 Yrs.	Papacy			Judgments	Papacy		7 Govts.	Pre-M
Years	Papacy					In Sackcloth		1260 Yrs.	Papacy				Papacy			Pre-M
Years	Papacy			Saracens	Turks	In Sackcloth		Pagan R.	Papacy	Protestant	Papacy		Papacy		7th Pope	Pre-M
Years								True Ch.	Papacy	Papacy		In Progress				Post-M
Years	Papacy			622-772 150-Sar.	997-1388 1281-1672			630-1890	Papacy	Papacy						Pre-M
	Papacy						France		Papacy			Future	Papacy	10 Kgdms.		Pre-M
Yrs. to Mill. To Res.	Papacy	(Celestial Signs Fulfilling)			391 Yrs. (1775) Ending	1260 Yrs.	France	1260 Yrs.	Papacy		Precede M.	In Progress	Papacy	10 Kgdms.	7 Govts.	Pre-M
	Papacy						Fr. Rev.		Papacy				In Progress	Papacy	10 Kgdms.		Pre-M
	Papacy					Slain	Fr. Rev.	Pagan R.	Papacy			In Progress	In Progress	Papacy		7 Mts.	Pre-M
	Papacy						Fr. Rev.	True Ch.	Papacy				In Progress	Papacy	10 Kgdms.		Pre-M

The predominant view of American writers on prophecy as a whole, prior to the nineteenth century, can be logically deduced from this tabular chart, and a balanced understanding obtained. For example, the Historical School view of the four progressive empires of prophecy and the tenfold division of the Roman fourth was virtually universal. Futurism was as yet unknown among Protestants. The Papacy as the prophesied Antichrist—the Little Horn of Daniel, the Man of Sin of Paul, and the Beast and Babylon of John the revelator—was likewise the practically universal view.

The year-day principle for all time periods, including even the 391 (or 396) years of the sixth trumpet, allocated to the Mohammedan Turks, was the common understanding. Even France as the "tenth part" of the Babylonian "city" of Europe, with the "earthquake" as the French Revolution upheaval, was the view set forth whenever mentioned. And premillennialism was predominant up until the nineteenth century, when many departures developed in popular American interpretation. Postmillennialism was largely unknown until the middle of the eighteenth century, and even then was rarely mentioned in writings on prophecy.

While the prophetic aspect of the 1755 Lisbon earthquake was clearly noted in England, it was similarly stressed in America. On the contrary, the 1780 darkening of the sun was noted only here in North America, where this celestial phenomenon was observed.

Other comparative surveys of these various lines may profitably be made by the interested investigator, or similar tabulations developed that will give the over-all picture.

A similar tabulation for Part II appears on pages 742, 743, dealing in similar fashion with sixty-two Old World Nineteenth-Century Advent Awakening writers. These two tabulations therefore summarize and visualize the over-all body of evidence for both Part I and Part II of Volume 3 of *Prophetic Faith of Our Fathers*.

first time had come into the historical picture of fulfillment.

Then began the encroachments on the clear premillennial advent teaching of the seventeenth century. First there was wholesome opposition to the Whitbyan postmillennial postulate. Then a gradual acceptance was spearheaded by Jonathan Edwards, who otherwise held to many orthodox positions but put the coming of Christ over to the *end* of the millennium. This deviation was destined to grow to formidable proportions in the early decades of the nineteenth century. It then came to be the focal point of fundamental clash and cleavage.

Along with the waning interest in prophecy which marked the latter half of the eighteenth century, must be placed the increasing skepticism that began to infiltrate the populace. And to these must be added the disruption caused by the Revolutionary War, with its serious curtailment of printing. The number of treatises on prophecy decreased, and those issued were now largely from clergymen. Most religious writings were of a more general character. It was like the greater stillness and the deeper darkness before the dawn.

Pens were largely silent on the prophetic theme, save for that narrower line of expositors who wrote with increasing clarity of understanding in the latter part of the eighteenth century. Interpreters were more conspicuous because less common. Postmillennialism was slowly on the gain, and gradually muffling the voice of premillennialism. Such was the setting for the nineteenth-century revival of interest in prophecy stimulated by the violent earthquake-upheaval of the French Revolution in obvious fulfillment of prophecy.

With the outbreak of the French Revolution, the "tenth part" of the city was declared by various writers actually to be falling, and the 1260 years in process of ending about that time. The plagues were believed to have begun, and to be already touching the Papacy and the Turk. The era of the last things was thought by many to be at hand. In this there was entire harmony with many European writers.[1]

---

[1] These are fully covered in Volume 2 of *Prophetic Faith*.

Then appears Spalding, "daystar" of the returning pre-millennial hope, stressing Babylon's fall, the celestial signs, the impending seventh trump, the falling away of France, Armageddon prior to the millennium, the 1335 year-days extending to the first resurrection, with New Jerusalem to be on earth. And he is followed by similar though isolated voices on the finale of prophecy, the last events, and the impending destruction of Antichrist. And the climax was reached with the witness of Timothy Dwight of Yale.

III. Summary of Early American Prophetic Interpretation

Through the accompanying tabular summarization, or charting, of the "Leading Views of the Principal American Writers on Prophecy" prior to the nineteenth century, an over-all picture emerges that is most illuminating. (See pages 252, 253.) Affording a scientific basis for analysis, certain impressive conclusions inevitably take shape therefrom in the mind. Well-defined deductions are inescapable that are of vital import in grasping the full picture of distinct advances in prophetic interpretation revealed in these first two centuries of American interpretation.

This earlier section of New World prophetic exposition has been, in the very nature of the case, similar to the Old World British and Continental exposition of the seventeenth and eighteenth centuries. The earliest writers on prophecy in America came from Britain, and of course brought their initial concepts of interpretation with them across the Atlantic. Theirs is the familiar pattern of European exposition of the seventeenth century, covered in Volume II of *Prophetic Faith*.

But as this group continued on in the new overseas colonies, they came to constitute a second, or paralleling, line of independent prophetic exposition witness. While their testimony had many similarities, yet they came to their own independent and sometimes different conclusions. In fact, there was comparative freedom from some misconceptions obtaining in Europe. Certain Old World trends—such as the inroads of rationalism, that cursed much of the theological thinking and prophetic interpretation of Germany in the eighteenth century, and affected England as well—at first made little headway in the American colonies. And the New World was largely free from the Preterist school of prophetic interpretation until the early nineteenth century. However, the return-of-the-Jews concept was woven all through the writings of the colonial interpreters, just as it was characteristic of many Old World expositors. But in the nineteenth century it became a point of cleavage.

The detailed evidence of the witnesses from 1800 to 1831, the date of William Miller's first sermon, is reserved for the final volume in the *Prophetic Faith of Our Fathers* series. There they will form the immediate background for the distinctive nineteenth-century Advent Movement, which is the objective of the final treatise, and the goal of our quest of the centuries. And only the leading expositions of the forty-three expositors listed are here tabulated. The new concept introduced from 1808 onward, concerning the 2300 years, in contrast to the scattered and hazy concepts prior to 1800, will be noted particularly. This is, in fact, one of the most significant features brought into focus by the new century.

While there were many minor writers on prophecy, covered in the preceding chapters of this volume, who are omitted from the chart because of space limitations, their expositions are usually more or less incidental—appearing in connection with other writings, or dealing with single aspects of prophecy. However, had they been included in the tabulation, these witnesses would not modify any general conclusions, but would rather intensify the main features of the over-all picture.

For example, virtually every minor American writer on prophecy recognized the Papacy as the Antichrist, predicted under various prophetic symbols—either the Little Horn, Man of Sin, Mystery of Iniquity, Beast, Babylon, or apocalyptic Harlot. Inclusion of their names would simply swell the list in those particular columns. The same unanimity applies to the year-day principle for the prophetic time periods of Daniel and the Apocalypse, or the Turk as involved in the sixth trumpet, etc. The list of leading writers here presented therefore gives a wholly fair cross section of the evidence.

We now set forth a comprehensive series of vital points, based on the chart, that need to be clearly noted ere we take leave of the stalwarts of early American days, and approach the climax of our investigation in the nineteenth century. These match to an impressive degree the positions held by European expositors during the same period. The major facts and similarities of the New World expositors, in comparison with the Old, are these:

1. The four empires of prophecy of Daniel 2, with the smiting stone as God's future but coming kingdom of glory, was uniformly held whenever expounded. This was even clearer in instances in the New World than in the Old.

2. The same standard series of empires in Daniel 7, with Rome as the fourth, and the Papacy as the Little Horn arising among the divisions of Rome, was one of the most pronounced and uniform characteristics of American, as well as European, exposition prior to the nineteenth century. (The Futurist view of an individual Jewish Antichrist was unknown among the Protestants of North America prior to the nineteenth century.)

3. The year-day principle for the 1260 days, as well as for all other time periods, was likewise the common view. The determining of the location of the 1260 years, chronologically, progressed toward a more accurate placement as the French Revolution period is entered, as with Old World calculators.

4. The hazy, variable, and only occasional discussion of the 2300 year-days—remarkably similar to the European uncertainty—in this same period—continued until the nineteenth century.

5. The same division of opinion as to whether the Turk or the Papacy is the culminating power of Daniel 11 obtains in the New as in the Old World.

17

6. Similar variableness in timing the 1290- and 1335-day periods is likewise observable—saving only that they are always recognized as year-days.

7. The same frequent application of the fifth and sixth trumpets to the Saracens and Turks appears as in Europe, and the "hour, day, month, and year" as a period of 391 (or 396) years has about the same proportionate frequency.

8. Similar recognition of France as the "tenth part of the city," that was to fall away from Rome, is found, as well as the slaying of the Witnesses near the close of the 1260 years. This was particularly true when the French Revolution was actually under way.

9. The virtually uniform application of the Papacy to the ten-horned beast from the sea is to be noted, but with two interpreters applying the second symbol of the two-horned beast from the earth to Protestantism, and several expounding the two horns as involving civil and ecclesiastical aspects. (In contrast, the majority of European writers considered the first beast to be pagan Rome, and the second beast papal Rome, as did Miller later in this country.)

10. The same common application of the plagues was to past judgments, or as in process of falling during the French Revolution, and not future—and with the seat of the Beast as Rome, and the drying up of the Euphrates as commonly applying to the Turk.

11. There was constant and uniform application of the woman of Revelation 17 to the Papacy, as in Europe. It is to be particularly noted that practically every writer on both sides of the Atlantic stresses this symbolism.

12. The premillennial concept of the second advent was commonly held on both sides of the Atlantic, until Whitby's postmillennial theory took root in the New World, with a growing conflict over the issue of a coming world betterment or an approaching world catastrophe.

13. The Lisbon earthquake of 1755 was similarly recognized in the New World as well as the Old as one of the series of

prophesied signs of the approaching end, with others awaited.

14. The Dark Day of 1780 was first awaited, and then observed and recognized by some in America as a sign of the approaching advent. But only in America, apparently, were men awaiting the falling of the stars as the next imminent celestial sign in the sequence.

15. Increasing allusions to the angelic messages of Revelation 14, the approaching end and advent, and even to the great day of atonement, occur as we close the eighteenth century.

SUMMARY OF THE EVIDENCE.—It therefore follows, from the evidence adduced, that for the first two centuries of American history the Papacy, as the prophesied Antichrist, was the universally reiterated concept among Protestants. And the paralleling year-day principle was the common and constant measuring rod for all prophetic time periods. Moreover, the 1260 year-days for the Papacy and the 391 years for the Turk were the common objects of calculation. On the other hand, a distinct epoch of interest in, and understanding of, the 2300 years, their inseparable relationship to the seventy weeks, and the terminus of the longer period to take place about 1844, is a characteristic confined to the nineteenth century and unknown to the first two centuries of colonial and early national interpretation. This pronounced development in emphasis is not without significance.

Such is the New World setting and summary of advancing prophetic interpretation, as we come to the threshold of the nineteenth century with its truly epochal developments.

PART II

NINETEENTH CENTURY
OLD WORLD
ADVENT AWAKENING

HARRY ANDERSON, ARTIST

THE ALBURY PARK PROPHETIC CONFERENCE OF 1826

The First Prophetic Conference in the Old World Advent Awakening Was Held in 1826 at Albury Park, Surrey, England. Here a Score of Prominent Heralds of the Second Advent and Able Students of the Prophecies Met to Compare Notes and Plan Advance Moves. The Painting Shows Drummond Addressing Chairman Hugh M'Neile, Seated at the Head of the Table, in the Large Library of Henry Drummond's Albury Park Villa. Joseph Wolff Is Seated Just Beyond M'Neile, at the Extreme Right Corner of the Table. Edward Irving Is the Second to Wolff's Right, and Daniel Wilson, Later Bishop of India, Is the Second to Irving's Right. An Epitome of This and Subsequent Albury Park Conferences.

CHAPTER FIFTEEN

Nineteenth-Century Revival of Prophetic Study

I. New Advent Awakening Becomes Impelling Force

As we turn back again to the Old World, and enter the portals of the nineteenth century in our quest for its witnesses on prophecy, a swelling chorus of voices becomes discernible. As the years pass, it is increasingly apparent that prophetic interpretation has entered upon a new and unfolding era. Interpreters gather up the neglected and rather generally forsaken positions of the Reformation writers, and draw upon the testimony of the early centuries, as they stride toward the climax of systematic prophetic exposition.

In each past epoch of obviously fulfilling major prophecy a host of witnesses have always appeared in different lands and languages to give their testimony. So in this new epoch we find them again, this time writing in English, Spanish, French, German, and Swedish, in the various countries of both the Old World and the New. A definite conviction develops that mankind has entered a new epoch—the era of the last things, the time of the end. Here, then, we have hope of finding the goal of our quest of the centuries.

The French Revolution was like the explosion of the long-pent-up forces of a volcano. The papal church and state were suddenly torn from their foundation and overwhelmed in the common ruin. The sudden and violent shock sent the Protestant church back to the prophecies. The exploits of Napoleon, with his attack on the Papacy and his temporary suppression of the Roman government, led many to wonder whether he were not the willful king of Daniel 11:36. The Napoleonic struggle, which for years absorbed the energies of Europe, came to a halt. It was the birth time of invention and of sharp advances in science. A secret dissatisfaction was spreading over society. A spirit of inquiry was abroad in the very air.

1. BREAKDOWN SUPERSEDED BY RETURNING CONVICTION.—Following upon the dominant place occupied by prophetic interpretation in the great Protestant Reformation century, had come the gradual breakdown and abandonment of the generally held Historical School positions on prophecy. These convictions had centered in the thesis that the Papacy of history was the Antichrist of prophecy. This growing repudiation was the aftermath of the Roman Catholic Counter-Reformation, with its clever counter-interpretation, adroitly set forth to parry the incriminating force of Protestant exposition.

The gradual acceptance by one group of Protestants of the Preterist Catholic scheme of interpretation—which had crowded all fulfillment back into the early centuries of the Christian Era —was matched by the boring inroads of Protestant rationalism, and its strangely revolutionary attitude toward the integrity and authority of Scripture, and its prophetic portions. So it came to pass that this second breakdown in interest and confidence in prophecy, now among Protestants, spread over Europe.

Meantime, inquiry into prophecy and its further development and understanding was confined to a narrow line of ardent students whose writings have fortunately been left for us, as disclosed in Volume 2. This period of general apathy was like the enveloping darkness that oppresses shortly before the break of day. There was now a deepening conviction that those expositors who, for more than a hundred years, had pointed to France as the scene of momentous events to occur about the end of the eighteenth century, and which would have disastrous effects upon Catholicism, had evidently had substantial prophetic ground for their expectations.

2. PROPHECY PROFFERS KEY TO TIMES.—Prophecy offered a key that might unlock the complex situation of the times. The study of prophecy—which had been the strength of the martyrs, the inspiration of the Reformers, and the support of the true witnesses of the centuries—was again revived.

In the early years of the nineteenth century, prophetic exposition was of a more general and vague character, such as G. S. Faber's *Dissertations* (1806).[1] But about 1812 the re-study of prophecy began to take on more definite shape. Lacunza's book had just been published in Spanish. In 1813 William Cuninghame's *Dissertations on the Seals and Trumpets* was issued, dating the 1260 years from the Code of Justinian to the French Revolution and the Code of Napoleon, which superseded the previous code. In 1815 J. H. Frere sent forth his *Combined View,* which came to have a leading place in one wing of the Historical School of prophecy group. In 1816 Lewis Way's *Letters* and Bayford's *Messiah's Kingdom* appeared —Bayford later, however, becoming a prominent member of the Catholic Apostolic Church.[2]

It is not without significance that in England, the very land which in the eighteenth century gave birth to the ruinous Whitbyan postmillennial theory, the counteracting antidote of premillennialism was revived in strength in the early nineteenth century. Postmillennialism had swept like a desolating flood over the Protestant churches, causing men to postpone the day of the Lord. To this had recently been added the pestilence of infidelity which reached its climax in the French Revolution. Now a vigorous counteraction had begun to set in.

With the renewed interest in prophecy, a far-reaching religious awakening rapidly took form and force in Great Britain, both within and outside of the Established Church. It spread to the European Continent and touched Asia Minor, Northern Africa, and Asia. Baptist, Wesleyan, and Anglican missionary societies sprang up. The British and Foreign Bible Society was

---

[1] These will all be noted in succeeding chapters.
[2] Edward Miller, *History and Doctrines of Irvingism,* vol. 1, pp. 10, 11.

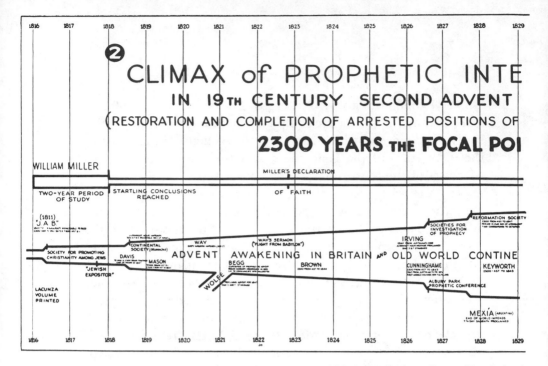

Only the First Half of Chart No. 2 Is Here Shown, Which in Its Entirety Covers Not Only the Nineteenth-Century Old World Advent Awakening but the New World Advent Movement as Well, With the 2300 Years as the New Focal Point of Study in Each. This Portion Indicates the Chronological Relationship of the British and European Awakening on Prophecy (Lower), to the Paralleling Beginning of Miller's Public Labors in America (Upper). In the European Section the Leading Organizations, Conferences, and Periodicals Between 1816 and 1844, Which Are

organized in 1804, with parallel movements on the Continent and in North America—those of the Old World slightly preceding the stirrings of the New. In it all the rebirth of the advent hope, coupled with an intensive restudy of the prophecies, supplied the new incentive to the recently launched missionary endeavor. A new epoch was under way.

3. HERALDED BY VOICE, PEN, AND CONFERENCE.—By voice and pen and study group the tidings of the near advent spread in ever-widening circles. More than a hundred important books on the premillennial advent and the prophecies appeared in the first four decades of the new century. Powerful preachers proclaimed the good news from prominent pulpits. Many local sermons, which have been preserved in printed form, warn that "the day of the Lord is near—the Judge eternal is coming! Prepare to meet thy God." [3]

---

[3] John Eggleston, *An Epistle to His Church*, p. 77.

266

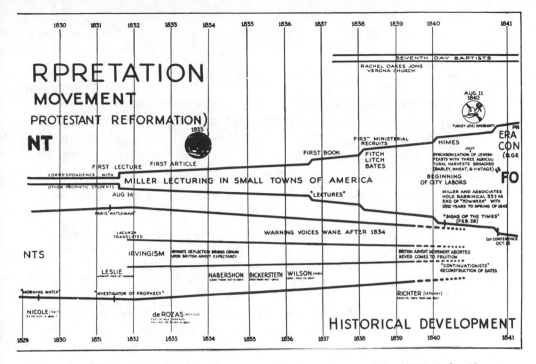

Only Indicated Here, Appear in Detail on a Later Chart. The Remaining Half of the Chart
Depicts the Full Development of the American Advent Movement. That, However, Is Reserved
for and Covered by the Next and Concluding Volume in the *Prophetic Faith of Our Fathers*
Series. The Slight Repetition of Those Portions of the Chart Nearest the Separating Space
Between the Pages Is to Facilitate the Reading of Each Page. The Purpose Is to Afford An
Over-All Picture. The Great Reduction Renders the Smallest Lettering Illegible.

One significant characteristic of this advent literature was
the custom of placing a quoted Scripture text on the title page
of the book, pamphlet, or tract. These were often as significant
as the treatises themselves. Among the oft-repeated favorites
were, "Fear God, and give glory to Him; for the hour of His
judgment is come," "Behold, He cometh with clouds," "Behold,
the Lord cometh with ten thousands of His saints"—and many
other related sentiments.

Old World men like Brown, Cuninghame, Frere, Mason,
Way, Begg, Pym, Noel, Bayford, Habershon, Nolan, Vaughan,
Hooper, Brooks, Tudor, Wolff, Keyworth, White, Addis, Irving,
Park, Croly, Bickersteth, Birks, Elliott, and a host of others
with whom we will shortly become acquainted, told it forth
in published form. Its amazing extent is visualized and can be
grasped from the chart of Old World Interpreters of Prophecy
in the nineteenth century on pages 270 and 271. Several

organizations and at least ten periodicals were launched in its support. Prophetic study groups and conferences were held in England, Scotland, Ireland, and France. The great advent awakening drew forth this comment from the contemporary essayist and historian, Thomas B. Macaulay (1800-1859)[4]:

"Many Christians believe that the Messiah will shortly establish a kingdom on the earth, and reign visibly over all its inhabitants. Whether this doctrine be orthodox or not we shall not here inquire. The number of people who hold it is very much greater than the number of Jews residing in England. Many of those who hold it are distinguished by rank, wealth, and ability. It is preached from pulpits, both of the Scottish and of the English church. Noblemen and members of parliament have written in defence of it." [5]

4. VOICES IN THE BOSOM OF CATHOLICISM.—Even more remarkable than the Protestant revival of emphasis upon the approaching advent was the rising of premillennial voices in the very bosom of the Catholic Church itself. Père Lambert, learned Dominican scholar in southern France at the turn of the century, renounced the papal theory of the millennium while yet in the church, and published an eloquent defense of the coming reign of Christ. And Manuel Lacunza, noted Spanish Jesuit of Chile and Italy, better known under the assumed name of Juan Josafat Ben-Ezra, abandoning the teachings of Bellarmine and Bossuet, gave to the world the celebrated *Venida del Mesias en Gloria y Magestad* (Coming of the Messiah in Glory and Majesty). This so fired the soul of Edward Irving that he translated it into English for the benefit of the rising advent cause in Britain.

Lacunza had concluded that the "false prophet" was the corrupted Catholic priesthood, and the apocalyptic Harlot the apostate Rome, while Lambert likewise believed that apocalyptic Babylon symbolized papal Rome and its priesthood. Thus in Catholic countries like France, Spain, Italy, Mexico, and throughout South America, fulfilling prophecy moved force-

---

[4] Educated for the bar, Macaulay turned to writing. Then he entered Parliament, becoming secretary of the Board of Control, and later legal adviser to the Supreme Council of India. Again returning to Parliament, he became Secretary for War, meantime writing his *History of England*. After a period as Paymaster General, he finally served again in Parliament.
[5] Thomas B. Macaulay, *Critical and Miscellaneous Essays* (1844), vol. 5, p. 324.

fully through Catholicism to call attention to the predictions of Daniel and John, after having been silenced so long by force.

5. OLD WORLD AWAKENING ANTEDATES AMERICAN MOVE-MENT.—The advent awakening in the Old World slightly ante-dated the rise of the distinctive advent movement in America, which did not really begin to gather momentum until about 1838. But the Old World awakening never became an integrated movement. It was strongly individualistic. There was little unification of position by the leaders. While there were warnings and entreaties, there was no general break or withdrawal from the churches. It was primarily an awakening. The development went so far and then stopped, and began to wane. It was like the glorious dawn that precedes the full glow of the morning sun, but it faded out before the high noon of the distinctive movement of these latter days filled the heavens of the New World.

II. 2300 Years Becomes Focal Point of Discussion

The approaching end of the 2300 years became the new focal point of much of the revived prophetic interest. It was so general that it runs like a golden thread through a large part of this extensive literature. It centered, the writers believed, around the prophesied cleansing of the sanctuary from the pollutions of popery and Mohammedanism, at the close of the 2300 years, which they held would terminate about 1843, 1844, or 1847.

No sooner, however, had the spotlight of study been shifted to the new positions of interest and concern—the 2300 years of Daniel 8:14 in newly discovered relationship to the seventy weeks of years of Daniel 9—than complications set in to vex and divide the growing group of expositors. One point of difference was the old argument that 2400 is really the correct rendering, rather than 2300. And further, some argued that the 2400 years should be dated from the time of the vision, a century earlier, rather than from the beginning of the seventy

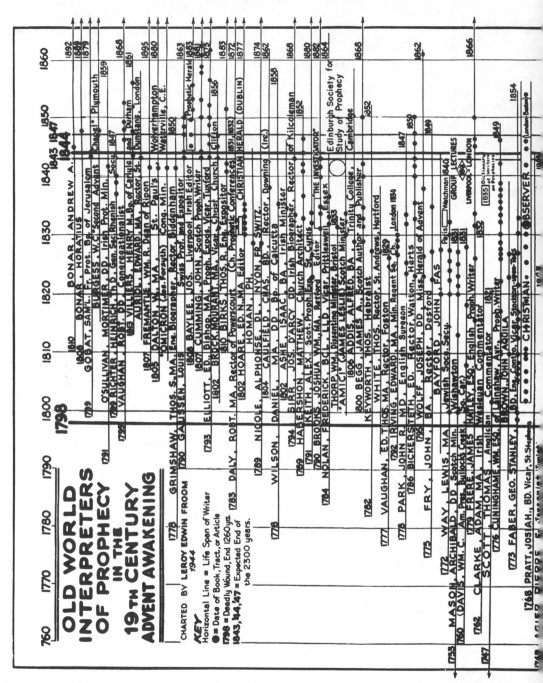

This Galaxy of Interpreters of Prophecy From 1798 Onward, in the Great Nineteenth-Century
Old World Advent Awakening, Is Here Presented in Chronological and Massed Sequence. The
Life Span and Intellectual Training and the Religious Affiliation or Vocation of the Individual

270

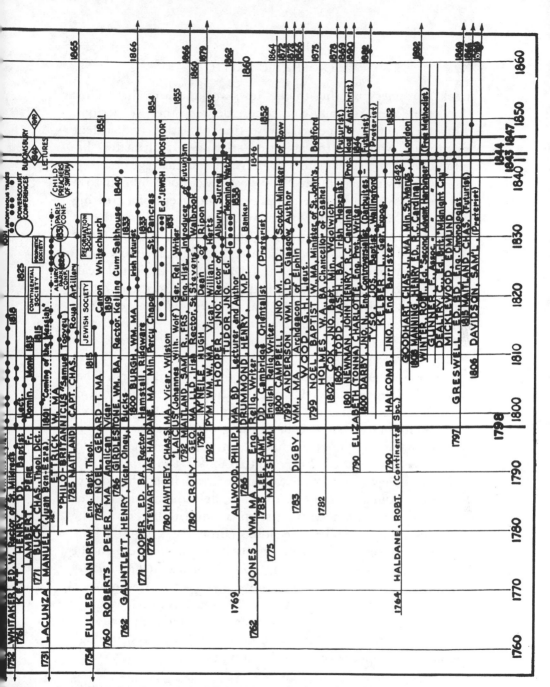

xpositors Are Indicated, as Well as the Dates of Their Many Writings. The Leading Prophetic
ocieties, Conferences, Periodicals, and Organizations for the Study and Propagation of the Proph-
cies All Appear in Their Appropriate Sequence and Relationship. Such Is the Over-All Picture

weeks' prophecy relating to the Jews and the Messiah. Thus
they severed entirely any connection between the two periods.
This theory was supported by a line of active and ardent
champions, who kept the agitation stirring. It ultimately became one of the chief points of division and cleavage.

This discussion of the 2300 years was not confined to a
few enthusiasts but became the prevailing concern of a growing
number of leading minds in religious thought. A third of a
century after Petri's revolutionary computation,[6] men in Great
Britain and America came separately to similar conclusions.[7]
That the prophetic time period of Daniel 8:14 indicated year-
days was accepted as an established principle. So the question
calling for a satisfactory answer was: *When did the 2300 years
begin, and consequently when would they end? And just what
was meant by this cleansing, or justification, of the sanctuary
that was to occur?*

1. HALES ASSERTS GENUINENESS OF 2300.—But first, what
of the rival reading of 2400 in the Theodotian translation of
Daniel in the Septuagint? Some, like Edward W. Whitaker,
in 1795, had favored the 2400 reading of the Vatican copy of
the Septuagint.[8] James Bicheno,[9] on the other hand, held
to the 2300, and dated the period from 481 B.C. to A.D. 1819,
when he believed Palestine would be freed from the foes of
the Jews. And with their restoration, he thought, the church
would be freed from Antichristian abominations.

Soon William Hales, the noted chronologer, signing himself the "Inspector," interested himself in the problem in the
prominent theological journal, *The Orthodox Churchman's
Magazine,* writing under the heading "Sacred Criticism." [10]
In this series Hales declared that the angel Gabriel was sent
to enable the prophet to "understand the oracle, and discern
the vision" (the grand prophetic period of 2300 days) through
the famous prophecy of the seventy weeks.

---

[6] See Volume 2 of *Prophetic Faith.*   [7] See tabulation on pp. 741, 742.
[8] Edward W. Whitaker, *General and Connected View of the Prophecies Relating to the
Times of the Gentiles,* pp. 272-277.   [9] James Bicheno, *The Signs of the Times,* p. 54.
[10] *The Orthodox Churchman's Magazine,* vols. 4-6, 1803, 1804. (Identified by internal
evidence.)

In one article Hales explicitly declared that "there is no other number in the Bible, whose genuineness is better ascertained than that of the 2300 days." [11] As to the interpretation, he added that he has adopted the position which Hans Wood, of Rossmead, Ireland, had brought forward but a few years before, that the "period of the 2300 days, begins along with that of the 70 weeks." [12] The remaining portion of 1810 days, he held, is distinguished by the three remarkable periods of 1260, 1290, and 1335 year-days, not running in succession as the divisions of the seventy weeks, "but partly synchronizing or coalescing with each other." [13] This same position Hales later confirmed in 1809, in his *New Analysis of Chronology*, declaring: "This chronological prophecy [of the 70 weeks] . . . was evidently designed to explain the foregoing vision, especially in its *chronological* part of the 2300 days." [14]

2. FABER AND FRERE CONTEND FOR 2400.—But what Hales had seemingly settled in 1804, G. Stanley Faber again questioned in 1806—whether "the 2300, the 2200, or the 2400 days, whichever of these three be the proper reading." [15] He also stated in a footnote that the sanctuary to be cleansed is the "spiritual sanctuary of the Christian Church," with the cleansing to consist of the overthrow of the papal Little Horn of Daniel 7 and the Mohammedan horn of Daniel 8.

Then, James Hatley Frere, in his *Combined View of the Prophecies*, in 1815, likewise accepted the reading of 2400 rather than 2300, beginning the longer period with the alleged time of the vision, in 553 B.C., and ending it in A.D. 1847. [16] Thus, curiously enough, the terminal year of Frere's *2400 years,* and of those who followed his exposition, nearly coincided with the larger group that held to 1843, 1844, or 1847 as the end of the *2300 years,* with the seventy weeks as the first portion. But the differences outweighed the similarities.

---

[11] *Ibid.*, February, 1804 (vol. 6), p. 75.
[12] *Ibid.*, p. 82.　　　　　　　　　　　　　　　　[13] *Ibid.*, p. 83.
[14] William Hales, *A New Analysis of Chronology*, vol. 2, p. 563 (on Daniel 9:27).
[15] G. Stanley Faber, *A Dissertation on the Prophecies*, vol. 1, pp. 224, 225.
[16] James Hatley Frere, *A Combined View of the Prophecies of Daniel, Esdras, and St. John*, pp. 246, 247. (Title page reproduced on p. 278.)

18

3. Cuninghame Holds 2400 Is Error.—William Cuning-hame, of Lainshaw, in *The Christian Observer* (1811) and in the several editions of his *Dissertation on the Seals and Trumpets,* clarified the whole question by showing that the 2400 years of the Vatican edition of the Septuagint was a "typographical error," as he avers:

"There is no support given to this various reading either by the genuine principles of Scriptural criticism, or by any other edition of the Seventy; for they all, with the exception of the Vatican edition, agree with the Hebrew Text." [17]

Cuninghame, the most prolific prophetic interpreter of the time, who made "truth his principal concern," wrote twenty-one treatises between 1802 and 1849. From 1807 onward he engaged Faber in controversy on this and other points, in the columns of *The Christian Observer.* He contended that the French Revolution had ushered in a new era, and declared himself in accord with those who held that the 1260-year period was to be dated from Justinian's decree. Cuninghame made an impressive interpretation of Daniel 7 in which he stressed the historical fulfillment of the papal casting of the truth to the ground, and practicing and prospering against it. [18]

4. "J.A.B." and Mason Establish 1843.—Although a clear statement on the joint beginning of the 2300 years and seventy weeks of years in 457 B.C., and the ending of the 2300 years in 1843, had appeared in 1810 in *The Christian Observer* [19] over the initials "J.A.B.," [20] it was the Scotch minister Archibald Mason who, in 1820, was chiefly responsible for refuting the arguments of William C. Davis, who dated the 2300 years from 453 B.C. to A.D. 1847. Mason contended for the terminal dates 457 B.C. and A.D. 1843, in his *Two Essays on Daniel's Prophetic Number of the Twenty-three hundred Days* (1820).

Able and influential writers in Great Britain joined in the discussion and quest for truth which centered, to no small

---

[17] William Cuninghame, *A Dissertation on the Seals and Trumpets of the Apocalypse* (2d ed.), p. 260 n. (Title page reproduced on p. 278.)
[18] Article in reply to Faber on the 1260 days, *The Christian Observer,* June, 1808 (vol. 7, no. 78), pp. 345-348.
[19] *Ibid.,* November, 1810 (vol. 9, no. 107), pp. 669, 670. (See illustration on p. 290.)
[20] All these witnesses will be noted later in detail.

degree, around this impressive number 2300. The organizations for the study and propagation of prophecy, which came into being, all touched upon it. Lewis Way reorganized the London Society to Promote Christianity Among the Jews, with *The Jewish Expositor* as its medium of communication and publicity. Discussions of the 2300 years are found in its pages. Henry Drummond, rich London banker and member of Parliament, became one of the most ardent promoters of prophetic research, founding the Continental Society in 1819 to lift the spiritual standard and foster prophetic study on the Continent. Emphasis on the 2300 years appears in its reports. In addition, Drummond was the finder and sponsor of Joseph Wolff, who became the intrepid herald of the advent and the prophecies throughout Asia. And Wolff based no small part of his appeal on this key prophecy.

5. DIFFERENCES DEEPEN OVER CONFLICTING POSITIONS.—
Frere's greatest acquisition was the winning of Edward Irving, the celebrated preacher in London. Gripped by the new-found prophetic truth, he became a powerful advocate, and likewise touched upon Daniel 8:14. But he followed Frere in the 2400 reading, dating it from the time of the vision to 1847. He applied Daniel 8 to the Mohammedan perversion, as a parallel to the Papacy on the West. And with it he taught the commonly held view of the restoration of the true worship in Jerusalem, when the Jews should be restored and converted. And like certain others, he believed that the 1335 years would end later, in 1867, when the resurrection of the righteous would take place.[21] This, too, was to make for confusion.

While Irving, Frere, and others held to the terminus of the 2400 years in 1847, Cuninghame, as early as 1826, in his *Scheme of Prophetic Arrangement,* came to endorse Archibald Mason's computation of the 2300 years as from 457 to 1843, definitely citing him as authority.[22] This endorsement raised

---

[21] Edward Irving, *Babylon and Infidelity Foredoomed of God*, vol. 2, pp. 209, 219.
[22] William Cuninghame, *The Scheme of Prophetic Arrangement of the Rev. Edward Irving and Mr. Frere*, pp. 80, 81.

the question of priority. In 1827 John A. Brown, in the Preface to *The Jew The Master-Key of the Apocalypse,* asked pointedly:

"Where, however does he [Cuninghame] find the opinion of such authors expressed, save in 'The Even-Tide,' and in a fugitive paper penned fourteen years since, by the same author [Brown himself], in which that circumstance was particularly stated." [23]

So it was evidently John A. Brown who signed himself merely "J.A.B." in *The Christian Observer* in 1810.[24] At this early date Brown recognized the integral connection between the 2300 years of Daniel 8 and the seventy weeks of Daniel 9, and synchronized the commencement of the 2300 years with that of the 490 years. In his *Even-Tide* (1823) he takes the clear position that the 2300 years, beginning in 457 B.C., would end in 1844, when he expected the cleansing to be fulfilled by the overthrow of the Mohammedan abomination and the restoration of the Jewish polity.[25]

6. ALBURY CONFERENCE SIDE-STEPS ISSUE.—Then in 1826, Henry Drummond, encouraged by Lewis Way, invited a number of ministers and laymen interested in prophetic study to meet in a conference at his villa in Albury Park, Surrey, to see "how far they coincided in understanding the mind of the Spirit on these momentous subjects." Mason was invited, but declined the long journey because of his advanced age. Nevertheless, he wrote out his thoughts on the various items. About twenty, however, accepted the invitation to be present. Among these were Lord Mandeville, Dodsworth, Marsh, Frere, Simons of Paul's Cray, Haldane Stewart, William Cuninghame, Edward Irving, Joseph Wolff, and C. S. Hawtrey, under the moderatorship of Hugh M'Neile. They spent six days in intensive study of the near advent, the prophecies of Daniel and the Apocalypse, the times of the Gentiles, the future condition of the Jews, and the duties of the church arising from these questions. This is impressively pictured in the frontispiece for

---

[23] John A. Brown, *The Jew The Master-Key of the Apocalypse,* p. vi.
[24] *The Christian Observer,* November, 1810 (vol. 9, no. 107), pp. 668-670.
[25] John A. Brown, *The Even-Tide,* p. xlii.

Part II of this volume.   Their conversations were epitomized in *Dialogues on Prophecy*.

All seemed agreed that the 1260 and 1290 days of Daniel were accomplished, and that the remaining years of the 1335 had begun.   At the conclusion of these, "the blessedness will be fully arrived."   During this time they were to look for the second advent of Christ in person to raise the dead bodies of the saints, and with them to reign on the earth.   Therefore great vigilance and fearless warring and righteousness was incumbent upon them.[26]   Certain questions were left open—whether 2300 and A.D. 1843, or 2400 and A.D. 1847 was the right number.

III. Conflicting Positions Over Closing Events

Throughout those decades there was much conflict of view and much debate over the opposing positions.   One group held that the terminus of the 2300 years, about 1843, 1844, or 1847, would mark the close of prophetic time, and that tremendous events would follow thereafter.   The other and larger group just as firmly held that 1843, 1844, or 1847 marked the terminus of the 2300 years.   But they taught that the 1290- and 1335-year periods, beginning synchronously with the 1260 years, would extend, respectively, thirty and seventy-five years beyond their close.

To such, the end of the 2300 years was simply a milestone, with the climactic and final events to follow more than two decades later.   Thus their eyes became increasingly fixed upon those future events, with relatively little heed to the nearer prophetic waymark of the close of the 2300 years.   It was there- fore left to the expositors of the Western World to clarify and unify these intriguing time periods.

1. VARYING VIEWPOINTS ON SEALS, TRUMPETS, AND WIT- NESSES.—In our attempt to obtain an over-all outline picture, let us note other differences that had a marked bearing on the fortunes of prophetic interpretation in this period.   Faber,

---

[26] Edward Irving, Preliminary Discourse by the Translator, in *The Coming of Messiah* (his translation of Manuel Lacunza's *La Venida del Mesias*, 1827 ed.), vol. 1, pp. clxxxviii ff.

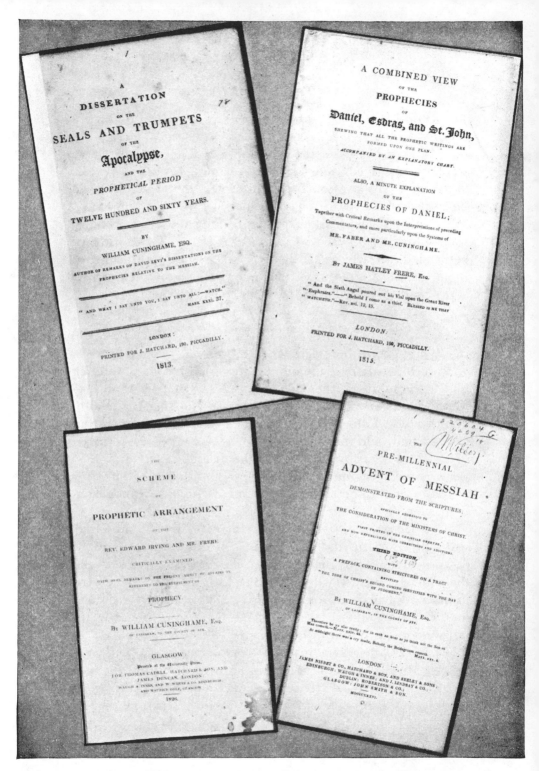

TWO DIVERGENT SCHOOLS OF INTERPRETATION DEVELOP

William Cuninghame, With His *Dissertation of the . . . Apocalypse* (1813), and J. H. Frere, With His *Combined View* (1815), Are Followed by Scores of Proponents of These Differing Schools of Thought, Largely Clustering Around Controversial Aspects of the 2300-Year Exposition

Cuninghame, and Frere were unquestionably the three most prominent expositors in Britain in the early part of the nineteenth century. These all began their writings on prophecy after the fury of the French Revolution had passed, and all three believed that the early vials of the seven last plagues had been poured out in the Revolution.

Faber saw the seven trumpets as an outgrowth of the seventh seal, just as he believed the seven vials were an outgrowth of the seventh trumpet.[27]   Thus, for him, the first six seals reached only to Constantine and the overthrow of heathenism in the fourth century.   Then the first six trumpets were fulfilled in the successive desolations of the Goths, Saracens, and Turks—and on to the French Revolution.   And the climactic power of the seventh head of the beast, as the willful king of Daniel 11, he considered to be infidelic or atheistic.   The "little book" he thought to be a supplemental prophecy forming chapters 10-14 of Revelation.

On the other hand, to Cuninghame the seals and trumpets were chronologically parallel, that is, beginning together, and each reaching from John's day to the great earthquake, ending together in the seventh seal and seventh trumpet, immediately before the great consummation—the seals prefiguring the history of the church, with the trumpets as the history of the secular Roman Empire in both West and East, much as Faber held them.

Frere, in disagreement with both, held that the seals depict the history of the Western secular Roman Empire, from John's day to the earthquake of the consummation, and the trumpets, in parallel chronology, that of the Eastern Empire, while the little book of Revelation 10 portrays the history of the church in chapters 10-14, likewise chronologically paralleling the former.   To Frere, the seventh head of the beast was Napoleon, while the Two Witnesses were clearly the Old and the New Testament, their death and resurrection being fulfilled in the French Revolution, from 1793 to 1797.

---

[27] This harks back to the position of Joseph Mede. See *Prophetic Faith*, Volume 2.

Sharp differences between these three leading expositors extended to other points.[28] Little wonder that students of prophecy should be perplexed by such discord. As a result, some came to distrust not only these expositors but the general positions and principles of the Historical School of Prophetic Interpretation.

2. BASIC CLASH OVER MILLENNIAL VIEWS.—In and through the play and counterplay of lesser differences among the heralds of the second advent near, there ran a deeper current of conflict with nominal Protestantism at large. It was the issue of evangelical premillennialism versus Whitbyan postmillennialism.[29] Against this more recent view of the postponement of the advent they presented an essentially united front.[30] Here was a clash of antagonistic expositional philosophies that was fundamental, for the two concepts were mutually exclusive. In fact, most of the opposition encountered by the preachers of the imminent advent was from advocates of this popular thousand-years-of-world-betterment theory now in ascendancy in the churches of the Old World as well as in those of the New.

A real battle developed in England over this millennial question, and over the general Protestant historical principles of interpretation.[31] When Irving translated the treatise of Lacunza into English and began fervently to preach Christ's premillennial advent, he found himself "painfully insulated" from most of his brethren in the ministry. But soon a great revival of premillennialism swept over Britain, which will be unfolded later in these pages.

3. RETURN OF THE JEWS PROMINENT.—Meantime, the reorganization of the Society to Promote Christianity Among the Jews brought the concept of the restoration and conversion of the Jews sharply to the forefront, and for a time its warmest

---

[28] Faber held the Two Witnesses to be the Waldenses and Albigenses, with their banishment from the valleys and their glorious return. Cuninghame believed them to be the Protestants against papal superstition, while Frere thought they were the two Testaments.
[29] Carefully covered in *Prophetic Faith*, Volume 2.
[30] While Faber held the Whitbyan view, Cuninghame and Frere, and virtually all other advent heralds, were stanch premillennialists.
[31] E. B. Elliott, *Horæ Apocalypticæ* (5th ed.), vol. 4, pp. 551, 552.

advocates were the premillennialists of Britain and the Continent—including such men as Way, Marsh, M'Neile, Pym, and Noel. In fact, this was one of the most prominent characteristics of the entire group of British expositors.

IV. Battle Over Fundamental Principles Ensues

Premillennial prophetic journals, such as *The Morning Watch* and *The Investigator,* appeared, and individual treatises by the score began to pour from the presses, reaching their peak in the early forties—with more than 150 separate works in the first half of the nineteenth century. Meantime Samuel R. Maitland, in his treatise of 1826, challenged the generally received year-day principle, as applied to the 1260 days of Daniel and the Apocalypse. In this he assailed the whole Protestant application of the symbols of the little horn and the beast of the Revelation—avowing that it was yet to be fulfilled in a personal and openly infidel Antichrist, with the days of his career as literal days.

In this view James Todd and William Burgh, of Ireland, joined. Thus the really epochal Catholic treatises of the Jesuit Lacunza and the Dominican Lambert were now countered by the professedly Protestant Maitland and Burgh, who were excusing the Papacy from the application while these two sons of the Roman church were applying it to their own papal Rome. Truly, it was an anomalous situation.

And still another factor began to operate to give fresh weight to anti-Protestant opinion—the Oxford Tracts, which began to be issued in 1833. The chief object of these writers was to de-Protestantize the Church of England.[32] Naturally enough, they took over the Futurist view of Antichrist, setting aside all application of the prophecies to the Roman Papacy. This left Protestantism hopelessly split, and the Papacy made good use of the efforts of the Oxford Tractators, as will likewise be noted later.

---

[32] *Ibid.*, p. 555; vol. 3, part 5, chap. 9.

Meanwhile the influx of German neology[33] into England was not without effect, with its Preterist apocalyptic scheme that had received great impetus under Eichhorn, Ewald, Heinrichs, and others.   Professor Lee of Cambridge adopted this Preterist view, and in America Professor Moses Stuart did likewise.   This, too, will be discussed later.

---

[33] Neology, it should be explained, is simply another name for rationalism.   It is an older and now obsolete term.   As then used, it meant the injection of new terms, and particularly the thrusting of new meanings into old words and phrasings—hence new views, that is, of a rationalistic character.

CHAPTER SIXTEEN

Panoramic Preview
of Developing Interpretations

I. "Christian Observer" Forum for Growing Prophetic Discussion

Perhaps no other printed medium of the time so uniquely revealed the growing interest in the prophecies and the progressive advances in exposition as did the staid London monthly *The Christian Observer*. Founded in 1802, edited by Josiah Pratt, vicar of St. Stephen's, and others, and issued by the members of the Established Church, it dealt frequently with prophecy from its very first volume. It was often the medium for the introduction of advanced positions in interpretation, as well as a forum for the free and frank discussion of differing viewpoints.

No more suitable vehicle is afforded through which to begin our tracing of the developments of prophetic interpretation from the turn of the century to the period of the prolific production of prophetic literature in the third and fourth decades. It pioneered the way until the various organizations came into being, prophetic conferences were called, and special periodicals were launched for the specific study of prophecy. It was a mirror of the times and afforded an effective medium for voicing the growing convictions of many.

It was, moreover, doubly unique in that an American edition, running article for article, was published at Boston, starting with the very first issue. For church periodicals, "Americans had to turn to the mother country, and Anglican churchmen naturally turned to the press of the Church of England." [1] As to its extent of circulation and influence in America, Morehouse adds:

"The *Christian Observer* was probably the most widely read of the English Church periodicals in America. Indeed in 1802 it began to be regularly reprinted in Boston, and thereafter for many years it had a considerable circulation in New England, New York, and other parts of this country. No attempts were made to adapt this publication to American conditions, and it paid little attention to American affairs, except when they were of a bizzare nature." [2]

Thus it was that the matters of concern to British students of prophecy were brought promptly and uniformly before many American readers. Let us now follow the unfolding discussion that appeared in its pages.

1. "JUVENIS" AVERS TURKISH 391 YEARS COMMONLY ACCEPTED.—In the initial volume for 1802, "Juvenis" [3] writes on "the prophecies relating to the Turk." He declares Revelation 9 to be "one of the clearest prophecies in Scripture, and most generally understood"; and without "any material discordance among the Protestant interpreters" from Brightman to Bishop Newton. [4] Juvenis speaks boldly of the "three hundred and ninety-one days, or prophetical years, during which they [the Turks] continue the slaughter of the third part of men." [5]

Nor does he find "any material disagreement" in their allocation of "the epoch of the victorious period of the Turks." Then he adds, "They all conclude this period, within the thirty last years of the seventeenth century; i.e. they fix the termination of the second woe (Rev. xi.14) in the termination of the seventeenth century." [6] On this basis he believes that the seventh trumpet has already sounded, and the "vials contained in it begun to be poured out." [7]

Juvenis also observes that "the fall of the tenth part of the city must have taken place about the end of the said woe,

---

[1] Clifford P. Morehouse, "Origins of the Episcopal Church Press from Colonial Days to 1840," in *Historical Magazine of the Protestant Episcopal Church*, September, 1942 (vol. 11, no. 3), p. 206.
[2] *Ibid.*, pp. 206, 207.   [3] Unidentified.
[4] *The Christian Observer*, December, 1802 (vol. 1, no. 12), p. 763.
[5] *Ibid.*   [6] *Ibid.*   [7] *Ibid.*, pp. 763, 764.

and the resurrection of the witnesses have been accomplished." [8]
He concludes by citing Eton[9] to the effect that the siege of
Vienna, in 1683, was the "last successful campaign of the Turks,"
and by quoting Sir Paul Rycaut to the effect that by 1698 the
Turks had "ceased to be a woe to Christendom." [10] Juvenis
adds that the success of the Christians over the Turks in 1697
led them to "fix a period" to the extension of the empire,
believing God did not intend them to extend it farther.

2. "E" AWAITS TURKEY'S END; NAPOLEON'S AMBITION
DOOMED.—Then in the January, 1804, *Observer,* "E" comments
on Daniel 11 and 12, applying Daniel 11:42 to the Turk's
stretching out his hand upon many countries in Asia, Europe,
and Africa. Verses 44 and 45 are placed as yet future, as
tidings out of the north ("possibly. . . Russia") leads Turkey
to plant his palace on the glorious holy mountain ("perhaps"
Mt. Sion, or Olivet), between the seas (the Dead and the
Mediterranean), where he shall come to his helpless end. "E"
concludes, "Herein seems to be predicted the future fall of
the Ottoman Empire." [11] Adverting to Bonaparte's triumphant
conquests, "E" declares that, in addition to Daniel 11, according to Daniel 2 and 7 "there were to be no more than
FOUR universal monarchies," and Bonaparte's efforts will prove
futile in attempting to establish a fifth.[12] He closes by referring to the current interest in the seven vials.

3. "TALIB" HOLDS 1260 YEARS ALREADY EXPIRED.—There
is further consideration by "C.L." in the January, 1805, issue,
of Mohammedanism in Revelation 9 and the Western apostasy
in chapters 10 to 18. But by 1807 an era of fuller discussion
and understanding of prophecy and its current fulfillments
dawns. In the November number, under the pen name of
"Talib," a layman—William Cuninghame, of Lainshaw, in
Ayrshire—challenges George Stanley Faber's interpretation

---

[8] *Ibid.,* p. 764.
[9] W. E. Eton, *A Survey of the Turkish Empire,* 3d ed., p. 188 ff.
[10] Sir Paul Rycaut, *The History of the Turks. Beginning With the Year 1679,* vol. 3, pp. 328, 557.
[11] *The Christian Observer,* January, 1804 (vol. 3, no. 25), pp. 11, 12.
[12] *Ibid.,* p. 12.

and timing of the 1260- and 2300-year periods, insisting that the 1260 years represent the spiritual tyranny of the Little Horn, followed by the judgment and taking away of its dominion, and this in turn by the "blessed state." [13] Contending that the saints in the body of the Roman Empire remained under the dominion of the Little Horn until the French Revolution, he concludes that "the 1260 years are, in fact, expired." [14]

4. DATES 1260 FROM JUSTINIAN; 2300 FROM VISION.—Although Cuninghame agrees with Faber that the 1260 years come within the 2300 years, he differs on the dating for each of the periods. The imperial letter of Justinian in 533 is taken to mark the beginning of the 1260 years,[15] which he ends in 1792. Cuninghame likewise rejects Faber's choice of 2200 instead of 2300 for Daniel 8:14,[16] but like Faber, he at this time still dates the period from the "vision of the ram and he-goat." [17] He dissents further from Faber by applying it to Romanism instead of to Mohammedanism.[18]

In the December issue Cuninghame continues with "auxiliary arguments" on the 1260 years, based on Christ's prophecy of Luke 21 (or Matthew 24). He holds that the "times of the gentiles" are the 1260- and 2300-year periods spoken of by Daniel. He lists the "unexampled" events of the past sixteen years in France, Austria, Germany, Italy, Switzerland, Spain, and Portugal as constituting signs of the latter times.[19] Coupled with this, Cuninghame holds that the entry upon the missionary epoch indicates that "the 1260 years are elapsed." [20] He adds that "none will deny that we live at a most momentous crisis." [21]

5. WHY HORN OF DANIEL 8 IS ROMAN, NOT MOHAMMEDAN.—Marshaling further reasons for applying the Little Horn of Daniel 8 to Romanism, and not to Mohammedanism, Cuninghame again speaks through the *Observer,* in 1808. His

[13] *Ibid.*, November, 1807 (vol. 6, no. 71), p. 701.
[14] *Ibid.*, p. 702.   [15] *Ibid.*, p. 703.   [16] *Ibid.*, p. 702.
[17] *Ibid.*, pp. 704, 705.   [18] *Ibid.*, p. 705.
[19] *Ibid.*, December, 1807 (vol. 6, no. 72), pp. 774, 775.
[20] *Ibid.*, pp. 776, 777.   [21] *Ibid.*, p. 777.

careful and logical reasoning concerning the 2300 years of Daniel 8 introduces a new era in the study of this particular prophecy.   He enunciates certain first principles.   Note them.

Cuninghame's first point is that this Little Horn "comes out of one of the four pre-existing horns" of the Macedonian kingdom, whereas Faber had applied it to Mohammedanism, "which arose more than six centuries after the fall of the last of the Macedonian kingdoms." [22]

Cuninghame then asks this searching question:

"How then can it be said that the Mohammedan empire, which was not *in existence* till the year of our Lord 622 (the date of the Hegirah), arose *at the end* of the Macedonian kingdoms, the last of which (Egypt) was annihilated by Caesar, in the year before Christ 30?" [23]

Cuninghame's second point is that "the history of Mohammedanism does not in any respect answer to the actions of the little horn," which was to take *"away the daily sacrifice, and cast down the place of his sanctuary."* [24]   If this is applied literally, he says, it "could only be accomplished while there was a literal sanctuary; i.e. before the destruction of Jerusalem and its temple."   But the "temple and city had been destroyed more than five centuries before the date of the Hegirah." However, in the *"symbolical* sense, the *church of Christ* is the *temple*, or *sanctuary*; and *the worship of this church, the daily sacrifice."*   This, he said, is the sense used in 2 Thessalonians 2. Cuninghame then makes two important statements:

"Of this temple, the daily sacrifice is taken away when this form of sound words no longer remains, and when the worship of God, through Christ alone, is corrupted and obscured, by superstitious veneration for the Virgin Mary and the saints, or by any species of creature worship. It then ceases to be the daily sacrifice ordained of God." [25]

"The *trampling this sanctuary under foot,* and *setting up the abomination of desolations in it,* signify the oppression of the visible church by some tyrannical and anti-christian power, set up, and exerting its authority, *within the church;* changing the times and laws of the church; lording it over the conscience of men, and persecuting all who dissent from it." [26]

[22] *Ibid.,* April, 1808 (vol. 7, no. 76), p. 209.
[23] *Ibid.,* p. 210.
[24] *Ibid.*
[25] *Ibid.,* p. 211.
[26] *Ibid.*

Then he concludes that "if this be the proper signification of the symbolical language in Daniel viii.11-13," these verses cannot apply to Mohammedanism, and adds:

"I deny that Mohammedism took away the *daily sacrifice* of the eastern church. That sacrifice was taken away, before the Moslems invaded the Greek empire, by the gross corruptions prevailing in the church, and by its superstitious veneration of the Virgin Mary and the saints. The *abomination of desolations* was set up in the Greek as well as the Latin church, by the Roman emperors, when they gave an antichristian precedence and tyrannical authority to the popes and patriarchs." [27]

Next comes his contention that while "Mohammedanism is an *opposing superstition*," it is a *"superstition* WITHOUT *the church,* and cannot therefore be an *abomination of desolations* IN *the church."* [28] Cuninghame pursues his argument by declaring that the predictions concerning the Mohammedan Saracens and Turks of the woe trumpets in Revelation 9 do not correspond with the specifications of Daniel 8. Such, he says, "are my reasons for rejecting Mr. Faber's interpretation." [29] On the contrary, he contends that the Romans became a horn arising out of the kingdom of Macedon, when it was reduced into a Roman province in the year 148 B.C. (sometimes now dated 146 B.C.) Therefore the rise of the Roman horn has the "precise chronological correspondence with that of Daniel's little horn of the he-goat." [30] The Roman horn magnified itself against the Prince of the host by crucifying the Lord of glory; then it took away the literal sacrifices of the Jews and cast down the literal sanctuary after it became Christian.

"It then *cast down the truth to the ground, and placed the abomination of desolations,* when it gave a tyrannical authority over the church of Christ to the popes and patriarchs, and established the creature worship of the Virgin Mary, the saints, and their images. And the Roman power has in every age destroyed the holy people, whether Jews or Christian saints." [31]

Under the type of the Apocalyptic beast which was, is not, and yet is, the Roman horn shall yet receive power with the ten kings for one hour. Then it shall be "broken without

---

[27] *Ibid.*   [28] *Ibid.* (Emphasis his.)   [29] *Ibid.*, p. 213.
[30] *Ibid.*   [31] *Ibid.*

hand, by that stone which is cut out of the mountain without hands." [32]   Such was the close, clear reasoning of Cuninghame in 1808.

6. WHY 1260 YEARS BEGIN WITH JUSTINIAN.—In January, 1810, "Talib" (Cuninghame) discusses further the issue of the Justinian (533) versus the Phocas (606) date for the beginning of the 1260 years.   He quotes from Paulus Diaconus, on the Phocas edict, showing that Phocas bestowed no new title upon Pope Boniface, merely confirming the title already conferred upon Pope John by Justinian, seventy-three years before. [33] Moreover, the pope in his official papers does not use the title "universal bishop," whereas the title, "head of the church," continues to be employed. [34]

7. "PHILO" IDENTIFIES EARTHQUAKE; DATES TRUMPETS.— The *Observer* records still further advances in 1810.   First, there is discussion by "Philo" [35] of the "earthquake" of Revelation 11 as the French Revolution, and France as the "tenth part of *the city,* or of the idolatrous kingdom of the Beast." [36] Philo's chief contribution, however, is on the fifth and sixth or Saracenic and Turkish trumpets of Revelation 9, with their 150- and 391-year periods, which he locates as 612-762 for the 150 years, and 1281-1672 for the 391 years. [37]

8. EVIDENCE FOR 533 AND 606 DATINGS.—Then Cuninghame, in the April number, presents further evidence from the sources on the authentic 533 Justinian decree as against the alleged 606 grant of Phocas, for the beginning of the 1260 years.   In behalf of the Justinian declaration, which recognized the right of the pope to the titles "*Head of the Church*" and "*Head of all the holy Priests of God,*" Cuninghame remarks:

"What is no less to be observed is, that this transaction took place precisely twelve hundred and sixty current years before the commencement of that awful series of political convulsions which have, in the short space of eighteen years since the fall of the French monarchy, almost completed the destruction of the papal power." [38]

---

[32] *Ibid.*
[34] *Ibid.*, pp. 16, 17.
[36] *Ibid.*, March, 1810 (vol. 9, no. 99), p. 133.
[37] *Ibid.*, p. 137.

[33] *Ibid.*, January, 1810 (vol. 9, no. 97), p. 16.
[35] Unidentified.
[38] *Ibid.*, April, 1810 (vol. 9, no. 100), p. 195.

19

EARLIEST OLD WORLD EXPOSITIONS ON END OF 2300 YEARS

"J. A. B." in 1810 Puts Period From 457 B.C. to A.D. 1843 (Upper Left); William C. Davis Fixes
Upon 453 to 1847 (Upper Right); Archibald Mason (Center Oval) in 1820 Corrects This to
457-1843 (Lower Left); and J. A. Brown Places the Terminus in 1844 (Lower Right); See Pages
474, 392, 400, and 405

After quoting the original Latin, Cuninghame leaves it for the reader to judge which is the one by which the saints and times and laws were delivered into the hands of the Papacy, and when the symbolical abomination of the desolation was set up in the church.[39]

In the May issue Faber gives his rejoinder, holding to his 606 "conjecture," as he calls it, but reaffirming their common belief in the French Revolution as the earthquake and France as the tenth part, or street, of the city.[40] In October, Cuninghame again defends this 2300 rendering of Daniel 8:14 as the reading of the original Hebrew, with the 2400 of the later Septuagint and the 2200 of Jerome's copies as obvious transcriber's errors. This rendering is also confirmed by the Syriac manuscript.[41] He then adds that Justinian, in his decree, declared the Virgin Mary to be the mother of God and pronounced an anathema against all deniers of this doctrine. Thus there was not only "recognition of the papal supremacy" but also "the establishment of idolatry in the visible church," for the giving to Mary of a portion of the honor and worship due only to God and Christ is idolatry.[42]

9. "J. A. B." ENDS 2300 YEARS IN 1843.—Now comes the introduction of a new method of dating the 2300 in a discussion by "J. A. B." [43] in the November, 1810, *Observer*. He notes Faber's attempt to have the 1260 years and the 2200 (Jerome's rendering) end together, and observes in passing that 1260 Mohammedan years of 354 days, from the Hegira in 622, would expire in 1843.[44] But this year, 1843, he holds, will introduce "one of the most memorable periods in Scripture history," when, without altering the 2300 of the received text, would come the close of this 2300-year period.[45]

J. A. B. contends that the 2300 years begin in 457 B.C., along with the seventy weeks, or 490 years of Daniel 9, and he stresses 457 B.C. as being "one of the most remarkable and

---

[39] *Ibid.*, p. 196.   [40] *Ibid.*, May, 1810 (vol. 9, no. 101), p. 257 ff.
[41] *Ibid.*, October, 1810 (vol. 9, no. 106), p. 600.   [42] *Ibid.*
[43] For discussion of John A. Brown, see pp. 404-408.
[44] *The Christian Observer*, November, 1810 (vol. 9, no. 107), p. 668.
[45] *Ibid.*, p. 669.

distinguished points of time in the whole Scripture chronology."
These 490 years reach to the cross, in Christ's thirty-third
year, and the remaining 1810 years of the 2300 "bring us to
the year 1843." [46] J. A. B. then looks "with ardent expectation
and holy hope" to the expiration of the prophecy in 1843
when "the 2300 years having been accomplished," the sanctuary
shall be cleansed. If it is necessary to have the 1260 years of
the papal Antichrist end with the 2300, then J. A. B. suggests
beginning them in 583, when the decree of the papal infallibility was promulgated, which would lead in 1260 years to
the same 1843. He closes by urging others, more competent,
to study and discuss the suggestion.[47] (Facsimile appears on
page 290.)

Thus, champions of the genuine 2300 years—versus the
faulty 2400 or 2200—arose, with advocacy of the application
of this period to Rome instead of to Mohammedanism. The
fundamental thesis of Petri and Wood[48]—that the seventy years
constitute the first segment of the 2300 years, and that the
two periods begin together—is again brought prominently
before the church and is destined to have an increasingly
important place in the thinking of those who participated in
the great Advent Awakening of the nineteenth century.

Soon Cuninghame's first book on prophecy appeared, *A
Dissertation on the Seals and the Trumpets of the Apocalypse*
(1813). The March, 1814, issue of the *Observer* gives a comprehensive book review,[49] agreeing in some points and disagree-
ing in others. The editor evidently accepts the 2300 rendering.[50]

10. BURN SHOWS TWO TESTAMENTS ARE TWO WITNESSES.
—In the August issue a military man, Major General A.
Burn, writes an illuminating defense of the Old and New
Testaments as the "Two Witnesses" in challenge of the Faber
position, citing the support of Napier, Brightman, and More.[51]
He holds that they are "the only true and faithful witnesses

---

[46] *Ibid.*   [47] *Ibid.*, p. 670.
[48] See full discussion in Volume 2 of *Prophetic Faith*.
[49] *The Christian Observer*, March, 1814 (vol. 13, no. 147), p. 163 ff.
[50] *Ibid.*, p. 172.   [51] *Ibid.*, August, 1814 (vol. 13, no. 152), p. 483.

for God," who will "instruct and illuminate the dark regions of earth, till the kingdoms of this world shall become the kingdoms of our God and of His Christ." [52]   Burn gives five reasons: Their name, *Testamenta,* means witnesses, and "they are they which testify of Me"; their number, two, signifies the two Testaments; their power is to pronounce plagues and judgments; their office is to prophesy or preach; and finally, they were to preach in sackcloth, and to be politically and symbolically slain for 1260 years. [53]

Thus they were during that "awful dark period" shut up in cloisters in a language unknown to the common people, to whom it was "death to read them in their mother tongue." [54] The climax of this argument is the recent formation of the Bible societies "for the express purpose of commissioning these two anointed ones to deliver their testimony pure and unadulterated to every human being under heaven."   Then he concludes:

"The 1260 years are expired, and the wonderful unexpected events that occur every day, announce the speedy approach of the Redeemer's reign upon earth." [55]

11. "C. E. S." Ends both 391 and 2300 in 1844.—In the June, 1818, *Observer,* "C. E. S." adverts to a small volume by Frederick Thruston, [56] which suggests that the 391 years and 15 days of the sixth trumpet extends from 1453 to 1844. C. E. S. advocates the likelihood of this dating, and cites Edward W. Whitaker [57] to the same end.   Several earlier men, such as Mede and Fleming, had *ended* the period in 1453, but the greater likelihood of its *commencing* then is here argued. The anxiety of all commentators to find the precise point of chronology that would mark the downfall of the Turkish Government is noted, as well as the "universal consent of interpreters, that the exhaustion of the Euphratean waters, produced by the effusion of the sixth vial, symbolizes the gradual dismemberment and subversion of the Ottoman Empire." [58] C. E. S.

---

[52] *Ibid.,* pp. 484, 485.   [53] *Ibid.,* p. 485.   [54] *Ibid.*   [55] *Ibid.,* p. 486.
[56] Frederick Thruston, *Researches into the Apocalyptic Little Book.*
[57] Edward W. Whitaker, *A General and Connected View of the Prophecies Relating to the Times of the Gentiles,* p. 146.
[58] *The Christian Observer,* June, 1818 (vol. 17, no. 198), p. 351.

also notes Turkish fears of Russia, as destined to drive them out of Europe. He likewise presents the year 1844 as the end of the 2300 years.[59]

12. "Senior" Dates 391-Year Period From 1299-1690.— In 1825 the *Observer* tabulated twelve new works on prophecy, including such authors as Way, Bayford, J. H. Stewart, Gauntlett, and Bickersteth.[60] Editorial comment stresses the two conflicting concepts of the millennium in the preceding century —that of Grotius on the one side, dating it from the era of Constantine, and of Mede on the other, dating it at the close of the prophetic periods, the seven vials, and the literal resurrection at the advent. In 1826 the dating of the 2300 was still being discussed.[61] And in a "Euphratean Vial" discussion by "Senior," [62] the remarkable agreement of Protestant interpreters is stressed that the fall of the Ottoman Empire is intended; the hour, day, month, and year, or 391 literal years of the sixth trumpet, are dated from 1299 and terminated in 1690—some "ending them in 1698." [63] But the writer says:

"The difference is of little consequence; and the less so, because both 1690 and 1698 witnessed successive and effectual degrees of the sentence pronounced upon the Ottomans, Thus far shall ye come, and no farther." [64]

13. Turkish Prophecy Continues to Agitate.—In 1827, we find various interesting views expressed. One correspondent notes the "running to and fro of many that knowledge (especially on prophetical subjects)" may be increased; another writer calls attention to the "extraordinary similarity" between the early Waldensian statement of faith and the Thirty-nine Articles of the Church of England, maintaining that the foundation of the latter may be traced to the former, some parts being "copied word for word from the Waldensian document," including the canonical list of the books of Scripture.[65] Again the prophecies on the Mohammedans are re-

[59] *Ibid.*, pp. 352-354.
[60] *Ibid.*, August, 1825 (vol. 25, no. 284), p. 489.
[61] *Ibid.*, B. Q. R., May, 1826 (vol. 26, no. 293), pp. 266-269.
[62] The same person who wrote as "Juvenis" in 1802.
[63] *Ibid.*, November, 1826 (vol. 26, no. 299), pp. 654, 655.
[64] *Ibid.*, p. 655. [65] *Ibid.*, May, 1827 (vol. 27, no. 305), pp. 272, 273.

hearsed by "Senior," as well as the Church of Rome as Antichrist and spiritual Babylon.[66] The premillennial aspect of the advent is also pressed in an article in the October issue.[67]

In February, 1828, a logical writer holds the plagues to be yet future, marshaling his reasons.[68] And "Senior" still insists that the "allotted" 391-year period of the sixth trumpet is from about 1300 to not later than 1697 or 1698.[69] He refers to a "host of witnesses" who hold the second woe ended "at the close of the seventeenth century." This he declares to be the "prevailing opinion." [70] Then "Epsilon" questions the necessity of the 1260 and 2300 years ending in the same year.[71]

14. "J. A. B." Reiterates Prior Stand on "1843."—"J. A. B." after silence in the *Observer* since October, 1810, when he first introduced the terminus of the 2300 years for 1843, again in 1828 launches into a detailed discussion of the chronology of the Jewish Passover, indulging in considerable arithmetic. After eighteen years he still holds that the 2300 years are to be recorded from the commission of Ezra in 457 b.c.[72]

15. "Observer" Creates Interest in Prophecy.—Mention is twice made of the conference at Albury Park for the study of prophecy, which had been reported in *The Record*.[73] Considerable space is given to Henry Drummond in the March *Observer* for a "Popular Introduction to the Study of the Apocalypse." [74] In introducing this, the editor says:

"A considerable portion of our pages, as our readers are aware, has for nearly thirty years been devoted to the important subject of prophecy, . . . fulfilled and unfulfilled, which has of late spread so widely, and excited so much of the inquiries of Christians of every communion." [75]

16. "D. M. P." Dates Turkish Period 1299 to 1690.— In a series of articles on the trumpets "D. M. P." writes on the first four as accomplishing the downfall of Western Rome

[66] *Ibid.*, August, 1827 (vol. 27, no. 308), pp. 462-465.
[67] *Ibid.*, October, 1827 (vol. 27, no. 310), pp. 592, 593.
[68] *Ibid.*, February, 1828 (vol. 28, no. 314), p. 66.
[69] *Ibid.*, p. 68.   [70] *Ibid.*, p. 69.   [71] *Ibid.*, p. 70.
[72] *Ibid.*, July, 1828 (vol. 28, no. 319), p. 415.
[73] *Ibid.*, December, 1828 (vol. 28, no. 324), p. 788; January, 1830 (vol. 30, no. 337), p. 56.
[74] *Ibid.*, March, 1830 (vol. 30, no. 339), pp. 130-142.
[75] *Ibid.*, p. 129.

and thereby preparing the way for the success of the caliphs in the East.[76] Stressing the date made famous by Gibbon—July 27, 1299[77]—he comes to the fall of Constantinople in 1453 and observes significantly:

"Once seated upon the imperial throne of the Caesars, the Turkish sultan assumed a new name and character among the kings of the earth, and his empire attained to such a colossal magnitude as to become for upwards of two centuries the scourge and terror of Christendom." [78]

Taking 1299 as the starting point, "D. M. P." therefore places the terminus of the 391 years in 1690, which was the last successful campaign of the Turks in Hungary. He then concludes with the remark, "But, whichever of the foregoing dates be preferred by the reader, he can hardly fail to acknowledge the accurate fulfilment of prophecy." [79]

17. THE CALL OUT OF BABYLON.—We note but one further development now, in the fifth decade of the century. In 1842 the issue of current compromises with Rome is sharply drawn, the purpose of many being to "unprotestantise our Church, and bring us back to Catholicity." A growing group was looking upon Romanism as a branch of Christ's Holy Catholic church, differing from Protestantism in unimportant matters, but constituting an older branch which retains things Protestantism has lost—the stem from which our Protestant branch once grew, and separation from which is to be regretted. To such, Rome is the "Saviour's holy home," and all are prodigal sons who have left the Father's house, and are feeding on husks, and ought without delay to return to the mansion where once we dwelt.[80]

The spell of such "magic of words" is to be dissolved "simply by telling the truth," and by "calling things by their right names." Instead of a church, a writer in the *Observer* contends that it is an apostasy, the mystery of iniquity, Babylon the great, from which we are to come out and be separate that we partake not of her sins and receive not of her plagues.[81]

---

[76] *Ibid.*, June, 1831 (vol. 31, no. 354), pp. 340, 341.
[77] *Ibid.*, August, 1831 (vol. 31, no. 356), p. 458.
[80] *Ibid.*, April, 1842 (vol. 5, no. 52), p. 198.

[78] *Ibid.*, p. 461.
[79] *Ibid.*, p. 463.
[81] *Ibid.*, pp. 198, 199.

Such is the remarkable record of the discussions on prophecy in this staid Church of England journal, in the interim before and while the leading books of the second, third, and fourth decades of this remarkable century of exposition were produced and the leading schools of interpretation were clearly developed. The stalwarts in the early discussions are thus before us, and from now on books on prophecy appear in increasing numbers, and other periodicals appear, largely founded for the discussion of prophecy.

II. Advent Heralds on the Continent and Beyond

The heavy tension in Europe preceding the outbreak of World War II made research work increasingly difficult, and curtailed our investigation of the Continental nineteenth-century witness on the revival of prophetic study.[82] This section is therefore incomplete and should have further study when conditions again become favorable. A few names and facts taken from notes during travels in 1938—but often without the customarily full investigation and documentation—must suffice for now and be supplemented later. However, even these help to round out the Continental picture. Various Continental writers recognized that the terrible judgments upon the Papacy during the French Revolution were evidence of the closing of the 1260 years, and of the approaching glorious deliverance of the church. But this transcendent event involved the proclamation of the last warning message of the everlasting gospel.

1. BENGEL'S FOLLOWERS HERALD IMMINENT ADVENT.—The large group of admirers and followers of Johann Bengel,[83] both in Germany and in other lands to which German colonists emigrated, perpetuated his expectation of the grand climax about 1836, on the supposition that the number 666 marked the

---

[82] The Munich crisis of 1938 brought research work in many of the Continental European libraries to a standstill. However, our investigation of British sources in the British Museum was virtually completed.
[83] Discussed in Volume 2 of *Prophetic Faith*.

years of papal supremacy. This is reflected in the writings
of a number of men between 1820 and 1835, such as Lindl,
Lilienstern, Leutwein, Stilling, Norke, Röhrborn, and Wurm.
A speech by the Hessian Landgrave Charles, before the Schles-
wig-Holstein Bible Society in 1829, stresses the advent as very
near, as indicated by the prophecies, when the resurrection
should occur and the millennium begin.[84]

A little earlier, Ignaz Lindl, who wrote *Leitfaden zur einfachen Erklärung der Apokalypse* (A Clue to a Simple Exposition of the Apocalypse) (1826),[85] began to expound the prophecies in Bavaria and Austria, thousands flocking to hear him in
1812-13.[86] Then Lindl, driven out of Bavaria, was called to St.
Petersburg by the czar, and became leader of the Pietists in
southern Russia. In 1820 Grossner of Düsseldorf as well as
other Protestants, was similarly called by Prince Galitzin of the
Ministry of Cults. But pressure was soon brought to bear by
Prince Metternich of Austria, and both Lindl and Grossner
had to leave, and the newly formed Russian Bible Society was
dissolved. However, thousands of German believers in the near
advent had sought shelter there ere the great storm should burst.
Grossner's efforts proved to be a forerunner of the Stundist
movement, with its "stunden," or hours for prayer and Bible
study, where the flame of the advent hope was nourished among
Germans and Russians.

Others, such as Pastor J. F. E. Sander, in *Versuch einer
Erklärung der Offenbarung* (Attempt to Explain the Revelation of John) (1829), changed from Bengel's 1836 date over to
1843, or possibly 1847.[87] Such men were admittedly influenced
by British writers on prophecy. In his preface Sander mentions
help he had received not only from Zobel and Lindl but from
recent books and pamphlets by English authors such as Irving,
Drummond, and Noel. He then refers to current political

---

[84] Reported in *The Christian Instructor*, June 29, 1830.
[85] See British Museum catalogue and Joshua W. Brooks, *Dictionary of Writers on the Prophecies*, p. liii.
[86] H. Dalton, *Johannes Grossner*, S. 149, 214, 258, 265, 278.
[87] J. F. E. Sander, *Versuch einer Erklärung der Offenbarung*, Johannis, S. 116; see also S. 66, 195.

and religious upheavals as evidence that "the last time is at the door," and that the kingdoms of this world were soon to become the kingdoms of Christ.[88]

On the other hand, C. T. Röhrborn in 1832, in *Höchst wichtige Weissagungen* (Most Important Prophecies), and Professor J. F. Wurm, of Stuttgart,[89] both held tentatively to Bengel's 1836 as the time of Christ's probable appearance. There was considerable acquaintance in Germany with current English writers on the prophecies and the advent. Lewis Way's *Thoughts on Scripture Expectations* was translated into the German in 1830.[90] W. A. HOLMES (1782-1843), of England, Chancellor of Cashel, in *The Time of the End,* as late as 1833 was almost the only British supporter of Bengel's 1836 date as the terminus of the 2300 years.

2. APPROACHING END OF 2300 YEARS AGITATED.—In 1805 and 1817 L. H. Kelber, Bavarian schoolmaster, issued *Vernünftige und schriftgemässe Gedanken über die Schöpfung und Dauer der Welt,*[91] in two parts, in which he counted the 2300 days as years, but ended them in his early expositions in 1793 when "the hour of temptation began," and hoped for the millennium of rest about 1836. But when, in 1835, he published a continuation of *Das Ende kommt* (The End Is Coming) he stated that Bengel missed his goal by seven years—that it should be 1843, not 1836. He based his work on Petri, who, just before the French Revolution, asserted that Christ's advent would not tarry beyond 1847.[92] As a result of conflict with the Lutherans over Antichrist, he wrote *Der Antichrist* (The Antichrist).

Heinrich Richter, missionary secretary of the Rhenish society, was likewise influenced by Petri's calculations. His Introduction to Daniel takes the position that the 2300 year-days begin with the seventy weeks, and terminate "1817 years

[88] *Ibid.,* S. ix.
[89] J. F. Wurm, *Ueber die Beweisgründe* (On the Proofs), S. 14.
[90] *Was hat die Christliche Kirche nach den Verheissungen der Heiligen Schrift zu erwarten?*
[91] *Rational and Scriptural Thoughts Concerning the Creation and Duration of the World.*
[92] L. H. Kelber, Introductory "Vorbericht," dated 1835, in *Das Ende Kommt* (1842 ed), pp. 4, 5.

after the 30th year of Christ or 1847 years after Christ's birth." [93]
And in volume 6 he plainly dates it as 1843. [94]

In Holland, H. Heintzpeter wrote two pamphlets, in 1819
and 1822, on *De groote Wereldgebeurtenissen,* or The Great
World Events (1842), endorsing Petri's calculation of the 2300
years as from 453 to 1847. [95] In Sweden many of the Pietists
were called "laesare," or readers, because of their diligent
reading of the prophecies. And because they raised their voices
in warning they were also called "ropare" (criers). Some were
imprisoned at Örebro. And children gave expositions of prophecy and exhorted to repentance in view of the soon-coming
Saviour and the hour of judgment, as will be duly noted in a
later chapter.

In Switzerland, Nicole, a lawyer near Nyon, and Professor Louis Gaussen, of Geneva, gave the same warning message,
based on the prophecies. Nicole's tract of 1829 is quoted in
the *Morning Watch.* [96] Assuming that the 2300 years, starting
with the seventy weeks, began in 454 B.C., they believed the
period would end by 1846-47, at the cleansing of the sanctuary.
When Gaussen was removed from his pulpit by the rationalist
professors, he became the center of a prophetic study circle in
Geneva. [97] Visiting Rome, he felt certain that Antichrist was
reigning there. He was called to a professorship in the newly
opened theological seminary at Geneva, where he gave his chief
attention to prophecy, and his lessons on the book of Daniel
were presented.

3. WITNESSES PENETRATE ASIA AND AFRICA.—These advent
witnesses, along with many others—such as Joseph Wolff in
Asia, Daniel Wilson in India, Samuel Gobat in Abyssinia—
sounding out over the Continent and penetrating Asia and
Africa, afford a fleeting glimpse of the advent emphasis, and its
ever-attendant prophetic exposition. The Old World Advent

---

[93] Heinrich Richter, *Erklärte Haus-Bibel,* Band IV, S. 749 ff. (Title page reproduced
on p. 378.)
[94] *Ibid.,* Band VI, S. 1089.
[95] H. Heintzpeter, *De groote Wereldgebeurtenissen,* bldz., 30.
[96] Discussed in a later chapter.
[97] *Samuel Gobat, . . . His Life and Work,* p. 43.

Awakening was more extensive and more intensive than many have been wont to realize. Its significance will grow upon us as we summon the individual and group witnesses. And the general emphasis upon the approaching end of the 2300 years will become increasingly impressive.

III. Determining the Dominant Prophetic Exposition

While these individual views on prophecy may at first appear independent and unrelated, there are certain common, or general, agreements upon basic positions that are most impressive. As with the colonial American writers, a tabulation of views of these Old World interpreters reveals a unity of teaching upon certain fundamentals that can rightly be called the dominant view of the expository group of Old World writers of the time. These include recognition of the four world powers of Babylon, Medo-Persia, Greece, and Rome in sequence, followed by Rome's breakup into ten divisions, and the Little Horn as the Papacy. Antichrist, as the historical Papacy, was recognized as revealed under the various symbols of Little Horn, Man of Sin, Beast, Babylon, and Harlot. Nothing could be more unanimous than this agreement.

The year-day principle was yet another universally proclaimed prophetic truth for all prophetic time periods. France as the tenth part of the "city," and the "earthquake" as the French Revolution, were frequently stressed. The Turk as the power of the sixth trumpet, with his time period of 391 years, was very generally held. And especially was the significance of the 2300 year-days, as beginning in the time of Persia and ending about 1843, 1844, or 1847, the new or added note, growing in volume and clarity. And along with this, there began to be coupled increasingly the declaration of the approaching hour of God's judgment, and the proclamation of the midnight cry, "Behold, the Bridegroom cometh."

Stripped of other details, upon which there were often marked differences, these larger aspects comprehend the common denominator of prophetic exposition—along with the imminent, personal, premillennial advent of Christ, when the righteous dead will rise and the eternal kingdom will be set up. That was the climax of all prophecy, the goal of all expectation, and the motivating power in all these organizations and their endeavors. These constitute the dominant prophetic exposition.

There was yet another commonly, yes, almost universally held position—the return of the Jews and their conversion before the end. This was a point of sharp division between the Old and the New World prophetic heralds, as will be unfolded later. Adherence to it definitely molded the concepts of the Old World group, coloring the understanding of the nature of the events to occur in connection with the ending of the 2300 years.

A comprehensive summary of the positions of all leading writers, and warranted conclusions drawn therefrom, will appear in our final chapter, where these points are visualized.

CHAPTER SEVENTEEN

Catholic Witness
Stirs Two Continents

I. A Clarion Voice From the Catholic Church

Before beginning our examination of the many Protestant witnesses, we shall first listen to two Catholic voices at the turn of the century. Just as the long and fateful 1260 years of papal spiritual supremacy over the churches was drawing to its dramatic close, a clarion voice rang out from the very shadows of the Vatican, destined to be heard halfway round the world. The Jesuit priest MANUEL LACUNZA called attention to the prophetic predictions of Daniel, Paul, and John, and sounded out once again the prophetic warning and appeal that had so long been silenced by force. He was the first voice; and the Dominican Père Lambert, of France, was the second. Not since the days of Joachim and the centuries preceding the Protestant Reformation had the like been heard. Now, from within the Roman communion, Catholic countries like Spain, France, and Italy, as well as virtually all of Mexico and South America, heard these prophetic voices in insistent tones.

Utterly disappointed and disillusioned by the absurdities and incongruities of the best-known Catholic expositors of millennial prophecy, Lacunza had recourse to Holy Scripture itself, and the light of the premillennial second advent broke upon him in all its impelling grandeur and simplicity. Like his contemporary, Lambert, the Dominican, he strongly urged investigators, especially those of the priesthood, to resort to the Book of God, which had been well-nigh consigned to oblivion. The two advents of Christ—the first in inconspicuous humility, and the second in glory and majesty—he presented as the two great focal points of all prophecy and the goal of all history. Such was the essence of Lacunza's burden and the theme of his message. Repeatedly he stressed the principle that those prophecies not fulfilled at the first advent will in verity be fulfilled at the second. His was an arresting voice, profoundly moving the Catholic and Protestant worlds alike.

From the days of Augustine onward the Catholic Church had held that Satan was bound by the first coming of Christ, that the millennium began either then or at the time of Constantine, and that the devil was loosed at the time of the assaults by Wyclif or Luther—or will be loosed when Antichrist shall appear in his final form. Lacunza came to see the error and unhistoricity of such a position, and turned back to the teachings of the early church, adopting the position of two literal resurrections separated by an interval of one thousand years.

The results of his extended investigation he wrote out in the form of a lengthy manuscript. But he could not get permission of the ecclesiastical authorities to print it. So when he was found dead in 1801, on the bank of the river which flows near Imola, Italy, where he resided, his book had not yet been published. But even in manuscript form it awakened many in Europe and South America to the fundamental truth that the second advent is to take place prior to the millennium —a truth not only utterly lost sight of in Roman Catholicism, but by now largely obscured in large sections of the great Protestant communions. This was due to the devastating inroads of the Whitbyan philosophy of world conversion, and of Christ's second coming at the *close* of the millennium. Lacunza's revolutionary position was squarely a confutation of that postmillennial theory, increasingly popular among Protestants.

The singularity and significance of Lacunza's contribution lay in its revolutionary interpretation—so far as Catholic positions were concerned—of Antichrist, and of his destruction at the *beginning* of the millennial period. This Lacunza placed as future and approaching, and introduced by the second, personal, premillennial advent of Christ, with the general resurrection of the wicked dead at the close. His thesis was therefore anathema to Rome. Later, when brought squarely and unavoidably before her for decision, it was consigned to the *Index Prohibitorum,* in harmony with her consistent position for centuries.

Political upheavals in Spain had weakened the grip of the church upon that unhappy land, and made favorable the printing of the first half-dozen editions. The power of the Inquisition was crippled and appeared about broken, so that it proved impotent to prohibit circulation and reading of the book. Final prohibition in all languages by the Sacred Congregation of the Index, at Rome, made authoritative by pontifical decree, thus brought the issue of the second advent, Antichrist, and tradition again squarely before the highest body of the Roman Church by one of her own learned and respected sons early in the nineteenth century.

Lacunza had challenged the inner heart of Catholic exposition, for he exalted the Bible above dogmatic tradition. His treatise also called a halt to the rapid retreat from the clear Protestant position on the advent. He identified Antichrist *not* as some individual blasphemer, to harass the church in the future, but as the "moral body" of apostasy. He expounded the temple of God as the Christian church, and taught that the two-horned beast is not an individual, but the Roman priesthood, which lend their aid to the consummation of apostasy.

The providential circumstances of the propagation of his book made it an instrument to give marked impetus to the study of the second advent in Britain among those Protestants already awakened to the study of the prophecies of Daniel and the Revelation. While there had been a small but steady line

20

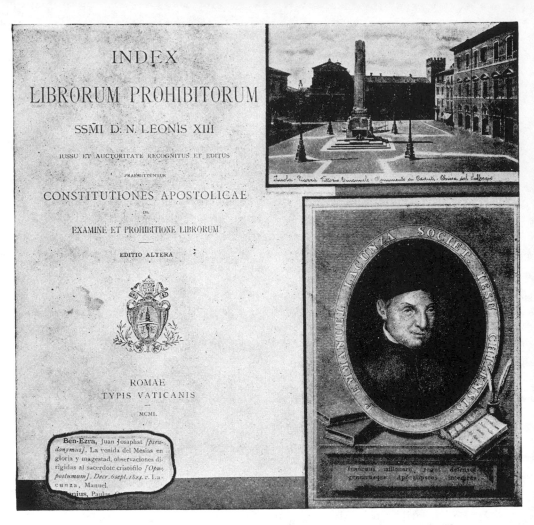

LACUNZA'S REVOLUTIONARY EXPOSITION PLACED ON INDEX

Manuel Lacunza (Lower Right), and the Church in Imola, Italy, Where He Lies Buried (Upper Right); Title Page of Official Vatican Copy of *Index Librorum Prohibitorum*, With Inset Item Listing Lacunza's Volume, Under Pseudonym "Ben-Ezra" (Left)

of Protestant students and writers on prophecy who held to premillennialism on the basis of an increasingly clear interpretation of the prophecies, symbols, and chronological periods (which features Lacunza but lightly touched), it was the province and accomplishment of Lacunza to clarify the whole premillennial issue, and to force home to open-minded Protestant prophetic students—as well as the closed minds of

306

Catholic theologians—this cardinal truth and principle.

Little wonder that Lacunza in the last quarter of the eighteenth century did not see all the light on prophetic interpretation that others in Great Britain, Germany, and North America saw and carried forward to increasing perfection—particularly a quarter century after his death. Lacunza's was a solitary voice almost from the shadows of the Vatican, just before the early dawn of the nineteenth-century revival of the advent hope and the beginning of the great second advent world movement that has since gone on with increasing force and volume.

Lacunza was verily one of God's chosen heralds. Moving Catholics and Protestants alike, his book was one of the greatest single influences to stir mankind to the nineteenth-century restudy of the prophecies, and exerted a profound influence, through Edward Irving, on the Albury Park Prophetic Conference of 1826. The true significance of Lacunza's life, witness, and influence cannot really be understood unless there is acquaintance with those providences, political upheavals, and ecclesiastical decrees that shaped the whole course of his life. These must now be noted in some detail.

II. Lacunza—Jesuit Herald of Second Advent

MANUEL DE LACUNZA, or Juan Josafat Ben-Ezra (1731-1801), Jesuit advent herald of Chile and Italy, was born in Santiago. Of substantial parentage, he received a careful religious education in letters, Latin grammar, and rhetoric at the Colegio Maximo, or Superior School, and was admitted to probation in the Jesuit Order in 1747, at the age of sixteen. Completing his two-year vows, he continued the study of philosophy and theology at Bucalemu, finishing with honors. As his third year of probation ended, he received sacred orders. Restive under the silence and retirement imposed by such a life, he was given the instructional and spiritual supervision of the younger students. But even this did not fully satisfy him, so he became a professor of Latin, and pursued studies in astronomy and geometry.[1]

Lacunza was celebrated locally as a preacher, and in 1766 took the four vows of the Jesuits. But in the autumn of 1767 he was expelled from Chile, with all members of the order, by decree of Charles III of Spain, which action involved all Spanish dominions. Lacunza went first to Cádiz, Spain, and then located at Imola, near Bologna, in central Italy, residing there until his death. He expressed no bitterness over his exile on strange soil, but in 1772 retired from the world, becoming an anchorite, or recluse, for the remainder of his days, holding converse only with his books. His frugal life was without comforts, as his living stipend was meager. To find relief from his disappointments, he began the study of the Fathers and then of the prophecies, reading all the commentaries he could find in a near-by convent. He was untiring in his application to study, constantly invoking the grace of the Holy Spirit. He lived a life of remarkable piety and prayer, spending five hours daily in such devotions. He solved the difficult questions that arose over texts by long seasons of prayer for divine illumination, in which his amanuensis, Father Gonzalez Carvajal, joined.

For thirty years Lacunza engaged in this profound study of the Holy Book, the writings of the Fathers, and theological interpreters. He compassed the entire Patrology—1,000 large volumes—to know, use, or refute the Fathers and the expositors. He made a scientific study of the Scriptures, formulating a comprehensive code. In 1779 he abandoned his trips to the libraries of Venice, Bologna, and Rome as without benefit, and devoted himself solely to the Scriptures.

His key to the prophecies was his discovery of the two comings of Christ. He separated the confusing parts, and emphasized the second advent at the *beginning* of the millennium.

---

[1] Bibliographical and historical data for this sketch are gathered from the most authoritative sources, including the sketches appearing in the introductions to the various editions of *La Venida.* Doubtless the most exhaustive and thoroughly documented treatise on Lacunza is a recent work by Alfred-Felix Vaucher titled *Une célébrité oubilée le P. Manuel de Lacunza y Díaz (1731-1801) de la Société de Jésus auteur de "La Venue du Messie en gloire et majesté"* (1941).

As to scholarship, he was never charged with inaccuracy, misquotation of authorities, or distortion. Thus his writing of *La Venida del Mesías en Gloria y Magestad* (The Coming of the Messiah in Glory and Majesty) neared completion, having occupied some twenty years.

In 1781 Ennodio Papia (the pseudonym used by Guiseppe Zoppi), published two books, *Apocalypse* and *Second Epoch of the Church*. In 1784 the *Second Epoch* was prohibited by the Sacred Congregation of the Index.[2] Lacunza dissented from Papia, contending that there are only two comings of Christ— the first in the flesh in lowly form at His incarnation, and the second in glory and majesty, soon. But he feared that his own production would likewise be placed on the *Index*. Thus *La Venida del Mesías en Gloria y Magestad* was brought forth in manuscript, in Spanish, under the pen name of Juan Josafat Ben-Ezra, a Christian Hebrew, and dedicated to "Christófilo" —lover of Christ. Fra Pablo gives the date, in introducing his "Critique" endorsing it, as about 1791, which was in the midst of the French Revolution.

Lacunza's treatise, produced almost under the shadows of the Vatican, reached Spain and South America in manuscript, arousing interest and admiration immediately. It soon became popular in manuscript form, and despite laborious hand duplication, had an amazing circulation all the way "from Havana to Cape Horn." It was translated into Latin and then Italian. Velez, erudite lawyer of the church in Buenos Aires, prepared an elaborate refutation, starting a long controversy. There were ardent friends and bitter opponents. Heated discussions ensued, of which Lacunza was aware. The discussion greatly stirred both Europe and South America. Meanwhile, Lacunza revised his manuscript and approved it for publication, as he deplored the imperfect copies circulating in Europe and in South American colonies.

---

[2] The Sacred Congregation of the Index is one of thirteen standing committees at the Vatican, each under the presidency of a cardinal, which aid the pope in the government of the church. It controls the censorship of Catholic writings, with official power of prohibition, though all decisions require pontifical approval. The *Index* contains the list of prohibited books.

Valdivieso sent his "Defense" of Ben-Ezra from Ravenna to Caballina, together with a manuscript copy translated from the Latin to Spanish. In 1799 the Jesuit Father Maneiro returned to Mexico, bearing an elegant Latin translation. Lacunza's description of the last days and the political conditions occurring, impressed the thoughtful, and the clergy "read it with avidity."

Lacunza's death was accidental, occurring in 1801. He was found dead on the bank of the river which flows near Imola. There were no printed editions of his treatise before his death. In 1802 D. Francisco Gil Lemos, lieutenant general of the Spanish Armada, had a manuscript copy in Spanish. When Napoleon overran Spain and took Ferdinand VII prisoner, Cádiz served as the capital of all Spain that had escaped French annexation. Besieged from February, 1810, to August, 1812, it was relieved by Wellington's victory at Salamanca, though Ferdinand VII was not restored until 1814. Under the interim government by the Cortes the Inquisition was abolished and some freedom of the press established. Thus the first edition of *La Venida,* bearing the name of Felipe Tolosa, came to be secretly printed near Cádiz, on the Isle of Leon, or San Fernando. Another Tolosa edition was printed in 1812, with a favorable censure by Fra Pablo de la Concepcion, the barefooted Carmelite.

III. Release of Treatise Stirs Two Continents

The turmoil created by the publication of the Lacunza treatise, and its really profound effect on two continents, is best seen by a rapid survey of the two decades following the initial printing. Assailed in 1813 by Friar Martinez in Italy, it nevertheless made proselytes in Italy and Spain. Opinion was sharply divided among the Jesuits, the Father General prohibiting the publication of opinion. Father Bestard, commissary general of the Order of St. Francis, in the Indies, warned vigorously against it, and attempted to stop its circulation in the various languages, becoming the archfoe of the

Lacunzan teachings and book. But it continued to be read and copied surreptitiously. A three-volume manuscript from Italy reached Havana, and marked Mexican interest developed in the new Spanish edition, while manuscript copies circulated continuously. The Cortes, or national legislature in Spain, expelled the bishops and banished the nuncio, and the second and third printings of the Tolosa, or Cádiz, edition appeared.

After Napoleon's reversal in Spain, Ferdinand VII returned and declared the decrees of the Cortes null and void, and re-established the Inquisition and the Jesuits. In 1816 the four-volume London edition of *La Venida* was printed at the expense of General Belgrano, diplomatic representative of the Argentine Republic, for distribution in his homeland. Meantime it was translated into other European languages. In 1818 the Mexican Inquisition[3] investigated copies circulated in Mexico but did not condemn them because of their popularity. The French 120-page compendium of Lacunza appeared, made by the Jansenist Agier, president of the Court of Appeals of Paris and writer on prophecy. The Paris *Chronique Religieuse* in 1819 recommended the acquisition of the book as full of light, and noted a Latin translation circulating in Italy.

By 1819 the Council of the General Inquisition of Spain ordered all copies collected, with reading prohibited pending full examination. Then the Mexican Inquisition prohibited the work "until properly certified," and the Spanish Inquisition warned against copies printed without permission of superiors. Nevertheless some copies were preserved in insubordination. The Peruvian Inquisition was also stirred over the Lacunzian doctrine, intense discussion ensuing in Mexico, Ecuador, Peru, Chile, Argentina, and Uruguay.

In 1820 the citizens of Cádiz secured renewal of the 1812 liberal constitution by a revolt which spread throughout the

---

[3] Court or tribunal for the discovery, examination, and punishment of heretics, with special judicial powers conferred on special judges. In Spain "it remained operative into the nineteenth century. . . . King Joseph Bonaparte abrogated it in 1808, but it was re-introduced by Ferdinand VII in 1814 and approved by Pius VII on certain conditions, among others the abolition of torture. It was definitely abolished by the Revolution of 1820."—*Catholic Encyclopedia*, vol. 8, art., "Inquisition," p. 37.

country. The Inquisition was again abolished—the prohibition
of the Lacunza work having been one of its last acts. The con-
vents were closed, and the freedom of the press was again
established.

In 1821-22 an edition appeared in Puebla, Mexico, and a
new Spanish edition was attempted at Granada, Spain. Archbishop de Palma's "reprobation" stressed Lacunza's violation
of the principle of the superiority of tradition, of not following
the church Fathers and the laws of the church. In 1823 he
was compelled to disclose in writing his reasons for censure.
He gave this censure in the form of five "Observations." "Sad
days for the Church of Spain," was the Catholic historian's
lament. Nevertheless, numerous priests accepted Lacunza's
views, and the book was received with favor in both religious and
literary circles.

The partisans of Lacunza were called new reformers, and
Lacunza was labeled an "innovator" and his contention a "new
idea." Meantime, Ferdinand VII (1808-20 and 1823-33), a
virtual prisoner since 1820, was released by the French army,
which suppressed liberalism and liberal constitutional government in Spain. Then, in 1824, Valdivieso's *Defense* of Lacunza,
written at Ravenna, was published in Mexico. Next, the Fran-
ciscan monk Bestard's vicious attack on Lacunza was printed
and a copy sent the pope, complaining that Lacunza insinuated
that the fulfillment of Revelation 13 and 17 is to be found in
the Roman priesthood and church. On the other hand, prominent Spanish theologians defended the book.

Then occurred the famous Cordova, Argentina, incident.
A well-known priest—probably Dean Funes—while preaching,
recommended Lacunza's book. A theological professor instantly
reproved the preacher, declaring the work heretical. The incident was denounced to the Sacred Congregation of the Index,
which received the informer and reproved the cathedral up-
roar. The Congregation of the Index appointed an official
examining committee of four. Fifteen censures resulted—the
leading ones being that Lacunza had exalted Scriptures above

tradition, had taught Antichrist was not a future individual, had not acceptably venerated Catholic exposition, and had invited criticism by writing in the vulgar tongue. The delicacy and difficulty of the decision was increased because Lacunza was dead.[4] But the solemn sentence was passed by the Congregation of the Index, and Pope Leo XII, on September 6, issued the formal decree—"Forbidden to be published in any language whatsoever."[5] By September 25 the decree was published and posted in the stipulated places.

But the conflict did not subside. The book was condemned by the Spanish friar Dos-Barrios, but commended by Vicar General Encina, of Toledo, seat of the primate of the Spanish church, with a favorable review by a Carmelite father. Secret societies read it with delight.[6] Then the five-volume Chamrobert edition appeared in Paris in 1825, and the five-volume Valdés edition in Mexico. Bestard's attempts to stop the circulation of the book were blessed by the pope, and Bestard was supported by eighty Spanish celebrities—archbishops, government officials, military and naval officers, educators, doctors, and noblemen.

In 1826 Edward Irving of London was profoundly affected by reading the 1812 Spanish edition, having on the previous Christmas preached his first sermon on the second advent. He then began to translate it into English. Then, later in 1826, the Ackermann London edition appeared, the best and most exact to be issued.[7] The Lacunza book became the subject of much discussion at the Albury Park Prophetic Conference. Secret societies in Spain continued to read the prohibited Lacunza, and it could not be silenced in South America.

In 1827 the Irving two-volume English translation was

---

[4] The procedure "provided that the matter should first be referred to the author himself, and his attention called to the objectionable passages. If the author then refused to deal with the congregation, or rejected the corrections that were required, the decree of condemnation was to be published."—*Catholic Encyclopedia*, vol. 13, art., "Roman Congregations," p. 143.
[5] Thus it stands on the official *Index Librorum Prohibitorum*; see "Ben-Ezra."
[6] Edward Irving, "Preliminary Discourse by the Translator" in Manuel Lacunza, *The Coming of Messiah* (Irving translation), vol. 1, pp. xv, xvi. Hereafter all references to *The Coming of Messiah* are to the Irving edition.
[7] Enrich, Chaneton, and Eyzaguirre each alludes to an edition in the United States; Enrich says, "after 1825," but no extant copy has been found. (See Vaucher, *op. cit.*, pp. 43, 46.)

published from the 1812 Cádiz printing, but checked with the 1826 Ackermann edition. In this way it became well and influentially known in Britain. Thus it had been translated into leading languages of Europe and had shaken the continent of South America, according to Ricci, while Chaneton says there was not an important town "from Havana to Cape Horn" to which Lacunza's book had not come. A one-volume abridged English edition was published in Dublin in 1833. And opinions in Mexico and South America continued to appear for and against Lacunza. Such was the turbulent career of this book, once having a really remarkable circulation, but now largely a forgotten volume. (Several early title pages, including a manuscript copy, reproduced on page 316.)

IV. Revives Early Church View on Millennium

1. FAVORABLE REPORT OF CARMELITE MONK.—The "Critique," a report of the work recommending publication, made by M. R. P. Fra Pablo, monk of the Barefooted Carmelite Order, to the vicar general of his order, and written at Cádiz, is most revealing. Dating his report December 17, 1812, he states that about twenty-one years prior, or about 1791, he had read Ben-Ezra's work in manuscript with deepest interest and had kept a copy constantly with him for frequent rereading.[8] He testifies to the author's profound study[9] and states that Lacunza's presentation had won his acceptance, though he was troubled over the number that hold the view of Augustine. But, he adds, "we know that this [Lacunza's] opinion is not new, but was held by the fathers of the first four centuries of the Christian era." [10]

That "the judgment of these first fathers should have been abandoned" he lays to the intermingling of errors and to veneration for Jerome and Augustine. However, "it came to lose ground, and at length to be given up." Then he adds, "The opinion has against it only the authority of the fathers and theologians from the end of the fourth century onward." [11]

---

[8] Manuel Lacunza, *The Coming of Messiah*, vol. 1, p. 3.
[9] *Ibid.*, p. 4.
[10] *Ibid.*, p. 5.
[11] *Ibid.*, p. 6.

And he holds that Lacunza's main point is that "Jesus Christ, with all the state of majesty and glory described to us in the divine books, is to come to our globe, not only to pronounce here definite sentence upon all the sons of Adam, but also, before the time of that judgment arrives, to reign in this world, and be acknowledged of all the nations of the earth together." [12]

Fra Pablo closes his report by declaring that Lacunza "infuses, moreover, into the mind a profound feeling of the truth of the Holy Scriptures, and draws to the perusal of them all believers, and especially the priests, to whom above all others belong the exact understanding and explanation of them." [13] Then he adds that the heart is filled with fear and trembling by the threatened calamity of the "holy church" being cast "into the outer darkness of infidelity in which they shall perish, forever lost to Christ Jesus the Saviour." [14]

2. Purpose: To Induce Study of Word.—In the dedication of his work "To The Messiah Jesus Christ," Lacunza says:

"I desire and purpose, to stir up, and even to oblige the priests to shake off the dust from their Bibles, inviting them to a new study and examination, a new and more attentive consideration of that Divine Book, which, though the book proper to the priesthood, as the instruments of his trade are to any artificer, appears in these times to have become to not a few of them the most useless of all books. What advantages might we not expect from this new study, were it possible to re-establish it among the priests, in themselves qualified, and by the church set apart for masters and teachers of the christian community!" [15]

In his Preface, Lacunza states that he did not wish to release his treatise to the reading public without first testing it upon learned men. But in this examination "a great curiosity" was aroused, and copies were made against his desire and widely circulated, even crossing the ocean to the Americas, "where they say it has caused no small stir." [16]

3. View Held in First Four Centuries.—Lacunza expressly states that his primary premise, of Christ's pre-millennial advent, "was so thought [held] during the first four centuries of

---

[12] *Ibid.*
[13] *Ibid.*, p. 8.
[14] *Ibid.*
[15] *Ibid.*, p. 9.
[16] *Ibid.*, p. 11.

LACUNZA'S *LA VENIDA* PRINTED IN MANY LANDS AND LANGUAGES

Appearing Initially in Manuscript Form in Europe and South America, It Was Printed First in Spain, at Cadiz (Upper Right), Then in England, France, Germany, Ireland, and Mexico, and Issued in Latin, Spanish, Italian, English, French, and German

the church; but the fourteen following centuries in which it has thought differently" have been given more weight.[17]

4. PRIESTHOOD SUBSTITUTES TRADITION FOR SCRIPTURE.— In his "Preliminary Discourse" Lacunza speaks of the peril that befell the Jewish church as their traditions swept aside the teachings of the Scriptures, and of the solemn parallel in the Christian church.[18] Then follows his serious indictment that the priesthood has fallen into "almost entire oblivion" as regards the Scriptures, leaning to the allegorical, mystical, and accommodated interpretation of the Scripture.

5. CHRIST TO RETURN AT APPOINTED TIME.—Plunging at once into the theme of the second advent, after having repudiated the current view, Lacunza says:

"Jesus Christ will return from heaven to the earth, when his time is come, when those times and seasons are arrived, *which the Father hath put in his own power. Acts i.7."* [19]

V. Views on Prophecy, Antichrist, Harlot, and Babylon

Lucunza's main argument concerns the establishment of his fundamental thesis—Christ's premillennial advent and subsequent glorious reign on earth. This he presents in a "masterly and convincing manner." [20] He wrote fearlessly on Antichrist, which has definite relationship to the millennium, for its destruction by Christ's coming was to precede and introduce it. Lacunza introduces the evidence of Daniel as well as that of the Apocalypse, though offering certain original and curious views on features of the symbols of the quadripartite image and the four wild beasts from the sea.

1. STONE KINGDOM TO SUCCEED DIVIDED EUROPE.—Lacunza included both Babylon and Persia under the head of gold, made the breast and arms of silver the Macedonian Empire, the brazen thighs as Roman, but the iron ten-toed legs, the Romano-Gothic professedly Christian kingdoms of "divided" Western Europe[21]

---

[17] *Ibid.,* p. 15. [18] *Ibid.,* pp. 25-27. [19] *Ibid.,* p. 57.
[20] E. B. Elliott, *Horæ Apocalypticæ* (5th ed.), vol. 4, p. 538 ff., where an excellent sketch of Lacunza's outline appears.
[21] Manuel Lacunza, *The Coming of Messiah,* vol. 1, pp. 137-141 (see William D. Smart's translated extracts, *A New Antichrist,* pp. 6-28).

—"Portugal, Spain, France, England, Germany, Poland, Hungary, Italy, Greece. In short, almost the whole of Europe, Asia Minor." [22] Thus he ends the prophecy as do others.

The stone without hands is the kingdom of Christ and His saints, that will utterly destroy the image in its last form. The significant point is that ten toes and the stone, as the final features of the outline, are essentially the same as the Protestant Historical position.

2. Continued Division Despite Intermarriages.—The agitation, movement, breaches, and combinations of the various parts of these kingdoms are then shown. [23] And the characteristic intermarriages of the rulers are likewise presented. But these kingdoms "though all contiguous to each other, as are the toes of the foot, set out by being divided and have continued divided, without interruption." [24]

3. Stone Kingdom Was Not Medieval Church.—The smiting by the stone and the filling of the earth by the mountain is by others, Lacunza says, regarded "as fully accomplished, and this great event as verified" [25] through the incarnation, with the mountain simply the "Christian church." [26] For authority, they cite one another. On the contrary, Lacunza contends that the two comings of Christ are "infinitely different" from each other, and we must not "confound that which belongs to the one with that which belongs to the other." [27] Lacunza declares that the "present church" has not "ruined, shivered, and pounded into dust and utterly consumed all the kingdoms figured in the statue, or in the toes of its feet," as demanded by the prophecy. [28] Then, he adds, "All this, and much more, which is in Scripture, must one day be verified, for till now they have not been verified." [29]

4. Announce Coming Kingdom to Earth's Sovereigns.—Then he speaks of this sacred obligation:

"To tell plainly and sincerely, all the existing sovereigns, that the kingdoms, principalities, powers, and lordships, are manifestly repre-

22 *Ibid.*, vol. 1, p. 141.   25 *Ibid.*, p. 146.   28 *Ibid.*, p. 151.
23 *Ibid.*, p. 142.   26 *Ibid.*, p. 142.   29 *Ibid.*, p. 152.
24 *Ibid.*, p. 143.   27 *Ibid.*, p. 148.

sented in the feet and toes of the statue, and to induce them with their own eyes to look into the Scriptures of truth. To tell them that their very kingdoms are the same which are immediately threatened with the blow of the stone." [30]

5. Curious Explanation of Four Beast-Kingdoms.—Lacunza's concept of the four beasts of Daniel 7 is novel and unsatisfactory. Noting the usual explanation of Daniel 7 as paralleling the kingdoms of Daniel 2, with the ten horns as the ten kingdoms,[31] he proposes another explanation. They are construed as four religions—idolatry, Mohammedanism, pseudo-Christianity, and anti-Christian deism, which is already unfolding itself to the world[32] in the French Revolution.

6. Antichrist Not an Individual but a Body.—To Lacunza, Antichrist was not an individual but was that embodied principle, power, or moral body which "dissolves" the faith of the church,[33] and which is to be destroyed by the second advent.[34] Lacunza analyzes and exposes the absurdity of the usual Romanist view of an individual Jew, of the tribe of Dan, born in Babylon, received of the Jews as Messiah, and conquering Jerusalem. Lacunza's protest against this standard Catholic position is very similar to the Protestant argument against such a hypothesis.[35] In certain features, however, Lacunza was a Futurist.

7. Antichrist Is Apostasy From the Church.—Lacunza then traces Antichrist, or the apocalyptic Beast, from its earliest germ as the mystery of iniquity in Paul's day, existing "by the side of and along with the mystical body of Christ." This defection will become more and more corrupt and apostate, century by century, till at length the apostasy is "entirely accomplished." [36] He then asks:

"Almost all the interpreters of the Apocalypse agree as to a general truth, that the terrible beast with the seven heads and ten horns, of which so much is said from the xiiith to the xixth chapters, is Antichrist himself. How then can this beast, and all the particular things spoken of it, be accommodated to, be possibly conceived of, an individual and singular person?" [37]

---

[30] *Ibid.*, p. 154.
[31] *Ibid.*, p. 155.
[32] *Ibid.*, pp. 164-173 (see Smart's version, pp. 29-50).
[33] *Ibid.*, pp. 197-199.
[34] *Ibid.*, pp. 196, 197.
[35] *Ibid.*, pp. 182-194, 204, 205.
[36] *Ibid.*, pp. 199, 200.
[37] *Ibid.*, p. 202.

8. Second Beast Symbolizes Roman Priesthood.—The second apocalyptic Beast, Lacunza says, is expounded by some as the false prophet of Antichrist—some individual person, perhaps an apostate bishop. But, holding the first beast to be a "moral body," he maintains that it is inconsistent to "conceive otherwise" of the second.[38] Then comes this really amazing declaration: "Now the new beast, this moral body composed of many seducers, will doubtless in those times prove infinitely more prejudicial than all the first beast, composed of seven heads, and armed with ten horns, every one of them crowned." [39] Expounding this contention, he adds:

"It is more than evident to every one who gives himself seriously to consider this metaphorical beast, that the whole of it is a prophecy of the miserable state in which the Christian church shall be in those times, and of the peril in which the greater number of believers shall be." [40]

And "fully persuaded of its truth, its importance, and even of its extreme necessity," Lacunza makes this dramatic announcement:

"Yes, my friend, our priesthood: this it is, and nothing else, which is here signified, and announced for the last times, under the metaphor of a beast with two horns like those of a lamb. Our priesthood, which like the good shepherd should defend the flock of Christ, and for it lay down their own lives, shall prove in those times its greatest scandal and most perilous snare." [41]

Small wonder there was consternation, and antipathy toward Lacunza's book!

9. Arraigns Priesthood for Perverse Character.— Charging that the iniquity, hypocrisy, and ambition of the Jewish priesthood in the time of Christ caused the rejection of Messiah at the first advent, he adds: "Has not the church of God in all times groaned under the load of many heresies, schisms, and scandals?" [42] Then he arraigns "the very priesthood of these times" as false shepherds:

"If still it appears too difficult to believe, that the christian priesthood of those times should be the only thing figured by the terrible

---

38 *Ibid.*, pp. 217, 218.   40 *Ibid.*   42 *Ibid.*, p. 221.
39 *Ibid.*, p. 219.   41 *Ibid.*, p. 220.

beast with two horns, reflect with new attention upon all the words and expressions of the prophecy, because nothing can be more distinct.... Tell me now, my friend, to what will all these things apply, think as you please, save to a wicked and perverse priesthood, such as that of the last times shall be? The doctors themselves acknowledge it to be so, they concede it in part, and this part once acknowledged, entitles us to ask the whole. Not finding any thing else to which they can apply what is said of the second beast, (besides that in the xvith and xixth chapters, the name of the false prophet is given to him) they commonly agree, that this beast or false prophet, will be some apostate bishop, full of iniquity, and diabolical malice, who shall stand on the side of Antichrist and accompany him in all his undertakings." [43]

"Sufficient then will it be, that the priesthood of these perilous times should be found in that same state, and with those same dispositions, in which the Hebrew priesthood were found at the time of Christ; that is to say, lukewarm, sensual, and worldly, without other desires, without other affections than belong to the earth, to the world, to the flesh, to self-love, wholly forgetful of Christ and of the gospel. All this seems intimated to me in that metaphorical expression which the Apostle makes use of, saying, that he saw this beast proceed or arise out of the earth." [44]

10. APOCALYPTIC HARLOT IS PAPAL, NOT PAGAN.—As to the apocalyptic Harlot of Revelation 17, Lacunza would fain omit discussion because of its delicacy and embarrassment, if that were not "to commit high treason against truth." [45] He observes that "the doctors do all agree, that the woman here spoken of is the city of Rome, in other times the capital of the greatest empire in the world, and now the capital and center of unity of the true Christian church." [46] Two opinions prevail: one, that "the prophecy was wholly accomplished, in past ages, in idolatrous and pagan Rome"; another, "that till this day it has not been fully accomplished; and [he] affirms that it will be accomplished in the times of Antichrist, in another Rome yet future, and very much changed from the present." [47]

Thus they have sought to "save the honour of the queen" by saying she has nought to fear—"the prophecy having been accomplished, many ages ago, upon pagan and idolatrous Rome," [48] or that it is "directed to other times yet to come, and

---

[43] *Ibid.*, pp. 223, 224.   [45] *Ibid.*, p. 239.   [47] *Ibid.*
[44] *Ibid.*, pp. 224, 225.   [46] *Ibid.*, p. 240.   [48] *Ibid.*

21

will not be verified upon the present Rome, upon Christian
Rome, upon Rome the head of the church of Christ, but upon
another Rome." [49]   These were, of course, the Preterist and
Futurist counterinterpretations introduced by the Jesuits in the
Counter Reformation.

Piling reason upon reason why these two positions are
untenable, Lacunza applies the symbol to the present corrupt
Christian church:

"What we say of the crimes of this woman [of Rev. 17], we say,
necessarily of her punishment also. Rome, not idolatrous but Christian,
not the head of the Roman empire but the head of Christendom, and
centre of unity of the true church of the living God, may very well,
without ceasing from this dignity, at some time or other incur the
guilt, and before God be held guilty of fornication with the kings of
the earth, and amenable to all its consequences. And in this there is
not any inconsistency, however much her defenders may shake the head." [50]

And in discussing the man of sin of 2 Thessalonians, Lacunza adds:

"The temple of God here spoken of, being then figurative and
spiritual, the whole mystery is thereby at once unlocked. The temple
of God whereof St. Paul speaketh, is nothing else than the church of
Christ, is nothing else than the congregation of all the faithful, is
nothing else than these believers united in one, who, as St. Peter
saith, 'as lively stones are built up a spiritual temple.' And this is the
temple of God, where the man of sin, the son of iniquity shall formally
sit, publicly shewing himself, and freely operating therein, as if he were
God: 'shewing himself that he is God.' And what may this mean?
What it means appears most clear and conformable to all which we
have observed above. It all proceeds towards one object without difficulty
or embarrassment. The man of sin, and son of perdition, is no other
in principle than a great number of true apostates, who having first
broken the bonds of Jesus, and disunited themselves from him, and so
verified in themselves what the apostle mentions first, *except there should
come a falling away first,* shall then unite into a moral body, and give
their labour to increase and strengthen it in all possible ways; and after
that has succeeded, shall rebel, and declare war against the same Jesus,
and against God his Father. Whence indeed to this man of sin the
name of Antichrist, or Contrachrist is given." [51]

Lacunza ends the discussion by this solemn declaration:

---

[49] *Ibid.*, p. 241.   [50] *Ibid.*, p. 252.   [51] *Ibid.*, p. 262.

"The particular things of which I treat are undeniably of the utmost importance, and of the utmost interest. While, on the other hand, the present system of things in the world, the actual estate of the Christian church, in many of its members, very like to that seventh angel of the Apocalypse, neither cold nor hot, Rev. iii.15. appear to cry loudly upon the ministers of religion, and to intreat them instantly to shake off sleep, to open their eyes, and to look about them and observe more attentively." [52]

This is not Rome pagan, he avers, but Rome Christian and papal, drunken in vain self-security, when actually on the eve of her utter destruction. If it be objected that she is the spouse of Christ, so, too, was old Jerusalem. But on the consummation of her apostasy, though without a heathen idol in her, she fell, and that without remedy. [53]

11. GREAT CITY IS PROFESSING CHRISTENDOM.—In his general view of the Apocalypse, Lacunza was still a Futurist, as were most Catholics. The seven-sealed Book is not clearly explained, nor is his conception of the woman of Revelation 12 clear. But the great city of Revelation 11 is professing Christendom. [54]

12. KINGDOM IS NOT YET COME.—Lacunza contends that present times demand a frank telling of the special message of God, not applicable in other times. [55] The kingdom of God, as indicated by the image-smiting stone that fills the earth, is not yet come. For that coming we ought to pray. [56]

13. BABYLON IS ROME ON THE TIBER.—Discussing the intent of Peter's term Babylon, Lacunza maintains that it is not literal Babylon on the Euphrates but Rome on the Tiber. [57] He calls attention to the fact that shortly before the execution of God's sentence against Babylon, a voice is heard counseling, "Come out of her, *My* people." [58]

14. TIME PERIODS ARE NOT UNDERSTOOD.—Of the prophetic time periods, Lacunza professes to know but little. The 1260 days—or forty-two months, or three and a half times—are the years during which the great tribulation of Antichrist among

[52] *Ibid.*, pp. 264, 265.   [53] *Ibid.*, pp. 248-253.
[54] *Ibid.*, vol. 2, p. 118; see Elliott, *op. cit.*, vol. 4, p. 542.
[55] Lacunza, *op. cit.*, p. 41.
[56] *Ibid.*, p. 44.   [57] *Ibid.*, p. 65.   [58] *Ibid.*, pp. 134, 135.

the Gentiles is to last.[59] The 1290 and 1335 days appeared "an impenetrable mystery." Perhaps, he suggested, the 1290 is shortened to the 1260 for the elect's sake.[60]

15. FOLLOWERS OF BEAST TO BE DESTROYED.—He declared that those who in any way gathered themselves together under the fourth beast of Daniel, or pertained to the two beasts of Revelation 13, were to be given to the burning flame.[61]

16. NEW EARTH AND JERUSALEM IMPENDING.—Lacunza believed the present heaven and earth would be destroyed, and a new heaven and earth of perfect beauty would ensue.[62] The paradisaical climate before the Flood would be restored,[63] the axis of the earth perhaps being restored to its original inclination.[64] He held that the New Jerusalem is a literal city to descend from God out of heaven.[65] Such were the astonishing views on prophecy of Lacunza the Jesuit.

VI. Lambert—Antichrist Is Roman Apostasy; Millennium Future

PÈRE BERNARD LAMBERT (d. 1813), Dominican monk of Province, southern France, was the second voice again bringing the millennial question to the forefront in Catholicism. His two-volume work on prophecy, *Exposition des predictions et des Promesses faites a l'Eglise pour les derniers temps de la Gentilité* (Expositions of the Predictions and Promises Made to the Church), appears to have been begun before the close of the eighteenth century,[66] completed about 1804, and published at Paris in 1806. So it was written after, though published before, Lacunza's treatise. It did not, however, have the circulation or the influence of the former.

Holding that the prevalent corruption and infidelity had reduced Christian faith to a "phantom," [67] Lambert observes that skeptics might well sneer at Christ's mission as a failure.

[59] *Ibid.*, p. 103.
[60] *Ibid.*, pp. 250, 251.
[61] *Ibid.*, pp. 216, 217.
[62] *Ibid.*, p. 231.
[63] *Ibid.*, pp. 232, 233.
[64] *Ibid.*, pp. 244, 245.
[65] *Ibid.*, pp. 258, 259.
[66] Le P. Bernard Lambert, *Exposition des predictions et des Promesses faites à l'Eglise pour les derniers temps de la Gentilité*, tom. 1, pp. 115, 56.
[67] *Ibid.*, pp. 22, 32, 53.

Lambert still held loosely to a Futurist Antichrist reigning for three and a half years, accompanied by Satan's loosing. But he, too, stresses the revolutionary view that the millennial reign of the saints is yet to come—to be introduced by the second personal advent of Christ, the destruction of Antichrist with his apostate church and Babylon, the resurrection of the saints and martyrs. Then the church will fill the earth, and Jerusalem will become the new center of light for a sabbatical period.[68] He based his beliefs on the multiple prophecies of Scripture.[69]

1. ROMAN POPE TO CONSUMMATE THE APOSTASY.—As E. B. Elliott (whose analysis I here follow) remarks, the propounded views were "new and strange for a Romanist." [70] Note them: The seven-hilled Babylon of the Apocalypse did *not* symbolize Pagan Rome, as Bossuet would have it. Nor did it symbolize Rome as falling into some new infidel apostasy, as Bellarmine had explained it. On the contrary, Lambert set forth the mystery of iniquity as the principle of corruption and perversion within the professing church, even back to apostolic days, that had grown through the centuries, nourished by the abuses, vices, errors, and impieties that had been admitted, and was at length to become the consummated *"apostasy,"* headed by a personal and papal Antichrist.[71]

While there have been many preparatory steps, Lambert avers that a Roman pope will head the consummated apostasy of Gentile Christendom, exacting divine honors and manifesting miraculous powers, and so fulfill the predictions of the man of sin and the apocalyptic Beast.[72]

2. FRENCH REVOLUTION HERALD OF CONSUMMATION. —Lambert believes that God will give special warnings of the near approach of the consummation. One such sign he thought to be the terrible infidelity of the French Revolution.[73] He also anticipated the coming and preaching of Elijah to both Jew and

---

[68] *Ibid.*, chapters 5 to 16.   [69] *Ibid.*, pp. 222, 223, 245.
[70] Elliott, *op. cit.*, vol. 4, p. 532.
[71] Lambert, *op. cit.*, tom. 2, pp. 318, 271. The explicit statements are quoted by Elliott, *op. cit.*, vol. 4, pp. 532, 533.
[72] Lambert, *op. cit.*, tom. 2, p. 314 ff.; also chap. 18.
[73] *Ibid.*, tom. 1, pp. 62-65, 71, 72.

Gentile.[74] Then, upon the consummation of the judgment,
Gentile Christendom would be destroyed by fire.[75] The scepter
would then revert to Jerusalem, which would be the center of
Isaiah's and John's new heaven and new earth.[76] Such is Elliott's
abstract of Lambert's teaching.[77]

3. SIGNS OF SIXTH SEAL ARE LITERAL.—As to certain details,
Lambert makes the signs of the sixth seal literal convulsions in
heaven and earth before the consummation.[78] The half hour's
silence is a brief respite before the last fearful trumpet judgments.[79] The French Revolution was like a trumpet peal of
alarm, "the *last* trumpet's alarm" to Christendom introductory
to the pouring out of the vials.[80]

4. ROMAN EMPIRE THE WITHHOLDING POWER.—The withholding power Lambert explains as the removal and division
into ten of the old Roman Empire, as the chronological sign and
epoch of the development of the man of sin.[81] Such were the
amazing views of the Dominican Father Lambert, at the turn
of the century, surpassed only by Lacunza's extended treatise
that attained such wide circulation.

---

[74] *Ibid.*, p. 171.   [75] *Ibid.*, pp. 100, 101.   [76] *Ibid.*, tom. 2, chap. 20.
[77] Elliott, *op. cit.*, vol. 4, pp. 532-535.
[78] Lambert, *op. cit.*, tom. 1, pp. 108, 117.
[79] *Ibid.*, p. 109.   [80] *Ibid.*, pp. 5, 72, 13, 14.   [81] *Ibid.*, tom. 2, p. 313 ff.

CHAPTER EIGHTEEN

Protestant Interpretation
Gathers Momentum

I. Papal Wound Introduces New Era

When Pius VI fell ill in 1797, Napoleon gave orders that in the event of his death no successor should be elected to his office, and that the Papacy should be "discontinued." [1] Rickaby observes, "No wonder that half Europe thought Napoleon's veto would be obeyed, and that with the Pope the Papacy was dead." [2] Leopold Ranke similarly says: It "now seemed that the papal power had been brought to a final close." [3]

The dethronement and captivity of Pope Pius VI, in 1798, by the sword of Berthier, had ended the 1260-year span from the elevation and liberation of the usurper Vigilius, in 538, by the arms of Belisarius and the gold of the Empress Theodora.[4] And when Pius VI died in French captivity, without a successor in sight, the outlook for the future of the Papacy seemed dark indeed. Thus G. Trevor wrote of it: "The papacy was extinct: not a vestige of its existence remained; and among all the Roman Catholic powers not a finger was stirred." [5]

However, Christian G. Thube, as noted in Volume 2, had warned that this was only a wound that would be healed.[6] And George Richards, in his Bampton Lecture for 1800, at Oxford

---

[1] Joseph Rickaby, S.J., *The Modern Papacy*, p. 1. [2] *Ibid.*
[3] Leopold Ranke, *The History of the Popes*, vol. 2, p. 459.
[4] See Volume 2 of *Prophetic Faith*.
[5] G. Trevor, *Rome From the Fall of the Western Empire*, p. 440.
[6] Christian G. Thube, *Das Buch des Propheten Daniels Neu übersekt und erklärt* (The Book of the Prophet Daniel newly translated and explained), p. 189.

University, on *The Divine Origin of Prophecy Illustrated and
Defended,* pointed to the close of the 1260 years as a most
striking fulfillment of prophetic exactness.[7] Thube says:

> "The French with the sword in their hands have exiled the pope
> and his cardinals totally from Rome, have destroyed the whole State
> of the Church, and erected a so-called Roman Free-State. . . . The present
> state of the papacy is this: that it has a wound from the sword, and
> nevertheless remains alive. How long this state will last thus, and in
> what the life of the papacy yet continuing will consist: that cannot yet be
> determined with certainty. The deadly wound will become healed again
> sooner or later. But how and by what it will be healed again, that likewise,
> we do not know before it will happen." [8]

Many others, as noted in Volume 2, declared that the
1260 years had ended. A new wave of prophetic study and exposition broke forth, and there was a general conviction among
such students that mankind had entered upon a new era—the
time of the last things.

II. Spotlight Shifts From Daniel 7 to Daniel 8

With the ending of the 1260 years of Daniel 7, allotted to
the exploits of the Little Horn, and brought to a close through
the French Revolution, the spotlight of prophetic interest and
concern moved from Daniel 7 over to Daniel 8, and the great
2300-year time period of verse 14. Over the span of the centuries prophetic study had shifted progressively from Rome,
the last of the four world powers, to Rome's divisions, then to
the identification of the little horn as the Papacy. And now,
after the close of the designated era of that Little Horn, only the
judgment scenes remain in the outline of Daniel 7. So, while
Daniel 7 and other prophecies are still of interest and concern,
the focal point of advanced study and discussion shifts to Daniel
8 after the French Revolution.

As we cross the threshold of the nineteenth century, many
of the treatises on prophecy by Protestant writers, from the very
first, deal with aspects of these 2300 years, particularly the closing

---

[7] George Richards, *The Divine Origin of Prophecy Illustrated and Defended,* p. 68.
[8] Christian G. Thube, *Anleitung zum richtigen Verstande der Offenbarung Johannis*
(Instruction for the Right Understanding of the Revelation of John), pp. 123, 124.

events. This period becomes the theme of principal inquiry by a growing number of earnest, competent students, seeking to determine the intent of the climax of this heretofore little-understood prophecy. It is a new emphasis. The correct dating of the period—its relation to other time periods, the accurate determination of its beginning year, the true length of the period itself, and the nature of the events to take place at its close, all become the quest of many minds and divers pens.

We shall now meet these men individually, first noting briefly their differing backgrounds, training, and achievements, and the events that had a bearing upon their study of prophecy, as well as their special contributions to the sum total of sound interpretation. Special note will be taken of their scholastic training, not to glorify learning or degrees, but to discover their mental caliber and competency for such exposition. Possessed of competent scholarship, these men were the intellectual peers of any in their day. They were not ignorant enthusiasts, but were unsurpassed in training, language, history, and theology, as well as in pulpit power and literary achievement.

And, as through the years men had come to sound conclusions through candid discussion of differing viewpoints, so this process for sifting and improvement becomes intensified in the nineteenth century. We shall begin with the early writers and follow progressively through the succeeding decades.

III. Hales—Dates Cross in 31 but Ends 2300 in 1880

The first Protestant expositor to be examined is WILLIAM HALES (1747-1831), famed for his *New Analysis of Chronology*, who was also a minister and an interpreter of prophecy. Born in Ireland, he was educated at Trinity College, Dublin, receiving his B.A. in 1768 and later his D.D. degree. After serving for a time as a tutor, he became a professor of Oriental languages, wearing a white wig to obviate objections of parents to his youthful appearance. Having taken orders in the Church of England in 1788, he resigned his professorship for the rectory,

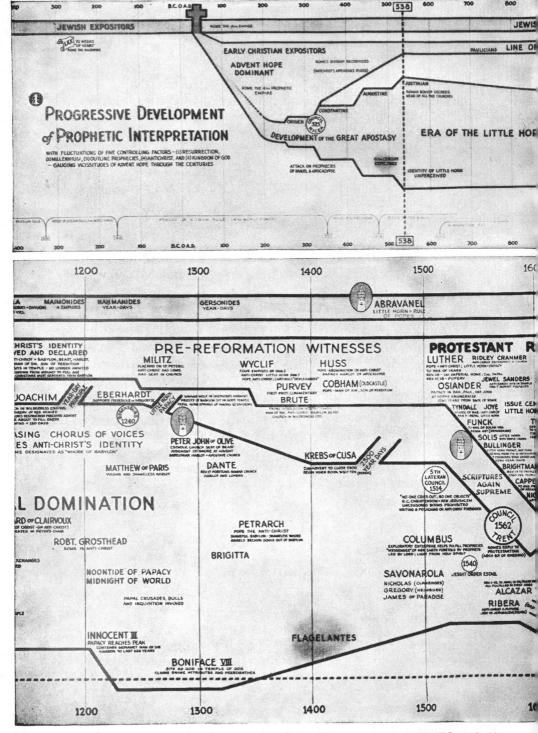

The Lower Chart Is an Enlargement of the Right-Hand Portion of the Upper Full-Length Chart. It Is Designed to Portray Nineteenth-Century Relationships and Sequences to the Developments of the Earlier Centuries Covered in *Prophetic Faith*, Volumes 1 and 2. The Particular Period of Present Study Is the Old World Advent Awakening, Involving the Proclamation of the Ending

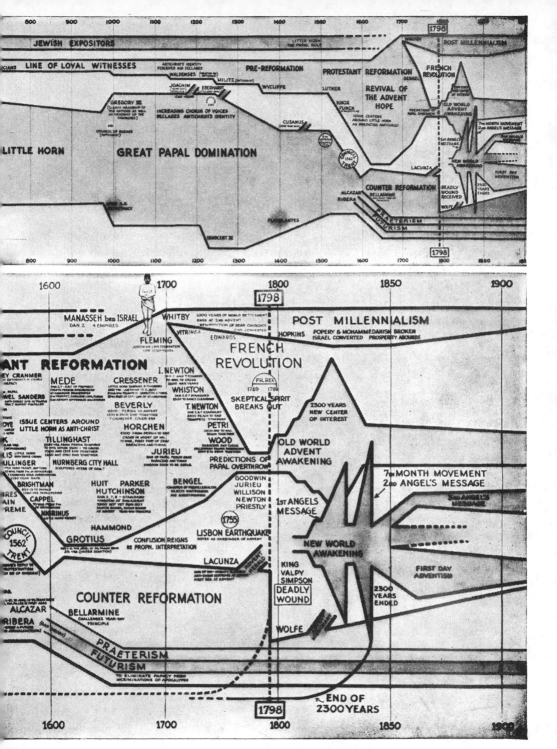

of the 2300 Years in 1843-44, With the Old World Phase Slightly Antedating but Reaching Its Climax in the New. The Details and Expansions of the Final Segment Appear on Pages 266, 267. The Slight Duplication of the Cuts Where the Pages Join Is to Facilitate the Complete Reading of Each. The Other Portions of the Lower Segment Appear in Volume 2.

where he lived in retirement. Here he devoted much of the
rest of his life to research and writing, in 1812 holding the chan-
cellorship of the diocese.[9]

Hales was author of twenty-two works. He wrote in the
fields of science, including astronomy, as well as in theology,
chronology, and prophecy. One of Hales' works was a vindication of Newton, and his *Dissertations on the Principal Prophecies* was issued in 1808. But back in 1803-04, writing under
the pen name of "The Inspector," he took issue with others in
a series of articles headed "Sacred Criticism" in *The Orthodox
Churchman's Magazine*, over the true number of Daniel 8:14—
whether 2400 or 2300.[10] Hales contended that the "2300" is
one of the best authenticated numbers in all Scripture.[11] In its
chronological position he followed Hans Wood of Rossmead,
Ireland,[12] holding the seventy weeks to be the first segment of
the 2300 years. This position he confirmed in his best-known
work, *A New Analysis of Chronology* (1809-1812), based on
original sources, and the result of twenty years' study. His
Synopsis of the Signs of the Times was published in 1817.

1. MAINTAINS STANDARD EXPOSITION OF DANIEL 2 AND 7.—
Quite a section of volume 2 of *A New Analysis of Chronology* is
devoted by Hales to an expository outline of the prophecies,
which form the setting and framework for his chronology. He
here shows the relationship and paralleling character of the
prophecies of Daniel 2, 7, 8, and 11. His chronology is thus
based upon Babylon, Persia, Grecia, Rome, and Rome's divisions, followed by the eternal kingdom of Christ.[13] The ten
kingdoms are tabulated as the Huns, Ostrogoths, Visigoths,
Franks, Vandals, Suevi, Burgundians, Heruli, Saxons, and
Longobards.[14] The little horn is declared to be the Papacy, and
the three uprooted horn-kingdoms are identified as the Heruli,
Ostrogoths, and Lombards.[15]

---

[9] *Dictionary of National Biography*, 1921-22 ed., vol. 8, p. 922. There is also an 1885-89
edition of this work; unless otherwise noted, all references are to the 1921 edition.
[10] *The Orthodox Churchman's Magazine*, 1803-1804, vols. 4-6.
[11] *Ibid.*, Feb., 1804 (vol. 6), p. 75.   [12] See Volume 2 of *Prophetic Faith*.
[13] William Hales, *A New Analysis of Chronology*, vol. 2, pp. 536-538.
[14] *Ibid.*, p. 537.   [15] *Ibid.*

2. MAKES 1880 TERMINUS OF 1260 AND 2300.—Hales' location of the time periods is odd and isolated among nineteenth-century writers. Though consistently applying the year-day principle, he terminates the 1260 and 2300 years in 1880. The origin and reason for this position will be noted later. But the 1260 years are located from A.D. 620 to 1880, and the 2300 are dated from 420 B.C. to A.D. 1880, with the seventy weeks as from 420 B.C. to A.D. 70.[16] The 1290 years he places from A.D. 70 to 1360—the time of Wyclif;[17] and the 1335 years are dated from A.D. 70 to 1405—the time of Huss.[18] These were all rather speculative.

3. CORRECTNESS OF 2300 VERSUS SEPTUAGINT 2400.—However, as to the reliability of the 2300-year figure of Daniel 8:14 as against the Septuagint 2400, Hales emphatically asserts, as the conclusion from extensive research:

"There is no number in the Bible whose genuineness is better ascertained than that of the 2300 days. It is found in all the printed Hebrew editions, in all the MSS. of *Kennicott* and *De Rossi's* collations, and in all the *ancient Versions*, except the *Vatican* copy of the Septuagint, which reads 2400, followed by Symmachus; and some copies noticed by *Jerom*, 2200; both evidently *literal* errors in excess and defect, which compensate each other, and confirm the mean, 2300." [19]

4. CRUCIFIXION IN MIDST OF WEEK IN A.D. 31.—Recognizing the seventy weeks as "weeks of years," and therefore "without doubt, 490 years," [20] Hales frankly discloses the origin of his unusual position in terminating the seventy weeks in A.D. 70— which leads to the extension of the 1800 remaining years of the 2300 period to 1880.[21] But the cross is securely placed in A.D. 31, in the *midst* of the one week of years, with the end year placed in 34 thus:

" '*After* the sixty-two weeks,' but not immediately, 'the MESSIAH was *cut off*'; for the sixty-two weeks expired in A.D. 14; and the *one* week, or *passion week*, in the midst of which OUR LORD was crucified, A.D. 31, began with his public ministry, A.D. 28, and ended with the martyrdom of *Stephen*, A.D. 34." [22]

---

[16] *Ibid.*, p. 537.
[17] *Ibid.*, pp. 538, 568-570.
[18] *Ibid.*, pp. 538, 570.
[19] *Ibid.*, p. 557.
[22] *Ibid.*, p. 564.
[20] *Ibid.*, p. 560.
[21] *Ibid.*

But along with his dating of the seventieth week, comes this curious interpretation of the segments of the seventy weeks. Though somewhat technical and tedious, his reasoning is well worth following:

"The *passion* week, therefore, began two [prophetic] weeks after the sixty-two weeks, or at the end of the sixty-four weeks; and there were five weeks, or thirty-five years, after the passion week, to the destruction of *Jerusalem*. So that the seventy weeks must be *chronologically* divided into sixty-four, one, and five weeks." [23]

5. BORROWED "ADJUSTMENT" SCHEME FROM WOOD.—The footnote to the foregoing statement, crediting Hans Wood[24] of Ireland with the origin of this scheme, is a statement of great importance to our study:

"This simple and ingenious adjustment of the *chronology* of the seventy weeks, considered as forming a branch of the 2300 days, was originally due to the sagacity of Hans Wood, Esq. of Rossmead in the county of Westmeath, Ireland, and published by him in an anonymous *Commentary on the Revelation of St. John*, London, 1787. Payne. 8vo. Whence I republished it in the *Inspector*, 8vo. 1799. And afterwards, in the *Orthodox Churchman's Magazine*, 1803; and now more correctly, 1809." [25]

6. EARLIEST PUBLISHING OF SCHEME IN 1799.—Hales' first employment of the scheme was in *The Inspector, or Select Literary Intelligence* (1799).[26] Here Hales ends the seventy weeks in A.D. 70.[27] Then he says it is "exactly 490 years from the assumed commencement of the 70 weeks, and also of the grand prophetic period of 2300 days, B.C. 420." [28]

But the three key dates of the "one week" are now set as of A.D. 27, 31, and 34, thus:

"And after the *sixty and two weeks*, before specified, as the largest division of the 70, was the ANOINTED [LEADER] '*cut off*' judicially, by an

[23] *Ibid.*
[24] Hans Wood's exposition, *The Revelation of St. John*, was issued with the pseudonym "Jn M——D" signed to the preface. The British Museum copy (680.d.4) has "Hans Wood" written on the preface page, just below the signature. The accuracy of this identification is likewise attested by Samuel Halkett and John Laing, *Dictionary of Anonymous and Pseudonymous English Literature*, vol. 5, p. 106, and by J. W. Brooks in his *Dictionary of Writers on the Prophecies*, p. xcv.
[25] Hales, *op. cit.*, vol. 2, pp. 564, 565. This quotation identifies "The Inspector" as Hales.
[26] For a good review of this volume see *The Gentleman's Magazine*, October, 1799, pp. 865-872.
[27] William Hales, *The Inspector, or Select Literary Intelligence*, p. 205.
[28] *Ibid.*, p. 206.

iniquitous sentence, *in the midst of the one week,* which formed the third and last division, and began with our Lord's Baptism, about A.D. 27.—'when he was beginning to be *thirty* years of age,' and commenced his mission, which lasted *three years and half* until his crucifixion, about A.D. 31.

"27. During this *one week,* which ended about A.D. 34 (about the martyrdom of *Stephen,*) a *new covenant* was established with many of the Jews, of every class; in the midst of which the Temple sacrifice was virtually abrogated by the *all-sufficient* sacrifice of *the Lamb of God that taketh away the sins* of the [repentant and believing] *world.*" [29]

In this he follows Wood by making a gap between the "62 weeks" and the "Passion Week." [30]

7. REPEATS A.D. 1880 DATING IN 1803.—In the series of articles in *The Orthodox Churchman's Magazine,* Hales, under his nom de plume "Inspector," says, in the August, 1803, issue, that the "attentive reader" of the "chronological prophecies of Daniel"—

"will find *internal evidence* the most cogent and irresistible, that this most famous prophecy will not be fulfilled, till the grand *prophetic period* of two thousand three hundred days (Dan. viii. 13-14.) shall be finished; which, according to my reckoning, will expire about A.D. 1880." [31]

8. TWO-HORNED BEAST IS MOHAMMEDANISM.—In the October issue Hales interprets the four beasts of Daniel 7 to symbolize the Babylonians, Medo-Persians, Macedo-Grecians, and Romans, with the Little Horn as the "Roman *Ecclesiastical* Power of the papacy," which plucked up three.[32] The "idolatries and corruptions" of the power of Daniel 11:36, 39 are likewise applied to the Papacy.[33] In his November article, Hales again stresses the "papal Antichrist" of Daniel 7, and identifies the first beast of Revelation 13 as the same.[34] But the second, or two-horned beast, he applies to the "Apostate *Greek* Church," centered in Constantinople, afterward succeeded by the "Apostate Mahometan church," with 666 as the number of Mohammed's name.[35]

29 *Ibid.,* p. 207.
30 *Ibid.,* p. 208.
31 *The Orthodox Churchman's Magazine,* August, 1803 (vol. 5), p. 80.
32 *Ibid.,* October, 1803 (vol. 5), pp. 214-216.
33 *Ibid.,* pp. 215, 216.
34 *Ibid.,* November, 1803 (vol. 5), pp. 280, 281.
35 *Ibid.,* p. 281.

9. BEGINNING OF 1260 COUNTED BACK FROM 1880.—On the assumption that the 1260 years end simultaneously with the 2300 years in 1880, Hales says:

"If then we count backwards 1260 years from A.D. 1880, their termination, as already shewn; it will give A.D. 620, for the commencement of this disastrous period of the sufferings of the *'two thoughtful witnesses;'* about the time of the adoption of the *Gregorian Liturgy* in the west, and of the publication of *Mahomet's* visions and revelations in the east." [36]

10. A.D. 620 COMPARED WITH EARLIER DATINGS.—Hales then tabulates the varied attempts of men in earlier generations to determine the beginning of the 1260 years—Whiston, 455 or 456; Isaac Newton, 378 or 379; King and Valpy, from 538,[37] and ending in 1798; and Bishop Newton, from 606.[38] Then Hales cites Hans Wood, the layman of Ireland, in these words:

"To this most sagacious and original expositor, perhaps, since the days of *Mede,* we owe the important *Chronological* adjustment of the three divisions of *Daniel's* seventy weeks; which I endeavoured to support and establish, in the INSPECTOR, 1798; the termination of the grand prophetic period of 2300 days in the year, A.D. 1880, and the commencement of the period of general persecution, A.D. 620, which I have here adopted; and I am now at liberty to divulge the name of this truly pious, learned, and respectable *Layman,* which his obstinate modesty forbad, during his lifetime, the late *Hans Wood,* Esq. of Rossmead, in the county of Westmeath, Ireland; who *is gone to his reward!"* [39]

Then Hales comments that the Romanists, "to elude the force of this prophecy," take the 1260 as a literal and future three and a half years. But he adds that the choice lies between Bishop Newton and Wood—"of which the latter is most comprehensive, as including the Mohametan, who surely is equally entitled to the palm of *persecution,* with his predecessor, the *Papal* antichrist." [40]

11. CHOOSES WOOD'S CALCULATION OUT OF MANY.—So in February, 1804, Hales made his initial declaration of the basic soundness of the 2300 years,[41] later repeated in his *New Analysis*

---

[36] *Ibid.,* December, 1803 (vol. 5), pp. 340, 341.
[37] See Volume 2 of *Prophetic Faith.*
[38] *The Orthodox Churchman's Magazine,* December, 1803 (vol. 5), **pp. 341, 342.**
[39] *Ibid.,* p. 342.   [40] *Ibid.,* p. 342.
[41] *Ibid.,* February, 1804 (vol. 6), p. 75.

of Chronology, as noted.   He then declares that "the end of the 2300 years is not yet come." [42]   As he comments on the attempts of others to fix their location, he adds: "The most judicious modern Critics, look forward to some future termination of the 2300 days, reckoning from different periods." [43]   Thus, while adopting the hypothesis of Hans Wood[44]—terminating the 2300 years in 1880, and embracing the 1260-, 1290-, and 1335-year periods— Hales steadfastly holds the passion week of years as of A.D. 27-8, 31, and 34, giving technical authorities in support.[45]   This is destined to be of great importance in our future quest.

IV. Buck's Dictionary—391-Year Period to End About 1844

Another early expositor was CHARLES BUCK (1771-1815), Independent minister and theological writer, who first served in Sheerness, then Hackney, and finally in London.[46]   Though the author of numerous works, he is remembered chiefly for his comprehensive *Theological Dictionary,* first appearing in 1802, but which passed through many reprints.   Under the heading "Mahometanism, sec. IV," Buck observes:

"From the aspect of Scripture prophecy, that, triumphant as this sect has been, it shall at last come to nought.   As it arose as a scourge to Christendom about the time that Antichrist obtained a temporal dominion, so it is not improbable but they will have their downfall nearly at the same period." [47]

Then, coming to the specific prophecy of Revelation 9, Buck makes this notable record in his *Dictionary* (also noting the witness of Newton, Mede, Gill, Simpson, Miller, and White for reference for the student of this portion of prophecy):

"The ninth chapter of Revelations seems to refer wholly to this imposture: 'The four angels were loosed,' says the prediction, 15th verse, 'which were prepared for an hour, and a day, and a month, and a year, for to slay the third part of men.'   This period in the language of prophecy, makes 391 years, which, being added to the year when the four angels were loosed, will bring us down to 1844, or there-

---

[42] *Ibid.,* p. 80.   [43] *Ibid.,* p. 81.   [44] *Ibid.,* p. 82.
[45] *Ibid.,* pp. 82, 83.
[46] See John Styles, *Memoirs and Remains of the Late Rev. Charles Buck,* pp. 310, 311; S. A. Allibone, *A Critical Dictionary of English Literature and British and American Authors,* p. 276.
[47] Charles Buck, *A Theological Dictionary,* 3d ed., pp. 64, 65.

abouts, for the final destruction of the Mahometan empire. It must be confessed, however, that, though the event is certain, the exact time cannot be easily ascertained." [48]

So at the very outset of the century this time period was in the forefront. This, too, will become increasingly a matter of emphasis.

V. Whitaker—Makes Little Contribution; Favors 2400

Passing mention should be made of EDWARD W. WHITAKER (1752-1818), Church of England clergyman and historian, who graduated from Christ Church, Oxford, in 1777. He was made rector of St. Johns, Clerkenwell, in 1778, then of St. Mildred's, London, and All Saints, Canterbury. From 1783 to his death he served as rector of St. Mary-de-Castro, Canterbury. He was founder of the Refuge for the Destitute, fostered a school, and was author of numerous works.[49] Among these were his *General and Connected View of the Prophecies Relating to the Times of the Gentiles* (1795), *Commentary on the Revelation of St. John* (1802), and *The Manual of Prophecy* (1808), as well as *A Complete System of Universal History* (1821). In prophetic interpretation Whitaker made little constructive contribution. He favored the Vatican Septuagint reading of 2400 for Daniel 8:14. He tried vainly to harmonize the 1260 days with this number by halving it. But he is frequently quoted, and his unfortunate emphasis of the 2400 reading exerted quite an influence.

VI. Faber—Blends Faulty Applications With Sound Principles

Of much prominence was GEORGE STANLEY FABER (1773-1854), "controversialist" prebendary of Salisbury Cathedral. He was born at Calverley, Yorkshire, the son of a minister. Educated at University College, Oxford, he received a B.A. in 1793, an M.A. in 1796, and a B.D. degree in 1803. Bampton lecturer

---

[48] *Ibid.*, p. 65.
[49] *Alumni Oxonienses*, 1715-1886, vol. 4, p. 1537; *Dictionary of National Biography*, vol. 21, p. 15.

in 1801, he was curate at Calverley from 1803 to 1805. He later served at Stockton-upon-Tees, Durham, and at Long Newton, where he remained twenty-one years. In 1830 he was made prebendary of Salisbury Cathedral. He was a stalwart advocate of the evangelical faith and the sole authority of Scripture as the rule of faith.

Faber belonged to the Historical School of prophetic interpretation, but brought the reinstated Napoleon of 1815 heavily into his scheme. Of profound learning, he was an uncompromising advocate of his convictions and conclusions. He was author of forty-two works, spanning a period of fifty-five years—from 1799 to 1853. He was the most voluminous religious writer of his generation, few having written so much or so long,[50] five columns being devoted to his works in the British Museum catalogue. His writings on prophecy were numerous and were the center of vigorous discussion for nearly half a century. One of his interesting books was *An Inquiry into the History and Theology of the Ancient Vallenses and Albigenses* (1838).

Many of his works were answered in print. Among those who wrote against him were Thomas Arnold, Shute Barrington (bishop of Durham), Christopher Bethell (bishop of Gloucester), George Corless, William Cuninghame, James H. Frere, Richard H. Graves, Thomas Harding (vicar of Bexley), F. C. Husenbeth, Samuel Lee, S. R. Maitland, N. Nisbett, Thomas P. Pantin, Le Pappe de Trévern, and E. W. Whitaker. So he was the center of continual controversy. The burden of his writing is indicated by the progression of titles:

Two Sermons before the University of Oxford, an attempt to explain by recent events five of the Seven Vials mentioned in the Revelations (1799); *A Dissertation on the Prophecies . . . Relative to the Great Period of 1260 Years* (1804); *Supplement to the Dissertation on the 1260 Years* (1806); *A General and Connected View of the Prophecies, Relative to the Conversion . . . of . . . Judah and Israel; the . . . Overthrow of the Antichris-*

---

[50] *The Gentleman's Magazine*, May, 1854, pp. 537-539; Allibone, *op. cit.*, pp. 573, 574; *Dictionary of National Biography*, vol. 6, pp. 975, 976.

tian Confederacy in . . . Palestine; and the . . . Diffusion of Christianity (1808); *Dissertation on the Prophecy Contained in Daniel IX.* (1811).

Another group continues the general theme: *Remarks on the Effusion of the Fifth Apocalyptic Vial and . . . the Restoration of the Imperial Revolutionary Government of France* (1815); *The Sacred Calendar of Prophecy: or a Dissertation on the Prophecies . . . of the Grand Period of Seven Times, and Especially of Its Second Moiety, or the Latter Three Times and a Half* (1828); *The Difficulties of Romanism* (1830); *Eight Dissertations on Prophetical Passages of Holy Scripture* (1845); *Letters on Tractarian Secessions to Popery* (1846); and *Napoleon III, Man of Prophecy* (1852).

In the Introduction to his *Dissertation on the Prophecies . . . Relative to the Great Period of the 1260 Years,* Faber maintains that "the interpretation of Prophecy knowledge is undoubtedly progressive," having been "gradually opened partly by the hand of time and partly by human labour undertaken in humble dependence upon the divine aid." [51] And as the "time of the end" comes, we may expect that "many will run to and fro and knowledge will be increased." In his first chapter Faber maintains that the persecutions of pagan Rome have nothing to do with the 1260 years, which are "the period of the dominance of the great Apostasy, and of the reign of the two little horns" of Daniel.[52]

1. MAINTAINS STANDARD VIEW FOR DANIEL 7.—The standard historical position on the four kingdoms of Babylon, Medo-Persia, Grecia, and Rome is held for Daniel 2 and 7, with the ten horns of the division, and the Little Horn as "the papacy," [53] "or spiritual kingdom of the Bishop of Rome." Faber follows Machiavelli and Bishop Lloyd for the listing and dating of the ten kingdoms.[54] The three horns plucked up to make way for it are tabulated as the Heruli, Ostrogoths, and Lombards.[55]

---

[51] George Stanley Faber, *A Dissertation on the Prophecies . . . Relative to the Great Period of the 1260 Years* (1807 ed.), vol. 1, p. v.
[52] *Ibid.,* p. 8.
[53] *Ibid.,* vol. 1, p. xxxiv, 154, 186.
[54] *Ibid.,* pp. 186, 187.
[55] *Ibid.,* pp. xxxiv, 183.

2. APPLIES LITTLE HORN OF DANIEL 8 TO MOHAMMEDAN-
ISM.—The usual interpretation of the Medo-Persian ram and
the Grecian goat is given, with Alexander as the great horn.[56]
But the little horn that became exceeding great, he avows, "relates to Mohammedanism." [57]

3. EXTENDS 1260 YEARS FROM 606 TO 1866.—Faber seeks to
apply the 1260 years to the "appointed hour" of both the papal
and the Mohammedan powers, and fixes upon 606 as the most
probable date that synchronizes for the two, as "the year 606 is
the most proper date of the Mohammedan imposture," when
Mohammed retired to the cave of Hera.[58] Likewise with 606
for the papal horn—"when *the Pope* was declared *Universal
Bishop and Supreme head of the Catholic Church,* it became a
mighty ecclesiastical empire." [59] This Mohammedan aspect explains his insistence upon the period 606-1866, rather than the
period from Justinian to the French Revolution.

4. TERMINATES 2300 WITH 1260 IN 1866.—Faber holds,
further, that the 2300 years of Daniel 8:14 and the 1260-year
periods both reach to the "time of the end" and "terminate
together *in the selfsame year.*" This he believes to be 1866.[60]
Expounding this, he adds:

> "It necessarily follows, that, *since the period of 2300 days,* and
> *the period of 1260 days,* both equally reach *to the time of the end,* or
> *to the end of the period of the wonders,* they both exactly terminate
> together. Thus it appears, that *the period of 1260 days* is in fact *the
> latter part of the greater period of 2300 days.*" [61]

Faber alludes to the variant readings of 2300 or 2400 but
does not argue for the merits of the 2400.[62] However, he does
say that the sanctuary was *"the spiritual sanctuary of the Christian church, not the literal sanctuary of the Jewish temple.* (See
Rev. xi. 1,2.)." [63] And Mohammedanism, in its spread, "took
away the *daily sacrifice* of praise and thanksgiving; polluted
the *spiritual sanctuary;* and presumed to magnify itself against

---

[56] *Ibid.*, pp. xxxv, 206.
[57] *Ibid.*, pp. xxv, 223.
[58] *Ibid.*, vol. 2, pp. 456, 461.
[59] *Ibid.*, p. 457.

[60] *Ibid.*, vol. 1, p. 459.
[61] *Ibid.*, p. 224.
[62] *Ibid.*, p. 225.
[63] *Ibid.*, p. 225 n.

even the *Prince of princes*." [64] The latter part of Daniel 11,
Faber applies to infidelic France. [65]

5. EARLY TRUMPETS REMOVE "LET" TO PAPAL DEVELOP-
MENT.—In volume 2, Faber deals with the first four trumpets
as preparing "the way for the man of sin" by taking away the
power which "prevented the revelation of the man of sin." [66]
These include Alaric and the Huns, Genseric and the Vandals,
and the "extinction of the line of Western Caesars." [67]

6. FIFTH TRUMPET SARACENS; SIXTH IS TURKISH.—The
fifth, or first-woe, trumpet, "in the East," is applied to "Mohammed with his Saracenic locusts," [68] for *"five prophetic months or
150 years."* [69] And the sixth, or second-woe, trumpet refers to
the four sultanies of the Turkish horsemen "loosed from the
river Euphrates" [70] for 391 years and 15 days. [71] This period he
terminates in 1672, at the siege of Cameniec. [72]

7. LITTLE BOOK THE RECORD OF APOSTASY.—Faber comprehends in the "contents of the little book" the "history of the
Western Apostacy" in Revelation 11 to 14. [73] He does not believe that the Two Witnesses are the Old and New Testaments,
but says that they are Christ's witnesses of the centuries. [74] The
woman of Revelation 12 is "the spiritual Church of true believers." [75]

8. TWO-HORNED BEAST SAME AS LITTLE HORN.—Faber
makes the ten-horned beast from the sea of Revelation 13 the
same as the fourth beast of Daniel 7. [76] And the two-horned
beast is not infidelic France but the "catholic spiritual empire of
the church of Rome, considered as including both the Pope his
head, and the regular and secular papal clergy his two lamb-like
horns." [77] *Latinus* is a name containing the number 666. [78]

9. IDENTITY OF SEVEN HEADS AND TEN HORNS.—The seven
heads he lists as kings, consuls, dictators, decemvirs, military

---

[64] *Ibid.*, p. 458.
[65] *Ibid.*, pp. xxxvi, xxxii, and chap. VI.
[66] *Ibid.*, vol. 2, pp. iii, 7.
[67] *Ibid.*, pp. iii, 8-22.
[68] *Ibid.*, pp. iv, 31.
[69] *Ibid.*, p. 459.
[70] *Ibid.*, pp. iv, 38.
[71] *Ibid.*, p. 459.
[72] *Ibid.*, vol. 2, p. 317; also *Supplement*, p. 72.
[73] *Ibid.*, pp. 45, 46.
[74] *Ibid.*, pp. v, 53-56.
[75] *Ibid.*, pp. vii, 126.
[76] *Ibid.*, pp. vii, 170.
[77] *Ibid.*, pp. ix, 259, 471.
[78] *Ibid.*, pp. x, 313.

tribunes, Augustan emperors, and Carlovingian Patricio-emperors. And the "ten primitive horns" are the Huns, Ostrogoths, Visigoths, Franks, Vandals, Sueves and Alans, Burgundians, Heruli, Saxons, and Lombards—with the Little Horn as *"the ecclesiastical kingdom of the Pope."* [79] The three horns plucked up were the Heruli, Ostrogoths, and Lombards.[80] The two-horned beast of Revelation 13 "occupies the place of the *little horn,* which is not mentioned by John." [81] However, the two-horned beast is made the same as the great scarlet whore—the "adulterous tyrannical church of Rome, or the spiritual catholic empire of the Pope." [82]

10. EARTHQUAKE AND VIALS IN FRENCH REVOLUTION.—Faber relegates the flying angels of Revelation 14 to the past—Lutheranism, Calvinism, and the Church of England reformations.[83] The seven vials are all poured out after August, 1792.[84] The great earthquake, or violent revolution, when a tenth part of the great Roman city fell, Faber applies to the French Revolution, breaking out in 1789.[85] The first shock of the "great earthquake" which overthrows the "tenth part of the Roman City," or French monarchy, struck in 1789.[86]

11. CALCULATING AND DATING THE SEVENTY WEEKS.—Faber's *Dissertation on the Prophecy Contained in Daniel IX.24-27; Generally Denominated the Prophecy of the Seventy Weeks* (1811) is a discussion of unusual clarity and value in certain sections. It concerns not only the choice of the seventh year of Artaxerxes for the initial year rather than the preceding decrees of Cyrus or Darius, but the nature of those years—whether solar or lunar. Much confusion had existed on this point, and the principle involved all time prophecy. He begins with a broad discussion of Jewish calendation and the methods of periodic monthly intercalation,[87] namely, lengthening the

[79] *Ibid.*, pp. 238, 239.
[80] *Ibid.*, p. 239.
[81] *Ibid.*
[82] *Ibid.*
[83] *Ibid.*, pp. x, xi, 336-342.
[85] *Ibid.*, pp. 94, 95.
[84] *Ibid.*, pp. xi, 351 ff.
[86] *Supplement*, pp. 78, 167. (This extensive and repetitious 106-page *Supplement* to Faber's *Dissertation . . . on the 1260 Years* was issued chiefly to meet the criticisms of Edward W. Whitaker. Nothing new appears.)
[87] George Stanley Faber, *Dissertation on the Prophecy Contained in Daniel IX.24-27,* pp. xiv, 9, 10, 38.

year by adding supernumerary days at the close in the month
Ve-Adar.[88] Arguing from the case of the two great Jewish festivals—the Passover fixed to the spring, and the Day of Atonement fixed to the autumn—Faber reaches this fundamental
conclusion: "The fixed nature of the great festivals proves, that
a *series* of such years must have been equal to a corresponding
series of solar years." [89] This principle is basic to sound interpretation.

12. JEWISH YEARS MUST EQUAL SOLAR YEARS.—This thesis,
he adds, is supported by Jackson, Prideaux, Sir Isaac Newton,
Blayney, and Davies.[90] And Faber repeats:

"A series of Jewish years must have been equal to a series of solar
years." [91]
"Whence it will follow, that the 490 years of the seventy weeks must,
either singly or collectively, be equal to 490 solar years." [92]

13. ALL PROPHETIC TIME FULFILLED IN SOLAR YEARS.—
While the Jewish years perpetually fluctuated in the exact
length, they always average the same number as the solar years,
so that the festivals of Nisan, or Abib (first month), and Tisri
(seventh month) did not circulate but were fixed.[93] Stressing,
then, that "the years of the seventy weeks are solar years," he
adds that "by a parity of argument we must likewise conclude,
that the 1260 years and the years of every numerical prophecy
are either *individually* solar years, or *collectively* solar years." [94]
Then comes the vital conclusion: *"No interpretation of the
prophecy, which is founded on the system of lunar or abbreviated years of either description, can be deemed admissible."* [95]

14. REASONS FOR THE SEVENTH OF ARTAXERXES.—Coming
next to the three decrees of the first year of Cyrus (536 B.C.),
the third year of Darius Hystaspes (519 B.C.), and the seventh
year of Artaxerxes Longimanus (458 B.C.), as well as the verbal
permission of the twentieth year of Artaxerxes,[96] Faber asserts

---

88 *Ibid.*, p. 75.
89 *Ibid.*, pp. xv, 47.
90 *Ibid.*, pp. xv, 49-65.
96 *Ibid.*, pp. xvi, 82-106.   These are tabulated on p. 107.
91 *Ibid.*, pp. xv, 75.
92 *Ibid.*, pp. xv, 76.
93 *Ibid.*, p. 75.
94 *Ibid.*, p. 77.
95 *Ibid.*, pp. xv, 77.

that no interpretation can be admitted that does not compute the seventy weeks from one of these established dates.[97] He then presents a series of objections to using the twentieth of Artaxerxes.[98] This method he pursues with each date, as well as citing their supporters.[99] After thorough examination he concludes that it must be dated from the decree of the seventh year of Artaxerxes Longimanus. "Therefore that decree must be the decree mentioned in the prophecy." [100]

Discussing the "cut off" feature, Faber notes Godwin's rendering of "cut out," and Mede's "allotted," or "cut out." [101] In the Appendix he gives the astronomical canon of Ptolemy, embracing the four groups of kings covering the prophetic kingdoms of Babylon, Medo-Persia, Greece, and Rome.[102]

15. PREDICTED DOWNFALL OF TURKEY.—Faber's final booklet, *The Predicted Downfall of The Turkish Power* (1853),[103] states at the very outset:

"With our best commentators, I consider the Downfall of the Ottoman Power to be clearly predicted in Scripture. Hence, whenever the destined time shall arrive, all the complications of modern political diplomacy will be found totally unable to prevent the Ruin of that once formidable Empire." [104]

Faber believes "its Dissolution *must* occur *before* the Close of the 1260 years," which he thinks had not yet come.[105] And this, he adds, would be marked by the restoration of the Jews. But "the Subversion of the Turkish Power will evidently occasion" the general war. Disturbed by news out of the East and North, the "Wilful Roman King" plants the tabernacles of his palaces between the seas in the glorious holy mountain, but he will come to his end with none to help.[106] Faber's major point is that "the Downfall of Turkey will be, at once, both the signal and the cause of this terrible war," [107] and will take place under the sixth vial.[108]

---

[97] *Ibid.*, pp. xvi, 107.   [99] *Ibid.*, pp. xvii, 136-224.   [101] *Ibid.*, pp. 232, 233.
[98] *Ibid.*, pp. xvii, 109-128.   [100] *Ibid.*, pp. xx, 299.   [102] *Ibid.*, pp. 430-432.
[103] Two editions were published in 1853 by the same publishers. The second edition bears the notation "with an appendix and other additions."
[104] George Stanley Faber, *The Predicted Downfall of The Turkish Power* (1st ed.), p.v.
[105] *Ibid.*, p. vi.   [106] *Ibid.*, pp. viii-x.   [107] *Ibid.*, p. x.
[108] *Ibid.*, pp. viii, x, 30.

16. SHRINKAGE OF TURKEY TABULATED.—Faber dates the 396 (391)[109] years of the Turkish woe trumpet from 1301 to 1697. From this time forward, he says, there has been a gradual and steady declension, and he lists the progressive recessions: 1699 —Treaty of Carlowicz, depriving the sultan of sway in Hungary and Transylvania; 1771—Crimea taken from Turkey; 1774— Treaty of Kainardge, securing independence of Tartars of Crimea, Bessarabia, and Kouban; 1784—Treaty at Constantinople, ending Ottoman sovereignty throughout these provinces; 1812—Treaty of Bucharest, giving Russia fortified places on left bank of the Danube; 1816—Servia detaches itself from Turkish Empire; 1821—Greek Insurrection led to independent Greek kingdom; 1829—Treaty of Adrianople, proclaiming independence of Moldavia, Servia, and Wallachia; 1830—the Sultan deprived of the suzerainty of Algeria; and 1840—Russia, Prussia, Austria, and England guarantee Egypt to Mehemet Ali.[110]

He observes, "By its exact and minute accomplishment of the prophecy of the Drying up of the Euphrates, it proves the correctness of the application of that prophecy to Turkey," and demonstrates the "principle of Symbolization." He adds, "We live in a period so pregnant with extraordinary events, that we may well be stirred up to no ordinary degree of seriousness." [111]

The entire volume is simply an unfolding of the outline given in the preface. After quoting one other point, we take leave of this final work:

"By the almost unanimous consent of commentators, the effect of the Sixth Trumpet, by loosing the Four Angels or Ottomanic Sultanies bound for a season in the region of the great river Euphrates, indicates the *Rise* of the Ottoman Power." [112]

Thus he concludes that "the Drying up of that same river indicates the Downfall of that same Empire." [113]

---

[109] 365 plus 30 plus 1, for 396, instead of 360 plus 30 plus 1, for the 391 years.
[110] *Ibid.*, pp. 30-32.
[111] *Ibid.* (2d ed.), p. 39.
[112] *Ibid.* (1st ed.), p. 22.
[113] *Ibid.*, pp. 22, 23.

CHAPTER NINETEEN

Growing Emphasis
on the Last Times

I. Commentator Scott—Expounds Standard Interpretation

Let us, without preliminaries, take the testimony of a number of expositors whose works were less conspicuous. THOMAS SCOTT (1747-1821), well-known Church of England commentator, was born in Lincolnshire. In 1772 he applied for religious orders. Fulfilling the conditions, he was ordained a deacon in 1772 and priest in 1773. He served as chaplain at Lock Hospital, London, and was appointed to several curacies. He studied Hebrew and became an able student of the Scriptures in the original. His life was lighted by an intense flame of piety. After transferring again to London he began the task of writing a commentary, commonly called *Scott's Bible*.

Financial difficulties and precarious health made its progress difficult, and in 1801 his health broke. After filling several pastoral posts he undertook the training of missionaries in 1807, continuing this endeavor until 1814, when his health completely gave way.[1] His writings were many, being collected into five volumes of *Works*, in 1805-08. Most noted, of course, is his well-known commentary. Scott is unique in that his exposition in this well-known commentary, is commonly accepted as the standard teaching of the time.

1. WEEKLY LECTURES ON SIGNS OF TIMES.—About the close of the French Revolution, Scott, in one of his sermons on the

---

[1] *Dictionary of National Biography*, vol. 17, pp. 1011-1013.

"Signs and Duties of the Times," declared it "incumbent" upon ministers to "look about them, to observe what is passing in the world, to mark the *signs of the times,* and as watchmen to warn the people of approaching danger." He declared that "the present times wear a most extraordinary appearance" and are "to a degree almost unparalleled in history." [2] This was part of a concerted effort by some of the London ministers for weekly lectures, by rotation in their several churches and chapels, on the signs and duties of the times, the Established Church joining with the nonconformists. [3] Such were among the feeble beginnings of the great awakening on systematic prophetic study and exposition soon to get under way.

2. IRON AND CLAY: SECULAR AND ECCLESIASTICAL ELE-MENTS.—In his popular notes and practical observations on the Bible, Scott presents the standard exposition of Daniel 2, from Daniel's day to the present time—the four recognized empires of prophecy, the division of Rome into ten, with the alliances and intermarriages, and the intermingled clay and iron representing the secular and ecclesiastical elements. The establishing of the kingdom of God as the "great mountain," he says, "yet remains to be accomplished." Then he adds, "We have in this dream a most extraordinary prophetical abstract of the most signal events, which would take place through the succeeding ages, nearly to the consummation of all things." [4]

3. PAPACY ARISES FROM ROME'S DIVISIONS.—Daniel 7 is presented as covering the same ground. The ten horns were the ten kingdoms. The little horn arising after and among them could not therefore be Antiochus Epiphanes. Rather, it is "the power of the Church and bishop of Rome," which seized and got possession of three of the kingdoms—the Exarchate of Ravenna, the kingdom of the Lombards, and the state of Rome. [5] The climax is "the coming of the Lord to destroy the kingdom of antichrist on earth," and this "will precede the introduction

2 Thomas Scott, *Theological Works,* vol. 2, p. 522.
3 *Ibid.,* pp. 526, 527.
4 *Scott's Bible,* notes on Dan. 2:38-45.
5 *Ibid.,* notes on Dan. 7:7, 8.

of the millennium." [6] The Papacy is clearly the little horn and the time of its domination 1260 years, at the end of which it will be "judged, condemned, and consumed." [7]

4. END OF 2300 YEARS NOT DISTANT.—On Daniel 8, Scott denies the rather common Antiochus Epiphanes application to the little horn, first holding the Romans, and later the Mohammedans, to be the power involved. In the culmination of the prophecy, the Antichristian power forecast shall be finally destroyed. The 2300 days "are put for years." Scott cites numerous authorities to the effect that the 2300 year-days are drawing toward their close, and concludes that no doubt their end "is not very distant." [8]

5. BEGINS SEVENTY WEEKS WITH ARTAXERXES.—Of Daniel 9 he writes that we here have "one of the most undeniable prophecies of Christ, and of His coming and salvation, that is found in the whole Old Testament." Then he adds, "It is universally allowed, that the seventy weeks here mentioned, mean seventy weeks of years, or what would be equivalent to seventy returns of the Sabbatical year; that is, four hundred and ninety years." [9] Referring to the different edicts—of Cyrus, Darius, and Artaxerxes—he fixes upon the possible seventh of Artaxerxes as the time generally regarded from which the "most eminent chronologers" had computed the period. [10]

6. TURKEY INTRODUCED INTO DANIEL 11.—In Daniel 11, Scott follows the line of Persian, Grecian, and Roman fulfillments with the apostasy of the Roman Antichrist in verses 36-39. Then an Eastern antichrist, "or Mohammedanism," is brought in from verse 40 onward, and in verses 44, 45, refers to tidings troubling the Turkish princes, with the "ruin of the eastern antichrist" not "far distant from that of the western; both of which seem to be predicted in this chapter." [11]

7. TURKISH TRUMPET (1281-1672); FRENCH REVOLUTION. —In the Apocalypse the first four trumpets relate to the "grad-

---

[6] *Ibid.*, verses 9-14.
[7] *Ibid.*
[8] *Ibid.*, notes on Dan. 8:13, 14.

[9] *Ibid.*, notes on Dan. 9:24.
[10] *Ibid.*, verses 25-27.
[11] *Ibid.*, verses 44, 45.

ual and complete subversion of the Roman empire," involving Alaric, Attila, and Genseric.[12] The fifth and sixth trumpets were the Saracens and the Turks, with their "391 years and fifteen days," which he extends from 1281 to 1672.[13] Due note is taken of France as the tenth part of the Antichristian city, and one of the ten kingdoms. And the earthquake is the French Revolution.[14]

8. TWO-HORNED BEAST IS ROMAN PAPACY.—On Revelation 13 he says, "All interpreters agree, that the Roman Empire, in some form or other, was here intended." Then he adds, "It is, therefore, absolutely certain, that the Roman power, as professing Christianity, and not that of pagan Rome, is meant." [15] The two-horned beast from the earth Scott believed to be "the emblem of the Roman hierarchy," the two horns probably signifying "the regular and secular clergy," [16] which beast is elsewhere called the "false prophet."

9. PAPAL BABYLON OF SEVEN HILLS.—In Revelation 17 the "woman was the emblem of the *church of Rome,* and the beast of the *temporal power* by which it hath been supported." [17] This is "Mystery, Babylon the great," and her religion the mystery of iniquity. The seven hills are also the seven forms of government, and the first six heads are kings, consuls, dictators, decemvirs, military tribunes, and emperors. The seventh head is papal, and its prescribed reign is 1260 years. Thus Scott was a careful and orthodox reflector of the standard Historical School of Protestant interpretation rather than an originator.

II. Fuller—Weekly Sermons on Apocalypse Throughout 1810

ANDREW FULLER (1754-1815), Baptist theologian, writer, and missionary advocate, of Ketteringham, England, was deeply exercised by religious questions in his boyhood. At sixteen he joined the Baptist church at Soham. His powers of exposition and exhortation were so marked that in 1775 he was called to

[12] *Ibid.*, notes on Rev. 8.
[13] *Ibid.*, notes on Rev. 9:13-15.
[14] *Ibid.*, notes on Rev. 11:13, 14.

[15] *Ibid.*, notes on Rev. 13:1.
[16] *Ibid.*, verses 11, 12.
[17] *Ibid.*, notes on Rev. 17:3-5.

the gospel ministry to serve his home church. Later, in 1782, he went to Kettering, where he remained until death. He was one of the founders of the Baptist Missionary Society, which was organized at Kettering in 1782. He was, in fact, its first secretary, with Carey as its first missionary. It was Fuller to whom Carey said, using the miner's phraseology, "I will go down (into the pit), if you will hold the rope." None was more concerned over missions than he. And the prophecies were a motivating factor.

Fuller was a man of great force and energy. Whatever he undertook he did with his might, and his controversial activities were constant. An able preacher and author, he wrote nine books, including *Expository Discourses on the Apocalypse,* published in 1815, the year of his death.[18] He also wrote numerous tracts, and contributed to various magazines. He received the degree of D.D. from both Princeton and Yale, but never used it.[19] It was Fuller who gave to William Cuninghame, of Lainshaw, Scotland, the idea that the seven last plagues were being poured out in the French Revolution. He had had it brought to his attention by Captain Charles Maitland.

As indicated by the title page, Fuller's *Expository Discourses on the Apocalypse* was originally preached to his Baptist congregation at Kettering throughout the year 1810,[20] with a vivid sense of dependence upon the enlightenment of the Holy Spirit. It was written under the consciousness that "the time is at hand," and because "the events of the present times" "called for a special attention to prophecy." Writing out his personal conclusions first, Fuller then consulted with other available writers. This in itself was significant. Finally, after frequently re-examining the manuscript over a five-year period, he sent it forth in 1815.[21]

1. SEVENTH SEAL EMBRACES ALL TRUMPETS.—In general, Fuller clings to Mede's old theory that the seventh seal contains

---

[18] Fuller's complete works were assembled in five volumes in 1837.
[19] *Dictionary of National Biography,* vol. 7, p. 750.
[20] Andrew Fuller, *Expository Discourses on the Apocalypse* in his *Complete Works* (London, 1837 ed.), vol. 3, pp. 385, 429.   [21] *Ibid.,* p. 436.

the whole of the trumpets, and the seventh trumpet, in turn, the whole of the seven vials.[22] And as the seals overthrew the pagan Roman Empire, so the trumpets overthrew the Christian,[23] the fifth and sixth representing the Saracens and Turks, by which both the Eastern Empire and church were overthrown. The earthquake of Revelation 11 is the upheaval in France, following the close of the sixth trumpet.[24] The sixth vial, producing Armageddon, involves the overthrow of Turkey.[25]

2. SARACENIC WOE (612-762); TURKISH WOE (1281-1672). —Fuller places the five months, or 150 years, of the Saracenic scourge from 612 to 762, when the Saracens ceased to extend their conquests and settled down peaceably in the countries conquered.[26] Their cavalry and their crownlike turbans seem to fulfill the symbolisms of the prophecy. The sixth, or Turkish woe, trumpet he begins in 1281 with the first "decided victory over the eastern Christians." The 391 years (the hour, day, month, and year), which he dates from 1281, lead past Othman in 1299, and the taking of Constantinople in 1453, to 1672, the year of their last victory over the Poles, and from which time they have been dwindling in power.[27] Their glittering harness and use of gunpowder are both foretold. Fuller held the seventh trumpet to be a kind of Jubilee, announcing the year of enlargement for the gospel as well as the pouring out of the plagues of devastation.[28]

3. FRENCH EARTHQUAKE-REVOLUTION IN TENTH OF CITY. —Revelation 10 deals with the Western, or Latin, apostasy, and the 1260 years of the apostasy.[29] Contending that the "earthquake" must denote a "revolution," the city the "Romish church, or the Apocalyptic Babylon," and the tenth part, or one of the ten horns, he says:

"I know of no event that seems to correspond so well with the prophecy as *the late revolution in France.* Thus it has been understood by some of the ablest expositors, and that for ages prior to the event."[30]

---

[22] *Ibid.*, p. 285.
[23] *Ibid.*, p. 287.
[24] *Ibid.*, pp. 287, 325.

[25] *Ibid.*, pp. 289, 290.
[26] *Ibid.*, p. 334.
[27] *Ibid.*, p. 336.

[28] *Ibid.*, p. 357.
[29] *Ibid.*, p. 338.
[30] *Ibid.*, p. 355.

Fuller then cites Goodwin (1639), Vitringa (1719), and Gill (1748), as this was being discussed in the current *Eclectic Review*.[31] He then observes:

"The revolution in France has truly been a moral earthquake, which has shaken the papal world to its center. One of the ten kingdoms which composed it, and that the principal one, has so fallen as at present to be a scourge rather than a support to it." [32]

4. FLEEING TO WILDERNESS INCLUDES AMERICA.—In Revelation 12 the woman represents the true church during the time of Antichristian corruption.[33] Referring to the second outburst of persecution, following the Protestant Reformation—the massacre of St. Bartholomew, in 1572; cruelties in the Piedmontese valleys, in 1655; and the revocation of the Edict of Nantes, in 1685—Fuller observes:

"If one place was more distingushed than another, as affording shelter for the woman at the time of this her *second flight*, I suspect it was *North America*, where the church of Christ has been nourished, and may continue to be nourished during the remainder of the 1260 years." [34]

5. SECOND BEAST SAME AS DANIEL'S LITTLE HORN.—The first beast of Revelation 13 is the Roman Empire, particularly in "its last or papal form," when the ten kingdoms have arisen. It is not, he believes, "the pope, or popedom, nor the church of Rome," but *"that secular power which has supported the church of Rome through the whole of her corrupt and bloody progress.* The beast is not the harlot, but that on which the harlot rides." [35] The second beast is the same as Daniel's little horn —"they appear to be one, and the same." As to the mark and name of the beast, Fuller conceives it to be "opposed" to "the seal of God." [36]

6. DRYING EUPHRATES IS DIMINISHING OF STRENGTH.—Applying the spheres of the various vials to the earth (continent) as France and Germany, the sea (maritime powers) as Spain and Portugal, and the fountains adjacent to Rome as Italy,

[31] *Eclectic Review*, February, 1814 (New Series, vol. 1), pp. 127-140.
[32] Fuller, *op. cit.*, p. 356.   [34] *Ibid.*, p. 366.   [36] *Ibid.*, p. 374.
[33] *Ibid.*, pp. 288, 364.   [35] *Ibid.*, p. 368.

23

Fuller says that the beast is the governments that supported the papal Antichrist. The sixth vial dries up the Euphrates, as Turkey "fitly expresses this diminution of strength and defence in a nation which issues in destruction." [37]

7. HARLOT CHURCH INFLUENCES MANY NATIONS.—Fuller discusses the Harlot of Revelation 17—"the opprobrious name given to the woman determines its reference to a corrupt and false church as opposed to the bride the Lamb's wife." [38] Her activities were not to be confined to a "single city or nation, but would extend over a number of nations." [39] Her attire and "meretricious ornaments" were those of no ordinary harlot. It was the ancient practice of harlots to put their names not only on their doors "but some of them upon their foreheads." This name on her forehead was expressive "not only of the general character of the antichristian church but of her impudence; practicing day by day the foulest and filthiest impostures, and yet calling herself the holy catholic church." [40]

Fuller closes by alluding, in a later note, to the strong tide in Europe in 1815 "In favour of old establishments, and so in favour of popery." And, he concludes, "the antichristian power may rise and fall repeatedly before it falls to rise no more." [41]

III. Commentator Clarke—Clear on Outlines; Confused on Periods

Another interpreter, whose commentaries were a household commonplace, was ADAM CLARKE (1762-1832), Irish Wesleyan preacher, commentator, and theologian, born in Londonderry, Ireland. Through the influence of Wesley, he completed his education at Kingswood School, near Bristol. Profoundly impressed to preach the gospel, he became a Methodist in 1778, and began to exhort. He passed through the stages of local and then regular preacher, and was appointed to his first circuit—of Bradford—in 1782. He labored in Ireland, Scotland, and the

---

[37] Ibid., p. 388.
[38] Ibid., p. 392.
[39] Ibid., pp. 393, 394.
[40] Ibid.
[41] Ibid., p. 430.

Channel and Shetland Islands. He became popular as a preacher and thrice filled the presidency of the Methodist body, in 1806, 1814, and 1822. After 1823, he resided chiefly in London.

Clarke was an assiduous scholar, putting in long hours on the classics, the early Fathers, and Oriental writers—in Hebrew, Syriac, Arabic, Persian, and Sanskrit. In 1807 he received an M.A. from the University of Aberdeen, and in 1808 an LL.D. He was a fellow of the Antiquarian Society, the Royal Irish, and other leading societies and institutes. The writer of numerous works, he is best known for his *Commentary* (1810-26) in several volumes.

1. PAPACY'S DEADLY WOUND OF 1798 SKINNED OVER.—On Daniel 2, Clarke gives the standard interpretation of the rise and fall of the four empires, then the ten divisions, and finally the fifth kingdom of the last days which "shall never have an end." The "Explanation" at the close of the chapter is quite explicit. The mingling of the clay and iron is by means of leagues and marital alliances.[42] Similarly, in Daniel 7 the four beasts are the identical four empires. The horns are the same divisions of Rome, and the little horn is "popedom." The year-day principle is applied to the 1260 days. But of this he says:

"If we knew precisely when the papal power began to exert itself in the *antichristian* way, then we could at once fix the time of its destruction. The *end* is probably not very distant; it has already been grievously shaken by the French. In 1798 the French republican army under General *Berthier* took possession of the city of Rome, and entirely superseded the whole papal power. This was a deadly wound, though at present it appears to be healed; but it is but *skinned over,* and a dreadful cicatrice remains." [43]

2. 2300 DAYS ARE YEARS; 70 WEEKS FROM ARTAXERXES.—On Daniel 8, after the Persian ram and the Grecian goat, the year-day principle is likewise applied to the 2300 days. But again he is not clear, suggesting that "if we date these years from the vision of the he-goat (Alexander's invading Asia), this was A.M. 3670, B.C. 334; and *two thousand three hundred* years

---

[42] Adam Clarke, *Commentary,* "Discourse on Nebuchadnezzar's Dream," following notes on Daniel 2.
[43] *Ibid.,* notes on Daniel 7:25.

from that time will reach to A.D. 1966, or *one hundred and forty-one years* from the present A.D. 1825." [44] However, Clarke dates the seventy weeks, or 490 years, from Artaxerxes' commission to Ezra. And in Daniel 11 he understands the Turk to be the king of the North, in verses 40-45. [45]

3. ENDS LAST PROPHETIC PERIODS IN TWENTIETH CENTURY. —In order to understand Daniel 12:9, he says, "we must wait 'till the time of the end;' and this, it appears from the foregoing calculations, will not arrive before the TWENTIETH CENTURY." [46] Clarke is still less clear on the Apocalypse, and as some of the notes are supplied by others, they will not be taken up here.

IV. Toovey—Ten-horned Beast, Papacy; Two-horned, France

Biographical data is lacking on PHILO BRITANNICUS (Samuel Toovey), [47] but his illustrated *Essay on the Prophecies of Daniel and the Revelation* (1813), was dedicated to the clergy of the Church of England, the Church of Rome, and every other denomination in England. It bears two texts on the title page, "God's Proclamation to Nations" (Jer. 18:7, 8), and "God's Commission to Ministers" (Eze. 3:17-22). Toovey later wrote *A Consideration of the Second Woe Trumpet about to End and the Third Woe that Will Follow Quickly* (1832).

1. LITTLE HORN HAS TRIPLE CROWN.—Graphic pictures tell the story. In the first drawing, effectively illustrating the *Essay on the Prophecies,* the ten-horned beast of Daniel is in an impressive pose. The three horns—the kingdom of Lombardy, the Exarchate of Ravenna, and the Principality of Rome —have already been uprooted, and the new horn of ecclesiastical Rome, surmounted by a triple crown, has appeared among the seven that remain. These are plainly named as Spain, France, Hungary, Portugal, Burgundy, Bohemia, and Naples—Rome continuing in papal form.

---

[44] *Ibid.,* notes on Daniel 8:14.
[45] *Ibid.,* notes on Daniel 11:40-45.
[46] *Ibid.,* notes on Daniel 12:9.
[47] See Samuel Halkett and John Laing, *Dictionary of Anonymous and Pseudonymous English Literature,* vol. 2, p. 201.

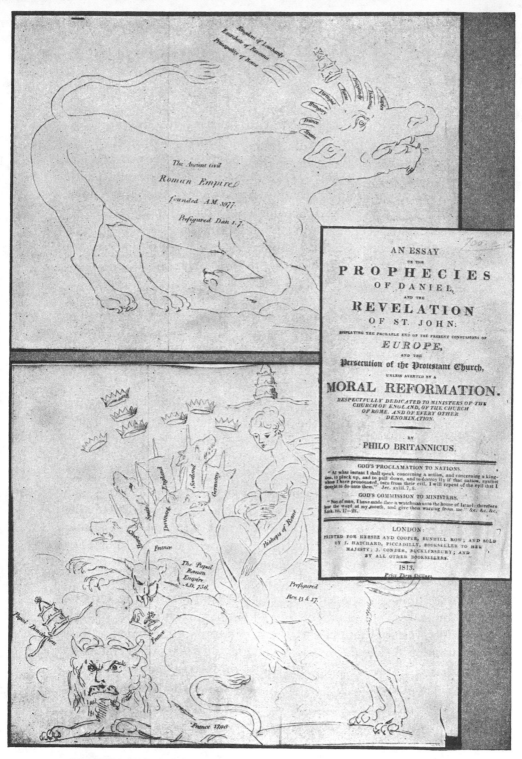

GRAPHIC PORTRAYALS IN PICTURES POPULARIZE PROPHECIES

The Samuel Toovey Treatise in 1813 Depicts the Papal Little Horn Uprooting the Three (Upper);
Pictures the Papal Church Seated on the Supporting Nations of Europe; and Conceives the Two-
horned Beast to Be France in 1798; Toovey Wrote Under the Pen Name Philo Britannicus (Right)

2. Tiara-crowned Woman Surmounts Europe.—The second concerns the seven-headed beast of Revelation 17, on which sits the woman with the same triple crown on her head and with the golden cup in her hand. Six heads are labeled kings, consuls, decemvirs, tribunes, dictators, emperors. But the woman surmounts seven progressive, or overlapping, mountains—much like a stack of pancakes, thin on the edges and thick in the middle. These hills or mountains are France, Portugal, Spain, Hungary, Sardinia, Bohemia, and Naples. The caption states that the eighth head is the pope, "prefiguring a second Stage of the Papal Power."

3. France Depicted as Two-horned Beast.—The third drawing shows the prancing beasts of Revelation 13 blended with the papal figure of Revelation 17 with her golden cup and triple crown. The heads of the beast, or "Papal Roman Empire," are labeled France, Hungary, Denmark, Spain, England, Scotland, Germany. The two-horned beast crawling up out of the earth has just tossed off "Papal Dominion" and "France" by its two horns, while the beast itself is labeled, "France, 1798." This is perhaps the first application of this symbol to France.

4. Little Horn Within Empire Confines.—Toovey's exposition is clear. The four mighty empires of prophecy, according to the agreement of both Protestant and papal commentators, are Assyria, Persia, Grecia, and Rome.[48] He then notes the inconsistency that "will not admit of the natural conclusions resulting from their own premises." He shows how Greece was conquered by Rome, Rome was at length divided into the lesser kingdoms by A.D. 476, and the papal Little Horn arose among them and after them,[49] and within the territory bound by the confines of the old Roman Empire of the West.[50] The presumptuous claims, the persecution of the saints, and the attempt to change God's times and laws through their traditions, creeds, and ceremonies for the allotted time period are mentioned. All this, he thought, would end in 1849.[51]

[48] Philo Britannicus (Samuel Toovey), *An Essay on the Prophecies of Daniel, and the Revelation of St. John,* p. 6.
[49] *Ibid.,* p. 7.   [50] *Ibid.*   [51] *Ibid.,* pp. 18, 19.

5. EVERLASTING KINGDOM CANNOT BE PAPACY.—Toovey dwells on the grandeur of the imminent judgment scene, and the approaching kingdom of God soon to be established. Reverting to Daniel 2, he points to the four metallic parts of the great image as representing the same four world powers, and comes to the kingdom that shall never be destroyed.[52] He states this everlasting kingdom cannot pertain to the Church of Rome, "for its authority has been destroyed by France."

6. FRANCE TO EFFECT PAPAL RESTORATION.—Turning to the two beasts of Revelation 13, Toovey declares the two-horned second beast "is now personated by France." [53]   Then he tries to find the 666 in Bonaparte's name. As the "first beast has been realized in the nature and events of the papal power," so France will "reinstate" the Papacy in all its former dominion and authority, and in the "accomplishment of the papal restoration by France," the prediction concerning the wounded head will be fulfilled.[54]

7. DEADLY WOUND GIVEN BY FRANCE.—Toovey held that "the revolution of France would suspend the power of the first papal beast (Rev. XIII), and by the deadly blow it would give to its supremacy would give free access to the light and truth of the scriptures, which could have no admission while the papal dominion existed." [55]

8. ESTABLISHMENT OF GOD'S KINGDOM ABOUT 1849.—After recapitulating the fulfillment of Daniel 7, the four empire-beasts and the ten horn-kingdoms and the papal Little Horn and the ultimate establishment of the kingdom of God about 1849,[56] he declares:

"We have seen, in our own experience, the fall of the first papal beast in St. John's vision, (chap. 13) his head wounded, and the beast become a wonder in his humiliation; and we have seen his power exercised by France, (presumptively the second beast in that vision,) who has realized most strikingly, the description of that hieroglyphic; and from the admitted and undoubted signification of the first beast, we have to apprehend that the second is as certainly personified in France,

---

52 *Ibid.*, pp. 20, 21.   54 *Ibid.*, pp. 36, 37.   56 *Ibid.*, pp. 65, 66.
53 *Ibid.*, p. 33.   55 *Ibid.*, p. 64.

who now exercises all the power of the first beast before him, and that he will reinstate the papal dominion." [57]

9. POLITICAL QUAKE IN FRANCE (TENTH OF CITY).—The great "political earthquake" of Revelation 11 is that which "convulsed Europe, and which threw down, in the monarchy of France, the tenth part of the papal city." [58]

10. RE-ESTABLISHMENT OF PAPAL POWER IN REVELATION 17. —In Revelation 17, Toovey applies the symbol to "the papal power re-established in its last stages of dominion," [59] which event will solve the mysterious paradox of that beast.

11. ETERNAL ESTABLISHMENT OF GOD'S KINGDOM.—The final event will be the receiving of His kingdom by the Son of man, when all other thrones will be cast down. Then will "the sacred volume of God's providence and salvation be open to the understanding of the whole earth." [60]

V. Captain Maitland—French Revolution Foretold; 1260 Years Ended

CHARLES DAVID MAITLAND (1785-1865), distinguished captain of the Royal Artillery, was for the last forty years of his life minister of St. James Chapel, Brighton. He received his education at St. Catharine's Hall, with a B.A. in 1834. [61] He was the father of Charles Maitland, author of the important *Apostles' School of Prophetic Interpretation* (1849), which will be noted later.

Although Captain Maitland wrote several books after entering the ministry, such as *The Parable of the Ten Virgins* (c. 1830) and *The History of Noah's Day . . . and the Coming of the Son of Man* (1832), [62] his most significant contributions were written in 1813 and 1814, before he studied for the ministry, while he was still a captain in the Royal Artillery. The first was *The History of the Beast of the Apocalypse* (1813). The second was titled *A Brief and Connected View of Prophecy:*

---

[57] *Ibid.*, p. 66.   [58] *Ibid.*   [59] *Ibid.*, p. 67.   [60] *Ibid.*
[61] Frederic Boase, *Modern English Biography*, vol. 6, supplement 3, p. 143.
[62] Joshua W. Brooks, *Dictionary of Writers on the Prophecies*, p. lvi.

Being An Exposition of the Second, Seventh, and Eighth Chapters of the Prophecy of Daniel; Together With the Sixteenth Chapter of Revelation (1814).

1. 1260 YEARS IN WILDERNESS ENDED.—In his *History of the Beast of the Apocalypse* the captain discusses Revelation 13-17. A frontispiece pictures the purple-clothed woman with a triple crown seated on the ten-horned, seven-headed beast. In the preface he agrees with the recently published position of William Cuninghame on the 1260 years, and his first work on the seals and trumpets.[63] Maitland asserts the Two Witnesses are the two Testaments—citing a pamphlet by another military man, General Burn, on *The Resurrection of the Two Witnesses* —with the 1260 years ending at the French Revolution, as "it can no longer be said of the Church, that she is hid in the wilderness."[64]

2. PROJECTS 1290 AND 1335 BEYOND THE 1260.—Maitland deals in the usual way with the Papacy as the Antichrist of the West, refers to the Mohammedan "false prophet" in the East, and the infidel power of Daniel 11:36-39, as well as the coming overthrow of papal Babylon.[65] Like Cuninghame, Maitland extends the 1290 years thirty years beyond the 1260, and the 1335 years forty-five years beyond the 1290,[66] at which time the millennial reign with Christ will begin.[67]

3. FRENCH REVOLUTION FORECAST BY MANY.—An extended book review of this brief work appears in the London *Eclectic Review*.[68] After commending a "military man" for his active interest in prophecy, it notes that Maitland had thought his exposition original concerning France as the instrument to break papal domination, and which events would reach their climax at the end of the 1290 years in the near future. The reviewer declares that many writers had "long ago depicted the prominent events arising out of the French Revolution,"

[63] Charles David Maitland, *The History of the Beast of the Apocalypse*, pp. iv, v.
[64] *Ibid.*, p. vii.   [66] *Ibid.*, p. 65.
[65] *Ibid.*, pp. 16, 64.   [67] *Ibid.*
[68] *Eclectic Review*, February, 1814 (New Series, vol. 1), pp. 127-140.

before they came to pass, "more clearly than he (Maitland) has done after the event." [69]

Starting with Napier, in 1593, the reviewer quotes a whole series of statements from Goodwin in 1639, Jurieu in 1686, an anonymous French writer in 1688, Cressener in 1689, Fleming in 1701, Vitringa in 1719, Daubuz in 1720, Willison in 1745, an anonymous English writer in 1747, and Bishop Newton. All these men, solely through the prophecy, applied the stipulations to yet future developments in France—the tenth part of the city, the street of the city, and the earthquake revolution. [70] Such were the extraordinary forecasts, the reviewer in the *Eclectic Review* observed, "before the event to which they point." [71] Such statements were evidently common knowledge.

4. STANDARD HISTORICAL VIEW OF DANIEL 7.—In his *Brief and Connected View of Prophecy,* Captain Maitland holds that the four beast-kingdoms of Daniel 7 are the "exact counterpart of the image in the first vision," [72] the ten horns being the same as the ten toes of the former prophecy. He gives the standard tabulation of the four beasts, [73] and names the ten horn-nations —Ostrogoths, Visigoths, Sueves and Alans, Vandals, Franks, Burgundians, Heruli and Thuringi, Saxons and Angles, Huns, and Lombards. [74]

5. 1260 YEARS OF PAPAL LITTLE HORN (533 TO 1792).— "This little horn," he continues, "which is the papal power, rose about the year 533." [75] The three horn-kingdoms plucked up to make way he names as the Ostrogoths, Heruli-Thuringi, and Lombards, who had attempted to establish themselves in Italy. [76] After discussing the prophesied characteristics of the Papacy, Maitland places the 1260 year-days from the Justinian acknowledgment of the pope's headship, in 533, to 1792, when the French support of the papal power fell away and the tenth part of the city fell. [77]

---

[69] *Ibid.*, p. 133.
[70] *Ibid.*, pp. 133-138.   [71] *Ibid.*, p. 138.
[72] Charles David Maitland, *A Brief and Connected View of Prophecy,* p. 16.
[73] *Ibid.*, pp. 16-18.   [74] *Ibid.*, p. 18.   [75] *Ibid.*, p. 19.
[76] *Ibid.*   [77] *Ibid.*, p. 21.

6. 2300 Years in Relation to 1260 and 1290.—Rather oddly, Maitland places the end of the 2300 years and the cleansing of the sanctuary, or "Gentile Temple," on the eve of the French Revolution, along with the close of the 1260 years.[78] This cleansing will be by means of the seven vials,[79] and will continue the thirty years, or till the close of the 1290 years and the destruction of the two abominations.   Maitland adds:

"The daily sacrifice of spiritual worship was taken out of the Gentile church, and the abomination that maketh desolate set up therein, in the year of our Lord 533.   From this period the saints were given into the hands of the Papal power, and permission was granted to that power to exercise dominion and tyrannize over them 1260 years.   (See Dan. vii. 25; and Rev. xiii. 5 to 8.)" [80]

7. Dates 2300 From Darius, 515 b.c.—The 2300 years, he believes, began with the Persian Empire[81] but are dated from the time of the dedication of the temple and the setting up of the daily sacrifice.[82]   This he simply places from the sixth year of Darius, 515 b.c.

8. Horn of Daniel 8 Papal Not Mohammedan.—Maitland denies that Mohammedanism is intended by the horn of Daniel 8, and concludes that "beyond a shadow of doubt" the "Roman power is the little horn of this vision." [83]

9. Heavenly Temple Opened at Seventh Trumpet.—According to Maitland the temple of God opened at the sounding of the seventh trumpet,[84] when the 1260 and 2300 years are expiring.[85]   The sixth vial involves the Turkish power and the four sultanies.[86]   Such were the understandings of a military officer in 1813 and 1814.

---

[78] *Ibid.*, pp. 24, 25, 49.
[79] *Ibid.*, p. 25.
[80] *Ibid.*, p. 27.
[81] *Ibid.*, p. 38.
[82] *Ibid.*, pp. 38, 39.
[83] *Ibid.*, p. 48.
[84] *Ibid.*, p. 50.
[85] *Ibid.*
[86] *Ibid.*, pp. 70, 71.

Twenty-three Hundred Years
Focal Point of Discussion

I. Cuninghame—Champion of the Number 2300

We now come to one of the most interesting, consistent, and continuous interpreters, WILLIAM CUNINGHAME, Esquire (1776-1849), of Lainshaw, Ayrshire. Thoughtful as a lad, with none too robust health, he had strong religious convictions even in his youth, when at school in Kensington, where he received most of his education. He later attended the University of Utrecht, going thence to India in the Bengal Civil Service. While he was there his religious convictions were deepened by contacts with the celebrated William Carey of Serampore and other Baptist missionaries. His first writing was done in India, where he issued a series of letters on *Evidences of Christianity,* published under the signature of "An Inquirer," and subsequently republished in England.

After the death of his father, and his succession to the estate at Lainshaw, Cuninghame returned to Scotland in 1804, and thenceforth until his death resided on his estate except for periodic visits to London. He was interested in scientific agriculture. But for the last forty years of his life he was "engrossingly occupied" with the writing of a series of twenty-one large and small works on prophecy and Biblical chronology,[1] for which he became widely and favorably known. He was also a participant in the important Albury Park Prophetic Conference in 1826.[2]

---

[1] Full list at close of *The Fulfilling of the Times of the Gentiles,* by William Cuninghame.
[2] Joshua W. Brooks, *Dictionary of Writers on the Prophecies,* p. lxxi.

Denominated the "learned layman" by Allibone, he has sometimes been erroneously confused with the clergyman William Cunningham, D.D., president of New College, Edinburgh.[3] But these were two distinct persons.[4] He never married, and the infirmity of gradually increasing deafness caused him to withdraw more and more from social and business contacts, and to devote all his time to prophetical and chronological studies. He was in the forefront of the discussions over the correctness of the 2300-versus-the-2400-years issue. The cause of missions was likewise dear to him, and he was a supporter of several religious societies, with special fondness for the London Society to Promote Christianity Among the Jews.

Under the pseudonym of "Talib"[5] he engaged for several years in discussion of religious topics in the London *Christian Observer,* as previously noted. His second book, *Dissertations on the Prophecies Relative to the Messiah,* published in 1810, was an answer to the learned Jew, David Levi. Issuance of his epochal *Dissertation on the Seals and Trumpets,* in 1813, attracted immediate attention. It received favorable notice in many critical religious journals, passing through four editions. Thenceforth his writings followed one after another in a constant stream. *The Apostasy of the Church of Rome, and the Identity of the Papal Power with the Man of Sin and Son of Perdition of St. Paul's Prophecy* (1818), constitutes another evidence of the fact that virtually every writer on prophecy also wrote on the papal Antichrist.

Several were controversial—his strictures against S. R. Maitland's newly projected Futurism, and Edward Irving's fallacious positions, as well as those of Frere and Faber.[6] As he advanced in years Cuninghame became more speculative and ran to mathematical calculations by cycles, trivial fractions, squares, and their combinations, as in *Supplement to the Scientific Chronol-*

---

[3] As in the case of Samuel Halkett and John Laing, *Dictionary of Anonymous and Pseudonymous English Literature,* vol. 7, p. 71, and vol. 5, p. 110.
[4] Joseph Irving, *The Book of Scotsmen,* p. 87.
[5] William Cushing, *Initials and Pseudonyms,* p. 143 (2d series).
[6] William Cuninghame, *A Critical Examination of Some of the Fundamental Principles of the Rev. George Stanley Faber's Sacred Calendar of Prophecy* (1829).

ogy of the Year 1839 (1840), and *The Fulfilling of the Times of the Gentiles, a Conspicuous Sign of the End* (1847).

At first Cuninghame was a communicant of the Established Church. But in 1822 he withdrew, giving his reasons in a pamphlet entitled *Narration of the Formation of a Congregational Church at Stewarton,* which town was near his estate in Ayrshire. Moreover, he became pastor of this church and continued to serve when at home until 1843. Then another minister was secured. Cuninghame left it with a commodious place of worship, a comfortable manse, and a suitable endowment for maintenance.[7]

1. BASIC PREMISES OF OUTLINE TIME PROPHECIES.—Cuninghame's *Dissertation on the Seals and Trumpets of the Apocalypse* (1813), dealing primarily with the 1260 years, grew out of the extended discussion with Faber in *The Christian Observer.* Writing "in the intervals of business," Cuninghame sets forth this basic premise:

"I take for granted, that the four beasts seen by Daniel in the seventh chapter of his prophecies, signify the Babylonian, Medo-Persian, Grecian, and Roman monarchies; and that the little horn of his fourth beast is a symbol of the papal power; and likewise that the Babylon of the Apocalypse is the church of Rome. These may be considered as *first principles* in the study of prophecy, of which no well-instructed protestant ought to be ignorant." [8]

The second axiomatic principle is that all time prophecy is to be understood as involving a day standing for a year.[9]

2. SEVEN SEALS EXTEND TO SECOND ADVENT.—Cuninghame rejected the theory that the seals were fulfilled in the early centuries and did not extend beyond the time of Constantine.[10] Instead, he placed the events of the sixth seal "immediately before the coming of the Son of Man." [11] The barbaric irruptions into Western Rome were represented by the early trumpets, beginning in 376, "preparatory to its partition among the ten kings." [12] Later the seven vials will bring the final destruction.[13]

---

[7] James Paterson, *History of the County of Ayr: with a genealogical account of the families of Ayrshire,* vol. 2, pp. 455, 456; Irving, *op. cit.,* p. 87.
[8] William Cuninghame, *Dissertation on the Seals and Trumpets of the Apocalypse,* p. v.
[9] *Ibid.,* pp. xii, xiii.   [11] *Ibid.,* p. 34.   [13] *Ibid.,* pp. 80, 81.
[10] *Ibid.,* pp. 1-58.   [12] *Ibid.,* p. 79.

3. SARACENIC WOE (612-762); TURKISH WOE (1302-1697).
—The fifth trumpet is "exactly applicable to the rise of the
Mahometan religion and power." [14]   Like the "great body of
commentators," he applies the fifth and sixth trumpets to the
Saracens and Turks, with the accepted time epochs of the 150
and 391 years.[15]   The 150 years are scheduled from 612 to 762,
and the 391 years allocated from 1302 to 1697, the battle of
Zenta, followed by the peace of Carlowitz.[16]

4. OPEN BOOK BELONGS TO TIME OF END.—The vision of
the angel with the open book "belongs, or is immediately introductory, to the time of the end, and of the seventh trumpet and
seven vials." [17]   The announcement of time no longer "seems to
be declared in reference to the finishing of the mysterious times
mentioned in the prophecy of Daniel," [18] when everything is
opened.   To "measure" is to take account of, or study, the
heavenly temple—court, holy place, and most holy.[19]

5. SEVENTH TRUMPET AT TIME OF ADVENT.—Cuninghame
held that "the sounding of the seventh angel in the Apocalypse
takes place at the same time as the coming of the Ancient of Days
in Daniel," when the Son of man descends from heaven, when
the enemies of the church are to be destroyed, and the saints
receive the kingdom.[20]

6. LAST PLAGUES LINKED TO HOLY OF HOLIES.—He looked
upon Revelation 11 as an epitome of the events unfolded in the
chapters to follow.[21]   The "opening of the holy of holies" in
heaven is, he held, "indicative of the near approach of that
glorious state of the church when the tabernacle of God shall be
with men." [22]   It also determines the timing of the seven vials of
wrath—the time of the seventh trumpet constituting part of
the third and last woe,[23] the Saracenic onslaught and the Turkish
invasion being the first and second woes.[24]

7. VIALS POURED OUT IN FRENCH REVOLUTION.—Cuninghame believed the vials to be in the process of pouring out in

[14] *Ibid.*, p. 94.
[15] *Ibid.*, pp. 94-104.
[16] *Ibid.*, pp. 144, 145.
[17] *Ibid.*, p. 107.
[18] *Ibid.*, p. 109.
[19] *Ibid.*, pp. 113-118.
[20] *Ibid.*, pp. 149, 150.
[21] *Ibid.*, p. 151.
[22] *Ibid.*, p. 152.
[23] *Ibid.*, pp. 152, 153.
[24] *Ibid.*, p. 155.

the French Revolution, citing the concurrence of other writers. He also believed that the ending of the 1260 years marked the beginning of the sounding of the seventh trumpet.[25]

8. VARIANT SYMBOLS FOR 1260 YEARS.—The woman of Revelation 12 is the true church in "concealment and invisibility," fed with heavenly manna for 1260 years, which period is also the forty-two months of Gentile occupation of the holy city, and of prophesying of the Witnesses in sackcloth.[26] The ten-horned beast from the sea (Revelation 13) is the same as Daniel's fourth beast—Rome. The little horn, he held, was represented by the second beast coming out of the earth.[27] In concurrence he cites Mede, Newton, Faber, Alcazar, Cressener, and Daubuz.[28] He lists the ten horns as the Visigoths, Suevi, Heruli, Franks, Burgundians, Saxons, Huns, Ostrogoths, Lombards, and Vandals,[29] and cites the notable speech on the Little Horn by Eberhard, archbishop of Salzburg, in 1240.[30] The seven heads are forms of government.

9. FIRST BEAST SECULAR; SECOND BEAST ECCLESIASTICAL.— Whereas the first beast is the secular power, the second represents the ecclesiastical Roman power, growing up silently and at first unheeded.[31] Cuninghame accepts the explanation of Irenaeus concerning *Lateinos* for the 666—with the Latin empire and church and ritual. In his *Apostasy of the Church of Rome*, he shows that "the Harlot Babylon the Great," of Revelation 17, "is a symbol of Papal Rome." He also notes that the "shocking enormities of the Romish Church" have been recorded by historians of her own communion, such as Fra Pablo, Sarpi, and L'Abbe Condillac.[32]

10. DATES 1260 YEARS FROM 533.—The 1260 years in their various listings, Cuninghame stoutly insists, refer to one and the same period, based on the year-day principle.[33] These all began

---

[25] *Ibid.*, pp. 157, 158.
[26] *Ibid.*, pp. 166, 167.
[27] *Ibid.*, p. 176.
[28] *Ibid.*, pp. 177, 178.
[29] *Ibid.*, p. 181.
[30] See Volume 2 of *Prophetic Faith*.
[31] *Ibid.*, pp. 191, 192.
[32] William Cuninghame, *The Apostasy of the Church of Rome*, pp. 146, 147.
[33] William Cuninghame, *Dissertations on the Seals and Trumpets*, pp. 208-214.

under the reign of Justinian and his issuance of the Civil Code, in which the pope is formally recognized as the head of all the holy churches and all the holy priests.[34] The same message concerning the primacy of the pope at Rome was conveyed to the patriarch of Constantinople.

"Thus the sentiments contained in them obtained the sanction of the supreme legislative authority of the empire: and in both epistles, the above titles were given to the pope." [35]

The pope's answer, likewise published in the code with the other documents, is equally important, showing that he understood the reference as formal recognition of the supremacy of the see of Rome. This was dated 533—the grant of Phocas in 606 being merely a renewal and confirmation of Justinian's bestowal.[36] Full citation of the Latin original is given in extended footnotes.[37]

11. ENDS 1260 YEARS IN 1792.—Similarly, Cuninghame gives his evidence for believing the period ended in 1792, at the French Revolution—listing the events involved in that tremendous upheaval as it affected the church, reaching the conclusion that the period had indeed ended.[38]

12. STRESSES INTEGRITY OF NUMBER 2300.—Discussing Christ's prophecy of Matthew 24, Cuninghame contends that all but the last events of this great outline have been fulfilled in the centuries traversed.[39] Next Cuninghame reviews the prophecy of Daniel 8—the Persian ram and the Grecian goat, and the mysterious 2300 years. Holding the exceeding great horn to be Rome, and the 2300 prophetical days to be years, at first he thought they were to be dated from 508 B.C., the commencement of the vision, to A.D. 1792—which he later changed to begin in 457 B.C. and to end in A.D. 1843. But Cuninghame takes full occasion to stress the soundness of the number 2300 in contrast to Jerome's 2200 and the later Septuagint 2400—all early Septuagints agreeing with the Hebrew text.[40]

---

34 *Ibid.*, p. 220.
35 *Ibid.*

36 *Ibid.*, pp. 220, 221.
37 *Ibid.*, pp. 222-230.
38 *Ibid.*, pp. 232-236.

39 *Ibid.*, pp. 277-286.
40 *Ibid.*, p. 287 n.

24

13. BEGINS 1260, 1290, 1335 SYNCHRONOUSLY.—In common
with Faber and some others, Cuninghame begins the 1260-,
1290-, and 1335-year periods together, so that he ends the 1290
and 1335 periods 30 and 75 years, respectively, beyond the ending of the first.[41] The close of the 1335 years he places in 1867,[42]
as the beginning of the millennium. This feature will be called
up for discussion later. He also leans to the restoration of the
Jews at the end of the 1290 years.[43]

14. PLACED JUDGMENT MESSAGE IN NINETEENTH CENTURY.
—On Revelation 14, Cuninghame holds that the 144,000 are
sealed "during the awful convulsions of the great earthquake." [44]
On this first angel preaching the everlasting gospel and proclaiming the hour of God's judgment, he denies the application by
some to Reformation times, not only because of the deciding
content of their preaching, but particularly for this reason:

"Neither could it be said, in consistence with truth, at the time
of the reformation, that 'the hour of God's judgment was come.' There
is nothing indefinite in the language of the Apocalypse. The hour of
God's judgment is a time well known, and exactly defined in the
chronological prophecies of Daniel and John. It is the period of the
judgment mentioned in Dan. vii.26, when the little horn, or the papacy,
is deprived of its power. It is likewise the time of the seventh trumpet,
and seven vials, in the Apocalypse, when God judgeth Babylon, and
destroyeth them who destroy the earth." [45]

Similarly, the second angel's message was "no less inappli-
cable to the time of the Reformation." [46]

15. LIVING IN TIME OF FIRST ANGEL.—Cuninghame then
asserts that the *first angel* represented no individual minister
"but a series of events in the church." He applies it to the then
present unparalleled emphasis in the preaching of the gospel,
and declares:

"This interesting prophecy seems now to be receiving its accomplishment, and will probably continue to be fulfilled with increasing clearness
during the remainder of the period into which we have entered." [47]

---

[41] *Ibid.*, p. 289.　　　　[44] *Ibid.*, p. 303.　　　　[45] *Ibid.*, pp. 308, 309.
[42] Diagram, accompanying 1843 (4th) edition.　　[46] *Ibid.*, p. 309.
[43] *Ibid.*, pp. 291, 293.　　　　　　　　　　[47] *Ibid.*, p. 311.

"We have also seen this preaching of the gospel, and distribution of the word, accompanied with a series of the most awful and tremendous judgments, which are at this moment speaking to us in the loudest manner, and calling on us to 'fear God, and give glory to him, for the hour of his judgment is come.' " [48]

16. SECOND AND THIRD ANGELS STILL FUTURE.—Cuninghame also holds that "the going forth of the *second angel* to declare the fall of Babylon seems to be still future, and of consequence also the preaching of the third angel." [49]   These he believes to be "synchronical."   Then comes the significant admonition, published—be it remembered—in 1813:

"The going forth of the second and third angels being thus future, it does not become us to form conjectures as to the manner in which this vision shall be accomplished." [50]

17. THIRD MESSAGE PRESAGES BEAST'S DESTRUCTION.—The "mission of the third angel," Cuninghame states, seems "immediately to precede the final destruction of the beast," and presages tremendous things, with the second advent following. [51]   The call to the marriage supper, the gathering of the elect, and the crushing wrath of God upon evildoers [52] are all involved.   The pouring out of the seven vials Cuninghame links with the opening of the holy of holies in heaven. [53]   The vials were being poured out, he holds, during the French Revolution.   The sixth involved the destruction of the Ottoman Turkish Empire, and all were to be grouped under the third woe.   Each is discussed at some length.   (Title page reproduced on page 278.)

18. STILL HOLDS ORIGINAL POSITION ON REVELATION 14.— All this was published, it should be remembered, in 1813.   Later editions of Cuninghame's *Dissertation on the Seals and Trumpets,* while expanded and perfected, did not call for serious revision.   Extensive documentary evidence is added for the 1260 years as from 533 to 1793.   Concerning his exposition of Revelation 14, he states that this was first written in 1812, and adds, "After an interval of 21 years I find nothing to alter in the

---

[48] *Ibid.,* pp. 311, 312.
[49] *Ibid.,* p. 312.
[50] *Ibid.,* p. 313.
[51] *Ibid.,* pp. 313-318.
[52] *Ibid.,* pp. 317-321.
[53] *Ibid.,* pp. 327-328.

principles of our exposition." [54]   Strengthening his former position that the message of the first angel was not given in Reformation times, he adds, virtually repeating his former words:

"Neither could it be said, in consistence with truth, at the time of the Reformation, that '*the hour of God's judgment was come.*' There is nothing indefinite in the language of the Apocalypse. The hour of God's judgment is a time well known, and exactly defined in the chronological prophecies of Daniel and John. It is the period of the judgment mentioned in Dan. vii.9-11, 26, when the BEAST is destroyed, and the LITTLE HORN, or the Papacy, is deprived of its power. It is likewise the time of the seventh trumpet, and the seven vials, in the Apocalypse, when God judgeth Babylon, and destroyeth them who destroy the earth." [55]

Then he enforces his earlier position on the first angel's message with this significant addition, the full force of which should not escape us:

"The foregoing view of the flight of the three angels was written in the year 1812; and I still adhere to it.

"To the general preaching of the everlasting Gospel by the *first angel,* there has, however, since that period been added the voice of *prophetic exposition,* which has gone forth in these kingdoms with a power unknown in former ages of the Church: and it has announced with unfaltering testimony, and in louder and yet louder sounds, *that the hour of God's judgment is come, and that the Lord is at hand.*

"I conceive, also, that, by the institution and work of our Continental and Reformation Societies, some preludious sounds of the voices of the second and third angels are heard, although I dare not yet think, that either of these angels has begun his flight." [56]

This clear discernment is noteworthy. There is intelligent understanding of the times.

In this later footnote Cuninghame says regretfully that the "voice of prophecy . . . has been, in some measure, quenched by Irvingism and Puseyism," which had but recently developed. Then he observes that "as we approach the season of *midnight,* when the Bridegroom comes," deep sleep will pervade the spiritual atmosphere, "intermingled only with the croaking of the three frogs, ch. xvi.15." [57]

---

[54] *Ibid.* (1843, or 4th ed.), p. 254.
[55] *Ibid.,* pp. 255, 256.
[56] *Ibid.,* p. 258.
[57] *Ibid.,* p. 258 n.

II. Meets Specious Fallacies and Makes Appeals

1. PROTESTS MYSTICAL INTERPRETATION OF ADVENT.—Brief notice must suffice for succeeding works. Cuninghame's *Pre-Millennial Advent of Christ Demonstrated From the Scriptures,* also of 1813, but appearing first in *The Christian Observer,* was primarily an appeal to the clergy. Deploring the popular attitude of the time, he declares that the Christian world is blinded by a "mystical application" concerning the advent.[58] Cuninghame contends that the time has arrived for a revival of the "primitive doctrine of the personal advent of the Messiah," that it is time to arouse a sleeping church to the significance of the "stupendous events" impending. It was published for the purpose of rescuing the doctrine of the glorious appearing from the low esteem into which it had been thrust by opponents.[59]

2. MEETS BURGH'S FUTURIST FALLACY.—In 1833 Cuninghame brought out the second edition of *The Apostasy of the Church of Rome,* with the title *The Church of Rome the Apostasy, and the Pope the Man of Sin and Son of Perdition of St. Paul's Prophecy.* The attempt of William Burgh, the Futurist, is exposed in this second edition, as having the deliberate purpose of attempting "to overthrow the whole scheme of Protestant interpretation, root and branch." [60]

3. CONFIRMS AUTHENTICITY OF JUSTINIAN'S DECREE.—Cuninghame's *Fulness of the Times* (1836) deals, in the preface, with Thomas Comber's charges in his *Roman Forgeries* (1673), that Justinian's edict-letter of 533 is a forgery. Citing Gothofredus, Gravina, Hothman, Baronius, and other witnesses, Cuninghame gives a scholarly and critical answer, with clear documentation for the authenticity of the citation.[61]

4. EARNEST APPEAL TO HEED ADVENT WARNING.—In his *Political Destiny of the Earth* (1833), Cuninghame meets some

---

[58] William Cuninghame, *The Pre-Millennial Advent of Christ Demonstrated From the Scriptures* (3d ed.), p. iv. (Title page reproduced on p. 278.)
[59] *Ibid.,* p. xv.
[60] William Cuninghame, *The Church of Rome the Apostasy, and the Pope the Man of Sin and Son of Perdition of St. Paul's Prophecy* (2d ed., 1833), Appendix, p. 51.
[61] William Cuninghame, *The Fulness of the Times,* pp. xi-xxi.

of the spiritualizing tendencies of the time that would depersonalize the second advent.   Here is his ringing declaration:

"If, then, as we certainly conclude, the Advent in Dan. vii.13, and Matt. xxiv.30, and Luke xxi.27, be our Lord's *personal coming* to judge the quick and the dead, since it has been seen that the 1260 years ended in the year 1792, and the Judgment of the ANCIENT OF DAYS, then began to sit, and the signs in the sun, moon, and stars, and distress of nations, and roaring of the sea and waves, or popular commotions, and the failing of men's hearts for fear, and the shaking of the powers of the political heavens or governments, are even now accomplishing before the eyes of every one who hath eyes to see, then it does most indubitably and incontrovertibly follow, that our Lord's coming with clouds is even *at the doors*; and as *that very generation,* to whom our Lord addressed his prophetic discourse, did witness its inchoate fulfilment in the awful destruction of Jerusalem, with circumstances of unparalleled wrath and misery on that people; so we believe that *this very generation,* before whose eyes the Lord is now spreading the multiplying signs of his approach, shall see his coming in his own glory, and the glory of the Father, and shall in vain call on the hills and the mountains to fall on them, and hide them from the wrath of the Lamb." [62]

On the basis of this premise he addresses himself to four classes—ministers, professors of religion, the careless and ungodly, and worldly politicians. To each he makes earnest appeal. Thus to ministers, as watchmen on the walls of Zion, appointed to sound the alarm, to know the hour of the night, and the proximity of the resurrection morn, he appeals to study the prophecies in order to discern the signs of the times:

"And if they who now have the high office of opening to their brethren the mysteries of the kingdom, desire to emerge from the condition of spiritual infancy, in which so many still remain, we tell them that they cannot advance a step beyond the first elements of the doctrine of Christ without the study of the prophetic word." [63]

Cuninghame stresses that "an awful crisis is now at hand," when the stone is about to smite the image on the feet:

"In other words, the time is at hand, when the Son of Man, with his Saints, shall be revealed in flaming fire, and shall abolish all earthly rule and authority, and establish his everlasting kingdom of peace and righteousness." [64]

---

[62] William Cuninghame, *The Political Destiny of the Earth* (3d ed., 1842), p. 25.
[63] *Ibid.,* p. 25.   [64] *Ibid.,* p. 26.

The professors of religion are reminded of the parable of the ten virgins, as he appeals to them not to treat "with levity or with scorn the annunciation of the *speedy Advent* and *glorious reign* of the Lord Jesus Christ." [65]   Next, speaking to the worldling who is hiding behind the indifference of the careless Christian, Cuninghame speaks of the terror of the advent to the ungodly, and makes this earnest plea:

"It is, indeed, the case that few of the ministers of Christ give heed to it, but on the other hand, you cannot but feel that we who hold it, do so with the Bible in our hands, and that we challenge our opponents to meet our arguments from the Word of God.   But this challenge is offered in vain.   Our adversaries are reduced to silence. Let every one, then, who has been leading a careless and ungodly life, into whose hands this Tract may fall, be persuaded not to neglect or despise the warning here given of the approach of the Son of Man with clouds, but let him instantly repent and turn to God, and believe in the Lord Jesus Christ, and he shall not only be saved from the wrath to come, but shall receive that spiritual illumination which will enable him to discern, whether this doctrine of the speedy advent of the Lord with all his saints, be the truth of God, or a fiction of our imagination." [66]

And finally, to the worldly politician he says:

"Let them all be warned that their schemes will end in utter disappointment.   The time is now at hand when all earthly authority must give place to that of the SAINTS OF THE MOST HIGH, and the shiftings of the political scenes witnessed in our own times, appear as it were to be the forerunners, of the entire prostration of wordly powers which is approaching." [67]

5. SCHOLARLY WITNESSES ATTEST PROPHETIC CERTAINTIES. —*Political Destiny* was really a survey of Daniel 2 and 7. [68]   Cuninghame asserts that Daniel's fourth beast, Paul's Man of Sin, and John's lamblike beast all describe the papal power. [69]   This statement he makes on the "nearly unanimous voice of the Protestant Churches," citing twenty-six leading names as illustrative. He next stresses the 1260 days as literal years from 533 to 1792. [70] In addition to Christian expositors, Cuninghame cites a large

---

[65] *Ibid.*, p. 27.   [66] *Ibid.*   [67] *Ibid.*
[68] William Cuninghame, *The Political Destiny of the Earth* (Philadelphia ed., 1840), Preface, p. v.
[69] *Ibid.*, p. viii.   [70] *Ibid.*, p. ix.

body of supporting Jewish writers—Saadia, Gaon, Jarchi (Rashi), Abarbanel, Moses ben Nachman, etc.[71]

The four empires of prophecy are outlined,[72] the ten divisions enumerated,[73] followed by identification of the papal Little Horn.[74] Finally the judgment scene, and the coming of the Son of man with the clouds of heaven is surveyed.[75] The "modern fancy of a *figurative coming* of the Son of Man" was declared unknown to the church of the early and Reformation centuries.[76]

To infidels—a fifth group—the prophetic procession of the centuries is passed in review, with its 1260-year period, and they are called upon to acknowledge and accept the foreknowledge of God.[77]

III. Revises Terminus of 2300 Years to 1843

The aggressive promotion of the particular interpretation of Edward Irving, popularizing the positions of his teacher, James Hatley Frere, led Cuninghame to issue *The Scheme of Prophetic Arrangement of the Rev. Edward Irving and Mr. Frere* in 1826. In a footnote at the close of the preface, Cuninghame says significantly, "Perhaps our Continental Societies are preparing the way for the accomplishment of the Prophetic warnings in Rev. xiv. 9-11." [78] And in chapter one he insists that, despite the "jarring and contending systems of the various interpreters of sacred prophecy," nevertheless "prophetic knowledge itself is evidently making rapid advances." [79]

1. LITTLE HORN OF DANIEL 8 ROMAN (NOT MOHAMMEDAN).—Cuninghame takes Irving to task chiefly for making the beast of Revelation 17, from the bottomless pit, to be infidel France, and for rendering Daniel 8:14, 2400 instead of 2300.[80] To show the unsoundness of this and related positions, he pays particular attention to the power of Daniel 8, asserting that

---

[71] *Ibid.*, pp. viii-xiv.   [74] *Ibid.*, pp. 23-29.   [76] *Ibid.*, pp. 34-40.
[72] *Ibid.*, pp. 16-21.   [75] *Ibid.*, pp. 29-33.   [77] *Ibid.*, pp. 45, 46.
[73] *Ibid.*, p. 22.
[78] William Cuninghame, *The Scheme of Prophetic Arrangement of the Rev. Edward Irving and Mr. Frere*, p. x n. (Title page reproduced on p. 278.)
[79] *Ibid.*, p. 1.   [80] *Ibid.*, pp. 18, 19.

though respectable authorities apply the little horn of Daniel 8 to Mohammedanism, names of equal weight counterbalance that position.[81] He shows that the acknowledged "theatre of the whole vision of Dan. viii," lies "wholly within the territories of the second and third empires of Daniel." [82] But the kingdom of Mohammed sprang up in Arabia, "which was never included in the empire of Alexander, and could not become a horn of the goat" until it had obtained possession of some of its territory.[83] This argument he pursues with clear reasoning and strong evidence.[84]

2. "DAILY" REMOVED BEFORE MOHAMMEDANISM AROSE.— Moreover, he holds that the little horn of Daniel 8 took away the daily sacrifice. But, he continues, "the daily sacrifice of the Eastern churches was taken away nearly a century before the appearance of Mahomed, and the abomination of desolation placed in them by the acts of the Roman emperors, in establishing the spiritual authority of the papal little horn and the idolatrous veneration of the virgin Mary and the saints." [85]

3. FALLACY OF THE 2400 YEARS ARGUMENT.—He next examines Irving's argument for the 2400 years—as from the time of the vision, supposedly in A.D. 553. Irving contends that 2300 years from this date would lead only to 1747, when nothing occurred, and that therefore the 2400 of the Septuagint, which would lead to 1847, is the true number, at which time the true worship will be restored in Jerusalem.[86] To this contention Cuninghame replies that such "calculation rests upon sand, for the number 2400 is not the reading of the Septuagint, as he supposes." [87] He then cites an array of authorities—including Prideau and Horne—showing that 2300 was the *original* Septuagint rendering. Only the Vatican edition of the later Theodotian translation of the Septuagint of Daniel so reads. On the contrary, the Complutensian (1514), the Aldine (1518), the Alexandrian (*c.* 1707 or 1720), and the Chisian all agree with the

---

[81] *Ibid.*, p. 63.
[82] *Ibid.*, p. 64.
[83] *Ibid.*
[84] *Ibid.*, p. 40 ff.
[87] *Ibid.*, p. 76.
[85] *Ibid.*, p. 70.
[86] *Ibid.*, p. 74.

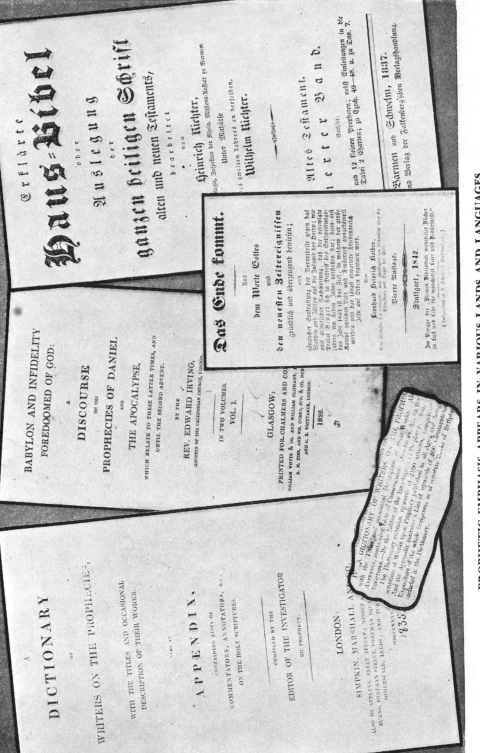

PROPHETIC EMPHASIS APPEARS IN VARIOUS LANDS AND LANGUAGES

Joshua Brooks' Remarkable *Dictionary of Writers on the Prophecies* (Left, With Inset), Tabulating Some 2100 Items; Title Page of a Noted Irving Discourse (Centre); and Two Well-known German Treatises on Prophecy by Kelber and Richter (Right)

Hebrew text of 2300.[88]   For these cogent reasons Cuninghame
rejects the 2400 rendering. [89]

The same argument was urged by Cuninghame at one of
the Albury Park Prophetic Conferences, as reported in *Dialogues
on Prophecy* (1828).[90]   After *Philalethes* [Lord Mandeville][91]
asks, "Does not Mr. Frere say that it ought to be 2400, and that
it is so in the Septuagint?"   Cuninghame gives this impressive
answer at the Council table:

"*Sophron.*—Yes, he does, but his position is quite untenable; and
he has subsequently abandoned it; p. 259.   The fact is, that our common
editions of the Greek Septuagint Bibles are printed after a copy in
which there was this typographical error; an error acknowledged to be such,
and what no scholar has dreamed of calling in question.   The edition of
the Greek Bible which is commonly used, is printed, as you will find
it stated in Prideaux, and Horne, not after that of the 70, but after
that of Theodotion, made about the end of the second century.   There
are three principal standard editions of the Septuagint Bible, all containing
the version of Daniel by Theodotion; viz. the Complutensian, published
in 1514; the Aldine, 1518; and the Vatican, 1587, from which the last
English editions of the 70 have been chiefly taken; to these three we may
add a fourth, being that of the Alexandrian text, published between 1707
and 1720.   Besides these, there is one called the Chisian, 1772, which contains the Greek text both of Theodotion and of the 70.   Of all these
six copies the Vatican alone reads 2400, all the rest agreeing with the
Hebrew and our English Bibles.   Moreover, the manuscript itself, in
the Vatican, from which the edition was printed, has 2300, and not 2400,
and therefore it is indisputable that the number 2400 is nothing but
a mis-print." [92]

Six years later the scholarly editor of *The Investigator, or
Monthly Expositor and Register, on Prophecy,* Joshua W.
Brooks, answering an inquiry from "W. G." in "The Septuagint Version *of the 2300 years,*" strongly supported Cuninghame's position:

"There is not a single *manuscript* known to be extant, whether
Hebrew or Greek, that sanctions the reading of 2400 days.   It rests
entirely upon a manifest *typographical error* of the Vatican EDITION,
taken from the Vatican manuscript; which the Chisian edition of Daniel

---

[88] *Ibid.*, pp. 76, 77.   [89] *Ibid.*, p. 78.
[90] Here called Sophron. See Brooks, *op. cit.*, p. lxxi.
[91] *Ibid.*
[92] *Dialogues on Prophecy*, vol. 1, pp. 326, 327.

notices, and says, that the Vatican *manuscript* reads 2300. W. G. will find this point fully discussed in 'The scheme of prophetic arrangement of the Rev. E. Irving and Mr. Frere critically examined, &c. by W. Cuninghame, Esq.' a small work, well worthy of a perusal." [93]

Still later, SAMUEL P. TREGELLES (1813-1875), eminent Greek scholar, critic, and author,[94] added a really final word.[95]

4. CLEANSING OF SANCTUARY AT TIME OF JUDGMENT.—Contending that "the abomination of desolation was placed in the sanctuary when the papal supremacy was established, together with the creature-worship of the virgin Mary and the saints," Cuninghame defines the cleansing as the execution of judgments upon the Gentiles and "the reestablishment in it [the sanctuary, or church] of the pure and spiritual worship of Jehovah." [96] And this would commence when "the time of the Judgment of Dan. vii.26 begins to sit for the destruction of the papal power." [97]

5. REVISES END OF 2300 TO 1843.—Then comes a manly revision by Cuninghame of his early position in dating the 2300 years, which had been "from the pushing of the Persian ram in the prosperous reign of Darius Hystaspes," to a terminus in 1792, at the close of the 1260 years. He now says, "It is very possible I may have been mistaken; for it is in itself equally probable that the 2300 years may terminate at the *complete cleansing* of the sanctuary in the day of Armageddon; and, in this case, the period must evidently commence at a later date than I have chosen." [98] He adds that if such should be the case—

"I am not aware of any more probable era which can be selected for their commencement than that which has been chosen by some recent writers,

---

[93] *The Investigator,* July, 1832 (vol. 1, no. 12), pp. 441. Signed ED[ITOR].
[94] Born at Falmouth, England, from 1838 to his death Tregelles devoted himself assiduously to the study of the New Testament text and related subjects. Author of several critical works, his *Greek New Testament, Edited from Ancient Authorities,* appeared in 1857, running through numerous editions. This work ranks with those of Tischendorf and Westcott and Hort, as one of the three great critical editions of the last century.
[95] He writes: "Some writers on prophecy have, in their explanations or interpretations of this vision, adopted the reading 'two thousand and *four* hundred days;' and in vindication of it, they have referred to the common printed copies of the LXX. version. In this book, however, the translation of Theodotion has been long substituted for the real LXX.: and further, although 'two thousand four hundred' is found in the common printed Greek copies, that is merely an erratum made in printing the Vatican edition of 1586, which has been habitually perpetuated. I looked [in 1845] at the passage in *the* Vatican MS., which the Roman edition professedly followed, and it reads exactly the same as the Hebrew text; so also does the *real* LXX. of Daniel. [So too Cardinal Mai's edition from the Vatican MS. which appeared in 1857.]" (S. P. Tregelles, *Remarks on the Prophetic Visions in the Book of Daniel,* p. 89 n.)
[96] William Cuninghame, *The Scheme of Prophetic Arrangement,* p. 79.
[97] *Ibid.*   [98] *Ibid.,* p. 80.

who suppose this period to have begun at the same time with the seventy weeks of Daniel, or in the year A.C.[99] 457, and, consequently, that it will terminate in the year 1843."[100]

Cuninghame recommends to the reader the "Mason of Wishawton" pamphlet "wherein he will find the subject treated more at large," and cites Mason's *Two Essays on Daniel's Prophetic Number of Two Thousand Three Hundred Days* (1820).[101] This was one of the earliest clear arguments in behalf of 1843. Cuninghame ends the chapter by observing:

"It does not appear to me that we can arrive at certainty on this point till the event shall make it clear. . . . An important end is in the mean while served, if by means of this and other prophetic numbers the attention of the church of God is kept awake, and in the position of earnest prayer, in the expectation of the stupendous events which are approaching."[102]

6. SYNCHRONIZES MATTHEW 24:14 AND REVELATION 14:6.— Still uncertain about the event to mark the close of the 1290 years, thirty years beyond the end of the 1260 years,[103] Cuninghame continues to hold that the final end will come forty-five years beyond that, or in $1792 + 30 + 45 = 1867$. That "end," he notes, is the same as of Matthew 24:14 when the witness of the preaching of the "gospel of the kingdom" shall be finished. Then the glorious advent of Christ shall take place in the clouds of heaven, to redeem His church and take the kingdom. And with this Cuninghame again ties in Revelation 14:6:

"Of this end, our Lord's words lead us to see that the immediate forerunner is to be an universal promulgation of the gospel, typified, also, by the flight of the Apocalyptical angel, chap. xiv.6. having the everlasting gospel to preach to all nations."[104]

This emphasis was now becoming a distinctive part of the prophetic and second advent emphasis.

IV. Astronomical Evidence Sustains 2300-Year Contention

In his *On the Jubilean Chronology of the Seventh Trumpet of the Apocalypse,* Cuninghame brought to the fore a unique

---

[99] *Ante Christum, ie.,* B.C.
[100] *Ibid.*
[101] To be considered in detail later.

[102] *Ibid.,* p. 81.
[103] *Ibid.,* p. 111.
[104] *Ibid.*

UNIQUE EVIDENCE FOR YEAR-DAY PRINCIPLE

Title Page of the De Chéseaux Volume Against the Starry Background That Was His Life Study.
His Impressive Deductions on the 1260 and 2300 Years as Celestial Periods Effectively Used by
Cuninghame to Sustain Year-Day Principle

line of evidence in confirmation of the year-day principle. The background was this: Nearly a century before, the Swiss astronomer M. Jean Philippe Loys de Chéseaux—correspondent of the Royal Academy of Sciences of Paris, foreign associate of the Academy at Göttingen, and author of various astronomical and mathematical works and tables—had been engaged in chronological research. And in order to fix the certainty of the date of the crucifixion, he was led to examine the book of Daniel.

M. de Chéseaux had been pondering a possible relationship between the prophetic periods of the 1260 and 2300 years, as the duration of certain predicted epochs, and the facts of astronomy —that is, the cyclical periods measuring the planetary revolutions in the heavens. To his amazement and delight he discovered that these periods comprise lunisolar cycles of remarkable perfection and accuracy, whose existence had been unknown to astronomers. He found that they are of one and the same character. He found, moreover, that the difference between these two periods, which is 1040 years—and which he called the "Daniel Cycle"—is the most accurate lunisolar cycle thus far discovered, harmonizing the revolutions of sun and moon. This he wrote out in "Remarques historiques, chronologiques, et astronomiques, sur quelques endroits du livre de Daniel" (Historical, Chronological, and Astronomical Remarks on Certain Parts of the Book of Daniel,[105] which was edited and published by his sons in 1754.

M. de Chéseaux here explains four kinds of cycles. Those—

1. Harmonizing the *solar day* and *solar year*.
2. Harmonizing the *solar year* and *lunar month*.
3. Harmonizing the *solar day* and *lunar month*.
4. Harmonizing all three—*day, month,* and *year*.

It had been almost impossible to find a cycle for this fourth class. But the 1260 years is such a cycle, with a remarkably small error. Then he had found that the 2300 years is even more perfect—the kind of cycle that had long been unsuccess-

---

[105] *Mémoires posthumes de Monsieur Jean Philippe Loys de Chéseaux, sur divers sujets, d'astronomie et de mathematiques avec de nouvelles tables très exactes des moyens mouvemens du Soleil, & de la Lune.*

fully sought by astronomers, a cycle "thirty times longer than the Period of Calippus," and having only "a seventeenth part of the error of that" ancient cycle, which error was "8h 12'." [106] The exact similarity of the slight error of these two cycles made de Chéseaux conclude that the difference between them—1040 years—ought to be a perfect cycle, free from error; and all the more remarkable as uniting all three kinds of cycles and "furnishing consequently a cycle of that fourth kind so long sought in vain." It proved to be even so. Then he says:

"This period of 1040 years, indicated indirectly by the Holy Ghost, *is a cycle at once solar, lunar, and diurnal or terrestrial of the most perfect accuracy.* I subsequently discovered two singular confirmations of this fact, which I will explain presently, when I have adduced all my purely astronomic proofs; may I in the meantime be permitted to give to this new cycle, the name of the DANIEL CYCLE." [107]

When de Chéseaux discovered the astronomical nature of this period, he regarded it as unmistakable proof of the inspiration of the book of Daniel. Such a cycle would never have been chosen by accident. And since it was not accidental, it must have been chosen by Him who timed the movements of the sun and moon in their orbits. [108]

M. de Chéseaux makes this further impressive statement:

"For several ages [centuries] the book of Daniel, and especially these passages of it, have been quoted and commented on by numerous and varied authors, so that it is impossible for a moment to call in question their antiquity. Who can have taught their author the marvellous relation of the periods he selected with soli-lunar revolutions? Is it possible, considering all these points, to fail to recognize in the author of the book of Daniel the Creator of the heavens and of their hosts, of the earth and the things that are therein?" [109]

Back in 1811 Cuninghame had noticed a reference to de Chéseaux's discoveries and had published the facts in a current *Christian Observer.* Then, in 1833, he wrote to the *Investigator,*

---

[106] *Ibid.,* p. 25.
[107] *Ibid.,* pp. 26, 27; translated freely in H. G. Guinness, *The Approaching End of the Age,* p. 403.
[108] De Chéseaux's results were checked at the time by Messrs. Mairan and Cassini, celebrated astronomers of the Royal Academy of Science of Paris, who declared them in harmony with astronomical fact.
[109] *Ibid.,* pp. 49-51; abridged in Guinness, *Romanism and the Reformation,* pp. 288, 289.

further describing the finding of the original work, which he had sought without success for twenty-two years. This fuller statement was then published as *On the Jubilean Chronology*. Professor Birks, of Cambridge, became much interested and wrote on it in 1843. And toward the end of the century H. Grattan Guinness made the fullest examination of all, Guinness' work being checked by Professor Adams of Cambridge.[110]

To Cuninghame these discoveries appeared as conclusive evidence that these prophetic numbers in Daniel are not literal days but *prophetic days* signifying *literal years*. Further, he believed that the 1260 years are a component part of the 2300 years. He felt that, in order to impress the church with their importance in measuring the epochs of the enemies of the church, they were not only announced to the church and confirmed by Gabriel with an oath, in the name of Him that liveth forever and ever (Dan. 12:7), but are engraved on the very system of the material universe, being "measures of the great revolutions of the diurnal, and lunar and solar periods of the heavens, these two numbers being, according to M. de Chéseaux, the only round numbers that are cyclical, and their difference 1040, a perfect cycle." [111] This was an impressive argument.

V. Frere—Champion of 2400 Rendering of Septuagint

On the opposite side of certain of these questions was JAMES HATLEY FRERE (1779-1866), controversialist writer on prophecy, born at Roydon, Norfolk, in England. His prophetic interpretations stirred considerable discussion on the part of expositors like G. S. Faber, William Cuninghame, and later by S. R. Maitland. He was likewise interested in educational questions, and about 1838 introduced a phonetic system for teaching the blind to read, and on which he wrote three books. He also devised an inexpensive method of stereotyping books, which was rather

---

[110] See T. R. Birks, *First Elements of Prophecy*, p. 372; H. G. Guinness, *The Approaching End of the Age*, pp. 399, 406; *History Unveiling Prophecy*, pp. 404, 405.
[111] William Cuninghame, *On The Jubilean Chronology of the Seventh Trumpet of the Apocalypse*, p. 31.

widely adopted.[112] Frere first began the study of the historical prophecies of Daniel and John about 1798, and to discuss the question with others in 1813.[113] This eventuated in his first book in 1815, *A Combined View of the Prophecies of Daniel, Esdras, and St. John.* (Title page reproduced on page 278.)

He was a gifted and logical writer, and author of eleven works, six of which were on Biblical prophecy. These, in addition to his *Combined View,* were *On the General Structure of the Apocalypse* (1826), *Eight Letters on the Prophecies* (1831), *The Harvest of the Earth* (1846), *The Great Continental Revolution* (1848), and *Notes, forming a Brief Interpretation of the Apocalypse* (1850). Though differing sharply from Faber and Cuninghame on certain features, he shared with them the view that the seventh trumpet had begun to sound in the French Revolution and that the seven vials were included in it—and that all this was in preparation for the imminent advent.

Frere was the leader of that school of interpretation holding that the correct number of Daniel 8:14 is 2400, on the basis of the Vatican Septuagint, instead of 2300. This 2400 years he dated from the alleged time of the vision, in 553 B.C., and therefore extended it to A.D. 1847.[114] The one seeming advantage of that end date was that it was in practical agreement with the 1843, 1844, and 1847 termini of the proponents of the 2300 years. The great disadvantage, on the other hand, was that the dating from the giving of the vision, was without regard to their relationship to the seventy weeks. The differences on these points opened the way for years of controversy, and ultimately led to uncertainty and disastrous abandonment, by many, of the whole prophetic scheme.

Attentive watch needs therefore to be kept of the unfolding conflict between advocates of the 2400-year school of exposition, and those of the 2300. Though the two reckonings ended at ap-

---

[112] *Dictionary of National Biography,* vol. 7, p. 706.
[113] James H. Frere, *The Great Continental Revolution, Marking the Expiration of the Times of the Gentiles, A.D. 1847-8,* pp. 6, 69; *A Combined View of the Prophecies of Daniel, Esdras, and St. John,* Preface, pp. iii, iv.
[114] James H. Frere, *A Combined View of the Prophecies of Daniel, Esdras, and St. John,* pp. 43, 246 ff., 260 ff.

proximately the same time, 1847—because some of the adherents to 2300 years missed the B.C. 4 factor, and began them in 453 B.C., and so ended them similarly in 1847—there were, nevertheless, basic differences. Though not original with Frere, the concept spread from him to Drummond, Wolff, and Irving. From the time of the 1826 Albury Conference onward, it came to symbolize a divergent wing—the Irvingites, who before long lost their prophetic bearings.

As noted, Frere's greatest acquisition was the winning of Edward Irving, one of the most celebrated preachers of London. Irving's studies with Frere opened a whole new world to him, with prophecy becoming the central theme of his thoughts, speech, and writing. This is frankly stated by Irving in the preface to his *Babylon and Infidelity Foredoomed* (1826).[115] (Facsimile reproduced on page 378.) Frere was a participant in the Albury Park Prophetic Conference discussions and was instrumental in forming the Society for the Investigation of Prophecy, in 1826.

1. SEALS IN THE WEST; TRUMPETS IN THE EAST.—Holding the usual interpretation of Daniel 2 and 7—the four empires, the ten divisions, the little horn as the Papacy, and the kingdom of God ensuing[116]—Frere believed that the seven seals of the Apocalypse depict the history of the Western Empire of Rome, while the seven trumpets parallel chronologically in the Eastern Empire.[117] The "Little Book Opened" he understood to be the history of the church.[118] He defines the prophetic symbols in a "Symbolical Dictionary" section.[119]

Frere followed the wake of Galloway in holding the Two Witnesses to be the Old and New Testaments, with their death and resurrection fulfilled in the French Revolution, with its renunciation of Christianity and its Toleration Edict of 1797.

2. 1290 AND 1335 EXTEND BEYOND 1260.—Basing his position on the year-day principle,[120] Frere likewise placed the 1260

---

[115] Edward Irving, *Babylon and Infidelity Foredoomed*, vol. 1, pp. iv-viii.
[116] James H. Frere, *A Combined View of the Prophecies of Daniel, Esdras, and St. John*, chaps. 2, 3. (The 10 kingdoms as variantly listed by Lloyd, Mede, and Newton are given.)
[117] *Ibid.*, pp. 11-13, 30, 34, 35.   [119] *Ibid.*, pp. 77-106.
[118] *Ibid.*, p. 13.   [120] *Ibid.*, pp. 90, 186.

years from 533 to 1792, the 1290 years from 533 to 1822-23, terminating with the close of the seven vials, and the 1335 years
from 533 to 1867, when he believed the millennial kingdom of
Christ should begin.   But the 2400 years, as noted, Frere allocates from 553 B.C. to A.D. 1847, when the sanctuary of the Eastern church should be cleansed from the corruption of Mohammedan superstition.[121]   The ram and the he-goat are, of course,
Medo-Persia and Grecia,[122] but Frere held the exceeding great
horn to be Mohammedanism.[123]

3. CONTRASTS SCHEMES OF FABER AND CUNINGHAME.—Frere
enters into a minute study of the leading positions on prophecy,
particularly the chronological relationship of the seals, trumpets,
and vials.[124]   Space precludes following his details.   He dia-
gramed the schemes of Faber and Cuninghame, showing how
Faber puts the seals *before* the trumpets, while Cuninghame
synchronizes them,[125] and capitalizes on their differences.   He
shows how Faber puts the 1260 years from 606 to 1866, while
Cuninghame places the 1260 years from 533-1792, the 1290
years (beginning synchronously with the 1260 in 533) extending
thirty years beyond, to 1822, and in the same way the 1335 years
reaching on to 1867.[126]   In the latter features, however, he was in
agreement with Cuninghame.

4. ENDS 2400 MIDWAY BETWEEN 1290 AND 1335.—Frere
holds tenaciously to the terminus of the 1260 years in 1792, the
1290 years in 1822, and the 1335 in 1867[127]—thus making the
year 1867 the focal point of his scheme, and having the 2400
years end midway between the 1822 and 1867 end dates for the
1290- and 1335-year periods respectively.   He is equally tenacious
—following Faber—in holding that the 2400 years begin in
553 B.C., the "third year of Belshazzar," and end in 1847.[128]

5. SOCIETIES PROCLAIMING JUDGMENT-HOUR MESSAGE.—
Sixteen years later, in 1831, after the Albury Park Confer-

---

[121] *Ibid.*, Explanatory Chart on "General Plan and Arrangement of the Prophecies,"
opposite title page; also pp. 37, 41, 42, 244.
[122] *Ibid.*, chap. 4.   [123] *Ibid.*, pp. 236-243.   [124] *Ibid.*, pp. 44-110.
[125] *Ibid.*, pp. 74, 75; also pp. 78, 79.
[126] *Ibid.*, pp. 75, 249, 256.   [127] *Ibid.*, p. 244.   [128] *Ibid.*, pp. 246-249.

ences, and after much discussion in the interim, Frere reiterates the same views of the prophetic periods and their dates in his *Eight Letters on the Prophecies, Relating to the Last Times.*[129] Discussing the flying angel of Revelation 14:6, Frere envisions in its symbolism the contemporary Bible and other societies, with the exaltation of the Two Testaments (Witnesses) after three and a half years of the denial of their authority under the French Revolution, as portrayed in Revelation 11.[130] This announcement of the hour of God's judgment is designed to prepare for the awful events impending, and to bring men to repentance, though others will be hardened.[131] So there were pronounced similarities.

6. PROPHETIC SOCIETIES FOREWARN BABYLON'S DOOM.— The second angel's prophetic proclamation, Frere holds, is to warn of the judgments to be visited upon the Papacy under the outpouring of the vials, and is being fulfilled in the "particular attention" being given to the prophecies and the warnings of numerous writers, and in such discourses and writings as Irving's *Babylon and Infidelity Foredoomed,*[132] and in those prophetic societies that meet weekly for the discussion of prophecy, with special annual meetings.[133] The whole earth, he continues, is to be "lightened with the glory of God through the study of his word of prophecy."[134]

7. REFORMATION SOCIETIES CALLING OUT OF BABYLON.— The third contemporary work of the church, as signified by the third angel of Revelation 14, is, he believed, "calling the elect people of God out of the mystic Babylon."[135] This emphasis was particularly manifest in Britain when in 1827 the Society "To Promote the Religious Principles of the Reformation" was formed, though it started originally through the attempts of a few clergymen in Ireland.

---

[129] James H. Frere, *Eight Letters on the Prophecies, Relating to the Last Times,* pp. 15, 28, 29.
[130] *Ibid.,* p. 60. [131] *Ibid.,* pp. 60, 61.
[132] Irving's discourse before the Continental Society, and afterward published.
[133] *Ibid.,* pp. 62, 63. [134] *Ibid.,* pp. 64, 65.
[135] *Ibid.,* pp. 66, 67; see also *Three Letters on the Prophecies* (1833), pp. 28, 29.

8. Time of Trouble and Armageddon Imminent.—Frere held that the last great conflict will center in Judea, according to Daniel 11:45.[136] And again Frere stresses the cleansing of the sanctuary in 1847, placing this event in the time of unexampled trouble of Daniel 12:1, which will mark the expiration of the "times of the Gentiles." Armageddon, he therefore contends, is not far distant.[137]

9. Vials Began With French Revolution.—In *The Harvest of the Earth* (1846), Frere places "the harvest" as "prior to the vintage of wrath." He emphasizes again the three societies to prepare the world for the final judgment—the Bible and the missionary organizations, the prophetic societies, and the Reformation societies, in their order of progressive fulfillment.[138]

Frere still held steadfastly to these basic positions in his last work, *The Great Continental Revolution, Marking the Expiration of the Times of the Gentiles, A.D. 1847-8* (1849). The 1260 years were set forth as from March, 533, to the abolition of royalty in the French Revolution in September, 1792, with the 1290 years closing in 1823 and the 1335 ending in 1867. The seven vials lead through the national profession of infidelity in France in 1792, the Reign of Terror in 1793-94, the overthrow of the papal government in Rome, 1796-98, the tyrannical reign of Napoleon, 1802-14, the army of occupation of France, 1815-18. And the sixth vial, in the Eastern Empire, involves the dismembering of the Turkish Empire, and in the Western Empire, the revolutions of Naples, Piedmont, Spain, and Portugal, in 1820-23.[139] One section, addressed to Dr. Joseph Wolff, still deals extensively with the 2400 reading versus the 2300, on the basis of the manuscript.[140]

---

[136] James H. Frere, *Eight Letters*, p. 76.
[137] *Ibid.*, pp. 76, 77.
[138] James H. Frere, *The Harvest of the Earth*, pp. 11-15.
[139] James H. Frere, *The Great Continental Revolution, Marking the Expiration of the Times of the Gentiles, A.D. 1847-8* (2d ed., 1849), "Tabular View of the Latter Times," facing opening page.
[140] *Ibid.*, pp. 66-69 (1848 ed.).

CHAPTER TWENTY-ONE

American Witness Injected Into Discussion

Inasmuch as an 1818 English reprint of the tractate on *The Millennium* by the American clergyman, W. C. Davis, of South Carolina, played an important part in the conclusions reached on the 2300 years by the influential Scotch minister, Archibald Mason, in 1820; and since this appears to be the only American work on the question at this early time which found its way into circulation in England, it seems desirable to include Davis' life sketch here, and the summary of his positions.

I. Davis of America—Seventy Weeks Grand Clue to 2300 Years

WILLIAM C. DAVIS, or Davies (1760-1831), Presbyterian minister of South Carolina, was trained for the ministry at Mt. Zion College, Winnsborough, South Carolina. Licensed to preach in 1787, he was ordained in 1789, and served the churches of Nazareth and Milford until 1792. For a time, following 1803, he was a stated missionary among the Catawba Indians. In 1806 he became pastor of Bullock's Creek church.[1] During that year he wrote *The Gospel Plan; or, A Systematical Treatise on the Leading Doctrines of Salvation* (1809), which drew upon him the charge of holding erroneous doctrine. Complaint was carried to the synod. The book was condemned in 1809, after a series of trials and hearings by the Presbyterian Church courts having jurisdiction.

---

[1] A full discussion of Davis appears in *Prophetic Faith*, Vol. 4.

Davis voluntarily withdrew from the Presbyterian Church in 1810, and organized the Independent Presbyterian Church, though he was formally deposed by the Concord Presbytery in 1811.[2] Thenceforth he labored diligently to build this Independent church in the Carolinas and in Tennessee, which was largely congregational in form of government. His followers perpetuated their separate church life until 1863, when this body was received into the Southern Presbyterian Church.[3] He wrote *A Solemn Appeal to the Impartial Public* (1812), and *Lectures on Paul's Epistle to the Romans* (published posthumously in 1858), as well as a *Catechism.*

Davis was the first American to set forth the proposition of the simultaneous beginning of the 2300 years and the seventy weeks of years. Published first in South Carolina, about 1808, while Davis was still pastor of Bullock's Creek, *The Millennium, or a Short Sketch of the Rise and Fall of Antichrist,* was later reprinted in England (1818), where it exerted a telling influence. It was noted by William Miller, in 1836,[4] as one of five key voices exemplifying the world-wide awakening on this prophetic time period, and in substantial agreement as to its time placement. Still later Davis issued another *Treatise on the Millennium* (1827), in which he reaffirmed in his declining years: "I am still in the full belief, that my calculation from Daniel is correct; and therefore I expect the Millennium to commence about the year 1847 or 1848."[5] He added that he often climbed to Pisgah's height to view the landscape, and rest contented, like Daniel, to go his way, hoping to stand in his lot at the end of days. (Facsimile reproduction appears on page 290.)

1. ANTICHRIST'S 1260 YEARS END AT ADVENT.—Davis' earlier pamphlet was obviously written between 1806 and 1810

[2] *Records of Concord Presbytery,* vol. 1, pp. 299, 332, 333.
[3] Sketch in *Constitution and Form of Government of the Independent Presbyterian Church in the United States of America;* McClintock and Strong, *Cyclopedia of Biblical, Theological, and Ecclesiastical Literature,* vol. 12, p. 257; William B. Sprague, *Annals of the American Pulpit,* vol. 4, pp. 122, 123.
[4] William Miller, *Evidence from Scirpture [sic] and History of the Second Coming of Christ, About the Year 1843,* p. 193. (Title page reproduced on p. 618).
[5] W. C. Davis, *A Treatise on the Millennium,* pp. 84, 85.

—probably in 1808—as it was while he was still pastor of Bullock's Creek. It deals with the prophecies of Daniel, Paul, and John concerning the papal Antichrist, the vials as fulfilled in the Reformation, and the French Revolution. He avers "the Pope, the man of sin, will be destroyed by the brightness and glory of his [Christ's] coming." [6] The length of the "reign of popery" is 1260 years, for "according to prophetic computation, we are to count a day for a year." [7] For this he cites Ezekiel 4, and then the three and a half times, the forty-two months, and the 1260 days as referring to the same period.

2. SEVENTY WEEKS FIRST PART OF 2300 YEARS.—Davis next turns to the 2300 years of Daniel 8:13, 14, declaring that the "cleansing of the sanctuary" means the restoration of the true worship of God to the church, or the beginning of the millennium. Here is his full statement:

"It must be evident that 'to the cleansing of the sanctuary,' means, to the commencement of the Millennium, when the true worship of God will be restored to the church. It is also evident that the 2300 days, are 2300 years, and consequently the end of these 2300 years must close the reign of popery." [8]

"Here we are to take special notice, that these 70 weeks are the first part of the 2300 years. Also, we are to notice that these 70 weeks were to be fulfilled on the Jews, before the Gentiles were connected with the church; therefore they relate solely to the Jewish nation, exclusively of the Gentiles." [9]

3. ACCOMPLISHMENTS OF THE SEVENTY WEEKS.—The reconciliation effected under the seventy weeks is the "atonement of the cross," the everlasting righteousness brought in is through the gospel dispensation, and the anointing of the most holy is Christ's ascension to heaven after the cross, "to sprinkle the most holy place with his own blood." [10] He again notes that the year-day principle for the seventy weeks means 490 years to Christ in the gospel dispensation. Remarking on the three divisions of the period, he points out that the sixty-second week will reach to "the time when he [Christ] should be publicly

[6] William C. Davis, *The Millennium, or a Short Sketch of the Rise and Fall of Antichrist,* p. 3.
[7] *Ibid.,* p. 4.   [8] *Ibid.,* p. 5.   [9] *Ibid.,* p. 6.
[10] *Ibid.,* pp. 6, 7.

inaugurated," at His baptism, when thirty years of age.[11] The last week of years, embracing His three and a half years of ministry, was marked by the cross in the midst, putting an end to all typical worship from Pentecost onward.[12] The remaining portion of the seventieth week was devoted to the preaching to the Jews.[13]

4. BASES CALCULATIONS FROM A.D. 30.—Basing his argument on A.D. 30 as the year when Christ was "30 years of age," and His crucifixion therefore in His "34th year," Davis calculates backward from the seventieth week (as from A.D. 30 to 37), instead of forward from a decree, and secures 453 B.C. as the beginning date.

"Christ was baptized when he was thirty years of age, and that he was crucified in his 34th year. So that when we add three years and a half, the remainder of the 70th week, we evidently see that Daniel's 70 weeks, or 490 years, come exactly to the thirty-seventh year of Christ. So that Daniel's 490 years, overrun the Christian era 37 years. We must therefore take the 37 years from 490, and the remainder is 453, and will coincide exactly with the birth of Christ." [14]

5. POSSIBLE FOUR-YEAR ERROR IN DATING VULGAR ERA.— He declares that there can be no mistake in this calculation— note this—"unless the Christian era be not exactly to the true date of the birth of Christ." [15] This point he repeats:

"If there be an error in my future calculation, it must be an error in the vulgar aera, not being correctly fixed to the time of the real birth of our Saviour. I know that it is generally thought that the vulgar aera is four years too late. If so, it will only bring on the Millennium four years sooner than I calculate, because I have to calculate by the vulgar aera, when the Scripture date ends, and I will of course be just so far wrong as the vulgar date differs from the true Scripture date." [16]

6. 2300 YEARS EMBRACE PERSIA, GREECE, ROME.—If the 1260 years of papal power date from 587 or 588, the addition of 1260 years equals 1848.[17] As to the soundness of the seventy weeks being the first part of the 2300 years, Davis says the

---

[11] *Ibid.*, pp. 7, 8.
[12] *Ibid.*, pp. 9, 10.
[13] *Ibid.*, p. 12.
[14] *Ibid.*, p. 16.
[17] *Ibid.*, pp. 17, 18.
[15] *Ibid.*, pp. 16, 17.
[16] *Ibid.*, p. 17.

seventy weeks are the angelic explanation of the dating of the 2300 years.[18] He reviews the symbols of Daniel 8—the Medo-Persian ram, the Grecian he-goat, Alexander as the notable horn, the four succeeding horns as the first divisions, and the exceeding great horn as the Roman Empire. The "vision of the Romans is carried on through the kingdom of popery until it is destroyed. It is evident that this vision comprehends the 2300 years, beginning in the reign of the Medes and Persians, and extending to the downfall of popery." [19]

7. SEVENTY WEEKS AT BEGINNING OF LONGER VISION.—When Gabriel came, Davis contends, it was to explain the longer vision. He therefore concludes:

"It must therefore appear that this second explanation, is an explanation of the same vision which contains the 2300 years, and where can we place these 490 years, but at the beginning of the vision." [20]

Holding that the 490 years, ending three and a half years after Pentecost, begin in 453 B.C., in the reign of the Persians, and comprehend the reign of the Persians from the decree to restore and rebuild Jerusalem—and on through the Grecian and Roman kingdoms—he states:

"But it is plain that the 2300 years also must begin at the same time, and extend through all those empires, to the close of the empire of popery; because the state of those very kingdoms is explained by the Angel under this very vision, the duration of which was proclaimed to be 2300 days, so that the very design of the 70 weeks was evidently to designate that first part of the vision, which would last until the calling of the Gentiles." [21]

8. GRAND CLUE: LIKE COLUMBUS'S TAPPED EGG.—This joint beginning Davis denominates as the "grand clue, on which the whole calculation is founded." [22] Asserting that if an absolutely accurate date for the beginning could be ascertained, then the exact ending could be known,[23] he tabulates his calculations and adds that it is not the vain venture of a productive imagination or bold conjecture. Referring to Columbus and the egg, Davis makes a unique point about his "clue."

---

[18] *Ibid.*, p. 19.   [19] *Ibid.*   [20] *Ibid.*, pp. 19, 20.
[21] *Ibid.*, p. 20.   [22] *Ibid.*, p. 21.   [23] *Ibid.*

"None of the gentlemen around the table could make it stand on its end, till Christopher gave it a tap on the table and shewed them how, and then they could all do it easily." [24]

"The only reason why divines have been so bewildered on this subject, is, because they have totally overlooked Daniel's 70th week, so accurately stated, and consequently had no number to direct their calculations." [25]

The influence exerted upon Mason by Davis will next be noted.

II. Mason—Dates Joint Beginning From 457 B.C.

ARCHIBALD MASON (1753-1831), of Wishawton, Scotland, was born in Bargody, Lanarkshire, of deeply religious parents. He was chosen to preach by the Reformed Presbyterian Church in 1783, and was ordained at Wishawton, Scotland, in 1787, where he ministered continuously for forty years. Andrew Symington, in his memoir, declares that Mason "longed for the glory of the latter days." [26] He was favorably known to the religious public through his eleven principal books, issued between 1793 and 1829. "In consideration of these writings" he "received in 1831 the degree of Doctor of Divinity from the College of Schenectady in North America." [27]

Though Mason was author of a dozen works, only four pertain to our quest. These, stretching over a period of fourteen years (1818-1827), show a definite progression in expanding interests and in accuracy of interpretation. His biographer states, "It was the very delight of his soul to preach Christ in the character of the Mediator," [28] one of his earliest books being on this theme. He constantly expounded the prophecies by word and pen. Says Symington:

"By these discourses he was brought into contact with that part of the religious community which had turned their attention particularly to the fulfillment of prophecy. While he enters with great ardour into the subject, he speaks with due submission in his calculations of times and avoids the extravagances into which not a few ran in these matters. He was invited to attend a meeting in the house of Henry Drummond, Esq. at

---

[24] *Ibid.*, p. 22.   [25] *Ibid.*, p. 23.
[26] Andrew Symington, *The Dismission, Rest, and Future Glory of the Good and Faithful Servant: Two Discourses, Preached . . . after the Funeral of the Rev. Archibald Mason, D.D.*, p. xii.
[27] *Ibid.*, p. xiii.   [28] *Ibid.*, pp. 49, 57.

Albury Park, on the 28th October, 1827 for a conference on prophetic subjects. His distance, advanced life, and other things, prevented his attendance, but he wrote remarks on the different topics of discussion and declared his sentiments about the coming of Christ at the destruction of anti-Christ, in agreement with what he published." [29]

1. PROPHETIC IDENTIFICATION OF ANTICHRIST.—Mason's first treatise to enter the field of prophetic exposition was issued in 1818—*An Inquiry Into the Times that Shall Be Fulfilled at Antichrist's Fall; the Church's Blessedness in Her Millennial Rest; The Signs that this Happy Season is at Hand; the Prophetic Numbers Contained in the 1335 Days; and the Christian's Duty, at this Interesting Crisis in Five Discourses.*[30] The initial discussion pertains to the soon-coming "stone" kingdom that smites the image of Daniel 2 on the feet of iron and clay.[31] At this time Antichrist's allotted reign will end, or be fulfilled. Mason cites Daniel 7:8, 21, 25, 2 Thessalonians 2:3, 4, Revelation 13:11ff., and Revelation 17. Of the papal Antichrist Mason says:

"These are some of the predictions concerning the rise, character, and conduct of the ecclesiastic beast of Rome. The history of the Romish church, and of the Popes who have been at the head of it, clearly shews, that, black and frightful as the representations are, they have not been exaggerated. It is not necessary that every feature in this prophetic drawing, should be found in this beast at his childhood, nor that they should all prominently appear in him in his old age; sufficient certainly it must be, if they are all applicable to him, in the course of his life and actings." [32]

These characteristics are: Rising among Rome's ten divisions, pretended vicarship of Christ, claim to infallibility, usurped power to depose and set up kings, hatred of true church, anathemas and edicts, cruel persecutions, worldly wisdom, and blasphemous names. He adds, "So do these inspired predictions delineate the abominations of popery." [33]

---

[29] *Ibid.*, pp. xiii, xiv.
[30] In the "new edition," 1821, this is combined with two other works, *An Appendix* (1818), and *Two Essays* (1820), under the title *The Church's Happy Prospect, and the Christian's Present Duty: Containing An Inquiry . . . in Five Discourses: With An Appendix to the Discourse on the Prophetic Numbers. Also Two Essays on Daniel's Prophetic Number of 2300 Days, and on the Christian's Duty to Inquire Into the Church's Deliverance.*
[31] Archibald Mason, *An Inquiry into the Times that Shall Be Fulfilled at Antichrist's Fall,* in *The Church's Happy Prospect, and the Christian's Present Duty,* p. 14.
[32] *Ibid.*, pp. 14, 15.
[33] *Ibid.*, pp. 15, 16.

2. VARIED ASPECTS UNDER SAME 1260 YEARS.—Mason asserts that the "time of his existence and power shall be fulfilled," because "those prophets whom the Lord employed to
foretell his rise and reign, predict also his fall and ruin." [34] Then
he quotes the words of Daniel, Paul, and John concerning the
fall of the system, adding:

"Such shall be the end of the lamb-horned, but dragon-mouthed beast,
which has successfully propagated error, idolatry, immorality, and persecution on the earth." [35]

The rather common concept of the two beasts of Revelation 13 is shared by Mason as "the secular and ecclesiastic" aspects involved in the Papacy.[36] Their time is the same as that
of the woman in the wilderness, the two witnesses prophesying
in sackcloth, and the prevailing power of the Little Horn. When
she is delivered from the power of the Horn, she emerges from
the wilderness and finishes her sackcloth witness. All these are
comprehended in the three and a half prophetic "times."

3. CONTEMPORARY RECOGNITION OF TIMES IS SIGN OF END.
—The contemporaneous running to and fro in, and understanding of, the prophecies concerning the end, is stressed:

"It is a certain mark of the time of the end, when many persons are
excited, in the providence of God, to employ their time and abilities in
the investigation of Divine predictions, in the observation of Divine providences, and in the application of the one to the other, that they may know,
and declare to the church, how far inspired prophecy is accomplished, by
the things that have come to pass in our days." [37]

Mason asserts that "we are bound to consider those things
as a sign that this happy season will soon arrive," because so
many are engaged in explaining these predictions.[38] In fact, he
declares, nothing of such "extent" and "perspicuity" has ever
appeared before, and must not go unrecognized as "a sign of
the coming of his kingdom." [39] Simeon, Anna, and Joseph of
Arimathaea were awaiting the first advent, and before that there
was the expectation of deliverance from the seventy years' captivity. So Mason pertinently adds:

34 *Ibid.*, p. 16.   36 *Ibid.*, pp. 16, 14, 80.   38 *Ibid.*
35 *Ibid.*   37 *Ibid.*, p. 75.   39 *Ibid.*, **pp. 75, 76.**

"When there is a very general expectation existing in the minds of believers, that Christ's kingdom, in her millennial glory, is soon to be established in the earth, we may consider it as a sign that this blessed deliverance is at hand. If the nature of this expectation, its extent among Christians, and the ground on which they rest their hope, are duly considered, it will appear to be an unquestionable sign, that the desired object is near—It is not a mere speculative opinion, or a bare conjecture; but it is a religious hope founded on the Divine promises, creating in them an earnest desire that God, for the glory of his name, and in mercy to immortal souls, would speedily send his gospel to the uttermost ends of the earth—This hope is also become very general among Christians, and multitudes of them are now looking for redemption to the church, and waiting for the kingdom of God.—The ground of their hope is the same with that of Daniel. Like that holy Prophet, they understand by the books of inspired prophecy, that the number of the years which God would accomplish in the desolations of his church is now coming to an end. The existence, therefore, of such an expectation in those who are truly religious and well informed, is a sign that the millennial day is at hand." [40]

4. 1335 CONTAINS THE 1260 AND 1290 YEARS.—Coming to the 1335 days in relation to the 1260 and 1290 contained within it, Mason holds that the 1335 days represent the gross number with respect "to the church's low condition, and to the reign and tyranny of the Antichristian horn." [41] To the 1260 he adds 30 for the 1290, and 45 more, or a total of 75, for the 1335 days. In this Mason begins with the 1260 days (42 months or three and a half times) "of the continuance of antichrist's power." [42] These "different representations describe a number of the same duration." He adds:

"The beautiful harmony of those descriptions of this number establishes the truth of this explanation of them, and shows that they describe a period of the same duration." [43]

5. TOUCHES PAPACY, JEWS, AND MILLENNIUM.—Each of these days is "the prophetic symbol for one year," according to Ezekiel 4. And the first number (1260) is the "time of the beast's war with the church, and of her depressed state," which must continue for the "long season of 1260 years." [44] Then Mason's argument continues:

---

[40] *Ibid.*, p. 77.
[41] *Ibid.*, p. 87.
[42] *Ibid.*, p. 88.
[43] *Ibid.*
[44] *Ibid.*, p. 89.

"Besides, there are two other numbers, which must be added to Daniel's 1260 years, one of 30, and another of 45 days, which must expire before the church's happy condition will begin. The 30 days must also signify 30 years, and the 45 days must represent 45 years; and these, being added together, form Daniel's gross number, of one thousand three hundred and five and thirty years." [45]

On the basis of Daniel 12, Mason connects the deliverance of the Jews with the close of the 1290 year-days—which begin with the taking away of the daily sacrifice and the setting up of the abomination.[46] Forty-five years after the close of the 1290 years—or at the end of the 1335 years—"the period of great blessedness shall then be introduced." [47]

"The last year of the 1335 years, will be the first year of the blessed millennium. It cannot begin sooner; for the church is not blessed till she wait and come to that year: It cannot be delayed till the following year; for when that year shall arrive, her blessedness shall begin." [48]

6. ENDS 1335 YEARS IN 1866-67.—Beginning the 1260 years with 533, Mason ends them in 1792 when the judgments begin to fall on the Papacy. The sequence of the three periods is:

"From 533 till 1792 inclusive of these years, we have Daniel's number of 1260 years. The 30 additional years, and the number of 1290 years, will terminate in 1822, when the public conversion and restoration of Israel will probably begin. The second additional number of 75 years and the gross number of 1335 will come to their end in 1867." [49]

In the *Appendix to an Inquiry Into the Prophetic Numbers Contained in The 1335 Days*, he repeats the argument.[50] This position he never abandoned.

7. SEVENTY WEEKS FIRST PART OF 2300 DAYS.—Mason's great contribution, however, was his *Two Essays on Daniel's Prophetic Number of Two Thousand Three Hundred Days; and on the Christian's Duty to Inquire into the Church's Deliverance* (1820). It was this treatise that had such a far-reaching influence upon the advent awakening on both sides of the Atlantic, and that was cited with admiration by the Millerites a score of years later. In discussing Daniel 8:13, 14, Mason first defines the terms involved:

---

[45] *Ibid.*
[46] *Ibid.*, p. 92.
[47] *Ibid.*
[48] *Ibid.*, p. 93.
[49] *Ibid.*, p. 96.
[50] *Ibid.*, p. 150.

"The daily sacrifice, in this vision, signifies the instituted worship of God in the church; and the desolation and treading down of the sanctuary and the host, means the error, superstition and idolatry, that were established instead of that worship. The question is an inquiry into the time that must elapse from the date of this number, to the time when the profanation of the sanctuary and the host shall come to an end, and the true worship of God shall be restored. This question is answered in the following words. 'Unto two thousand and three hundred days.' The answer also describes the event which will take place at the expiration of those days; and assures us, upon the veracity of that God whose servant the angel was, of the certainty of that event, 'Then shall the sanctuary be cleansed.'" [51]

Mason first rejects the opinion of Magnus Friedrich Roos in *Exposition of the Prophecies of Daniel,* who interprets this text to mean 2300 Jewish evening and morning sacrifices on 1150 whole days.[52] He takes similar exception to Bicheno and Faber.[53] He then sets forth the view that the visions of the 2300 days of Daniel 8 and the seventy weeks of Daniel 9 began "at the same time." [54]   (Title page of *Two Essays* is on page 290.)

8. BOTH VISIONS BEGIN WITH PERSIA.—Mason contends "that the clearness of the latter number is intended to remove the obscurity of the former; that the seventy weeks are the first part of the 2300 days; and that both numbers commenced at the same time." [55]   He adds that the 2300 days is the only number that begins under the Jewish dispensation and "extends to the time of the end." Also, the same angel explains both visions.[56] The "reasonableness and probability" of this thesis assumes the proportions of a "certainty." This is followed by clear reasoning on the very structure and historical demands of Daniel 8 and 9. The vision of the Persian ram and Grecian goat begins with Persia, and the seventy weeks begin with the command of a Persian king—the Babylonian kingdom having passed.[57] And both visions refer to the sanctuary—the vision of Daniel 8

---

[51] Archibald Mason, *Two Essays on Daniel's Prophetic Number of Two Thousand Three Hundred Days; and on the Christian's Duty to Inquire Into the Church's Deliverance* (Newburgh, 1820 ed.), p. 6.

[52] Magnus Friedr. Roos, *Auslegung der Weissagungen Daniels, die in die Zeit des Neuen Testaments hineinreichen, nebst ihrer Vergleichung mit der Offenbarung Johannis,* pp. 205, 206.

[53] Archibald Mason, *Two Essays of Daniel's Prophetic Number of Two Thousand Three Hundred Days,* p. 8.

[54] *Ibid.,* p. 10.   [56] *Ibid.,* pp. 10, 11.

[55] *Ibid.*   [57] *Ibid.,* p. 12.

to show the desolation and cleansing of the sanctuary, and the vision of the ninth an answer to his prayer for light to "shine upon thy sanctuary." [58]　And the 2300 days is not connected with any other period but the seventy weeks. It has to do with the popish pollutions of the sanctuary. [59]

9. SEVENTY WEEKS BEGIN WITH ARTAXERXES' DECREE.— Mason now mentions the pamphlet he had "lately seen" by William C. Davis, of South Carolina, which was first published in America, and "republished in 1818, at Workington, in the North of England." [60]　Concerning Davis' basic contention that the 2300 days commenced with Daniel's seventy weeks, Mason frankly states: "In this opinion I am constrained to concur. Though there are some things in his manner of calculating them, with which I do not agree." [61]

Mason criticizes Davis' failure to notice the decree as marking the beginning of the seventy weeks, "but arbitrarily fixes its termination in the 37th year of the Christian era." [62] On the contrary Mason insists that it should be in this wise:

"The decree of the Persian king, mentioned in this prophecy, must be the decree of Artaxerxes given to Ezra, in the seventh year of that monarch's reign. The decrees of Cyrus and Darius were too early, and the decree of Artaxerxes, in the twentieth year of his reign, given to Nehemiah, was too late, for answering the prediction.—Artaxerxes issued his decree to Ezra, in the 457th year before Christ. If we add to this number 33 years, which was our Redeemer's age at his crucifixion, we have 490 years." [63]

10. 457 B.C. SUBTRACTED FROM 2300 LEAVES A.D. 1843.— Discussing the component parts of the seventy weeks and the crucifixion of Christ in A.D. 33, in the midst of the seventieth week—which began with the public baptism of Jesus—Mason comes to his climax in clear reasoning on the time feature. Having shown that the 2300 days and seventy weeks begin together he continues:

"The two thousand three hundred years began four hundred and ninety years before the death of our Lord Jesus Christ, and four hundred and fifty-seven years before his birth, at which the Christian era com-

---

[58] *Ibid.*, p. 13.　　[60] *Ibid.*, p. 9.　　[62] *Ibid.*, p. 16.
[59] *Ibid.*, p. 8.　　[61] *Ibid.*　　[63] *Ibid.*

menced. If we subtract 457 from 2300, the remainder will give that year in the Christian era, when the 2300 years will expire. By this simple operation, we find that this number will end in 1843. In that year, the Lord's sanctuary shall be cleansed, the church and the nations will be delivered from the abominations of the Mother of Harlots, and Popery will perish from the earth." [64]

11. FANCIFUL ANALOGY LEADS TO 1866.—Instead of drawing upon the Day of Atonement type for the intent of the "cleansing of the sanctuary," Mason cites 2 Chronicles 29:3, 15, 17-19 concerning the physical cleansing of the pollutions of the earthly sanctuary in the time of Hezekiah.[65] The pollutions under Ahaz were taken as a type of the pollutions under Romanism. But this was clustered about the celebration of the Passover in the first month. And Mason develops another idea:

"May not those twenty-four days, which elapsed between the cleansing of the temple and the keeping of that passover, be an emblem of the twenty-four years, which will intervene between 1843, when the church will be delivered from popery, and 1867, when the blessed millennium will begin?" [66]

12. STRANGE ALLOCATION OF "666 YEARS."—Another curious bit of reckoning is that "from the year 133, before Christ, when the Roman Empire became an Asiatic state, till A.D. 533, when the emperor Justinian constituted the Bishop of Rome the head over all the churches, there were 666 years." [67] Then Mason reverts to his early formula:

"From 533 till 1792 inclusive, we have Daniel's 1260 years, when the judgment began to sit, and the vials to be poured out. From 1792 till 1822, Daniel's number of 30 years [1290] is fulfilled. By adding 45 years to 1822 [the 1335 years], we are brought to 1867." [68]

But he ends with repetition of this strong note:

"Daniel's 2300 years, commencing with the 70 weeks, in the 457th year before Christ, will terminate in A.D. 1843, when the sanctuary will be cleansed from popish abominations." [69]

13. SIXTH VIAL INVOLVES TURKISH OVERTHROW.—Mason's final work, *Remarks on the Sixth Vial, Symbolizing the Fall of the Turkish Empire* (1827), contends:

---

[64] *Ibid.*, p. 21; see also p. 54.
[65] *Ibid.* (3d ed.), in *The Church's Happy Prospect*, pp. 175-177.
[66] *Ibid.*, p. 178.   [67] *Ibid.*, p. 206.   [68] *Ibid.*   [69] *Ibid.*, p. 207.

"It is universally agreed, I believe, that this trumpet predicts the rise, the power, the ravages, the cruelty, and the conquests of the Turks. To no other system will the particular parts of the prediction apply; but in it every circumstance in the prophetic description has been realized." [70]

In both the trumpets and the vials the Euphrates is the place of origin and must refer to the same thing. Both refer to the Turkish Empire. This Mohammedan Turkish power is spoken of as the "eastern antichrist," as the Papacy is the Western. The Turkish Empire must fall before the Man of Sin shall go into perdition, and the predictions of the sixth vial must be accomplished before the complete fall of the Papacy, Babylon the Great. Thus:

"As the fall of Turkey will prepare the way of the eastern nations, so the fall of Popery will prepare the way of the western nations, to come to the brightness of our Redeemer's rising in the east." [71]

III. Brown—First Introduces Then Undermines 1844 Date

While Frere held to the concept that the 2400 years of the Vatican Septuagint would end about 1847, as early as 1826 Cuninghame, in his scheme of prophetic arrangement, had endorsed Mason's computation of the 2300 years appearing in his *Two Essays on Daniel's Prophetic Number*. Mason had fixed upon 1843 as the correct terminus, with "the complete cleansing of the sanctuary in the day of Armageddon." [72]

This endorsement by Cuninghame of Mason's calculation as the first to fix upon 1843, raised the issue of priority in the discovery. In 1827 JOHN AQUILA BROWN, [73] in the preface to *The Jew, the Master-Key of the Apocalypse* (1827), refers to Cuninghame's progression in understanding the 2300-year period, and calls attention to his own two-volume *The Even-Tide; or, Last Triumph of the Blessed and Only Potentate, the King of Kings, and Lord of Lords; Being a Development of the Mysteries of Daniel and St. John*, published in 1823. This

---

[70] Archibald Mason, *Remarks on the Sixth Vial, Symbolizing the Fall of the Turkish Empire*, p. 8.
[71] *Ibid.*, p. 17.
[72] William Cuninghame, *The Scheme of Prophetic Arrangement of the Rev. Edward Irving and Mr. Frere Critically Examined*, p. 80.
[73] Unfortunately no biographical data on Brown is thus far available.

had expressly set the date limits as 457 B.C. and A.D. 1843. But, behind that, he refers to "a fugitive paper penned fourteen years since, by the same author" [74]—that is, by himself, which obviously was *The Christian Observer* item of November, 1810.[75]

It therefore seems evident that this remarkable statement in *The Christian Observer* of November, 1810 (vol. 9, no. 107), was by John A. Brown, inasmuch as it was signed "J.A.B.," and no record has been found of any other writer on prophecy at that period bearing those initials.[76]

1. FOUNDATION LAID FOR "CONTINUATIONISM."—The title page of Brown's *Even-Tide* of 1823, sets forth his scheme of time prophecy, illustrated by a simple diagram within. The 391, 1260, 1290, 1335, 2300, and 2520 year "Lines of Time" are noted, and the year 1844 is set forth as the time of the "destruction of the papal power," and the "triumph of the Jewish kingdom." But the years 1873 and 1917 are also introduced as the end dates for the "extirpation of Mohammedanism" and the "close of the judgment," respectively. And this is not only on the basis of extension of the other time periods beyond 1844, but by a double-dating application of the 2300 years, as from 428 B.C. to A.D. 1873.[77] The 1917 date was taken from the 2520 years, or "seven times," of Nebuchadnezzar's tree, from 604 B.C. to A.D. 1917. Thus another stone was laid on the foundation of the "continuationist," or successive application, theories that later became prominent among advent heralds of Britain. This tended to minimize the 1843 or 1844 date and fix the mind on the later dates. (Title page reproduced on page 290.)

2. THREE LINES END IN 1844.—However, Brown is very clear in choosing the decree of 457 B.C., at the time of Ezra, as a "fit epoch from whence to calculate the period of cleansing the sanctuary." [78] This, he says, "points to a period when alone the sanctuary will be effectually cleansed,—namely, at the ex-

[74] John A. Brown, *The Jew, the Master-Key of the Apocalypse*, pp. vi, vii.
[75] See pp. 274, 276, 291, 292 of the present work.
[76] James A. Begg did not begin his writing until 1829.
[77] John A. Brown, *The Even-Tide*, vol. 1, Preface, pp. XLII, XLIII.
[78] Ibid., p. 126.

piration of the 2300 years." [79] Brown holds that it will not be
cleansed so long as "Mohammedism still reigns in its precincts."
Brown therefore makes a threefold ending in 1844—the "391
solar years of the sixth trumpet or Turkish Woe," from 1453
to 1844; the "1260 solar years papal assumption of the doctrine
of infallibility," from 584 to 1844, and "2300 solar years of
Ezra's Decree to the incipient cleansing of the sanctuary"—
457 B.C. to A.D. 1844. Thus he says:

> "A similar event is naturally to be expected from the use of the same
> terms; and, under the latter branch of the prophecy of Daniel, the very
> same desolation is predicted, as well as the close of the oppression deter-
> mined, within the period of the 2300 years; for it is not a simple cleansing
> of the sanctuary, spiritually considered, which is then to take place, but
> the revival also of the power of the host, which had been trodden down;
> and must occur in the same year as the revival of the witnesses, and the
> cessation of the Turkish woe, as well as the ceasing to scatter the power of
> the holy people. The exit of the 2300 years, consistently with other por-
> tions of prophecy, must therefore find its place in the same year, 1844." [80]

3. 2300 YEARS BEGIN WITH PERSIA.—Brown notes that
the vision of Daniel 8 begins with the time of the Persian ram. [81]
This was explained by the same angel, Gabriel, in chapter 9,
and "he [Daniel] could not be ignorant that, in prophetical
language, a day stood for a year." Daniel therefore understood
the seventy weeks to be "a further revelation of the same subject." [82] Brown then contends that Daniel 8 and 9 have "a positive connection with the eleventh" and "these several revelations
have one common link of union." [83]

4. LIMITS 2300 YEARS TO HOLY LAND.—But Brown makes
the 2300 years refer "chiefly, if not wholly, to the Jewish sanctuary, Jerusalem and Palestine, or the Holy Land." [84] The connection with the seventy weeks—first with the death of Christ
in A.D. 34, which he places at the end of the seventieth week—is
stated thus:

> "From the promulgation of Ezra's commission, . . . 457 B.C. to the end
> of the seventy weeks, or death of Christ in his thirty-fourth year, four
> hundred and ninety years terminate A.C. [A.D.] 34.

---

[79] *Ibid.*
[80] *Ibid.*, p. 127.
[81] *Ibid.*, p. 128.
[82] *Ibid.*, p. 129.
[83] *Ibid.*, p. 134.
[84] *Ibid.*, p. 135.

"From the death of Christ, in his thirty-fourth year, to the end of the period of desolation, and close of the period of the two thousand and three hundred years, and consequent cleansing of the sanctuary, eighteen hundred and ten years, the remaining portion of that period terminate 1844." [85]

5. DATES 1260 YEARS FROM 584 TO 1844.—The 1260 years of the Papacy, which Brown also makes to be the "two-horned beast," end with "the hour of the harlot's judgment; and the beast falls at Armageddon, with his ten kings in 1844." [86] This period he sets as from 584 to 1844.[87]

6. EXTENDS 1290 YEARS FROM 622 TO 1873.—The 1290 years are placed from "the first setting up of the Mohammedan abomination to its final eradication, and the revival of pure and undefiled religion throughout the world." This Brown begins in A.D. 622, and terminates in "A.D. 1873, in the Battle of Gog and Magog, the period of the second judgment on Christ's descent from heaven, and the general resurrection." [88]

7. 1335 YEARS DATED 622 TO 1917.—The "destruction of every enemy, and their final and everlasting punishment; the destroying of the veil spread over all nations; the eradication of the curse, and the glorious and eternal reign of Messiah upon earth," Brown puts at the close of the 1335 years, which he places from A.D. 622 to 1917.[89]

In his later volume Brown takes note of Irving's translation of Lacunza. He expresses regret that the Lacunzan notion of Antichrist was retained in the English translation.[90] The angel of Revelation 14, with the message of verses 6 and 7, Brown curiously limits to Palestine and the Turkish area.[91] The second angel's message he limits to "Babylon or the Papal Harlot, viz. in Italy, and the third Germany and France, for these are represented by the Beast and his Image." [92] In a footnote he takes issue with the contention of *"Crito"* (J. H. Frere),[93] in Drummond's *Dialogues of Prophecy*, that these three angels are sym-

[85] *Ibid.*, pp. 135, 136.   [87] *Ibid.*, p. XLI.   [89] *Ibid.*, p. XVIII.
[86] *Ibid.*, Preface, p. XL.   [88] *Ibid.*, p. XLII.
[90] John A. Brown, *The Jew, the Master-Key of the Apocalypse*, p. xvi n.
[91] *Ibid.*, p. 96.
[92] *Ibid.*, p. 97.
[93] Joshua W. Brooks, *A Dictionary of Writers on the Prophecies*, p. lxxi.

bolic of societies or organizations for the proclamation of the
last events and the coming of the kingdom.[94]

Thus were strengthened the foundations of that continuationist, or successive, application of prophetic fulfillment that
would shift the expectation forward, away from the initial
date of 1844 to later events in an over-all scheme.

IV. Roberts—Dates 2400 Years From 553 to 1847

PETER ROBERTS (1760-1819), Anglican vicar, writer, and
antiquary, was educated at Trinity College, Dublin, from which
he received his M.A. in 1793. He remained to study Oriental
languages and astronomy, then became a tutor.   Entering Anglican orders, he served as rector and vicar in several churches,
including Madeley and Halkin.[95] He wrote numerous histories,
and produced a volume on the *Church of Rome* (1809). Finally,
the year before his death he wrote *A Manual of Prophecy*
(1818).

1. THE PAPAL TYRANNY IN DANIEL 7.—This "comparative
view of the prophecies" takes the standard historical position
on Daniel 2 and 7, stressing the ten kingdoms of Europe as
the "divisions of the western empire." Roberts also calls attention to the fact that at the time of the breakup, and also about
800 and at 1240, there always seem to be about ten divisions,
citing Bishop Newton's list.[96] The Little Horn is the "papal
power.   Its spirit is tyranny, its object universal dominion,
and its policy Roman." [97]   Due note is taken of its blasphemies.
And its 1260-year dating is from the sixth century till the late
conquest of Italy by the French.[98]

2. DATES 2400 FROM TIME OF VISION (553).—Roberts
likewise follows Frere in adopting the 2400 of the Vatican Septuagint for Daniel 8:14, instead of 2300, dating the years from
the assumed time of the vision in the third year of Belshazzar

---

[94] John A. Brown, *The Jew, the Master-Key*, p. 97.
[95] *Alumni Dublinenses*, 1593-1860, p. 706; *The Gentleman's Magazine*, August, 1819
(vol. 89, part 2), p. 181; *Dictionary of National Biography*, vol. 16, p. 1275.
[96] Peter Roberts, *A Manual of Prophecy*, pp. 37, 38.
[97] *Ibid.*, p. 39.   [98] *Ibid.*, pp. 39-41.

in 553 B.C. and so terminating the period in 1847. He also anticipates that the fall of Mohammedanism will accomplish its fulfillment.[99]

V. Bayford—The Judgment-Hour Angel Flying

JOHN BAYFORD, F.A.S.[100] was most active in the Society for Promoting Christianity Among the Jews, and with Henry Drummond was one of the joint patrons[101] of Joseph Wolff, making possible his extensive missionary journeys. He also edited Wolff's *Missionary Journal and Memoirs* (1824). Bayford was a participant in the Albury Park Prophetic Conferences of 1826 and onward.[102] His part in the published *Dialogues on Prophecy* appeared under the pseudonym "Evander."[103] Later, when the Catholic Apostolic (or Irvingite) Church was formed, Bayford, along with Drummond, came to have a leading part.[104]

1. STANDARD EXPOSITION OF DANIEL 2 AND 7.—Bayford's *Messiah's Kingdom, or, A Brief Inquiry Concerning What is Revealed in Scripture, Relative to the Fact, the Time, the Signs, and the Circumstances of the Second Advent* (1820), bore on the title page the text Revelation 14:7. It covered the leading prophecies of Daniel and the Revelation. The standard exposition of the four empires of Daniel 2, a divided Europe, and finally the stone kingdom of Messiah, is followed by the standard interpretation of Daniel 7.[105] Bayford follows Machiavelli's list of the ten horn-kingdoms, and applies the Little Horn to the ecclesiastical power of the Bishop of Rome, with the three horns as those divisions making way for the ecclesiastical states of the Papacy.[106]

2. 1260 YEARS (529-1789) AND 1290 AND 1335.—The 1260 year-days are put from 529 to 1789.[107] The differential between

---

[99] *Ibid.*, pp. 50, 51.   [100] Little biographical data available.
[101] *Travels and Adventures of the Rev. Joseph Wolff*, pp. 481, 482.
[102] Edward Miller, *History and Doctrines of Irvingism*, vol. 1, p. 41.
[103] Brooks, *op. cit.*, p. lxxi.
[104] Miller, *op. cit.*, vol. 1, p. 11; Robert Baxter, *Irvingism, in Its Rise, Progress, and Present State*, p. 15.
[105] John Bayford, *Messiah's Kingdom, or, A Brief Inquiry Concerning What is Revealed in Scripture, Relative to the Fact, the Time, the Signs, and the Circumstances of the Second Advent of the Lord Jesus Christ*, pp. 64, 65.
[106] *Ibid.*, pp. 68-70.   [107] *Ibid.*, p. 71.

the 1260 and 1290 and 1335 years is taken as the time required to accomplish "the great wonders—cleansing the church from every unclean thing, and to restore Jew and Gentile, as Judah and Israel." [108]

3. DAILY SACRIFICE: BLOOD OF LAMB OF GOD.—Of the daily sacrifice of Daniel 8:11-14, and the trampling power, Bayford says, "The daily sacrifice which he hath taken away, is doubtless the Lamb of God, the blood of which, the Mahometan tramples underfoot, counting it an unholy thing." [109]

4. 2300-YEAR PROBLEM (POSSIBLY 481-1819).—Of the dating of this treading underfoot, Bayford is not clear. The 2300 are assuredly years, but their commencement is difficult to determine. And some have applied it to popery, others to Mohammedanism. No connection is made with the seventy weeks, to which he gives the standard interpretation. [110] Bayford adds:

"From the commencement to the close of the vision, there will be 2,300 years, at which time, the Church of Christ being cleansed from all impurity, the Millennial dispensation will commence: for it should be recollected, that the sanctuary cannot be cleansed until the Lord comes to his temple, as Malachi iii. intimates. The exact commencement of the vision is not defined clearly, lest men should know the seasons, which God keepeth in his own power; and many different opinions have been maintained by different commentators." [111]

But it is not from the time of the vision, and not from 555 B.C., for 2300 would end in 1747—not in 1847 as the advocates for the 2400 years place it. He seeks to eliminate improbabilities:

"The event has certainly made it manifest, that the commencement is not to be computed from the time when the prophet saw the vision, for that was the third year of Belshazzar, or before Christ 553, which gives the close at the year 1747, when the changes foretold, did not in any respect take place." [112]

A possible date, suggested by some, is 481 B.C.—that of the expedition of Xerxes against Greece. Time will put speculation to test:

"If this should be the date, the vision terminates in the year 1819, being

[108] *Ibid.*, pp. 110, 111.
[109] *Ibid.*, p. 82.
[112] *Ibid.*, pp. 83, 84; see also pp. 280, 281.
[110] *Ibid.*, pp. 90, 91.
[111] *Ibid.*, p. 83; see also p. 85.

thirty years from the French revolution, and 1290 years from the setting up of the power of Popery, according to the scheme which is given in p. 71. Whenever the appointed epoch shall arrive, events will speak for themselves; and a few months may be sufficient to bring to its test, the date that is now suggested. Our opinion, therefore, may well be suspended for a short time; and it may be sufficient to search for another date, when this is found not to be the true one." [113]

5. PAPACY PLACED IN DANIEL 11:36 FF.—Bayford puts the Papacy in Daniel 11, from verse 36 onward, dissenting from Faber, who suggests France.[114] The magnification referred to in verse 37 is his blasphemous assumptions and false intercessors and mediators in verse 38.[115]

6. THE CHURCHES AND THE TRUMPETS.—Coming to the Apocalypse, Bayford deals with the four sets of symbols—candlesticks, seals, trumpets, and vials. The seven churches are the "seven principal epochs, or periods of the church," and disclose its spiritual condition.[116] Of the present state Bayford observes that it is more or less apparent that "the church is *now* in Laodicea," [117] with the final judgments impending at the second advent. The fifth and sixth trumpets represent the Saracenic and Ottoman judgments upon the Greek Empire.[118] The five months, or 150 years, are placed from 612 to 762, and the 391 years of the sixth trumpet from 1281 to 1672.[119]

7. THE WILD BEAST IS THE PAPACY.—The second wild Beast of Revelation 13 is the "ecclesiastical power arising from out of the earth, or from out of a carnal and worldly profession of christianity, connecting itself with the civil power of the ten kingdoms, gaining the ascendency over it." [120] The paralleling of the fourth monarchy symbols of Daniel 2, 7, and 11— the legs and feet of the image, the fourth beast, and Little Horn, and the willful king who exalts himself above even God —is matched by the dragon, the wild beast, and the scarlet-colored beast in Revelation 12, 13, and 17.[121] The seven heads

---

[113] *Ibid.*, p. 84. (Bayford's book, published in 1820, was evidently written in 1819 or 1818.)

[114] *Ibid.*, p. 103 ff.
[115] *Ibid.*, pp. 104, 105.
[116] *Ibid.*, p. 127 ff.

[117] *Ibid.*, p. 148.
[118] *Ibid.*, p. 172.
[119] *Ibid.*, pp. 187, 189.

[120] *Ibid.*, p. 228.
[121] *Ibid.*, p. 224.

are kings, consuls, dictators, decemviri, military tribunes, triumviri, and emperors.[122]   And the time of making war with the
saints is from Justinian to 1789.[123]

8. VICARIUS FILII DEI "HARDLY SATISFACTORY."—As to the
number of the beast—666—*Latinus* and *Vicarius Filii Dei* have
been suggested; but Bayford declares them "hardly satisfactory,"
and adds, "The true name remains yet to be discovered." [124]

9. THE HOUR OF GOD'S JUDGMENT IMPENDS.—Again we
note the contemporary application of the angels of Revelation
14. Verses 1-5 are applied to the church of the Reformation,
having just emerged from popery.   Verses 6 and 7 are applied
to the Bible societies and similar organizations, from 1803
onward.[125] Of this angel, Bayford says:

"When the event takes place, which is signified by this symbol, the day
of the Lord's judgment is actually at hand, for the angel cries unto all men,
'Fear God, and give glory to him, for the hour of his judgment is come.' " [126]

10. SECOND AND THIRD MESSAGES THEN FUTURE.—But of
the second angel's message Bayford says:

"Whether the two angels who are spoken of, are yet future, it is not
easy to determine." [127]
"If these two angels are, indeed, made manifest, the fulfillment may
probably be traced in the general stir which is now seen to have taken
place, throughout many parts of Christendom, evincing an universal and an
increasing sense of the corruptions of the Romish Church." [128]

11. THE SECOND ADVENT NEAR AT HAND.—Stressing the
future but imminent character of these events, as preparatory to
the event of the second advent of verses 14-20, he says:

"The circumstances, however, are as yet but imperfectly known; and
it may require that the events should be more fully developed, before an
opinion is hazarded, as to whether this portion of the prophecy has, or has
not been accomplished.   A short period, however, may decide: for all
things seem preparing for the great event, which is announced in the
following verses." [129]

Bayford then stresses the "tremendous day" of the Lord,
when He shall descend from heaven. He then deals with the

---

122 *Ibid.*, p. 215   125 *Ibid.*, pp. 232-234.   128 *Ibid.*, p. 236.
123 *Ibid.*, p. 227.   126 *Ibid.*, p. 283.   129 *Ibid.*, pp. 236, 237.
124 *Ibid.*, p. 230.   127 *Ibid.*, p. 235.

1260, 1290, 1335, and 2300 years—the 2300 years must end with one of the other periods, possibly in 1819.[130]

12. Two Resurrections Mark the Millennium.—The three unclean spirits from heathenism, the Papacy, and infidelity have already gone into action. The old papal power is in resurgence, recovering its lost powers and prerogatives.[131] The millennium, to be introduced by the second advent, is bounded by the two resurrections—one at the beginning, the other at the close.[132]

---

[130] *Ibid.*, pp. 279, 281.   [131] *Ibid.*, pp. 254, 255.   [132] *Ibid.*, p. 327 ff.

THE

JEWISH EXPOSITOR,

AND

FRIEND OF ISRAEL:

CONTAINING

MONTHLY COMMUNICATIONS RESPECTING THE JEWS,

AND THE

Proceedings of the London Society.

אקים את־סכת דויד הנפלת׃ Amos ix. 11.
Οὐκ ἀπώσατο ὁ Θεὸς τὸν λαὸν αὐτοῦ. Πᾶς Ἰσραὴλ σωθήσεται.
Rom. xi. 2. 26.

VOL. VII.—1822.

London:

Printed by A. Macintosh, 20, Great New Street, Gough Square.

PUBLISHED BY OGLE, DUNCAN, AND CO. PATERNOSTER ROW;
SOLD AT THE LONDON SOCIETY'S DEPOSITORY, 10, WARDROBE PLACE,
DOCTORS' COMMONS; BY SEELEY, FLEET STREET;
AND HATCHARD, PICCADILLY.

THE

MORNING WATCH;

OR

QUARTERLY JOURNAL ON PROPHECY,

AND

THEOLOGICAL REVIEW.

WATCHMAN, WHAT OF THE NIGHT! WATCHMAN, WHAT OF THE NIGHT!
THE WATCHMAN SAID, THE MORNING COMETH, AND ALSO THE NIGHT: IF
YE WILL INQUIRE, INQUIRE YE: RETURN, COME. ISAI. XXI. 11, 12.

[Edited by John Tudor, Ed.]

VOL. I.—1829.

LONDON:

PRINTED BY ELLERTON AND HENDERSON,
GOUGH SQUARE.

PUBLISHED BY JAMES NISBET, BERNERS STREET.

1830.

THE

CHRISTIAN HERALD:

A Monthly Magazine,

CHIEFLY ON SUBJECTS CONNECTED WITH

PROPHECY.

EDITED BY A CLERGYMAN OF THE ESTABLISHED CHURCH.

"The words are closed up and sealed TILL THE TIME OF THE END."—
"Many shall run to and fro, and knowledge shall be increased."
DANIEL XII.

VOL. I.

FOR THE YEAR 1830.

DUBLIN.

RICHARD MOORE TIMS, 85, GRAFTON-STREET.
SOLD IN LONDON, BY JAMES NISBET, 21, BERNER'S-STREET.
To be had of all Booksellers.
M.DCCC.XXX.

THE

INVESTIGATOR,

OR

MONTHLY

EXPOSITOR AND REGISTER,

OF

PROPHECY.

VOL. I.

1831-2.

LONDON:

SIMPKIN AND MARSHALL.

ENTIRE JOURNALS DEVOTED TO PROPHETIC INVESTIGATION

These, and Others Not Pictured, Were Launched to Foster Interest and Understanding of the
Prophecies Relating to the Last Days, and the Imminent Advent Was Forecast by Them. The
2300 Years Was Constantly Noted (See pages 416, 501, 579, and 599.)

CHAPTER TWENTY-TWO

Jewish Society and Journal Launched

We now enter a new era in the development of the Old World Advent Awakening. Heretofore the heralding voices had been largely unrelated—a man here and one there, independently writing and preaching as conviction moved him. There had been no concerted action. Now they began to associate and to organize to further their common purpose. Various groups were formed to study and to spread their united conclusions. Before this, only the already established religious journals had carried occasional articles on prophecy. Now periodicals primarily devoted to the carrying of the message of the approaching advent and the prophetic evidences therefor began to be launched. It was the dawn of a new day, bringing a new impetus to the themes that had already gripped the hearts of many. About the first of these organizers was Lewis Way, whose interesting career we now view.

I. Way—Pioneer Herald of the Imminent Advent

LEWIS WAY (1772-1840), of Stansted Park, was born at Bucks, England, and educated at Merton College, Oxford, receiving his B.A. in 1794 and his M.A. in 1796. In 1797 he was called to the bar by the Inner Temple and served for a time as a barrister-at-law, settling at Stansted Park in 1805.[1] An unre-

---

[1] *Alumni Oxonienses* 1715-1886, vol. 4, p. 1514; *Dictionary of National Biography*, vol. 6, pp. 81, 82; *The Jewish Encyclopedia*, vol. 12, pp. 477, 478; Joseph Wolff, *Travels and Adventures of the Rev. Joseph Wolff*, pp. 80, 81; *The Gentleman's Magazine*, June, 1840 (New Series, vol. 13), p. 663; *Jewish Intelligence*, March and June, 1840 (vol. 6), pp. 55-57, 152-153.

lated stranger by the name of John Way left him the extraordinary legacy of £300,000 to be used "for the glory of God." [2] Lewis Way immediately left his former life and took Anglican orders to devote his life thenceforth to the welfare of the Jews. These, he believed, must be evangelized before the second advent, which he held to be imminent. He was convinced that the Jews must return to their ancestral homeland, and believed that "the conversion of the Jews would perhaps be the first effect" of the latter rain.[3]

Way had heard of a society founded by Joseph Samuel C. F. Frey in 1808, for converting the Jews, that was now much in debt. He offered to liquidate the indebtedness if the management were turned over. This was done, and the journal of the organization, *The Jewish Expositor,* edited by C. S. Hawtrey, was taken over in September, 1817, to promote the project. Springing from the parent London society, a large number of auxiliary societies spread all over England. Every shire had its own organization.[4] A similar extension covered Scotland,[5] and there was a strong society in Berlin.[6] More than that, American affiliates were organized, with prominent men in leadership, and a journal, *Israel's Advocate,* similar to *The Jewish Expositor,* was launched in America in January, 1823. In London men like William Wilberforce, the preacher; Sir Thomas Baring; Charles Simeon, of Cambridge; William Marsh, the preacher; [7] and Henry Drummond, the banker,[8] were prominent promoters.

In 1817 Way and some associates left England for the Continent, traveling through Holland and Germany to Russia. One object was to study the condition of the Jews, to inquire into their "sentiments concerning the expected Messiah," to distrib-

<hr/>

[2] A. M. W. Stirling, *The Ways of Yesterday,* pp. 91-120. A fascinating recital of Way's life and work, which also touches upon many of his associates in heralding the advent.
[3] *The Christian Observer,* October, 1821 (vol. 20, no. 10), pp. 605, 606.
[4] See full details in *The Jewish Expositor,* November, 1826 (vol. 11), pp. 436-439, 472-476. (Title page reproduced on p. 414.)
[5] *Ibid.,* March, 1827 (vol. 12), pp. 116-119.
[6] *Ibid.,* April, 1822 (vol. 8), pp. 165-169.
[7] WILLIAM MARSH (1775-1864) was an impressive evangelical preacher and friend of Charles Simeon. A graduate of St. Edmond Hall, Oxford, with an M.A. in 1807, he became curate of St. Lawrence, Reading, and then rector of St. Thomas, Birmingham, where he came to be known as "Millennial Marsh." In 1837 he was appointed to the deanery of Bridgenorth. In 1839 he became incumbent of St. Mary, Leamington. See *Dictionary of National Biography,* vol. 12, p. 1103.
[8] To be studied in detail later. See p. 435 ff.

ute Hebrew New Testaments to them, and to prepare the way for missions among them. The other purpose was to awaken the sympathetic interest of Christians toward the Jews.[9] In Berlin, Way enlisted the interest of the English ambassador, Sir George Ross, and through him conferred with the crown prince, and in Russia he was received sympathetically by Czar Alexander I, who invited him to lay the matter of Jewish civil and social welfare before the impending Congress of Aix-La-Chapelle.[10] Alexander, who had already partially emancipated the Russian Jews, showed his interest by issuing two ukases assuring all baptized Jews of government protection, and promising them land for farming.[11]

On October 5, 1818, at Aix-La-Chapelle, Way presented to Czar Alexander a petition, addressed to the allied rulers of Europe, and a memorial, which so impressed Alexander that he referred it to the conference. In the protocol dated November 21, 1818, signed by all the plenipotentiaries, the principle of the emancipation of the Jews was recognized, and the memorial mentioned, without the merits of the case being entered into.[12]

It was while traveling in the steppes of Russia that Way formulated his convictions on the soon return of Christ. These were published under the pseudonym Basilicus,[13] in *The Jewish Expositor* (1820-22), and were later issued in booklet form as *Thoughts on the Scriptural Expectations of the Christian Church* (1823). His concepts of prophecy will be duly noted. Way met Joseph Wolff in 1819 and, with Henry Drummond's assistance, sent him to the University of Cambridge as the Jewish Society's protégé.[14] His associations with other heralds of the approaching advent will unfold as the story progresses, and as these other men are introduced.

---

[9] *The Jewish Expositor*, September, 1817 (vol. 2), p. 358; Lewis Way, *A Letter, Addressed to the Right Reverend the Lord Bishop of St. David's*, pp. 15, 16.
[10] Max J. Kohler, *Jewish Rights at the Congresses of Vienna (1814-1815) and Aix-La-Chapelle (1818)*, p. 88; Stirling, *op. cit.*, p. 148.
[11] *The Jewish Encyclopedia*, vol. 1, p. 346, vol. 12, p. 478.
[12] Kohler, *op. cit.*, pp. 50-56. *Mémoires sur l'état des Israélites* (1819) contains the petition, memorial, report thereon, and other related items. Way stressed the Jewish relationship to prophecy and its fulfillment.
[13] Samuel Halkett and John Laing, *Dictionary of Anonymous and Pseudonymous English Literature*, vol. 6, p. 41.
[14] Joseph Wolff, *Travels and Adventures*, pp. 80-82.

Way traveled considerably in Europe and in the Holy Land. In 1823, when in Rome, he preached to the English congregation on the ancient Waldenses.[15] He founded the Marboeuf (English Reformed) Chapel in Paris, financed by Drummond, which was completed by his son, also a minister. While residing there in 1824, he wrote a remarkable discursive poem of 364 pages entitled *Palingenesia, the World to Come.*[16]

By 1826 his Paris home had become the center of an ever-widening circle of influence.[17] He also issued *The Watchman* in Paris in 1831, a little journal devoted to the discussion of the welfare of the church, the exposition of prophecy, and the report of weekly meetings of the interested at his residence for the study of the prophecies concerning the second advent.[18]

So first Way was instrumental in reorganizing, in 1817, the Society for Promoting Christianity Amongst the Jews composed largely of Christians, which sent Wolff forth on his travels and to which he reported through *The Jewish Expositor.* Second, he was a prominent participant in the Continental Society, as will soon be apparent. And then he was instrumental in effecting the formation of the Reformation Society, in 1837, as will be also noted later. He was always stressing the restoration of the Jews, which was inseparably tied to the advent expectancy in the British Advent Awakening.

1. GRAND TERMINUS OF 1260, 1290, AND 1335 YEARS (1866). —While in Rotterdam, on his 1817 trip on the Continent, Way conversed with Rabbi Joseph Leyman on the prophetic basis for expecting the soon coming of the Messiah. Way describes the rabbi's inquiry and his response, in letters to *The Jewish Expositor.*[19]

"This brought us to the question of time; and we soon got deep into Daniel's weeks and days. The rabbi said he was not satisfied with any of the calculations of the targumists or rabbins, because all their times were past; and he requested I would tell him how we interpreted the passage of Daniel xii.12, relating to the 1335 days; upon which I referred him to

---

[15] Lewis Way, *The Household of Faith.*
[16] On authorship, see Halkett and Laing, *op. cit.*, vol. 4, p. 292.
[17] Stirling, *op. cit.*, p. 281.
[18] *The Watchman*, May 7, 1831 (vol. 1, nos. 1 and 2), p. 4.
[19] *The Jewish Expositor*, January, 1818 (vol. 3, no. 1), pp. 75-79.

Dan. vii.25. and explained 'the time and times and dividing of time' as three years and a half, or forty-two months, or 1260 days, (that is, prophetical years,) at the end of which the judgment should sit on the last enemies of the church, and the dominion be given to the power mentioned in ver. 13, 14, of the same chapter. I then shewed, that—supposing this period to terminate, according to christian calculations, about the year 1791,—30 years added, according to Dan. xii.11, would bring the 1290 days to the year 1821 or 2, and, adding 45 years, would bring the blessing of the 12th verse, to the year 1866; which was the point he requested to be ascertained." [20]

2. 2300 Years From Vision Under Darius.

—Way then discusses the relation of the 2300 years of Daniel 8:14 to the problem, which he believes will lead to at least the restoration of the Jews:

"Supposing Daniel to refer to the year 509 or 508 as the commencement of the vision, or to have written at *that* time (when he certainly was at the court of Darius) then the termination of the period would fall in the year 1791 or 2, at the same time with the supposed termination of the other period of 1260 years, or 'time, times, and half time,'

	509	and	508
	1791		1792
	2300		2300

"The Rabbi said, 'It is possible, I cannot dispute it.'—The above was drawn out in parallel lines with the Jewish computation of time, and left for his consideration." [21]

3. Two Mysteries Approaching Their Climax.

—Way's *Thoughts on the Scriptural Expectations of the Christian Church* which ran intermittently through *The Jewish Expositor* between January, 1820, and May, 1822, concern the following: The second advent, first resurrection, end of the world, world to come, restitution of all things, kingdom of Israel, and types, prophecies, and parables. It begins with a discussion of the two mysteries—the secular arm checking the "mystery of iniquity"; and the other to be accomplished by the "renovation of a distracted world," and the "triumphant establishment of the kingdom of God." [22]

---

[20] *Ibid.*, p. 78.
[21] *Ibid.*, pp. 78, 79.

[22] *Ibid.*, January, 1820 (vol. 5, no. 1), p. 24.

LEWIS WAY DECLARES THE JUDGMENT HOUR NEAR

Through London Pamphlet (Upper Left), Paris Periodical (Upper Right), and Extensive Poem (Lower Pair), Lawyer Lewis Way (Center Oval) Proclaims the Approaching Advent Near, and Founds the Society to Herald It to the Jews (*Jewish Expositor*—Pictured on Page 414)

4. Now in Feet of Clay; Stone Is the Next.—The first advent was revealed through Daniel 9 and the seventy weeks, but the vision of Daniel 8 would not be understood till the "time of the end," when the "wise shall understand." The great outline of prophecy in Daniel 2 comprehends the successive revolutions of universal empire from Babylon onward, under the symbol of the metallic man, as is generally understood. Then he adds:

"We are concerned at present only with the feet and toes of the image composed of iron and clay, and these will be allowed to represent the Roman Empire in its last divided state, partly strong as iron, partly weak as clay, but divided into ten kingdoms at least." [23]

The setting up of God's kingdom by supernatural means, "without hands," is to take place at the second advent:

"The stone smites the image on the feet, or last divided state of the Roman Empire, and breaks the rest of the image in pieces. It may be doubted, whether this figure can properly represent the first advent of our Lord, as the Empire was not then in its divided state, but it seems to be referred by Christ himself to the judgments attending or preceding his second appearance." [24]

This, Way says, will be at the close of the "times of the Gentiles."

5. Advent Follows Destruction of Beast.—Further details appear on Daniel 7 in relation to the advent:

"The Roman Empire is there designated by a beast with ten horns, in the midst of which a little horn arises speaking great words. The beast is slain, his body destroyed and given to the flame, and then follows, 'I saw in the night visions,' and behold one like 'the Son of Man came with the clouds of Heaven.' St. Paul says, 'The Lord Himself shall descend from Heaven,' 1 Thess. iv.16. but not till 'that Wicked be revealed, whom the Lord shall consume with the Spirit of his mouth, and shall destroy with the brightness of his coming.' (2 Thess. ii.8.)" [25]

6. Two Resurrections Bound Thousand Years.—After discussing the first resurrection at the premillennial second advent, Way writes that "the general resurrection appears to take place before 'the white throne and him that sat on it,' at the

---

[23] *Ibid.*, p. 28 (1823 pamphlet reprint, p. 12).
[24] *Ibid.* (pamphlet, pp. 12, 13).
[25] *Ibid.*, p. 29 (pamphlet, p. 13).

expiration of the thousand years, when death and hell give up their dead." [26]

7. FINAL JUDGMENT-HOUR CRY STRESSED.—Like others simultaneously in different parts of the world, Way is constrained to notice and to stress the "judgment hour" cry. He closes with these thoughts:

"It is just before the fall of Babylon, that the apostle 'saw another angel fly in the midst of heaven, having *the everlasting gospel* to preach unto them that dwell on the earth, and to every nation, and kindred, and tongue, and people, saying with a loud voice, Fear God and give glory to him, for *the hour of his judgment* is come.' " [27]

"*This gospel of the kingdom* (the gospel of the age to come), will be preached to all the world before the end: that is, the end of the present dispensation, for as Christ appeared 'once in the end of the world,' (the Jewish oeconomy) to put away sin, so 'to them that look for him shall he appear a second time (in the end of this world, the present Christian era) without sin unto salvation,' and then will 'his kingdom come, and his will be done, on earth.' " [28]

8. SATAN NOT YET BOUND FOR MILLENNIUM.—Four years later, in 1824, while ministering in Paris, Way produced his monumental poem "The World to Come," composed of six books, taking in every phase of the great conflict between Christ and Satan. In book 2 Way contends that Satan is not yet bound, that the harvest is at the advent, and that the vintage is identified with judgments on the Roman state and church. It begins:

"Hail! mighty angel! whose extended hand
Holdeth the key of Hades! with a chain
Of adamantine force prepar'd to bind
Satan that ancient serpent, Dragon call'd,
And Devil, and in holy writ esteem'd
God of this present world, wherein he rules
In princely council, and in papal chair
Proud of his usurpation; hasten down,
And seal his destiny, and shut him up
In Tophet thus ordained, deep and large
With stream of brimstone kindled, in the pit,
The bottomless! that he no more deceive
Nations or men, until a thousand years
Of peace on earth have run their promis'd course." [29]

---

[26] *Ibid.* (pamphlet), p. 27.   [27] *Ibid.*, p. 113.   [28] *Ibid.*
[29] Lewis Way, *Palingenesia, the World to Come*, book 2, pp. 37, 38.

Paying his respects to the false Augustinian theory of a millennium back in the early centuries from the first advent, or from Constantine, Way says:

> "There are who deem such period took its rise
> In days of sainted Helena, or reign
> Of Trinobantian Constantine, when first
> A christian monarch sat on Caesar's throne.
> Is Satan then a pris'ner? doth he not
> Roam still at large throughout his realm of air
> A roaring lion seeking out his prey,
> Insatiate of destruction? Was he bound
> When Europe gather'd a misguided host
> To consecrated standard of the cross,
> And at the call of one enthusiast
> Sent forth her myriads to the holy land?
> Clothing religion's meek and modest form
> (Mistaken guise of christian chivalry!)
> In all the pomp and circumstance of war!" [30]

> "Was Satan bound, when that tribunal dread
> Reproach and terror of the christian world,
> First deem'd it *Act of Faith* to burn alive
> All who disclaim'd its superstitious rites?
> When he who went about in doing good,
> Found most who then profess'd to follow him,
> Not healing sick, or preaching to the poor,
> His precious gospel; but amassing wealth
> To swell a convent's treasury, and glut
> Some overgrown and pamper'd Hierarch
> With product of indulg'd and licens'd sin.
> And where is Satan now? in chains below
> Or yet at large? Methinks, he knoweth well
> His time is short, because he rageth so." [31]

9. DESCENDS TO CLEFT MOUNT OF OLIVES.—Book 3 emphasizes the personal advent and identifies the day of judgment and one thousand years "with the new Jerusalem state and kingdom of the Stone at the close of the fourth monarchy."

> "Blessed is he that watcheth! they that keep
> Their garments undefiled, while their Lord
> Prepareth them a place,—behold! he comes

---

[30] *Ibid.*, pp. 38, 39.
[31] *Ibid.*, p. 39.

To take them to himself, that where he is
They also may be—Thus his word declares
He will Himself descend, and glorify
The place of his own *feet*, for they shall stand
Upon the mount before Jerusalem!
And in that day when Olivet shall cleave." [32]

10. GREAT HIGH PRIEST AND TRUE TABERNACLE.—Book 4
is addressed to Christ as High Priest in the true tabernacle and
emphasizes the redemption of the body at Christ's second advent.

"Blessed and only Potentate! though now
Dwelling in light of glory, whereunto
No mortal eye can penetrate! by faith
We follow thee where thou art entered
Our intercessor, and our Great High Priest
Of *good things yet to come*, within the veil
Of the true tabernacle! Once for all
While yet the temple stood, in time thus call'd,
End of the world." [33]

11. FEAR GOD: THE HOUR OF JUDGMENT.—Book 6 stresses
the unsealed book, as many run to and fro and understand the
end.[34]   The six thousand years and the seventh thousand years
of rest are noted, and the coming of the Lord to execute judgment on the disobedient.[35]   It closes with prophetic triumph,
and an application of Revelation 14.   Note it:

"THE EVERLASTING GOSPEL—tidings glad
To ev'ry nation, kindred, people, tongue,
For all shall hear, tho FEW should heed the call
Of that swift Messenger, on eagle wing
Flying thro midst of Heaven! warning thus
A WORLD that lieth in THE WICKED ONE!
'Fear GOD! and give Him glory! for HIS DAY
Of judgment is at hand!   O! worship Him
Maker of all things, Heaven, Earth and Sea!'
THE RIGHTEOUS JUDGE, THE KING FOR EVERMORE,
Sitteth between the Cherubim! his words
Are true and faithful: spoken thus to JOHN!
BEHOLD! AND WRITE THOU!   I MAKE ALL THINGS NEW!" [36]

---

[32] *Ibid.*, book 3, argument on opening page.
[33] *Ibid.*, book 4, argument on opening page.
[34] *Ibid.*, p. 206.   [35] *Ibid.*, pp. 206, 207.   [36] *Ibid.*, p. 264.

12. Weekly Meetings to Study Prophecy.—Way's paper, *The Watchman,* will be more fully noted later. Beginning as a weekly, it was changed to a monthly, and later was called *The Gallican Watchman.*[37] It contains expositions of Bible truth given every Friday night.[38] Then it tells of weekly meetings every Wednesday afternoon for the study of the prophecies "relative to the Lord's glorious appearing"—stressing the fact that the epoch is at hand, and will be followed by the thousand years.[39] Note is taken of the work of the Paris branch of the Continental Society, and distress is expressed over the Irving fanaticism in 1831.[40]

13. Jansenist Interest in the Advent.—Special notice is taken of the society of one hundred Jansenist women in Paris, existent from the time of Louis XIV, cherishing from their ancestors "an indubitable persuasion of Christ's second coming to establish his personal reign upon earth." [41] The spread of the advent belief, the signs of the times, and Babylon's consciousness of her coming "dissolution," and the interest on the part of Catholics, are all noted. [42] There is also prominent mention of Lacunza (Ben-Ezra) and his *La Venida del Mesías en Gloria y Magestad,* and the English translation by Irving, particular mention being made of the exposition of Daniel 2 and the divided kingdom unlike the preceding four.[43]

Other statements will appear in the recital of other organizations, in which Way participated, such as the meetings of the Continental Society.

II. *Jewish Expositor* Discusses Prophetic Periods and Symbols

We now turn to the second journal in which discussion of the prophecies appeared, and for the launching of which Way was responsible. Although *The Jewish Expositor and Friend of Israel,* published in London and edited by C. S. Hawtrey, was established primarily for other purposes, the exposition of

[37] See *The Gallican Watchman,* October 8, 1831 (vol. 2, no. 1).
[38] *The Watchman,* May 7, 1831 (vol. 1, nos. 1, 2), pp. 1-3.
[39] *Ibid.,* pp. 4, 5.   [41] *Ibid.,* p. 47.
[40] *Ibid.,* p. 37.   [42] *Ibid.,* pp. 48, 49.   [43] *Ibid.,* pp. 58, 59.

prophecy periodically crept into its pages. Thus back in August, 1816, "B" contended that the little horn of Daniel 8 and the willful king of Daniel 11:36 refer to Mohammed and his successors. He held, further, that the 1260 and the 2300 years end together, and that these events are tied in with the drying up of the river Euphrates.[44]

Then P. Bolton, in the November, 1819, number, after enumerating the four great empires of prophecy and the ten divisions of the fourth, interprets the little horn of Daniel 7 as the Papacy, and places the 1260 years from 533 to 1793.[45] The "earthquake" of Revelation 11 he declares to be the French Revolution, and France the tenth part of the city Babylon. But the little horn of Daniel 8 he expounds as Mohammed, and the 1260- and 2300-year periods he strangely ends together in 1868.[46]

1. "C. C." DATES 2300 (457-1843); 1290 (508-1798).—In the October, 1820, issue "C. C." impressively places the seventy weeks as from Ezra's commission in 457 B.C. to the A.D. 33 cross, and the 2300 years from 457 B.C. to the cleansing of the sanctuary in 1843. Moreover, he advances the interesting position that the 1290 years are dated from A.D. 508 to 1798, when the French expelled the pope from Rome[47]—about the first to suggest such a dating for this specific period.

2. "T. B." WOULD DATE 2400 FROM 553 TO 1847.—In the November, 1825, issue a report of the proceedings of the London Society for Promoting Christianity Among the Jews speaks of the 1260 days as years, for "a day means a year," and the three and a half times as three and a half prophetic years of 360 days, or "1260 natural years." This is the period of the little horn that arose after the ten horns were established.[48] Then "T. B.," in the April, 1828, issue, citing Horne, adopts the Frere and Irving dating from the alleged time of the vision, for the 2400 years, which he places as from 553 B.C. to A.D. 1847.[49]

[44] *The Jewish Expositor*, August, 1816 (vol. 1), pp. 315, 316.
[45] *Ibid.*, November, 1819 (vol. 4), pp. 421, 471-473.
[46] *Ibid.*, p. 473.
[47] *Ibid.*, October, 1820 (vol. 5), pp. 386, 387.
[48] *Ibid.*, November, 1825 (vol. 10), p. 415.
[49] *Ibid.*, April, 1828 (vol. 13), p. 131.

3. "J. G. O." ENDS 2300, 391, AND 1290 ALL IN 1844.—In volume 1 of the new series for 1831 mention is made that the term "generation" (*genea*) means race.[50] And in volume 2, for 1832, the unidentified "J. G. O." stresses 1844 as the focal point for the 2300 years, starting from 457 B.C., as well as for the 391 years of the Turkish woe, dated from the fall of Constantinople in 1453, and so reaching to 1844. Then, finally, he takes 553 or 554 for the beginning of the 1260 years of papal tyranny, and ends them similarly in 1814, with the thirty additional years, to the end of the 1290 years, likewise extending to 1844.[51] The millennium, he believed, would follow shortly thereafter.[52]

4. CUNINGHAME SUMMARIZES WITNESS ON FOUR EMPIRES.— Considerable note is taken of several then-recent books by the Futurist S. R. Maitland, and the strictures of William Cuninghame against Frere's positions.[53] In volume 3, for 1833, Cuninghame writes concerning the virtually unanimous consent of the Jewish and Christian churches "for more than eighteen centuries," in identifying the four empires as "Babylon, Persia, Greece, and Rome." In support he cites the Targum of Jonathan ben Uzziel, and the Jewish writers Abarbanel, Kimchi, and David Levi. Then in the Christian category. Irenaeus, Hippolytus, Lactantius, Chrysostum, Cyril of Jerusalem, and Jerome are listed. And from more recent times he names Mede, Sir Isaac Newton, More, Brightman, Cressener, Daubuz, Whiston, Lloyd, and Bishop Newton.[54]

5. PROPHETIC PERIODS DRAWN FROM CYCLES OF UNIVERSE. —Then Cuninghame cites the unique witness of de Chéseaux, noted eighteenth-century Swiss astronomer, on the numbers 1260 and 2300, and particularly their difference—1040—as "astronomical cycles, bringing into harmony *solar* and *diurnal* time." [55] His argument is interesting and impressive, leading to three conclusions: 1. These prophetic numbers are mystical days, signifying years, not literal days. 2. The 1260 years are a com-

---

[50] *Ibid.*, 1831 (vol. 1, new series), p. 54.
[51] *Ibid.*, 1832 (vol. 2), pp. 402, 403.
[52] *Ibid.*, p. 404.
[53] *Ibid.*, p. 427.
[54] *Ibid.*, 1833 (vol. 3), pp. 56, 57.
[55] *Ibid.*, p. 59.

ponent part of the 2300 years. 3. In order to impress the church with the unspeakable importance of these prophetic numbers, they were not only announced with a solemn oath (Dan. 12:7), but are engraved in the very system of the universe, being taken from the measures of the "great revolutions of the Diurnal and Monthly and Annual periods of the heavens." [56]

6. "E" DEFENDS CORRECTNESS OF 2300 NUMERAL.—Finally "E" rises to a strong defense of the 2300 years, as against the suggested 2400, and observes, "There is probably no numeral in the Scriptures the correctness of which may be more entirely relied on." [57] But not yet certain as to the dating, he suggests the span of 480 B.C. to A.D. 1820, on the supposition that this terminus involves "the cleansing either of Christian countries or the Jewish sanctuary from the Mohammedan yoke." [58] Thus the 2300 years penetrates every medium employed for the discussion of prophecy.

Because of Hawtrey's editorship, we shall here note his part in the picture.

III. Hawtrey—Advent and Resurrection Begin Millennium

CHARLES S. HAWTREY (1780-1831), secretary of the Society for Promoting Christianity Among the Jews, and editor of *The Jewish Expositor*, was educated at Oriel College, Oxford, with a B.A. in 1801 and an M.A. in 1813. Curate of Holyrood, Southampton, and vicar of Wilston, Monmouth, in 1805, he became minister of the Episcopal Chapel for the Jews, at Bethnal Green. [59] In the roster of officers and trustees in the *Summary Account of the Origin, Proceedings, and Success of the London Society for Promoting Christianity Among the Jews,* Sir Thomas Baring, M.P., is president; Henry Drummond and Lewis Way are among the vice-presidents, and Hawtrey is the first of the three secretaries. (Title page reproduced on page 444.)

1. RESURRECTION MARKS BEGINNING OF MILLENNIUM.— A part from his editorial writing in *The Jewish Expositor,* Haw-

---

[56] *Ibid.*   [57] *Ibid.*, p. 30.   [58] *Ibid.*, pp. 32, 33.
[59] *Alumni Oxonienses*, 1715-1886, vol. 2, p. 631.

trey wrote *The Nature of the First Resurrection,* in 1826, with the anonymous signature, "A Spiritual Watchman." [60] In this treatise, which was originally a sermon, he stresses the "literal resurrection of the saints." [61] As to the "time," he says, "It will take place at the *commencement,* and not at the close of the millennium, or that period designated as 'a thousand years.' " And as to the "circumstances of it," Hawtrey adds, "It is equally manifest that it will be *preceded* by the personal coming and appearance of the Saviour in his glory." [62] Contrasting the spiritual reign of Christ between His ascension and His second advent, he says:

"But Scripture abundantly testifies that he shall at length appear in person, to reign visibly and gloriously over his church. In the preceding chapter, therefore, there is a most magnificent description of his personal appearance before the first resurrection actually commences." [63]

A series of four lectures delivered in 1830, in which the papal apostasy and the fateful year 1792 were stressed, he likewise published anonymously as a tract, *The Pre-millennial Personal Advent of Christ,* "By a Spiritual Watchman."

2. Events Focusing at the Advent.—The blending of true and false concepts concerning this event is further attested by a note following the quoted statement, making the second advent to be "synchronical" not only with the first resurrection of the dead and the translation of the saints, but with the fall of Babylon, the destruction of all opposing enemies, the restoration of the Jews, and the conversion of the world. [64]

IV. Gauntlett—Expounds Apocalypse Weekly for Two Years

Henry Gauntlett (1762-1833), vicar of Olney, Bucks, was born in Wiltshire and schooled at West Lavington. Ordained in 1786, he became a curate at Tilshead. He filled a number of curacies until 1811, when he became vicar of Olney. He was a close friend of Roland Hill and, with John Newton and Thomas

---

[60] Identified in Joshua W. Brooks, *A Dictionary of Writers on the Prophecies,* p. xxxix.
[61] Charles S. Hawtrey, *The Nature of the First Resurrection,* p. 10.
[62] *Ibid.*   [63] *Ibid.,* p. 11.   [64] *Ibid.*

Scott, strongly supported the evangelical revival in the English church. Gauntlett tells, in the preface of his *Exposition of the Book of Revelation* (1821),[65] how in 1817 he was asked to substitute for a scheduled speaker on the prophecies before the Society for the Promotion of Christianity Among the Jews. As the result, his own interest was deeply aroused in prophecy, and this in turn led to a series of forty-four discourses on the Apocalypse to his own congregation, throughout 1819 and 1820—a most unusual and significant occurrence.

Gauntlett firmly believed that the larger portion of the prophetic outlines "have now actually been fulfilled," and that the remaining portions, "of the highest interest and consequence to the Church, are undoubtedly on the eve of their completion." [66] He urged that the Apocalypse be studied by statesmen as well as by clergymen. An extraordinarily representative list of subscribers is appended to his book—about a thousand in all—nearly half of whom were clergymen of prominence, and the rest writers on prophecy, educators, and men of affairs in the national life.

1. 1260-YEAR REIGN OF PAPAL ANTICHRIST.—Gauntlett views "the popish hierarchy as Antichrist," believing this to be the chief burden of the Apocalypse. He declares:

"Protestantism considers Popery as antichristianity and believes that the popish hierarchy is consigned to perdition by the great Head of the Church, after it has held its destined usurped reign of 1260 years." [67]

2. SEVEN TRUMPETS ENFOLDED IN SEVENTH SEAL.—A summary of Gauntlett's entire exposition is given in a six-page "Brief Outline . . . noting the chapters, verses, and chronology." [68] The first six seals he believes to be confined to the first four centuries, to the time of Constantine,[69] with the seventh seal expanded into the seven trumpets. The first trumpet he allocates to the Gothic invasion, the second to Attila and the Huns, the third to the Vandals, and the fourth to the "extinction of the imperial and other subsequent forms of government in the western empire." [70]

---

[65] Two editions in same year.
[66] Henry Gauntlett, *An Exposition of the Book of Revelation*, p. xxxii
[67] *Ibid.*, p. xxxvi.   [68] *Ibid.*, pp. xli-xlvii.   [69] *Ibid.*, pp. xli, xlii.
[70] *Ibid.*, pp. xlii, xliii.

The fifth, or first woe, trumpet he assigns to the Mohammedan imposture, beginning in the seventh century, and the sixth trumpet to the Ottoman Turks from 1281 onward. [71]

3. Makes Two-horned Beast Same as Little Horn.—

The 1260 years Gauntlett places between 606 and 1866, embracing the period of the Two Witnesses and the church in the wilderness.[72] The ten-horned beast of Revelation 13 is interpreted as the "papal persecuting Roman empire," by which the antichristian church has all along been supported, with "the two-horned beast of the earth denoting the Roman hierarchy, or papal church." [73] This he holds to be the same as the little horn of Daniel 7, only given as a separate symbol by John.[74]

4. Seventh Vial Afflictions Under French Revolution.

—Gauntlett begins the angelic messages of Revelation 14 around the time of the Reformation, and extends them to the great consummation.[75] The seven vials are applied to the afflictions under the French Revolution, from 1789 onward, with the sixth vial, having "reference to Mahomedism and the Turkish nation," as "yet future." [76]

5. Fifth Trumpet, 612-762; Sixth Trumpet, 1281-1672.—

Gauntlett's premise all the way through is that Rome is the fourth prophetic empire, divided into ten parts, or nations, with the papal Antichrist following.[77] But popery, the "western antichrist," opened the way for Mohammedanism, the "eastern antichrist." [78] The five prophetic months, or 150 years, of the fifth trumpet, he places from 612 to 762, or from the time Mohammed "publicly propagated his imposture." [79] As in all prophetic time, the day stands for the year, and this is the period selected by most prophetic writers.[80] The 391 years of the sixth woe Gauntlett dates from 1281, "the first conquest of the Turks over the Christians," to 1672, "the last success by which they extended their dominions." [81] He follows Bishop Newton in saying that

---

[71] *Ibid.*, xliii.
[72] *Ibid.*, p. xliv.
[73] *Ibid.*
[74] *Ibid.*, p. 201.

[75] *Ibid.*, p. xli.
[76] *Ibid.*, pp. xlvi, 255-278.
[77] *Ibid.*, p. 112.
[78] *Ibid.*, p. 118.

[79] *Ibid.*, pp. 119, 120, 123
[80] *Ibid.*, p. 123.
[81] *Ibid.*, p. 127.

if they only knew the exact date of the first event, "the exactness
of the fifteen days might be found." [82]

6. SEVEN FORMS OF GOVERNMENT; TEN KINGDOMS.—Gauntlett is not clear on the earthquake of Revelation 11, but the
dragon of chapter 12 is clearly pagan Rome, with the seven heads
as the commonly accepted forms of government, and the ten
horns as the nations into which the empire was later divided. [83]
He believed that the seven vials would be poured out before the
termination of the 1260 years, which he had placed in 1866. So
he begins the seven vials with the French Revolution, in 1789. [84]

7. PAPAL SYMBOL OF REVELATION 17.—The "great whore"
of Revelation 17 refers "without doubt," he asserts, to Rome
papal. [85] He notes the seven hills, or mountains, of Rome [86] as
prefiguring the seven forms of government, [87] which are discussed
at much length.

8. DESTRUCTION OF POPERY AND MOHAMMEDANISM PRE-
CEDES MILLENNIUM.—Gauntlett does not attempt to date the
millennium, but alludes to those who attempt to extend the
close of the 1290 and 1335 years beyond the terminus of the 1260
years. If this papal period be dated from 606 to 1866, then the
added seventy-five years would lead to 1941, he remarks. [88] But
he gives no endorsement to this view. Gauntlett, as a stanch
premillennialist, holds that before the millennium begins,
popery and Mohammedanism are to be destroyed. [89] He also
holds that the conversion of the Jews is involved. At the close
of the millennium, Satan is loosed for the little season. Such
was the scope of Gauntlett's unusual Sunday evening sermons,
covering the years 1819 and 1820.

V. Girdlestone—2300 Years Applied to Mohammedan Rule

WILLIAM E. GIRDLESTONE (1786-1840), rector of Kelling
cum Salthouse, Norfolk, was born in Norwich. Educated at
Gonville and Caius College, where he was an honor student, he

---

[82] *Ibid.*, p. 128.
[83] *Ibid.*, p. 176.
[84] *Ibid.*, p. 257.

[85] *Ibid.*, p. 283.
[86] *Ibid.*, p. 291.
[87] *Ibid.*, pp. 291-293.

[88] *Ibid.*, p. 358.
[89] *Ibid.*, p. 360.

afterward spent a period in the army. Ordained a deacon, and then becoming a priest in 1814, he served continuously as rector of Kelling cum Salthouse from 1821 till his death, in 1840.[90]

1. MOHAMMEDANISM, LITTLE HORN OF DANIEL 8.—In his *Observations on the Visions of Daniel, and on ... the Revelation of St. John* (1820),[91] Girdlestone holds the standard view of the four prophetic empires of Daniel 2 and 7, Babylon dropping out of the depiction in Daniel 8. But the tyrannical power of the "exceeding great" horn, Girdlestone applies to Mohammedanism.[92] In Daniel 9 the prophet cheers his people with the promise of the Messiah, and specifies the time of His coming. In Daniel 11, the power of the Romans is stressed, and Antichrist in his Roman as well as his Mohammedan phases is depicted.[93]

2. 2300 YEARS MOHAMMEDAN RULE END 1965.—His time calculations were quite unusual. Holding, orthodoxly enough, to the 1260-, 1290-, 1335-, and 2300-day periods as years, Girdlestone applies the first three periods to Mohammedanism. Beginning them together in 630, he ends the 1260 years in 1890, the 1290 in 1920, and the 1335 in 1965, when the 2300 years of Mohammedan dominance would also end, and the sanctuary be cleansed.[94] This curious calculation is premised on beginning the 2300 years when Alexander was made captain of the Grecian army against Persia, which would lead to 1965 as the terminus of the 2300 in the "blessed time" and the cleansing of the sanctuary.[95]

---

[90] John Venn, *Biographical History of Gonville and Caius College*, vol. 2 (1713-1897), p. 140.
[91] His *Notes on the Apocalypse* (1847) is simply an expansion of earlier notes.
[92] William E. Girdlestone, *Observations on the Visions of Daniel, and on . . . the Revelation of St. John*, p. 2.
[93] *Ibid.*, p. 3.   [94] *Ibid.*, p. 59.   [95] *Ibid.*, pp. 60, 61.

PRINCIPALS AT THE ALBURY PARK PROPHETIC CONFERENCE

Banker Henry Drummond (Left), in Whose Spacious Albury Park Villa the First Prophetic Conference Was Held (Upper Center). The Presiding Officer Was Hugh M'Neile (Right). Below (Center) Is the Catholic Apostolic Church Later Erected by Drummond's Funds

CHAPTER TWENTY THREE

Continental Society
and Albury Conference

I. Drummond—Patron of Advent-awakening Organizations

ANOTHER great organizer and promoter of group study and action was HENRY DRUMMOND (1786-1860), banker and member of Parliament. Educated at Harrow and Christ Church, Oxford, he became an active partner in his father's bank at Charing Cross in London. He toured Russia in 1807, and served as a member of Parliament for Plympton Earles from 1810 to 1813. He was intimate with Pitt and other leading statesmen of his time. Whenever he rose to speak in Parliament, there was a hush of expectation owing to his high character, wealth, and scholarship. He was an authority on currency and scientific agriculture, a shrewd debater, and a daring wit. Young Drummond had the highest offices of the state open to him.[1]

Then, in June, 1817, "satiated with the empty frivolities of the fashionable world," and constrained by Christ's counsel to the rich young ruler, he broke up his hunting establishment and sold his Grange, that he might devote his whole life to Christian service. Drummond seceded from the Church of England and joined the evangelicals by immersion. With his wife he started on his way to the Holy Land in 1817, to orient himself to his new relationships. A terrific storm caused the

---

[1] *Dictionary of National Biography*, vol. 6, pp. 28, 29; Washington Wilks, *Edward Irving*, pp. 184, 185; *The Gentleman's Magazine*, April, 1860 (New Series, vol. 8), p. 414; Edward Miller, *The History and Doctrines of Irvingism*, vol. 1, p. 30 ff.; William Jones, *Biographical Sketch of the Rev. Edward Irving*, p. 204 ff.

ship to put into the port of Genoa, and his wife appealed to him not to attempt to complete the trip.

He had heard of the difficulties of Robert Haldane at Geneva,[2] and being invited by Professor Gaussen of Geneva, he joined Haldane in the movement against the Arian tendencies of the Consistory at Geneva. His wealth and zeal made him so formidable a power that he was summoned before the Consistory, or Council of State. He therefore withdrew just across the border into France, carrying on the work of reform from there. Circulating Martin's version of the Scriptures, instead of the one corrupted by the Arian clergy, he encouraged the ministers ejected by the Venerable Company to form a separate body. Because of his concern over the Geneva situation, Drummond helped form the Continental Society in 1819, of which we shall hear later, and sustained it with his own means. This brought him into contact with Edward Irving.

While still at Geneva he also became interested in Joseph Wolff, son of a Jewish rabbi, then a student in the Papal College of Missionary Propaganda, at Rome, whom he persuaded to leave Rome, and whose patron he became, financing his extensive missionary trips, which began in 1821,[3] under the auspices of the Society to Promote Christianity Amongst the Jews. In 1826 the notable Albury Park Prophetic Conference was held in his palatial home in Surrey.[4] He was to be found wherever there was activity in the great Advent Awakening.

He supported the prophetic journal *The Morning Watch* (1829-30), was editor and sponsor of *Dialogues on Prophecy* (3 volumes), was author of *Introduction to the Study of the Apocalypse* (1830), *Social Duties on Christian Principles* (1839), *Conditions of the Agricultural Classes* (1842), and participated in the production of some ninety books and pamphlets. Drummond was unsparing in his exposure of the iniquities of Ro-

---

[2] Alexander Haldane, *The Lives of Robert Haldane . . . and His Brother, James Alexander Haldane*, p. 426 ff.
[3] *Travels and Adventures of the Rev. Joseph Wolff*, pp. 61-65; A. M. W. Stirling, *The Ways of Yesterday*, p. 204 ff.; Miller, *op. cit.*, p. 31.
[4] Miller, *op. cit.*, pp. 35-45. See frontispiece for Part II in this volume of *Prophetic Faith*, p. 262, where the conference is pictured.

manism. In 1825 he founded the professorship of political economy at Oxford, and became a Fellow of the Royal Society in 1839.

Later he became one of the founders of the Catholic and Apostolic, or Irvingite, Church,[5] serving as pastor at Albury in 1832, and having charge of their interests in Scotland and Switzerland until his death. He built the Irvingite church at Albury in 1854, at the cost of £16,000, sustaining it with his own means, and erected a parish house in 1841. In 1847 he again entered Parliament, representing West Surrey thenceforward until his death, and was a frequent speaker. His *Speeches in Parliament,* volume 1, contains 131 speeches. His personal views on prophecy are on record.

1. SCOPE OF THE SEALS AND TRUMPETS.—Drummond's *Introduction to the Study of the Apocalypse* gives a comprehensive survey of the leading prophetic outlines and symbols. The seven seals, he believes, trace the course of the Christian church through the centuries from purity to apostasy, with the sixth as "the punishment of the papacy, beginning at the French Revolution," and the seventh "when a similar event destroys all Christendom."[6]

The trumpets, he holds, represent the barbarian scourgings of the West. The fifth and sixth trumpets "are almost unanimously believed to represent the armies of the faith of the Mohammedan imposture, the Saracens and Turks, who destroyed 'the third part,' of the Roman Empire, extirpated the name of Christianity, and still hold the 'land of Immanuel.' "[7] The Euphrates rises in the country from which the Saracens sprang, after the apostate Mohammed had "entered upon his pretended mission." The power represented by the Euphrates wanes again under the sixth vial of Revelation 16.[8] The seventh trumpet completes the mysterious proceedings of God; and time is superseded by the "countless ages of eternity." The

[5] Robert Baxter, *Irvingism,* pp. xi-xv.
[6] Henry Drummond, *Introduction to the Study of the Apocalypse,* p. 8.
[7] *Ibid.,* p. 9.
[8] *Ibid.,* p. 17.

seven plagues, Drummond holds, are component parts of the
seventh trumpet.[9]

2. MESSAGES OF REVELATION 14 BEING PROCLAIMED.—
Furthermore, in Revelation 12 the woman is the church, and
the child is Christ Jesus. The beast of Revelation 13 is Rome,
and the 144,000 are "undefiled with the Papal harlot," having
"come out of the false church." [10] The "works enumerated"
in the angelic messages of Revelation 14, have been going on
for thirty years. Societies have been sending out the everlasting
gospel; the testimony that Babylon is about to fall has been
given and God's people have been called to come out of her.
The chapter ends with the coming of the Son of man at the
close of the harvest.[11] Application of these angelic messages to
movements and organizations of the time became increasingly
common among Drummond and his associates.

3. PLAGUES AFFECT PAPACY AND TURKEY.—The plagues
are the detailed parts of the seventh trumpet, Drummond points
out, like the seventh sounding of the trumpet at Jericho, with
its seven blasts.[12] The fifth vial is concentrated on the throne
of the papal beast, and the sixth symbolizes the exhaustion of
the Turkish power.[13] Drummond makes particular reference
to the fleet of Protestant England, the fleet of Catholic France,
and the fleet of Greek Catholic Russia joining in 1830 to sweep
the crescent "off the face of the deep." [14]

4. REIGNS WITH SAINTS ON THIS PLANET.—The final scenes
concern the war of the great day of God Almighty, when Christ
gathers His people at the beginning of the millennium, as
He comes to the judgment upon Babylon. Then will follow
the triumphant reign of Christ with His church on this planet.[15]
Two helpful diagram-maps outline the boundaries of the four
kingdoms of Babylon, Medo-Persia, Greece, and Rome. Then
the Roman Empire is pictured as it was overrun by the papal
apostasy in the West and the Mohammedan apostasy in the
East.

9 *Ibid.*, p. 9.   10 *Ibid.*, pp. 10, 11.   11 *Ibid.*, p. 11.
12 *Ibid.*, p. 12.   13 *Ibid.*, p. 13.   14 *Ibid.*, p. 14.   15 *Ibid.*, p. 16.

But before continuing with Drummond we must pause long enough to present the part played by Haldane.

II. Haldane—Contender at Geneva Over Apocrypha

ROBERT HALDANE (1764-1842) was born in London, inheriting large property holdings. His early life was spent in the British Navy. He went through the French Revolution, but was shortly afterward converted, and devoted his life to missionary endeavor. He sought to go to India, but when permission was refused by the East India Company, he joined Roland Hill and others in spreading the evangelical revival in Scotland. Haldane seceded from the Established Church, and at his own expense erected a place of worship under the name of the Tabernacle. He also organized a theological school in Paris. He next turned his attention to the evangelization of Africa, taking twenty-four young natives from Sierra Leone and giving them a Christian education. His personal labors awakened an interest in southern France. Then he turned his attention to Geneva and Montauban, taking a prominent part in the management of the newly formed Continental Society, and the Bible Society of Edinburgh.[16]

Haldane was prominent in the current controversy over the Apocrypha, which he found had been appended to the Toulouse Bible. Discussion was followed by public rupture with the British and Foreign Bible Society, as he believed the supremacy and integrity of the Bible was at stake—the Bible Society having been founded on the principle of an excluded Apocrypha. This led to the establishment of the Edinburgh organization.[17]

III. Continental Society—Formed to Herald Judgment Hour

While still at Geneva, Haldane contemplated formation of a Continental Society, but Drummond actually set the plan in

---

[16] *Dictionary of National Biography*, vol. 8, p. 898.
[17] Haldane, *op. cit.*, pp. 484-507; *The Gentleman's Magazine*, February, 1843 (New Series, vol. 19), p. 222.

motion, when the Venerable Company in Geneva refused ordination to those who would not submit to its position regarding the deity of Christ.[18] So Drummond dispatched a mission of these deposed ministers to Alsace. The society was fully organized in 1819, M. Mejanel, one of the first representatives, having been expelled from Geneva in 1818, and with him Henri Pyt and others who had broken with the Arian Consistory.[19] The society arranged for the training of missionary students, Haldane devoting much of his time to the furtherance of the society on the Continent. The Edinburgh Auxiliary was formed in 1821.

The unique character and witness of the society can perhaps best be seen by sketching its annual reports. The first report of the Continental Society for the Diffusion of Religious Knowledge—which was its full name—was issued in 1819. These annual reports were not for "general use" but for the "private information of the Secretaries and Members of the Committees of Auxiliary Societies," [20] and were confidential in character. The organization was formed to meet the still-prevalent infidelity in France and Italy, the inroads of Socinianism or Arianism in the Geneva church, and the attempt to impose the Toulouse version of the Scriptures, containing the Apocrypha, upon the French Reformed Churches in Switzerland, France, and Holland. Another threat to be countered was the infiltration of "German Neology" into the great universities of Germany as well as the development of a mystic spiritism among the illiterate.[21] The supreme motive, however, was to herald the impending judgment hour, as will become increasingly evident. (Title page reproduced on page 444.)

The second report lists Sir Thomas Baring, M.P., as president, with Henry Drummond and Lewis Way as two of six vice-presidents, and John Bayford and Joseph Wolff among the committee of eighteen. It states that its "arduous task" is that

---

[18] Haldane, *op. cit.*, p. 454.
[19] *Ibid.*, pp. 454, 455.
[20] *Proceedings of the Continental Society, . . . Eighth year, 1825-1826,* slip pasted on title page.
[21] *First Report of the Continental Society,* 1819, pp. 4-6.

of "exposing the corruptions of Christianity." [22] For this reason, "unbroken silence" concerning "names of persons and places" is necessary to avoid defeat of its objectives, and possible danger to the society's agents.[23] The "rules and regulations" state:

"I. The object of this Society is to assist Local Native Ministers in preaching the Gospel, and in distributing Bibles, Testaments, and Religious Publications over the Continent of Europe; but without the design of establishing any distinct sect or party." [24]

1. ORGANIZED AT TIME MARKED OUT BY PROPHECY.—The business of the society was to be conducted at monthly meetings "in or near London." Its committee was chosen yearly at the annual meeting, held each May. The object of the organization was reiterated by the president, in the fourth annual meeting, as being "to preach the everlasting gospel." In moving the adoption of the report, Lewis Way, in his opening remarks, stresses the times as marked out in prophecy, and the society's mission as calling men "out of the mystical Babylon." [25]

"This Society yields to none in general importance, but stands preeminent, with respect to the time, in which its plans are to be carried into effect. There is a time for all things; and I think this is the very time marked out by prophecy, and determined by the circumstances of Europe, when this Society ought to commence a scriptural crusade under that sacred commission, for which you have the highest authority above all other societies, at the present moment, with respect to the spiritual world, *to call its members out of the mystical Babylon.* That is the foundation, on which this Society ought to rest, and, if built on this foundation, stand it must: it must accomplish the very end, for which God has established it." [26]

2. HOUR OF GOD'S JUDGMENT IS COME.—After dilating upon the corruption of Christianity on the Continent, the prevalence of infidelity and the philosophical heresy of neology, Way refers to the "latter rain" and the harvesttime, and states that "the time is really come to pull down Antichrist." Then follows this remarkable declaration concerning the hour of God's judgment:

---

[22] *Second Report of the Continental Society,* 1820, p. 3.
[23] *Ibid.*
[24] *Proceedings of the Continental Society, . . . Fourth Year, 1821-1822,* p. 30.
[25] *Ibid.,* p. 33.
[26] *Ibid.,* pp. 33, 34.

"You have heard the gospel mentioned as *everlasting;* . . . but that word is never applied to any other gospel than that gospel to be preached now, for a specific and peculiar purpose, to pull down Babylon; and, it must be the everlasting gospel, not the gospel according to *Calvin,* or according to *Luther,* but the gospel according to St. John; that is the gospel, that will pull down the strong holds of Satan, and lay them in the dust . . . you will find that, immediately after the gospel is preached to all nations, great Babylon will fall; because the hour of God's judgment will be come. Now, the hour of God's judgment is inseparably connected, by St. Paul, with the appearance and kingdom of our Lord Jesus Christ." [27]

3. CHRIST'S KINGDOM SUCCEEDS BABYLON'S FALL.—Then Way immediately expands his meaning of the time and the message:

"I am not now preaching a sermon, but giving you an outline, that you may see what prophecy relates to, when it tells you that, as Jerusalem was destroyed, for rejecting the Saviour, and the kingdom passed over to the fourth Monarchy, *that* Empire now having served the purpose of the Almighty, as a rod and an axe, in his hand, to cut down that people, and to scatter them on the face of the earth, then Babylon itself shall fall: and what is to succeed to that? why, the kingdom of Christ upon earth." [28]

Holding that this includes the conversion of the Jews, Way closes by referring to *"the stone cut out of the mountain without hands,"* and declares, "This Society stands *pre-eminent,* on account of *the time.* I believe *now* is the time, *or never:* therefore, work while you can." [29]

4. BABYLON INCLUDES MORE THAN PAPAL ROME.—One of the characteristics of the large annual meeting was the anniversary sermon. In 1822 this was preached by Lewis Way, on "The Flight Out of Babylon." He held that great Babylon of the Apocalypse is the apostate condition of the Christian "church at large," and is not restricted to "papal Rome." [30] Way stressed the responsibility not merely of reclaiming infidel France, proving the deity of Christ to the sophists of Germany, accelerating the ruin of papal hierarchy, and rebuilding the tabernacle of David, but of warning and teaching every man of the impending "time of the Lord's vengeance" and "re-

[27] *Ibid.,* p. 36.   [28] *Ibid.*   [29] *Ibid.,* p. 37.

[30] *Ibid.,* pp. viii, ix.

demption," immediately preceding and introductory to His "second revelation in glory."[31] Here we catch a glimpse of the motivating concept of the organization.

5. MAP OF PROPHECY INDICATES LAST DAYS.—Way stresses the prophecy of Daniel 12:1, concerning the unparalleled "time of trouble," which he applies to "this time," according to those who had "made the prophetical Scriptures" their special study.[32] This "map of prophecy" includes the "last day scoffers" of Peter and Jude, and the repetition of the violence of the days of Noah.[33] Then Way declares, "The lamp of the Reformation, once shining with such lustre amid the darkness of Popery, is well nigh gone out for lack of oil."[34]

6. WINDS HELD BRIEFLY FOR SEALING WORK.—Along with this, Way notes the growing expectation of the approaching manifestation of the Redeemer, also the unclean spirits gathering the world to the battle of the great day of God Almighty.[35] But the vial of final wrath is still restrained. Way concludes:

"How seasonable then is the proclamation! 'Flee out of the midst of Babylon, and deliver every man his soul: be not cut off in her iniquity;' though this be a day of vengeance, it is a day of mercy. The winds of heaven seem to be withheld for a season, that the servants of God may be sealed,—that a great multitude may be gathered to stand before the throne, and sing the song of salvation to God and to the Lamb. The pacification of Europe has opened a door of entrance for the dissemination of Protestant Bibles, and a door of utterance may open of its own accord, to Protestant Preachers."[36]

7. VERY EXISTENCE OF SOCIETIES A SIGN OF TIMES.—In the Eighth Report, for 1826, Henry Drummond contends that the "very existence" of the Bible Societies, the Societies to Promote Christianity Amongst the Jews, and the Continental Societies is among the distinct "signs of the *latter times;* by which expression I mean those days which immediately precede the establishment of that universal kingdom."[37] The object of the society, he re-iterates, is to call people out of Babylon.

[31] *Ibid.*, pp. xiii-xvi.   [33] *Ibid.*, pp. xviii, xix.   [35] *Ibid.*, pp. xix, xx.
[32] *Ibid.*, pp. xvi, xvii.   [34] *Ibid.*, p. xix.   [36] *Ibid.*, pp. xx, xxi.
[37] *Proceedings of the Continental . . . Eighth Year, 1825-1826,* p. 33.

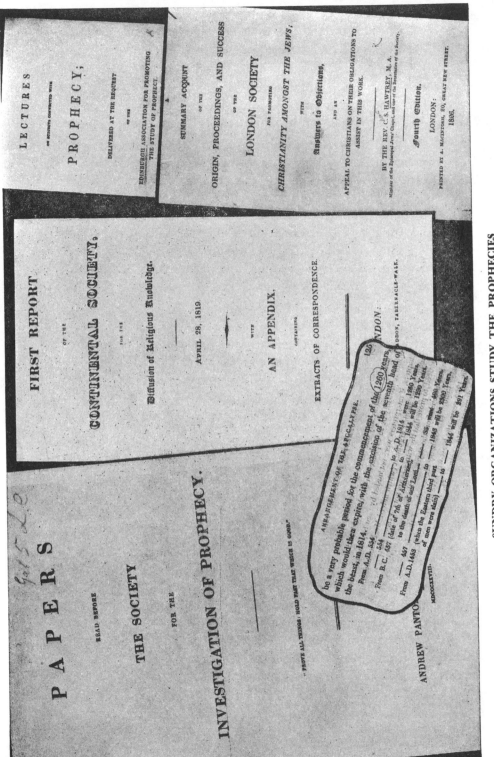

SUNDRY ORGANIZATIONS STUDY THE PROPHECIES

The Society for the Investigation of Prophecy (Left, With Inset) Stresses the Years 1843-44; Another Fosters Their Study on the Continent (Center); Others of a Local Lecture Nature Appear (Upper Right). Among the First Organized Was the Society to Spread These Teachings Among the Jews (Lower Right)

8. Society to Herald Great Judgment Hour.—Lewis Way makes a second remarkable address. Noting the *"positive irreligion"* of the Continent, which stimulated the formation of the Continental Society, Way warns against the danger of Protestant relapse, and notes the spirit and state of Babylon. He admonishes against passing all the charges on to the Roman church. Coming again to their great mission, he says:

"The term *'everlasting Gospel'* is never used but once in the Scriptures, and as some societies have taken to themselves a resemblance to that angel who flies through the midst of heaven to declare it, I call on Bible Societies, on Missionary Societies, and on Continental Societies, and on every one who may desire to be placed in the situation of that holy angel, to carry the commission of that angel with them, and what is *that?* It has never been carried yet, as far as I am aware, in its full sense and application. It is to be found, if you will refer to the next verse, where many of our friends always stop, 'Fear God, and give glory to Him for the Hour of His Judgment is come.' Here is the commission of the angel, and it should be that of every society bearing a missionary character, and composed of believers in the Lord Jesus Christ." [38]

9. Prophecy a Divinely Appointed Calendar.—Way urges that the specific work of the society rests "on the analogy of prophecy"; further, that "this is the time" to send missionaries to declare "the fall of Babylon." As to the way by which the time may be known, he avers that God made "a calendar for His people."[39] Prophecy is our guiding light. As Daniel knew by books when the Jews were to come out of Babylon, so those "living in 'the time of the end' " should know the nearness of "Christ's coming from heaven." We are to preach not only against the iniquities of the Church of Rome but on the coming marriage of the Lamb. "This is the time in which we are now living, and this is the language of prophecy both in the Old and New Testament." [40]

10. If Society Is Unfaithful, God Will Call Other Heralds.—Way then dilates first on the proclamation, "Fear God, for the hour of His Judgment is come," then on "Babylon is fallen," and finally on "Come out of her, my people." [41]

---

[38] *Ibid.*, p. 39.
[39] *Ibid.*

[40] *Ibid.*, p. 40.
[41] *Ibid.*

That triple cry, he declares, is sounding forth. Now come the
almost prophetic words addressed to the society—words that
should be remembered by us as we come to later developments:

> "I will say, in reference to this Society, that whether it is done by
> you or not, the command will be proclaimed. And if you do not preach
> it, it will be preached by others, as a witness; though it will not be believed.
> For the Gospel of the kingdom, the glorious kingdom of the Lord God
> Almighty, in the person of his Son Jesus Christ, is to be preached to all
> nations, as a testimony against, if not for them." [42]

11. TIME TO RESCUE FROM THE BURNING HOUSE.—Hugh
M'Neile, whom we shall meet again, also speaks of "powerful
witnesses" in behalf of the great truth of the Lord's second
coming,[43] and calls for a bold yet appealing declaration of the
sins of Babylon. M'Neile continues:

> "I am, Sir, I repeat, decidedly of opinion, that not only should the
> Gospel be preached in Babylon, winning souls by its attractive loveliness;
> but that these, and statements such as these should be reiterated with
> affectionate earnestness: that seeing multitudes of our fellow-creatures care-
> lessly dwelling in a burning house, we should not only call to them, 'Behold
> here is a safe habitation to fly to:' but also 'Behold! your house is on
> fire.' Sir, the fire is gaining upon this house, for the coming of the Lord
> draweth nigh. Now, therefore, is the time for the voice of the Continental
> Society to be raised, and cry aloud; not consulting the carnal policy of
> man's boasted prudence." [44]

In the eleventh report, for 1829, Horatio Montague stresses
that "Popery is the Apocalyptic Babylon," [45] with the Continental Society raising the cry, "Come out of her, my people," as
he refers to the papal "Beast of the Apocalypse." [46]

So the real purpose of the society is most apparent.

12. REPUDIATE BOTH PROTESTANT AND ROMAN APOSTASY.—
The twelfth report, of 1830, shows an expansion of officers, with
The Honorable John James Strutt as president, and Drummond,
Way, and Lord Mandeville among the twelve vice-presidents,
J. H. Frere and the Haldane brothers on the committee of
twenty-three, and Hugh M'Neile as one of the secretaries. Wil-
liam Cuninghame and Henri Pyt presented the following:

---

[42] *Ibid.*, pp. 40, 41.
[43] *Ibid.*, p. 52.
[45] *Proceedings of tne Continental Society,* . . . *Eleventh Year, 1828-1829,* p. 28.
[44] *Ibid.*, pp. 52, 53.
[46] *Ibid.*, p. 29.

"Resolved Unanimously,

"II. That this Meeting, contemplating the enormities of the great apostasy of Rome, and the insidious and deceiving artifices of those who have embraced heresies (no less injurious) under the fair name of Protestantism, while both are blinding the minds of the children of men, do resolve, by God's grace, to keep clear of each, and to make no peace with either; as the only ground on which they can possibly be of service, in convincing his children, and calling them out from the fellowship of both." [47]

The unchanging keynote of the society is again stressed in the motion of Henry Drummond:

"Resolved unanimously,

"III. That this Meeting, impressed with the thought that the day of labour is far spent, and must soon close; and that to be instrumental in the accomplishment of Jehovah's purposes of grace to his people is the highest honour and greatest interest of his Church, do recognize the great duty and privilege of raising the cry throughout apostate Christendom, 'Come out of her, my people, that ye be not partakers of her sins, and that ye receive not of her plagues.' " [48]

It will be observed that participants in the Jewish Society are likewise active in this organization.

13. "IMPENDING DAY OF LORD" KEYNOTE IN 1836.—By 1836 the Continental Society's name was changed to the European Missionary Society, with Edward Bickersteth giving the annual address in this "eighteenth year" of the organization. The near advent of the day of the Lord was still the keynote, when God will "visibly and manifestly work his mighty acts," rectifying every wrong under which the earth now groans, punishing evildoers, regenerating the earth by fire, judging all men, and the bringing in of the new heavens and earth. [49]

That day, Bickersteth declares, is the breaking up of kingdoms and churches by the final events of Daniel 2, when the stone smites the image, and all is broken to pieces, "explicitly interpreted by the angel as pointing out Christ's *kingdom breaking in pieces all* the previous *kingdoms,* and then *standing for ever."* [50] This accomplishes the complete overthrow of popery,

---

[47] *Proceedings of the Continental Society,* . . . *Twelfth Year, 1829-1830,* p. 3.
[48] *Ibid.*
[49] *Proceedings of the European Missionary Society,* . . . *Eighteenth Year,* 1835-6, p. 16
[50] *Ibid.*

Mohammedanism, infidelity, and every opposing kingdom. It is introduced by the time of trouble, and, Bickersteth adds, by the deliverance of the Jews.[51]

14. THE SIGNS AND ORDER OF EVENTS.—The signs in the sun, moon, and stars are manifest, and the sign of the Son of man, as He appears in the heavens to raise the dead and change the living saints, is near at hand.[52] The beast and the kings of the earth and their armies, "in their rage, enmity, and blindness," make war against the Lord. Judgments are poured out on Antichrist and his adherents.[53] Satan is then to be bound, and Christ will begin His "glorious millennial reign, with his saints, over the earth." [54] Finally, Satan is loosed for a little season; then he is cast into the lake of fire, the impenitent with him, and the eternal kingdom begins.[55]

15. SECOND ADVENT PRECEDES MILLENNIUM.—The actual advent, Bickersteth holds, does not begin the day of the Lord, but is clearly included within it.[56] It is represented as near at hand. So he concludes, "It is then, in my view, impossible that there can be a certain period of 1,000 years before its coming." [57] Premillennialism is axiomatic with this group.

16. NOT PRESUMPTION TO DISCERN SIGNS OF TIMES.— Bickersteth feels that during the 1800 years of the Christian Era the large part of the Apocalypse has been fulfilled. He concludes:

"The present preaching of the Gospel to the Gentiles—the unprecedented excitement among the Jews—the series of judgments poured out on Europe in the last forty years—the decay of the resources of the Turkish empire, answering to the *drying up of the Euphrates*—the unclean spirits now abroad—the shaking of every thing through the earth—have all one voice testifying the approach of the day of the Lord. The chronological Prophecies, given to the Church to help her to discern the times, confirm this view." [58]

He affirms that they are living on the "borders" of that great upheaval. It is therefore not "presumption to discern *the*

---

[51] *Ibid.*, pp. 16, 17. [54] *Ibid.*, pp. 18, 19. [57] *Ibid.*, p. 20.
[52] *Ibid.*, p. 17. [55] *Ibid.*, p. 19. [58] *Ibid.*
[53] *Ibid.*, pp. 17, 18. [56] *Ibid.*

signs of the times; it is not humility to be unacquainted with prophecy; but it is, in the view of our Lord, hypocrisy to pretend to religion, and yet to neglect the signs of the times." And again the refrain is sounded forth:

"This Society has been formed, in the conviction of the evil state of Europe through its apostacy from the true God, to aid the faithful ministers and servants of Christ in their labours to bring men to repent, to fear God, and give glory to him, that they may escape the Divine judgments in the quickly coming day of wrath." [59]

So prophecy permeated every consideration, and motivated every action. The terms of Revelation 14 were constantly invoked.

IV. First Prophetic Conference Meets at Albury Park

In a desire to compare views and to gain a better and more united understanding of the prophecies pertaining to the times, groups of expositors held periodic meetings in the summer of 1826. Then, upon suggestion of Lewis Way, Henry Drummond invited by letter certain ministers and laymen whom he believed would be interested in assembling toward the close of the year for a full week of uninterrupted study and discussion. Twenty students of prophecy responded to the first call, Joseph Wolff being among the number, and Hugh M'Neile, rector of the parish of Albury, serving as moderator.[60]

Thus the first Prophetic Conference in the Old World Advent Awakening came to pass—the first of its kind, apparently, in the modern history of the church. Drummond's luxurious villa at Albury Park, near Guildford, in Surrey, reached by an easy drive through the woods, was admirably suited for such an assemblage. It provided shady, secluded walks for contemplation or discussion.[61] The participants were vitally interested in the immediate features of fulfilling prophecy and were anxious to work out satisfying applications for divergent points.

---

[59] *Ibid.*, p. 27.
[60] A graphic painting of this epochal conference appears as the frontispiece of Part II in this volume on p. 262.
[61] Miller, *op. cit.*, pp. 35, 36.

These conferences were repeated annually until 1830. Forty-four individuals in all attended one or more, representing various churches and communions. The interchurch character of the group is revealed by the fact that nineteen were clergymen of the Church of England, one a Moravian, two Dissenting ministers, four ministers of the Established Church of Scotland, eleven were English laymen, one a Scotch Presbyterian layman, and six others were of undetermined persuasion.[62] Well-known names included Drummond, M'Neile, Cuninghame, Wolff, Irving, Daniel Wilson (afterward Bishop of Calcutta), Frere, Hawtrey, Vaughan, Bayford, Stewart, Simons, Marsh, John Tudor (later editor of *The Morning Watch*), and Lord Mandeville.[63]

The 1827 meeting was more largely attended than the 1826 gathering, and the interpretations of prophecy appear to have taken a more definite turn—focalizing upon the coming advent and the millennium, the "times and seasons," and the return of the Jews. The apocalyptic vials were believed to have been poured out on Rome in 1798, and the Lord's return was expected in 1847.[64] The 1828 session was not so well attended, but the current war with Turkey was eagerly watched as an indication of the near approach of the end. The later vials were taken as foreshadowing the proximity of the battle of Armageddon. Prophetic time was believed to have almost expired.[65]

A delightfully intimate picture of the first Albury Conference appears in a six-page "Postscript" [66] by Irving, appended to his 138-page translator's "Preliminary Discourse" to Lacunza's *Coming of Messiah,* which he had hoped to submit as his 1826 "Christmas offering to the church." [67] The desire of these prophetic students to "compare their views" as regards the

---

[62] *Ibid.,* p. 40.
[63] *Travels and Adventures of the Rev. Joseph Wolff,* p. 234; Miller, *op. cit.,* pp. 40, 41.
[64] Miller, *op. cit.,* p. 42.
[65] *Ibid.,* p. 43; *Dialogues on Prophecy,* vol. 2, pp. 12-14. The first 150 pages of this volume are devoted to a general discussion of the nearness of Armageddon.
[66] Edward Irving, "Preliminary Discourse," in Manuel Lacunza, *Coming of Messiah,* vol. 1, pp. clxxxviii-cxciv.
[67] *Ibid.,* p. clxxxviii.

"present crisis," and to discuss "great prophetic questions, which do at present most instantly concern Christendom," [68] are outlined.

Six full days, from Thursday to the succeeding Friday, were spent in "close and laborious examination of the scriptures," on the times of the Gentiles, the Jews, the prophetic visions of Daniel and the Apocalypse, the second advent, and the "duties to the church and the world arising out of the same." [69] No official report was issued, so it would not bear any "stamp of authority," that the church "might not take offence." [70] But Irving stresses the unity of the view on the times of the Gentiles, the restoration of the Jews, and the conclusion of the present dispensation in great judgments. All agreed that the day of the Lord was "hard at hand, yea even at the very door." [71] Then he adds:

"All agreeing that in the view of these things, there was required of us the greatest vigilance at our several posts, and the most fearless constancy in affectionately warning and preaching righteousness to all; according as they are admonished be [by] our Lord in the sixth vial, under which it was the universal opinion we are now living, ready for the last great and concluding vial of wrath." [72]

There were three sessions daily—one before breakfast, the principal session between breakfast and dinner, and the third in the evening. In the morning they came together for an hour precisely at eight, "as early as we could well see." This was a devotional period, marked by prayer and seeking God for wisdom and light. It was led by a minister appointed in advance, who based his study solely upon Scripture. The participants all sat around a large table in the library, taking notes on the outline. [73] Breakfast followed, during the two-hour intermission, that they "might each one try and prove himself before the Lord, upon the great questions at issue, and that we might come together with convictions, not with uncertain persuasions, and speak from the conscience, not from present impressions." [74]

At eleven o'clock they reassembled. After again seeking

[68] Ibid.
[69] Ibid., p. clxxxix.
[70] Ibid., p. cxc.
[71] Ibid., pp. clxxxix, cxc.
[72] Ibid., p. cxc.
[73] Ibid., pp. cxc, cxci.
[74] Ibid., p. cxci.

God for divine favor, the moderator asked each to express his convictions on the subject presented in the morning study. All had taken notes on these discussions.

"No appeal was allowed but to the scriptures, of which the originals lay before us, in the interpretation of which, if any question arose, we had the most learned eastern scholar perhaps in the world to appeal to, and a native Hebrew, I mean Joseph Wolff." [75]

Four or five hours were spent in this way—each one expressing his opinion before the meeting broke up. When weary, they "refreshed" themselves with prayer, "which also we regarded as our main defence against Satan." [76] The period closed with an "offering of thanksgiving," by one of the clerical brethren. After dinner they proceeded, beginning at seven o'clock, to "winding up and concluding the whole subject." [77] In this evening session they were familiarly seated around the fire of the "great library-room," but still under the guidance of the moderator, and all taking notes. [78]

At this time any question or difficulty that had arisen during the day might be propounded, the questions being directed to the one who had given the study, and anyone was heard that was "able to resolve it." This final session of the day broke up "towards eleven o'clock," with the singing of a hymn and a prayer. [79] Irving comments:

"Such were the six days we spent under the holy and hospitable roof of Albury house, within the chime of the church bell, and surrounded by the most picturesque and beautiful forms of nature; but the sweetest spot was that council-room where I met the servants of the Lord, the wise virgins waiting with oil in their lamps for the bridegroom, and a sweeter still was that secret chamber where I met in the Spirit my Lord and master whom I hope soon to meet in the flesh." [80]

Breaking forth into verse, Irving sings out:

"O Albury! most honoured of the King
And Potentate of heaven; whose presence here
We daily look for!   In thy silent halls
His servants sought, and found such harmony

---

[75] *Ibid.*   [76] *Ibid.*   [77] *Ibid.*, pp. cxci, cxcii.
[78] Drummond's notes were subsequently issued in *Dialogues on Prophecy*, which we shall examine shortly.
[79] *Ibid.*, p. cxcii.   [80] *Ibid.*

Of blessed expectation, as did fill
Their hearts with lively joy: as if they'd caught
The glory of the cloud which bore their Lord,
Or heard the silver-toned trump of jubilee
Sound his arrival through the vault of heaven.
From thy retreat, as from the lonely watch-tower,
We had certain tidings of the coming night,
And of the coming day. The one to brace
Our hearts with dauntless resolution,
All sufferings to endure in his behalf,
Who for our souls did bear the ascendant dire
Of Satan's hour and power of darkness.
The other to delight our hearts with thoughts
And dearest joys which are not known to those
Contemptuous and unfaithful servants,
Who think not of the promise long delayed
Of thy most glorious coming, gracious Lord!
For me, and for these brethren's sake I pray,

"That the sweet odour of those hallowed hours
May never from our souls depart, till thou
Our glorious King thy standard in the heavens
Unfurlest, and command'st the Archangel strong
To make the silver-toned trump of jubilee
Sound thine arrival through the vault of heaven,
And quicken life within the hollow tomb." [81]

"So singeth my soul," he declares, as he gives form to "these sweetest recollections of my life." Declaring "the doctrine maketh most winged speed" among some, he expresses distress over the indifference of the Church of Scotland.[82] Commenting on the "harmony and unanimity" of these "long and laborious sessions" of the conference, he says:

"Of which assembly the least that I can say is this, that no council, from that first which convened at Jerusalem until this time, seemed more governed, and conducted, and inspired by a Spirit of holy communion." [83]

Then he adds:

"But alas! that church to which I owe my reverence as to a mother, a bountiful though somewhat a stern mother to me, giveth little heed that I can hear of, to this great immediate overwhelming truth. Do thou bless, O Lord, this second attempt of her unworthy son to awaken some of her fathers, some of her doctors, some of her ministers, some of her elders, some

---

[81] *Ibid.*   [82] *Ibid.*, pp. cxcii, cxciii.   [83] *Ibid.*, p. cxciii.

of her members, yea all, yea all, Oh my God, if so it might be pleasing in thy sight and according to thy will." [84]

Recalling the glories of the good confession and martyrdom of the earlier Scotch church, he cries out from his "lonely watch-tower," where the Lord had stationed him, for strength to make known to the church "whatever I hear and see." [85]

V. M'Neile—Stresses Call Out of Babylon

HUGH M'NEILE (1795-1879), dean of Ripon, was born at Ballycastle, Antrim. Educated at Trinity College, Dublin, he received his B.A. in 1815, his M.A. in 1821, and his B.D. and D.D. degrees in 1847. He had studied for the bar at Kings Inn, Dublin, but severe illness overtook him in Switzerland in 1816, where his life was saved. This turned his mind to the ministry, and in 1820 he was ordained to the curacy of Stranorlar. While preaching at Percy Chapel, in London, he attracted the attention of Henry Drummond, who in 1822 presented to him the rectory of Albury, in Surrey, where Drummond lived. While at Albury, M'Neile frequently preached in London, chiefly at St. Clement Danes Church, his eloquence invariably attracting large congregations. In 1834 he was appointed curate of St. Jude's, Liverpool, and received the canonry at Chester Cathedral. In 1868 he was transferred to the deanery of Ripon. [86]

M'Neile held strongly evangelical opinions and strenuously opposed the Church of Rome. His vigorous public utterances involved him in frequent public discussions and much newspaper warfare. He wrote a dozen volumes, including *The Times of the Gentiles* (1828), *Popular Lectures on the Prophecies relative to the Jewish Nation* (1830), *Prospects of the Jews,* and *Every Eye Shall See Him.* He was a participant in the Continental Society proceedings and presided at the Albury Park Prophetic Conference in 1826.

1. SEPARATE FROM THE ABOMINATIONS OF BABYLON.— M'Neile's *The Abominations of Babylon* sermon was delivered

---

[84] *Ibid.*   [85] *Ibid.*
[86] *Dictionary of National Biography,* vol. 12, p. 690.

before the Continental Society in 1826. Based on Revelation 18:4, it defines Babylon as not only *"Popery* in general," [87] but "the mother of harlots"—embracing under one general term "the whole of the anti-Christian systems of the western empire." From these the people of God are to be called out. "It is the province of the CONTINENTAL SOCIETY to carry it through the length and breadth of Babylon." [88]

He points out that the early church, though undaunted by pagan persecution, fell under the emoluments and glories of the world lavished upon it by Constantine. The sole authority of the Word was laid aside, and the opinions and traditions of men substituted. The church was made the interpreter. The Reformation at length restored the Bible standard and swept away the human rubbish. But, alas, the spirit of the Reformation "has fled," and "the spirit of popery permeates the ecclesiastical councils." From this spirit the people of God are to come out. "Half separations will not do." There is to be no compromise with subtle infidelity. [89]

2. BABYLON EXPRESSLY DEFINED AS PAPACY.—Another sermon, *The Character of the Church of Rome,* at St. Andrews, Liverpool, in 1836, is based on the prophetic picture of Revelation 17. Again identifying "persecuting, blasphemous" Babylon, M'Neile asks and answers thus: "Where, and what is that power? The answer is, POPERY!" He adds:

"There has been nothing at all like it, except Popery; and nothing conceivable can be more like it, than Popery has been, and is, and must continue, until the glorious appearing of a greater than Cyrus, the true everlasting destroyer of all persecutors, and deliverer of all Saints." [90]

VI. *Dialogues*—Composite View of Prophetic Emphasis

As previously noted, the three-volume *Dialogues on Prophecy* (1828, 1829) contains the views of the participants of the Albury Park Prophetic Conferences, beginning in 1826,

---

[87] Hugh M'Neile, *The Abominations of Babylon,* p. 3.
[88] *Ibid.,* p. 4.
[89] *Ibid.,* pp. 4-8.
[90] Hugh M'Neile, *The Character of the Church of Rome,* p. 37.

as drawn from their conversations and writings.[91] All who were present had written on, or had been engaged in, the discussion of the prophecies. At the close of the sessions "perfect unanimity was ultimately found to prevail" [92] upon a number of points. These are the more significant for our quest because they now represent a united group view. And the premillennial advent was the primary issue at the root of their controversies with others.

1. UNITED ON SIX-POINT PROPHETIC INTERPRETATION.—Their clearly defined six-point platform needs to be noted:

a. That the present Christian dispensation is "not to pass insensibly into the millennial state by gradual increase of the preaching of the gospel; but that it is to be terminated by judgments, ending in the destruction of this visible church and polity."

b. That "during the time these judgments are falling upon Christendom" the Jews will be restored to their own land.

c. That the "judgments will fall principally" upon Christendom.

d. That the "termination of these judgments" will be succeeded by the millennium.

e. That the second advent "precedes or takes place at the commencement of the Millennium."

f. That the 1260 years "commence in the reign of Justinian and terminate at the French Revolution," the seven vials then begin to be poured out, and the advent is therefore soon at hand.[93]

Fictitious names appear in the colloquy. But their identity is disclosed by J. W. Brooks in his *Dictionary of Writers on the Prophecies,*[94] and a list of the participants also occurs in Miller's *History and Doctrines of Irvingism.*[95]

2. JUDGMENT-HOUR MESSAGE FREQUENTLY CITED.—However, the statements were not always made by the person just

---

[91] *Dialogues on Prophecy,* vol. 1, p. i; Joshua W. Brooks, *A Dictionary of Writers on the Prophecies,* pp. lxxi, xcvi; a critical review of volume 3 appears in *The Christian Observer,* October, 1829 (vol. 29, no. 334), pp. 625-627.
[92] *Dialogues on Prophecy,* vol. 1, p. ii.
[93] *Ibid.,* pp. ii, iii.
[94] Brooks, *op. cit.,* p. lxxi.
[95] Miller, *op. cit.,* pp. 40, 41.

at the time or in the order presented in the *Dialogues*. Various religious magazines charged that the positions taken at the conference were "novel," "heretical," and a "modern invention." But others, equally prominent, joined in certain of their conclusions; so the critics contradicted one another.[96] The names of the great expositors of the past are frequently cited in the *Dialogues*—such as Mede, Newton, Cressener, Whiston, King —as well as contemporary opinion, like that of Cuninghame, Frere, Bayford, Brown, etc.,[97] several of whom were present. Frequent reference is made to the angelic message of Revelation 14, "Fear God, and give glory to him, for the hour of his judgment is come," and its contemporary fulfillment by the various societies—Bible, Jewish, Continental, etc.[98] The church at large, however, is declared to be "in a state of practical unbelief" on the premillennial second advent.[99]

3. SUNDRY SYMBOLS—FRANCE, TURKEY, AND PAPACY.— They said that Daniel 11 is obviously a literal prophecy of a "succession of individuals," but has not yet had an exposition that has received "the general consent of the church." [100] But the four empires of Daniel 2 are frequently mentioned as having an established interpretation, with Rome as the fourth world power, and the ten divisions still in existence.[101] The termination of the 1260 years at the French Revolution, or earthquake, is another generally accepted axiom.[102] A "new era" clearly began with the French Revolution. The fifth vial had been poured out on Rome, and the sixth is the drying up of the Turkish Euphrates.[103] The symbolic little horn of Daniel 7 is always "the papacy." [104]

4. 2300 YEARS TO END IN 1843 OR 1847.— The controversy over the 2300 years, or 2400 as Frere contends, was taken up, and defense of the 2300 is made by Sophron (Cuninghame), and the number 2400 is shown to be "nothing but a mis-print." [105]

[96] *Dialogues on Prophecy*, vol. 1, p. ix.
[97] *Ibid.*, pp. 72, 270.
[98] *Ibid.*, pp. 72, 134.
[99] *Ibid.*, p. 179.
[100] *Ibid.*, pp. 271, 272.

[101] *Ibid.*, p. 278.
[102] *Ibid.*, pp. 180, 296, 297, 311, 341.
[103] *Ibid.*, p. 314.
[104] *Ibid.*, pp. 322, 323.
[105] *Ibid.*, pp. 326, 327.

Philalethes (Lord Mandeville) then asks how the 2300 are to be dated. Anastasius (Drummond) answers by citing the various Persian decrees, and declaring for that of Artaxerxes Longimanus, with 453 B.C. and A.D. 1847 as the beginning and end years.[106] But he also notes Mason's advocacy of 457 B.C., which would end the period in 1843. The 1290 and 1335 years are set forth as extending thirty and seventy-five years, respectively, beyond the close of the 1260 years, with which they are started simultaneously.[107]

Crito (Frere) also mentions the five months, or 150 years, of the Saracenic woe, and the Jubilee of jubilees, or 2450 years, from B.C. 603 to 1847, while Anastasius speaks of the "seven times," or 2520 years, of the Gentiles.[108]

5. MIDNIGHT CRY FROM A HUNDRED PULPITS.—Volume 2 of the *Dialogues,* likewise appearing in 1828, continues the discussion of Turkey's predicted disintegration, and again notes the signs which presage the second advent, especially how Europe has been torn by the wars following the French Revolution. Then comes this impressive declaration by Sophron (Cuninghame), on the extent of the "cry" at that time:

"The midnight cry which awakens the virgins, can be nothing but a company of preachers, proclaiming the coming of the Bridegroom, and that cry has been made.

"Philalethes.—How can it be said that that cry has been made by a company of preachers when so few of them believe it?

"Sophron.—I could name, nevertheless, above one hundred pulpits in London, and various parts of England, in which the cry has been clearly and loudly made; and there is scarcely an individual in the kingdom that has not heard of it." [109]

6. MESSAGES OF REVELATION 14 BEING GIVEN.—Aristo (Irving) states: "All agree that the thirteenth [of Revelation] relates to the Papacy. The twelfth chapter describes the Dragon, or Pagan period of the church's history; and the fourteenth gives the state of the true church in opposition to the two former." [110] The favored band of Revelation 14:1-5 is comprised of those

---

106 *Ibid.,* pp. 328, 329.   108 *Ibid.,* pp. 334, 335.   110 *Ibid.,* p. 43.
107 *Ibid.,* p. 330.   109 *Ibid.,* vol. 2, pp. 17, 18.

"not defiled with papal harlotries." The successive angels do not simply follow after the preceding has ceased, "but rather going along with, like waves rolling on each other," and so may be "nearly synchronical." [111] There is reference not only to the Continental Society in London but to its auxiliaries in Ireland, France, and Prussia, together with Reformation Societies then all over Ireland, as well as a society of clergymen in London established "on purpose to preach against popery." [112]

Almost incidentally, in another connection, the impressive suggestion is dropped by Valerius, who has not been identified:

"The High Priest coming out of the Holy of Holies, having changed his robes and put on the shining garments, can represent nothing but Christ coming out of heaven in glory, without the sins of the people." [113]

This position became predominant in the American Advent Movement in 1844, as will be seen when that is discussed.

7. LIVING IN TOE PERIOD OF IMAGE.—Aristo (Irving) rehearses Daniel's famous prophecy of the colossal image, naming the four world powers and referring to the "ten Gothic Kingdoms." He adds:

"This statue is now in the toes; and in the battle of Armageddon, these, and all the rest of it, are ground into dust, by the smiting of the stone cut out without hands." [114]

And Daniel 7 represents "the same fourfold succession of brutal power." But with it the restoration of the Jews is pressed, as they are identified with the kings of the East, to come as the symbolic Euphrates is dried up.[115]

8. OMINOUS SILENCE ON ADVENT BROKEN.—The bulk of volume 3 of the *Dialogues,* published in 1829, which closes the series, has little on prophecy. Nearly thirty pages are devoted to the Day of Atonement and the attendant Feast of Tabernacles.[116] The world outline of Daniel 2 is repeated, with particular emphasis on the geographical location of each of the four kingdoms, and how for centuries "papal iniquity," Mohammedanism, and now infidelity have raged. Anastasius (Drum-

---

[111] *Ibid.*
[112] *Ibid.*, p. 44.
[113] *Ibid.*, p. 93.
[114] *Ibid.*, p. 121.
[115] *Ibid.*, pp. 121-125.
[116] *Ibid.*, vol. 3, p. 120 ff.

mond) adds that 5,768,900 infidel volumes had been circulated within twelve years,[117] and the vengeance of the Papacy is on.[118] But now, "all on a sudden, in so many parts, He [Christ] has made His church to break the ominous silence, and speak of His Appearing. It is not for nought, nor is it for disappointment, that He opened unto us His prophecy, and given [gave] us to speak of His kingdom." [119]

9. EARLY CHURCH MADE LOVE TO KINGS.—The early church "could not bear the prosperity of being established over the Roman Empire." Then it was that she "forgot that she was a widow; she forgot that her husband was absent in the heavens, and was to appear again for the justification; she made love to the kings of the earth and gave herself to them." [120] But God has raised up witnesses concerning the coming destruction of the "Antichristian papacy" at the second advent, when the great Judge will come to redress these wrongs. But now Protestantism has ceased her protests, and the majority neither look nor pray for that coming of the Son of man.[121] Such is the tenor of these *Dialogues on Prophecy,* representing the discussions at the Albury Park Prophetic Conferences.

---

[117] *Ibid.,* pp. 421, 422.   [119] *Ibid.,* p. 435.   [121] *Ibid.,* p. 452.
[118] *Ibid.,* p. 423.   [120] *Ibid.,* pp. 451, 452.

CHAPTER TWENTY-FOUR

Wolff: Ambassador of the Coming Kingdom

JOSEPH WOLFF, likewise of the Advent Awakening, was a most unique character. He was the world's most noted missionary traveler and linguist of his generation. Of Jewish birth, Catholic education, and finally Protestant persuasion and adoption, he was born in Germany, educated in a half dozen countries, and at last was naturalized in England. These factors, together with his marriage to Lady Georgiana Walpole, daughter of the Earl of Oxford, and his financial backing, provided by the banker Henry Drummond, opened the door of access even to England's nobility, as he became known throughout the world because of his trips to inner Asia. While he wrote no books on prophecy, probably no other individual ever traveled so widely as he in witnessing to the prophetic aspect of the second advent before such varied classes and diversified nationalities.

Accomplished in fourteen languages and expert in about six, Wolff preached to Jews, Turks, Parsis, Hindus, Chaldeans, Armenians, and Syrians—to mention but a few—and testified before pashas, sheiks, shahs, kings, and queens, and even American Presidents, as well as the humblest natives. He was the missionary representative of the London Society to Promote Christianity Amongst the Jews, and a major participant in the Albury Park Prophetic Conference. It is essential that we trace his career with unusual detail, as his life was intertwined with the leading influences and the most distinguished characters of the nineteenth-century Old World Advent Awakening.

461

WOLFF PENETRATES INNERMOST RECESSES OF ISLAM

This Intrepid Herald of the Returning Messiah Traveled More Widely Than Any Other Man of His Time to Announce the Soon-coming Second Advent Throughout Asia, Asia Minor, Africa, Europe, and America. Where He Spoke Before the Assembled Congress

Joshua W. Brooks, editor of *The Investigator,* declares that "no individual has perhaps given greater publicity to the doctrine of the *Second Coming.*" [1] From 1821 to 1827 Wolff's travel was sponsored by Henry Drummond and John Bayford, who met his expenses, while from 1827 to 1831 he went forth as a regular missionary of the London Society. But in 1828 he relinquished his support[2] by the society, though still accountable to them, to avoid the twitting of the Jews, who accused him of mercenary motives, and to show that love was his only motive.[3]

In the *Journal of the Rev. Joseph Wolff* (1839), presented as a series of letters to Sir Thomas Baring, president of the Society to Promote Christianity Amongst the Jews, Wolff states in the Preface that he had "traversed the most barbarous countries for eighteen years, without protection of any European authority whatsoever, and . . . [had] been sold as a slave, thrice condemned to death, attacked with cholera and typhus fever, and almost every Asiatic fever in existence, and bastinadoed and starved." [4] His heart-cries for godliness, power, and perseverance[5] reveal the secret of his influence. Despite his tremendous record of travel and versatility, curiously enough Wolff could not ride a horse or a donkey, swim, cook his own "victuals," sit cross-legged, or shave himself.[6]

Let us note the high lights in the varied career of this odd genius.[7]

I. Wolff—Advent Herald on Four Continents

JOSEPH WOLFF (1795-1862), Jewish Christian "missionary to the world," was born in Bavaria, but was immediately after taken to Prussia by his father, who was a rabbi. His strict

---

[1] *The Investigator, or Monthly Expositor and Register, on Prophecy,* April, 1836 (New Series, no. 2, vol. 5, no. 44), p. 88.
[2] *Travels and Adventures of the Rev. Joseph Wolff,* p. 599.
[3] *The Jewish Expositor,* February, 1828 (vol. 13), p. 64.
[4] *Journal of the Rev. Joseph Wolff,* p. vi.
[5] *Missionary Journal and Memoir, of the Rev. Joseph Wolff,* pp. 207, 325; first published serially in *The Jewish Expositor.*
[6] *Travels and Adventures,* pp. 284, 85, 234.
[7] The ordination sermon, preached by Bishop Doane, not only gives a clear sketch of Wolff's life but tabulates about the most complete list of the places visited in the peregrinations of Wolff. (George Washington Doane, *The Apostolical Commission, the Missionary Charter of the Church,* pp. 23, 24.) An impressive map of the places visited by Wolff in his extensive travels appears in H. P. Palmer's *Joseph Wolff,* p. 8.

Hebrew training began when he was only four, and he was early taught that the Jews generally were awaiting the soon-coming Messiah. He was also taught to regard Christians as idolatrous worshipers of crosses of wood. He was sent to a Christian school to learn German, but at home he listened to the rabbis discussing the coming of Messiah. Soon he began to wonder about Christ, and at eight received favorable impressions of Christianity from Spiess, the Lutheran village barber-surgeon, from whom the Wolffs secured milk.

Directed to watch the milking so nothing forbidden would be added by the servant, Joseph would weary of the stable and converse with Spiess about the Messiah. Through reading the forbidden chapter, Isaiah 53, he was finally persuaded that Jesus was the prophesied Messiah, and told the Lutheran minister of his desire to become a Christian. But at home, fearing punishment, he remained silent, for his parents were concerned lest he turn from the faith of his fathers.[8]

Jewish Deists soon began to inject doubt into young Wolff's mind concerning the inspiration of Moses and the validity of the Jewish ceremonies, and his rabbinical prejudices were shaken by these skeptical Jews. Joseph now began the study of Latin, Greek, and Hebrew. At eleven he was sent to the Protestant Lyceum at Stuttgart, then to an uncle at Bamberg, where a Roman Catholic Latin and history teacher instilled further principles of Christianity. Joseph determined to become a Christian, declaring his intention publicly. His father threatened to disown him if he did so. He fled to Frankfort to escape Jewish persecution, and was befriended by a Catholic shepherd[9] who not only gave him shelter and prayed for him but divided with Wolff his meager funds, and sent him on his way with a practical lesson in Christianity.

Young Wolff wished to become a preacher of the gospel, but a rationalist Protestant professor at Frankfort discounted Christian baptism and membership. His father having died,

---

[8] *Missionary Journal and Memoir*, pp. 5, 6; *Travels and Adventures*, pp. 2-6; Frederic Boase, *Modern English Biography*, vol. 3, cols. 1458, 1459.
[9] *Missionary Journal and Memoir*, pp. 7, 8; *Travels and Adventures*, p. 9.

Wolff received Christian instruction from Professor Knapp, at Halle, and continued to be persecuted by the Jews. In 1810 he visited Prague, Bohemia, with testimonials from Halle. But the Catholics were suspicious of him because he was a Jew. Penniless in Vienna, Wolff was befriended by an Austrian officer. This was followed by a disappointing six weeks in a Benedictine monastery, where he was persecuted because of his race.[10]

1. BAPTIZED INTO CATHOLICISM AT SEVENTEEN.—He went to Munich for six months, where he clashed with Jewish professors and found the Protestant professors all rationalists. Disgusted now with Protestantism, Wolff was provided by Catholic priests with early and later Catholic writings showing the distinctions between Catholicism and Protestantism. At Anspach other rationalist Protestant professors discouraged him from becoming a Christian, so he determined to be baptized a Catholic. In 1811, at Saxe Weimar, after studying the Latin classics and natural history under a pantheist, and meeting noted skeptical philosophers, he went to a monastery at Heidelberg, then studied at a Swiss monastery. Finally at Prague, after instruction in a Benedictine convent, he was baptized a Catholic at the age of seventeen.[11]

In 1813 Wolff began the study of Arabic, Syriac, and Chaldean, and attended theological lectures at Vienna for a year and a half. Here he formed the friendship of such noted scholars as Von Hammer, Kopitar, Jahn, Von Schlegel, Körner, Von Penkler, Werner, and Hofbauer, the superior-general of the Redemptorists—similar to the Jesuits— (this order being just then abolished for a time). Later he returned to Vienna and began to translate the Bible into German, the excellence of which was admitted by several scholars.[12]

In 1815, after lecturing on Hebrew before the University of Landshut, Wolff accepted the invitation of Frederick Leopold, Count of Stolberg, a truly pious Catholic, to visit him

---

[10] *Missionary Journal and Memoir*, pp. 8-10; *Travels and Adventures*, p. 9.
[11] *Missionary Journal and Memoir*, pp. 11-13; *Travels and Adventures*, pp. 9-11.
[12] *Missionary Journal and Memoir*, pp. 13-15; *Travels and Adventures*, pp. 15, 25.

at Westphalia. Stolberg was not a believer in the grosser things of Catholicism—the immaculate conception, the worship of saints, the infallibility of the pope, the bodily ascension of the Virgin, or the Inquisition and the crusades. He was, moreover, a constant reader of the Bible, believed in the power of Christ and His resurrection, considered Huss a martyr, and regarded Luther highly.[13]

Wolff attended Leopold's school, partook of his sentiments, and continued translating the Scriptures. He entered the Protestant University at Tübingen, where he studied Oriental theology for nearly two years through the liberality of Prince Dalberg—chiefly Oriental languages, Arabic and Persian, ecclesiastical history, with Biblical exegesis under Professors Stuedal, Schnurrer, and Flatt. Here he disputed with the professors in favor of "Stolberg" Catholicism. And here he made the acquaintance of other noted philosophers and scholars.[14]

Wolff left Tübingen in 1816 and proceeded toward Rome. On the way he visited Fribourg, Switzerland. The head of the Redemptorists there took away his Hebrew Bible, because it was printed in heretical Amsterdam. Grieved at the loss, he secured another from a Protestant preacher. The Redemptorist head at Valais then took this second Hebrew Bible away from him, because it was printed at Leipzig. But Wolff regained it by stealth.[15]

When he reached Milan, the professors and librarians of the Ambrosian library provided him with introductions to Cardinal Vendoni. At Turin he met a number of scholars and diplomats, and finally, after passing through Genoa and Pisa, he arrived at Rome, seeking out Abbot Ostini, professor of ecclesiastical history at the Collegio Romano, who informed Pius VII of Wolff's arrival. He was introduced to the pope by Monsignor Testa, and conversed about Stolberg, Schlegel, and

---

13 *Travels and Adventures*, pp. 25-30.   14 *Ibid.*, pp. 33-35.
15 *Ibid.*, pp. 38-40. This Bible he kept throughout his period at the Collegio Romano and the Propaganda, studying for examinations from it. When he was banished from Rome, it was left behind in the confusion. It was recovered years later—in 1837—on his American visit, from Roman Catholic Bishop Kendrick, of Philadelphia, former fellow student with Wolff at Rome, who said, "Take back your own." This he kept throughout the remainder of his life.

Hoffbauer. He showed the pope his Hebrew Bible, telling of its adventures, and the pope desired him to read from it.[16]

2. Conflict in the Propaganda at Rome.—Wolff was now placed by the pope in the Collegio Romano, in 1816, pending the re-establishment of the Propaganda.[17] Conflict over the Reformation was evaded in the church history class, but trouble began as Wolff challenged the infallibility of the general councils, transubstantiation, the infallibility of the pope above the councils, the immaculate conception, and the right of the church to burn heretics.

Important Roman Catholic College of the Propaganda, in Rome, Attended by the Dynamic Joseph Wolff Before His Withdrawal to Train for Heralding the Advent to Many Nations

The situation became critical because of Wolff's boldness in expressing his opinions on these delicate subjects. He discovered the Christianity of Rome sharply at variance with that of the Stolberg family. The litanies to the Virgin, the pretended miracles, the suppression of Scriptures, and the inconsistency with the simplicity of Christ, all distressed him. His conscience

16 Missionary Journal and Memoir, pp. 20-23; Travels and Adventures, pp. 40-46.
17 During the exile of Pius VII at Fontainbleau, the Collegio Urbano della Propaganda Fide was used as a barracks by the French soldiers. On the return of the pope in 1814, its restoration was begun, but not completed until 1817 (Travels, p. 46, note).

revolted, and he protested openly, contemplating precipitous flight.[18]

In January, 1818, Wolff was transferred to the new College of Missionary Propaganda, pursuing his studies there. The appointment of a new scholastic rector eased the situation, and Wolff received minor orders. Here he met Henry Drummond, his future patron, who came to Rome to see Wolff.[19] Wolff was in the midst of a sharp dispute with the rector of the Propaganda over the right of the church to burn heretics—which Wolff denied on the basis of the command "Thou shalt not kill." The rector defended it, because seventeen popes had declared it proper. "Then," replied Wolff, "seventeen Popes have done wrong." During the entire conversation Drummond stood outside the door and listened. Because of such a stand, Drummond declared he would "remain Wolff's friend to his dying hour, though all England should trample upon him!" Speaking to Wolff, he said, "Wolff, go with me to England"; but Wolff was not ready.[20] Later he wrote, "Wolff, come out of Babylon." [21]

Wolff's contact with the Protestant Drummond brought him under the scrutiny of the Inquisition. Cardinal Litta, however, opened a way of escape for Wolff through an appointment from Rome to Vienna.[22] But he was sent away by the pope's express decree, banished as recusant, lest he taint the students with his sentiments. The cardinal carried out the order with tears, and Wolff was escorted out of Rome at three o'clock one morning by twenty-five gendarmes.[23]

For months afterward, he was cruelly treated at Vienna.[24] Then he was sent to the convent of Val-sainte, where he was kept in durance for seven months among the Liguorians, an order much like the Jesuits. At Salzburg he met the Oriental scholar Sandbichler, who first directed his attention to the study of unfulfilled prophecy and the Apocalypse.[25]

---

[18] *Missionary Journal and Memoir*, pp. 25-32; *Travels and Adventures*, pp. 48-52, 57, 58.
[19] Drummond had disposed of his elaborate estates and started for the Holy Land. A storm forced the ship into Genoa, and his wife besought him not to proceed to the Holy Land. He stopped at Rome while en route to Geneva, whither he went to aid Haldane. See p. 435.
[20] *Missionary Journal and Memoir*, p. 34; *Travels and Adventures*, pp. 60, 61.
[21] *Travels and Adventures*, pp. 62, 63.   [22] *Ibid.*, pp. 64, 65.
[23] *Ibid.*, p. 65.   [24] *Ibid.*, pp. 69, 70.   [25] *Ibid.*, pp. 70-72.

3. ACCEPTS DRUMMOND'S INVITATION TO LONDON.—Convinced of his fundamental differences with the Catholic Church, Wolff obtained a dismissal in 1819, thus being "cast off" by the "mother of his adoption." At Lausanne he met a messenger from Drummond with another urge to come to London, which offer he now accepted.[26] After reaching Paris he made the rest of the journey with Robert Haldane, a friend of Drummond, recently come from Switzerland, who laid before him the doctrine of justification by faith.[27]

Arriving in London in 1819, at the age of twenty-three, Wolff was introduced to London friends by Drummond, particularly to Lewis Way,[28] secretary of the London Society for the Promotion of Christianity Amongst the Jews. He was immediately taken over by the society for training as one of its missionary representatives. He was given two years of further training at King's College, Cambridge, with separate instruction in theology by Charles Simeon, and in Persian, Chaldean, and Arabic by Samuel Lee.[29] Wolff threw himself into the program with ardor, often rising at 2 A.M. After visiting various Protestant churches he became a member of the Church of England by joining the Episcopal Chapel, of which Hawtrey was pastor.[30]

In 1821 Wolff became a charter student of the newly formed Stansted Seminary,[31] in Sussex. Further Biblical instruction on the points at issue between Jews and Christians followed. The study of Hebrew, Greek, Latin, and modern languages was likewise continued, with foreign scholars to aid in the finishing touches in these languages. Thus the students were to be prepared for their task as traveling missionaries for the Society to Promote Christianity Amongst the Jews.[32] After eight months of this, eagerness to enter upon his missionary career led Wolff to proceed to Palestine in 1821, under the financial patronage of Henry Drummond and John Bayford.[33]

---

[26] *Ibid.*, pp. 76, 77.   [27] *Ibid.*, p. 78.   [28] *Ibid.*, pp. 80, 81.
[29] *Missionary Journal and Memoir*, pp. 51, 52; *Travels and Adventures*, pp. 83-87.
[30] *Travels and Adventures*, p. 79.
[31] At first with but eight students. *The Jewish Expositor*, June, 1822 (vol. 7), p. 220.
[32] *Travels and Adventures*, pp. 88, 89.
[33] *Missionary Journal and Memoir*, p. 52; *Travels and Adventures*, pp. 88, 89, 481, 482.

4. ENTERS UPON EVENTFUL MISSIONARY CAREER.—Wolff's
missionary labors from 1821 to 1826 included Palestine, Egypt,
the Sinaitic Peninsula, Mesopotamia, Persia, the Crimea,
Georgia, and the Ottoman Empire. He stressed the second
advent and made constant reports through *The Jewish Expositor.* In his ardor he sometimes sat up all night reading and expounding the Scriptures to the Jews in Jerusalem.[34] In 1823 he
promoted schools for Armenian, Persian, and Jewish children,
and in 1824 published his *Missionary Journal and Memoir.* Part
of the time he carried a printing press with him, provided by
Drummond.[35]

Between the years 1826 and 1830 Wolff was traveling continuously throughout England, Scotland, Ireland, Holland, Germany, the Mediterranean, Malta, the Greek Islands, Egypt, Jerusalem, and Cyprus, with reports continuing in *The Jewish
Expositor.* He was constantly on the lookout for the lost tribes
as the "kings of the East." [36] In 1827 he married Georgiana
Mary, daughter of Horatio Walpole, Earl of Oxford, their acquaintance having been fostered by Irving. In the same year
Wolff was naturalized as an Englishman before both the House
of Lords and the House of Commons.[37]

Between 1831 and 1834 his travels covered Turkey, Persia,
Turkestan, Bokhara, Balkh, Afghanistan, Cashmere, Hindustan,
and the Red Sea. In 1831 he was seeking the lost tribes in the
126 Afghan villages visited.[38] In 1833, in the kingdom of Oude,
he preached the imminent advent of Christ. And in 1835 his
Researches and Missionary Labours, dedicated to J. H. Frere,
was issued as a report of his travels during the preceding four
years.

Between 1835 and 1838 Wolff was traveling again—in
Gibraltar, Malta, Egypt, Mt. Sinai, Jiddah, Masowah (Africa),
Kamazien, Tigre, Abyssinia, Bombay, St. Helena, and finally in

[34] *The Jewish Expositor,* December, 1823 (vol. 8), p. 483.
[35] *Ibid.,* April, 1823 (vol. 8), p. 160; *Missionary Journal and Memoir,* p. 331.
[36] Joseph Wolff, *Researches and Missionary Labours Among the Jews, Mohammedans,
and Other Sects,* Preface.
[37] *Travels and Adventures,* p. 238.
[38] *Journal of the Rev. Joseph Wolff for the Year 1831,* p. 55. Not to be confused with
Journal of the Rev. Joseph Wolff (1839).

the United States and England. In 1837 he was ordained a deacon of the Church of England by Bishop G. W. Doane, in Newark, New Jersey, and he preached in Philadelphia, Baltimore, and Washington.[39] In December he preached before a joint session of the Congress of the United States, as well as the legislatures of New Jersey and Pennsylvania.[40] Also he received the degree of D.D. from St. John's College, Annapolis, Maryland.

In 1838 Wolff was ordained a Church of England priest by the bishop of Dromore, Ireland, and made rector of Linthwaite, Yorkshire. He received an LL.D. from the University of Dublin in the same year.[41] In 1839 he issued his *Journal of the Rev. Joseph Wolff,* and in 1843 made a second dangerous journey to Bokhara to ascertain the fate of two British officers. At Constantinople, on the final journey, he was still preaching on Christ's personal coming and reign,[42] and in 1845 published the *Narrative of a Mission to Bokhara,* and was made vicar of Ile Brewers. Finally, in 1860, he published his large *Travels and Adventures of the Rev. Joseph Wolff,* and died while contemplating a new and still harder missionary journey.[43]

II. Heralds 1847 Advent in All Travels

1. DISTRIBUTES BIBLES AND DISCOURSES ADVENT TRUTH.— In all his travels Wolff was constantly distributing Bibles and tracts among rabbis and priests, and to all who would receive them.[44] The Caraite Jews[45] especially received them "with gladness and gratitude, as they did the Old Testament."[46] He discussed Bible truth with the leading Jews, Mohammedans, Protestants, and Roman and Greek Catholics of the various communities, as well as with the diplomats. Two samples of Wolff's

---

[39] *Travels and Adventures,* p. 517.
[40] *Journal,* pp. 398, 399.
[43] *Dr. Wolff's New Mission* (1860).
[44] *Travels and Adventures,* pp. 286, 291, 332; *The Jewish Expositor,* August, 1822 (vol. 7), p. 214.
[41] *Travels and Adventures,* p. 520.
[42] *Ibid.,* p. 530.
[45] He frequently speaks of the Caraites (or Coraeem) as "anti-traditional" Jews. (*Travels and Adventures,* pp. 210, 228, 229.) These will have an important place in Volume 4 of *Prophetic Faith.*
[46] *Missionary Journal and Memoir,* p. 279.

teaching and preaching on the coming Messiah, must suffice.

Beginning with a discussion, on his first journey, with the ship's officers and a Welsh Methodist minister, he repeatedly applied the prophecy of Daniel 9 to the first advent, and he also cited Daniel on the second advent.[47]   To a Jew he said:

> "The prophet is here speaking of the second coming of our Lord; of that time which Jesus Christ himself predicteth; of that time, when the Son of man shall come in his glory, and all the holy angels with him; when he shall sit upon the throne of his glory; and before him all nations shall be gathered: and he shall separate them one from another, as a shepherd divideth the sheep from the goats." [48]

He expressed his joy in the second advent in a sermon:

> "Let this be our sincere prayer. 'Come, Lord Jesus, come quickly.' . . . What a beautiful song we shall hear, from a whole ransomed creation, when He shall come! . . . THE BRIDEGROOM COMETH.   He cometh! He cometh! 'He cometh to judge the earth; with righteousness shall He judge the world, and the people with equity.' " [49]

On his last mission to Bokhara, in 1843-45, the Persian banditti of the Khan of Khorasaun made him a slave, with the design of selling him to the Turkoman chiefs, but they finally set him free, declaring him their guest and sending the Arabic Bibles he gave them to their mullahs. Concerning his activities while at Meshad under those circumstances, Wolff wrote:

> "I fixed on their tents public proclamations, announcing to them the second coming of Christ in Glory and Majesty, called on them to repent of their evil doings, and especially exhorted them to give up the practice of making slaves of the Persians." [50]

2. PARTICIPANT AT ALBURY PARK CONFERENCE.—In 1826, when Wolff was back in England, Drummond and Irving sent for him to come to London, then to Albury Park to attend the important first Prophetic Conference. Wolff lists the leading participants and the characteristics of the conference, remarking about "each person speaking out his peculiar views." [51]

3. CITES PROPHECIES TO JEW AND BEDOUIN ALIKE.—Wolff quotes a letter which he wrote to the Jews at Alexandria, upon

[47] *Ibid.*, pp. 53, 54, 140, 239.   [48] *Ibid.*, p. 195.   [49] *The Pulpit*, vol. 34, p. 146.
[50] Joseph Wolff, *Narrative of a Mission to Bokhara* (1843-1845), p. 62.
[51] *Travels and Adventures*, p. 234.

one of his visits there, in 1828. He stresses the imminence of the return of the Messiah and the restoration of the Jews to the favor of God. As proof, Wolff cites the prophecies of the first advent that were fulfilled: the scepter has departed from Judah; the seventy weeks of Daniel have expired; Jesus was born in Bethlehem; He was born as the son of a virgin; He confessed Himself to be the Son of God before the high priest; and He was a stone of stumbling and a rock of offence to the house of Israel.[52]

In another letter, to Sir Thomas Baring, Wolff recites a discussion with the Bedouins who visited his tent near Cairo. They inquired, "When will Christ come?" Wolff answered, "In a very few years." Then he referred to the numbers in Daniel and the portentous signs of the times, showing "the restitution of all things cannot be very far off"—as witness rationalism in Germany, infidelity in France, and atheism in Spain.[53]

4. Looks for Second Advent in 1847.—In conversation with the Goosh-Bekee at Bokhara, representing the king of Bokhara, Emeer[54] Almooneneen, in 1832, Wolff witnessed concerning Christ and His second advent. After stating, "This Bible is my occupation," Wolff said:

"He died for our sins, rose again, went to Heaven, when he shall come again, according to my opinion, in the year 1847, and reign at Jerusalem 1000 years." [55]

Certain members of the Jewish Society in London, it should be added, took exception to Wolff's emphasis of the advent in 1847, at the beginning of the millennial period, and protested.[56]

5. Placards Announce Advent for 1847.—Wolff pressed the second advent before his hearers in all his travels, stressing the year 1847 as the date of Christ's return. He had a rather dramatic experience at Alexandria. To test out, in this instance, "how far one may go in preaching the gospel to Turks, without exposing one's life to danger," he executed the following:

---

[52] *Journal*, pp. 119-123.
[53] *Ibid.*, pp. 184, 185.
[54] Variously spelled Amir, Emeer, and Emir.
[55] *Researches and Missionary Labours*, p. 131.
[56] *The Christian Observer*, February, 1830 (vol. 30, no. 338), p. 97; (vol. 30, supplement, 1830), pp. 800, 801.

"I wrote proclamations to Turks, and Jews, and Christians, in the Arabic language; in which I exhorted them to believe in the Lord Jesus Christ, to be the Son of God, to have died for our sins on the cross, to have risen again, and that, according to my conviction produced by the reading of Daniel, he will come again in the year 1847; when the Jews shall look on Him whom they have pierced and mourn; when he shall restore them to Jerusalem, where he will reign over them with his saints; then the Turkish empire shall fall, and be destroyed. I exhorted them, therefore, to repent and believe in Jesus Christ." [57]

These public proclamations he posted on the walls in the various streets of Alexandria. As a result, several Turks of high position came to hear what he had to say. Jews came also, as did Protestants. Discussions lasted for hours, as he preached Christ and distributed Bibles and Testaments in their own languages. This resulted in correspondence with officials in which Wolff "proclaimed to them Christ crucified, and at the same time the judgment over the Turkish Power." [58] Wolff reported all this through a letter to his friends, published in the London *Morning Herald*,[59] as he did not fail to capitalize on the press. A "great sensation" resulted from one of his letters to the mufti of the capital. In fact, such a stir followed that the British consul urged Wolff to leave Alexandria.

6. LUCKNOW MUSSELMAN CHALLENGES 2300 YEARS.—In 1833, at Lucknow, in the kingdom of Oude, the Musselman Moulvees (Emeer Sayd Ahmed, Mujtehed of the Sheah), wrote Wolff a truly remarkable response. In a previous communication Wolff had maintained from Daniel 8 that "Christ would descend upon the earth after twenty-three hundred years from the time of Daniel, which was 453 years before Christ; that having deducted 453 from 2300, there remained 1847; and the present year is 1833, from which the latter sum having been deducted there remained 14 years,[60] which is the period of Christ's coming." [61]

The Emeer challenged this interpretation with a remark-

---

[57] *Monthly Intelligence of The Proceedings of the London Society,* December, 1830 (vol. 1), pp. 181, 182.
[58] *Ibid.,* p. 182.   [59] Sept. 5, 1829.
[60] On the "14 years" see correspondence with D. Manoel de Portugal Castro (1833), *Researches and Missionary Labours,* p. 312.
[61] *Ibid.,* pp. 258, 259.

able grasp of the issues, contending that (1) in the prophecy Christ's coming is not alluded to; (2) the dating 453 is not proved; (3) the 2300 are days, not years; (4) to fix upon the year is contrary to Christ's declaration that no man knows the day or hour; (5) wars and "rumors" are not any particular sign; (6) the flying angel does not refer to the propagation of the gospel; and (7) the New Testament is not the Word of God.[62]

7. MESSIAH'S ADVENT FOLLOWS FOUR WORLD POWERS.—It is highly desirable to note Wolff's explicit answer, for we have here his exposition of prophecy:

"The contents of Daniel ii, and again vii.1-28, are a fourfold succession of kingdoms, which should arise out of the earth, but which should not endure for ever; whereas the kingdom of the *Son of Man and his saints,* of whom Daniel speaks, *should endure for ever.* That the 'Son of Man, coming in the clouds of heaven,' mentioned in verse 13, is Christ the *expected Messiah,* is not only admitted by Christians and Jewish commentators, but must be likewise admitted by you, as an orthodox Mohammedan; for according to the Koran and your Hadees, Christ, not Mohammed, went in the form of the *Son of Man* to heaven, and therefore he only can return in that form." [63]

8. SANCTUARY CLEANSED AT SECOND ADVENT.—Then Wolff continues, leading directly to the 2300 years and the cleansing of the sanctuary:

"The eighth and following chapters of Daniel contain a succession of events which shall precede and follow the coming of that *Son of Man;* one of them is in chapter viii.14: 'That the sanctuary should be cleansed,' i.e. Jerusalem, called in Hebrew a name which the Jews gave to that place from time immemorial, and on which account it was called by the Mohammedans *Kudus,* i.e. *holy.* It is therefore clear that the cleansing of the sanctuary shall be concomitant with *those wonders* (vii.13.), when the four empires shall be broken to pieces by that 'Stone' which shall descend from heaven, i.e. the *Son of Man,* in order that He, the Lord of glory, may enter into that cleansed sanctuary. By that 'Ram, He-Goat,' etc., to which you allude, are here meant different Kings, which is explained in the text itself, i.e. of the Babylonian, Persian, Grecian, and Roman empires." [64]

9. YEAR-DAY APPLICATION TO DANIEL'S PROPHECIES.—As to the issue of the prophetic days as years, Wolff says:

---

[62] *Ibid.*, pp. 258-262. [63] *Ibid.*, p. 262. [64] *Ibid.*, pp. 262, 263.

"I answer, that by a *prophetic day*, a year is meant, that is clear by Ezekiel iv.4, 5. And that Daniel took this method of counting *days* for *years*, according to Ezekiel, his contemporary, is clear by Daniel ix.; for both profane and sacred history teach us that 'from the going forth of the commandment to restore and to build Jerusalem, unto the Messiah, and the cutting off of the Messiah,' as many years did elapse as Daniel prophesied days should elapse. (Daniel ix.25, 26) You cited above English authorities without giving their names; I now give you English authorities with their names, i.e. the famous Doctor Scott in his answer to the Jewish Rabbi Crool; Doctor Mant, in his commentary of the Bible; Newton, Hooper, etc. and I would quote also the Italian and Spanish authors, Cornelius a Lapide, Bellarmin, and Ben Ezra." [65]

10. APPROACH OF ADVENT HERALDED BY SIGNS.—Concerning Matthew 24:36, Wolff's method of answering questions is disclosed:

"Did our Lord say that that day and hour should *never* be known? Did he not give us signs of the times, in order that we may know at least the *approach* of his coming, as one knows the approach of the summer by the fig tree putting forth its leaves? Matth. xxiv.32. Are we never to know that period, whilst He himself exhorteth us not only to read Daniel the Prophet, but to understand it? and in that very Daniel, where it is said that the words were shut up to the time of the end (which was the case in his time), and 'that many shall run to and fro,' (an Hebrew expression for observing and thinking upon the time,) 'and *knowledge* (regarding that time) shall be increased. Daniel xii.4. Besides this, our Lord does not intend to say by this, that the *approach* of the time shall not be known, but that the *exact* 'day and *hour* knoweth no man;' enough, he does say, shall be known by the signs of the times to induce us to prepare for his coming, as Noah prepared the ark; (for he compares those days to the days of Noah, Matt. xxiv.37-41.) Enough is revealed to us in the Scripture, to know by all that has come to pass in the Eastern and Western Roman empires, that He, Christ, will soon set up the ark of his Church, as the only possible place of safety." [66]

11. PROCLAIMS SECOND ADVENT TO KING OF OUDE.—And to the king of Oude himself Wolff wrote this appeal:

"My earnest wish is, that your Majesty and your whole court should enquire into the truth of the Gospel of our Lord Jesus Christ, with prayer and supplication; and your Majesty will be then convinced that Jesus Christ was the Son of God, born of the Virgin Mary, by the power of the Holy Spirit; and that the fulness of the Godhead was in Him bodily; and that He died for our sins, rose again, and went to heaven; from whence he will come again in the clouds of heaven. In believing this glorious

---

[65] *Ibid.*, p. 263.   [66] *Ibid.*, pp. 263, 264.

doctrine, your Majesty will experience joy, peace and love in your own heart, and begin to diffuse among your Majesty's subjects, that peace, joy, and love by means of which your Majesty will become the father spiritual and temporal of your subjects; and your Majesty will one day shine like the stars, and like the brightness of the firmament for ever and ever.

"Your Majesty's most obedient and humble servant,

"Joseph Wolff, Missionary." [67]

After summarizing the results of his travels, Wolff speaks of the "divers instruments" God is employing for "overturning, overturning, overturning, until He comes whose right it is." [68]

12. HERALDS 1847 ADVENT THROUGHOUT INDIA.—In 1833, when Wolff was in Calcutta, Mr. Dealtry, afterward bishop of Madras, had him lecture "on the personal reign of Christ, and state his proofs for believing that Christ would come upon the earth in 1847." Wolff did it with such modesty that he "gained the affection of all." [69] That Wolff held and proclaimed the advent-in-1847 concept in all his travels is evidenced by a letter to Wolff from the viceroy of Goa, dated November 6, 1833:

"You assure that the said Old and New Testament, which contain the glorious news of the establishment of our Lord Jesus Christ's personal reign on earth, in the city of Jerusalem, fourteen years hence [1847], is presented for my edification." [70]

13. PREACHES ADVENT TO MUHAMED ALI'S MINISTER.—In 1836, when Wolff was in Cairo, he had a conference with Boghos Bey, minister of Muhamed Ali. Of this Wolff says:

"I had one day a conference with Boghos Youssuf Bey, minister to Muhamed Ali; he told me a great deal of the activity of his master, the Vice Roy, and his son, *Ibrahim Pasha;* that both devote very few hours to sleep, and that *Ibrahim Pasha* had lately taken thirty thousand fire arms. from the Druses in the mildest manner, so that the Christians of Damascus, and throughout Syria, and even Jews, enjoy the most perfect liberty, and were no longer molested by the Turks. Boghos also informed me that people are sent to Muhamed Ali from Daghestaun. I preached to him (Boghos) the second coming of our Lord, and shewed to him Isaiah xix." [71]

Following this he preached to the British residents at Alexandria.

---

[67] *Ibid.,* p. 272.
[68] *Ibid.,* pp. 337, 338.
[69] *Travels and Adventures,* p. 429.

[70] *Ibid.,* p. 466.
[71] *Journal,* pp. 293, 294.

"On the 31st January I preached to the British Inhabitants of *Alexandria,* on the restoration of the earth to its original beauty and glory, under the government of Jesus Christ and His Saints, when the Lord again shall look down upon the earth, and say, '*Behold it is very good,*' when the curse shall be taken away from her, and peace and good will toward men shall prevail." [72]

14. CLASHES WITH THE CATHOLIC FAITH.—Wolff's distribution of Bibles drew upon him hostile Catholic bulls and anathemas from Rome in 1825, as well as prohibitory Turkish firmans, which were read at Constantinople and Aleppo, chiefly because he was a "Bible Man," circulating the Scriptures in the vulgar tongue, and especially without the Apocrypha. The bull specifies "One Wolf, of Bamberg," who had once been "expelled from the college in this city," and had "miserably gone astray," condemning him for infusing deadly heresy, and for attempting to establish a college at Antoura.[73] Members were forbidden to communicate with him, under pain of excommunication.[74]

Wolff later capitalized upon his banishment from Rome in 1818, in a printed *Letter Addressed to the Citizens of Rome* (1849). He warned that the overturning foretold in Ezekiel 21 "has commenced, and it will continue until He come whose right it is." [75] Boldly declaring popery to be "a lie," that can never be reformed, but has to be destroyed,[76] he urged them to read the writings of Savonarola, and "above all, publish translations of the Spanish work of the Jesuit Lacunza on the Coming of Christ in *Majesty* and *Glory,* in which work the downfall of the Pope is predicted." [77] He designated himself, "Formerly Pupil of the Collegio Urbano della Propaganda at Rome."

[72] *Ibid.,* p. 294.
[73] In 1822, while in the mountains of Lebanon, he had sought to negotiate with the Maronite bishop for the turning over of the vacated convent Kurka to Drummond and Bayford for the establishment of a college at Aleppo. (*The Jewish Expositor,* September, 1822 [vol. 7]; *Missionary Journal and Memoir,* pp. 224, 292, 297, 302.) One of Wolff's procedures, in his travels in Syria, Arabia, and Persia, was to create among the natives a desire for schools where they could be taught languages by competent teachers from England. Thus, in 1825, at Bussora and Bushire such schools were established in vacant houses for seventy children of all faiths, the Scriptures being read daily, under the patronage of Captain Taylor. (*The Christian Observer,* July, 1826 [vol. 26, no. 295], p. 442; "Eighteenth Report of the London Society," p. 29.) Drummond and Bayford furnished the schoolbooks and materials, and subscriptions were received from the public. (*The Christian Observer,* July, 1826 [vol. 26, no. 295], p. 443.)
[74] *The Jewish Expositor,* February, 1825 (vol. 10), pp. 100-103.
[75] Joseph Wolff, *Letter Addressed to the Citizens of Rome,* p. 6.
[76] *Ibid.,* p. 8.
[77] *Ibid.,* p. 9.

In 1822 Wolff declared the pope to be Antichrist, as is seen in his discussion with Catholic priests on Mount Lebanon, where he says, "I showed that the Pope is Antichrist. 2 Thess. ii. 3, 4." [78] In his appeal to the Jews of Great Britain he arraigned the pollutions and perversions of the Church of Rome, and summoned them to "come out of Babylon and be separate." [79] Wolff also made strictures on the Protestant apostasy, and in 1831 referred to the Jewish Society as "that mystical Babylon in Wardrobe Place," [80] Wardrobe Place being the headquarters of the Jewish Society.

15. PREACHES ADVENT BEFORE AMERICAN CONGRESS.—At the time of Wolff's visit to America, the *Congressional Globe* of December 18, 1837, recorded the motion of ex-President John Quincy Adams in the House of Representatives for the use of the hall for a lecture by Joseph Wolff. In his remarks Adams called him "one of the most remarkable men living on the earth at this time," telling of his background and his life devoted to "the propagation of that gospel throughout the world," and how "he has visited every part of the world." Stating that he had heard one of his lectures, Adams declared, "A more profound, closely-reasoned, and convincing argument upon the proofs of Christianity, than that contained in the lecture to which he had alluded, it had never been his lot to listen to." [81] The motion was passed, and Wolff preached to the assembled Congress and the clergy of Washington.

In expressing his gratitude for this unusual privilege in a letter printed in the *National Intelligencer*, addressed "to the Honorable Members of Congress," Wolff thanked them that he had been permitted to speak before them "the truth of the everlasting Gospel, and illustrate that great truth as experienced by me during my peregrinations from the Thames to the Oxus, to the Ganges, the wilderness of Arabia, and the mountains of

---

[78] *Missionary Journal and Memoir*, p. 215; also *The Jewish Expositor*, September, 1826 (vol. 11), p. 352. Later in life, when his missionary travels were over, Wolff adopted the Futurist view of Antichrist (*Travels and Adventures*, p. 237).
[79] *The Jewish Expositor*, March, 1827 (vol. 12), pp. 96, 97.
[80] *The Morning Watch*, March, 1832 (vol. 5, no. 1), p. 233.
[81] *The National Intelligencer* (Washington, D.C.), Dec. 16, 1837; *Journal*, pp. 398, 399.

Abyssinia." At the close he repeated his affectionate regards for such "hospitality, kindness, and attention, and into whose ears I was enabled to sound the words: 'Behold He comes in clouds descending, once for poor sinners slain.'" He signed it, significantly enough, "Joseph Wolff, Missionary to all the nations." [82]

16. PROCLAIMS SECOND ADVENT TO AMERICAN HEARERS.—In his farewell letter to Bishop Doane (Episcopalian) he declared, before leaving the American shores, that "an invisible power had continually carried me from land to land, and from sea to sea, to preach the tidings of salvation, and the second coming of our Lord in glory and majesty." [83] And to his American hearers in New Jersey, Pennsylvania, and Maryland, he expressed heartfelt appreciation for having "been allowed to proclaim to you the coming glory, and personal reign of Jesus Christ, upon the throne of his father David. I have been allowed to point out to you His humiliation upon Calvary, and his future glory at Jerusalem, when his feet shall stand upon the Mount of Olives." [84] Challenged on his interpretations, he gave this clear answer in defense of the historical and literal interpretation of prophecy:

"Whether I am right or wrong in regard to my literal interpretation of prophecy must be determined, not by any letter written at Calcutta, but by the grammatical construction of Holy Writ, and by the interpretation of its figures and symbols, for the purpose of bringing out of those figures and symbols not a *Platonic mysticism,* but the corresponding physical, historical, and literal meaning." [85]

17. VIEWS WIDELY DISCUSSED IN THE PRESS.—Much space and publicity were given to Wolff's travels and views at the time of his American visit, through both the secular[86] and the religious press.[87] Some of these were reports, and some were published letters from Wolff to the editors. He was charged by some with believing in Irving's tongues movement, which he categorically denied.[88] Just before he left America in 1837 someone asked

---

[82] *Ibid.,* Dec. 21, 1837.   [83] *The Missionary,* Dec. 30, 1837, p. 207.   [84] *Ibid.*
[85] Letter to the editor, *The Churchman,* Sept. 30, 1837.
[86] *New York Observer,* Sept. 16, 1837, p. 146; *New York American,* Sept. 25 and 26, 1837; see also *New York Commercial Advertiser* and *Newark Daily Advertiser.*
[87] *The Missionary,* Sept. 23 and 30, and Dec. 30, 1837; *The Churchman,* Sept. 30, 1837.
[88] Letter to the editor, *The Churchman,* Sept. 30, 1837; see also *Travels and Adventures,* p. 485, regarding attitude in England.

Wolff, "What will you say, Mr. Wolff, when 1847 arrives, if the millennium does not commence?" "Why, I shall say," he replied, with inimitable simplicity, "that Joseph Wolff was mistaken." [89]

While Wolff in the earlier years of his travels stressed the prophetic dates, in later life he gave up the positions formerly held on the 1260 years, and the papal Antichrist, and finally on the 1847 date for the advent.[90]

18. CHALLENGED AS TO "VISIONS" OF CHRIST.—Challenged as to certain "visions," he related how once, when discouraged over his work out in Bokhara, "suddenly a splendor covered the room, and the voice 'Jesus enters!' thundered in my ears. I saw suddenly Jesus standing upon a throne surrounded by little children, mercifully and kindly looking at them. I fell down, and worshipped, and the vision disappeared." [91] Again, in Malta, when similarly "very much cast down," then "suddenly my room was transfigured and I believe I was in New Jerusalem. Jesus Christ, surrounded by Abraham, Isaac, and Jacob, and the Apostles, walked about the street." [92] But Wolff said nothing about these incidents except when asked, holding that he was called to preach Christ crucified, not personal experiences.

19. ARAB EXPECTANCY OVER RETURNING MESSIAH.—In his travels in Bokhara, in 1839, Wolff reports this remarkable expectancy in that vicinity. "The Arabs of this place [Hodeyda] have a book called *Seera*, which treats of the second coming of Christ, and his reign in glory." [93] Of another place he records:

"I spent six days with the children of Rechab (Beni Arhab). They drink no wine, plant no vineyard, sow no seed, live in tents, and remember the word of Jonadab the son of Rechab. With them were children of Israel of the Tribe of Dan, who reside near Terim in Hatramawt, who expect, in common with the children of Rechab, the speedy arrival of the Messiah in the clouds of heaven." [94]

---

[89] *The Missionary*, Dec. 30, 1837, p. 206.
[90] *Travels and Adventures*, pp. 250, 272, 407, 429, 566, 595.
[91] Letter in the *Calcutta Journal*, dated June 4, 1833, in *The Churchman*, Sept. 30, 1837.
[92] *Ibid.*; see *Travels and Adventures*, pp. 381, 517.
[93] Joseph Wolff, *Narrative of a Mission to Bokhara, in the Years 1843-1845*, p. 51.
[94] *Ibid.*, p. 52.

CHAPTER TWENTY-FIVE

Medley of Voices in Swelling Chorus

France now provides two additional witnesses—the Catholic Jansenist Judge Agier and the Protestant Bishop Gobat of Jerusalem.   Utterly different in their testimony, they nevertheless form part of the medley of voices in the swelling chorus on the approaching advent.   And to these is to be added the Swiss lawyer and statesman Nicole, who discussed and defended the 2300 years with unusual understanding.   Then John Fry, English clergyman, completes the quartet of this chapter.   With two of these men, as with many of their predecessors, the 2300 years is the theme of discussion.   We turn first to the noted Jansenist jurist.

I. Judge Agier—Jezebel Is the Jesuits; Beast Is Christian Rome

Again we hear a voice from the fringes of Catholicism.   It is PIERRE JEAN AGIER (1748-1823), the French jurist, of the Jansenist sect, speaking forth.   He had been president of the dread Tribunal of the French Revolution in 1795, and then vice-president of the Tribunal of Appeals of Paris, in 1802, and had published several legal works.   But he had begun the study of Hebrew when forty years of age and had become a recognized commentator and translator of Scripture.[1]   It was he who translated the French abridgment of Lacunza.   Then, in 1818, he wrote a treatise on the second advent, and also one on the prophecies

---

[1] John M'Clintock and James Strong, *Cyclopedia of Biblical, Theological, and Ecclesiastical Literature*, vol. 1, p. 103.

concerning Jesus Christ and the church, in 1819.[2] His *New Version of the Hebrew Prophets* appeared in 1820-23. But his crowning work was a two-volume *Commentaire sur l'Apocalypse* (Commentary on the Apocalypse) in 1823. Agier applied the "Seven Apocalyptic Letters" of Revelation 2 and 3 to the "seven ages, or successive stages of the church."[3]

1. "JEZEBEL" INDICATES THE JESUIT ORDER.—Agier identifies the Ephesus period with apostolic times. The Jezebel of the Thyatira church he pointedly applies to the Jesuits. He says:

OLD HEADQUARTERS OF JANSENISTS IN FRANCE
Ruins of Old Jansenist Monastery Near Paris (Left and Right), and Books (Center) of This Catholic Sect, Setting Forth Their Belief in the Second Advent and the Approaching Destruction of Babylon

"Who is this Jezebel? Alas! the coincidence of the times speaks loud enough. It is that too famous Society organized at the very time when the council of Trent was convened; an infernal Society which was not well-known until about the time of its destruction, and to which nothing in history can be compared. The name of that impious queen Jezebel fits it exactly. A queen, whose goal is a universal monarchy, pretending to serve popes and kings, while, in reality, making them serve her and appropriating their power. She claimed to be a Prophetess, professing lofty ideas about religion, even considering the Fathers as befogged, while reducing faith to mere forms and veiling the essentials. What important truth in morals or doctrine did she not assail when she deemed it expe-

---

[2] *Vues sur le second avénement de Jésus-Christ* (1818); *Prophéties concernant Jésus-Christ et l'Eglise, éparses dans les Livres saints* (1819).
[3] *Commentaire sur l'Apocalypse*, vol. 1, p. 71.

dient? What worthy and useful men in all lands did she not persecute
when they were contrary to her? Never, since the beginning of Christianity, did Satan have more zealous sectarians or more efficient instruments
of deception." [4]

2. SEALS SIMILARLY COVER CHRISTIAN ERA.—The first seal
is interpreted as "the first age of the church," ending in 313.[5]
The second seal is the "internal divisions" that superseded the
"attacks from without." [6] The others follow.

3. YEAR-DAY APPLIED TO FIVE MONTHS.—To the "five long
months" of the fifth trumpet he applies the year-day principle
but recognizes difficulty in placing them. He also makes the
locusts the Jesuit order,[7] as others had done occasionally.

4. FRENCH REVOLUTION TURNS INQUIRERS TO PROPHECIES.—
In volume 2, Agier discusses the quest for an explanation of the
Apocalypse at the time of the French Revolution.

"In 1793, a new disaster, the explosion of infidelity and its frightful
consequences, turned the minds of the people once more and most de-
voutly to this extraordinary resource held in reserve by Providence. I
remember the general impression made by this unexpected event. People
turned fervently to the Holy Books, finding neither comfort nor peace
anywhere else. Interpreters were consulted. Aged people, who were
supposed to know more about such matters, were appealed to; and a worthy
ecclesiastic, whom I often mentioned, and who was still alive (M.
Samson), was repeatedly compelled, in order to comply with the wishes
of his parish, to expound his views on the Apocalypse, of which he had
made a life-long study." [8]

5. THE SEAT OF THE BEAST IS ROME.—Discussing "the
beast" of Revelation 13, that fulfilled the "designs of the
dragon," Agier declares it to be "a reunion of Daniel's four
beasts," with the characteristics of the lion, bear, and leopard.
The ten horns are the same, representing kings.[9] The chief
difficulty is the failure to mention the little horn, but John
"points it out with equivalent terms." The fifth vial is poured
out on the throne of the beast, "which is also the city of Rome,
where Antichrist will undoubtedly locate." [10]

[4] Ibid., p. 78.
[5] Ibid., p. 118.
[6] Ibid., p. 119.
[7] Ibid., p. 198.
[8] Ibid., vol. 2, p. 7.
[9] Ibid., p. 24.
[10] Ibid., p. 25.

6. NOT PAGAN BUT CHRISTIAN ROME.—Fornication with the kings of the earth indicates "reciprocal favors, concordats and treaties." [11] And the Catholic Agier plainly declares there is no one who does not immediately recognize in this picture the city of Rome, seated on the seven mountains, reigning over the kings of earth.[12] Then in a footnote he challenges Bossuet's claim that it is pagan Rome, holding instead that it is "Christian Rome," [13] with further defections to come. Then comes this remarkable statement:

"We must not, therefore, allow our eyes to be blinded by the respect and filial attachment we have for a church which is still our mother, nor by the regard which we may harbor for the noble city in which she dwells. Truth must retain its rights. And after all that has been said, the city of Rome meant by the prophecy, is and remains Christian Rome, the Rome of today, or, at least, such as it will be at the time the prophecy is fulfilled." [14]

Such is the unusual note added by the Jansenist Agier. Unquestionably he was influenced by Lacunza's positions, with which he was familiar, and whose treatise he had translated. In any event his was one of the swelling chorus of voices in the Great Awakening.

II. Bishop Gobat—Studies Turkish Prophecy With Boghos Bey

SAMUEL GOBAT (1799-1879), native of French Switzerland, and later bishop of the United Church of England and Ireland in Jerusalem, was born in Crémine. He was piously inclined as a child, but at nine began to doubt passages in the Bible, and from his eleventh to his twentieth year was an infidel. In 1818 he was converted, and desired an education. So, from 1821 to 1825 he entered upon missionary training, first in the Missionary Institution of Basel. From there he went to Paris to study Arabic, and in 1825 proceeded to London.

During this training period lifelong friendships were formed with such heralds of the advent as Professor Louis Gaussen, of Geneva; Lewis Way, of London; Bishop Daniel Wilson,

---

[11] *Ibid.*, p. 123.
[12] *Ibid.*

[13] *Ibid.*, pp. 123, 124.
[14] *Ibid.*, p. 124.

of Calcutta; Josiah Pratt, of the London Missionary Society; and Gerard Noel. All these men, it should be noted, were actively interested in the study and exposition of prophecy.[15] Gobat's own interest in the prophecies was a natural result. He also became acquainted with the expositor Edward Bickersteth. Gobat labored as a missionary in Abyssinia from 1830 to 1836, where he met Joseph Wolff.[16] Then he went to Malta, helping in the revision of the Arabic Bible and serving as director of the Church Missionary Press.[17]

While at Malta, Gobat helped translate Keith's *Fulfilment of Prophecy,* checking on the correctness of the rendering by two Arabic scholars.[18] But prior to this, after his ordination and call to Abyssinia, Gobat was detained for three years at Alexandria, Egypt, where he made some significant contacts while engaged in further language study. One of these was with Boghos Bey, first minister to Mohammed Ali, viceroy of Egypt, with whom he spent many evenings in studying the Bible, "often till past midnight." [19] He also attempted "Bible-meetings" with the "infidel Europeans," in French and German as well as English, announcing these publicly by placards.[20] But his crowd was thinned by the Roman Catholic priests' threat of excommunication for those who attended.

Meantime his studies with Boghos Bey continued. One evening, in 1828—

"We had been discussing prophecy, and thought to have discovered that the Turkish empire was soon to be destroyed. I looked at these prophecies with a theological eye—he [Boghos Bey] from a political point of view; so that, although we seemed to have the same idea, we did not fully understand one another. After leaving Alexandria I thought little more about it, till five years later, on my first return from Abyssinia in 1833, I called upon Boghos Bey. Hearing that I was at the door, he came smiling to meet me, and said at once, 'Do you remember that evening when we conversed upon prophecy? A few days afterwards I communicated our views to Mohammed Ali, and read those prophecies with him. The conse-

[15] *Samuel Gobat, Bishop of Jerusalem. His Life and Work,* pp. 42, 43, 158.
[16] *Ibid.,* pp. 161, 177-179.
[17] *Dictionaire Historique & Biographique de la Suisse,* tome 3, p. 472; Robert Baird, biographical sketch in Gobat's *Journal of Three Years' Residence in Abyssinia,* p. xvi.
[18] *Samuel Gobat,* p. vi.
[19] *Ibid.,* p. 88.   [20] *Ibid.,* p. 90.

quence was that he immediately resolved upon attacking the Sublime Porte; and this is the origin of our conquest of Syria.' So great a fire may one spark kindle." [21]

Such was one of the strange by-products of prophetic study by Gobat in old Egypt.

III. Swiss Lawyer Nicole—Cogent Reasoning on 2300 Years

One of the most illuminating illustrations of the extent to which intelligent discussion of Daniel 8:14 was being conducted in various lands of the Old World, is to be found in a tract by a prominent Swiss lawyer, which was reprinted in *The Morning Watch* (London). ALPHONSE M. F. NICOLE (1789-1874), doctor of jurisprudence and lawyer of Nyon (Canton de Vaude), French Switzerland, served as deputy in the Grand Council from 1814 to 1835, and was deputy to the Federal Diet in 1832,[22] which legislative bodies correspond to the House of Representatives and the Senate in the United States Congress.

In the midst of his busy life this prominent civic leader made a valuable contribution in French under the title *Recherche sur Daniel viii.13, 14* (Research Work on Daniel 8:13, 14). The title itself had significance. Nicole takes note of the contention that the number in Daniel 8:14 should read 2400 instead of 2300, and that the period represented should be dated from the time of the vision, and therefore would end in 1847. In refutation, Nicole contends that it is "dangerous to put aside the number [2300] given in the original text." [23] In lieu of the weak arguments proffered, he offers a "more natural or normal interpretation." [24]

1. BEGINS WITH PERSIA; NOT BABYLON OR GRECIA.—Nicole's argument can best be grasped by noting each of his four points: "1. *It is impossible to date the beginning of this period from the moment when Daniel had the vision.*" [25] He supports this proposition by the fact that the vision starts with Persia,[26]

---

[21] *Ibid.*, p. 94.
[22] *Dictionaire Historique & Biographique de la Suisse*, tome 5, p. 142.
[23] Alphonse Nicole, "Recherche sur Daniel viii.13,14," *The Morning Watch*, September, 1829 (vol. 1, no. 3), p. 350.
[24] *Ibid.*, p. 350.   [25] *Ibid.*   [26] *Ibid.*

symbolized by the ram, and not with Babylon, which was still in existence when Daniel had the vision, with no mention of the overthrow. Instead, Daniel "begins his explanation at a time when this kingdom [Persia] already existed in strength and greatness." [27]

Nicole's second argument is equally pertinent: "2. *It is impossible to date the beginning of this period from the time when the kingdom of the Medes and Persians was overthrown by Alexander.*" [28] This, he says, is "proved by reasoning inversely." The vision does not begin with the struggle between the Persian ram and the Grecian goat. Rather, that is "included in the period of the 2300 years," which contains the "total of the events noted by the prophecy." [29]

2. BEGINS AT REBUILDING OF JERUSALEM AND TEMPLE.—An alternative dating, based on the 2300 years, is introduced by Nicole's third point: "3. *It is possible to place the beginning of this period at the complete reestablishment of the Jewish worship after the return from the Babylonian captivity.*" [30] The perfect agreement with the "historical part of the prophecy" is stressed. Thus the vision begins with Medo-Persia "already existing in its full strength," under which the Jews "returned to Palestine, rebuilt the temple, and then rebuilt the walls of Jerusalem." [31] Daniel 8:13 gives a "summary of all events symbolically represented in the vision," and deals with the "state of the church of God and of Jesus Christ during the time which should precede the purification of the sanctuary." The vision "divides all of the history into two parts"— the "length of time of the continual sacrifice," and then later the length of the "desolation," involving the sanctuary. The combined length of "these two periods, added one to the other and taken together," will be 2300 years, "after which the sanctuary shall be purified." [32]

This simple and literal interpretation leads Nicole to the suggestion as to the date for beginning the 2300 years, namely,

[27] *Ibid.*, p. 351.   [29] *Ibid.*   [31] *Ibid.*
[28] *Ibid.*   [30] *Ibid.*   [32] *Ibid.*, p. 352.

from "the end of the indignation" (verse 19), or Babylonian captivity, and the return of the Jews from Babylon to Jerusalem, and the "complete reestablishment of the religious services in the holy city." [33] Then, he asserts, will begin the 2300 years.

3. STARTS UNDER ARTAXERXES; NOT CYRUS OR DARIUS.— Finally, under the heading, "4. *More precise research of the beginning of the end of the 2300 years under consideration,*" Nicole contends that the restoration of the worship was not complete in the first phase under Cyrus, so that could not be the starting point. The same reasons "oblige us to reject" the dedication of the second temple under Darius, in 575 B.C. This, therefore, leaves the reign of Artaxerxes upon which to "focus our attention." [34] Such dating, he adds, "merits the most exact examination." The expiration of 2300 years from that date would occur "not very far from the time in which we live." [35]

Referring to the decrees issued to Ezra and Nehemiah, Nicole notes that only at this time was the Holy City raised up from its ruins and surrounded by new walls, with the worship of God established in a "stable manner." This, then, was the beginning of the "seventy weeks of years," during which the Mosaic worship would last, and would close "with the cessation of the sacrifice and the oblation." [36] Therefore, with the 2300 years dated from the reign of Artaxerxes, "the end of the 2300 years should follow in the year 1846 or 1847 of our era," when "the faithful will be able to hope to see accomplished the purification of the sanctuary." [37]

Such is the close reasoning on the true number and dating of the 2300 years which the French lawyer Nicole of Nyon injected in 1829 into the widespread discussion of prophecy.

IV. Fry—Dates 2300 Years 457-1844; Extends Other Periods

JOHN FRY (1775-1849), rector of Desford, Leicester, was a graduate of University College, Oxford.[38] He was the author

---

[33] *Ibid.*
[34] *Ibid.*, p. 353.
[35] *Ibid.*
[36] *Ibid.*
[37] *Ibid.*
[38] *Alumni Oxonienses*, vol. 2, p. 499; *The Gentleman's Magazine*, August, 1849 (New Series, vol. 32), p. 216.

of numerous books on prophecy, including *The Second Advent;
or, the Glorious Epiphany of Our Lord Jesus Christ* (1822),
The Epochs of Daniel's Prophetic Numbers Fixed (1828), and
*Observations on the Unfulfilled Prophecies of Scripture, which
Are Yet to Have Their Accomplishment Before the Coming
of the Lord in Glory, or at the Establishment of His Everlasting
Kingdom* (1835). The previous writing of *A Short History of
the Church of Christ* (1825), designed for schools, gave him
a clear grasp of the historical counterpart of prophecy. Fry is an
example of revision and progression of view in the thirteen years
elapsing between his earliest and latest volumes. His clarity,
and the comprehensive scope of his expositions, as well as his
later revisions, and his emphasis of 1844 call for a rather close
tracing of his positions. Though they may be a bit tedious, they
exemplify the interpretation of the times and the processes of
reasoning employed.

1. EARLY UNCERTAINTY IN DATING 2300 YEARS.—Fry, who
cites Sir Isaac Newton on his title page, from the first follows
the standard interpretation of the four empires of prophecy,
and the western divisions of the fourth, for Daniel 2 and 7.[39]
He follows Machiavelli and Bishop Lloyd's list of the ten primary
kingdoms. The Ostrogoths, Heruli, and Lombards are the
three plucked up.[40] Persia and Grecia are the powers of Daniel
8, with Mohammedanism as the conspicuous horn.[41] On the
2300 years of Daniel 8:14, Fry shows that by dating from the
alleged year of the vision, 553 B.C., 2300 years leads to 1747.
But at that time "the sanctuary has in no sense been cleansed,
either in the west, or in the east, or on the holy mountains of
Palestine." [42]

This indicated a later date for the commencement of the
period. Hale's testimony to the genuineness of the 2300 is
cited,[43] as also the adoption of the 2400 by Faber and Frere—
2400 from 553 B.C. leading to A.D. 1847. On this, Fry takes no

[39] John Fry, *The Second Advent; or, The Glorious Epiphany of Our Lord Jesus Christ*,
vol. 2, pp. 1-28.
[40] *Ibid.*, pp. 15-19.   [41] *Ibid.*, pp. 29-34.   [42] *Ibid.*, p. 44.
[43] *Ibid.*, pp. 45, 46.

personal position in his 1822 volume. But the seventy weeks, or 490 years, he unhesitatingly puts from 457 B.C. to the year A.D. 33, at which latter date he places the crucifixion.[44]

2. EXTENDS CLOSE OF 1290 AND 1335 BEYOND 2300.—Fry is also uncertain, at this early date, as to how and when to date the 1290- and 1335-year periods.[45] But he looks upon the taking away of the daily as the "same thing as 'giving the saints,' or the 'times and the laws,' into the hand of the Little Horn of the fourth beast," and that the interruption of the temple service is the same as the "triumph of the papal idolatry" over the principle and provision of early Christianity.[46] So he concludes that "thirty years after the close of the little horn's triumphant reign," will be some notable happening, and forty-five years beyond that "comes the happy era for which you long." [47] In any event, he avers, "we are somewhere about the termination of this period—are near approaching it, or perhaps have actually passed it." [48]

3. NOT POSITIVE ON DATING OF 1260 YEARS.—After Asserting the propriety of studying and discussing these numbers, he asks when the Papacy assumed its power, and says:

"Could we fix with certainty on this, of all epochas most important, then could we say with confidence: date from that epocha 1260 years, and you will see the papacy cease to have 'the saints,' or 'the times and laws,' in its hand or power; date 30 years from that era, and you will witness another remarkable occurrence: and if you have but the happiness to reach, in your prolonged earthly pilgrimage, five-and-forty years beyond the expiration of that thirty, you will see the advent of Messiah's kingdom, and the end of all these wonders." [49]

He cites the various beginning dates assigned to it by men in the past—365, 410, 455, 529, 533, 540, 606, and on into the eighth century. He says he has not yet reached his own conclusions, but expresses the opinion that "the expiration of this period of 1260 years will alone show when it began." [50] He inclines, however, to Cuninghame's 533-1793 dating. The 1290

[44] Ibid., p. 47.
[45] Ibid., p. 88.
[46] Ibid., p. 89.
[47] Ibid., pp. 89, 90.
[50] Ibid., p. 92.
[48] Ibid., p. 90.
[49] Ibid., pp. 90, 91.

years would then reach to 1823, and the forty-five years beyond that epoch, "that is, in the year of our Lord 1868, the hope of Israel, and of all the ends of the earth, appears." [51] Therefore the cleansing, or vindicating, of the sanctuary "may shortly be expected to be developed." [52] The time is "fast approaching."

4. APPLICATION AND TIMING OF TRUMPETS.—On the trumpets, the first four are the emigrations of the barbarians—Alaric and his Goths, Genseric and the Vandals, Attila and the Huns forming the first three. [53] The fifth is the Saracens for five prophetic months (150 years), from 612-762. [54] The sixth is the Ottoman Turks, the prophetic hour, day, month, and year (391 years), being from 1281 to 1672. [55]

5. FRANCE TENTH OF CITY; BEAST, THE PAPACY.—With others, Fry believed the tenth part of the city, that fell under the blow of the earthquake, to be France casting off the papal yoke with violence. Thus the whole papal city was "shaken to its very foundations." [56] And as captive Greece subdued her Roman conqueror, so Rome in turn "cast the fetters of a moral captivity upon the fierce invaders of the North." [57] And the beast of Revelation 13 is the same as Rome's papal Little Horn of Daniel 7. [58]

6. SIXTH (TURKISH) VIAL YET FUTURE.—Not wholly certain the first four vials can be shown to have been fulfilled in recent European history, Fry is sure that the sixth—the drying up of the Euphrates, or "Ottoman Turks"—is "still future." [59]

7. PAPACY IN WEST; MOHAMMEDANISM IN EAST.—In his later *Observations on the Unfulfilled Prophecies of Scripture,* Fry places on the title page the text, "The great day of the Lord is near, and hasteth greatly, even the voice of the day of the Lord." Discussing the latter part of Daniel 11, he holds that the last of the four empires of Daniel 2 and 7 is there portrayed, to be followed by the kingdom of the saints. "Chittim" means

[51] *Ibid.,* p. 93.   [53] *Ibid.,* pp. 334, 341.   [55] *Ibid.,* pp. 354-357.
[52] *Ibid.,* p. 94.   [54] *Ibid.,* p. 351.   [56] *Ibid.,* pp. 381, 382.
[57] *Ibid.,* p. 394, citing Hallam's *State of Europe During the Middle Ages.*
[58] *Ibid.,* p. 404.   [59] *Ibid.,* p. 437.

Rome, and "the development of an apostasy from the true religion" parallels the exaltation of the "wicked one." [60] He notes the prior parceling out of the Roman Empire, represented by the ten toes and the ten horns. The exceeding great horn of Daniel 8, Fry still believed to be the eastern, or Mohammedan, power. [61]

8. REVELATION 14:6 IN PROCESS OF FULFILLMENT.—Section Four deals with the predicted "Signs of the Approaching Day of the Lord," among which he places the special "preaching of the gospel of the kingdom," which he felt was "beginning to be accomplished," citing Revelation 14:6. He speaks regretfully of some who were futilely "thinking to prepare a Millennium for themselves, under the present dispensation." [62] And he declares that many "will be enlightened to see the bearing of the word of prophecy upon the times on which we are fallen: the proclamation will go forth, 'Fear God, and give glory to him; for the hour of his judgment is come.' " [63] Fry adds, interestingly, that "the epithet 'everlasting,' applied to the 'Gospel of the kingdom' is peculiar to this passage, and seems to intimate the introduction of a dispensation of the kingdom which shall be forever." This all takes place before the great and terrible day of the Lord. [64]

9. REVELATION 17; OVERTURNING OF PAPAL SUPREMACY.— The hating of the whore, in Revelation 17, denotes "the overturning of the supremacy and dominion of the Roman church, which the kingdoms of the western empire had borne for so many ages as a beast of burden." This is to take place before, or at least before the close of, the pouring out of the last vial of judgment. [65]

10. GIBBON BEST EXPOSITOR OF TRUMPETS.—In an Appendix of this later work, in interpreting the first six trumpets, Fry states, "I have been convinced for many years, that the infidel historian, Gibbon, is the best of all expositors," and that "the era of the six trumpets, agrees with his era of 'the fall of the

---

[60] John Fry, *Observations on the Unfulfilled Prophecies of Scripture*, p. 24.
[61] *Ibid.*, p. 25.   [63] *Ibid.*, p. 36.   [65] *Ibid.*, p. 37.
[62] *Ibid.*, p. 35.   [64] *Ibid.*

Roman empire' both in the west and in the east." Moreover, he feels that the fall in the West is symbolized by the first four, with "the fifth and sixth the fall of the Roman power in the east." [66] He again identifies the first three trumpets as Alaric and his Goths about 395, Genseric and his Vandals about 429, and Attila and his Huns about 433. [67] After the fourth, a "break in the prophecy is strongly marked in the vision"—the angelic announcement of the three woes to follow. The fifth is the Mohammedan Saracens, and the sixth the Mohammedan Turks. [68]

11. 1260 YEARS FOLLOW BREAKUP OF ROME.—The beginning of the 1260 years Fry places "after the destructive inroads of the barbarian nations." The papal Little Horn of Daniel 7 is the "prime mover in the war made on the saints." [69]

12. SEVEN TIMES OF GENTILES (677 B.C. TO A.D. 1844).— Holding to the clear principle that in prophetic time a day stands for a year, Fry indicates that the "seven times of the Gentiles," or 2520 years, dated from the captivity of Manasseh, in 677 B.C., "would close in the year of our Lord 1844." [70] This expression—"times of the Gentiles"—he adds, had "caught the attention" of many expositors. [71]

13. 2300 YEARS—457 B.C. TO A.D. 1844.—And the 2300 years of Daniel 8, "on the same scale so many years," Fry now clearly begins from "the same epocha" as the seventy weeks of Daniel 9—from the going forth of the decree to restore Jerusalem in 457 B.C. Then he adds with positiveness: "If the twenty-three hundred years are to be dated from the same epoch, (adding one for the year of the era) they also terminate A.D. 1844." [72]

14. 391-YEAR PERIOD MAY END 1844.—In addition to these two, both terminating in 1844, Fry adds that the 391 years of Revelation 9:15 may also be "dated from the establishment of the Mohomedan Turks at Constantinople." The number of days, counted on the common scale, may also terminate in the

66 *Ibid.*, p. 349.   68 *Ibid.*, p. 350.   70 *Ibid.*, pp. 370, 373.
67 *Ibid.*   69 *Ibid.*, pp. 358, 359.   71 *Ibid.*, p. 369.
      72 *Ibid.*, p. 370.

year A.D. 1844.[73] The fractional part of the year is also noted as of the "hour."

15. MOHAMMEDANS ALSO EXPECT CHRIST TO REVISIT THE EARTH.—Fry calls attention, moreover, to the remarkable fact that "the Mohammedans in various parts of the world, have their expectations fixed on the same year, A.D. 1844." [74] This was on the basis of the 1200th year from the Hegira, when, many believed, "Jesus Christ shall revisit the earth, and when all men shall be of one faith." [75] Then Fry concludes:

"Whether we shall or shall not be led by our best inductions from the prophecies of the Scriptures, to conclude that the year A.D. 1844, be the actual period of the coming of our Lord in glory—as the Mahomedans suppose to make us all of their religion.—For they say that, though Mahomed is the greater prophet, and his religion the only true one; yet that Mahomed is not risen from the dead, but that Jesus is, and that in his person this visitation is to take place. This coincidence in the expectation of so large a body of mankind, with the general prospects of the people who wait for redemption in the Church of Christ, is certainly not to be disregarded. Something very similar was the case, from whatever cause, in respect of the whole civilized world, at or near the epoch of the first advent." [76]

16. CLEANSING OF SANCTUARY APPLIED TO JERUSALEM.— The impressive implications of 1844 on the basis of such calculations, leads Fry to this discussion of the cleansing of the sanctuary:

"It is, indeed, a matter of the most awful inquiry,—on the assumption that this hypothesis which directs our attention to A.D. 1844, is true— what expectation can be formed from the holy Scriptures respecting the events of that epoch. It is said in Daniel, chapter viii.14, in connection with the expiration of the two thousand three hundred days—'then shall the sanctuary be cleansed.' The original is 'justified,'—in the sense I should suppose of—vindicated in the claim of asserted rights or granted privilege. This seems to apply to the site of the holy temple of Jerusalem: this cleansing or justifying of the sanctuary may, therefore, predict in unfulfilled prophecy, the circumstances attending the possession of Jerusalem, by that *first* restoration of Judah, and colonization of Palestine." [77]

Others, Fry says, are of the opinion "that this 'cleansing of the sanctuary,' should rather be referred to this last vindication

[73] *Ibid.,* p. 371.   [75] *Ibid.*   [77] *Ibid.,* p. 372.
[74] *Ibid.*   [76] *Ibid.,* pp. 371, 372.

of the holy city from the grasp of the last oppressor, and the actual possession of the mountain of the Lord's house, by the entrance of the divine presence, as described in the prophet Ezekiel." [78]

17. 1260 YEARS FROM SIXTH TO NINETEENTH CENTURY.— Fry contends that the restored and newly regulated government of Justinian afforded, in a special manner, a "model for the future spiritual monarchy of Papal Rome," and that "the canonical government of the Court of Rome, was the image of the civil or temporal sovereignty of the restored empire." [79] Now follows this unique statement of view concerning the chronology of the 1260 years:

"This constitution coming into operation in the latter part of the sixth century, and continuing its sway among the Roman Catholic nations till towards the close of the eighteenth centuary [sic], when it begins with violence to be exchanged for new principles of legislation and government, has marked a cycle of twelve hundred and sixty years, which, since its determination in the French Revolution, has escaped the attention of few commentators of the scripture prophecies." [80]

18. 1260 YEARS (537-1797); 1290 TO 1827; 1335 TO 1872.— Coming to the 1290 and 1335 days of Daniel 12:11, from the taking away of the daily sacrifice, as from the time of the restoration of the supreme authority of Justinian,[81] Fry offers the period 537-1797 for the 1260 years:

"In the year 537, the year after the armies of Justinian had taken possession of Rome for the first time, November 17th, Bishop Sylverius by his order, or that of the wretched empress Theodora, was spoiled of his pontifical character, and immediately led into exile in the habit of a common monk, where it is said, he died by hunger. By command of the same authority, the Clergy of Rome proceeded to the choice of a new Bishop, and after *solemn invocation of the Holy Ghost,* elected the deacon Vigilius, who had purchased this promotion 'by a bribe of two hundred pounds of gold.' " [82]

"If this should be the violation and abomination spoken of in the prophecy, from which the mystic days are to be dated, as of course anticipate the last mentioned dates sixteen years. From A. D. 537, the cycle of twelve hundred and sixty years, which brings us to A. D. 1797, is very remarkably terminated; this year was the last of the reign of Pope Pius VI. A. D. 1793

---

[78] *Ibid.,* p. 373.
[79] *Ibid.,* p. 376.
[80] *Ibid.*
[81] *Ibid.,* p. 378.
[82] *Ibid.,* p. 379.

[1798], February 15th, the Roman people proclaimed their independence, 'the tree of liberty,' as they called it, 'was planted in the capitol.' "[83]

"Thirty years extended out from this epocha, brings us to the latter part of 1827."[84] And "on this hypothesis," "the last forty-five years must be dated from 1827 or 1828, directing us to A.D. 1872 or 1873, for the blessed era intimated by Daniel."[85] The arrival of these years, beginning with 1844, Fry solemnly concludes, "must be expected with feelings of deepest interest, by all who are 'looking for this great day of the Lord.' "[86]

Be it noted, however, that while 1844 is mentioned, the climax of Fry's expectations is shifted over to the early seventies.

---

[83] *Ibid.*
[84] *Ibid.*, pp. 379. 380.

[85] *Ibid.*, p. 380.
[86] *Ibid.*

CHAPTER TWENTY-SIX

Prophetic Society and the Morning Watch

The growing advent and prophetic awakening now takes on added form and force as the Society for the Investigation of Prophecy is launched in England, and the Reformation Society in Ireland gets under way. Along with these is to be noted the rather pretentious quarterly *The Morning Watch,* which begins to exert considerable influence. Meantime, editors, historians, and clergymen continue to add their testimony. Note the picture.

I. Society Formed to Investigate Last-Day Prophecies

James H. Frere in 1826 conceived the idea of forming the Society for the Investigation of Prophecy. He wrote out suggestive rules for such an organization and prepared an opening address. He even obtained the consent of Edward Irving, a frequent visitor at his house, James Stratton, and Thomas White—all ministers—to become members of such a prophetic study group. Then the thought occurred to him that if God really desired such an organization formed He would also impress someone else with its need. So he let the matter rest.

Not long after, Lewis Way, then minister of the English church in Paris, came to England on a visit, and sent word that he wished to see Irving. Frere accompanied him. Way at once told Irving, Hawtrey, secretary of the Society for Promoting Christianity Amongst the Jews, and Frere, of his burden to "impress upon the church the duty of studying the Prophetic Scriptures with reference to the Second Coming of Our Lord." After obtaining their consent to join in such an endeavor, Way secured lodgings near Frere, that they might study the Apocalypse together. And under Way's signature the summons was sent out for the first meeting of its kind in June, 1826.[1]

So the Society for the Investigation of Prophecy came into being, formed for the express purpose of studying "the speedy coming of our Lord, and the judgments about to come upon the Empire, and the Apostate Church, of Rome," and in believed fulfillment of the demand of Revelation 14:8 and 18:3.[2] Periodic meetings and prepared papers were part of the plan. This was now the third organization—along with the Society for the Promotion of Christianity Amongst the Jews and the Continental Society—having kindred objectives, and all concerned over the prophecies.

The Prophecy Investigation Society was still flourishing in 1848. A four-page "Private" notification slip lists all members and officers, as of May, 1848. It tabulates thirteen governing "Rules," and gives the subjects and speakers of the large *semi-annual* meeting for April, with notification of a similar meeting in November. The three-day spring conference is scheduled, beginning April 24, at St. George's, Bloomsbury. A whole series of *semiweekly* lectures at St. George's for the "Spring Course" is also tabulated, with subjects and speakers listed between February 23 and April 24, 1849.[3] Meetings in the homes of the various members are also scheduled, the "President for the day" being the clergyman at whose house the meeting was to be held. The one to speak was given a month's notice.

The Rules limit the membership to fifty, one fifth of whom might be laymen. In addition to such familiar names as Birks, Haldane Stewart, Pym, Marsh, Bickersteth, White, Baylee, Frere, Hoare, Brock, Elliott, and M'Neile, are many other cler-

---

[1] James H. Frere, *Great Continental Revolution*, pp. 85-87.
[2] *Ibid.*, pp. 86, 87.
[3] Apparently these were held annually over a long period. Published collections for several different years are referred to as the "Bloomsbury lectures" under Bickersteth and others.

gymen, including the Bishop of Cashel. These were stationed
all over Britain. Among the members were the Duke of Manchester, Sir Thomas Blomfield, and J. P. Plumptre, M. P. Several
naval and military leaders are included—Rear Admiral Hope,
Capt. F. E. V. Harcourt, R.N., and Capt. John Trotter of the
army.

The "subjects for investigation" all bear on prophecy, the
impending crisis, and the second advent, the coming kingdom
being the keynote.

II. Irish Reformation Society Calls "Out of Rome"

The Reformation Society, formed in 1827, was designed to
play its part in fulfillment of the prophesied angelic messages
of Revelation 14. It resulted in the successful preaching of the
gospel in Ireland and succeeded in calling out many from the
Church of Rome.[4]

III. White—Ends 1290, 2300, and 391 in 1843-44

THOMAS WHITE,[5] rector of St. Andrews, Hertford, and minister of Welbeck Chapel, St. Marylebone, was the writer of the
closing paper in a series of seven read in 1828 before this Society
for the Investigation of Prophecy. It was titled "Diagram and
Observation Intended to Illustrate the Arrangement and assist
the Exposition of the Apocalypse." Citing G. S. Faber, Thomas
Gisborne, J. A. Brown, and William Cuninghame on the dating
of the 1260 years—whether from 533 to 1793, or otherwise—
White contends that Justinian was not successful in the recovery
of authority over the Western Empire until the overthrow of
the Gothic kingdom in 554 by the success of Narses.[6]

So he suggests the 1260 years as from 554 to 1814, and the
1290 as from 554 to 1844—which year is to White the pivotal
date of the prophetic numbers. (Title page and inset reproduced on page 444.) Here is his unique tabulation, making

---

[4] *Ibid.*, p. 87.   [5] Biographical data not yet available.
[6] *Papers Read Before the Society for the Investigation of Prophecy* (1828), p. 124. The
other papers were by John Tudor, Henry Drummond, John Thompson, M.D., and
T. W. Chevalier.

1844 the terminal point of the 1290-, 2300-, and 391-year periods:

"From A.D. 554 _____ to A.D. 1814 were 1260 Years.

—— 554 _____ to —— 1844 will be 1290 Years.

From B.C. 457 (date of 7th of Artaxerxes), to the death —— 33 were 490 Years.
of our Lord

—— 457 _____ to —— 1843 will be 2300 Years.

From A.D. 1453 (when the Eastern
third part of men to —— 1844 will be 391 Years." [7]
were slain)

On the 391 years of the Turkish woe, White believes they should be dated not from Turkey's "first rise" but "from its triumph over the Eastern Empire; and that it marks out the time during which that empire shall continue to be slain, and the duration of the second woe." [8] He questions the position of many who place the termination sometime before the French Revolution, and observes:

"I am very much of the opinion that the Turkish power is yet a woe, both to Jews and Christians; and that it will continue to be so until its downfall. Present appearances make that downfall seem nearer than the above calculation leads me to anticipate; but it is not difficult to suppose that causes, such as have hitherto prevented that most desirable consummation, may yet retard it for seventeen years." [9]

So, following the exegesis that would end the 391 years approximately with the 2300 years, White dates the beginning of this longer time period synchronously with the seventy weeks in 457 B.C. And he terminates it in 1843—another in the growing list of expositors holding such a position.

IV. *Morning Watch*—Stresses Last Events and 2300-Year Terminus

Most voluminous of the periodicals dealing with prophecy was the ponderous "Quarterly Journal on Prophecy and Theological Review," called *The Morning Watch,* issued from 1829 to 1833. It was edited by John Tudor and financed by Henry Drummond. "Its first volumes contain many valuable essays: the latter volumes were almost exclusively devoted to the doctrines and transactions of the *Irvingites*." [10] Thus the prophetic views of Albury Park were steadily disseminated.

---

[7] *Ibid.*, p. 125.   [8] *Ibid.*   [9] *Ibid.*
[10] Joshua W. Brooks, *Dictionary of Writers on the Prophecies*, p. cvi.

The 735 pages of the first volume were a reflector of a large segment of the interpretations of the time. Regrettably, many of the contributors use only initials or pseudonyms that cannot always be identified. In their various styles they exalt prophecy as God's beacon light to men, and stress sound methods of studying and interpreting prophecy. Such discussions as "The Times and Seasons" superimpose the whole scheme of the Apocalypse upon the Old Testament feasts, from the Passover in the first Jewish month, and its accompanying wave-sheaf, on through the Feast of Weeks, and finally to the Feast of Trumpets, Day of Atonement, and Feast of Tabernacles. The imagery, or scenery, is taken almost wholly from the tabernacle erected by Moses. Thus a framework is formed for the gospel dispensation.[11]

1. HOMAN OUTLINES END IN 1843-44.—In the June issue a brief note by PH. HOMAN[12] cites four prophecies that he believes would terminate about 1843. These are (1) the seven times, or 2520 years, from the captivity of Israel by Esarhaddon, in the reign of Manasseh in 677 B.C., which "will be found to terminate in A.D. 1843"; (2) the 2300 years to the cleansing of the sanctuary, from "the decree for restoring the civil and ecclesiastical polity of the Jews," from the seventh year of Artaxerxes, A.D. 457; "consequently, the 2300 days, reckoned from this, terminate in A.D. 1843"; (3) restoration of Israel will take place in the Jubilee, and, according to the computations of many chronologers, the next year of Jubilee will occur in 1843 or 1844; (4) the 391 years of the Ottoman power—an hour, day, month, and year, from the capture of Constantinople in 1453 to 1844.[13] The restoration of Israel is anticipated at that time.

2. REVELATION 14 PICTURES LAST-DAY EVENTS.—In the September number the integrity of the Apocalypse, its transmission through the centuries, and the soundness of premillennialism are stressed.[14] Of Revelation 14, Tudor writes that this is "that portion of the Revelation which the slightest inspection shews to be the most important of the whole book. It begins with the visitation on

[11] *The Morning Watch*, March, 1829 (vol. 1, no. 1), pp. 43, 44.
[12] Biographical data not available at this writing.
[13] *Ibid.*, June, 1829 (vol. 1, no. 2), pp. 271, 272.
[14] *Ibid.*, September, 1829 (vol. 1, no. 3), p. 273.

Babylon, and runs on to the overthrow of all the powers of evil, to make way for the kingdom of Christ. All the preceding revelations point onwards to this time; and all the Old-Testament Prophets look forward to it, as 'the last days,' 'the time of the end,' 'the day of the Lord,' etc." [15]

This, he declares, is the time when prophecy is unsealed, and this time of the unsealing is also the announcement of the coming of Christ previous to His actual coming.[16] This follows the expiration of the 1260 years.[17]

Earnest dissent from the Futurist S. R. Maitland's *Inquiry* on the 1260 years is voiced in the form of a book review. With keen logic and incisive words Maitland's positions on literal time are analyzed and overthrown. Though it is devoted chiefly to the 1260 year-days, the 2300 year-days are also discussed and defended, and the incongruity of Maitland's position is exposed.[18]

3. Gradual Development of Prophetic Interpretation. —The December issue presents a comprehensive picture of "the gradual Unfolding of Prophecy." This traces the growing understanding of prophecy throughout the Christian Era, along with each advancing fulfillment of prophecy. With this are the perversions in the time of Origen and Constantine, and later the fallacy of postmillennialism, from Grotius and Hammond onward. The early awakening on prophecy, around the thirteenth and fourteenth centuries, is portrayed with bold but accurate strokes. The witness of Arnoldus de Nova Villa (1250), Grosthead (1250), Laurence (1260), Petrus Johannis (1290), Militzius (1366), Wyclif (1371), Brute (1391), and Wimbledon (1389) is cited.[19] Then John Tudor, editor of *The Morning Watch,* observes, "These extracts may suffice to shew how truly, in the general, these confessors understood the prophecies of Antichrist." [20]

This is followed by writers like Brightman (1616), Mede, More, Sir Isaac Newton, and Whiston.[21] Then expositors from

---

[15] *Ibid.*, p. 294.
[16] *Ibid.*
[19] See Volume 2 of *Prophetic Faith.*
[20] *The Morning Watch,* December, 1829 (vol. 1, no. 4), pp. 531-537. Tudor will be presented more fully later in this chapter.
[21] *Ibid.*, pp. 537-539.

[17] *Ibid.*, p. 296.
[18] *Ibid.*, pp. 509-518.

the French Revolution onward are listed, including Bicheno, Whitaker, Towers, Faber, Cuninghame, Frere, Way, Bayford, and Irving. Tudor again stresses the "typical application of the set times of the Jewish year to the order of events declared in the prophecies." [22] This gives to probability the "stamp of certainty."

4. LAST EVENTS IN DAY OF ATONEMENT SETTING.—In further "Interpretation of the Apocalypse," the 1260 years are allocated from Justinian's Code in 533 to 1793 in the French Revolution and the Napoleonic Code. [23] The sealing work of Revelation 7 is described thus:

"The sealed ones are gathered when Christ comes from without the veil (Heb. IX.28) denoting the Day of Atonement, when the high priest came out the last time from the holy of holies." [24]

The Day of Atonement and the Feast of Tabernacles following are connected with "the *remnant* of the woman's seed with whom the dragon went to make war."

These two feasts—of Atonement and Tabernacles—the writer continues, are tied in with the events between the French Revolution and the end. These give notice of the Lord's coming sufficient to warn the world. The events of the seventh seal Christ shall enact in person—the seventh trumpet, seventh seal, and seventh vial all being fulfilled at the same time. The writer maintains that "all the imagery in this poem was taken from the Day of Atonement"—the golden censer, the incense, the deep affliction, the temple opened, and the ark seen "indicating the opening of the veil on the day of atonement." [25] This is an impressive emphasis, of which more will be heard later.

5. TURK'S WANE FOLLOWING 391-YEAR PERIOD.—The trumpets are held to be the invasion of the northern barbarians, with the fifth the Saracens, and the sixth the Turks for "391 years and a fraction"—a time "capable of being fixed with the greatest accuracy." The wasting away of the Turkish power "we daily

22 *Ibid.*, p. 541.
23 *Ibid.*, pp. 547, 550.
24 *Ibid.*, p. 555.
25 *Ibid.*, pp. 555, 556.

behold," which is preparing the way for the third woe.[26] The Two Witnesses are declared to be the two Testaments, and the three and a half years of their slaying began in 1793,[27] with France as the "tenth part of the city." [28] Revelation 12 is the history of the persecutions of the true church; and Revelation 13, the history of the papal Antichrist, with the usual explanation of the heads and horns.[29] And the two-horned beast is thought to be another picture of the same, only in his infidelic form.[30]

6. SEVEN CHURCHES EXTEND TO ADVENT.—In volume 2 (1830), the periods of the seven churches are distributed thus: (1) Ephesus, to the persecution by Nero, A.D. 64; (2) Smyrna, till the accession of Constantine, in 324; (3) Pergamos, the interval between elevation of Constantine and the rise of the Little Horn at the beginning of the 1260 years; (4) Thyatira, the testimony against the Papacy during the 1260 years; (5) Sardis, from the end of the 1260 years until the preparation for the coming of the Lord; (6) Philadelphia, the period of the preparation, until the Lord comes in the air and meets His saints, changed and risen; (7) Laodicea—the "only one yet entirely future"— the church during the great tribulation between the coming of the Lord and the establishment of His throne.[31]

7. 2300 YEARS END IN 1843 OR 1847.—Again treating on the time periods leading to the "time of the end," The Morning Watch says that the period of the 2300 years "appears to end about the year 1847," though allusion is made to the extension of the 1290 and 1335 years, with the latter terminating in 1867.[32] In volume 3 (1831) the ending of the 1260 years in 1798, at the "deposition of the Pope," is mentioned by "F" as the preference of some, with the terminus of the 2300 years in 1843 or 1847, at the re-establishment of true worship at Jerusalem.[33] With it is noted the drying up of Turkey that has long been under way. Still further discussion occurs in volume 5 (1832) on the "Sacred

---

[26] Ibid., pp. 557, 558.   [28] Ibid., p. 563.   [30] Ibid., pp. 569-571.
[27] Ibid., pp. 562, 563.   [29] Ibid., pp. 564-568.
[31] Ibid., September, 1830 (vol. 2, no. 2), p. 510.
[32] Ibid., December, 1830 (vol. 2, no. 4), pp. 916, 917.
[33] Ibid., June, 1831 (vol. 3, no. 2), p. 472.

Numbers." The relation of the 2300 years and the seventy weeks brings this impressive editorial statement:

"The first number given is 2300 years (viii.14), which includes the time of both advents; the second number given is 490 years, or 70 weeks (ix.24), which includes the time of the First Advent only. Both these numbers must have the same commencement, for the second is declared to be given to enable Daniel to understand the meaning of the first." [34]

The 1810 years which remain beyond the seventy weeks, end in A.D. 1847. The ending of the 1260-year papal period in 1793[35] is repeated.

8. PROTESTANTISM INCLUDED UNDER "BABYLON."—There is an increasing tendency to place nominal Protestantism within the confines of Babylon. Thus: "Babylon is christendom, in all its parts, and under all its denominations of Papal, and Protestant, and Dissenter." [36] In the later volumes the nature of Christ, spiritual gifts, speaking with tongues, and the now-developed Irvingism have increasing space and attention. Acrimony comes in to mar the discussions, and the editor ends its issuance.

V. Editor Tudor—"This Is Our Day of Atonement"

JOHN TUDOR (d. 1862) is listed in the British Museum catalogue as one-time editor of the *Church of England Quarterly Review*. He was one of the initial members of the Society for the Investigation of Prophecy, and later editor of *The Morning Watch* (1829-33). Tudor was also one of the forty-four men who attended annually the Albury Park Prophetic Conferences (1826-30) to discuss the fulfillment of prophecy. In 1833 he became an elder, and in 1835 an apostle in the Catholic Apostolic Church.[37]

His is the first of the papers read before the Society for the Investigation of Prophecy in 1828. He was author of *Brief Interpretation of Revelation* (1833), and *Prophetic Character of*

---

[34] *Ibid.*, June, 1832 (vol. 5, no. 2), p. 276.   [35] *Ibid.*, pp. 278-280.
[36] *Ibid.*, December, 1832 (vol. 6, no. 2), p. 282.
[37] Frederic Boase, *Modern English Biography*, vol. 3, col. 1032; Edward Miller, *The History and Doctrines of Irvingism*, vol. 1, p. 15.

Revelation (1858).   In discussing "The Structure of the Apocalypse," he takes as axiomatic the four empires of prophecy and the year-day principle for the 1260 years, and the pouring out of the seven vials, or plagues, as connected with the sealing and the harvest.[38]

1. TWO TESTAMENTS SLAIN IN FRENCH REVOLUTION.—The 1260 years of the treading down of the Holy City, when the church is in the wilderness, and the Witnesses, or Old and New Testaments, are in sackcloth, is when they are "degraded from their proper dignity, kept from the people, and prohibited from being had in any other version than the Vulgate, a dead language." [39]   The slaying of the Witnesses Tudor ties to the "time of the French Revolution," "their office as witness being cut short by the infidel beast," before the preaching of the "everlasting gospel" of Revelation 14.[40]

2. THIS PERIOD OUR DAY OF ATONEMENT.—When the last vial is poured out, Tudor adds, the voice from heaven cries, "It is done," and the kingdoms of the world become the kingdoms of our Lord.   Now comes this remarkable statement likening the time they had reached to the Day of Atonement:

"The temple of God is then opened, and the ark of his testament seen, xi.19; and the voice issues from *the throne,* xvi.17; both expressions equally denoting the holy of holies, which was only entered once a year, on the day of atonement.   This period is therefore our day of atonement, and requires our particular notice, to know what events we may expect, answering to the type.

"The day of atonement, called in the Mishna, THE DAY (Joma), was the strictest of the Mosaic fasts, and observed annually on the 10th of Tisri. All the morning was employed by the High Priest in sacrifices; first to atone for his own sins, then for the sins of the people: among which the two goats, one of which became the scape goat, was a form of sacrifice peculiar to this day.   But the most important ordinance of the day was the High Priest's entrance, then and on no other occasion, within the vail of the holy of holies.   After the sacrifices, he put on his white linen garments, and, taking a censer full of coals from the brazen altar, strewed incense thereon, and entered with a cloud of smoke.   This was the turning point of the day.   During his disappearance, the people gave every demonstration of sorrow; but as soon as he had offered the incense, he changed the

---

[38] *Papers Read Before the Society for the Investigation of Prophecy,* p. 6.
[39] *Ibid.,* p. 7.   [40] *Ibid.,* p. 8.

linen for the gorgeous priestly garments, and, coming forth to the people, turned their sorrow into joy; and from that time in the year of release did the jubilee begin." [41]

3. CLIMAXES WITH REAPPEARANCE OF ABSENT LORD.— Applying the type, Tudor says the Christian "doth yet feel it a time of humiliation and mourning for his absent Lord. But unto them that look for him, shall he appear the second time without sin unto salvation." [42] And he feels that the turning point is when the temple, or tabernacle, is opened and the ark is seen. After describing the tabernacle and its furniture and the daily and yearly service,[43] Tudor deals with the command to measure the temple and court where the worshipers assembled, which was "cast out," or made common and unholy, its enclosure removed by the professing but apostate church for forty-two months.[44] During this time the true temple remains invisible, and the apostate woman attires herself with purple and scarlet, and takes up her golden cup. Then, says Tudor:

"At the conclusion of the forty-two months, when the judgment on this apostasy begins, a true visible church is brought forth, consisting of the 144,000 sealed ones, vii.4, who stand on mount Zion, and follow the Lamb whithersoever he goeth." [45]

4. HARVEST AND VINTAGE FOLLOWED BY JUBILEE.—Tudor next discusses the harvesting of the wheat and the burning of the tares—the latter synchronizing with the destruction of Babylon.[46] Then he considers the vintage, which concluded the operations of the Jewish sacred year, and is "the closing event of our present dispensation." The vintage, continues Tudor, "was immediately succeeded by the feast of tabernacles, 15 Tisri"— Tisri "answering nearly to October." [47] Tudor then expounds the types and antitype, and how at the close of the Day of Atonement they began returning to their "alienated possessions and suspended liberty; and could keep the feast of tabernacles on the 15th." [48] This was the climax of the series.

5. THE SEALING AND THE MARK INDICATED.—The types are pressed still further:

---

[41] *Ibid.*, p. 9.   [43] *Ibid.*, p. 10.   [45] *Ibid.*   [47] *Ibid.*, p. 18.
[42] *Ibid.*, pp. 9, 10.   [44] *Ibid.*, p. 11.   [46] *Ibid.*, p. 16.   [48] *Ibid.*

"When the ark came up out of the wilderness, the first act, after cross-ing Jordan, was the renewal of the covenant at Gilgal, Jos. v.; so when the wilderness state of the church in the Apocalypse has expired, the first act is the sealing a true church, vii.1, xiv.1, xv.2. But the sealing includes protection also, and therefore alludes to the marking the foreheads of those men who sigh and cry for the abominations of the land, Ezek. ix. 4." [49]

6. HERALDING THE COMING BRIDEGROOM.—The ancient judgments on Babylon—the captivity, the drying up of its river for Cyrus, and the capture, setting the captives free—Tudor presents as symbolizing the fall of Babylon, the cry to come out of her, her plagues coming in a day, her destruction by fire, her merchants lamenting, as set forth in Revelation 18 and 19. [50] Then comes Tudor's next remarkable statement:

"If these things be so, and I think it certain that they are so; our situa-tion in the prophetic series of events is brought within narrow limits, and our duties are clear and obvious. We live under the sixth vial, the prepara-tion for the great day of God Almighty, xiv.14. 'The second woe is past, and behold the third woe cometh quickly,' xi.14. The seventh vial impends over our heads, at whose effusion the cry shall be heard, 'It is done,' xvi.17. The seventh angel is preparing; and 'when he shall begin to sound, the mystery of God shall be finished,' x.7. The Gospel of the kingdom has well nigh gone round the earth, and 'then shall the end be,' Matt. xxiv.14. 'The fig tree beginneth to put forth its leaves, shewing that summer is at hand,' Matt. xxiv.32. The cry is raised among the virgins, 'Behold the bridegroom cometh,' Matt. xxv.6. The lord is returning from a far country, to reckon with his servants, 19." [51]

7. SOUNDS CALL OUT OF BABYLON.—Tudor's conclusion is an appeal for his readers not to be like the auditors of Noah, heedless of the message; or like Sodom, indifferent to the gather-ing tempest of fire. The plagues of Babylon will come in one hour, and fiery judgment—"therefore come out of her my people." Watch, he admonishes, lest the Master of the house coming suddenly, find you sleeping. [52]

VI. Historian Jones—Depicts Fate of Papal Antichrist

Besides those organized into study groups were individuals like WILLIAM JONES (1762-1846), Baptist religious writer, who

[49] Ibid., p. 19.
[50] Ibid., p. 20.

[51] Ibid., p. 21.
[52] Ibid., pp. 21, 22.

was born in Lancashire. He was a bookseller before he became pastor of the Scotch Baptist church at Finsbury, London, where he served until his death. He was the author of numerous able works, among which were a helpful *History of the Waldenses* (1811), a *History of the Christian Church* (1816), and a well-known *Biblical Encyclopedia* (1816), as well as a *Dictionary of Christian Biography* (1829). His *Lectures on the Apocalypse* appeared in 1830. Jones thus had an unusual historical background acquaintance for his expositions of prophecy.[53] Upon this he drafted constantly.

1. ROMAN PAGANISM RETARDS PAPAL APOSTASY.—In his *History of the Christian Church*, of 1816, Jones quotes extensively from the Waldensian "Treatise concerning Antichrist," with all its applications to the Papacy of the prophetic symbols of Daniel, Paul, and John. He cites their apology and their protest, and the persecutions visited upon them, as well as the admissions of their enemies. Jones tells the story of the Antichristian apostasy, particularly as a fulfillment of 2 Thessalonians 2, at first kept back by the hindering restraint of the pagan Roman government. He maintains that Antichrist arose and corrupted the early Christian church, and will be destroyed by the brightness of the Lord's coming, when the cities of the nations fall. This is the continuing keynote of the volume.[54]

2. EXPOSITION OF SYMBOLS IN CYCLOPEDIA.—In his popular *Biblical Cyclopedia* many of the fundamental interpretations appear under such topics as "Antichrist," "Babylon," "Daniel," "Locust," "Millennium," "Persia," and "Revelation." Detailed exposition of the prophetic symbols was thus upon the general reference shelf. For example, under "Antichrist," the seven-hilled seat of its residence, the blend of ecclesiastical and political power, its persecuting character, its length of continuance on the year-day principle, and other features were set forth with

[53] *Dictionary of National Biography*, vol. 10, pp. 1066, 1067.
[54] William Jones, *The History of the Christian Church*, . . . *Including the Very Interesting Account of the Waldenses and the Albigenses.* Volume 2 is largely given over to the teachings and tribulations of the Waldenses, showing their relationship to the Wyclifite and Hussite positions. After a full recital of their persecutions, Jones tells of the final surcease of open hostilities.

clarity and force.[55] This continued with discussions on the "rise and ravages of the Turks" as the sixth trumpet, the French Revolution "earthquake" and France as the tenth part of the city, the two beasts of Revelation 13 with the first as secular Rome and the second as the hierarchy or false church itself, which is contemporary, and all along acts in concert with the first or secular beast.[56] This was all standard teaching.

3. STANDARD POSITION ON DANIEL 2 AND 7.—Jones' *Lectures on the Apocalypse,* of 1830, was occasioned by the issuance of Drummond's *Dialogues on Prophecy* (1827), which in turn was the result of the Albury Park Conferences. Jones had been associated with Drummond in the establishment of the Continental Society. Now Drummond places with him the first volume of Irving's translation of Ben-Ezra for perusal. This, with the awakened interest in prophecy on the part of many able men, and the apathy and scorn of others concerning prophecy, as well as the compromises on the part of not a few who would *"meet Antichrist half-way,"* [57] moved Jones to write.

In his discussion of the trumpets of Revelation 8, Jones diverts to the identity of the four beasts of Daniel 7, stoutly maintaining that they symbolize Babylon, Medo-Persia, Greece, and Rome, with the various features incident.[58] These in turn are identical with the four parts of the image of Daniel 2, only in Daniel 7 Antichrist is introduced as the "Little Horn,"[59] springing up among the "ten distinct kingdoms."

4. DISMEMBERMENT ACCOMPLISHED BY EARLY TRUMPETS.— These horn-kingdoms were the same as the divided state of the feet and toes of the image, accomplished by the incursions of the northern barbarians. These invasions were indicated in the Apocalypse by the first four trumpets of Revelation 8.[60] Under the fourth, with Odoacer, comes the extinction of the Western Empire,[61] and the ten kingdoms resulting are listed.

---

[55] William Jones, *Biblical Cyclopedia* (1824 ed.), vol. 1, art. "Antichrist."
[56] *Ibid.,* vol. 2, art. "Revelation."
[57] William Jones, *Lectures on the Apocalypse,* pp. iv-vii.
[58] *Ibid.,* pp. 286, 287.   [60] *Ibid.,* pp. 290-304.
[59] *Ibid.,* pp. 288, 310, 311.   [61] *Ibid.,* pp. 304, 305.

5. Papal Little Horn for 1260 Years.—Returning to the little horn of Daniel 7, Jones applies the symbol to the popes of Rome and discusses the blaspheming, persecuting, and lawless character of the Papacy, treating the three and a half times of flourishing as 1260 years of dominance in scattering the people of God.[62]

6. Fifth Trumpet Papal; Sixth Turkish.—Jones differs from many in holding that the fifth trumpet, or first woe, applied to Antichrist, or the kingdom of the clergy; but he agrees that the sixth trumpet applies to the Mohammedan Turks,[63] with their subversion approaching.[64]

7. Two Witnesses Are the Two Testaments.—On the Two Witnesses of Revelation 11, Jones holds that they denote the Old and New Testaments. These "testified of Christ and his kingdom in opposition to Antichrist and *his* kingdom."[65] Although the seventh trumpet will mark the doom of Antichrist and his supporters, it will be "a kind of *jubilee*-trumpet," announcing the time of the church's "enlargement and deliverance from captivity."[66]

8. Second Beast Same as Little Horn.—Holding the woman of Revelation 12 to be the church, and the man-child to be Christ Jesus, Jones applies the dragon to Imperial Rome.[67] The two beasts of Revelation 13 he believes to be the secular and ecclesiastical aspects of Antichrist,[68] the second beast being the same as Daniel's Little Horn,[69] with its "terrible engine of antichristian tyranny," the spiritual courts of the Inquisition.[70]

9. Papal Babylon Is Ecclesiastical Rome.—In Revelation 17 the seven mountains upon which the fallen church sits are the seven forms of government,[71] and the ten horns are the same ten kingdoms of the divided Rome of the former chapters.[72] Jones then ties together the whole picture of the multiple symbols of Antichrist in this one comprehensive statement:

[62] *Ibid.*, pp. 310, 311.
[63] *Ibid.*, p. 332.
[64] *Ibid.*, p. 378.
[65] *Ibid.*, pp. 368, 369.
[66] *Ibid.*, p. 379.
[67] *Ibid.*, p. 401.
[68] *Ibid.*, p. 426.
[69] *Ibid.*, p. 427.
[70] *Ibid.*, p. 429.
[71] *Ibid.*, p. 510.
[72] *Ibid.*, p. 511.

"Can we be at any loss, then, in recognizing Daniel's little horn, and Paul's Man of sin, in the woman enthroned in the midst of the mystical Babylon? What ecclesiastical domination has Rome ever known, save that of the papacy? What heresy has ever so copied the trappings of the harlot, or so beguiled the rulers and the people of the earth into the practice of irreligious and idolatrous devices? The name engraven on the brow of christian Rome, as it is called, and engraven alike by history and prophecy, is 'Mystery, Babylon the great, the mother of harlots, and of the abominations of the earth!!' " [73]

Jones' understanding of prophecy gave new meaning to his church history and led him to seek for hidden features that otherwise would have passed unnoticed. Contrariwise, his familiarity with church history made his expositions of prophecy more sound and clear than were those without such a background. Thus knowledge enhanced knowledge.

---

[73] *Ibid.*, p. 514.

CHAPTER TWENTY-SEVEN

Irving's Contribution
Marred by "Utterances"

I. Irving—Brilliant Triumphs End in Tragic Shadows

EDWARD IRVING (1792-1834), most colorful figure in the British Advent Awakening, was born in west Scotland. Brilliant in schoolwork and religiously inclined, he attended the Presbyterian seceders church in his boyhood. He was graduated from the Edinburgh University in 1809, and became master of the mathematical school at Haddington in 1810, while studying for the ministry. In 1812 he was made master of a newly established academy at Kirkcaldy, and it was there that he formed close friendship with Thomas Carlyle, who had been called to head an opposing school. In 1815 Irving obtained a license to preach, but in 1818 he resigned his schoolwork and repaired to Edinburgh, where he continued his studies, his favorite being church history.

In 1819 he found another opportunity to preach, and soon Dr. Joseph Chalmers arranged for Irving to be his associate at St. John's, Glasgow, where he was ordained. Feeling himself entirely eclipsed by Chalmers, Irving accepted an invitation to a chapel in Hatton Garden, London, in 1822.[1] Piety was his outstanding characteristic; fasting and prayer, his habit. Deep sympathy and understanding of their joys and sorrows endeared him to his people. He was ever the minister, ever the ambassador for God.

[1] *Fraser's Magazine,* January, 1835 (vol. 11, no. 61), pp. 99-103; *Dictionary of National Biography,* vol. 10, pp. 489-493.

Irving's oratory, plus his good reputation from Glasgow, soon filled the little chapel with the most brilliant members of London society.[2] It was there that Drummond was attracted to him. Crowds flocked to hear Irving. Men of letters and rank attended. The seats were occupied for hours in advance, with admission by ticket only. The speaker was tall and stately, with bushy black hair hanging down in ringlets. He possessed a deep voice with a broad Scotch accent and had a solemn manner and impressive gestures. From the very first a tone of authority

London's Famous Regent Square Presbyterian Church Echoed to the Prophetic Expositions of the Distinguished Pulpit Orator Edward Irving

characterized his preaching. Just at this time the fervor of the great Advent Awakening was spreading, and the events of the French Revolution were regarded generally as a fulfillment of prophecy. The impending end of the world was anticipated,[3] and the advent note rose from many a pulpit. Though interested earlier in the prophecies concerning the advent, Irving's entire absorption in them dates from 1826, when he became

[2] Robert Baxter, *Irvingism, in Its Rise, Progress, and Present State* (2d ed.), p. 5.
[3] Edward Miller, *The History and Doctrines of Irvingism*, vol. 2, pp. 2-5.

acquainted with Lacunza's book on the coming of Christ and resolved to translate it.

Irving had a revulsion against the narrow ecclesiasticism of his day. He yearned for a mighty cure for the grievous diseases of the world. The first result of this concern was a three-hour sermon preached before the Continental Society, and published in 1826 under the title *Babylon and Infidelity Foredoomed of God*. It was a popularization of Frere's expositions in his *Combined View*.

Meantime Irving's congregation had grown to be large and wealthy, and was housed in a new church in Regent Square.[4] There a thousand persons packed the church Sunday after Sunday to hear Irving's extended expositions of prophecy. In 1828 he undertook a tour of Scotland to proclaim the imminence of the advent. The overcrowded galleries of the largest churches could not accommodate the crowds, where he was heard with enthusiasm. The people of Edinburgh came out to hear him at five o'clock in the morning. At Holywood and Dunscourse he preached to open-air congregations of 10,000 to 12,000.[5] Early in 1829 *The Morning Watch*, the quarterly journal on unfulfilled prophecy, was established by members of the Albury Conference.

Another journey to Scotland followed in 1830. But Irving's tract on *The Orthodox and Catholic Doctrine of our Lord's Human Nature* (1830) brought charges of heresy. Irving stopped his writing and with weeping and prayer examined his heart anew. But he was persuaded of his own soundness. Then the "unknown tongues" were first manifest in his congregation in October, 1831. The discourse was interrupted by an outbreak of the "utterances." Controversy developed over the origin of the phenomenon—whether of divine or demonic possession. The attempted prosecution for heresy in December, 1830, had led to Irving's withdrawal from the jurisdiction of the London Presbytery. But he was soon removed from his pulpit

[4] See John Hair, *Regent Square, Eighty Years of a London Congregation*, and J. C. S. Brough, *The Centenary of Regent Square, 1827-1927*.
[5] Washington Wilks, *Edward Irving*, pp. 188, 189, 203.

by the church trustees, in 1832.[6]   The larger part of the congregation—about 800—adhered to him and were forced to seek temporary quarters.   They then formed the "Holy Catholic Apostolic Church," popularly known as the Irvingite church.

Irving was deprived of his status as a clergyman in the Church of Scotland after an ecclesiastical trial in 1833, by the presbytery of Annan, on the charge of heresy.   After traveling in Scotland, preaching to crowds in the open air, he returned to London to find himself suspended, virtually deposed by his own congregation, and occupying a minor position.   His health declined rapidly, and he died in Glasgow in 1834.   All the ministers of Glasgow attended his funeral service, as that of a minister of Christ.

He was one of the pre-eminent Christians of his time, with a spirit of humility, consecration, and spiritual perception which most of his contemporaries neither possessed nor were capable of assessing.   He was "other worldly" but never a fanatic.[7]   His humility and his tolerance betrayed him into allowing, and in some degree countenancing, the excesses into which some of his followers ran.   His oversolicitude led him to fear to grieve the Holy Spirit, which he thought might have inspired the "tongues" and the healing.   But he himself never "spoke with tongues" nor assumed to heal by magnetic power.[8]

The Irvingite church still survives, with a fine Gothic structure built by Drummond in 1854.   Irving was one of the most striking ecclesiastical figures of his generation, of high character, and exempt from every taint of charlatanism.[9]

---

[6] *The Trial of the Rev. Edward Irving*, pp. 87, 88 (A shorthand report).
[7] See Lillian W. Kelley, "Edward Irving, . . . a Portrait," *The Journal of the Presbyterian Historical Society of England*, May, 1932 (vol. 5, no. 1), pp. 21-30.
[8] Thomas Carlyle was Irving's friend, and wrote: "One who knew him well, and may with good cause love him, has said: 'But for Irving, I had never known what the communion of man with man means.   His was the freest, brotherliest, bravest human soul mine ever came in contact with: I call him, on the whole, the best man I have ever (after trial enough) found in this world, or now hope to find.' "   ("Death of the Rev. Edward Irving," *Critical and Miscellaneous Essays*, vol. 4, p. 82.)   But Carlyle's eulogy did more to damage Irving's reputation than the attacks of his foes.
   A fine tribute to Irving was paid by the Presbytery of London North a century after his death.   "Edward Irving was a man misled by false lights; but he was not himself false to what he believed to be the light.   He was deceived; but he was not dishonest.   He listened to voices which were not of truth; but he was sincere when he declared that he was condemned because he 'refused to allow the voice of the Spirit of God to be silenced.' "   (*Presbyterian Messenger*, December, 1934.)   See also Jean C. Root, *Edward Irving, Man, Preacher, Prophet.* (Picture appears on p. 515.)
[9] *Fraser's Magazine*, January, 1835 (vol. 11, no. 61), pp. 99, 100.

II. Providences Behind the Translation of Lacunza

The Lacunza, or Ben-Ezra, volume—*La Venida del Mesias en Gloria y Magestad*—printed in Cádiz, Spain, during the brief period of freedom enjoyed under the government of the Cortes, was suppressed as soon as the Inquisition recovered its power. In 1816 a large Spanish edition was printed in England for circulation in South America exclusively, with no copies retained in England. Later Agier's abridgment could be had in France, where Lewis Way, the English clergyman in Paris, saw it.

Meanwhile a Church of England clergyman who was laboring in Spain brought back a copy of an early edition to England. It became the subject of correspondence among the persons afterward assembled and represented at the Albury Park Conference, and plans were laid to translate portions of it into English.

While this was going on, Lewis Way, who for some time "standing in his watchtower" in his English pulpit in Paris, had been "crying aloud the Advent truth," came to England to regain his health. Hearing of the prophetic sermons of Irving, who on Christmas, 1825, had begun to preach regularly on the second advent, he asked a friend to take notes on Irving's messages and give them to him for study. It so happened that this friend was the very one who had much to do with the revision of the partial translations of Lacunza. So the notes of Irving's discourses and the pages of Lacunza often met on the same table in London, on their way to their different destinations. Noting the substantial agreement of the two, this friend brought the "Ben-Ezra" volume to Irving, who had been studying Spanish. Irving was gripped by its clear message, and determined that it should be translated in entirety. Recognizing it as a master work, he sought to learn the identity of "Ben-Ezra, a Hebrew Christian." Then Way came to London and met Irving. Discussing the theme of mutual interest, Way told of the great treatise of the Spanish Jesuit Lacunza, which he had seen only in

the French abridgment, while Irving related the plans for translating Ben-Ezra.   To the surprise of both, the information
arrived that Ben-Ezra was none other than Lacunza.[10]

Then an unexpected opportunity came to Irving. Grieving
over the recent death of his child, and being none too well, he
was urged by his congregation to take a summer's rest in the
country.   The two opportunities joined, and resulted in his
undertaking the full translation.

He "prevented the dawning of the morning," and ended his
task for the day only when the shades of evening made further
work impossible.[11]   When his eyes and hands failed, his wife
became eyes and hands for him.   Thus they labored to make it
their 1826 Christmas offering for the church.[12] Just before he
finished the translation, he obtained a copy of the more accurate
1826 Ackermann edition, which enabled him to collate it with
the 1812 edition.[13]

It was while engaged in the translation of Lacunza's book
that Irving was invited to the Albury Park Prophetic Conference, where the participants decided to combine their forces
and convert a guerrilla warfare into a more general or regular
campaign.[14]   This "worthy old Jesuit," as Irving denominates
Lacunza, was one of God's people in the midst of Babylon.[15] And
this was the more impressed upon Irving as he had come to sense
the "antichristian condition of most, I had almost said all, the
Protestant churches abroad." [16]

Irving began the dedication of his English translation with
the expression of this soul burden:

"My soul is greatly afflicted because of the present unawakened and
even dead condition of all the churches, with respect to the coming of our
Lord Jesus Christ, which draweth nigh, and which, as I believe, is close
at hand." [17]

He then told how he felt it his duty to translate this Spanish
volume that demonstrated from Scripture "the erroneousness

[10] Edward Irving, "The Translator's Preliminary Discourse," in *The Coming of Messiah*
(his English version of Lacunza's *La Venida*), vol. 1, pp. xvi-xx.
[11] Wilks, *op. cit.*, pp. 273-275.
[12] Edward Irving, "Preliminary Discourse."   [15] Irving, *op. cit.*, p. xxiii.
[13] *Ibid.*, p. xxi.   [16] *Ibid.*, p. xxiv.
[14] Miller, *op. cit.*, vol. 1, pp. 28, 29.   [17] *Ibid.*, p. i.

of the opinion, almost universally entertained amongst us."
In his early study and preaching, Irving had paid little attention
to the prophecies of the advent. Then his eyes were opened, but
he deliberated further for months, to be sure he was not in error.
His first book, *Babylon and Infidelity Foredoomed of God,* in
1826, was the result of his study.[18] Then having "broken
ground," he felt it necessary to take strong defensive positions.
Among these was the belief that "the first droppings" of the
latter rain were discerned in the religious revivals of recent
years.[19]

Irving's translation of Lacunza was published in 1827. By
the summer of 1829 he had written a second volume, on *Daniel,*
and had helped to launch *The Morning Watch.*

III. Interpretation of Symbols and Time Prophecies

1. FIRST BLOW STRUCK FOR BABYLON'S FALL.—In *Babylon
and Infidelity Foredoomed of God,* which was dedicated to
J. Hatley Frere, Irving tells frankly how he became Frere's pupil,
"to be instructed in prophecy according to your ideas thereof." [20]
Delivered originally before an annual Continental Society
meeting, this lengthy address shows the progress of infidelity,
rising upon the ruins of superstition. Irving holds that infidelity was the instrument striking the "first blow of Babylon's fall,"
thirty-three years before (in 1793), with both destined to fall
together in the "approaching battle of Armageddon." [21]

Irving contends that "this is that generation, and this is
that time" to "address the Church concerning many other things
connected with the second coming of the Lord," of which "she
is utterly oblivious," and he appeals to his brethren in the ministry to make it their "most serious and solemn consideration." [22]

2. WIDESPREAD EXPECTATION OF ADVENT.—At the beginning of his discourse Irving makes this statement about the gen-

[18] *Ibid.,* pp. iii, iv.
[19] *Ibid.,* p. v.
[20] Edward Irving, *Babylon and Infidelity Foredoomed of God,* vol. 1, p. vi.
[21] *Ibid.,* p. xii.   [22] *Ibid.,* pp. xii, xiii.

eral expectation among students of prophecy concerning the impending papal downfall and the second advent.

"The Papacy no sooner arose out of the bishopric of Rome, than the true Church at once recognized it to be the beast of the Apocalypse, and testified against it, with a more uniform consent than in these accommodating days we are willing to do. And now that the downfal of that power is hard at hand, which is the next great event of revelation, there is beginning to prevail a great consent among the exact interpreters of prophecy concerning the same, and a constant expectation amongst the spiritual, of the second coming of the Lord, which is to follow." [23]

3. GENERAL CONSENT CONCERNING PAPAL HORN.—In Irving's comments on the "four main streams" of Daniel's prophecy—Daniel 2, 7, 8, and 11—each is set forth as adding details to the others.[24] The four kingdoms of Daniel 7 are universally recognized. And this "universal consent" involves identification of the Little Horn as "the PAPAL POWER, which arose at the time that the Roman empire split into ten kingdoms." [25] The 1260 days are also by common consent recognized as being years of papal supremacy over the saints. They must begin after the appearance of the ten, with Justinian's Code in A.D. 533.[26] Much evidence is adduced to establish this initial date. From that time "great strides towards absolute supremacy" followed.[27]

4. 1260 YEARS DATED FROM 533 TO 1792.—Irving holds that there can be no reasonable doubt as to the 533 beginning of the 1260 years, and he asserts repeatedly that they ended in 1792, through the French Revolution.[28] He believes that the 1290 years extend thirty years beyond 1792-93, and that the 1335 years terminate another forty-five years beyond that date. All periods of trouble would then end, at which time the blessing of the earth would be fully come.[29] The seven trumpets are given the usual application—the first four to the barbarian invasions, and the Saracens and Turks as the fifth and sixth woe trumpets on the Eastern Empire.[30] The seven vials are likewise interpreted as having begun with the French Revolution.[31]

---

[23] *Ibid.*, vol. 1, p. 26.   [25] *Ibid.*, pp. 57-60.   [27] *Ibid.*, pp. 110, 111.
[24] *Ibid.*, pp. 49-51.   [26] *Ibid.*, pp. 75-82, 86.
[28] *Ibid.*, pp. 114, 115, 127, 132, 150, 165, 216.   [30] *Ibid.*, pp. 195, 196.
[29] *Ibid.*, pp. 174, 175, 253, 257.   [31] *Ibid.*, pp. 220-249.

5. 2400 YEARS FROM 553 B.C. TO A.D. 1847.—On Daniel 8:14, Irving follows his mentor, Frere, in preferring the 2400 of the Septuagint to the 2300 of the Hebrew. This period he begins with the alleged date of the vision, which he puts at 553 B.C., with the 2400 years terminating in 1847. He connects with this the conversion of the Jews.[32] So he says:

"Therefore we adopt the reading of the Septuagint, and expect that true worship will be restored in Jerusalem in the year 1847. And if true worship be restored in Jerusalem at that time, we know that the Jews, as a people, must have been restored before that time, and not only restored, but converted." [33]

The pollution of the sanctuary is from the Arabian imposture, Mohammedanism, which power is already beginning to break.[34]

6. ENDS 1290 IN 1823; 1335 IN 1867.—Irving likewise ends the 1290 years in 1823,[35] and the 1335 years in 1867.[36] This conclusion stirs Irving deeply, as he exclaims:

"How near is this! Within the lifetime of a man—to this generation— to thine own children, O reader!—perhaps to thine own self—to these eyes which now direct this pen that writes." [37]

7. JUDGMENT HOUR THE CLIMACTIC SIGN.—The signs foretold "even now have passed," or may be seen "passing, before us" [38]—the scourging of the ten kingdoms, the Man of Sin in rags and tatters, the Turk about to be deprived of his power, the decay of faith among Protestants.[39] Finally, as the climax of all the signs, Irving leads up to this dramatic declaration concerning the flying angel of Revelation 14:6, 7:

"The angel of the ministry of the Gospel, who, as he flies, continueth to say with a loud voice, 'Fear God, and give glory to him; for the hour of his judgment is come.' The day of his wrath, is the years from the ending of the Papal period till the coming of Christ; the hour of his judgment, is the very coming of Christ; and when the angel of the seventh vial hath emptied his vial, the great voice comes forth from the midst of heaven's throne, saying, 'It is done;' or, The end is come. Wherefore, we surely conclude, that, if the angel hath well nigh finished his circuit through the

32 Ibid., pp. 258, 259; vol. 2, pp. 222-225.
33 Ibid., vol. 1, p. 259.
34 Ibid., vol. 2, pp. 222, 223.
35 Ibid., p. 215.
36 Ibid., pp. 218, 219.
37 Ibid., pp. 225, 226.
38 Ibid., p. 242.
39 Ibid., pp. 272, 273.

heavens, and the Holy Scriptures have been well nigh translated into all languages, the hour of God's judgment is come, and the end of all these things is at hand." [40]

8. PERIODS END WITHIN GENERATION LIVING.—In his *Last Days,* issued in 1828, Irving contends that the world has indeed reached the last days. He dwells on the prophesied characteristics of the time and the time periods of Daniel—the 1260 years of the papal period, the 1290, and the 1335.[41] Then he says:

"There can be little doubt that the one thousand two hundred and sixty days concluded in the year 1792, and the thirty additional days in the year 1823, we are already entered upon the last days, and the ordinary life of a man will carry many of us to the end of them." [42]

Then follows an allusion to the "four successive monarchies" of Daniel 2 and the destruction of them by the "fifth monarchy of Messiah,"—the stone smiting the image.[43]

9. THE LITTLE HORN IS THE PAPACY.—Irving's bulky *Exposition of the Book of Revelation in a Series of Lectures* (1831) is largely in the field of spiritual lessons, with little historical exposition. Only occasional references appear. Thus, after alluding to the three former beasts of Daniel 7, Irving refers to the "destruction of the fourth beast, or Western Roman Empire, into the ten Gothic kingdoms subsisting, that is, Papal Europe, with fiery judgment, because of its obedience to that usurper of Divine dignities, the Pope, symbolized by the little horn." Then he discusses the "activity of God, in human affairs," and God's "purpose at length to give the kingdoms unto the Son of Man." [44]

10. TWO BEASTS SYMBOLIZE ROME IMPERIAL AND PAPAL.— In discussing the sequence and characteristics of the seven churches, Irving leads from pagan Rome on through papal Rome. Satan's earlier efforts against the Christian church were succeeded by the period of Thyatira, as Satan gave his power,

---

[40] *Ibid.,* p. 295.
[41] Edward Irving, *The Last Days; A Discourse on the Evil Character of These Our Times,* pp. 22-24.
[42] *Ibid.,* p. 24.   [43] *Ibid.,* pp. 24, 25.
[44] Edward Irving, *Exposition of the Book of Revelation,* p. 237 (pagination continues through four volumes bound as two).

seat, and authority to the beast.[45]   The two beasts of Revelation
13 are the two phases of Rome, imperial and papal, the latter
the image of the former.   This chapter presents the "full-length
portraiture and completed form" of Antichrist.[46]

11. ADULTERESS SPOUSE IS APOSTATE CHURCH.—In a later
portrayal of the perversion of the church, Irving contrasts the
"chaste and beautiful spouse of Christ," of Revelation 12, who
fled into the wilderness to escape the persecution of the Beast
for the 1260 years, with the seduced church exhibited in the
"base concubine" and the "adultress spouse" of the kings of the
earth, drunk with the blood of saints.   Such is the "transfiguration of the church"—"the transition from the state of the
church of Smyrna to the state of the church of Thyatira." [47]   This
is the "great apostasy into which the ten kingdoms of the Western Roman Empire" have fallen.[48]   The exposition breaks off at
this point.

IV. Acceptance of Utterances Deception Brings Eclipse

Between 1828 and 1834 Great Britain was deeply stirred
by the Advent Awakening.   Palestine seemed in the process of
being liberated from the Turkish yoke, and men thought the
way would thus be opened for the anticipated return of the Jews.
Meantime Irving and others laid stress on the restoration of the
gifts of the Spirit before the end, and held that bodily infirmity,
as a direct infliction of Satan, was to be healed by faith and
prayer.   He was therefore greatly interested in the formation of
the brotherhood organized in 1827 by J. Haldane Stewart, following publication of his tract urging united prayer that there
might be a fresh outpouring of the Holy Spirit.

During Irving's extensive tours throughout his native Scotland, chiefly to proclaim the near advent and to urge the necessary preparation, he won the three Bonars at Edinburgh.   Horatius Bonar (1808-1889) was then but twenty-one.   In Scotland
premillennialism was strange and unwelcome to the Scottish

---

[45] *Ibid.*, p. 540.   [47] *Ibid.*, p. 615.
[46] *Ibid.*, pp. 540, 541.   [48] *Ibid.*, p. 618.

churchmen of the day, and a stigma was attached to all who received the doctrine. But Horatius disseminated the doctrine by voice and pen, and was for years editor of *The Quarterly Journal of Prophecy*. His poetical contributions were so numerous that he was styled the "hymnist of the advent." Andrew Bonar wrote *Redemption Drawing Nigh*.

Irving had meantime developed the view that Christ came in fallen and sinful flesh, with like appetites and desires, and that the work of the Spirit was to subdue and keep under all the motions of the flesh, which it effectually did. And this very work, he reasoned, the Holy Spirit is to do in man until he is made entirely free from sin. Coupled with this was the belief that the full and miraculous gifts of the Spirit ought to abide in the church, and men fail to possess them only from want of faith, and that they should pray earnestly and continually for these gifts. This position provoked attacks upon Irving from all quarters,[49] and discussions of spiritual gifts in both periodicals and books, by such men as M'Neile, Pym,[50] Noel, and Leslie.

These considerations now formed the continual theme of his discourses. And it was at this juncture that the "utterances" appeared, first in Scotland and then in London, in 1831, and were received as the gift of prophecy.[51] During Irving's first tour of Scotland some young women had been healed by prayer.[52] Later when supernatural manifestations began to appear, they claimed to have the gift of tongues. A favorable report from a delegation of Irving's congregation[53] led to the organization of meetings to seek the restoration of the gifts.

Despair of the world's conversion by the ordinary methods of evangelization, and the expectation of supernatural manifestations as a prelude to Christ's second advent, laid the foundation for acceptance.[54] From the union of these several factors the

---

[49] Robert Baxter, *op. cit.*, p. 8.
[50] *The Morning Watch*, June, 1832 (vol. 5, no. 2), pp. 430-440; also September, 1832 (vol. 6, no. 1), pp. 222-224.
[51] Baxter, *op. cit.*, p. 10.
[52] *The Christian Observer*, November, 1830 (vol. 30, no. 347), pp. 708, 709.
[53] *The Morning Watch*, September, 1830 (vol. 2, no. 3), pp. 659-664; December, 1830 (vol. 2, no. 4), pp. 869-873.
[54] Wilks, *op. cit.*, p. 203.

Catholic Apostolic Church came forth. When Irving heard of Scottish women speaking in unknown tongues, he thought of the disciples on the day of Pentecost and suspected no travesty of the repetition of that wondrous story. Several influential members of Irving's congregation went to Scotland to examine the evidence.[55] The leader brought back a good report, and Irving failed to detect imposture.[56]

Entirely new arrangements in Irving's congregation were introduced by direction of the utterances, and the ministry of "angels," "apostles," "prophets," and "elders" was recognized. Unleavened bread was substituted for leavened in the communion service. Irving was directed by these voices to suspend his ministry until his reordination in 1833. Drummond was made not only an angel of the church and one of the twelve apostles, but both Drummond and Bayford were among the prophets, with Irving only an angel. Prayer meetings were held every morning at six o'clock—including the winter season.[57] The utterances were regarded as the gifts of prophecy, and gifts of healing were also claimed.[58] His congregation and his best friends having forsaken him, the last five years of Irving's life were cast in deepening shadows, and he died of tuberculosis and a broken heart in 1834.

V. Baptist Noel Discusses the Phenomenon

1. MIRACULOUS GIFTS WITHDRAWN FOR CENTURIES.—In 1831, at the time of the "tongues" manifestation in Irving's church, which became the theme of considerable discussion in religious circles, Baptist Noel wrote *Remarks on the Revival of Miraculous Powers in the Church.* He was then minister of St. John's Chapel, Bedford Row. In this he contended that "miraculous powers have for many ages been withdrawn from the church." He said that supernatural answers to prayer had

---

[55] *Ibid.,* p. 204; Miller, *op. cit.,* p. 61; *The Morning Watch,* December, 1830 (vol. 2, no. 4), pp. 869-873.
[56] *The Morning Watch,* September, 1830 (vol. 2, no. 3), pp. 659-664; December, 1830 (vol. 2, no. 4), p. 850 ff.
[57] Baxter, *op. cit.,* pp. 11-16.
[58] *Ibid.,* pp. 17-25.

often occurred as the "immediate and sovereign work of God," but that this was "totally distinct from the effect of a gift to be habitually exercised by men." In apostolic days the miraculous powers were constantly exercised. But for centuries any miracles had been "insulated cases," "wrought immediately by God," and not "systematically," with men receiving the power to work them.[59]

2. ARGUMENT FROM JOEL 2 EXAMINED.—Discussing the argument from Joel 2:28, 29, Noel refers to the partial fulfillment at Pentecost but stresses the fact that it was not universal, though the text might seem to imply it.[60] Not all received the gift of prophecy, but it was limited to "some." [61] The promise was therefore limited, and not unconditional. Stressing the fact also that the early gifts were limited to the gifted persons, Noel shows that among the most eminent Christians of the centuries—the Waldenses, Wyclif, Huss, Luther, Calvin, Bullinger—none believed miraculous gifts were operative in their day.[62] Only "Roman-Catholic traffickers in wonders" were the exception.[63]

3. DELUDED BY RELIGIOUS EXCITEMENT.—Noel felt that nothing, therefore, in the history of the gifts, in the promises of Scripture, or in the circumstances of the church warranted the position now taken by some. What they called faith was more properly called "enthusiasm." [64] Not denying the possibility, he nevertheless declined to accept the so-called "gift of tongues," for God "never yet set the seal of miracles to error." The "foreign tongues spoken in the primitive church were always intelligible to the speakers," [65] were a sign to unbelievers, and none exercised the gift of tongues without an interpretation. Noel therefore concluded:

"All that has happened, therefore, among these pious persons, so far from justifying an expectation of the gifts, only proves how completely even the most pious persons may be deluded by an enthusiastic excitement. I am very far from the disposition to hold them up to scorn, feeling more

---

[59] Baptist W. Noel, *Remarks on the Revival of Miraculous Powers in the Church*, p. 3.
[60] *Ibid.*, p. 10.   [62] *Ibid.*, pp. 16-18.   [64] *Ibid.*, p. 28.
[61] *Ibid.*, pp. 10, 11.   [63] *Ibid.*, pp. 18, 19.   [65] *Ibid.*, p. 29.

sympathy with an honest though hurtful enthusiasm, than I can with a sour and supercilious orthodoxy." [66]

VI. Stewart—Everlasting Gospel Angel Now Flying

JAMES HALDANE STEWART (1776-1854), English theologian and writer, and rector of Limpsfield, Surrey, was born in Boston, Massachusetts. He was educated at Exeter College, Oxford, receiving a B.A. in 1806 and an M.A. in 1811. From 1812 to 1830 he served as minister of Percy Chapel, then was vicar of Great Ouseburne and curate of St. Bridget, Liverpool, from 1830 to 1846.[67] He was also chaplain to the Marquis of Bute and the Earl of Breadalbane. Stewart was a participant in the 1826 Albury Park Prophetic Conference,[68] having written in 1825 *A Practical View of the Redeemer's Advent*. His *Watchfulness Against the Dangers of the Present Times* was based on the former.

1. FIVE VIALS OUTPOURED IN FRENCH REVOLUTION.—Stewart's *Practical View of the Redeemer's Advent* was originally given as a series of discourses. In one of these, entitled "Reasons for Expecting," in discussing the seven last plagues, or vials, of wrath, he holds that "five of these vials of the wrath of God were poured out during the late [French] revolutionary war; and that we are now entering upon the sixth vial." [69] In support he invites candid comparison of the "striking similarity" of symbolical language of the vials and the dreadful calamities of the period. These he looks upon as "tremendous judgments falling upon the men which had the 'mark of the beast,' or upon Papal countries." [70]

2. SIXTH VIAL EXHAUSTION OF TURKEY.—The "river Euphrates" of the sixth vial, Stewart holds to be "the symbol of the Turks, who are the followers and successors of Mohammed." In

[66] *Ibid.*
[67] Frederic Boase, *Modern English Biography*, vol. 6, suppl. 3, col. 623.
[68] Joshua W. Brooks, *Dictionary of Writers on the Prophecies*, p. lxxi; Boase, *op. cit.*, vol. 6, suppl. 3, col. 623.
[69] James Haldane Stewart, *A Practical View of the Redeemer's Advent*, p. 158; he cites "Faber, Gauntlett, and others."
[70] *Ibid.*

proof he alludes to "the rise of that people, in Rev. ix.14." [71] The drying up is the "gradual exhaustion of their power," the symbol being "taken from the literal drying up of the river Euphrates" when Cyrus entered Babylon. And this was to be so the "kings of the East" might be prepared—these being the "remnant of Judah and Israel." [72] Coupled with all this is the gathering of the world to the battle of the great day of God that is to "terminate the contest between God and all his enemies." [73]

3. INDICATES DAY OF JUDGMENT IMPENDS.—Stewart avers that the gradual exhaustion of Turkey is "at this moment accomplishing," every year seeing new defections among their tributary governments. Then he adds, "The late movements in Turkey lead many among them to conclude that the Day of Judgment is at hand; and they believe, that, before that day, Mohammedanism will be almost abolished." [74] The crescent is no longer the appropriate banner, but "a planet in the wane."

4. EVERLASTING GOSPEL ANGEL FLYING.—In discussing the flying angel of Revelation 14:7 with the judgment-hour message, Stewart says this "refers to the last times," though he thinks the "hour of his Judgment," means "temporal judgments upon His enemies," not the great day of judgment.[75] And these judgments synchronize with the wide and rapid preaching of the gospel, symbolized by the "*flying* in the midst of heaven." The "whole church of Christ is at this time in motion," whereas thirty years previously (1795) their missionary exertions were confined to two institutions: The Society for the Promotion of Christian Knowledge, and The Society for the Propagation of the Gospel.[76] Now forty-one societies exist for the single purpose of spreading the gospel of the kingdom.

5. 1260 YEARS OF PAPAL OPPRESSION.—In this same connection Stewart touches upon the 1260 years of the "papal power" as the "man of sin," which was to oppress the church of Christ,[77] for this long period, but likewise involving the Mohammedan power, which dates its acts from the year of the Hegira.

---

[71] *Ibid.*, p. 159.
[72] *Ibid.*
[72] *Ibid.*
[74] *Ibid.*, p. 162.
[75] *Ibid.*, pp. 170, 171.
[76] *Ibid.*, pp. 171, 172.
[77] *Ibid.*, pp. 176, 177.

VII. Gerard Noel—Smiting by the Stone Impends

GERARD THOMAS NOEL (1782-1851), of Richwood, English dissenting minister and writer, was educated at Edinburgh and at Trinity College, Cambridge, receiving his B.A. in 1805 and his M.A. in 1808. After taking orders he served as curate in several places. Later he left the Anglicans and joined the Baptists. He was a close friend of Wilberforce and wrote a number of books on prophecy.[78] Beginning with his sermon given before the London Society for Promoting Christianity Amongst the Jews (1810), and *The Day at Hand* (1818), he wrote *A Brief Enquiry into the Prospects of the Church . . . in Connexion with the Second Advent* (1828), *Extracts on Prophecy, Chiefly the Approaching Advent and Kingdom of Christ* (1835), *Lectures on points in the Controversy between Romanists and Protestants* (1836), and *Christian Missions to Heathen Nations* (1842).

1. HISTORY FORMS COUNTERPART OF PROPHECY.—Noel's *Brief Enquiry* deals with the premillennial establishment of the kingdom of Christ. Sharing the view of virtually all his associates, he declares that the image of Daniel 2 "foretells a succession of monarchies, the last of which, when broken into TEN parts, is smitten to shivers by the STONE cut out of the mountain." [79] The second vision, that of the four beasts, "foretells the same succession of FOUR monarchies," the same ten divisions and the "eleventh," and then depicts his work. These prophecies "no human hand could have traced, because no human mind could thus have pierced through the dark and interfolded veils of futurity." [80] Noel calls on the reader to compare the prophecy with the history, and to marvel at the accuracy.

2. STONE TO SMITE AMID PRESENT DIVISIONS.—After naming the four empires, and the ten divisions, and "the sanguinary Papacy," he declares that the judgment has already begun to sit, and the papal throne to totter as "the kingdom of the Son of God hastens to the hour of its manifestation, alike to the con-

---

[78] *Dictionary of National Biography*, vol. 14, pp. 536, 537.
[79] Gerard Thomas Noel (Philadelphia, 1840 ed.), *A Brief Enquiry*, p. 35.
[80] *Ibid.*

fusion of his foes, and to the joy and glory of his saints." [81] Such is the prophesied fifth monarchy. As to the designated time he adds:

"Let the wicked tremble; let the wicked mourn; let the wicked believe, repent, and live! Yet a little while, and these prophecies will attest the fidelity of Him who uttered them! Christian! the last tempest may soon gather around thee, but, 'be of good cheer.' 'Lift up thy head, for thy redemption draweth nigh.' " [82]

Concerning the time when the stone smites the Roman image, Noel declares:

"We find that the 'stone cut out from the mountain' does *not* smite *the legs* of the image, which *legs* represent the *unbroken* or *imperial* form of the Roman Empire, but it smites upon the *feet,* that is, upon the Roman Empire in its *divided state,* or when broken into the ten kingdoms. It is *'in the days of these kings'* that the stone smites the Roman image." [83]

3. RESURRECTION PRECEDES THE MILLENNIUM.—Noel boldly takes the position that the resurrection of the saints precedes the millennium, in order that the resurrected saints may reign with Christ during the thousand-year period.

4. 1260 YEARS, ENDING 1792, PRECEDE KINGDOM.—Having thus made an "outline of those great events which appear to lie depicted on the map of prophecy," [84] Noel comes to the "times and seasons," and the "chronology of the period, in which we live." According to Daniel 2, the advent will take place *"during the divided* state of the Roman Empire." [85] And according to Daniel 7, it will be after the period of the "spiritual despotism" of the Little Horn, its three and a half times, or 1260 days, or prophetic years.[86] After noting the parallel time periods in Revelation, Noel dates the 1260 years from the Justinian grant of 533, down to 1792. In support he quotes extensively from Cuninghame.[87]

5. CUMULATIVE SIGNS OF TIMES AND WORLD'S APATHY.— The cumulative signs of the time of Matthew 24 and Joel 2 he then portrays, with the "political convulsions" foretold. Last

---

[81] *Ibid.*, p. 36.
[82] *Ibid.*, pp. 36, 37.
[83] *Ibid.*, p. 37.
[84] *Ibid.*, p. 98.
[87] *Ibid.*, pp. 101, 102.
[85] *Ibid.*, p. 99.
[86] *Ibid.*

of all he alludes to that sealing message of the angel of Revelation 7, the "remnant of the election of his grace." [88]   These identify "the present time to be the hour of approaching mercy to the church, and of destruction to its foes." [89]   Noel then stresses the "insensibility of the world to the warning voice of Christ"—the scoffing of the days of Noah repeated.   Vividly he portrays the ancient scene:

"During one hundred and twenty years did the warning voice of God utter its mournful accents, and intreat a cessation in the work of ungodliness and sin.   The accents were scattered to the desert air; they reached no rebel heart of man.   The shortness of time, the approach of death, the brooding darkness of the gathering storm, interrupted not the career of sensuality, the progress of licentiousness, nor the noise of mirth.   They eat, they drank; 'the harp, and the viol, and the tabret, and melody, were in their feasts;' they formed alliances; they built up many a domestic dwelling-place; they coveted individual and national renown; but 'they regarded not the work of the Lord,' nor knew 'the operation of his hands.'   They ridiculed the prophetic record.   They smiled in idle scorn, while the Prophet built and surveyed his ark, an appointed refuge from the approaching wrath!   But the insensibility of man delayed not the purpose of God; the neglected warning cancelled not the recorded purpose; the mirth of the criminal arrested not the hand of the executioner; the horizon blackened; the tempest burst; and the human population lay buried beneath the waves!" [90]

---

[88] *Ibid.*, pp. 105-107.   [89] *Ibid.*, p. 107.   [90] *Ibid.*, pp. 109, 110.

CHAPTER TWENTY-EIGHT

Futurist Interpretation
Enters the Picture

A new and alien note is soon to be projected into the field of prophetic interpretation—the Futurist view of the prophecies concerning Antichrist. Prior to 1826 this Roman Catholic view, first set forth by Francisco Ribera to counter the Reformation exposition, had found no acceptance among Protestants. Now it is taken up by an Anglican, bringing confusion to some, but driving other students of prophecy to deeper examination of the basic principles of interpretation. Stalwarts soon arise to defend the standard Protestant principles of interpretation. But first note two further adherents to the Historical School view, who wrote in 1825.

I. Doctor Park—391-Year Turkish Woe Ends in 1844

JOHN R. PARK, M.D. (1778-1847), surgeon and theologian, was born in Liverpool. He received his M.D. from Jesus College, Cambridge, in 1818, and his F.R.C.S. in 1819. He delivered the Gulstonian Lectures in 1821, and not only wrote numerous works on medical science and the pathology of fever but produced several thoughtful treatises on prophecy.[1] In 1825 the "much enlarged" second edition of his *Concise Exposition of the Apocalypse, So Far as the Prophecies Are Fulfilled* appeared, with another edition in 1826. This was followed by his *Amicable Controversy with a Jewish Rabbi on Messiah's Coming*

---

[1] *Dictionary of National Biography*, vol. 15, p. 218.

(1832). In his preliminary *History of Christianity* Doctor Park epitomizes the history of Christianity, century by century, first tracing the rise of Mohammedanism in the East and then the course of the Papacy in the West.

1. Trumpets Involve Mohammedan Inroads.—Park stresses the "miracle of prophecy," but is especially concerned with the "three septenaries" of the seals, trumpets, and vials. The seals describe the "gradual corruption, and, at length, almost total extinction of true Christianity." The trumpets "treat of the rise, progress, and final establishment of the dominion" of the Eastern Antichrist.[2] Especially does he emphasize the 150 years of the Saracen and the 391 years of the Turk, established "on the ruins of Christianity in the East."[3]

2. Papacy in West; Mohammedan in East.—Touching upon the "seventh century," in the historical section, Park says:

"We have now reached an eventful period in the history of our religion, marked by two momentous occurrences, one, the establishment of the Papal hierarchy, and the other, the rise of Mahammedism. As these form the most prominent features in the picture of Antichristian domination, so they are distinguished in the prophetic history, by descriptions more minute and circumstantial than any others that occur." [4]

Park calls the alleged "prophet of God"—

"the most extraordinary enthusiast that had yet appeared upon earth; this was Mahomet, the founder of the religion which bears his name, and of the Saracen empire, which in the short space of 150 years, extended itself over the greater part of Asia, and no inconsiderable portion of Europe and Africa." [5]

3. Saracenic Inroads From 612 to 762.—As the prophetic interpretations are more comprehensive in the *Concise Exposition* section, we will pursue them there. The 150 years,

---

[2] John R. Park, *A Concise Exposition of the Apocalypse*, pp. 2, 3. "Prefixed" to or appearing first, within the same covers but with separate pagination is Park's 89-page combined *The History of Christianity Epitomised:* and *A Vocabulary of the Symbolical Language, With Scriptural Authority for Their Interpretation.* Their purpose was to "supply deficiencies" in the 108-page *Exposition* following, and to give opportunity for "other additions." (General preface, p. v.) The 1826 edition, titled *A New Exposition of the Apocalypse*, is identical in paging and content with the 1825 *A Concise Exposition of the Apocalypse*, the *Epitome* and *Vocabulary.*
[3] *Ibid.*
[4] John R. Park, *History of Christianity Epitomised*, p. 25.   [5] *Ibid.*, p. 26.

or five prophetical months of the Saracenic fifth trumpet, Park delimits as from 612 to 762.[6] Of this woe he says:

"The Saracens were alike armed for controversy and for battle, with the Koran and the sword. One was their breastplate in argument, the other gave them victory in war.

"The tail, as the noxious part, denotes their poisonous doctrine, by which they prevailed as much as by the sword. Their doctrine and dominion kept pace together for 150 years." [7]

He adds that Mohammedanism owed its rise to the "darkness and ignorance which enveloped the Christian world," and to the "corruptions which disfigured the pure religion of Jesus."

4. TURKISH 391 YEARS FROM 1453 TO 1844.—The Saracens paved the way for their Turkish successors. The 391-year period of domination over the Greek Empire, Park placed from 1453 to 1844. While the locusts torment, the horses kill; the gospel was banished; "the Koran alone remained." [8] The comparison of East and West is stated thus:

"These 1260 years of impure worship in the West, are cotemporaneous with a similar period already noticed in the East. If computed from the year 606, which seems to be most distinctly marked as the commencement of the papal hierarchy, it will terminate in 1866, by adding 1260 years; whereas the Eastern apostasy appeared destined to prevail from 612 to 1844. Thus the two will be almost exactly cotemporaneous." [9]

The Two Witnesses, Park adds incidentally in his comment, "mean the prophets of the Old and New Testament." [10]

5. BEAST'S REIGN PLACED FROM 606 TO 1866.—Coming to the ten-horned beast from the sea, Park says:

"The sea signifies the Western Gentiles; the beast an idolatrous, tyrannical empire; his horns are the kingdoms composing that empire; his heads are seven successive forms of government ruling over the empire." [11]

With the agility of a leopard, the grasp of a bear, and the bite of a lion, its power is derived from Satan, and Rome is the seat of the beast. The seven heads are kings, consuls, dictators, decemvirs, military tribunes, emperors, and popes. The horns

---

[6] John R. Park, A Concise Exposition of the Apocalypse, p. 22.
[7] Ibid., p. 23.   [9] Ibid., p. 32.   [11] Ibid., p. 42.
[8] Ibid., p. 26.   [10] Ibid., p. 33.

are the Machiavellian list. The dating of the reign of the beast is again put as 606-1866.[12]

6. TWO HORNS OF BEAST: TWO ORDERS OF CLERGY.—The two-horned beast from the land is similarly dated, and is defined as "the Romish ecclesiastical empire; nominally Christian, really Antichristian. Supported by two orders of clergy, monks and priests." [13]

7. FIFTH VIAL POURED OUT IN FRENCH REVOLUTION.— Advancing to the vials, Park dates the fifth vial from 1750 to 1800. He contends that it has fallen directly upon the throne of the beast, and avers it "can be no other than that terrible explosion of the French revolution." He then adds:

"The evils of this great convulsion, moral, political, and religious, have strikingly fulfilled the prophecy, and fallen upon the throne of the beast; for they have been almost exclusively visited upon those countries where the Romish faith predominated, as Italy, Austria, Spain, Portugal, and France." [14]

8. SIXTH VIAL SPELLS OTTOMAN FALL.—The sixth vial is placed from 1800 to 1850, and involved the "downfal of the Ottoman Empire."

"The drying up of the Euphrates, (in evident allusion to the dominion established by the Euphratean horsemen under the Sixth Trumpet), is a metaphor that appears singularly appropriate to the gradual manner in which the Ottoman Empire is now dwindling away. And as the Eastern and Western Apostacy arose at the same time, so it here appears that they are destined to fall together." [15]

9. WOMAN IN PURPLE IS LATIN CHURCH.—The woman of Revelation 17, in "gaudy attire and meretricious ornaments," and in striking contrast to the woman of Revelation 12 adorned with the "heavenly luminaries," is the "Latin Church." [16] The ten horns are the ten kingdoms, which were "not yet in existence" when the prophecy was given.[17]

Such is the comprehensive viewpoint of this prophecy-studying physician in this intensive time.

---

[12] *Ibid.*, pp. 42, 43.
[13] *Ibid.*, p. 46.
[14] *Ibid.*, p. 61.
[15] *Ibid.*, p. 62.
[16] *Ibid.*, p. 64.
[17] *Ibid.*, p. 65.

II. Cooper—Messages of Revelation 14 Follow 1792

EDWARD COOPER (1771-1833), rector of Ridgware and Yoxall, Stafford, was educated at All-Souls College, Oxford, from which he received a B.A. degree in 1792.[18] Cooper's *Crisis* was an attempt to show the "prospects and the duties" of the church in the light of the "signs of the times" and the "predicted desolations of the Papal Kingdoms."[19] The three English editions of Cooper's work are dated 1825 (2 eds.) and 1826, with an American edition in 1827. Prophecy had long been his favorite study.[20] Occasionally he wrote upon it in some periodical under an assumed name.

1. 1260 YEARS FROM 533 TO 1792.—A comprehensive chart visualizes Cooper's entire scheme.[21] He places the 1260 years from Justinian's edict in 533 to 1792—following William Cuninghame.[22] And the 1260 years under its various equivalents "exclusively refers to the domination of the Papal power in the Roman or Western Empire." Thus:

"It is during the 1260 years, that, according to Daniel, the saints were to be given into the hands of the little (Papal) Horn: and that, according to St. John, the Holy City was to be trodden down under foot of the Gentiles, and the two witnesses were to prophesy in sackcloth, and the woman was to be nourished in the wilderness, and the ten-horned beast was to continue to make war: all symbols of the depression of the true Church, and of the tyrannical power exercised over it in the Western empire."[23]

2. 2300 YEARS (UNDATED) ASSIGNED TO MOHAMMEDANISM. —But Cooper allocates the 2300 years to the "successive desolations of the Eastern empire and church by the Saracens and Turks."[24] While they have two separate assigned time periods (the 150 and 391 years), nothing, he feels, ties these in with the 2300 years, which he leaves undated, and the drying up of the Turkish Euphrates continues on apace. The 391 years Cooper dates from 1327, and terminates with the peace of Passarowitz in 1718.[25]

[18] *Alumni Oxonienses*, 1715-1886, vol. 1, p. 292.
[19] Edward Cooper, *The Crisis*, title page.
[20] *Ibid.*, preface, p. iii.   [22] *Ibid.*, p. vi.
[21] *Ibid.*, p. xvii.   [23] *Ibid.*, p. x.

[24] *Ibid.*
[25] *Ibid.*, pp. x-xii.

3. REASONS FOR DATING 1260 YEARS FROM 533.—Cooper holds that the period of the 1260 years, beginning under the Emperor Justinian, represented the duration of papal power and prosperity, not its total "existence." [26] He stresses the promulgation of Justinian's pronouncements not only to the Bishop of Rome but to the Patriarch of Constantinople, both of which documents recognize the pretensions of the former. These documents were "all unrolled at full length, by Justinian himself, in the volume of civil law; and thus obtained the stamp of public and legislative authority, as the laws of the Empire." [27] Thus it "may be justly considered that the Saints were virtually delivered into the hand of the Little Horn." [28]

4. OVER-ALL PICTURE OF PROPHECIES CHARTED.—The simplest way to grasp the Cooper over-all exposition of prophecy is to note his comprehensive "prophetical chart," measuring about sixteen by eighteen inches. To the left is a perpendicular column in which are listed from top to bottom, Daniel 2, 7, 8, 9, 10-12, and in Revelation the seals, trumpets, witnesses, vials, dragon and woman, and the two beasts. Running horizontally at right angles to this left column of the various prophecies, are segments representing the advancing centuries, with Babylon (603-539 B.C.), Persia (539-331), Grecia (331-167), and Rome, beginning 167 B.C., spanning the B.C. and A.C. centuries, with the 1260 years from 533 to 1792.

5. 1867 MADE THE GREAT FOCAL POINT.—The time of the end, Cooper says, is from A.D. 1792 + 30 years + 45, culminating in 1867, and introducing the millennium. Thus, under Daniel 2, running horizontally from the Babylonian head of gold, each subsequent division leads on to the next, with the stone smiting the image in 1867.[29] Thus 1867 is made the great focal point, the terminal date, for all prophetic lines. Similarly he has the corresponding four beasts of Daniel 7, the Little Horn wearing out the saints for the 1260 years (533 to 1792),

---

[26] Ibid., p. 27.
[27] Ibid., p. 31.
[28] Ibid.
[29] Ibid., chart facing p. xvii.

the taking away of his dominion in 1792, and the saints possessing the kingdom in 1867. Daniel 8 begins with the Persian ram, and follows with the Grecian goat, and the Mohammedan power trampling on Christianity and propagating its false religion by the sword,[30] taking away the daily and casting the sanctuary down, with the sanctuary cleansed by 1867.

6. 70 WEEKS (457 B.C.-A.D. 33); WILLFUL KING, NAPOLEON.—Daniel 9 starts the seventy weeks in 457 B.C., with Messiah cut off in A.D. 33. Daniel 11 is similarly carried through Persia, Grecia, and Rome, with Napoleon for Daniel 11:36, and the time of trouble followed by the time of blessedness in 1867. The latter chapters of the book are largely devoted to this proposition.

7. SARACENIC WOE (150 YEARS); TURKISH WOE (391 YEARS).—The seven seals cover the church dispensation. The seven trumpets are visitations upon the Roman Empire—the first four being the barbarian irruptions against Western Rome in 376, 395, 441, and 455. The fifth trumpet is the Saracenic attack on the Eastern Empire, 533-762, and the sixth is the Turkish conquests from 1327 to 1718 (the peace of Passarowitz),[31] as noted.

8. TWO BEASTS: SECULAR AND ECCLESIASTICAL ROME.— The woman in the wilderness is "the true church."[32] The two beasts of Revelation 13 constitute the secular and the ecclesiastical Roman power.[33]

9. MESSAGES OF REVELATION 14 FOLLOW 1792.—The three messages of Revelation 14, it is to be noted, are placed following 1792, representing the diffusion of the prophetic message on the approaching destruction of Antichristian Rome and the triumph of Christ's kingdom. The binding of Satan is placed in 1867, followed by the "progressive increase of real Christianity throughout the world: the Earth shall be filled with the Glory of the Lord."

---

[30] *Ibid.*, note 9 on chart.
[31] *Ibid.*, pp. xi, xii. These periods are shown on the chart.
[32] *Ibid.*, note 10 on chart.
[33] *Ibid.*, notes 81 and 82 on chart.

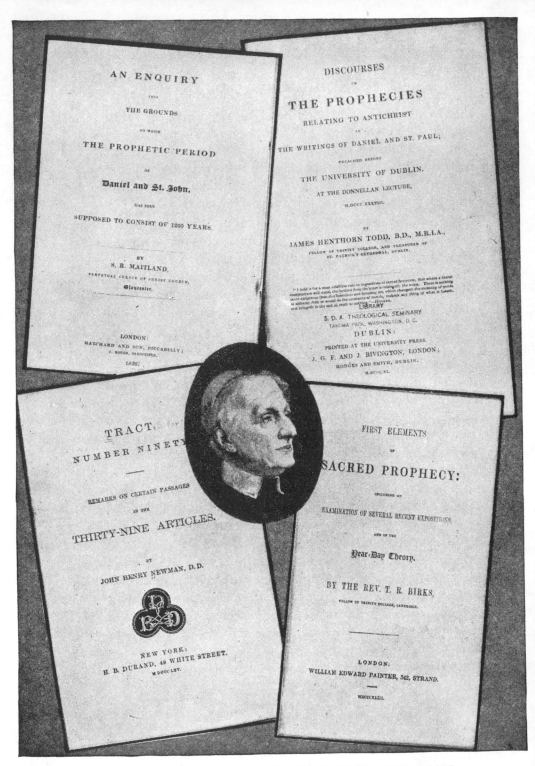

FUTURISM ATTACKS YEAR-DAY AND EXPLAINS ANTICHRIST

First Protestant Espousal of Ribera's Catholic Futurism by S. R. Maitland in 1826 (Upper Left) ; Supported by J. H. Todd's Treatise (Upper Right), Which Furnished the Covering Argument for the Retreat of J. H. Newman (Center Oval) Into Catholicism Through the Oxford Movement and Tractarianism (Lower Left); T. R. Birks Defends Historical Positions (Lower Right)

III. Maitland—Projector of Futurism Among Protestants

We now come to the first Protestant to accept the Riberan interpretation of Antichrist, SAMUEL R. MAITLAND (1792-1866), historical critic and author of some fifty books. Born in London, the child of nonconformist parents, he was mainly self-educated, though he attended St. Johns and Trinity College. He then studied law at Inner Temple. Though he abandoned the profession, his legal studies left an indelible impress upon his mind and method. In 1821 Maitland was admitted to deacons' orders, and in 1823 he became curate of Christ Church, Gloucester.

Toward the close of his incumbency at Christ Church, religious circles throughout England became deeply moved by Irving and others who were proclaiming an interpretation of prophecy based on the year-day principle. So in 1826 Maitland published a seventy-two-page pamphlet entitled *An Enquiry into the Grounds on which the Prophetic Period of Daniel and St. John, Has Been Supposed to Consist of 1260 Years.* This attracted considerable attention and initiated a "paper war" between the two schools of interpretation that continued for years.[34] (Title page reproduced on page 540.)

This was followed by *A Second Enquiry* (1829). Maitland also wrote *An Attempt to Elucidate the Prophecies Concerning Antichrist* (1830). As the issue involved the orthodoxy, or Protestantism, of the Waldenses and Albigenses that the historian Milner had claimed among the prophesied "Heavenly Witnesses" of the Middle Ages, Maitland produced an elaborate work, *Facts and Documents Illustrative of the History, Doctrine, and Rites of the Ancient Albigenses and Waldenses* (1830). It may be well to note that attacks on the Historical School of interpretation, with its year-day principle, have often been coupled with attacks on the Waldenses.[35] Meanwhile, Maitland had become deeply interested in the conversion of the Jews,

---

[34] *Dictionary of National Biography*, vol. 12, p. 816.
[35] This issue over the Waldenses is fully discussed in Volume 2 of *Prophetic Faith*.

and in 1828 he made an extensive journey throughout France, Germany, Prussia, Russia, and Poland to study their condition.

In 1835 Maitland began contributing monthly to the *British Magazine,* which articles eventuated in two volumes, one in 1844 entitled *The Dark Ages,* and the other *The Reformation in England.* In 1838 Archbishop Howley appointed him librarian and keeper of the manuscripts at Lambeth. This office afforded him opportunity for research, which resulted in his having the honorary degree of D.D. conferred upon him. He edited the *British Magazine* from 1839 to 1849.

Maitland incurred the deep dislike of the Evangelical party by his severe handling of their leaders and his merciless criticism of the historian Milner,[36] the martyrologist Foxe, and many others. He was often attacked in print,[37] and in turn took up the cudgels with William Cuninghame and others.[38] A. W. Hutton declared that his "keen critical instinct sometimes led him to an excessive historical scepticism." [39] It was inevitable that he should gain the ill will of the Evangelicals; he was also oddly the "object of suspicion to the Tractarians." [40] It should be noted that he had contempt for much of the general concept of the "Reformation as a religious movement." [41] His reactionary interpretations of prophecy follow.

1. Convinced the 1260 Are Natural Days.—In his 1826 *Enquiry,* Maitland took his stand against the vital year-day principle and flatly declared:

"After much consideration, I feel convinced that, '*the time, times, and dividing of time;* Dan. vii.25:' '*Time, times, and a half;*' Dan. xii.7: '*Time, times, and half a time;*' Rev. xii.14: '*Forty and two months;*' Rev. xi. ii—xiii.5: '*The thousand two hundred and threescore days;* Rev. xi.3: are not mystical phrases relating to a period of 1260 *years;* but, according to their plain meaning, denote a period of 1260 *natural days.*" [42]

---

[36] See Samuel R. Maitland, *A Letter . . . with Strictures on Milner's "Church History."*
[37] *Dictionary of National Biography,* vol. 12, p. 816.
[38] Samuel R. Maitland, *The 1260 Days,* in *Reply to the Strictures of William Cuninghame* (1834).
[39] Such as Samuel R. Maitland's *Reply to an Enquiry on . . . 1260 Years* (1828), *Letter to the Rev. Wm. Digby . . . on the 1260 days* (1831).
[40] Samuel R. Maitland, *Essays on Subjects Connected with the Reformation in England,* p. xi.
[41] *Ibid.,* p. xiv.
[42] Samuel R. Maitland, *An Enquiry into the Grounds on which the Prophetic Period of Daniel and St. John, Has Been Supposed to Consist of 1260 Years,* p. 2.

2. ROME'S DIVISIONS AND MOHAMMEDANISM NOT INVOLVED.
—Maitland maintains the position that the difficulties had arisen
from treating the prophecies of Daniel and St. John as "chronological" prophecies, fulfilling through the centuries. He asserts: "It appears to me that these predictions relate to things
which were still future," particularly the predictions of Antichrist.[43] He elaborates:

"I have no faith therefore in the applications of prophecy to the
ten Gothic kingdoms, or the delusions of Mahomet, the overthrow of
the French Monarchy, or the Turkish Empire. I believe that the Scripture
prophecies do not (unless it may be incidentally) throw any light on the
state of things either in the Church or in the world, before the breaking
out, or to say the utmost, the introductory circumstances, of the Apostasy.
The main subject is, I believe, the great and final conflict between the God
of heaven and the god of this world—between the Redeemer and the
Destroyer of man—between Christ and Antichrist." [44]

3. SAYS TERMS OF PROPHECY NOT MET BY POPE.—Maitland capitalizes upon the admitted variations among prophetic
interpreters on these time periods, and other details, and then
rejects them all. His favorite device is to play Faber against
other writers, thus to bring a question upon all. His *Second
Enquiry,* in 1829, includes remarks on an adverse review in
the *Christian Guardian,* and maintains that the pope does not
meet the terms of the prophecy.[45]

4. HOLDS FOURTH EMPIRE NOT ROME.—His *Attempt to
Elucidate the Prophecies Concerning Antichrist* was directed
against J. H. Frere. In this he plays the expectation of the early
church—which had no concept of the year-day principle for
the longer time periods—over against the Protestant Reformation interpretation, and rejects the application to the pope.[46]
Maitland denies that the fourth empire of Daniel 2 is Rome.[47]
And he makes the 2300 days literal time.[48]

But no sooner had this alien note been sounded than chal-
lengers arose, and stanch defenders of the old view took the

[43] Samuel R. Maitland, *An Attempt to Elucidate the Prophecies,* p. 3.
[44] *Ibid.,* p. 4.
[45] Samuel R. Maitland, *Second Enquiry,* p. 78.
[46] Samuel R. Maitland, *An Attempt to Elucidate the Prophecies,* pp. 2, 3.
[47] *Ibid.,* p. 8.   [48] *Ibid.,* p. 34.

field. Conflicts increased and cleavages became more pronounced with the passing years. It should be borne in mind that Futurism among Protestants was unknown in the Reformation and post-Reformation centuries. Only Catholics, who had introduced it, held it until now.

IV. Croly—Confines 1260 Years to Papacy (533-1793)

The first strong voice to be lifted against the Futurist innovation was that of GEORGE CROLY (1780-1860), Irish author and expositor. He was born in Dublin and educated at Trinity College, Dublin, where he distinguished himself as a classical scholar and public speaker. After receiving his M.A. degree he was ordained in 1804, and installed in a curacy in northern Ireland. The obscurity of his situation was distasteful to him, however, and he moved to London and devoted himself chiefly to literary pursuits. He became critic writer on the *New Times* and was a contributor to the *Literary Gazette* and *Blackwood's Magazine.*

The editor of the *Gazette* sought to procure Croly a church preferment, but his efforts failed, because Croly was confounded with a converted Roman Catholic priest of nearly the same name. Croly accordingly continued to devote himself to literature, producing *Paris in 1815, Angel of the World, May Fair* (1820), *Tales of St. Bernard,* (1822), and many others. His collected poems were published in 1830.[49] But his scholarly commentary on *The Apocalypse of St. John* was issued in the midst of it all—in 1827. Later, in 1848, as rector of the Church of St. Steven, Walbrook, he wrote *Popery the Antichrist.* In this, Croly took note of the serious attempt "of late" to "take the brand of Antichrist from Popery" by applying it either to the past or the future.[50] Then he epitomized the main arguments of his larger work.

Croly's *Apocalypse of St. John,* bore the comprehensive subtitle, "Prophecy of the Rise, Progress, and Fall of the Church

---

[49] *Dictionary of National Biography,* vol. 5, pp. 135, 136.
[50] George Croly, *Popery the Antichrist,* p. 8.

of Rome; the Inquisition; the Revolution of France, the universal war; and the final triumph of Christianity." The Preface stated, "Christianity declared the one true Mediator; Popery was its corruption, by substituting many false mediators for the true." [51] Here are the leading features of the Croly exposition.

1. SLAYING OF TWO WITNESSES ENDS 1260 YEARS.— Croly's interest was aroused by the slaying of the Two Witnesses of Revelation 11, in connection with the "abjuration of religion by a government and people," which event was to come at the conclusion of the 1260 years. This he believed to have occurred in 1793. Reckoning back 1260 years, he was brought to 533. Noting Bishop Newton and Dr. Mann of Charter-House, he turned to Baronius and found "Justinian's grant of supremacy to the pope" formally fixed to that period, while the subsequent "grant of Phocas," in 606, was "nothing beyond a confirmation of the grant of Justinian." [52]

2. 1260 YEARS PLACED FROM 533 TO 1793.—Croly observes that the reason for the frequent adoption of the 606 date "seemed to be its convenient coincidence with the rise of Mahometanism." [53] Laying aside the commentators, Croly tied his interpretation to this 533-1793 placing of the 1260-year epoch. Later he found that many others had done the same. [54]

3. MAKES SEALS, TRUMPETS, AND VIALS CONTEMPORANEOUS. —Croly makes the seals, trumpets, and vials "nearly contemporaneous," and excludes the Greek Empire and the Mohammedan invasion. [55] The ten days of persecution in the Smyrnian period are the "ten years' persecution" from 303 to 313, as "days are in prophetic language *years*." [56] The seals spread over the entire Christian Era, [57] with the third seal (the black horse and the balances) as "the prophecy of the popedom" from the sixth century on, [58] and the fourth seal as the French Revolution, climaxing in 1793. [59] The sixth seal is set forth as "the

[51] George Croly, *Apocalypse of St. John*, Preface, p. 1.
[52] *Ibid.*, Introduction, pp. 12, 13.
[53] *Ibid.*, p. 13.   [55] *Ibid.*, p. 41.
[54] *Ibid.*, p. 14.   [56] *Ibid.*, pp. 54, 55, 67.
[57] *Ibid.*, table, p. 69.
[58] *Ibid.*, pp. 82-87.
[59] *Ibid.*, pp. 87-89.

35

prophecy of the universal war." [60] Beginning the trumpets, however, in the thirteenth century, Croly confines them to the papal affliction of the church. [61]

4. Two Witnesses the Old and New Testaments.—Croly denominates Revelation 10 as "The Propagation of the Gospel," and interprets the "little Book" as the Bible. [62] He notes the various predictions of the 1260-year period, [63] and considers the Two Witnesses the Old and New Testaments. [64] He gives details and documentation for the 533 date—the circumstances and specifications of the Justinian letter to Pope John, the letter to Epiphanius, Archbishop of Constantinople, announcing the primacy of the Roman bishop, and the supporting statements of the rest of the Code. [65] These conclusions follow:

"The supremacy of the Pope had by those mandates and edicts received the fullest sanction that could be given by the authority of the master of the Roman world. But the yoke sat uneasily on the Bishop of Constantinople; and on the death of Justinian the supremacy was utterly denied." [66]

"That Phocas repressed the claim of the Bishop of Constantinople is beyond a doubt. But the highest authorities among the civilians and annalists of Rome spurn the idea that Phocas was the founder of the supremacy of Rome; they ascend to Justinian as the only legitimate source, and rightly date the title from the memorable year 533." [67]

Croly recites the events of 1793, which set aside the provisions of 533, giving a detailed depiction. [68]

5. France the Tenth Part; Three and a Half Days (1793-97).—The "political earthquake" of Revelation 11, and the fall of the "tenth part" of the city, is applied to the upheaval in France. [69] And the era of the stupendous triumph of the Bible is portrayed, after the three and a half years of its repression in France, "from November, 1793 till June, 1797." [70]

6. Symbols of True and False Church.—Croly calls Revelation 12 "the vision of the church" under pagan and then papal persecution. [71] During the latter the church is fed

---

[60] Ibid., pp. 92-95.
[61] Ibid., pp. 109-138.
[62] Ibid., pp. 151-158.
[63] Ibid., p. 161.
[64] Ibid., p. 162.
[65] Ibid., pp. 165-174.
[66] Ibid., pp. 169, 170.
[67] Ibid., p. 171.
[68] Ibid., pp. 174-176.
[69] Ibid., pp. 178-180.
[70] Ibid., p. 181.
[71] Ibid., p. 200.

1260 years in the wilderness place prepared of God,[72] or from 533 to 1793. The floods are persecution, under the crusades and the Inquisition.[73] In Revelation 13 the Papacy is "shown in its full action," [74] receiving the ancient capital of paganism and its power and authority. The two-horned beast is set forth as the Inquisition under the Dominican order,[75] with the number 666 as the year of the birth of the Inquisition, i.e., A.D. 533 + 666 = 1198, when the Inquisition was launched.[76]

7. TEN HORNS NAMED AND DATED.—The ten horns are those named by Machiavelli and Bishop Lloyd—the Huns (356), Ostrogoths (377), Visigoths (378), Franks (407), Vandals (407), Sueves and Alans (407), Burgundians (407), Heruli and Turingi (476), Saxons and Angles (476), and Lombards (526),[77] according with the kings of Daniel 7.

8. ANGELIC MESSAGES ARE STEPS TO TRIUMPH.—Revelation 14 is portrayed as "the church triumphant." [78] The angelic messages portray the steps by which the triumph is accomplished —the Bible evidence that "the time of the final catastrophe is at hand, 'the hour of His judgment is come.' " [79]

9. FALL OF PAPAL ROME PORTRAYED.—Revelation 17 portrays the "fall of papal Rome." [80] The fallen woman is "corrupted Christendom," "stained and intoxicated with the blood of the people of God." [81] The seven heads are the "seven hills" of Rome, and the ten kingdoms are contemporaneous, and shall turn against popedom.[82] The thousand years is "entirely future," [83] with Revelation 21 and 22 as "the church triumphant." [84]

The remaining portion of the treatise (pages 286-470) is historical, tracing first the pagan persecutions,[85] then the barbarian invasions,[86] and next the details of the rise and dominance of the Papacy.[87] Then follow details of the Inquisition,[88]

[72] *Ibid.*, pp. 204-208.
[73] *Ibid.*, pp. 209, 210.
[74] *Ibid.*, pp. 212-214.
[75] *Ibid.*, pp. 218-221.
[76] *Ibid.*, pp. 222-228, 236-249.
[77] *Ibid.*, pp. 229, 230.

[78] *Ibid.*, p. 249.
[79] *Ibid.*, p. 252.
[80] *Ibid.*, p. 254.
[81] *Ibid.*, p. 257.
[82] *Ibid.*, p. 262.

[83] *Ibid.*, p. 275.
[84] *Ibid.*, pp. 276-285.
[85] *Ibid.*, pp. 286-289.
[86] *Ibid.*, pp. 318-334.
[87] *Ibid.*, pp. 334-369.
[88] *Ibid.*, pp. 370-398.

and lastly the French Revolution.[89]   In this, much detailed data
of importance is given, with the climax in the seizure of Pius VI
in February, 1798, his banishment, and his death in exile.[90]
Such was the scope of this impressive treatise by a lawyer-
preacher outside the special circle of study groups and heralds
of the advent.

V. Vaughan—No Cleansing of Sanctuary Expected Before 1843

Still another defensive voice was that of EDWARD T.
VAUGHAN (1777-1829), vicar of St. Martin's, Leicester. He was
educated at Rugby and then at Trinity College, Cambridge,
from which he received a B.A. in 1796 and an M.A. in 1799.
Then he became vicar of St. Martin's, Leicester, and rector of
Foston, Leicestershire.[91]   His sermon on the second advent,
called *The Church's Expectation* (1828), was preached in 1827
before the Society for Promoting Christian Knowledge. He
said that in the past his eyes had been holden on the prophecies,
but now the prophecies shone forth in midday luster.

1. CHAMPIONS HISTORICAL SCHOOL OF INTERPRETA-
TION.—Vaughan opposes the Antiochus Epiphanes theory and
the scheme of literal time for the prophetic periods. From
Jerome to Bishop Newton, Porphyry's scheme has often been
refuted. Antiochus is made "a general receipt for all ails." [92]
Vaughan speaks of the nobility, the naturalness, and the ease
of the Historical scheme of prophetic interpretation "from the
first establishment of the Persian empire to the general resurrection." [93]   The time of the end represents a definite period.
The stone that smites the image is Christ, the Little Horn of
the fourth beast is the Papacy, but the little horn of the Ram
and He-Goat, in Daniel 8, is made the Turk.

2. CLEANSING OF SANCTUARY INVOLVES JERUSALEM.—
Vaughan holds that immediately after the tribulation, when the

[89] *Ibid.*, pp. 415-446.   [90] *Ibid.*, pp. 425-427.
[91] Frederic Boase, *Modern English Biography*, vol. 6, suppl. 3, col. 736; *Admissions to Trinity College, Cambridge*, 1701-1800, vol. 3, p. 327.
[92] Edward T. Vaughan, *The Church's Expectation*, p. 48. (Title page on p. 550.)
[93] *Ibid.*, p. 49.

"times of the Gentiles" are fulfilled, and Jerusalem and its temple are no longer trodden underfoot of the Gentiles, then "the sanctuary shall have been cleansed." [94] Then will come the signs foretold, the great tribulation, the Gentile judgment, the shaking of the nations, "which is closed by the Lord's terrible but most welcome appearing." [95] Thus, continues Vaughan, "a clear date has been vouchsafed; viz. 2300 years from a notorious epoch." This "cleansing of the sanctuary," he feels, is "the delivering up of the Jewish City and Temple from Gentile into Jewish hands." [96]

3. Not Looked for Until 1843.—No one knows just how soon "the preparation for this beginning of the consummation shall be made manifest." When, in 1827, the navies of Great Britain, France, and Russia struck an unprecedented blow at the Turkish navy at Navarino, many were looking for the "courier who may announce a Christian possessor of Constantinople." [97] Then Vaughan adds the significant sentence, "Howbeit I do not look for the completion of this sign till 1843." In this he concurred with twoscore other leaders who had fixed upon this approximate date.

4. Sixth Vial Involves Same Expectation.—Moreover, Revelation 16 "leads us to precisely the same expectation." Vaughan continues:

"The *sixth* vial of judgment comprehends the drying up of the Euphrates, that the way of the Kings of The East—the rightful Sovereigns—God's kings—may be prepared; and synchronously with it, the preparation of the kings of the earth, (the Papal earth,) and of the whole world, (all the nations of Christendom,) for the last conflict: and the *seventh* comprehends those very judgments which are thus to be introduced." [98]

5. Dates 1260 Years From Justinian's Edict.—Before closing his discourse Vaughan speaks of the "great keys" which God has put in our hands, "viz. Daniel's prophecies, and the Revelation of John the Divine." And on the 1260 years he says, "I can find nothing which satisfies me as to the commence-

[96] *Ibid.*
[95] *Ibid.*, p. 53.
[98] *Ibid.*
[94] *Ibid.*, p. 52.
[97] *Ibid.*

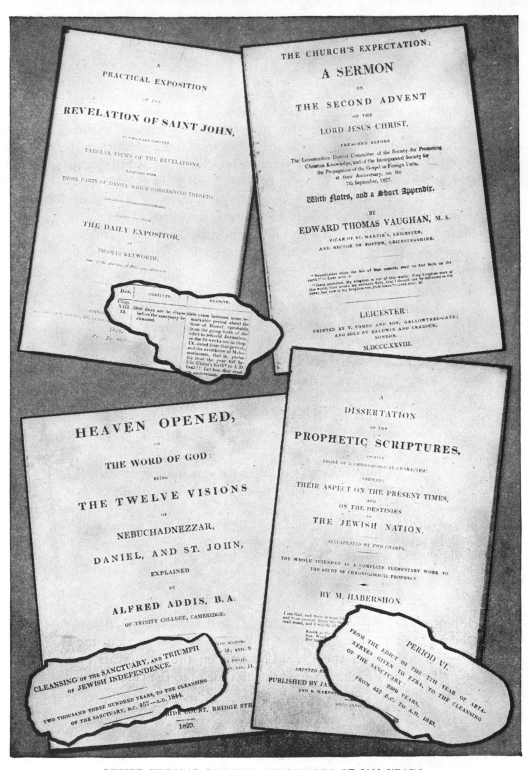

OTHER TYPICAL BRITISH EXPOSITORS OF 2300 YEARS

Thomas Keyworth in 1828 (Upper Left, With Inset) Places 2300 Years from 457 B.C. to A.D. 1843;
E. T. Vaughan in 1828 (Upper Right) Takes the Same Position; Alfred Addis in 1829 (Lower
Left) Puts the Period in a Chapter Heading, "B.C. 457-A.D. 1844"; and Matthew Habershon in
1834 (Lower Right) Allocates Period VI "From 457 B.C. to A.D. 1843"

ment of the 1260 years, like the edicts of Justinian."[99] He prefers the span of 537 to 1797 for this period.

VI. Keyworth—Dates 2300 Years From 457 B.C. to A.D. 1843

The tide of exposition rolls on. Another able expositor was THOMAS KEYWORTH (1782-1852), well-known Hebraist, who was born in Nottingham. Keyworth went to London as a young man, where he was converted from Unitarianism and entered Cheshunt College to prepare for the Congregational ministry. After serving in several churches he finally went to London, and from 1842 to 1851 was at Aston Tirrold, Berkshire. Modest and simple, he was actively interested in the poor and in the promotion of missionary activity.[100] He was widely praised for his valuable *Principia Hebraica* (1817). In the field of interpretation he wrote *A Practical Exposition of the Revelation of St. John* (1828), which was also well received.

This treatise is in the form of a terse comment, with a concluding "Tabular View" of the prophetic symbols of Revelation compared with Daniel. Keyworth introduced his exposition by declaring incisively that it was "a *duty* for the watchmen of Sion to sound an alarm in the Holy Mountain."[101] Then he observed: *"There never was a time since the beginning of the world,* (except when Messiah was about to appear as the man of sorrows), *when events so interesting were about to occur, as at the present moment."* [102] (Title page reproduced on page 550.)

1. PAPAL ROME'S POWER 1260 YEARS.—Stalwartly proclaiming the Historical School view and the standard interpretation of the four empires, he wrote clearly of the division of Rome and the papal Antichrist following. And while the dragon of Revelation 12 was pagan Rome, it transferred its power to the ten kingdoms of the leopard beast for the 1260 years.[103]

---

[99] *Ibid.*, pp. 58, 59.
[100] *Dictionary of National Biography*, vol. 11, p. 88.
[101] Thomas Keyworth, *A Practical Exposition of the Revelation of St. John*, Introduction, unpaged. [102] *Ibid.* [103] *Ibid.*, p. 40.

2. LAMB-HORNED BEAST REPRESENTS PAPACY.—As the leopard beast represents the temporal tyranny in support of popery "throughout the ten kingdoms," so, he thought, the "lamb-horned beast represents the *ecclesiastical* or religious tyranny, exercised by the papistical clergy." [104] Keyworth is frankly uncertain as to the 666, and the three angels of Revelation 14 are relegated to the past.

3. LEADING DATES OF ERA TABULATED.—Keyworth tabulates the leading dates of the Christian Era: 303-313, as the terrible "ten days" of prophesied persecution; 410, Alaric and the Goths; 451, Attila and the Huns; 455, Genseric and the Vandals; 476, the empire overthrow, and the rise of "the distinct kingdoms, or, governments," as denoted by the ten toes and horns of Daniel 2 and 7 and Revelation 13 and 17; 606 the recognition of the power of the pope as universal bishop; 1204, the establishment of the Inquisition; 1453, the supplanting of the Saracens by the Turks; 1517, the beginning of the reformation from popery by Luther. [105]

4. FIRST FOUR TRUMPETS OVERTHROW ROME.—In perpendicular columns in his "Tabular View," he parallels the symbols and the meaning. Thus, for the first four trumpets, Alaric and the Goths—and on through the Huns and Vandals, and the total overthrow of the empire. [106]

5. SARACENIC WOE, 612-762; TURKISH WOE, 1281-1672.— The fifth trumpet of locusts, *"emblematical* of Mahomet and his successors," for the five months (150 years), was from 612 to 762. And the sixth trumpet—the Turkish establishment for the hour, day, month, and year as 391 years and 15 days—was from 1281 to 1672. [107] The 1260 years as set forth in Revelation 12, 13, and 17, reach perhaps from 606 to 1866, [108] with the seventh trumpet, or third woe, beginning the millennium perhaps in 1866. [109]

6. LITTLE HORN CORRESPONDS TO TWO-HORNED BEAST.— In comparing the corresponding parts of Daniel and the Revela-

---

104 *Ibid.*, pp. 41, 44, 45.   106 *Ibid.*, pp. 69, 70.   108 *Ibid.*
105 *Ibid.*, pp. 65-68.   107 *Ibid.*, p. 70.   109 *Ibid.*

tion, Keyworth puts the ten toes and the ten horns of Daniel over against the ten horns of Revelation 12 and 13—meaning the ten kingdoms.[110] The little horn uproots three horns, and in comparison the papal tiara has three crowns.[111] The little horn of Daniel 7 and the two-horned beast of Revelation 13 are paired as symbolic of the pope and popery.[112]

7. SATAN BOUND AND KINGDOM ESTABLISHED.—The judging of the Little Horn by the Ancient of Days is preceded by the seven vials "about to be poured out." [113] The time, times, and half a time of Daniel and the forty-two months and 1260 years of Revelation are identical. The Son of man taking the dominion, and Satan bound for 1,000 years,[114] are synchronous.

8. MOHAMMEDANISM IN DANIEL 8 AND REVELATION 9.— The taking away of the daily sacrifice by the fierce horn of Daniel 8 is paired with the locusts of Revelation 9, or Mohammedanism.[115]

9. 2300 YEARS FROM 457 B.C. TO A.D. 1843.—As the climax of the series, to his expression "2300 days are to elapse before the sanctuary be cleansed," Keyworth adds this impressive statement (reproduced with title page on page 550):

"2300 years between some remarkable period about the time of Daniel, (probably from the going forth of the edict to rebuild Jerusalem, as the 70 weeks are in chap. IX. dated from that period,) and the overthrow of Mahommedanism, that is, probably from the year 457 before Christ's birth to A.D. 1843!! Let him that readeth understand." [116]

As a further detail he makes this comment on the relationship of the seventy weeks and the 2300 days:

"Our Lord was crucified about A.D. 33, now 33 added to 457, make 490, and 70 weeks of years, (i.e. 7 times 70) amount to 490, consequently 457 years before Christ's birth is the commencement of Daniel's 70 weeks, and probably of these 2300 days." [117]

10. EXTENDS 1290 AND 1335 YEARS BEYOND 1260.—The time of "unequalled trouble," of Daniel 12 Keyworth then pairs

[110] *Ibid.*, p. 72.
[111] *Ibid.*, p. 73.
[112] *Ibid.*
[113] *Ibid.*
[114] *Ibid.*
[115] *Ibid.*
[116] *Ibid.*, p. 74.
[117] *Ibid.*

with the outpouring of the seven vials of Revelation 16. And in common with not a few, he extends the close of the 1290 years beyond the end of the 1260 years. And the 1335, in turn, he projects slightly beyond the terminus of the 1290 years. Such is the tabular picture painted by Keyworth.

CHAPTER TWENTY-NINE

Sabbatarian Note Sounded
in Prophetic Circles

Amid the continuing emphasis on the 2300 years by individual expositors and local groups of earnest students gathering in different places to study or expound the prophecies, we reach the year 1829. Then one of the Scottish writers introduces the Sabbatarian question into the prophetic circles. Merely noted here, it will be developed in a later chapter. But let us look first at another of the group meetings, and then at other individual writers. We will then come to Begg, the Sabbatarian.

I. Congregational Ministerial Association Studies Prophecies

Ministerial groups of various persuasions, in different places, as well as distinctive organizations, were studying the prophecies. For example, there was an address by ROBERT VAUGHAN [1] before the Monthly Association of Congregational Ministers and Churches, published at their request. Given at Hanover Chapel, Peckham, in 1829, *The Nature and Duration of the Papal Apostacy* comprises a comprehensive survey of the prophecies of Daniel, Paul, and John, and depicts the "impressive outline" of the centuries. These are associated "with

---

[1] ROBERT VAUGHAN (1795-1868), Congregational minister, was pastor at Worcester (1819-25) and Kensington (1825). He was professor of history at London University (1834-39), receiving a D.D. from Glasgow in 1836 for distinguished service. From 1843 to 1857 Vaughan was president and professor of theology of Lancashire Independent College, and president of the British Congregational union in 1846. In his later years he served as pastor at Uxbridge and Torquay, and founded and edited the *British Quarterly*, from 1845 to 1865. (*Dictionary of National Biography*, vol. 20, p. 175; Frederic Boase, *Modern English Biography*, vol. 3, col. 1081.)

nearly everything that has been, that is, and that shall be." [2]
We pause but for two points.

1. PROPHETIC OUTLINE OF WORLD HISTORY.—The "four
empires that should succeed each other," in Daniel 2, are named
and described. [3] The paralleling four beasts of Daniel 7, with
the ten horn-kingdoms appearing "at the same time" within
the Roman Empire, [4] are portrayed. The Little Horn, uprooting
three, with eyes and mouth denoting "watchfulness, and policy,"
has its identity demonstrated "by the events of history," as
"the character of the papal government became strikingly conformable to the predictions of the prophet." "The visions
of Daniel present a sublime outline of this world's history." [5]

2. PAPAL BABYLON TO PERISH AT ADVENT.—In Revelation
17, Rome was the "only city ruling the kings of the earth,"
standing on seven mountains, or with seven successive governments. "Can we be at any loss then in recognizing Daniel's
Little Horn, and St. Paul's Man of sin, in the Woman enthroned
in the midst of the mystical Babylon? What ecclesiastical
domination has Rome ever known, save that of the papacy?" [6]
All three portrayals present the same fate—the Wicked One
consumed by the brightness of the Redeemer's coming, and
Babylon the great to fall. [7] And the period of duration leads
into a discussion of the 533-Justinian versus the 606-Phocas
date for its beginning. [8]

II. Addis—1843 the Grand Focal Point of All Prophecy

ALFRED ADDIS (b. 1806), graduate of Trinity College,
Cambridge, in 1827 [9] wrote *Heaven Opened* (1829), with the
subtitle stating that it covers the "twelve visions of Nebuchadnezzar, Daniel, and St. John." The next year he produced
The Theory of Prophecy (1830). His *Concise View of the Language, Scheme, and Spirit of the Chronological Prophets,* follow-

---

[2] Robert Vaughan, *The Nature and Duration of the Papal Apostasy,* p. 50.
[3] *Ibid.,* pp. 50, 51.   [5] *Ibid.,* pp. 52, 53.   [7] *Ibid.,* p. 63.
[4] *Ibid.,* p. 51.   [6] *Ibid.,* p. 62.   [8] *Ibid.,* pp. 68, 69.
[9] *Admissions to Trinity College, Cambridge, 1701-1800,* vol. 4, p. 225.

ing a year later, holds essentially the same positions and uses the same diagrams. (Title page reproduced on page 550.) Here are his positions.

1. HOLDS HISTORICAL VIEW OF FOUR KINGDOMS.—In the great outline prophecies Addis concurred with the Historical School view of Daniel 2, with the Babylonic-Assyrian golden head from 680 B.C., the Medo-Persian silver breast and arms, from 536 B.C., the Grecian brass belly and thighs, from 331 B.C., and the two iron legs of Rome, from 168 B.C. The feet are the divided European kingdoms.[10]

2. PAPAL ELEVENTH HORN (553-1813) FOLLOWS ROME'S DIVISIONS.—The paralleling four beasts of Daniel 7 represented the same world kingdoms, with the division of the fourth into ten horn-kingdoms and the eleventh horn as the papal power.[11] These ten kings he lists as the Huns, Ostrogoths, Visigoths, Franks, Vandals, Alans, Burgundians, Heruli and Thuringia, Saxons and Angles, and Langobards.[12] The 1260 days are rated as years in harmony with all prophetic time[13]—the "tyranny of the pope" rather uniquely placed from 553, the date of the plucking up of the Ostrogothic horn by Justinian's generals, when the East and West were reunited, to the end of intolerance in 1813.[14]

3. 2300 YEARS DATED FROM 457 B.C. TO A.D. 1843.—The ram of Daniel 8 is Medo-Persia,[15] and the he-goat is Grecia. The desolation of the sanctuary for 2300 years is placed as beginning in 457 B.C.[16] The 490 years extend from 457 B.C. to A.D. 33.[17] The seventh week is placed from A.D. 26 to 33.[18] The cleansing of the sanctuary at the end of the 2300 years Addis locates in 1843.[19] This is, in fact, his focal date, as it occurs again and again.

4. SEVENTY WEEKS THE KEY UNLOCKING 2300 YEARS.—An entire section is devoted to the 2300 years, and is titled, "Cleansing of the Sanctuary, and Triumph of Jewish Independence," with the running title, at the top of the page, "Cleansing of the

---

10 Alfred Addis, *Heaven Opened*, pp. 4-14.
11 *Ibid.*, pp. 313, 314, 4-6. 14 *Ibid.*, pp. 14, 314. 17 *Ibid.*, pp. 6, 169.
12 *Ibid.*, p. 314. 15 *Ibid.*, p. 4. 18 *Ibid.*, pp. 320, 321.
13 *Ibid.*, p. 169. 16 *Ibid.* 19 *Ibid.*, p. 22.

Sanctuary, B.C. 457-A.D. 1844." [20]   This Addis convincingly
places from the "perfect reestablishment of the religious affairs
of the Jews by Artaxerxes, B.C. 457." [21]   The 2300-year period
ends when "the church is sanctified and *cleansed* with the wash-
ing of water by the word, and presented to Christ a glorious
church, not having spot or wrinkle or any such thing. . . . Eph.
v.26, 27; Rev. xxi.2; xix.7." [22]   The *"ostensible* key" to Daniel
8:14, he asserts, is furnished by the 490 years of Daniel 9, which
reach to Messiah and are dated from 457 B.C. [23] Then Addis adds:

> "But as the 487 years expired A.D. 30, at the commencement of
> our Lord's ministry, the remaining 1813, or the whole 2300, will expire
> A.D. 1843." [24]

5. ANTICHRIST'S OPPOSITION ENDS AT SANCTUARY'S CLEANS-
ING.—As preliminary to his discussion of the 2300 years, Addis
expatiates upon the Church of Rome's policy of using priestcraft to play upon the "credulity of the vulgar," as did the pagan
hierarchy before them.   Here is perhaps the most pertinent
and striking section in the entire book:

> "Elate with their power the Caesars and their decemvirate have exalted
> themselves above all laws human and divine. They have sat in the seat of
> Christ, enforcing their own dogmas of religion by the arm of their power;
> and in the midst of peace have destroyed many, who possessed the truth, by
> sword, by flame, by captivity, and by spoil many days.   Their existence
> has been a continual opposition to the Prince of princes, truth itself,
> Christ, from the time of his temporal crucifixion under Pontius Pilate to
> the present time: and they have thus incontestably shown themselves to be
> that Anti-Christ which should appear. But the desolation of the church
> must have an end; the autocracy of the civil power in the affairs of those
> who are Christ's must be swept away, and the Sanctuary be cleansed. The
> re-establishment of God's people after the seventy years' captivity, and
> their subsequent scattering were, together, to last 2300 years. In the
> year B.C. 457, they were re-established by Artaxerxes under Messiah as
> sole Leader; and their scattering will consequently be accomplished A.D.
> 1843." [25]

6. ENDS 1290 YEARS WITH 2300 IN 1843.—The "seven
times" of the Gentiles, or 2520 years, Addis dates from 680 B.C. to
A.D. 1840. [26] And the vision of Daniel 11 he carries down through

---

[20] *Ibid.*, p. 116 ff.   [22] *Ibid.*, p. 175.   [25] *Ibid.*, p. 320.
[21] *Ibid.*, p. 174.   [23] *Ibid.*, p. 176.   [26] *Ibid.*, pp. 4, 20.
                          [24] *Ibid.*

Persia, Grecia, Rome, and the divisions,[27] with the 1290 years of Daniel 12 dated from 553, and terminating with the 2300 years in 1843-44,[28] when also the Little Horn is broken without hand.[29] The "fall of the Roman Church" in 1843 is repeatedly noted.[30] Thus he reasons: "This abomination will therefore be set up A.D. 553; and the 1290 years will begin from thence, and consequently expire, A.D. 1843." [31] While Addis ends the 1290 years with the 2300 in 1843, he begins the 1335 years with this latter time, and therefore extends this prophetic period [32] on through the millennium.

7. FIFTH TRUMPET, SARACENS; 6TH VIAL, OTTOMAN DISSOLUTION.—Addis begins the seven heads of the "dragon and sea beast," with Babylon,[33] and places the church-woman in the wilderness from A.D. 553, with the Two Witnesses as the opposers of the "corrupt papacy." [34] The fifth trumpet is the Saracenic conquest, with the "five months," or 150 years, dated from 786 to 936.[35] The falling of a tenth part of the "city" and the pouring out of the vials in the French Revolution are noted.[36] The fifth vial was poured out on the seat of the Papacy, and the sixth pertains to the "dissolution of the Ottoman Empire." [37]

8. LAST EVENTS ALL FOCALIZED ON 1843.—The climactic date of 1843 is presented by Addis in tabular form under the heading: "VII. The Era of the Seventh Trumpet, Seventh Thunder, Seventh Vial, Third Woe, Millennium, and general Judgment." [38]

Here is placed the establishment of the mountain kingdom, the second advent, the Beast committed to the burning flame, the Little Horn broken, the sanctuary cleansed, the commencement of the 1335 years, the great multitude coming out of tribulation, the time of judging the dead, the treading of the wine press, the deliverance of the church, the desolation of the Whore, the first resurrection. The second resurrection and the

---

27 *Ibid.*, pp. 4-14.
28 *Ibid.*, pp. 14, 177, 179, 192, 320.
29 *Ibid.*, p. 22.
30 *Ibid.*, pp. 406-409, 413, 414, 424, 431.
31 *Ibid.*, p. 179.
32 *Ibid.*, pp. 22, 192.
33 *Ibid.*, p. 5 ff.
34 *Ibid.*, pp. 14, 15.
35 *Ibid.*, pp. 15, 193.
36 *Ibid.*, p. 21.
37 *Ibid.*
38 *Ibid.*, pp. 22, 23.

destruction of the wicked come at the end of the thousand years.[39] While Addis does not connect the three angels' messages of Revelation 14 with the prophetic organizations, as did some, he specifically ends the witness of each message in 1843 as the consummation of the Reformation, and he ties the thrusting in of the sharp sickle to the "signal overthrow" of the Papacy.[40] Such is the over-all picture presented by Addis.

III. Begg—Shares Mason's and Cuninghame's Views

JAMES A. BEGG (1800-1868), Scottish writer on prophecy and promulgator of the seventh-day Sabbath, was born in Paisley. His father was a teacher and provided him a liberal education. He was apprenticed to the printing trade, at which he worked for some time. Then he became a bookseller and stationer in Glasgow. He was also "the publisher of a considerable number of works on doctrinal, prophetical, and other Bible subjects," a persevering student, even to his old age. He excelled in the literary use of the English tongue, and rose to a recognized place among the prophetic authors of his time.[41]

Well known in his field, Begg was conspicuous in his love for the Bible and for historical and Scriptural research. While especially fond of the prophecies, he also lectured on geology, creation, and the Flood. In his earlier life he was an adherent of the Reformed Presbyterian Church of Scotland. But he came to differ from that church on the question of the prophecies. The second premillennial coming of Christ gripped his heart, and in 1829 he published *A Connected View of Some of the Scriptural Evidence of the Redeemer's Speedy Personal Return.* In 1831 he published *The Scriptural Argument for the Coming of the Lord, Letters to a Minister of the Gospel, on his and other Interpretations of our Saviour's Predictions of His Return,* and *Christ's Speedy Return in Glory.* In 1832 he wrote a pamphlet, *True Cause of Prevalence of Pestilence,* and in 1835 he

---

[39] *Ibid.*   [40] *Ibid.*, pp. 406-412.
[41] William Fulton, "James A. Begg, A Memorial Discourse," prefixed to *Summary of Doctrines Taught in Christian Meeting House, . . . Glasgow, by the Late James A. Begg;* see *The Sabbath Recorder,* May 13 and 20, 1869 (vol. 25, nos. 20, 21), pp. 77, 85.

published *Extracts on Prophecy, Chiefly the Approaching Advent and Kingdom of Christ.* In this he quotes from thirty prominent expositors.

Begg was very clear and explicit on the Little Horn as being the papal Antichrist and the Babylon of the prophecies upon whom tremendous judgments were due. Toward the end of his life, however, he drifted into the Futurist view of an individual antichrist yet to come. In common with most British expositors, he stressed the literal restoration of Israel. He also looked forward to the overthrow of Turkey. Among the signs of the approaching end he included spiritism. William Anderson, of Glasgow, spoke highly of Begg's proclamation of "the truth of the kingdom" in western Scotland.[42]

His last book was titled *An Examination of the Authority for a Change of the Weekly Sabbath at the Resurrection of Christ* (1850), which brought him prominently before the public. Beginning about 1832, soon after the publishing of his first book on prophecy, Begg began the observance of the seventh-day Sabbath.[43] His espousal of the Sabbath and his personal observance of it thereafter until his death; his contact with the Millerite *Signs of the Times* in 1840, just after it was started; his offer of articles on the continuing obligation of the seventh-day Sabbath, which they declined; his first communications in the Seventh Day Baptist *Sabbath Recorder* of New York in May, 1845;[44] his articles on "The Original Sabbath Unchanged" in *The Recorder,* beginning November 13, 1845;[45] his publication of *An Examination of the Authority for a Change of the Weekly Sabbath;* and his baptism in Glasgow, on July 7, 1853, by J. W. Morton, Seventh Day Baptist minister of Plainfield, New Jersey —all form part of a fascinating and unique story.

This will be dealt with more fully in connection with the revival of the Sabbath at the time of the expanding Advent Movement in America from 1844 onward.[46] It appears that Begg

[42] William Anderson, *An Apology for Millennial Doctrine,* Part 1 (1830), p. 63, note.
[43] Letter from J. A. Begg to Editor George B. Utter, *The Sabbath Recorder,* May 1, 1845 (vol. 1, no. 45).
[44] *Ibid.*   [45] *The Sabbath Recorder* (vol. 2, no. 21).
[46] To appear in Volume 4 of *Prophetic Faith.*

was convinced of the binding obligation of the seventh-day Sabbath by the study of the Word itself, and not initially from contact with Seventh Day Baptists.[47]

1. REGRETS QUIBBLE OVER 2300 YEARS.—Begg's "earliest acquaintance with Unfulfilled Prophecy"[48] was derived from Archibald Mason, his fellow countryman, to whose "occasional pulpit ministrations"[49] he was indebted. His *Connected View* was a reply to a series of antagonistic articles in the *Christian Instructor*. He makes frequent allusions to Cuninghame's writings, as well as those of Faber, Way, Drummond, Irving, and Keith. He extolls the study of prophecy, stressing its potential value to the Jews for determining the time of Messiah's first appearance and the protection of the early church from loss in the destruction of Jerusalem.[50]

At the very outset Begg regrets Irving's unfortunate reference to the Septuagint variation of 2400 instead of 2300. Begg indicates that the original Septuagint reads 2300 for determining the "mighty year of God's glory." Such quibbling attitudes, he says, throw "unnecessary doubt upon the certainty of the 'times' revealed," and he makes supporting reference to Cuninghame's clear evidences.[51]

2. ANTICHRIST DESTROYED BEFORE SECOND ADVENT.—Begg holds that Antichrist will be destroyed *before* the millennium[52]—destroyed by the brightness of Christ's second coming according to Paul. In Daniel 7, after the four empires, the ten nations into which Rome was divided appear, the period of the Little Horn, or "Papal Antichrist," is followed by the destruction of the Beast with the horns.[53]

3. OTHER SYMBOLS OF DESTRUCTION FOR PAPACY.—The same destruction is visited by the angel with the seven vials, under the sixth of which the Turkish Empire is dried up, and by the last of which Antichrist is destroyed as well.[54] Begg also

---

[47] In this conclusion Corliss F. Randolph, president of the Seventh Day Baptist Historical Society, concurs, as in his letter to the writer, dated "Maplewood, N.J., Feb. 11, 1935."
[48] James A. Begg, *Connected View* (1830 ed.), pp. ix, 142.
[49] *Ibid.*, pp. viii, xiii, 36, 79, 87, 141.
[50] *Ibid.*, pp. 18, 19.   [51] *Ibid.*, p. 18, n.   [53] *Ibid.*, pp. 148, 149, 190
[52] *Ibid.*, pp. 143, 191.   [54] *Ibid.*, pp. 150, 243.

places the angel of Revelation 14:6, 7, with the "hour of God's judgments," just before the destruction of mystic Babylon.[55] And with this he lists the final overthrow by the ten horns which have power one hour with the Beast.[56]

4. PROGRESSIVE OUTLINE OF DANIEL 7.—The first resurrection, Begg avers, introduces the thousand years. The prophetic outline back of the millennium is thus described:

"The seventh chapter [of Daniel] contains, as we have seen in speaking of the destruction of Antichrist, a prediction of four great empires which should exist from the beginning of the captivity till the Millennium. From three of these, viz. the Babylonish, the Persian, and the Grecian, the extensive dominion has long since passed away; and as it was predicted of the fourth or Roman empire, that 'the ten horns out of this kingdom are ten kings that shall arise,' so was it divided into ten kingdoms, forming the present European dynasties, in which state it has continued many centuries. The rise of Antichrist was predicted, as a little horn growing up among these horns or kingdoms; on account of whose blasphemies, thrones of judgment for his destruction are represented as being at length set by the Ancient of Days." [57]

5. STANDARD OUTLINE OF DANIEL 2.—In Daniel 2, "the same four monarchies are represented as the various parts of one great image, the Roman empire forming the legs and feet, and its subdivision into the present European kingdoms being here witnessed in the ten toes." [58] The mingling of the iron and clay is "by royal intermarriages." Then Begg concludes:

"But the whole shall be broken to pieces when Christ shall come in the clouds of heaven for the establishment of that Kingdom which 'shall not be left to other people.' " [59]

This synchronizes with the sounding of the seventh angel, when the kingdoms of this world become the kingdoms of our Lord and of His Christ, and when the downfall of Babylon is announced by the heavenly shout of triumph.[60]

6. BRITAIN ONE OF THE TEN HORNS AND TOES.—Britain, Begg asserts, "forms one of the kingdoms symbolized by 'the ten horns' of the fourth beast, or Roman empire," of Daniel 7,[61]

---

[55] Ibid., p. 152.
[56] Ibid., pp. 152, 153.
[57] Ibid., pp. 190, 191.
[58] Ibid., p. 192.
[61] Ibid., p. 232.
[59] Ibid., p. 193.
[60] Ibid.

which beast is to be given to the burning flame. It forms "one also of the ten toes of Nebuchadnezzar's great image, which was *'broken to pieces* together.' " [62] And Britain, he adds, is one of the ten kings of Revelation 17: "Thus is Britain included in the destruction which shall overtake the ungodly nations." [63]

7. TURKEY'S OVERTHROW IN DANIEL 11.—Not only does Turkey constitute the special objective of the sixth vial, [64] but Begg brings it in Daniel 11 thus:

"Daniel, in predicting the final overthrow of the Ottoman power (this application being generally admitted, we stop not to notice the grounds on which it is made,) foretold that *'tidings out of the East and out of the North shall trouble him. Dan. xi.44." [65]

IV. Hooper—2300 Ends in 1847; Angelic Messenger Flying

The persistent and even predominant interest in the 2300 years is attested again by the next two expositors—both rectors in the Church of England. The first is JOHN HOOPER, curate of Westbury, Wilts, and then rector of Albury, in Surrey. [66] He was author of a number of works on prophecy and the advent. In 1829 he wrote *The Doctrine of the Second Advent,* an address to the members of the Church of England. Then followed *The Present Crisis,* while he was still at Westbury. Equally stressing the imminent advent, both treatises had texts on the title pages on understanding the times, the imperativeness of prophecy, the nearness of the kingdom of God, and the soon-coming advent. In 1844 he wrote *A Word in Season;* then *Apocalypsis; or, The Revelation of Jesus Christ,* and *The Kingdom of God* in 1846, *The Advent* in 1847, as well as lesser items.

1. STANDARD POSITION ON DANIEL'S OUTLINES.—Hooper presents a terse but clear outline of the empires of the great metallic image of Daniel 2, the feet and toes of the Western Roman Empire, "waiting the fall of that stone, which shall grind it to powder." [67] Then follows the impressive paralleling prophecy of Daniel 7, with the Little Horn as "none other than the

---

[62] *Ibid.*
[63] *Ibid.,* pp. 232, 233.
[64] *Ibid.,* p. 243.
[66] Further biographical data unavailable.
[65] *Ibid.,* p. 246 (italics his).
[67] John Hooper, *The Doctrine of the Second Advent,* pp. 9, 10.

Pope or Antichrist." [68] Attention is given to the message of Revelation 14, calling out the chosen ones from the "church of Rome, 'the mother of harlots and abominations of the whole earth.' " [69] The 1260 years are dated from 533 to 1793, when the judgment upon the Papacy began. The 1290 years extend to 1823, and the 1335 years continue to 1868. [70]

2. DATES 2300 YEARS FROM 453 B.C. TO A.D. 1847.—Hooper places the finishing of the mystery of God and the full establishment of His kingdom at the end of the 1335 years. [71] But his main argument concerns Daniel 8:14 and the ending of the "2300 days or years." Hooper refers to the diversity of dates for the terminal point, owing to the difficulty in determining its commencement. The seventy weeks, he continues, "clearly specify some great public transaction, from which we are to commence dating"—the command to restore and rebuild Jerusalem. [72] This he dates from the complete re-establishment of the daily sacrifice, which was effected in the time of Ezra, and, according to Horne, in 453 B.C. [73] This ends the period in 1847, with its climactic events:

"If we date, then, from this epoch, it will bring us to the year of our Lord 1847: 'Then shall the sanctuary be cleansed.' B.C. 453, + A.D. 1847 = 2300. Now this cleansing of the sanctuary must include the seventh or last vial, which brings the great and terrible day of the Lord, when he shall come with his holy ones to take vengeance on the wicked adversary, who perishes at the battle of Armageddon." [74]

3. MIGHTY EVENTS MARK INTERVENING TIME.—If the foregoing calculation be correct, Hooper continues, "in about 18 years from the present time, (1829), the sanctuary or Jerusalem will be cleansed." [75] And during the intervening period "mighty events" would occur—the drying up, or gradual consumption, of the Turkish power, the restoration of the lost tribes of Israel, and the total destruction of Babylon the great, culminating in "the coming of our Lord with all his saints." [76] Thus he concludes:

---

[68] *Ibid.*, pp. 10, 11.   [71] *Ibid.*, p. 36.   [74] *Ibid.*
[69] *Ibid.*, p. 22.   [72] *Ibid.*   [75] *Ibid.*
[70] *Ibid.*, pp. 34, 35.   [73] *Ibid.*   [76] *Ibid.*, pp. 37, 38.

"The glorious manifestation, therefore, of the Son of Man cannot be far distant! and the awful judgments, which are invariably spoken of throughout the Prophets, as preceding his advent—may be daily, yea, hourly expected." [77]

4. Signs of Imminent End Include Turkey.—Listing next the prophetic signs of Matthew 24—the gospel to all nations, famines, pestilences, earthquakes, distress of nations, and overturning of governments—Hooper asserts that these "began to take place at the French Revolution." Then the luminaries of the political heavens of the Roman earth were eclipsed. The "entire overthrow of the ten kingdoms," he believes to be at hand.[78] He thinks this will be the last sign before the appearance of Christ. The seven vials, he holds, are in process of being poured out, with the fulfilling of the sixth involving the "gradual exhaustion" of the Turkish Empire.

5. Harbingers of the Second Advent.—Hooper's second treatise, *The Present Crisis,* begins by commenting on the general conviction that humanity had arrived at some great crisis hour of history. The Bible presents its character, and sets forth present conditions as a sign of the "*speedy* and glorious appearing of the Son of Man," involving "the restoration of the Jews—the destruction of antichrist and the resurrection of the saints." [79]

Hooper purposes to show the "striking correspondence" between the prophetic declarations and the "present times." [80] He lists the preaching of the gospel to all nations, the abounding of iniquity, the degenerate state of the church, the scoffers at the advent, the distress of nations, the churches being admonished of the near approach of the Bridegroom, the ending of the 1260 years, the sounding of the seventh trumpet, and the drying up of the mystic Euphrates. These, he declares, are among the "harbingers of the glorious appearing of the Son of Man,—of the resurrection of his saints,—and of his millennial glory." [81]

6. Phenomenal Missions Advance a Sign.—Hooper cites the unparalleled spread of the gospel to the world—how more

---

[77] *Ibid.*, p. 38.
[78] *Ibid.*, pp. 38, 39.
[79] John Hooper, *The Present Crisis*, p. 3.
[80] *Ibid.*, p. 4.
[81] *Ibid.*, pp. 4, 5.

had been accomplished in the last thirty-five years than through-out the previous Christian Era.[82] The light thrown upon the prophetic word is then stressed, as "many run to and fro, and knowledge is increased." Never since the first advent has the prophetic Word been "so much studied." [83] He adds:

"'The *Revelation* of Jesus Christ,' contained in the Apocalypse, shewing the coming of the Just One, with all his saints, to the destruction of the apostate nations, is now made so plain to the church, that none can, or, at least, ought to be ignorant of it." [84]

"The opening, then, and unfolding of the prophetic word, is another convincing proof that we are arrived at the end of the age; the unsealing of prophecy, and the revelation of the 'mystery of God,' being reserved unto *the time of the end*,' Dan. xii.9; Rev. x.7." [85]

7. The Flying Angel in Fulfillment.—Of the admonish-ing of the church he says:

"The ministers of Jehovah have proclaimed, 'Behold the Bridegroom cometh!' and as certainly as the cry has been made, so certainly will the Bridegroom come." [86]

Not until the "great political earthquake" of 1792 was the church "aroused from her slumbers," when she began earnestly to fulfill His long-neglected command.[87] Then follow these remarkable statements:

"Who cannot perceive in all this the fulfilment of the apocalyptic vision,—'the angel flying through the midst of heaven, having the ever-lasting gospel to preach to them that dwell upon the earth, and to every nation, and kindred, and tongue, and people? Rev. xiv.6. And what fol-lows? Another angel, saying, Babylon is fallen, is fallen! A third calls upon the nations to separate from her fornications,—the Son of man is seen sitting on a white cloud,—the harvest of earth is reaped." [88]

"The fact of the wide, rapid, and almost universal spread of the gospel, is one of the signs of the present times, which is 'a witness to the nations' of the approaching downfall of Babylon, and of the glorious coming of the Son of man. Reader, hast thou embraced the great salvation revealed in the gospel? If not, delay no longer to seek this one thing needful; rest not till thou hast found peace with God, through our Lord Jesus Christ,—till this gospel, which is travelling over the world as the messenger of mercy, prove the power of God to the salvation of thy soul." [89]

---

82 *Ibid.*, p. 5.
83 *Ibid.*, p. 17.
84 *Ibid.*, pp. 17, 18.
85 *Ibid.*, p. 18.
86 *Ibid.*, p. 19.
87 *Ibid.*, p. 5.
88 *Ibid.*, p. 6.
89 *Ibid.*, p. 7.

In former times the church was looking for the advent, but because of the "apparent delay," it had "fallen asleep." But during this "night of sleep," Hooper says, "the church has been aroused by an alarm of the Bridegroom's approach." [90]

8. 1260 YEARS (533-1792) HAD ENDED.—Hooper emphasizes the "expiration of the 1260 prophetic days or years," during which the saints of the Most High had been given into the hands of the Papacy, the holy city trodden underfoot, the witnesses prophesied in sackcloth, and the church preserved in the wilderness. This is his comment:

"The events of 1792, marked the *termination* of this period; then the people of God were delivered from the persecuting power of the papacy; popery received its mortal wound, and could no longer trample the servants of the Redeemer under foot; the slaying of the witnesses, (viz. the Old and New Testament,) under the *infidel* ascendancy—their subsequent resurrection—their ascent to heaven, or the patronage they received from kingly power, proved that they had completed the number of their days, in which they were to prophecy in sackcloth, Rev. xi.7-12." [91]

This is further confirmed, he continues, by the earthquake which took place in the same hour "when the tenth part of the papal city (viz. France) fell." [92]

9. 1290 YEARS ENDED; 1335 SOON EXPIRING.—The vials, he believes, began to be poured out in 1792, as with the ending of the 1260 years *"time* should be no longer." So in the thirty-seven years since 1792, the 1290 years had expired, and entry had been made into the 1335 years. So he concludes that they are living "beyond the 1260 years." [93] Thus he holds that the seventh trump began to sound in 1792,[94] and during its sounding "the first resurrection is to take place, and the bodies of the living saints are to be changed." [95] Then he bursts forth:

"Oh! what a glorious sight will the manifestation of the sons of God be! each made like unto Christ's glorified body, shining with united and eternal splendour, like the brightness of the firmament, and as the stars forever and ever." [96]

---

[90] *Ibid.*, p. 19.
[91] *Ibid.*, pp. 19, 20.
[92] *Ibid.*, p. 20.
[93] *Ibid.*, p. 22.
[96] *Ibid.*
[94] *Ibid.*, p. 23.
[95] *Ibid.*, p. 24.

10. Exhaustion of Turkey Followed by Babylon's Fall.
—He says in conclusion, "The drying up, therefore, of the
mystic River Euphrates, by which is signified, the exhaustion
of the power and strength of the Turkish Empire, will lead to
the destruction of Babylon the great, the mother of harlots and
abominations of the earth." [97]

Hooper's work on the Apocalypse simply reiterates the
positions of his previous books—the imminence of the advent,
the important place occupied by the 2300 years in determining
the time, and by the 2300 years and the 70 weeks for the Jews
beginning together in 453 b.c., and the longer period ending in
1847. [98]

11. New Prophetic Era Began in 1793.—His final tractate, *The Advent* (1847), stresses the phenomenal opening of
the prophetic word "from the time of that great prophetic era,
1793." As truly as the "political earthquake" of the French
Revolution shook the world, so have the people of God been
awakened, as by a voice from heaven, "declaring the coming
morning." A ray of light "gleamed along the prophetic horizon," and men betook themselves to the study of prophecy,
"declaring that a new era had arrived," the advent was soon
expected, when the dead in Christ must be raised. [99] The prophetic basis for the nearness of the advent is stressed—the 1260
years "clearly terminated in 1793," with the commencement of
the "season of the Redeemer's advent."

12. Cleansing of Sanctuary Already Begun.—Moreover,
Hooper adds, the great prophetic number of 2300 years, to close
with the cleansing of the sanctuary, or Christian church, "terminates as clearly at the period in which we are now living." And
he adds, "Who shall venture to say that that cleansing has not
already commenced?" [100] He dates all these signs of the last days
from 1793 onward, [101] believing mankind had entered the last
"generation." Then he adds:

---

[97] *Ibid.*, p. 25. [100] *Ibid.*, p. 21. [101] *Ibid.*, p. 25.
[98] John Hooper, *Apocalypsis; or, The Revelation*, pp. 23, 24.
[99] John Hooper, *The Advent*, pp. 15, 20.

"If the interpretation, therefore, which has been given of these signs be correct—if they really began to appear A.D. 1793—the coming of the Lord must be near indeed; for, according to this view of the prophecy, the present generation which has witnessed these signs will not pass away till the Son of Man be come." [102]

V. Pym—70 Weeks Begin the 2300 Years (453-1847)

The second at this time to stress the same 2300-year prophecy is WILLIAM W. PYM (1792-1852), who was educated at St. Johns, Cambridge, and received a B.A. in 1813 and an M.A. in 1816. From 1816 until his death he was vicar of Willian, Herts.[103] He wrote several small works, occupying a column in the British Museum catalogue. Their scope is evident from the titles: *Thoughts on Millenarianism* (1829),[104] *Inquiry Concerning Spiritual Gifts* (1832), and *A Word of Warning in the Last Days* (1835), which had two American editions, in 1837 and 1839. Then came *The Restitution of all Things* (1843), *The Doctrine of the New Testament on the Time of the Second Advent* (1843), *The Judgment and Kingdom of Christ* (1843), and *Watch: a Call to Every Man* (1848). He wrote the Introduction to *Good Things to Come,* the 1847 collection of Bloomsbury lectures by twelve clergymen. Finally, in 1851, he wrote *The City of Confusion to be Contrasted with the Heavenly Zion.*

Pym affords an interesting example of progressive change in prophetic interpretation. According to the Preface of his *Word of Warning,* he reached a time, several years prior, "when it pleased God to incline mine heart to receive these doctrines." Then, in 1829, he felt constrained to send forth his *Thoughts on Millenarianism* to help "warn the world" of the "speedy appearing" of Christ. But at that time his emphasis was upon the 1335-year time prophecy, which he then thought would terminate in 1867. But by 1835 his mind had been directed to the 2300 years, as beginning synchronously with the seventy weeks and terminating in 1847, by which time he expected the advent.

[102] *Ibid.,* p. 27.
[103] *The Gentleman's Magazine,* November, 1852 (New Series, vol. 38), p. 545; Frederic Boase, *Modern English Biography,* vol. 6, Supp. 3, cols. 440, 441.
[104] Two replies appeared in 1836.

Pym's *Word of Warning* was one of the British works publicized in the earliest issues of the American Millerite *Signs of the Times,* in 1840.[105]

1. LITTLE HORN, PAPACY; 1260 YEARS, 533-1793.—In his treatise on the millennium, which brings into small compass pertinent extracts from the Fathers, Pym taught the standard positions on Daniel 2 and 7. The little horn of chapter 7 is the Papacy, to be destroyed by the brightness of Christ's second advent. According to his reckoning the 1260 years date from Justinian's imperial edict in 533, and thus reach to 1793 and the French Revolution, which gave the Papacy a blow from which it had not then recovered.[106]

2. 1335 YEARS EXTENDED SEVENTY-FIVE YEARS BEYOND.— Pym then deals with the three prophetic time periods of Daniel 12—each based on the year-day principle. Beginning the three numbers synchronously, he extends the 1290 and 1335 years thirty and seventy-five years, respectively, beyond the terminus of the 1260 years in 1793—thus ending the 1335 in 1867.[107] Referring to entirely different calculations by others, he says, "The predicted events, which are to take place as the ushering in of the Millennium, *are nearer than is commonly supposed,* and that in very deed *the Coming of the Lord draweth nigh.*"[108] He then tabulates a prophetic "time" as a year, a prophetic "day" as fulfilled in a natural year, a prophetic "year" of twelve prophetic months as twelve prophetic months of thirty prophetic days[109]—therefore a prophetic year stands for 360 natural years.

3. DISCOVERS ONE KEY DATE FOR SECOND ADVENT.—His *Word of Warning,* with three scriptures on the advent appearing on the title page, was widely quoted in both Britain and America. In the Preface he states that for twenty years (or beginning in 1815) he had been connected with the British and Foreign Bible Society. But since he had accepted the doctrine of the second advent—which in no way diminished his activities in the

---

[105] *Signs of the Times* (Boston), December 15, 1840 (vol. 1, no. 18), p. 146.
[106] William W. Pym, *Thoughts on Millenarianism,* pp. 30, 31.
[107] *Ibid.,* p. 32.   [108] *Ibid.,* p. 33 (italics his).
[109] *Ibid.*

British and Foreign Bible Society—he felt it to be his duty to
warn the world by the preaching of the "everlasting gospel" concerning the speedy appearing of Christ.

He frankly states that his "views respecting the *Scripture
dates* were not so clear, at the time of writing the former work,
as they now are." [110]   That which clarified it all was the new
understanding of Daniel 8 in the light of Daniel 9.   Here he
found the key date that would unlock or govern the advent.   For
this he is indebted to another who wished his name withheld.

"*One date may be ascertained correctly;* and by means of this one
correct date we are enabled to ascertain the year, in which the restoration
of the seed of Abraham shall be accomplished; and by that the time,
before which the Second Advent of the Lord must have taken place." [111]

4. SEVENTY WEEKS BEGIN SYNCHRONOUSLY WITH 2300.—
The persecuting horn of chapter 8 is so similar to the Roman,
or papal, Little Horn of chapter 7 that he is led "to connect them
both in time and character."   Gabriel is sent to Daniel in chapter
9, verse 23, to explain the mysterious time vision of chapter 8.
The seventy weeks, or 490 years, were to be separated from the
2300, thus:

"To enable Daniel to understand the vision, he is told first to separate
seventy weeks, or 490 days, as a portion of the 2300 days of the preceding
chapter, 'determined on his people,' during which time the Jews should
remain in possession of the favour of God, after their return from Babylon.   He then tells him what would be done for the Jewish people during
these seventy weeks, or 490 days: the sum of which is to seal up the vision
and prophecy, and to anoint the Most Holy, ver. 24." [112]

And from the fact that the angel made known the dating of
the seventy weeks from the "commandment to restore and to
build Jerusalem," Pym concludes:

"The *seventy weeks commencing with the giving forth of this commandment, the 2300 days of the vision in the preceding chapter commence
also at the same time.*   For it is to be remembered that what is here stated
is avowedly an explanation of a preceding vision." [113]

---

[110] William W. Pym, *Word of Warning in the Last Days* (1839 American ed.), pp. vi, vii.
[111] *Ibid.*, p. 24 (1837 American ed.).
[112] *Ibid.*, p. 24.
[113] *Ibid.*, pp. 24, 25.

5. OVERSPREADING ABOMINATIONS FOLLOW SEVENTY WEEKS.—Pym then discusses the component divisions of the seventy weeks—seven weeks (or forty-nine years), for the rebuilding of Jerusalem; and before the close of the next sixty-two weeks (or 434 years) Messiah would have come; with the last week (of seven years) characterized by the cutting off of Messiah "some time in that week," along with the cessation of the sacrifices pointing forward to the Messiah.   Then comes this impressive statement:

"Then, by the overspreading of abominations the sanctuary is again made desolate, until the consummation of the remainder of the 2300 days, when that determined shall be poured upon the desolator [ix.27], and he shall then be broken without hand. (vii.25.)" [114]

6. 2300 CANNOT BE LITERAL DAYS.—He next buttresses the principle that in these numbers days must be "put for *years,*" citing Ezekiel 4.   He observes that as literal days do not agree with the demands of the seventy weeks, neither will they with the 2300, for this reason:

"For the first events of that vision, which consist only of the fightings between the Ram and the Goat, occupy five reigns of the kings of Persia, down to Alexander, king of Grecia: a period much too long to be included in 2300 days.   It is moreover declared that the events of this vision should continue until the cleansing of the sanctuary [viii.14.], which is declared to be the last end of the indignation [viii.17. 19.]   But as the Jews are still scattered over the earth, and their city and temple are not yet rebuilt, we know that the last end of the indignation is not yet come; and therefore that the 2300 days or years are not yet fulfilled.   The time of fulfilment is evidently that time spoken of in all the prophets, when God will cleanse both his people and his sanctuary." [115]

7. COMMENCEMENT FIXED BY MIDWEEK CRUCIFIXION.—To determine the common commencement, Pym says:

"But these numbers in both chapters of Daniel being thus proved by *internal* evidence to be years, and both having the same commencement, as being *one vision*, it remains to fix, by *internal* evidence also what was this commencement.   For as there were manifestly three commandments by Cyrus, Darius, and Artaxerxes [Ezra vi.4], so we cannot, by external evidence, ascertain which of these commandments is the one to which the seventy weeks apply." [116]

---

[114] *Ibid.*, p. 25.   [115] *Ibid.*   [116] *Ibid.*, pp. 25, 26.

The "fixed point" by which to determine the correct date is "the cutting off of Messiah in the *midst* of the last week." [117]

8. SEVENTIETH WEEK DATED A.D. 30 TO 37.—Taking the position that Christ began preaching when He was thirty years of age, and preached three and a half years; and the disciples preached to the Jews for three and a half years more, he dates the seventieth week thus:

"The covenant therefore is the Gospel covenant, and the last week of the seventy are those seven years which began when Christ was thirty years old, and finished A.D. 37, at the conversion of Cornelius. Sixty-nine weeks, or 483 years, have therefore to be reckoned back from the 30th year of Christ for the commencement of the seventy weeks, which deducting 30 from 483, makes before Christ 453; or, which is the same thing, 490 years, i.e. 70 weeks from A.D. 37." [118]

9. 2300 YEARS FROM 453 TO 1847.—Coming now to the vital relationship between the seventy weeks and the terminus of the 2300 years and the event involved, he says:

"But if the seventy weeks begin 453 years before the incarnation of Christ, the 2300 beginning at the same time, *we ascertain their termination* merely by deducting the years before the incarnation: which leaves A.D. 1847 as the time when the sanctuary shall be cleansed, and the vision be accomplished: *the last end of the indignation.*

"And this last end shall be *the consequence* of the second coming of Christ, as we have already seen; therefore before the end, i.e. A.D. 1847, Christ shall have come." [119]

10. SECOND ADVENT EXPECTED BY 1847.—While the day and hour is not made known, writes Pym, the completion of the work Christ came to do "is declared in these numbers," which lead to the time of trouble, the first resurrection, the scattering of the holy people, and the breaking of the last kingdom by the "*stone cut out without hand,*" as stated in Daniel 2.[120] Then comes this clear-cut conclusion:

"From the data, furnished entirely by this prophecy, we have ascertained, That the year of our Lord 1847 is the time appointed by Jehovah for the restoration and re-establishment of the seed of Abraham in the land, which he sware unto their fathers. From various passages of holy writ the next advent of the Lord must precede that restoration: from

[117] *Ibid.*, p. 26.　　　　　　　　[119] *Ibid.*
[118] *Ibid.*　　　　　　　　　　　[120] *Ibid.*

which it follows, *That the Second Advent of the Lord Jesus Christ must have taken place before the year 1847.* This is a calculation which a child may comprehend: it rests upon no uncertainty of human speculations, or upon corrupted or doubtful chronology, but upon one scriptural date connected with our own reckoning of time." [121]

Pym closes chapter 3 with an appeal to the Christian church to be "warned of their Lord's approach, 'lest coming suddenly he find them sleeping.' " [122]   Chapter 4 summarizes the various prophecies concerning Christ's first advent, showing how they were all fulfilled in the first advent.   His conclusion and summation come in chapter 6.   Appealing to the reader to allow these arguments to have their due weight, he reminds him that this is "present truth":

"*That the coming of our Lord draws nigh;* and so nigh, that *before* the year 1847, *the Scripture leads us to conclude,* it will have taken place. We speak not of the day or hour of that event; but, this we say, that by one unquestioned and unquestionable part of the chronology of the Bible, which has been placed beyond the power of man to corrupt, or in any way alter, (see Chap. III.) we are taught *the time, when one predicted event shall occur,* which event, *the same Scriptures teach us,* shall take place *after the Lord be come.*" [123]

11. Connects Return of Jews With 1847.—Pym connects the standing up of Michael with the cleansing of the sanctuary from its pollutions, for the "seed of Abraham" shall be "restored to their own land."   This, he reiterates—

"will take place in 1810 years from the end of the seventy weeks, or from three years and a half after Messiah shall have been cut off, in other words, from A.D. 37: for 1810, added to 490, i.e. to 70 weeks of years, equals 2300; and 1810 years from the year of our Lord 37 brings us to A.D. 1847." [124]

He deliberately refrains from stressing those aspects of "millenarian" doctrine "at which the finger of scorn is pointed" —the personal reign, the descent of the New Jerusalem, the many mansions, and even the doctrine of the new heaven and new earth—but stresses the one point *"that the national conversion of Israel and Judah are to be brought about only by the appearing of the Lord Jesus Christ."* [125]

---

[121] *Ibid.*, p. 27.
[122] *Ibid.*

[123] *Ibid.*, pp. 38, 39.
[124] *Ibid.*, p. 39.

[125] *Ibid.*, p. 40.

12. RETURN OF LORD EXPECTED WITHIN TWELVE YEARS.—
Referring to "much opposition, both from without and from
within," Pym makes this appeal:

"That the return of the Lord Jesus Christ to our earth, whenever it
take place, shall have for one of its objects to judge the world, every believer in the Bible will confess. If then we have the slightest reason to
suspect, that this judgment may take place before twelve short years have
completed their course [1835-47], 'what manner of persons ought we to
be in all holy conversation and godliness?' (2 Pet. iii.11.) But what manner
of persons are we? That is the important question. Are we living as
if we believed so awful an event to be at hand?" [126]

13. SEVEN TIMES OF GENTILES (673 B.C.-A.D. 1847).—
Finally, with an allusion to Habershon's and Cuninghame's
works, Pym speaks of the "seven times," or 2520 years of Leviti-
cus 26, as embracing the 2300 and having the same termination.

"In other words, the judgments threatened by Moses, which should last
during the seven times, or 2520 years; and the judgments revealed to
Daniel, which should come to an end by the cleansing of the sanctuary after
2300 years, must have one and the same termination. The 2300 years being
a portion of the greater number 2520. It has been already stated, and
that statement was drawn from the vision, and explanation of the vision
given to Daniel by Gabriel, that, according to the vulgar computation, the
period of 2300 years will expire in A.D. 1847." [127]

In his search for the beginning of the 2520 years Pym notes
the dates of Horne, Usher, Calmet, Prideaux, Hales, Cuninghame, and Bell, which all come within the space of four years.
Taking Hales' 673 B.C. date, he concludes: "For 1847 + 673 =
2520 years, or 7 times." [128] To Pym it appeared as "clear as if
written with a sun-beam," that the 2300 and 2520 years end
together with the expiration of the "times of the Gentiles." [129]
He declares himself "much strengthened" by reading Cuninghame's strictures on the Irving and Frere fallacious scheme of
Prophetic Arrangement.

14. INCLINES TO 2300 YEARS FROM 457 B.C. TO A.D. 1843.—
Pym is impressed by the argument that would begin the 2300
years in 457 B.C., and end them in 1843—four years earlier than

126 *Ibid.*, pp. 40, 41.   128 *Ibid.*
127 *Ibid.*, p. 48.   129 *Ibid.*, p. 49.

1847. To this he was now leaning, as we lose sight of him.

"Now, should it turn out to be as I have now supposed, that the 2300 years end at the *complete cleansing* of the sanctuary, in the day of Armageddon, I am not aware of any more probable era, which can be selected, for their commencement, than that which has been chosen by some recent writers, who suppose this period to have begun at the same time with the seventy weeks of Daniel, or in the year B.C. 457, and, consequently, that it will terminate in the year 1843." [130]

VI. Allwood—Apocalyptic Beast Is Papal Rome

There is nothing new presented by PHILIP ALLWOOD (1769-1838), lecturer and author. He was educated at St. Paul's and Harwich, and then at Magdalen College, Cambridge, from which he received a B.A. in 1791, an M.A. in 1794, and a B.D. in 1802.[131] He was author of *Twelve Lectures on the Prophecies Relating to the Christian Church, and especially to the Apostasy of Papal Rome* (1815). He also wrote *A Key to the Revelation of St. John, the Divine* (1829), bearing the text "Blessed is he that readeth . . . for the time is at hand."

1. JOHN'S BEAST SAME AS DANIEL'S LITTLE HORN.—Following the general interpretations of the time, Allwood believed the ten horns of the beast of Revelation 13 to be the ten kingdoms "which were to spring up within the limits of the *Western* Empire, after the division of the whole Empire into two parts in the year 365." [132] The seven heads are the seven forms of Roman government, and the crowns on the horns "demonstrate that these ten kingdoms were so many *absolute* and *independent* sovereignties." [133] After the wounding of the imperial beast, it was succeeded by that "spiritual dominion which is denominated the 'Little Horn' by Daniel, and 'the Beast of the Earth' by St. John." It is none other than "the BISHOP *of* ROME, that *spiritual tyrant,* who, in the year 606, was placed supreme over the Church of God, into whose hands, 'the saints of the MOST HIGH' " were then given.[134]

---

[130] *Ibid.*
[131] *Alumni Cantabrigienses,* part 2, vol. 1, p. 45; *The Gentleman's Magazine,* June, 1838 (New Series, vol. 9), p. 664.
[132] Philip Allwood, *A Key to the Revelation of St. John, the Divine,* vol. 1, p. 571.
[133] *Ibid.*   [134] *Ibid.,* p. 580.

2. Second Beast Embraces Priestly Orders.—As the first beast was the "temporal Roman Empire," so he held that the two horns of the second, or ecclesiastic, beast represent the *"regular* and *secular Orders* in *the Romish Church,* which is *the spiritual Empire* here intended." [135]

---

[135] *Ibid.*, p. 599.

CHAPTER THIRTY

Irish Heralds
Launch Prophetic Journal

The year 1830 opens with one hundred Protestant heralds of the advent in Catholic Ireland. By voice and pen they stress the prophecies in the same familiar vein as elsewhere—2300 years and all. And prophetic conferences are held. In Scotland, too, the testimony is given. Then Preterism joins Futurism to bring increasing challenge and attempted confusion to the Historical School of interpretation. Of the answering responses, some are clear; others are hazy. We turn first to Ireland.

I. Dublin *Christian Herald* Proclaims Advent Prophecies

The launching of *The Christian Herald* in 1830, in the very heart of Roman Catholic Ireland, was quite a venture. Edited by EDWARD NEWENHAM HOARE (1802-1877),[1] rector of St. Lawrence, Limerick, and minister of the Episcopal Chapel attached to the Blind Asylum, this Irish monthly started without sponsors, capital, or subscribers. It was forthwith attacked by other magazines, but was aided by upwards of one hundred clergymen of the Established Church. It was a venture of faith, and the result of a conviction that the church must be stirred and the truth of the second advent proclaimed.[2] The opening editorial stresses the concurrence of conviction, both from the "prophetic numbers" and the "signs of the times," that the

---

[1] Biographical data lacking.
[2] *The Christian Herald*, vol. 1, Preface, pp. [iii], iv.

advent is near, even at the doors.[3]   (Title page reproduced on page 414.)

After rehearsing the story of the advent hope of the early church, and its loss throughout the Dark Ages, when "the abominations of 'the mother of harlots' covered all Christendom," the *Herald* tells how gleams of advent and prophetic light broke upon the Waldenses and Lollards, and finally burst forth in great fullness during the Reformation, after which it was brought into disrepute by fanatics.   But now, once more, the doctrine of the premillennial advent of Christ has been revived, and is again suffering a renewed attack by Satan.[4]

1. "R.H." IDENTIFIES TIME AS PHILADELPHIA PERIOD.—In volume 1, by means of a diagram, "R.H." identifies the seven periods of the Christian church as symbolized by the seven churches of Revelation 2 and 3; Ephesus is the apostolic age; Smyrna, persecution under pagan Rome; Pergamos, temporal prosperity under Constantine; Thyatira, papal persecution of the martyrs in the Dark Ages; Sardis, the sixteenth-century Reformation; Philadelphia, spiritual emphasis in the early nineteenth century; and Laodicea, the time of great declension prior to the second advent and the judgment of Antichrist. He thus identifies his own time as that of Philadelphia, and believes that the advent is drawing near.[5]

After denying the spiritual concept of the resurrection as "but the step to a new life," the *Herald* sets forth a first literal resurrection of the saints "at the Second Advent of Christ, and the other not for a thousand years after." [6]

2. DIVISIONS OF ROME REFUSE TO ADHERE.—In the July issue begins a detailed editorial exposition of Daniel 2, with the standard four empires of Babylon, Medo-Persia, Greece, and Rome.[7]   Much attention is given to the divided state of the feet, still existing and destined to "so continue, as we shall presently see, till the second advent." [8]   Broken up by the "hordes of

---

[3] *Ibid.*, January, 1830 (vol. 1, no. 1), p. 1.
[4] *Ibid.*, pp. 6, 7.
[5] *Ibid.*, April, 1830 (vol. 1, no. 4), p. 56.
[6] *Ibid.*, May, 1830 (vol. 1, no. 5), p. 65.
[7] *Ibid.*, pp. 100, 101.
[8] *Ibid.*, p. 102.

barbarians," the empire "at length came to be divided into TEN kingdoms." There is stress of the fact that this is all in the "west of Europe; (exclusive of that part which the Romans conquered from the three preceding empires)." [9]

Despite the admixture of potter's clay and the "continual jealousies, the endless feuds, the bitter animosities, and the bloody and long protracted wars," there nevertheless was the strength of iron, as in the reigns of Charlemagne, Charles V, "and we may add, during the late reign of the usurper Bonaparte." [10] But "these ten kingdoms could never again be made to coalesce, or adhere together, so as to form one united and unbroken body."

"This has been attempted; efforts have been made to this end, and of late years especially, a great attempt was made for this purpose, when Bonaparte established the French INDIVISIBLE empire, as it was called; but see how soon it was crushed to pieces." [11]

The mingling of the seed of men was "the INTERMARRIAGES of the royal families of Europe into one another." [12]

3. IDENTIFYING MARKS OF PAPAL LITTLE HORN.—The August issue continues with Daniel 7. Again the standard historical interpretation appears, with great detail, such as the sea of nations, the strength and dignity of Babylon symbolized by the king of beasts and the king of birds, the rough and savage bear of the empire of the Medes, with the Persians ascendant. [13] In the next number the nondescript fourth empire of Rome, and its ten divisions, continues—the plucking up of the Duchy of Rome, the Exarchate of Ravenna, and the kingdom of Lombardy, to make way for the pope and his successors.

Thus did "Popedom become the eighth little horn of the fourth beast," with the pope wearing the triple crown of the three plucked up. [14] The papal eyes of cunning are noted, and the "noisy and blustering" mouth thundering forth bulls and anathemas, excommunicating princes, absolving subjects, and boasting supremacy. The great words include the claim of

---

[9] *Ibid.*
[10] *Ibid.*, p. 103.
[11] *Ibid.*
[12] *Ibid.*
[13] *Ibid.*, August, 1830 (vol. 1, no. 8), pp. 117-120.
[14] *Ibid.*, September, 1830 (vol. 1, no. 9), p. 142.

infallibility and the assumption of divine attributes and titles. The special time period of 1260 years is noted.[15]

4. CONTINENTAL SOCIETY GIVING REVELATION 14 TO TEN KINGDOMS.—Laudatory emphasis is given to the Continental Society, its purpose, needs, and accomplishments, in the light of German neology and French infidelity. Its field of operation is "Babylon; throughout the streets of which (i.e. the various kingdoms into which Christendom is divided)" its message is to be given. To these, the heralds of the society send the cry, "Come out of her my people." This cry should "resound from hill to hill, throughout the nations of Europe; this is the warning voice, which by the mouth of her heralds she would proclaim at the head of every street of the great city of Babylon." [16] These and similar societies are editorially regarded as "the fulfilment of the vision of the angel having the everlasting Gospel to preach, to all nations under heaven (Rev. xiv.6), so do we regard the Continental Society as the voice which cried aloud, previous to the downfall of Babylon (Ch. xviii.4)." [17] Here is a paragraph that gives the heart of it all:

"Those kingdoms, which constitute the sphere of this society's operations, are the ten horns of the fourth beast which Daniel saw; the ten toes of Nebuchadnezzar's image. Destruction, fearful, sudden and complete awaits them; the stone cut out without hands is ready to fall upon them and to crush them to atoms; their doom is fixed, and soon shall they be made as 'the chaff of the summer threshing floors;'—the deluge of fire is about to be poured upon them, and their place shall no more be found. Upon their ruins shall be established the kingdom of our Lord and of his Christ; and then shall the transgressors be rooted out, and the meek shall inherit the earth." [18]

5. CHARLOTTE ELIZABETH'S PROPHETIC POEM.—The September issue closes with a prophetic poem by Charlotte Elizabeth, then living in Ireland. The first twelve lines read:

> "When from scattered lands afar
> Speeds the voice of rumour'd war,
> Nations in tumultuous pride
> Heav'd like Ocean's roaring tide

---

[15] *Ibid.*, pp. 143, 144.   [16] *Ibid.*, p. 155.   [17] *Ibid.*
[18] *Ibid.*

When the Solar splendours fail
And the Crescent waxeth pale,
And the pow'rs that starlike reign,
Sink dishonour'd to the plain.
World! do thou the signal dread;
We exalt the drooping head
We uplift th' expectant eye,
Our redemption draweth nigh." [19]

The witness of this talented writer will be noted later.

6. JUDGMENT PRECEDES ADVENT; 1260 YEARS BEGIN 533.—
In the October number the exposition of Daniel 7 continues,
with the judgment scene as the one that *"precedes* the second
coming of Christ, which is described in *verse* 13, and therefore
cannot be the *last judgment* which shall be conducted by Him,
after that His coming again." "The judgment here described
precedes the millennium," and it is "followed by *the general
judgment of all."* [20] The 1260 years that mark "the duration
of the power of the little horn" must be dated from some event
when "extraordinary power was given to the little horn." [21]
Holding that both the grant of the Greek emperor Phocas, in
606, and the grant of Pepin, in 755, came too late, the editor
fixes upon the edict of Justinian in 533, as leading 1260 years
later to the French Revolution in 1793. [22] The visit of Edward
Irving from London to Dublin, and his lectures in large halls,
are noted with approval, [23] and the Scottish J. A. Begg's new
book *Christ's Return in Glory* is favorably reviewed. [24]

7. DIGBY ON PROPHETIC DATES AND PAPAL REVIVAL.—
Volume 2, for 1831, begins by stressing the "awful doom" that
awaits the horns of the fourth Beast, the "toes of Nebuchadnezzar's image," and "the judgments about to crush them to
dust." [25] Drummond's *Dialogues on Prophecy* is noted, [26] as
are also the travels of Joseph Wolff. [27] In July the testimonies
of the early church Fathers on the millennium are given, with
documentation. [28] One writer, in August, prefers the 2400 of

---

[19] *Ibid.*, p. 156.   [24] *Ibid.*
[20] *Ibid.*, October, 1830 (vol. 1, no. 10), p. 158.
[21] *Ibid.*, p. 159.   [25] *Ibid.*, January, 1831 (vol. 2, no. 13), p. 1.
[22] *Ibid.*, pp. 160, 161.   [26] *Ibid.*, p. 15.
[23] *Ibid.*, p. 176.   [27] *Ibid.*, March, 1831 (vol. 2, no. 15), p. 59.
[28] *Ibid.*, July, 1831 (vol. 2, no. 19), pp. 162-167.

the Septuagint instead of 2300, for Daniel 8:14, and dates the period from 553 B.C. to A.D. 1847, as the time of Mohammedanism's triumph over the churches of the East.[29]

William Digby, who had been present at the Powerscourt House meeting for the consideration of prophecy, dates the 490 years from the decree of Artaxerxes Longimanus, and the 1260 years from 533 to 1793, for the "masterpiece Popery." [30] He remarks that the papal Jezebel, "when she has a new sort of lovers—the children of her former ones—to court, has painted her face to look like a blooming beauty of the XIXth century, and tired her head with the cap of liberty." [31] The times are evil and the people confused—except those who are "instructed by the prophets" from the great "calendar of prophecy," and who know the times will wax worse until the second advent.[32]

8. "H.F." ON SIGNS OF TIMES AND CHRISTENDOM AS "CITY." —"H.F." presents a sketch, in tabulated form, of the signs of the "Last Days"—revolutions, commotion, wars, earthquakes, plagues, famines, increase of wickedness, decay of true religion, gradual wasting away of Turkey, increase of infidelity, anarchy, and popery, general circulation of the Scriptures (Rev. 24: 6, 7), increased light on prophecy (Dan. 12:4, 9, 10), renewal of spiritual gifts, despoiling of the Catholic Church, and restoration of the Jews.[33] The great city of Revelation 16 is the nations of Christendom, since "in the 11th chapter of the Revelation, the Revolution of France is designated as the falling of the tenth part of the city." [34]

9. TWO ORGANIZATIONS FOR STUDY OF PROPHECY.—Two unique organizations for the study of prophecy are then noted. The first is the Paisley (Scotland) Society for the Investigation of Prophecy, instituted in October, 1830,[35] with its "Regulations" for appointments, and its procedure.[36] Paisley was where James A. Begg resided. The second is the Powerscourt House four-day meeting on prophecy in October, with three sessions daily,

[29] *Ibid.*, August, 1831 (vol. 2, no. 20), pp. 180, 181.
[30] *Ibid.*, December, 1831 (vol. 2, no. 24), pp. 270-273.
[31] *Ibid.*, p. 274.
[32] *Ibid.*, pp. 274, 275.
[33] *Ibid.*, pp. 275-279.
[34] *Ibid.*, p. 279.
[35] *Ibid.*, p. 282.
[36] *Ibid.*, pp. 283-286.

under the chairmanship of Robert Daly, rector of Powers-court[37]—one of the leading topics being the 1260 year-days.[38]

10. SEVENTY WEEKS AND 2300 DAYS.—In volume 3, for 1832, appears an important editorial discussion of the relationship of the 2300 years to the seventy weeks of years. To the question "How long shall be the vision?" the answer is, "Seventy weeks are determined (or 'cut off' from a larger portion of time)."[39] It is here argued that there are two parts to the question, and the second—the sanctuary and the host to be trodden under-foot—is the result of the former. Seventy weeks of years are appointed for accomplishing the former part; and that will leave 1810 years for the accomplishment of the rest of the vision.[40] Then comes this clear bit of reasoning:

"If now the fulfilment of the former portion of 70 weeks has proved to be years, we come to the conclusion that the latter number of 1810 is also years; to be dated from the fulfilment of the former; namely, the crucifixion and ascension of Messiah. Thus 1810 added to A.D. 33, makes A.D. 1843 the date for the cleansing of the sanctuary."[41]

Discussions by J. H. Frere[42] and J. N. Darby[43] appear, and there is notice of a second series of meetings for the discussion of prophecy at Powerscourt House, centering chiefly on the gifts and on Antichrist.[44]

11. SHRINKING EUPHRATES IS TURKISH DISINTEGRATION.—In volume 4, for 1833, the concept of an individual infidel anti-christ in the last days is increasingly emphasized by one group of contributors.[45] Notice is also given of the 1833 Curry abridg-ment of Irving's English translation of Ben-Ezra, published at Dublin.[46] But the item of greatest significance in this volume

[37] These periodic discussions continued over several years under the chairmanship of Robert Daly, bishop of Cashel. The meetings were held every second Tuesday, during the summers, with two or three sessions daily. Lady Powerscourt filled her house with prominent clergymen of every denomination from England, Scotland, and Ireland—among them Edward Irving. Difficult questions were propounded. They sought agreement upon the "great features," and expected disagreement upon "minor details." So deep was Lady Powerscourt's interest that she had consulted all available books on the subject. (*Personal Recollections of the Right Rev. Robert Daly, D.D.*, pp. 18-23; *Letters and Papers by the Late Theodosia A. Viscountess Powerscourt*, pp. x, xi.)
[38] *The Christian Herald*, December, 1831 (vol. 2, no. 24), p. 287.
[39] *Ibid.*, September, 1832 (vol. 3, no. 31), pp. 190, 191.
[40] *Ibid.*, p. 194.
[41] *Ibid.*
[42] *Ibid.*, December, 1832 (vol. 3, no. 32), p. 258.
[43] *Ibid.*, p. 281.
[44] *Ibid.*, pp. 290, 291.
[46] *Ibid.*, pp. 52, 216.
[45] Such as Frere in *The Christian Herald*, March, 1833 (vol. 4, no. 33), pp. 50-52.

concerns the "drying up of the Euphrates." [47] The horn of Daniel 7 is held to be the Papacy in the Western Empire, and the horn of Daniel 8 is set forth as the Mohammedan, or Turkish, power in the Eastern Empire, destined to "come to an end." "The glory of the Ottoman empire has long been on the wane. The waters of the great river Euphrates have been gradually drying up." [48] Then follows a list of its losses and retrenchments.

12. 1843 ENDING CONNECTED WITH OTTOMAN FALL.—By the exhaustion of the Euphratean waters preparation will be made for the gathering together of the confederacy of the beast, the false prophet, and the ten kings of the Latin earth, "to their own destruction at Armageddon." [49] But this is connected by Hoare, the editor, with the return of the Jews, the "kings of the East," to their own land of Palestine. [50] As one of the events connected therewith, the editor places the termination of the 2300-year prophecy, which had its beginning with the seventh of Artaxerxes, in 457 B.C. Then he says:

"If we reckon the 2300 days as years, we shall find the period terminates in A.D. 1843. Whether this be the true method of calculation a few years will prove." [51]

Then he adds that various "learned men" had been led to expect this event at different periods from 1840 to 1847. [52] With this he connects the wasting away of the Ottoman Empire. [53] While we may not know the day or hour, the wise know when the coming of the Lord is near. Dissenting note is taken editorially of the supernatural manifestations in Irving's London church. [54] On the other hand, Futurist contributors seek to disparage the papal Antichrist concept and the year-day principle. [55]

13. CONFLICTS AND APATHY END "HERALD'S" CAREER.— Volume 5, for 1834-35, brings this unique journal to a close. Agi-

---

[47] *Ibid.*, June, 1833 (vol. 4, no. 34), p. 53 ff.
[48] *Ibid.*, p. 53.
[49] *Ibid.*, p. 54.
[50] *Ibid.*, pp. 54, 55.
[54] *Ibid.*, p. 108 ff; also September, 1833 (vol. 4, no. 35), p. 208.
[55] *Ibid.*, pp. 194-199, 250, 251.

[51] *Ibid.*, p. 58.
[52] *Ibid.*
[53] *Ibid.*, p. 59.

tation by the Futurists, a waning interest, and a diminishing subscription list brought about its demise. Challenges increased on the year-day principle,[56] on the papal Antichrist,[57] and on the 533 Justinian edict constituting the pope the "head of all the churches." [58] The editor observes that belief in millenarian doctrines appeared confined at first to men "distinguished for orthodoxy in doctrine, and freedom from the spirit of dissent." [59] But now extremism had arisen with "mutual recriminations." And "prejudice against the study of prophecy" had increased and had "deterred many inquirers from the consideration of the subject." As a result there had been a "decrease in circulation of such works as this, treating on Prophecy," and "these have withdrawn their support." [60] So with a warning that the devil would seek to "divert your minds from the subject of the Lord's second Advent," Editor Hoare says, "Finally, brethren, farewell." [61]

II. Digby—Champion of Historical Year-Day Principle

WILLIAM DIGBY (1783-1866), Irish archdeacon of Elphin from 1809 to 1823, was educated at the University of Dublin, with an M.A. in 1820.[62] He wrote *A Treatise on the 1260 Days of Daniel and Saint John: Being an Attempt to Establish the Conclusion That They Are Years; and also to Fix the Date of Their Commencement and Termination* (1831). This was occasioned by S. R. Maitland's attempt to overthrow the year-day principle and to thrust Antichrist into the future. Later he published *Appeal to the Roman Catholic Priesthood of Ireland* (1845).

1. PAPAL HORN ASCENDANT OVER DIVISIONS.—With forceful logic and substantiating facts Digby establishes the partitioning of the Roman fourth world power "into ten separate sovereignties," followed by "the rise of a new power of a different character—an ecclesiastical character," that "should soon swal-

---

[56] *Ibid.*, March, 1834 (vol. 5, no. 37), p. 32 ff. [61] *Ibid.*, pp. 220, 221.
[57] *Ibid.*, pp. 36, 37. [59] *Ibid.*, July, 1835 (vol. 5, no. 40), p. 217.
[58] *Ibid.*, p. 132. [60] *Ibid.*, p. 218, 219.
[62] *Alumni Dublinenses*, 1593-1860, p. 229; Frederic Boase, *op. cit.*, vol. 6, Supp. 2, col. 106.

low up the temporalities of some" and afterward "succeed in obtaining an evil ascendant over the whole." [63]

2. ALL PARTIES AGREE ROME WAS PARTITIONED.—This power would stand until the Ancient of days would come, and the judgment would sit. The time period of this ecclesiastical phase is not days but years. On the division of Rome into ten kingdoms all opposition parties agree—the papal Machiavelli, the infidel Gibbon, and the Protestants Mede and Isaac Newton. [64]

3. PAPAL USURPER'S PERIOD 1260 YEARS.—Scouting the Jesuit counterinterpretation of Futurism, now obtruding into Protestantism, Digby affirms that the papal usurper has assumed the place of prophet, priest, and king, and that the beast of Revelation 13, connected with the city of Rome, has long ago made his appearance. [65] The destruction of the empire has *"long since* been accomplished"; therefore the "days" of the Gothic kings "are not natural days," but years, [66] and the 1260 days are years.

4. 2300 YEARS BEGIN WITH SEVENTY WEEKS; 457 B.C.— Similarly, the 2300 days, relating to the pollution and eventual cleansing of the sanctuary, are years, beginning synchronously with the seventy weeks.

"Is it not then more reasonable to date its commencement from the commencement of the restoration of that sanctuary in the days of Ezra, which will make it to commence SYNCHRONICALLY with another vision of the same Daniel, respecting the same sanctuary; I mean the vision of the seventy weeks, which I suppose that R.D. will allow to have commenced with the seventh year of Artaxerxes Longimanus, and to have terminated (making an allowance for the error of four years which has crept into the common reckoning of the Christian era) Anno Domini 33." [67]

Upon the "understanding the 2300 days to mean years," he declares:

"The time for the cleansing of the sanctuary at Jerusalem has not yet arrived—nor will it for sixteen years yet to come, (making the same allowance again for the error of four years in the chronology.)" [68]

---

[63] William Digby, *A Treatise on the 1260 Days*, p. 4.
[64] *Ibid.*, pp. 4, 5.   [66] *Ibid.*, pp. 7, 8.   [68] *Ibid.*, p. 9.
[65] *Ibid.*, pp. 6, 7.   [67] *Ibid.*, pp. 8, 9.

5. TERMINUS OF 2300 YEARS ABOUT 1843.—In other words, A.D. 1831 + 16 = 1847, and 1847 — 4 = 1843. Digby then contends that the 2300 years should be connected with "that lesser calendar of prophecy," the 70 weeks, or 490 years. Therefore, "after the expiration of 2300 years from the same memorable period," of 457 B.C., the Redeemer shall come to Zion, to consume His enemies with the rod of His mouth, as He comes in the "clouds of heaven, and with all the angels of God as His worshipping attendants." [69] Thus he concludes:

"Then, as Daniel says, shall the sanctuary, after its long continued desolation and treading down beneath the horses hoofs of the robbers of the wilderness, be cleansed—and cleansed, to be polluted no more for ever!" [70]

To this Digby joins the "exhaustion of the Ottoman power," making way for the homeward move of the Jews. When these things are coming to pass, the expiration of the 2300 years is at hand, and is of probable occurrence "within about a dozen years, or a little more, from the present period" [71]—in other words, 1831 + 12 = 1843, or "a little more."

6. 1260 YEARS DATED FROM 533 TO 1793.—Challenging Maitland's denial of the 1260 year-days to begin "shortly after the ten Gothic horns had sprouted forth" from the fourth beast, Digby refers to the clear understanding of Wyclif, Luther, Jewell, and Mede concerning the papal Antichrist as the "foredoomed Babylon of the New Testament." He speaks of the witness pouring forth from "burning lips and burning pens" of true Protestants, in contrast to present "Protestants of a feebler spirit." [72] He declares that the 1260 days are years, beginning with Justinian's decree of 533 recognizing the pope as head of all true churches "by sending bishops to him as ambassadors." [73] This period is not dated from the early inception of the Papacy, or from the beginning of its temporal sovereignty, but from the bestowal of spiritual authority by "Justinian the personator of the dragon"—and Justinian reigned in both East

[69] Ibid., pp. 9, 10.
[70] Ibid., p. 10.
[71] Ibid.
[72] Ibid., pp. 11, 14, 15.
[73] Ibid., p. 26.

and West, and was promulgator of the laws commonly accepted.[74] A second confirmation of the year-day principle comes from the ending of the 1260 days in 1793 during the French Revolution.[75] And "Babylon the Great is spiritually fallen already." [76]

7. SEVEN TIMES (2520) FROM 723 B.C. TO A.D. 1793.—Moreover, 1260 years is the second half of the times of the Gentiles dated from 723 B.C.[77] Then he submits the following, as he is unwilling to hold a position that is untenable:

"I wish to know, what can be advanced against these things, so as to constitute a valid, or even plausible ground of objection to the above scheme of interpretation being admitted." [78]

8. TEN DIVISIONS: THE THREE AND THE SEVEN.—Regarding the partitioning of Western Rome, and the diversity in the listing of the ten toes and ten horns of Daniel 2 and 7, some contend that there could be no variation in the names.[79] According to Daniel 7:8, three were to be plucked up before the mysterious eleventh. These Digby lists as the Herulo-Turingi, the Ostrogoths, and the Lombards.[80]

This leaves "only seven Gothico-Roman kingdoms to inquire after." [81] These must be primary kingdoms that have been perpetuated. These Digby lists as the Vandals, Suevi, Alans, Burgundians, Franks, Visigoths, and Anglo-Saxons. These are the ones listed by the "greater majority of the historians, or commentators." [82] In support he mentions Machiavelli, Mede, Lloyd, Isaac Newton, Bishop Newton, Whiston, and Faber.[83] That is the Irish archdeacon's concept.

III. Leslie—Heralds of the Judgment Hour Sounding

JAMES LESLIE,[84] of Edinburgh, simply signed himself "Amici" in his eleven-page *Circular Letter on the Revolution in Europe,* now with a twelve-page Appendix in the third edition. It is addressed "To All Christian Ministers and People in Great

---

[74] *Ibid.*, pp. 26, 27.
[75] *Ibid.*, pp. 34, 35.
[76] *Ibid.*, p. 38.
[77] *Ibid.*, pp. 38, 39.

[78] *Ibid.*, p. 39.
[79] *Ibid.*, p. 72.
[80] *Ibid.*, pp. 73, 74.
[81] *Ibid.*, p. 74.

[82] *Ibid.*, p. 76.
[83] *Ibid.*, p. 81.
[84] Biographical data lacking.

Britain." The previous editions had been distributed just in Edinburgh alone through the "unusual mode" of house-to-house visitation, as a means of discovering the interest of the people.

"Accordingly, beginning a course of visiting from house to house, and taking each family in a land, he left a copy with each, informing them that they should have the reading of it gratis, and if pleased with it, they might keep it at a small price. By these means all were warned of the great and dreadful things coming on the world, and our own country." [85]

1. JUDGMENT-HOUR CRY HAS BEGUN.—The result of such a canvass of sentiment was that "almost every other family or person kept them, and paid for them, except the very poor ones, to whom he freely bestowed them." [86] Stressing the fact of general belief in the second advent, but with decided differences as to the time, manner, and attendant circumstances, Leslie emphasizes the nearness of Christ's return and makes the impressive declaration:

"Several ministers and others in Britain have called, and are now calling the attention of their countrymen to the 'signs of the times.' The cry has gone forth, 'Fear God and give glory to him, for the hour of his judgment is come,' and many have attended to the warning. But it is also too true that many treat it with scorn, or looking upon it as wild, fanatical, bold, and presumptuous, attempt to dissuade others from listening to it." [87]

2. FRENCH REVOLUTION EARTHQUAKE ENDED 1260 YEARS.— Leslie describes the time as an "ominous silence" or an "interval of peace," before the bursting of the storm, during the "pouring out of the sixth vial on the Mahometan power in Europe and Asia." [88] The earthquake of the seventh vial was taken to be a "political revolution," soon to follow after the French Revolution, which closed the 1260 years. [89] In support, he cites Irving's Preliminary Discourse to his version of Ben-Ezra: "We now stand (i.e. 1827) upon the very edge and lip of the seventh vial, which is to consumate all wrath, and make a full end of the indignation." [90] He also cites the appeal of the Glas-

---

[85] James Leslie, *Circular Letter on the Revolution in Europe*, p. 2.
[86] *Ibid.*
[87] *Ibid.*
[88] *Ibid.*, p. 6.
[89] *Ibid.*, p. 7.
[90] *Ibid.*

gow minister, William Anderson, in *Apology for Millennial Doctrine*,[91] on the time of respite before the coming judgments.

3. SIXTH SEAL OPENED; EUPHRATES DRYING UP.—Satan's rule is nearly ended, Leslie continues; the time of retribution is at hand. The signs of the times all indicate it—"The *volcanoes of France* having begun again to smoke, threatening an erruption." The French Revolution, at the opening of the sixth seal, commenced the work of terror. But "in the midst of the desolation, the elements are marvellously ordered into a calm, till the servants of God have been sealed."[92] But the "suspension of the storm we enjoy at present . . . *cannot be continued much longer.*" Next Leslie cites John Hooper's *Present Crisis,* on the drying up of the mystic river Euphrates, or "ruin of the Turkish empire," as a sign of the imminent appearance of our Lord.[93]

4. ONE HUNDRED IRISH HERALDS OF ADVENT.—The concluding sentence reveals the number of Protestant ministers in Ireland proclaiming Christ's coming:

"I feel happy in acquainting you that about 100 protestant ministers in Ireland are proclaiming his [Christ's] coming, and perhaps there are near half as many in England, but Oh! how few in Scotland! May they be greatly increased!"[94]

5. PROTESTS IRVING'S TONGUES MOVEMENT.—In 1832, in a *Letter to the Rev. Edward Irving,* Leslie upbraids Irving's recent course "concerning the gift of tongues," this having given "great offence to the serious and reflecting part of my countrymen,"[95] because of his prominence in the exposition of prophecy and the heralding of the advent. So Leslie bears "public testimony" against "these your errors."

6. SHAKING OF NATIONS UNDER WAY.—In the following year, in *The Shaking of the Nations,* an essay on the causes of divine judgments—with the text "And I will shake all nations;

---

[91] *Ibid.*, pp. 7, 8.
[92] *Ibid.*, p. 8, citing Anderson's *Apology For Millennial Doctrine.*
[93] *Ibid.*, 1829 ed., p. 26.
[94] *Ibid.*, p. 23. This agrees with the Dublin *Christian Herald* statement. See p. 579.
[95] James Leslie, *Letter to the Rev. Edward Irving,* p. 14.

and the Desire of all nations shall come," on the title page—
Leslie declares, "There never was a time since the world began,
wherein it was more shaken than at present." [96] Yet, he adds,
mankind in general seems "quite insensible as to what may be
the ultimate or concluding part of this woeful drama thus acting
upon the stage of this wicked world." Satan contrives to get the
minds of men so engrossed with "human plans of reformation
for the better government of church and state" as to lose sight
of the design God has in view. [97] Referring parenthetically to the
odium brought upon the advent truth by the Irvingites, Leslie
says:

"It is true indeed that the religious world has much reason for being
displeased with some, who, after having begun to sound the trumpet of
alarm in Britain, have also commenced sounding a trumpet of strange
tongues, as they thought, or of miracle-working powers." [98]

7. THREE SPIRITS: PAGAN, PAPAL, AND INFIDEL.—Adverting again to Haggai, Leslie holds that many now seek the fulfillment in the second advent and the destruction of all things. [99]
With this he places Joel 3:16, showing that the great shaking
occurs at the second advent. And along with that he stresses
the three unclean spirits that, just before the day of God,
gather the nations for Armageddon, [100] just as they operated in
France before the great Revolution. Then the spirit of the
pagan dragon joined that of the corrupted papal priestcraft,
and these in turn were joined by the spirit of infidelity. Now,
in 1830, they have broken out again. The shock is felt in
Spain, Italy, Poland, Austria, and England. [101]

8. UNITE TO SUPPORT BEAST BRIEFLY.—The throne of
Mohammedanism is also shaking, Leslie continues. And Russia
in the north begins to bestir herself, hoping to gain much
out of the struggle. The same shaking is also operating in the
different churches as well as states. Then comes to pass St.
John's prediction, "These have one mind, and shall give their
power and strength unto the beast." [102]

---

[96] James Leslie, *The Shaking of the Nations*, p. 4.
[97] *Ibid.*, pp. 4, 5.   [99] *Ibid.*, p. 6.   [101] *Ibid.*, pp. 8, 9.
[98] *Ibid.*   [100] *Ibid.*, p. 8.   [102] *Ibid.*, p. 9.

9. ALL 1260-YEAR PERIODS ARE IDENTICAL.—After remarking that the common idea of a spiritual coming of Christ had been conveyed to Protestants through the impure channel of the church of Rome, Leslie turns to the 1260 years. He says:

"The time of the continuance of the head of that church to oppress the saints, is clearly pointed out by Daniel and St. John, Daniel gives us a time, times, and the dividing of time, in chapter vii. verse 25. John refers to the same oppression, 1st, Under the figure of two witnesses prophecying in sackcloth (Rev. xi.3,) 1260 days. 2d, Under the figure of a woman nourished in a wilderness for a time, times, and a half, Rev. xii.14. The same oppression is referred to in chapter xiii. verse 5, and the *time*, 42 months. All commentators agree, that these periods must be understood prophetically; so that 1260 days are so many years, and that 42 months, at the rate of 30 days to each month, amount to the same portion of time; and that *time, times, and the dividing of time,* is just the same." [103]

10. PAPAL 1260-YEAR PERIOD (531-1792).—Addressing himself to the time of this period, when the saints were put under the Little Horn's power, Leslie states:

"Now the Roman Emperor, Justinian, had that power, he only having the spiritual, as well as the temporal power of the empire; and this he did by an edict, bearing date A.D. 532. 'He gave full power to the Bishop of Rome to settle all controversies, by which he is declared Head of the Church, and infallible in all matters of faith,' &c. Counting forward, then, from that date, 1260 years brings us down to 1792, the eventful period of the French Revolution. At that time the Roman Catholic religion was publicly proscribed, her ministers insulted, and her temples profaned by the French infidels; and to complete the degradation, the holy city was assaulted and taken, and the Pope himself carried away captive. And that which is very remarkable, the two French officers in the chief command of the military sent by Napoleon Bonaparte upon this exploit, were called, the one LUTHER, and the other CALVIN! and with orders to tell his Holiness, that '*his kingdom was at an end!*' " [104]

11. HAVE ENTERED UPON THE LATTER DAYS.—While the pope recovered his temporal powers for a time, he never recovered his spiritual authority, and will be destroyed at the second advent. Thus, Leslie says, Daniel's prophecy was fulfilled. The judgment shall sit, and they shall "take away his dominion to consume and to destroy it unto the end." The

---

[103] *Ibid.*, p. 33.   [104] *Ibid.*

"end" being "the END of the four Gentile Monarchs, or the END of the present dispensation," he concludes that we are "ENTERED UPON THE 'LATTER DAYS.' "[105]

IV. Campbell—"The Hour of God's Judgment Is Come"

The prophetic message of Revelation 14:6 became the text, or the burden, of many a sermon. An example appears in *The Everlasting Gospel* (1830), a sermon preached by the Scottish minister JOHN M'CLEOD CAMPBELL (1800-72),[106] of Row, Dumbartonshire, in April, 1830. It was preached in The Floating Chapel, at Greenock and "taken in shorthand." Pressing upon the hour of God's judgment and the need to "fear God and to give him glory," he insists that they are living in the last days of the dispensation. Here are his words:

"I would now say to you, this night, 'fear God and give him glory, for the hour of his judgment is come,' in a strict and literal sense. We are now at the close of that last day, concerning which the apostle says, 'Hereby we know that it is the last time.' At the beginning of this day, of the Gentile dispensation, the Apostle said, 'we know that the ends of the world have come upon us.' The ends of the world had come upon them, but we are just at the evening of that last day—we are at the last hour of that last day; and it is very nigh, very nigh, even at the door. My dear hearers, I beseech you to consider, that it is just near at hand, at the very door, according to all who have studied this matter, and have sought the teaching of God; (and God desires that we should see what is before us, and not be groping in the dark,) that they are all of one mind; that that period commonly called the millenium—the reign of Christ—is just at hand."[107]

Most earnestly he appeals for the voice of prayer and the humbling of heart that will transform and prepare the life that the coming wrath may be escaped.[108] His closing words are: "O that you understood these things! 'Fear God and give glory to him, for the hour of his judgment is come.' " Amen![109]

---

[105] *Ibid.*, p. 34.
[106] Educated at Glasgow, 1811-20, and then at Edinburgh, he became a licentiate in the Church of Scotland. He was minister of Row in 1825, but was ejected for "heresy" in 1830. He preached in the highlands from 1830 to 1832, and was minister of a congregation in Glasgow from 1833 to 1859, receiving a D.D. degree from the University of Glasgow. (*Dictionary of National Biography*, vol. 3, pp. 840, 841.)
[107] John M'Cleod Campbell, *The Everlasting Gospel*, pp. 28, 29.
[108] *Ibid.*, pp. 31, 32.   [109] *Ibid.*, p. 32.

V. Preterist Lee—Ends Prophecies With Jerusalem's and
Rome's Fall

The projection of the Preterist view into the discussion in 1830, by SAMUEL LEE (1783-1852)—noted Orientalist and professor of Arabic and of Hebrew at Cambridge,[110] and rector of Barley, Hertfordshire (later canon of Bristol)—brought the three post-Reformation schools of interpretation again into definite conflict—the Historicist, Futurist, and Preterist. Preterism had become well-nigh dominant in the rationalistic universities of Germany.[111]   And now the noted linguist, Lee, under whom Wolff studied at Cambridge, espoused it.   His *Events and Times of the Visions of Daniel and St. John,* first published in 1830, is strictly Preterist; that is, all the specifications of Daniel and the Apocalypse were allegedly fulfilled in the downfall of pagan Rome and the overthrow of Jewry.

A general résumé must suffice: Lee builds nearly everything around the seventy weeks of Daniel 9, not as a definite chronological term but as an indefinite period.   He makes the three and a half times of Daniel 7 coincident with the last of Daniel's seventy mystical weeks, and comprehends within it the two catastrophes—first the fall of Jerusalem and the reprobate Jewish nation, and then the heathen Roman as God's instrument for desolating Jerusalem.   So the three and a half times is the last half of Daniel's seventieth week.[112]

In the Apocalypse the seals, trumpets, and vials are synchronous, according to Lee, and are compassed in this elastic seventieth week—the fourth seal referring to Jerusalem's fall in the middle of the week, the fifth to the pagan persecutions. The trumpets likewise depict the fall of the Jews.   The witnesses testify in the first three and a half days of the seventieth week, and are assailed in the latter three and a half days by the heathen Roman power, the beast from the abyss.   Christ is the

---

[110] One of the most profound linguists of his time and "master of 18 languages," he held various churchly posts and was author of numerous books.
[111] Such scholars as Hernnschneider, Eichhorn, Hug, Heinrichs, Hartig, Herder, Ewald, Bleek, and De Wette, with Professor Moses Stuart in America, and Dr. Samuel Davidson in England.   For detailed study see E. B. Elliott, *Horæ Apocalypticæ* (5th ed.), vol. 4, pp. 565-594.
[112] Samuel Lee, *Events and Times of the Visions of Daniel,* 1851 ed., pp. 69, 70.

child of the church of Revelation 12, and the persecution of the beast of Revelation 13 is under heathen Rome, from Domitian to Diocletian inclusive.

Thus the devil is loosed for a little season, Lee holds, as is depicted by the sixth trumpet—the hour, day, month, and year being the same as the three and a half times. Finally, the compassing of the beloved city and the destruction of Satan and his hosts signify the fall of the pagan Roman power, with the apocalyptic new heavens and new earth, the Christian church after Constantine. So the 1,000 years constitute "the apostolic period." Such was Lee's strange and yet familiar Preterist view of prophecy, which was as yet shared by relatively few in Britain.

VI. Anderson—Sixth Seal Began at French Revolution

WILLIAM ANDERSON (1799-1873), Scotch Presbyterian minister and author, was born at Kilsyth. He served as pastor of the John Street Presbyterian congregation of Glasgow almost continuously from 1822 to 1873, receiving an LL.D. degree from the University of Glasgow in 1850.[113] He was a strong advocate of the separation of church and state. An entire column of entries of his books appears in the British Museum catalogue. His *Apology for Millennial Doctrine* (1830) entreats its readers to take heed, holding that the sixth seal began its work of terror at the French Revolution.[114] He carried a heavy burden for others, that they might be heirs of the first resurrection, believing that the sealing of the servants of God was under way.

1. MULTIPLE EVENTS MARK SECOND ADVENT.—Anderson's *Apology* was written when he was serving as minister of the Relief Church, Glasgow. He begins by declaring that the destruction of the powers of Europe, the desolation of the Turkish Empire, and the destruction of popery will accompany the second advent. He declares, further, that the two literal resurrections, first the righteous and then the wicked, bound the

---

[113] *Roll of the Graduates of the University of Glasgow*, p. 282.
[114] William Anderson, *An Apology for Millennial Doctrine*, part 1, pp. 38, 41.

millennial period. And then the earth will be renovated, rectified, and beautified forever."[115] This, he declares, will begin to come to pass "when the Image of which Nebuchadnezzar dreamed shall be broken in pieces, Satan enchained, and the greatness of the kingdom under the whole heaven given to the Son of Man." [116]

2. SEVENTH VIAL SOON TO BE OUTPOURED.—Lifting his voice in warning of coming upheavals, he adds that "at the opening of the sixth seal (Rev. vi.12), the French Revolution commenced its work of terror," citing Cuninghame on the seals and trumpets.[117] He contends, moreover, that the sealing work is effected by that angel having the everlasting gospel to preach to all nations, followed by the next angel announcing the fall of Babylon.[118] Then he adds:

"The vial of wrath, the seventh, the last, the most woeful, is brimming high ready to be outpoured; and presently the season of peace shall have closed, for the recording of the names of those who shall be heirs of the First Resurrection." [119]

3. PRIMITIVE MILLENNIAL VIEW REVIVAL.—Calling the roll of the centuries, Anderson cites the blighting influence of Cerinthus, who perverted the early millennial view. The abuse spread until it became a curse. Then came other perversions under the apostate church.[120] At last the millennial truth that had been depressed for centuries sprang up again at the Reformation, along with the revival of the study of the Revelation.[121]

4. FIFTH EMPIRE OF DANIEL 7 IMPENDS.—In his closing section Anderson gives this terse exposition of Daniel 7:

"The Vision recorded in the seventh chapter of the book of Daniel, terminates in the same manner as does the Dream recorded in the second chapter. The four empires of Babylon, Medo-Persia, Greece, and Rome,—respectively symbolized by the Lion, the Bear, the Leopard, and the Monster,—having been overthrown and destroyed, the Fifth empire in the succession is the Kingdom of Heaven." [122]

---

115 *Ibid.*, pp. 1, 2.   118 *Ibid.*, p. 40.   121 *Ibid.*, part 2, p. 48.
116 *Ibid.*, p. 7.   119 *Ibid.*, p. 41.   122 *Ibid.*
117 *Ibid.*, p. 39 n.   120 *Ibid.*, pp. 4, 9, 50.

CHAPTER THIRTY-ONE

Prophetic Investigator
and Dictionary of Writers

Now comes the last of the leading prophetic journals, *The Investigator,* followed by the unique *Dictionary of Writers on the Prophecies,* both published in London. Anonymous tracts echo the advent message. Meetings for the study of prophecy convene in different cities. The familiar pattern of the prophecies appears, including the 2300 years. The Day of Atonement type is stressed again. The midnight cry is sounding from a thousand voices, declares a Bristol clergyman. Echoes of Bengel's positions are heard, and finally the testimony of another military man is given. We first note the strong witness of the journal edited by J. W. Brooks.

I. *The Investigator*—Reviewer of Prophetic Study; Herald of Advent

Another prophetic journal, *The Investigator, or Monthly Expositor and Register, on Prophecy,* edited by Joshua W. Brooks, was published from 1831 to 1836. One of the ablest of the various prophetic journals, in addition to its articles on prophecy and book reviews of current prophetic works, it gave news notes on current developments. Among the contributors are many of the most aggressive current expositors, though often of differing views, such as Begg, Cuninghame, Frere, Maitland, Birks, and Wolff. Here are noted Haldane and Drummond's Continental Society, and the Reformation Society. And Way's

599

Paris *Watchman,* as well as weekly meetings for the study of prophecy in the French capital, are chronicled. There is discussion of the anticipated revival of the gifts of the Spirit before the advent, and announcement of the appearance of *The Morning Watch.* There are also periodic discussions of the 2300 years. And the last volume closes with an invaluable *Dictionary of Writers on the Prophecies,* compiled by Brooks, the editor.

One of the earliest articles, "On the Duty of Prophetical Investigation and Discussion," asserts:

"The times are such as men of all parties and all opinions allow to be awfully portentous, and to bespeak some crisis to be impending; and all christians will confess, that prophecy alone is the only source from which we are likely to obtain light as to the result." [1]

1. VARIOUS MEETINGS FOR STUDY OF PROPHECY.—"Meetings for the discussion of prophecy" are reported for Birmingham, Leicester, with eighteen clergymen present, with word that "similar meetings, though on a smaller scale, have come to our knowledge in various places." [2] Lewis Way's monthly periodical, *The Watchman,* "chiefly devoted to the subject of Prophecy," is noted for Paris, where weekly meetings for the study of prophecy are in progress. A citation concerns the views of the Jansenists, a Catholic sect, which holds "sentiments which approximate to evangelical Protestantism" on Christ's second coming. [3] Then there is a terse answer to an inquiry on the question of 2300 or 2400 as the editor replies:

"There is not a single *manuscript* known to be extant, whether Hebrew or Greek, that sanctions the reading of 2400 days. It rests entirely upon a manifest *typographical error* of the Vatican Edition, taken from the Vatican manuscript." [4]

2. CLEANSING OF SANCTUARY IN 1843.—In volume 2 (1833) of *The Investigator* the editor discusses the "Progress of Prophetical Inquiry," from the time of Origen to his own day. He remarks that some are deterred "from its contemplation" by the

---

[1] *The Investigator,* August, 1831 (vol. 1, no. 1), p. 11.
[2] *Ibid.,* September, 1831 (vol. 1, no. 2), p. 52.
[3] *Ibid.,* November, 1831 (vol. 1, no. 4), p. 114.
[4] *Ibid.,* July, 1832 (vol. 1, no. 12), p. 441.

"obloquy and odium" created by the few.[5] In the June issue of 1833, "C.S." writes on the anticipated time of the commencement of the millennium. One of the most important factors mentioned is the cleansing of the sanctuary, which he takes to be Jerusalem or Palestine, thus involving the fact and place of Mohammedanism. He conceives the 2300-year time period to begin in 456 B.C., with the seventy weeks as the first part.[6] Thus it will end in 1843.

In volume 3 (1833), there is further discussion of the 2300 years, whether it involves the actions of the Western Antichrist or the Eastern, or Mohammedan, power.[7]

3. FRANCE IS TENTH PART OF CITY.—The fulfillment of the fall of the "tenth part of the city," by France in the French Revolution, is presented by Editor Brooks. He shows that this was the opinion of Cocceius in 1655, Goodwin in 1683, Cressener in 1690, then Whiston, Willison, and Taylor between 1745 and 1770, as well as of Bishop Newton. For the position that France was the "street of the city," he cites Vitringa, Jurieu, and John Bird in 1747, as well as Towers later. And for the earthquake as the French Revolution, Brooks cites Mede, More, Vitringa, and Fleming in 1700.[8]

4. JUDGMENT-HOUR MESSAGE SOUNDING.—In volume 4 (1834) appears a book review of WILLIAM ANTHONY HOLMES' *The Time of the End* (1833). Holmes places the end in 1836 on the basis of Bengel's calculation, followed by Wesley, at which point he terminates the 2300 years as well as other periods.[9]

"Nemo" discusses Revelation 12-14, holding the Papacy to be the second beast, from the earth, with the two horns representing civil and ecclesiastical power. The judgment-hour message of Revelation 14:6, 7, draws forth this significant comment: "A small voice has already been heard foretelling ap-

---

[5] *Ibid.*, January, 1833 (vol. 2, no. 6), p. 201.
[6] *Ibid.*, June, 1833 (vol. 2, no. 11), p. 401.
[7] *Ibid.*, September, 1833 (vol. 3, no. 2), p. 29.
[8] *Ibid.*, December, 1833 (vol. 3, no. 5), pp. 150-155.
[9] *Ibid.*, December, 1834 (vol. 4, part 2), pp. 109, 116.

proaching judgments, but a loud voice will soon resound we trust from many pulpits in this privileged land." [10]

5. CONTROVERSIES BETWEEN EXPOSITORS INCREASE.—Several editorial book reviews appear, approving Cuninghame's writings and pointing out fundamental weakness in Frere's and Irving's works. [11] One of the serious challenges was on the 2400- versus the 2300-year contention, though Wolff's claims of supporting Hebrew manuscripts are noted. [12] Brooks expresses concern over the increasing controversies between writers on prophecy and their acrimony, and over developments among the Irvingites. [13]

6. 1836 STIMULATES EXPECTATIONS OF CRISIS.—Because of Bengel's former expectation for the year 1836, in which date he had been followed by many, including John Wesley and W. A. Holmes, [14] volume 5 (for 1836) brings forth editorial comment about that, as well as the expectation for that year found among the dervishes of Persia by Joseph Wolff. [15] This, together with the approaching end of the 6,000 years, had stimulated the "general expectation of some great crisis being at hand," irrespective of difference of detail or of the precise year. [16]

A review of John Henry Browne's *The Time of the End* quotes him as contending that mankind had entered that fateful period. The evidence cited included increase of prophetic knowledge or understanding (Dan. 12:4), the deepening last-day apostasy, the proclamation of the judgment-hour message (Rev. 14:6, 7)—the very existence of which was a "sign of the times"—and the drying up of the Euphrates. [17]

---

[10] *Ibid.*, June, 1835 (vol. 4, part 4), pp. 344, 345. This substitution of "judgments" for the judgment is to be noted, for it characterizes the view of a number, as will be recalled.
[11] *Ibid.*, p. 354 ff.
[12] *Ibid.*, p. 355 (referring to p. 315).   [13] *Ibid.*, pp. 364, 367.
[14] W. A. HOLMES, B.A., was chancellor of Cashel. His book, *The Time of the End,* which was the result of a "series of lectures," begins the "seven times" (2520 years) with the captivity of Manasseh, under Esarhaddon in 685 B.C., which would end this period in 1835-36. (Pages 60, 61.) Then the kingdoms of this world should become the kingdoms of our Lord. With this he places the 2300 years from the 7th of Artaxerxes, which he dates in 456 B.C., and to which he adds nine years—or 465 from 2300, which he likewise brings to 1835-36, when the sanctuary should be cleansed, the Jews restored, and the kingdom of Christ established for a thousand years. (Pages 93, 94.) Holmes contends that the sanctuary cannot be cleansed so long as the Mosque of Omar stands on Mount Moriah, surmounted by the crescent. The year 1836 was also looked upon as the Jubilee of Jubilees, from the entry and possession of Canaan, in 1448 B.C. (Pages 96, 97.) Then in 1836 all prophecies would be fulfilled.
[15] *The Investigator*, January, 1836 (vol. 5, no. 43, New Series, no. 1), p. 5.
[16] *Ibid.*, p. 7.   [17] *Ibid.*, pp. 41-43.

7. CONTINUING EMPHASIS ON 1847 AND 1843.—Reviewing Joseph Wolff's *Researches and Missionary Labours* (1831), Brooks asserts:

"No individual has perhaps given greater publicity to the doctrine of the *Second Coming* of the Lord Jesus Christ, than has this well known Missionary to the world. Wheresoever he goes, he proclaims the approaching advent of the Messiah in glory, together with various other circumstances of the prophetic word, which he conceives will be the accompaniments or the immediate precursors of the day of God." [18]

He notes especially Wolff's stressing of 1847 in his discussions springing up in his travels, as the year of the approaching advent.[19] Brooks also reviews Habershon on the chronological prophecies, who boldly presses 1843 as the grand terminus not only of the 2300 years (457 B.C. to A.D. 1843) but of the "seven times" (2520 years) from 677 B.C. to A.D. 1843. The 1260 years are placed from 533 to 1793, with the 1290 and 1335 extending beyond.[20] Then the editor announces the sudden but unavoidable termination of *The Investigator,* but not without a parting appeal for preparation for "the coming of our Lord Jesus Christ." [21] But let us seek a closer view of Brooks.

II. Brooks—Champions Historical View and Premillennialism

JOSHUA WILLIAM BROOKS (1790-1882), prebendary of Lincoln Cathedral, author, and editor of *The Investigator,* as well as compiler of *A Dictionary of Writers on the Prophecies,* was prominent in prophetic exposition circles between 1831 and 1844. Though information is lacking as to his early life and education, we find him rector of East Retford, 1821-27, rector of Grove, 1827-43, and vicar of St. Mary's, Nottingham, 1843-64, also rural dean 1855-64. Then he was prebendary of the Lincoln Cathedral from 1858 until his death in 1882.[22]

One and a half columns are needed to list the works of

---

[18] *Ibid.*, April, 1836 (vol. 5, no. 44, New Series, no. 2), p. 88.
[19] *Ibid.*, p. 91.
[20] *Ibid.*, July, 1836 (vol. 5, no. 45, New Series, no. 3), pp. 158, 159.
[21] *Ibid.*, October, 1836 (vol. 5, no. 46, New Series, no. 4), p. 228.
[22] Frederic Boase, *Modern English Biography,* vol. 1, col. 420.

Brooks in the British Museum catalogue. He compiled *A Dictionary of Writers on the Prophecies* toward the close of his editorship of *The Investigator* (1831-36). He wrote the widely read *Abdiel's Essays on the Advent and Kingdom of Christ* (1834), as well as *Elements of Prophetical Interpretation* (1836), *The History of the Hebrew Nation* (1841), and "The Signs of the Second Advent" (1843) in *The Second Coming, the Judgment and the Kingdom of Christ,* one of the collections of Bloomsbury lectures. He was, moreover, a prominent participant in the Edinburgh Association for Promoting the Study of Prophecy, his contributions thereto, for 1841, being published as its *First Series* of *Lectures on Subjects Connected with Prophecy.*

1. PREMILLENNIALISM PROPHETIC ISSUE OF THE HOUR.— Brooks' *Essays on the Advent and Kingdom of Christ* deals with the purpose and propriety of prophecy. After touching upon the prophecies of the first advent, Brooks comes to the vicissitudes that befell the premillennial interpretation through the centuries of the Christian Era—oft thrown into the background and upon other occasions brought into disrepute by fanatical friends, but ultimately firmly and soundly established in the great Reformation bodies.[23] And now, after further diversions by Whitby's postmillennial theory, it has come again to the forefront in the nineteenth century. He declares the most vital issue of the hour to be the premillennial or postmillennial advent.[24]

2. GODDESS OF REASON DEPRIVED OF REASON.—Brooks advocated with conviction and force the premise that the French Revolution inaugurated the period of the outpouring of the seven vials, destined to destroy the apocalyptic beast and Babylon.[25] In connection with the excesses of the Revolution he reveals the tragic anticlimax to the infamous episode of "public homage offered to a harlot, who was deified as the goddess of reason." He writes:

---

[23] Joshua W. Brooks, *Essays on the Advent and Kingdom of Christ* (Philadelphia, 1840-1841 ed.), [Part 1], pp. 5-12.
[24] *Ibid.*, pp. 13, 106, 107.
[25] *Ibid.* (London, 1843 ed.), p. 198.

"In the Paris papers of August 1st, 1817, is the announcement of the death of this wretched female, the infamous Theroigne de Mericourt in the hospital for pauper lunatics of Saltpetriere, 'where (say the Journals) she had lived unpitied and unknown.' Thus, by a striking retribution, this unhappy woman who had received adoration as the goddess of reason, was for the last twenty years of her life deprived of reason; and she who was by the multitude worshipped as a divinity, was abandoned by the same multitude to the contempt and miseries of pauperism!" [26]

3. Midnight Cry Ringing in Nineteenth Century.—
In *Elements of Prophetical Interpretation,* Brooks traces the fluctuating positions of the church throughout the Christian Era on the fundamental principles of prophetic interpretation. From the generally held premillennial view of the early church, on to the "new allegorizing system," between the time of Origen and that of Jerome,[27] Brooks gives a systematic discussion of the "Voice of the Church" in those crucial centuries.

He then presents an impressive picture of the nineteenth century Advent Awakening as the conviction of a great impending crisis grips scores of minds "in Great Britain, and the Continent." It was "unequivocally premillennarian," and resembled the midnight cry of the parable: "Behold the Bridegroom cometh." With but few exceptions, Brooks adds, "there is scarcely to be found a writer on prophecy of any eminence in the present century, who is not looking for the pre-millennial advent." [28] A veritable galaxy of premillennial writers had arisen, and at least eight periodicals were exclusively or chiefly devoted to the exposition of prophecy—the *Jewish Expositor, The Morning Watch, The Christian Herald, The Investigator, The Christian Witness, The Christian Record, The Watchman,* and *The Expositor of Prophecy.*[29]

Many of these writers were in the Established Church, though others were scattered through the Dissenter groups, and many were laymen.[30] The leading ones are named.

---

[26] *Ibid.,* p. 199 n.
[27] Joshua W. Brooks, *Elements of Prophetical Interpretation,* pp. 55-61.
[28] *Ibid.,* pp. 104, 105.
[29] *Ibid.,* p. 105. There were several other periodicals devoting space to the consideration of prophecy.
[30] *Ibid.,* pp. 105-107.

4. WATCHMAN'S DUTY TO HERALD ADVENT.—In a chapter on "The Judgment," Brooks declares:

"It is the duty of *all* to call upon thee 'to fear God and give glory to Him, for the hour of his Judgment is come;' (Rev. xiv.7.) but more especially is it the duty of God's *ministers*. They are placed as watchmen in Israel to discern the signs of the times, and to look out whether it be a sword coming or peace; and if it be a *sword* coming, and the watchman 'blow not the trumpet, and the people be not warned; if the sword come and take away any person from among them, he is taken away in his iniquity; but—his blood will I require at the watchman's hand.' (Ezek. xxxiii.6.)" [31]

5. "ANTICHRIST" PREDOMINANTLY APPLIED TO PAPACY.— The chapter "On the Antichrist" discusses the essential unanimity of the historical "Protestant application of the Man of Sin to Popery, and of Babylon to Papal Rome." [32] He alludes to many other expositors who, while applying the little horn of Daniel 7 to the Western Antichrist, or the Papacy, also apply the horn of Daniel 8 to Mohammedanism, or the Eastern antichrist, [33] and those so holding are named.

6. YEAR-DAY PRINCIPLE AND 1260 YEARS FROM 533.—In the chapter "On Time Mystically Expressed" the development of the year-day principle is discussed, Mede being one of the principal earlier champions. [34] The section "On the Antichrist" most carefully traces the historical position of the church in the past—discussing Joachim, Eberhard, Bernard of Clairvaux, Olivi, and the Reformers. [35] The Western and Eastern Antichrist concept is again touched, [36] and the various attempts to fathom the 666 are noted in "The Name of the Beast," whether years, a date, or a name. [37] A large list of prophetic expositors completes the volume. [38]

On "The Chronological Prophecies," the evidence in behalf of the 1260 year-days, as from 533, is presented, and the adherents are again named. [39]

---

[31] *Ibid.*, p. 230.
[32] *Ibid.*, p. 390.
[35] *Ibid.*, pp. 370-381. On all these see volumes 1 and 2 of *Prophetic Faith*.
[36] *Ibid.*, pp. 391-401.
[37] *Ibid.*, pp. 436-443.
[33] *Ibid.*, pp. 391-400.
[34] *Ibid.*, p. 353.
[38] *Ibid.*, pp. 502-506.
[39] *Ibid.*, pp. 472-474.

III. Dictionary of Prophetic Writers Produced

Brooks' *Dictionary of Writers on the Prophecies* contains "upwards of 2,100 titles," with "occasional descriptions" of treatises, together with 500 commentaries on whole books of Scripture issued up to 1834. Author, title, place and name of publisher, and editor are given in alphabetical sequence. Originally published as an appendix to the *Investigator,* it is incomparable in the whole range of prophetic literature. Compassing not only British authors, but German, American, French, and Spanish as well, it reaches back to embrace and antedate the Reformation. The earlier titles are, of course, in Latin. As a safeguard, Brooks had the work checked by the learned expositors Edward Bickersteth and W. W. Pym.[40]

Editorship of the *Investigator* and authorship of prophetic works, as well as favorable location in London, gave Brooks access to an amazing number of writings on the prophecies.[41] It was such access and such familiarity with the full body of prophetic witness that helped hold the sounder British writers on prophecy and the advent so clearly on their course. Their progression was marked in the abandonment of the obvious faults of the earlier positions, and in the new and insistent emphasis on the 2300 years, as terminating in 1843, 1844, or 1847. (Title page of *Dictionary* reproduced on page 378.)

IV. Anonymous Tracts Echo the Advent Message

Between 1831 and 1833 numerous anonymous tracts appeared on the second advent and the prophecies. One was titled *The End of All Things Is at Hand.*[42] After giving a survey of world conditions as signs of the times, including the drying up of Turkey, the author comes to the prophecy of Daniel 2. An interesting pictorial illustration presents progressively the head

---

[40] Joshua W. Brooks, *Dictionary of Writers on the Prophecies,* preface, pp. 1, 2.
[41] Although the Advent Source Collection, housed in the Seventh-day Adventist Theological Seminary, Washington, D.C., now has a far larger and more comprehensive assemblage of photostats, microfilms, and originals, this *Dictionary* is invaluable to the investigator, and a marvel for its time.
[42] Undated, but evidently about 1831.

of gold, breast and arms of silver, etc. After naming the first three kingdoms, he notes the "iron sway" of Rome and the fact that but one act yet remains—the destruction of the nations and the setting up of the kingdom of God.[43] The writer closes his evidence with the question, "Are these things so or not?" This is a question that thousands were asking.

Another was titled *The Scriptural Doctrine of the Second Advent* (1833), as presented before "one of the Associations of the Edinburgh Young Men's Society." The events attending the advent are portrayed, two of the subheads reading, *"ii. The Lord cometh to destroy Antichrist,"* and *"iii. The Lord cometh to destroy the Fourth Monarchy, or Apostate Christendom."* [44]

Still another tract was an 1832 reprint of extracts from Martin Luther's sermon on *The Signs of Christ's Coming, and of the Last Day* (1832).

The last tract that will be noted is one headed *Ye Know Not When the Master of the House Cometh* (1832). Though these tracts were printed in different places, their emphasis was almost identical. They hold a unique place in the swelling chorus of advent witnesses.

V. Nolan—Stresses Day of Atonement and Jubilee Types

FREDERICK NOLAN (1784-1864), noted linguist and theologian, was born in Dublin. He was a student at Trinity College, Dublin, and received a B.C.L. and a D.C.L. from Oxford, and later an LL.D. Ordained in 1806, and serving in several curacies, he is usually identified as the vicar of Prittlewell, Essex. He was prominent and active, became a fellow of the Royal Society in 1832, and preached the Bampton Lectures in 1833, the Boyle Lectures in 1834, and the Warburton Lectures in 1833-36.[45]

Nolan was author of several works of a critical and expositional nature, as well as of some against the corruptions of the

---

[43] *The End of All Things Is at Hand*, pp. 20, 21.
[44] *The Scriptural Doctrine of the Second Advent*, pp. 24, 25.
[45] *Dictionary of National Biography*, vol, 14, p. 540.

church of Rome.   The leading titles were *Inquiry into the Integrity of the Greek Vulgate, or Received Text* (1815), *The Expectation Formed by the Assyrians that a Great Deliverer Would Appear about the Time of Our Lord's Advent* (1826), *The Time of the Millennium Investigated* (1831), *The Analogy of Revelation and Science* (1833),[46] and *The Chronological Prophecies* (1837).[47]   In addition, he wrote numerous introductions to modern languages—French, German, Italian, Spanish, etc.   Nolan was stanchly evangelical and strongly opposed to the pro-Catholic Oxford Movement.   He frequently appeared before learned societies, as with "On the Antiquity and Connexion of the Early Cycles," [48] to which he annexes six chronological tables after the example of Scaliger and Petavius, in which the first year of Artaxerxes I appears as 465 b.c.[49]

1. SEVENTH SEAL IMAGERY DERIVED FROM ATONEMENT.—In his *Time of the Millennium* (1831), Nolan notes the 6,000-year argument, with the seventh thousand years as a Sabbath of rest, which originated with the rabbinical Jews, "passed into the Christian Church," and was adopted by the early Fathers.[50] These he cites in detail.[51]   The imagery of the seventh seal, he contends, was derived from the great Day of Atonement and the Jubilee.[52]   "The analogy between this description, and the service of the Temple, upon one of the most solemn festivals of the Mosaic ceremonial, is so obvious that it has often excited the attention of the antiquary and scholar." [53]

2. DAY OF ATONEMENT AND HOLY OF HOLIES.—Nolan stresses the frequent allusions to the "Temple of God" opened in heaven, the ark of the tabernacle, the altar, and the incense. (Revelation 9 and 15.)   These scenes, he insists, represent occurrences "within the precincts of the same celestial structure." [54] Reference is made not only to the "daily service" but to the "peculiar solemnity" of the services on the *great day of Atone-*

---

[46] Bampton Lectures, before the University of Oxford.   [47] Warburton Lectures.
[48] *Transactions of the Royal Society of Literature*, vol. 3, pp. 1-70.
[49] *Ibid.*, p. 70.
[50] Frederick Nolan, *The Time of the Millennium*, pp. 7-15.
[51] *Ibid.*, p. 17.   [53] *Ibid.*, pp. 108, 109.
[52] *Ibid.*, pp. 14, 15, 108.   [54] *Ibid.*, p. 110.

ment," performed "by the high priest, in the holiest place of the Temple," and celebrated in the seventh month.[55]

3. GREAT SABBATISM CALLED THE MILLENNIUM.—Noting also the system of septenaries, with the sabbath of days, of weeks, and of months, the Jews also had their sabbaths of years, and a great sabbath of the septennial period termed the Jubilee. This commenced on the great Day of Atonement and was ushered in with the sound of trumpets. This was "considered a type of that great sabbatism to which we give the name of the Millennium." [56] Such is the "exact correspondence" between the earthly and the heavenly services of the tabernacle.

4. GOD'S THRONE IN HOLY OF HOLIES.—On the tenth day of the seventh month the high priest went alone into the holy of holies with the golden censor, hidden from the congregation, and this holy of holies with its ark and mercy-seat represented God's throne.[57] Such is the "key to the mystic sense of the heavenly service," with Christ as our ministering priest.[58]

5. TRUMPETS HERALD ATONEMENT-JUBILEE.—The opening of the seventh seal then indicates the opening of the millennium, and the Jubilee.[59] And these transcendent events "are alike represented to commence with the great Day of Atonement." Moreover, "an indissoluble link seems to bind them together in the rite of the sounding of the trumpets"—the Day of Atonement, and the Jubilee.[60]

6. NOT CLEAR ON CHRONOLOGICAL PROPHECIES.—In a later work, however, on *The Chronological Prophecies* (1837), Nolan writes without much clarity or conviction on the time periods. On Daniel 8:14 he remarks that instead of the simple word "day," the compound expression "mornings and evenings" is used. Because of this he reduces the number 2300 by one half, or to 1150.[61] And the 666 and 1260 years he makes consecutive, "and computed from the destruction of Jerusalem." [62]

---

55 *Ibid.*
56 *Ibid.*, pp. 110, 111.
57 *Ibid.*, p. 115.
58 *Ibid.*, pp. 117, 118.
59 *Ibid.*, pp. 120, 121.
60 *Ibid.*, p. 121.
61 Frederick Nolan, *The Chronological Prophecies*, p. 117.
62 *Ibid.*, p. 276.

VI. Thorp—Sounding of Midnight Cry Heralds the End

WILLIAM THORP (d. 1833),[63] dissenting minister at Bristol, wrote a number of works as listed in the British Museum catalogue. The title having a vital bearing upon our quest is *The Destinies of the British Empire, and the Duties of British Christians at the Present Crisis,* published in 1831. It was originally a series of lectures. Not only is revealed the keen interest of many in the "awfully neglected" study of prophecy, but the strong antagonism of others toward its exposition is set forth by this sentence in the Preface:

"Those excellent men, who in modern times have directed their attention to the study of the sacred prophecies, have been vilified, misrepresented, and held up to public derision as fools, fanatics, and maniacs." [64]

Thorp then cites Sir Isaac Newton as saying that about the time of the end, in all probability "a body of men will be raised up, who will turn their attention to the prophecies, and insist upon their literal interpretation, in the midst of much clamour and opposition." [65]

1. SIGNS SHED LIGHT ON PROPHETICAL DATES.—Holding clearly to the Historical scheme of prophetic interpretation for the great "chronological prophecies of Daniel, and the Apocalypse," Thorp stresses certain "signs" given "as harbingers, announcing the speedy appearance of the Son of Man, in the power and glory of his kingdom." [66]   Then he says further:

"By comparing the signs of the times with the numerical prophecies, we may know, with certainty, when the awful and glorious day of the Lord is rapidly advancing upon us. The great and broad outlines of prophecy are obvious to every man who is exercised in the study of the prophetical writings, long before the predicted events are fulfilled." [67]

Stressing the "considerable obscurity" that rests upon the "prophetical dates," until the consummation should be near, he makes his declaration:

---

[63] *The Gentleman's Magazine,* Supplement to Jan.-June, 1833, vol. 103, part 1, p. 650.
[64] William Thorp, *The Destinies of the British Empire, and the Duties of British Christians at the Present Crisis,* p. iv.
[65] *Ibid.,* p. v.
[66] *Ibid.,* p. 142.   [67] *Ibid.,* pp. 142, 143.

"Thus the prophecies of Daniel were closed up and sealed till the time of the end, when the book was to be opened, the seals were to be removed, the mysterious dates were to be developed, many were to run to and fro, and prophetical knowledge was to be increased. The period here foretold, is that in which we are now living; for never since the time of the Reformation has there been such deep and intense attention paid to the sacred prophecies as within the last thirty or forty years. The seals are now being removed, the signs of the times shed a light on the prophetical dates, the prophetical dates reflect their light upon the signs of the times." [68]

Thorp emphasizes this mutual help of the signs of the times "on the prophetical dates," and the prophetical dates upon the signs of the times.

"The general or discursive predictions lend their beams also to the general stock of information; and, altogether, form a concentrated body of light, visible and conspicuous to all, except to those who are wilfully blind." [69]

2. DOWNFALL OF PAPACY AND TURK IMPENDS.—Among the signs, or precursors, "announcing the speedy approach of the great day of the Lord," Thorp places first the "present concussion of the nations." Announcing that mankind had entered a new era, with revolution again on the march, he declares that these "mighty revolutions" will terminate in "the downfall of the papal kingdoms in the western Roman empire; in the annihilation of the Turkish," the "destruction of the heathen nations," and the "universal establishment of the millennial kingdom of our Redeemer." [70] Then he adds:

"The simultaneous shaking of all the provinces of the Ottoman empire with the convulsions of all the kingdoms of the papacy, is another sign that the day of God is advancing. Popery and Mohammedanism—the great eastern and western apostacies, rose about the same time; and, about the same time, according to the spirit of prophecy, they may be expected to fall in one common ruin." [71]

3. INFIDELIC SCOURGE FORETOLD IN DANIEL.—The "fearful progress of infidelity" is given as "another prognostic" of the nearness of the end. He continues:

---

[68] *Ibid.*, p. 143.
[69] *Ibid.*, pp. 143, 144.

[70] *Ibid.*, p. 144
[71] *Ibid.*, pp. 144, 145.

"Daniel foretold, that when the reign of papal superstition was nearly over; at the time of the end, an infidel power should arise, and do according to his will; that he should exalt himself and magnify himself above every god, and speak marvellous things against the God of gods; and should prosper till the indignation be accomplished. And have we not seen in these latter days an atheistical monster rising out of the foetid and vermin-producing marshes of the mother of harlots, in a neighbouring country; possessed and goaded on by infernal furies, breaking down the thrones and overturning the altars of papal superstition; stalking abroad among the nations, with portentous strides; trampling upon every thing sacred and divine; shaking the foundations, and tearing the very elements of society." [72]

4. WORLD PROCLAMATION OF GOSPEL FINAL SIGN.—After referring to the "re-ingrafting of the Jews," Thorp next presents the gospel to the heathen world as the next sign of the end of the age:

"The propagation of the gospel in heathen lands, to prepare a place for the church beyond the limits of the papal empire, before it is broken in pieces and annihilated, is another sign indicating the nearness of that day. For the gospel of the kingdom, our Lord has told us, must be preached in all the world, as a witness to all nations; not, you will observe, for the conversion of all nations—for this glorious and immense accession to the kingdom of our Redeemer is an achievement reserved for the millennial age—but as a witness to all nations: and when this witness has gone its rounds, then the end of the age, or the present state of things, shall come." [73]

5. SYMBOLICAL ANGEL NOW ON THE WING.—Thorp points to the societies and organizations bringing this about, and couches it all in the prophetic setting of Revelation 14 as one of the final signs:

"The symbolical angel of the Apocalypse, flying in the midst of heaven, and shaking eternal blessings from his wings, having the everlasting gospel to preach to them that dwell upon the earth. This remarkable sign, moving with speed and majesty in the spiritual heaven of the universal church, and indicating the coming of the Lord, is visible to all nations; for the symbolical angel takes wing immediately before the days of vengeance." [74]

6. SLEEPING CHURCH AROUSED BY HERALDED RETURN.—Thorp finally presents the last sign as within the church itself. He refers to the parable of the virgins as one of several concern-

---

[72] *Ibid.*, p. 145.   [73] *Ibid.*, pp. 148, 149.   [74] *Ibid.*, p. 149.

ing the second advent, where the state of the church is presented. Stressing the cry at midnight, "Behold, the bridegroom cometh," he says:

"The whole professing church, both real Christians and hypocrites, is thus represented as falling asleep while the Lord delayeth his coming, and roused from its death-like lethargy by the annunciation of his return." [75]

7. MIDNIGHT CRY NOW BEING HEARD.—Asserting that the parable characterizes the "present state of the professing church," he declares:

"That circumstance is in itself a proof that the time is near at hand. The midnight cry is now heard; is not his coming, therefore, near, very near; even at the door?" [76]

8. COURSE OF 1260 YEARS HAS NEARLY RUN OUT.—Noting the sneer of professing Christians as well as the taunts of infidel scoffers, in asking, Where is the promise of His coming? Thorp stresses this very condition as a sign of the near advent, along with the signs among the nations, in the papal church, the Ottoman Empire, and the upsurge of infidelity, as well as the proclamation of the gospel.[77]   To these he adds:

"The death-like slumber of the church; and the midnight cry that has recently been raised, and that is now ringing in the ears of an infidel world, and a sleeping church; all indicate that the 1260 years have nearly, at least, run out their course. And when ye see these things, know that the kingdom of heaven is at hand. Of that day and that hour knoweth no man; but we may know with certainty, by these signs and these prophecies, that it is fast approaching." [78]

9. MIDNIGHT CRY SOUNDED BY THOUSAND VOICES.—Then comes this remarkable assertion:

"To conclude, the midnight cry is now heard, from a thousand voices; behold the bridegroom cometh; he comes in clouds of flaming fire, with all his mighty angels taking vengeance. But who may abide the day of his coming? Not the unbelieving and impenitent; they shall suddenly be destroyed, and that without remedy. Not the hypocrite and the formalist, roused from their fatal delusions, when it is too late; like the foolish virgins, they shall find the gates of mercy for ever closed against them.

---

[75] *Ibid.*, p. 157.   [77] *Ibid.*, pp. 158, 159.
[76] *Ibid.*   [78] *Ibid.*, p. 159.

Who shall stand when he appeareth? They who wait for him, and who love his appearing, and his kingdom." [79]

Thorp closes with this searching appeal:

"Go ye out to meet him; shake off the lethargy with which you are oppressed; gird your loins; trim your lamps, keep them ever burning and shining; be watchful, be sober, and hope unto the end, for the grace which shall be brought unto you at the revelation of Jesus Christ. Behold, he cometh in clouds of glory! PREPARE MY SOUL TO MEET HIM!" [80]

VII. Lieutenant Wood—Living in Last Segment of Time

LIEUTENANT G. H. WOOD,[81] another military man, wrote *The Believer's Guide to the Study of Unfulfilled Prophecy* in 1829, dealing with the great "Gentile apostasy," the second advent, and Christ's millennial reign. The "result of a long and diligent study," it seeks to bring "into one connected view" the prophetic evidence.

A glance over its twenty-four chapters reveals its scope— the great apostasy, the second coming, the destruction of the wicked, the saving of the elect, the resurrection of the righteous dead, the change of the living saints, and the certainty of the near approach of the advent. Then follow the ascension and preservation from the fiery judgments, the millennial reign of the saints, the present earth reduced by fire becoming the new earth wherein the righteous dwell, the loosing of Satan for a short season at the end of the millennium, the general resurrection of the dead, the last judgment, and finally the everlasting kingdom established on this earth.[82]

1. GREAT APOSTASY FOLLOWED BY "TIME OF END."—The great apostasy, taking place during the "times of the Gentiles," leads into the "time of the end," the last time, the last days, or end of the world as variously called. Numerous scriptures are cited in support.[83] The signs of the second advent are numerous, he avers, and are to be studied and understood, and he cites the admonitions of Christ, Paul, and Peter.

---

[79] *Ibid.*, pp. 159, 160.   [80] *Ibid.*, p. 160.   [81] No biographical data available.
[82] G. H. Wood, *The Believer's Guide to the Study of Unfulfilled Prophecy*, Preface and Contents, pp. ii-iv.   [83] *Ibid.*, p. 1 ff.

2. 1260 Years, Papal Power; 2300 Years, Jewish Oppression.—As to the time periods, the "1260 days of years"
are "the time of the power of the papacy," or "oppression of
the Christian Church by antichrist." [84] The 2300 days of years,
of Daniel 8:14, are set forth as involving the "treading down
of the Jews, and their restoration with that of the elect remnant
of the Christian church, after the destruction of their enemies." [85]
No dates are suggested, but familiarity with the positions of
others is evidenced, and agreement with them is obvious. And
along with the Antichristian apostasy, the Mohammedan oppression is mentioned.[86]

3. In Last Segment of Prophetic Time.—Allusion is
also made to the view of some that the 1290 years ended in
1823, and the last period, the 1335, is "supposed to end A.D.
1868," when the millennial blessedness shall have begun. The
events of the latter part of Daniel, Wood holds, have been in part
fulfilled by the French Revolution, and we now stand at the
point of Revelation 16:13, when the unclean spirits are to go
out of the mouth of the pagan dragon, the infidel beast, and
the papal false prophet. The vials are already being poured
out, and the second advent will occur immediately after the
drying up of the Euphrates, or the "total destruction of the
Ottoman power and empire." [87]

4. Resurrection and Translation Accompany Advent.
—Wood held clearly to the literal resurrection of the body
at the second advent, and to living with Christ on the renewed
earth during the millennium. He was also clear on the changing and immortalizing of the bodies of the living saints at the
second advent, citing many texts. In an appendix he marshals
the supporting testimony of the Fathers of the primitive church,
the reformers, and the pastors of the Church of England.

---

[84] *Ibid.*, pp. 24, 25.   [85] *Ibid.*, p. 26.   [86] *Ibid.*
[87] *Ibid.*, pp. 26, 27; see also p. 41.

CHAPTER THIRTY-TWO

Bishop Wilson
Ends 2300 Years in 1847

Most impressive is the fact that in far-off Madras, India, the bishop of Calcutta published a tractate on the 2300 years of Daniel 8, in 1836. Keith arises strongly to defend the year-day principle under attack from Futurist and Preterist alike. Cox and Sirr expound effectively. And Habershon, the architect, makes 1843 the focal point of the 2300 years. So the increasing stream of witnesses flows on. Here is their testimony.

I. Bishop Wilson—Dates End of 2300 Years in 1847

DANIEL WILSON (1778-1858), well-known bishop of Calcutta, India, was apprenticed at fourteen to a silk manufacturer. He worked from 6 A.M. till 8 P.M., but instead of seeking recreation, he spent two hours each night studying Latin and Greek, and writing essays on Scriptural subjects. In 1797, at the age of seventeen, he was soundly converted, adopting Calvinistic views. This brought to him a new outlook on life and a desire to enter the ministry. At last his father consented and sent him to Oxford, but its religious life at the time was at a low ebb. Deficient in the classics, Wilson spent whole nights in study, and graduated with first honors, receiving his B.A. in 1802, and his M.A. in 1804.[1]

Having begun his ministry as curate at Chobham (or Cob-

---

[1] Josiah Bateman, *The Life of Daniel Wilson, D.D.;* John N. Norton, *Life of Bishop Wilson; Dictionary of National Biography,* vol. 21, pp. 558-560.

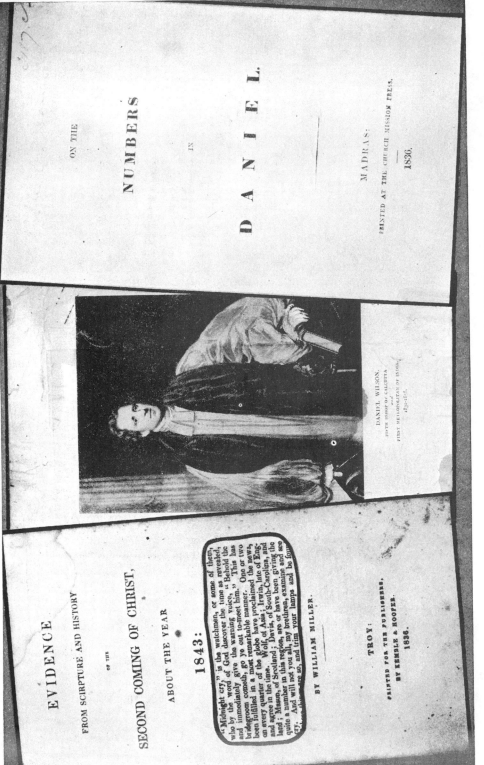

MILLER TREATISE MATCHED BY WILSON EXPOSITION

William Miller's First Book on Prophetic Evidences (Left), Issued in the New World in 1836, Tells of Similar Heralds in Other Lands (Inset);
Daniel Wilson's Treatise (Right) Issued in India, Likewise in 1836, Was One of the Growing Chorus of Voices

ham), he returned to Oxford to tutor in St. Edmund's Hall while ministering among the farming people. Eventually he was made vice-principal of St. Edmund's. In 1811 he went to St. John's Chapel, London, where he remained till 1824, and where his reputation as an Evangelical preacher increased so greatly that the church had to be enlarged. A breakdown from over-work was followed by his vicarage of St. Mary's of Islington. Wilson was ever a hard worker and a powerful organizer, building no fewer than three large churches, providing for the spiritual needs of about 6,000 parishioners.

He took a deep interest in church missionary and Bible Society work. His wife died in 1827, and he gladly responded to the call to India in 1832, in which year he also received a D.D. degree and was consecrated Bishop of Calcutta. His service in India was successful and fruitful, but in 1845 he was compelled to return to England for a rest because of jungle fever. Though on sick leave, he preached sixty-one sermons, in many of them referring to the Tractarian Movement,[2] and inveighing against it as Romanizing the Church.

Wilson was the author of many works, six columns in the British Museum catalogue being devoted to his books and to books about him. Some were: *Catholic Emancipation and Protestant Responsibility* (1829); *Popery Unchanged; Preaching Christ Among the Jews;* and "Observations on 'Tract 90' by J. H. Newman," an appendix to *The Sufficiency of Holy Scripture as the Rule of Faith,* 2d. ed., Calcutta, 1841. He was a participant in early Albury Park Prophetic Conferences,[3] but withdrew from the last conference or two before leaving for India. He preached a total of 5,806 sermons, frequently dwelling upon prophecy. (Wilson's portrait and the title page of his treatise on Daniel appear on the opposite page.)

1. 2300 DAYS COMMENCE SYNCHRONOUSLY WITH SEVENTY WEEKS.—Wilson's tractate *On the Numbers in Daniel* (1836)[4]

[2] Eyre Chatterton, *History of the Church of England in India,* chap. 11.
[3] Edward Miller, *History and Doctrines of Irvingism,* pp. 40, 41, 44.
[4] Attributed by various writers to him, though not mentioned in Bateman's *The Life of Daniel Wilson.*

is remarkable for the clarity of its reasoning and its impressive conclusions on the dating of the time periods. The focal point of Wilson's interest and investigation was the 2300 years of Daniel 8:14. To understand this number, Wilson relates how Daniel was "first told to separate seventy weeks, or 490 days, as a portion of the 2,300 days of the preceding chapter," for the Jews, during which they would "remain in the favour of God." [5]

The order of events of the seventy weeks is portrayed by Daniel, the first being the prophesied command to restore and build Jerusalem. Wilson then makes this impressive deduction: .

"Therefore the seventy weeks commencing with the given [giving] forth of this commandment; the 2300 days of the preceding vision, commence also at the same time, for *the visions are one.*" [6]

2. DAYS OF BOTH PERIODS ARE YEARS.—After the rebuilding of Jerusalem, which would occupy seven weeks, or forty-nine days, and after sixty-two subsequent weeks, or 434 days, Messiah would come and be cut off, and the sacrifices and oblations of the Mosaic law would cease. Then by the overspreading of abominations, the sanctuary will again be made desolate, until the consummation of the 2300 days. This proves, Wilson argues, that "those numbers meant that days are put for *years.*" Then the desolation should be broken without hand. (Dan. 8:25.)[7] Now he adds, "As literal days will not agree with the seventy weeks, so neither will it agree with the 2300 days of Chapter VIII." [8]

3. 2300 YEARS FROM 453 B.C. TO A.D. 1847.—Wilson therefore takes the stand that "the 2300 years are not yet fulfilled," as they reach to "the last end of the indignation." He then seeks for that beginning decree for the dating, citing the three decrees of Cyrus, Darius, and Artaxerxes.[9] Dating the seventieth week of years from A.D. 30 to 37, and deducting 483 years, he

5 Daniel Wilson, *On The Numbers in Daniel,* p. 10.
6 *Ibid.*   7 *Ibid.*   9 *Ibid.*
                                  8 *Ibid.,* p. 11.

arrives back at 453 B.C. by that familiar method.[10] Then follows this conclusion:

"But if the seventy weeks begin 453 years before the Incarnation, the 2300 beginning at the same time, we ascertain their termination merely by deducting the years before the incarnation, leaving A.D. 1847, as the time when the sanctuary shall be cleansed, and the vision be accomplished—the *last end of the indignation.*

"And this last end shall be the *consequence* of the second coming of Christ, as we have already seen in looking to Daniel's expectations; and therefore, *before the end, Christ shall have already come.*"[11]

4. LOOKED FOR RESURRECTION "WITHIN 14 YEARS."—Recognizing that "no man knoweth" the day nor the hour when He cometh, Wilson reasoned that these numbers nevertheless bring one to the time of the last things, the standing up of Michael, the time of trouble, the first resurrection, and the breaking up of the oppressor by the stone cut out without hand. To prove that the 2300 years "come to their conclusion in 1847" no other data are needed save the demands of the prophecy and the fact that "Christ was born 1835 years ago," "and crucified in the thirty-fourth hear [year] of his age."[12] According to promise, Daniel was to stand in his lot, being raised from the dead to receive the inheritance promised to Abraham and his seed, "at the *end* of the days, which *end* is within fourteen years of the present time."[13]

5. DESTRUCTION OF ANTICHRIST AT SECOND ADVENT.—A period of great tribulation will precede the second advent, and the "signs shall thicken as the times draw nearer the end."[14] The return of the Jews is, of course, mentioned, and the fall of Turkey is stressed—the steady loss of its territory being already under way. The meeting place of hostile powers is Palestine and Syria, with the coming storm hushed but for the season.[15] As the enemies of Christ are gathered under Antichrist, who is symbolized by the little horns of Daniel 7:8 and 8:9, his actions are further described in chapter 11: "The actings of this Antichrist are declared in the latter part of Daniel xi.36, to the

10 *Ibid.*, p. 12.
11 *Ibid.*
12 *Ibid.*, pp. 12, 13.
13 *Ibid.*, p. 13.
14 *Ibid.*, p. 14.
15 *Ibid.*, p. 15.

end; and he is brought to his end in the glorious holy mountain, which is at Jerusalem." [16]

6. PRESENT MESSAGE TO CHURCH IN REVELATION 14.— Wilson describes the descent of Christ to stand on Mount Olivet and the destruction of His enemies as portrayed in 2 Thessalonians 2:8 and Revelation 19:11. This whole series of judgments, Wilson says, is forewarned in the instructions to the church in Revelation 14. Christ's waiting people are gathered to Him, and He totally destroys His enemies. This brief but remarkable treatise from India on the approaching close of the 2300 years and the cleansing of the sanctuary then concludes with this statement:

"This whole period will be accomplished before the year 1847; and thus the probable beginning of it is brought very near indeed: it may begin in the course of the present year, for all the preparatory signs are around us. And though we know not the day, nor the hour, when it shall actually begin, the time for watching and waiting is come; every thing we see speaks in the plainest terms,—*Prepare to meet thy God.*" [17]

II. Keith—Establishes Papal Little Horn and Year-Day

ALEXANDER KEITH (1791-1880), Scottish writer on prophecy, and minister of St. Cyrus, Kincardineshire, from 1816 to 1840, was born in Aberdeenshire. He was educated at Marischal College and the University of Aberdeen, from which he received a B.A. in 1809 and a D.D. in 1833. He was licensed by the presbytery in 1813 and ordained in 1816. In 1839 he was sent to Palestine and Eastern Europe as a member of the commission to inquire into the state of the Jews, and again visited Palestine in 1844. Joining the Free Church secession movement of Scotland, he had his name removed from the roll of the established church in 1843.[18]

Keith was distinguished as an author, writing several books on the fulfillment of prophecy. The first important book was *Evidence of the Truth of the Christian Religion, Derived From*

---

[16] *Ibid.*, p. 18.   [17] *Ibid.*, p. 19.
[18] *Dictionary of National Biography*, vol. 10, pp. 1203, 1204.

the Literal Fulfilment of Prophecy (1828). It was patterned after the work of Bishop Newton.[19] The popular interest in prophecy at this time may be gauged by the fact that this work ran through forty editions, and was published in a number of other tongues. Keith wrote one of the strong defenses of the year-day principle to meet the spreading fallacies of the Futurist interpretation. In 1826 he penned, in two volumes, *The Signs of the Times, as Denoted by the Fulfilment of Historical Predictions,* and later *The Harmony of Prophecy; or, Scriptural Illustrations of the Apocalypse* (1851). His most elaborate work was *History and Destiny of the World and of the Church* (1861).

1. FIRST VOLUME, ON OLD TESTAMENT PROPHECY.—Keith's first important book, *Evidence of the Truth of the Christian Religion,* deals solely with Old Testament prophecies, and is concerned chiefly with the prophecies of the first advent, the destruction of Jerusalem and other cities—such as Babylon and Tyre—and the woes on the Jews.[20] The time of the Messiah's advent is given on the basis of the seventy weeks, which time period is dated from the seventh of Artaxerxes to the death of Christ.[21] Keith's exposition became a standard in its field. The outline prophecy of Daniel 11 is also noted—covering Persia, Grecia, Rome, Antichrist, and finally the Turk.[22] But on this it is very brief.

2. HORN OF DANIEL 8 INTERPRETED AS MOHAMMEDANISM.— *The Signs of the Times* ably compasses the visions of Daniel 2, 7, 8, and 11.[23] Then come the seals and trumpets of the Apocalypse, the cloud-clothed, rainbow-crowned angel, the Two Witnesses, the sun-clothed woman, the two beasts, and lastly the seven vials.[24] The standard position on the four kingdoms is maintained by Keith, together with the year-day principle.[25] The Persian ram, the Grecian goat, and its four horn divisions

---

[19] See J. W. Brooks, *Dictionary of Writers on the Prophecies,* pp. xlvii, xlviii.
[20] Alexander Keith, *Evidence of the Truth of the Christian Religion* (1832 ed.), chaps. 1-7.
[21] *Ibid.,* p. 29.
[22] *Ibid.,* pp. 265-273.
[23] Alexander Keith, *The Signs of the Times* (1832 ed.), chaps. 2-8, pp. 10-167, 657-661.
[24] *Ibid.,* chaps. 9-29, pp. 168-656; 661-673.
[25] *Ibid.,* pp. 10-23, 657.

are given, but with Mohammedanism as the exceeding great horn.[26] In Daniel 11 the Papacy is given a prominent place from verse 35 onward, with Turkey introduced in verse 40.[27]

3. DIFFERS ON SEALS; CONCURS ON TRUMPETS.—In his exposition of the Apocalypse and its seals, Keith differs from others in applying the second seal to Mohammedanism and the third to "popery" in the Dark Ages, with infidelity for the fourth. The sixth seal is believed not yet fulfilled.[28] He gives the standard interpretations of the trumpets: the first, Alaric and the Goths; the second, Genseric and the Vandals; the third, Attila and the Huns; and the fourth, Theodoric and the Ostrogoths.[29] The fifth trumpet is the Saracens for their allotted time period;[30] and the sixth trumpet, the Turks that were bound in the Euphrates but loosed for 396 years,[31] dated from 1057 to 1453.[32]

4. 1260 YEARS OF PAPACY 529-33 TO 1789-93.—Keith interprets the angel of Revelation 10 as the Reformation,[33] and the two witnesses are those who testified for God throughout the 1260 years.[34] The woman of Revelation 12 presents the history of the church.[35] The two beasts of Revelation 13 are the commonly interpreted imperial Rome and the papal Rome that succeeded it.[36] And the 1260 years of the papal power are dated from 529-33 to 1789-93.[37]

5. JUSTINIAN'S DECREE SELECTED FROM FOUR.—Keith distinguishes sharply between the edicts of the emperors Gratian and Valentinian, in 378-79, those of Theodosius and Valentinian III, in 445, and the final authorization by Justinian in his imperial letter of 533 and the confirmations of the *Novellae*, simply renewed by Phocas in 606.[38] Such is his succinct reasoning and marshaled evidence, drawn much from Croly, in behalf of the beginning of the 1260 years under Justinian. The vials, extending from 1782 to 1831, are applied to the French Revolution, the

---

[26] *Ibid.*, pp. 23-43, 657.
[27] *Ibid.*, pp. 81-167, 660, 661.
[28] *Ibid.*, pp. 168-216, 661-663.
[29] *Ibid.*, pp. 217-269, 663-665.
[30] *Ibid.*, pp. 269-298, 665, 666.
[31] 396=365+30+1.
[32] *Ibid.*, pp. 298-359, 666, 667.

[33] *Ibid.*, pp. 362-393, 668, 669.
[34] *Ibid.*, pp. 393-410, 669.
[35] *Ibid.*, pp. 410-425, 669.
[36] *Ibid.*, pp. 425-445, 670.
[37] *Ibid.*, pp. 445-451, 640.
[38] *Ibid.*, pp. 91-98.

fifth vial being directed against the Catholic kingdoms, and the sixth against Turkey, and involving its disintegration.[39]

6. 2300 YEARS DATED FROM 480 B.C. TO A.D. 1820.—At the very close Keith discusses the ending of the 2300 years and the cleansing of the sanctuary through the related delivery of Jerusalem from Mohammedan tyranny—"the place of which was trodden down by the Turks." [40] He oddly dates the beginning from the invasion of Greece by Xerxes, in 480 B.C., and ends it in A.D. 1820.[41] The thirty years between the expiration of the 1260 and the 1290 years are taken as an interval leading to the completion of the 2300 years.[42] Then follows this meaningful statement:

"May we not look again to the times and the seasons that are passed, and see whether the period may not be commenced for the cleansing of the sanctuary as well as of the sitting of the judgment? We have seen how, after a time of previous repose, uninterrupted and accumulating calamities have beset the Turkish empire, 'melted away' its armies, 'drained' its population, and depopulated its cities, since the year 1820." [43]

7. FINAL EVENTS, ADVENT, AND NEW EARTH.—In his *The Harmony of Prophecy*, Keith emphasizes the fulfillment of the sixth seal at the very end of human affairs—at the time of the second advent, when Babylon comes in remembrance before God.[44] The seventh trump is placed at the same time, together with the harvest and wine press, and the first resurrection.[45] Then follows a paralleling of certain prophecies of Christ, Moses, David, Isaiah, and Habakkuk, with those of the Revelation.[46] The last part of the work discusses the kingdom, and the two resurrections, separated by the thousand years.[47] Then follow the executive judgment and the new earth.[48]

8. LITTLE HORN'S IDENTITY ESTABLISHED BY EVIDENCE.—Keith's last and most pretentious work, *The History and Destiny of the World and of the Church*, deals entirely with the four empires of prophecy in Daniel and the Apocalypse, indentifying

---

[39] *Ibid.*, pp. 461-656, 671-673.
[40] *Ibid.*, pp. 636-639.
[41] *Ibid.*, pp. 638, 639.
[42] *Ibid.*, p. 641.
[43] *Ibid.*, p. 639.
[44] Alexander Keith, *The Harmony of Prophecy*, pp. 56, 57.
[45] *Ibid.*, pp. 72-75.
[46] *Ibid.*, pp. 100-289.
[47] *Ibid.*, p. 290 ff.
[48] *Ibid.*, p. 385 ff.

Daniel's fourth power with John's dragon and beast, and Daniel's little horn with the two-horned beast of John's vision—both representing the Roman apostasy and the woman in purple and scarlet. This treatise is thoroughly documented, and illustrated with coins and medallions from Grecia onward. There is much detailed history of great value in critical study.

He gives paralleling columns of the texts in Daniel 2 and 7, and Revelation 12, 13, and 17, bearing on Rome,[49] and deals similarly with the papal Antichrist, in Daniel 7 and 11, 2 Thessalonians 2, and Revelation 13 and 17.[50] Papal medallions illustrate the terms and specifications of the "eyes" of the horn,[51] and the boastful and blasphemous claims.[52] In support of the fearful persecutions there are extensive footnote excerpts from the sources.[53] The time of the Little Horn is still set as from 529-33 to 1789-93.[54]

9. PAPAL IDENTITY CONFIRMED BY MEDALLIONS.—The witness of the Roman Catholics is constantly drawn upon to establish the fulfillment of particular specifications of Daniel 7 and 11, 2 Thessalonians 2, and Revelation 13 and 17.[55] The beasts of Revelation are minutely compared with the fourth beast of Daniel,[56] in the light of Romish declarations and claims. All through these chapters authentic medallions illustrate the contentions.[57] Even the garments of scarlet and purple of Revelation 17 are illustrated in color.[58] Altogether it is a scholarly and really classical work—establishing beyond peradventure the thesis that the Papacy is the power symbolized by Daniel, Paul, and John.

III. Cox—Opposers Crushed Ere Kingdom Established

JOHN COX (1802-1878) was a dissenting Baptist minister of Woolwich. He wrote *A Millenarian's Answer of the Hope That Is in Him* (3d ed., 1832), and *Thoughts on the Coming*

---

[49] Alexander Keith, *The History and Destiny of the World and of the Church*, p. 132.
[50] *Ibid.*, p. 148.   [53] *Ibid.*, pp. 198, 199.   [56] *Ibid.*, pp. 330-349.
[51] *Ibid.*, pp. 167, 168. [54] *Ibid.*, pp. 209-217.   [57] *Ibid.*, pp. 350-403.
[52] *Ibid.*, pp. 174, 175. [55] *Ibid.*, pp. 229-313.   [58] *Ibid.*, pp. 420, 432.

and Kingdom of Our Lord Jesus Christ (2d ed., 1839). In the latter book Cox notes with regret the "strong tide of prejudice" against the premillennial coming of Christ, the first resurrection, the reign of the saints with Christ, and the renovation of creation—so strong that "many good people will scarcely hear these things mentioned." [59]   Throughout his pages Cox alludes frequently to Cuninghame, Way, Begg, Bickersteth, and other expositors.

1. POPERY MUST FIRST BE OVERTURNED.—This work, strongly and conclusively maintaining the premillennial view, is devoted largely to the "events which must occur previous to the setting up of the kingdom of Christ." [60]   First, "Popery must be entirely destroyed." [61]   Denominating the Papacy "Satan's masterpiece," [62] Cox surveys the various symbols, beginning with the appellation of "Babylon," in Revelation 17. [63]

It is also the little horn of Daniel 7, subduing three kings, and wearing out the saints for a period of 1260 years. [64]   It is the second beast of Revelation 13—the first being the Roman Empire—and is the same as the false prophet of Revelation 19. Then the infidelic upheaval of the French Revolution is noted in Revelation 11. [65]   But it is after the career of the Papacy that the Son of man comes in the clouds, as indicated in Daniel 7, Matthew 24, and other scriptures, especially 2 Thessalonians 2. [66]

2. MOHAMMEDANISM MUST NEXT BE DESTROYED.—Second, Mohammedanism must also be destroyed. [67]   Revelation 9 describes "the character and actions of the dreadful power"—the Saracens in verses 1-11, and the Turks in verses 12-21. Some consider its destruction also indicated in Daniel 11:36-45. [68]   Cox mentions the difference of view regarding the horn of Daniel 8, some holding it to be Mohammedanism. But the clearest reference of all is in Revelation 16. The "sixth trumpet calls the Turks into political existence," and the "sixth vial extermi-

[59] John Cox, *Thoughts on the Coming and Kingdom of Our Lord Jesus Christ* (Philadelphia, 1842 ed.), Preface, p. v.
[60] *Ibid.*, p. 26.
[61] *Ibid.*, p. 27.
[62] *Ibid.*
[63] *Ibid.*, p. 28.
[64] *Ibid.*, pp. 32, 36.
[65] *Ibid.*, pp. 33-35.
[66] *Ibid.*, p. 36.
[67] *Ibid.*, p. 37.
[68] *Ibid.*, p. 38.

nates their power from the prophetical earth." [69]   The Euphrates in both instances stands for the Turkish power.

3. DESTRUCTION OF TEN KINGDOMS PRECEDES.—The destruction of the ten kingdoms is the next major premillennial event Cox marshals. In this he enumerates the four powers of Daniel 7—Babylon, Medo-Persia, Grecia, and Rome, which latter still continues in the nations of Europe.[70] And in Daniel 2 the same outline terminates with the stone smiting the toes of the image, and filling the earth.[71] Armageddon will occur at this time.[72] And as is customary with virtually all English writers of this period, Cox includes the return of the Jews.[73]

4. BINDING OF SATAN PRECEDES MILLENNIUM.—Lastly, Cox lists the "binding of Satan." This event will not take place in the present dispensation, but at the beginning of the next.[74] Such is the prophetic picture painted by Cox in discussing the coming and kingdom of Christ.

5. BEAST'S DESTRUCTION AND THE FIRST RESURRECTION.—In his *Millenarian's Answer of the Hope That Is in Him,* Cox sets forth, as the first proposition of his premillennial hope, the destruction of Antichrist, "with all its abettors and helpers," and the crushing of all tyrannical governments—particularly those "which constitute the last Beast of Daniel, or the Roman Empire." [75] He holds that the resurrection of the righteous will precede, and the general resurrection follow, the thousand years.[76] These points he elaborates.

6. PROPHETIC DEPICTION OF PAPACY.—In discussing Daniel 7, Cox declares it to be a "history of the prophetic earth," from Babylon on to the establishment of the kingdom of Christ. The same four powers of Babylon, Medo-Persia, Grecia, and Rome, the ten divisions, and the little horn, with its period of three and a half times, draws this comment: "It is allowed on all hands that the papacy is clearly pointed out in this description." [77]

---

[69] *Ibid.*, pp. 38, 39.   [71] *Ibid.*, p. 40.   [73] *Ibid.*, p. 44.
[70] *Ibid.*, pp. 39, 40. 42.   [72] *Ibid.*   [74] *Ibid.*, pp. 57, 58.
[75] John Cox, *A Millenarian's Answer of the Hope That Is in Him* (Philadelphia, 1840 ed.), p. 3.
[76] *Ibid.*, pp. 3, 4.   [77] *Ibid.*, pp. 7, 8.

7. DESOLATION OF KINGDOMS AND RUIN OF TURK.—The second personal advent of Christ will accompany the desolation of earthly kingdoms, "including the papal power whose abominations are the grand cause of this destruction." [78]   And the power of the latter part of Daniel 11 may be the Turk, which will come to his end with none to help.[79]

8. PROPHETIC EVENTS OF THE FIRST AND SECOND ADVENTS.— The prophecy of the seventy weeks, leading to the first advent with its attendant features, is duly noted, and then the prophecies of the second advent.[80]   Next, the numerous passages bearing on the events clustering around the second advent and the millennium are discussed at length.[81]

9. PREMILLENNIALISM IS HISTORIC HOPE OF CHURCH.—The last part of the pamphlet traces the history of premillennialism from the early centuries onward.   In order to show the sentiments of the Reformers, Cox cites the Catechism of the Church of England, of 1553, which declares the stone is not yet hewed out of the mountain to bring to nought the image of Daniel 2, and Antichrist is not yet slain.[82]   Similarly the Baptist Confession of 1660 is quoted in support of premillennialism.[83]

From there he passes on to the time of Mede, Twisse, Ussher, Isaac Newton, Goodwin, Hussey, Gill, Toplady, and many others.   In other words, premillennialism was "received by the primitive church, and has been espoused by the wisest and best of mankind."   And now the leading topic of the faithful is that "he will come again to set up a kingdom, to avenge his church, and reign with his saints," despite the doubts of the scoffer and the contrary assertions of false stewards.[84]   So Cox was an undeviating premillennialist.

IV. Sirr—Resurrection Grand Accompaniment of Advent

JOSEPH D'ARCY SIRR (1794-1868), Irish biographer, was a graduate of Trinity College, Dublin, receiving a B.A. in 1812.

---

[78] Ibid., pp. 8, 9.
[79] Ibid., p. 11.
[80] Ibid., p. 12.
[81] Ibid., pp. 13-24.
[84] Ibid., pp. 45-48.
[82] Ibid., pp. 38, 39.
[83] Ibid., p. 40.

an M.A. in 1823, and the B.D. and D.D. degrees in 1843. He was rector of Ringwood, Morestead, and Kilcoleman, Ireland. He was author of several religious works, including a useful "Life of Archbishop Usher" [85] prefixed to the archbishop's *Religion of the Ancient Irish* (1835). Sirr's three books on prophecy were *The Deluge a Type of the Conflagration* (1832), *The First Resurrection Considered* (1833), and *Westport Darbyism Exposed* (1843).

1. FIRST RESURRECTION ACCOMPANIES ADVENT.—The writing of *The First Resurrection* was occasioned by a treatise published by a Mr. H. Gipps, LL.B. Sirr replied by asserting that the second advent strain runs all through the Old Testament, as well as the New, and supported his contention with a comprehensive survey of textual evidence.[86] Chiefest among his ten arguments is the one that the first resurrection is the grand accompaniment of the second advent.[87] After introducing the millennium Sirr turns to a discussion of the parables bearing on the advent.[88] Then he takes up the transfiguration as a type of the Coming One.[89]

2. PAPAL JEZEBEL DESTROYED AT ADVENT.—The prophetic symbols of Daniel, Paul, and John are frequently brought into the picture. In discussing the Jezebel of the Thyatira church of Revelation 2, Sirr asserts she is the "very counterpart" of the "woman that rideth the beast, Rev. xvii. She is the apostate church, with whom spiritual fornication is committed." And "she is to be desolated by the *ten horns*." And from all this, Sirr adds, "it is quite obvious that it is to the second advent of the Lord Jesus we are referred." [90] He declares that the conditions of the Laodicean church also represent the "last days" before the second advent.[91]

3. JEWISH RACE NOT TO PASS TILL FULFILLMENT.—In an appendix, answering a query concerning the statement, "This

---

[85] *Alumni Dublinenses*, 1593-1860, p. 754; *The Gentleman's Magazine*, May, 1868 (vol. 233, part 1); *Dictionary of National Biography*, vol. 18, p. 317.
[86] Joseph D'Arcy Sirr, *The First Resurrection Considered* (Philadelphia, 1841 ed.), pp. 5-35.　　[87] *Ibid.*, p. 15 ff.　　[88] *Ibid.*, p. 36 ff.
[89] *Ibid.*, p. 58 ff.　　[90] *Ibid.*, p. 69.　　[91] *Ibid.*, p. 71.

generation shall not pass," in Christ's great prophecy, Sirr attempts to show from a number of similar uses of the original Greek term (genea) that it indicates the "Jewish Race," which would not pass till the full accomplishment—and pointing to their remarkable continuance as a race for nearly eighteen centuries.[92] They would be preserved through all the long desolations, and not cease from being a distinct race while being trodden down by the Gentile powers, even under the Inquisition —and would so continue till the day of the appearance of the Son of man.

4. WHY FOURTH EMPIRE (ROME) IS CALLED BABYLON.— Discussing the "prophetic earth," symbolized by the statue of Daniel 2—the Babylonian, Medo-Persian, Grecian, and Latin, or Roman, kingdoms—Sirr remarks: "These different kings and kingdoms being represented by the component parts of a human body of gigantic size" are marked with "coexistence and connexion" of the parts.   That, he avers, is why Rome is called Babylon.

"From this mode of considering these four kingdoms (viz. the Babylonian, the Medo-Persian, the Grecian and the Roman)—as component parts of one larger kingdom, it results that both in the Old and in the New Testaments, Rome (which is represented by the legs and feet of the image) is called Babylon, (which is the head of it:) Because, in the mind of the Holy Spirit, which embraces, under one glance, the whole series of the times of the kingdoms represented in the image, the empire of Babylon was but the beginning of the Roman empire, as the head was but the upper part of the image, while the Roman empire in its turn was nothing else but Babylon in its development, as the legs and feet were but the completion of the image." [93]

Then he refers to the succession of angels with the varying messages, as Babylon is brought to judgment and hopeless ruin.[94]

5. LANGUAGE DETERMINES DISTINCTIVE EMPIRE LIMITS.— Sirr's comments on the distinctive geographical location of each of the four monarchies, as determined by the languages peculiar to each, are interesting.   First, there came the Chaldean, then the Persian, and next the Greek, throughout Egypt, Syria, Asia

---

[92] Ibid., pp. 160, 161.   [93] Ibid., p. 165.   [94] Ibid., p. 166 n.

Minor, Thrace, and Macedonia as far as the Danube. Finally, the Latin prevailed in Africa as far as Mount Atlas, and in Europe from the west bank of the Rhine and the whole right bank of the Danube to the Mediterranean to the ocean. The French, Italian, Spanish, and Portuguese are simply so many different corruptions of the Latin, and the religious worship in these countries is performed in Latin by the Roman Catholics.[95]

6. KINGDOM TO SAINTS FOLLOWS SATAN'S BINDING.—Sirr concludes by showing that the Catholic Church has sought to usurp God's kingdom and church. But when the devil is bound at the beginning of the millennium, at the advent, then the dominion and greatness of the kingdom shall be given to the saints forever.[96]

V. Architect Habershon—1843 Focal Point of 2300 Years

MATTHEW HABERSHON (1789-1852), noted church architect and able lay writer on prophecy, designed churches at various places in Derbyshire. In 1806 he connected with Atkinson, the architect, and was an occasional exhibitor at the Royal Academy between 1807 and 1827. Soon after this he became deeply interested in prophecy. In 1842 he visited Jerusalem in behalf of the London Society for Promoting Christianity Amongst the Jews—an object which also greatly interested him —to arrange for the erection of the Anglican Cathedral and other buildings connected with the mission. On his way home in 1843 the king of Prussia conferred on him the great gold medal for achievement in science and literature.[97]

Habershon appeared as a new and able defender of the 2300-year interpretation. A sober-minded writer, building on the solid terra firma of historical and chronological fact, he stressed the continual fulfillment of prophecy before the eyes of men. His chart of Scripture prophecy was most comprehensive. He made 1843-44 the focal point of the 2300 years, and

95 *Ibid.*, p. 167.   96 *Ibid.*, p. 170.
97 *Dictionary of National Biography*, vol. 8, p. 856.

of the 391 as well, but had the 1335 years extend seventy-five years beyond.

Habershon was author of seven books on prophecy, and was widely quoted by others, such as Pym and Bickersteth. The titles indicate the scope: *A Dissertation on the Prophetic Scriptures* (1834), *A Guide to the Study of Chronological Prophecy* (1835), *Premillennial Hymns* (1836), *An Epitome of Prophetic Truth* (1841), *An Historical Exposition of Prophecies of the Revelation of St; John, shewing their connection with Those of Daniel* (1841), *Two Remarkable Signs of the Times* (1842), *The Shadows of the Evening: or the Signs of the Lord's Speedy Return* (1845). He also wrote a memoir of the author and a preface to Charles Daubuz's *Symbolical Dictionary* (1842).

1. 2300 YEARS DATED FROM 457 B.C. TO A.D. 1843.—In his *Historical Dissertation on the Prophetic Scriptures of the Old Testament*, Habershon deals in "Period VI" with the 2300 years, charting them "from 457 B.C. TO A.D. 1843," and beginning them with the "Edict of the seventh year of Artaxerxes, 457." [98] Noting the antecedent decrees of Cyrus and Darius, Habershon says:

"I have no hesitation in giving it the preference on this occasion; and therefore consider the edict given to Ezra, as that from which the commencement of these 2300 years ought to be dated." [99]

2. ENDS SEVEN TIMES OF GENTILES IN 1843.—Habershon ties in the seven times (or 2520 years) with the 2300 years by beginning the longer period in 677 B.C.:

"The final termination of the 'seven times' was proved to correspond exactly to this year—that is, 2520 years, reckoned from 677 B.C. the date of Israel's final ruin; and 2300 years, reckoned from Ezra's commission in 457 B.C., both terminate in the year 1843." [100]

Observing that this leads to the "time of the end," he concludes:

"The mere probability of such great events being now so near, should excite us all to increasing watchfulness, and an anxiety to possess an interest in that only ark of safety which is to be found in the Gospel." [101]

---

[98] Matthew Habershon, *A Dissertation on the Prophetic Scriptures*, p. 290.
[99] *Ibid.*, p. 293.   [100] *Ibid.*   [101] *Ibid.*, p. 294.

3. PLACES 1260 YEARS FROM 533 TO 1793.—"Period VII," the "great period of 1260 years," Habershon puts "from A.D. 533 to 1793." [102] After noting four possible starting points, he records his choice of 533, citing Cuninghame and Croly.

"In choosing between these two I feel no hesitation, with the great majority of modern commentators, in giving a preference to the one of the Emperor Justinian, rather than that of Phocas; and assigning the date of his edict, which was March 533, as the true and proper commencement of this period, and the time when the saints were delivered or 'given' into the hands of the Pope." [103]

4. TABULAR DATING OF KEY PROPHETIC EVENTS.—In a table of key dates at the close of his work, Habershon lists among other dates, 677-76 B.C. ("Esarhaddon carries away the small remnant of Israel . . . and thus totally and finally destroys the kingdom of Israel from being a nation"), as "the commencement of 'the times of the Gentiles,' " or 2520 years. [104] Later on comes 457-56 B.C. ("celebrated decree of Artaxerxes Longimanus king of Persia to Ezra"). Under this Habershon lists:

"1. The commencement of the 'Fourth Period,' or the 490 years' prophecy of Daniel, to the death of Christ.
"2. The commencement of the 'Sixth Period,' or the 2300 years, to the restoration of the Jews and cleansing of the sanctuary." [105]

Under A.D. 33-34 ("The Death of Christ") he writes, "This great event forms the termination of the 'Fourth Period,' or the 490 years of Daniel." [106]

Then, following the years 396, 433, 439, and 476 for the first four trumpets, [107] the date 533 ("the edict of the Emperor Justinian constituting the Pope head of all the holy churches; thus giving the 'saints into his hands' ") is given as the "commencement of the Great Period of 1260 years." [108] The year 1453 (the capture of Constantinople) is noted as the time of the "sounding of the Sixth Trumpet." [109]

The year 1793 ("the full maturity of the French Revolution," the Reign of Terror) is given as the termination of the

---

[102] *Ibid.*, p. 295.
[103] *Ibid.*, p. 327.
[104] *Ibid.*, p. 444.
[105] *Ibid.*, p. 446.
[106] *Ibid.*, p. 447.
[107] *Ibid.*, pp. 447, 448.
[108] *Ibid.*, p. 448.
[109] *Ibid.*, p. 449.

1260 years,[110] and 1843-44 (termination of the 2300 years) is noted as "the fall of the 'little horn' of Mohammedanism—the cleansing of the Jewish Sanctuary." [111]

5. SUPPLEMENTAL DATES ARE LISTED.—In the second, or 1840, edition, the chapter arrangement is perfected and the statements amplified, but the arguments and the datings remain the same. With the 1260 years there is also a tabulation of 1260 years from the formation of the ten papal kingdoms "to their common destruction," as from 583-84 to 1843-44. Chapter 10, which is devoted to detailed and conclusive evidence for the 533 beginning of the 1260 years of the papal era, cites many of the ablest past and contemporary expositors.[112] Various tabulations, such as Ptolemy's king list, and that of the Eastern and Western Roman emperors, are helpful.[113] A comprehensive chart plots the relationship of the "times of the Gentiles," the 2300 years, as well as the seventy weeks beginning synchronously with the 2300 years, the fifth and sixth woe periods, and the 1260 years. As with others, Habershon extends the 1290- and the 1335-year periods beyond the synchronous close of the 1260-, 2300-, and 391-year periods, suggesting possible dates.[114]

6. BACKGROUND FOR TRUMPETS IN DANIEL 7 AND 8.—In his *Historical Exposition of the Prophecies of the Revelation of St; John,* Habershon confines himself largely to the seals and the trumpets. In the Introduction he alludes to Rome as the fourth empire, the ten divisions, the springing up of the "little papal Horn" in the midst of the ten, in Daniel 7, and of the "Mohammedan little horn" of Daniel 8.[115] The French Revolution is included under the "present signs of the Times," along with the breaking of the Mohammedan little horn "without hand." [116]

7. SEVEN SEALS DEPICT APOSTASY IN CHURCH.—Coming to the seals, Habershon depicts them as "showing the gradual progress of the frightful apostasy of the church of Christ," [117] and

[110] *Ibid.,* p. 450.
[111] *Ibid.,* p. 451.
[112] Matthew Habershon, *An Historical Dissertation on the Prophetic Scriptures* (1840 ed.), pp. xxxii, 229-273.
[115] Matthew Habershon, *An Historical Exposition of the Prophecies of the Revelation of St; John,* pp. xx, xxi.
[116] *Ibid.,* p. xxi.
[113] *Ibid.,* pp. 401-407.
[114] *Ibid.,* insert in 1842 ed.
[117] *Ibid.,* p. 49.

therefore covering the Christian Era. First, the triumph of Christianity, and then the corruption of the church, in the first four seals.[118] Then, under the fifth and sixth seals, the "partial recovery of the church at the Reformation," followed by "the actings of infidelity as exhibited in the consequences of the French Revolution." [119] The seventh seal creates—

"a solemn pause—the nations awaiting in anxious and tremulous suspense the blow that is to cause their extinction, the extinction of the ten-king-domed Roman empire—and with that, that of the great image of Daniel, the last of the Gentile monarchies of the world!" [120]

8. EARLY TRUMPETS BARBARIAN INVASION OF ROME.—Habershon defines the seven trumpets as "the judgments of God upon the [Western] Roman empire" by the "terrible invasions of the Goths, Vandals, Huns, and other Barbarians." [121] Contending that the trumpet is a "signal of hostile invasion," he gives the customary exposition of the first four trumpets as involving Alaric and his Goths, Attila and the Huns, Genseric and his Vandals, and Odoacer and the Heruli. [122]

9. FIFTH TRUMPET IS SARACENIC WOE (612-762).—The fifth trumpet is portrayed as the "judgments of God upon the [Eastern] Roman Empire, by the Saracens, or the rise of Mahomet." [123] This first of the woe trumpets, which were to be proclaimed to all the inhabitants of the earth, "plainly intimates that the calamities of the remaining trumpets shall be greater and more terrible, and refer to events of yet higher importance, than the former ones." [124] Citing the testimony of Gibbon, "decided enemy of Christianity," he quotes: *Mahomet, with the sword in one hand and the Koran in the other, erected his throne on the ruins of Christianity and of Rome.* [125] After expounding the various characteristics, Habershon times their "five months," or 150 years, from 612 to 762.[126]

10. SIXTH TRUMPET OSMANLI TURKS (1453-1844).—The sixth trumpet, or second woe, Habershon expounds as "the rise

[118] *Ibid.*, pp. 49-59.
[119] *Ibid.*, pp. 71, 86.
[120] *Ibid.*, p. 113.

[121] *Ibid.*, p. 117.
[122] *Ibid.*, pp. 128-143.
[123] *Ibid.*, p. 145.

[124] *Ibid.*, p. 146.
[125] *Ibid.*, pp. 148, 149.
[126] *Ibid.*, p. 167.

and establishment of the Turks, or Ottomans." [127]   Later he adds,
"It may indeed be said, that there is no one part of the Revelation in which there exists so unanimous an agreement as that
the Turks were the second woe." [128]   The "restraint caused by
the crusades" being removed, the Ottoman Empire arose in the
latter part of the thirteenth century, and Habershon notes Gibbon's famous date of July 27, 1299, for Othman's invasion of
Nicomedia.[129]   After the defeat of the Latins and the Tartars,
the fall of Constantinople was accomplished in 1453.[130]   Habershon comments on the "precision and minuteness" with which
the period of its continuance is made.   The very omission of a
week in the formula "shews design," and he states:

> "The usual mode of prophetic computation, which has already been
> explained and applied, is still to be adhered to.   This will bring the hour,
> the day, the month, and the year, to 391 prophetic days, which are conse-
> quently to be considered as years." [131]

11. Hour, Day, Month, and Year Is 391 Years.—After expounding the various symbolic expressions, Habershon says of
the appointed duration:

> "It is not extravagant to believe, that that fall may take place at the
> termination of the period, as set forth in this prophecy; and which termina-
> tion, reckoning 391 years ('the hour, and the day, and the month, and the
> year,') from the fall of Constantinople on the 29th May 1453, will happen
> in June 1844." [132]

Habershon then brings the fall of the Papacy into connection with "the ceasing of the sixth trumpet; and with the opening of the seventh seal." [133]   He applies the "time shall be no
longer" to the close of the prophetic period of the 1260 years.[134]

12. All Evidences Point to 1844.—The great revolution,
as the tenth part of the city falls, discloses *the events of the
French Revolution.*" [135]   Habershon now awaits the close of the
391 years, as dated from 1453.   "No period of time," he avers,
"appears to be more clearly marked." [136]

[127] *Ibid.*, p. 171.
[128] *Ibid.*, p. 297.
[129] *Ibid.*, p. 182.

[130] *Ibid.*, p. 184.
[131] *Ibid.*, p. 185.
[132] *Ibid.*, p. 194.
[136] *Ibid.*, p. 281.

[133] *Ibid.*, p. 199.
[134] *Ibid.*, p. 208.
[135] *Ibid.*, p. 277.

"There appears to be no presumption in the attempt to direct the anxious mind to the chronological periods which God has given, and to inquire how far they support these anticipations. I have done so, as have likewise almost all that have gone before me in these studies; and the results of my inquiries, as they run throughout the whole of this work, and as they appear in the chronological chart in my former work, must, by this time, be familiar to the reader. It will be perceived they all point to a very early period, the year 1844; and although it is fashionable to object to the fixing of dates, yet so long as it is said, 'things that are revealed belong to us and to our children for ever,' I see not on what sufficient ground." [137]

In support he quotes Charles Buck in his *Theological Dictionary*, published more than thirty years before:

"The late Rev. Charles Buck, in his valuable Theological Dictionary, published above thirty years ago, seems to have seen it aright; and I mention it more especially, as being the opinion of a Dissenting minister of high consideration. 'The four angels were loosed, says the prediction, verse 18th, which were prepared for an hour, and a day, and a month, and a year, for to slay the third part of men. This period, in the language of prophecy, makes 391 years, which being added to the year when the four angels were loosed, (prepared) will bring us down to 1844, or thereabouts, for the final destruction of the Mahometan empire.' " [138]

13. DANIEL INVOLVED IN CLOSING SCENES.—Habershon concludes by discussing the third woe as involving "the last solemn judgment on the Western nations," as well as the first resurrection—then the establishment of the kingdom of Christ." [139] In this connection he introduces the closing scenes of Daniel 11,[140] and the last great struggle of Revelation 19.[141]

14. ENDS TURKISH 391 YEARS IN 1844.—In the introduction to *Pre-Millennial Hymns* (1841), "An Epitome of Prophetic Truth" Habershon refers to the prophecies as having "latterly occupied the solemn consideration of many among us," and as having attracted "the deep attention of the church at the present time, under a persuasion that the accomplishment of judgments predicted is nigh at hand, and will be witnessed by the existing generation." [142] Alluding to his own day as within the "time of the end," and the close of the 2300 years in 1844, he

---

[137] *Ibid.*, pp. 285, 286.   [139] *Ibid.*, p. 289.   [141] *Ibid.*, pp. 307, 308.
[138] *Ibid.*, p. 287.   [140] *Ibid.*, pp. 300, 311.
[142] Matthew Habershon, "An Epitome of Prophetic Truth," in *Pre-Millennial Hymns* (2d ed.), p. 1.

again adverts to the 391 years of the Turkish woe.[143] This he once more dates from the fall of Constantinople in 1453, with the 391 years extending to 1844.[144]

15. FINAL EVENTS OF PROPHECY IMPEND.—Habershon then observes:

"Taking for granted that such calculation is correct, the time will then have arrived when 'the second woe will be past,' and the moment of which it is emphatically said, 'Behold, the third woe cometh quickly.' " [145]

The last woe will bring with it the fall of the papal kingdom, at the same general time as the fall of the Ottoman power. This being true, " 'the great Tribulation' must be very near its commencement!" [146]

The revealing titles of the hymns include "The Word of Prophecy," "The two Witnesses," "The Sealing of the People of God," "The Kingdom of the 'Beast,' " "The Doom of the 'Beast,' " "The 'Man of Sin,' " "The Church in the Wilderness," "The Lord is at Hand," "The Bridegroom cometh," "Babylon the Great," "The Fall of Babylon," "The Battle of Armageddon," "Christ the King of Glory," and "The New Jerusalem." Surely, this was a unique hymnal, supporting the spoken and written advent message. This, be it remembered, was the witness of an architect.

---

[143] *Ibid.*, pp. 15, 16.   [144] *Ibid.*, p. 46.   [145] *Ibid.*
                                     [146] *Ibid.*, p. 47.

CHAPTER THIRTY-THREE

A Feminine Touch
on the Prophecies

I. Charlotte Elizabeth—Weaves Prophetic Thread Through Writings

CHARLOTTE ELIZABETH [Tonna][1] (1790-1846), gifted miscellaneous writer and editor, was born in Norwich, her father being an English rector. In her youth she was deprived of her sight for months following eyestrain from excessive study. Leaning toward a literary vocation, she resolved to become a novel writer. But her plans were changed when she married Captain George Phelan and later moved to Ireland. While there she wrote a tract for the Dublin Tract Society. Then she began to write in earnest, under her given names. After five years in Ireland she moved to Clifton, where she continued her literary work.

Charlotte Elizabeth is listed as the author of thirty works, two and a half columns being required in the British Museum catalogue for her numerous writings, some of which involved much research. In 1834 she founded the *Christian Lady's Magazine,* which she continued to edit until her death. In 1837 she published an abridgment of Foxe's *Book of Martyrs,* in two volumes. She was editor of the *Protestant Annual* in 1840, and of the *Protestant Magazine* from 1841 until her death in 1846.

She was a "very successful religious writer,"[2] and her in-

---

[1] Née Browne; married Captain Phelan, then Tonna.
[2] Obituary, *The Gentleman's Magazine,* October, 1846 (New Series, vol. 26), p. 433; Lewis H. J. Tonna, *A Memoir of Charlotte Elizabeth,* pp. 10, 11.

fluence was widely felt. Strongly Evangelical in her views, she wrote a number of anti-Catholic tracts and Orange songs, including "The Maiden City," which became quite popular.[3] Because of her hostility to the Church of Rome, some of her works were placed on the *Index Expurgatorius*.[4] Her writings were denounced and forbidden by the archbishop of Sienna. Her last work was *War With the Saints*—the story of the crusades against the Albigenses and Waldenses. She possessed a rather elegant pen style and was one of the very few women in Britain to write on prophecy in the nineteenth-century Advent Awakening. She suffered from cancer the last eighteen months of her life, at which time she developed a roll-of-paper apparatus for her writing, so that her manuscripts were literally written "by the yard." [5]

In her *Personal Recollections,* in 1841, Charlotte Elizabeth tells first of her opposition to, and then of her wholehearted acceptance of, premillennialism.[6] Her paths had crossed those of Joseph Wolff, missionary herald of the advent. There was a struggle in England over greater British recognition of the Papacy—the "healing measure" of 1829.[7] The wrong of renewing "the ancient alliance with Antichrist," and of giving "the priests of Baal authority to legislate for the ordering of God's temple," [8] roused her to action. In her conclusions she was influenced by the protests of Hugh M'Neile, who "always proceeded on the simple fact that Popery is Antichrist." [9]

In 1829 she told how the gospel had been preached in Britain in early days, probably by an apostle, and an independent church established. Opposition developed "to the Romish delegate, Augustine [in the fifth century], when he was deputed to incorporate this country in the growing mass of papal dependencies." [10] Then, she adds, "Rome, not then arrived at the full stature of the Apocalyptic Beast, prevailed." And, "once sub-

---

[3] *Dictionary of National Biography*, vol. 19, p. 961.
[4] *The Gentleman's Magazine*, October, 1846 (New Series, vol. 26), p. 433.
[5] Charlotte Elizabeth [Tonna], *War With the Saints*, Preface, in the *Works of Charlotte Elizabeth* (1850 ed.), vol. 1.
[6] Charlotte Elizabeth, *Personal Recollections* (1842 ed.), pp. 202-206.
[7] *Ibid.*, p. 298.
[8] *Ibid.*, p. 229.
[9] *Ibid.*, p. 235.
[10] *Ibid.*, p. 226.

jugated, England lay at the foot of the Popes, from generation to generation, with now and then a movement towards free-dom." [11] After recounting the fluctuating fortunes of the days of Henry VIII, Bloody Mary, Elizabeth, and James I, followed by Charles I, she expresses her alarm at the prospect of new capitu-lations.[12]

In London ministers like Howels and Irving had been active in preaching down such heresy. Both men were bold and direct in dealing with the perils of popery, and influenced her thinking.[13] Charlotte Elizabeth was also greatly strengthened by her work of abridging into two volumes the large English martyrology by Foxe.[14] Especially impressed with Irving, she could not at first go along with his teaching on the advent.[15] She still believed the first resurrection to be mystical—"of the souls of the martyrs, whose spirits were to animate the happy race of believers during a thousand years." [16] Finally, the inconsist-encies of it all became untenable.

Gripped by the truth of the imminent advent, she tells of the "efforts the enemy has made to stifle this doctrine." For example, the "check" given by the later defections of Irvingism was "very great." [17] Accepting the advent truth, and its pro-phetic setting, she thenceforth weaves this theme, like a golden thread, through her subsequent writing. Thus she says:

"We are looking in breathless anxiety for the next movement among the powers of Europe, in reference to the east. Since the great blow was struck at Navarino, the drying up of the Euphrates has been progressive and without a pause. A sudden movement among the mountaineers of Syria has brought all Europe into the Land of Promise as a battle-field; and though only the preliminary alarm has yet sounded, in comparison with what is to follow, still there is a general impression even among those who would scoff at the mention of Armageddon, that in the very spot pointed out by Scripture will the great conflict of warring kingdoms take place. Blessed are they that watch!" [18]

1. "PROTESTANT MAGAZINE" GIVES PROPHETIC SLANT.—As its name might suggest, *The Protestant Magazine*, edited by

---

[11] *Ibid.*, pp. 226, 227.
[12] *Ibid.*, pp. 227, 229.
[13] *Ibid.*, pp. 252, 253.
[14] *Ibid.*, p. 301.
[15] *Ibid.*, p. 253.
[16] *Ibid.*, p. 257.
[17] *Ibid.*, p. 259.
[18] *Ibid.*, pp. 299, 300.

Charlotte Elizabeth, carried a monthly article dealing with the prophetic side of the "apostasy of the Church of Rome." [19] In one issue the writer states that the face of Rome carries on it "the characteristic lineaments of Antichrist," [20] and the prophetic symbols are presented in support. In a personal article, "Leaves from an Old Almanac," the editor writes, "The drunken harlot by whom the apostasy was typified, bore on her forehead the word 'MYSTERY.' " [21] Book reviews of works on prophecy were frequent,[22] and the witness of the reformers on prophecy is recited.[23] Forthright and fearless, Charlotte Elizabeth declares that when she accepted the editorship of *The Protestant Magazine* she "threw away the scabbard of that spiritual sword with which a combat was to be waged against the Papal Antichrist." [24] Such was the witness of a journal outside the prophetic expositor class.

2. PROPHETIC DEPICTIONS APPLIED TO PAPACY.—In Charlotte Elizabeth's last work, titled *War With the Saints,* written while she was fatally ill with cancer, chapter 2 portrays vividly the power, wealth, and grandeur of the Papacy under the ambitious Innocent III. Here are sample sentences: "You see before you the Man of Sin, the Son of Perdition, engaged in his foreshown work of opposing and exalting himself." "Beneath him, and around him, swell the seven hills of 'that great city which ruleth over the kings of the earth.' " "There, where the river of mystic Babylon, the Tiber, rolls sluggishly along. . . ." [25] And again, in describing the beast of the Apocalypse which is to make war with the saints, and to overcome them, she identifies it as in "every way identical with papal Rome." [26] She stands in amazement that, with the solemn truths of inspired prophecy before them, "historians of the past, or politicians of the present

[19] *The Protestant Magazine,* June, 1840, through December, 1841.
[20] *Ibid.,* March, 1841 (vol. 3), p. 74; August, 1841 (vol. 3), p. 255.
[21] *Ibid.,* July, 1841 (vol. 3), p. 220.
[22] *Ibid.,* July, 1841 (vol. 3), p. 245. Review of *The Apostasy Predicted by St. Paul,* by Mortimer O'Sullivan.
[23] *Ibid.,* August, 1841 (vol. 3), p. 259.
[24] *Ibid.,* November, 1841 (vol. 3), p. 365.
[25] Charlotte Elizabeth, *War With the Saints,* in *The Works of Charlotte Elizabeth,* (1850 ed.), vol. 1, p. 775.
[26] *Ibid.,* p. 785.

days, can deal with this subject as with any ordinary matter, where natural causes produce natural effects." [27]

3. WEARS OUT SAINTS FOR ALLOTTED PERIOD.—The chapter on "The Wearing Out" details the devisings of Innocent III in turning the machinery of the Inquisition on the Albigenses and Waldenses of Piedmont for their extirpation. The prophetic application is based on the "predicted reign" of Daniel's Little Horn, which would wear out the saints for "a time, and times, and half a time." [28]   And John, she adds, sees the same power warring against the saints, with "the Great Harlot, seated on that beast," drunken with the blood of saints—the martyrs of Jesus Christ. Then the witness of Christ Himself is cited, as His followers were to be delivered up, afflicted, and killed. "Thus, we observe, first, that for a certain allotted period, the man of sin was to have dominion." "Such is the infallible portraiture of the condition, and the destiny of the people of God during the reign of Antichrist." [29]

4. UNPRECEDENTED TROUBLE BEFORE THE END.—In *Principalities and Powers in Heavenly Places*, Section IX deals with "Satanic Wrath, as the End Draws Near." [30]   Declaring that through inspired prophecy the history of the future is no less certain than the history of the past, Charlotte Elizabeth refers to the unprecedented trouble predicted for the world just before the end. Of this she writes:

"This is mentioned as taking place at the time of the destruction of what we have every reason to believe is the Turkish empire; and synchronizing with the duration of that empire, is the period of 1260 days mentioned in Rev. xii.6." [31]

While oppression has marked its past history, yet just before the end "we are led to expect a very great accession of devilish power at that time, when the Lord is approaching to destroy that Deceiver with the brightness of His coming." [32]

---

[27] *Ibid.*   [29] *Ibid.*, p. 869.
[28] *Ibid.*, pp. 839-869.
[30] Charlotte Elizabeth, *Principalities and Powers in Heavenly Places,* in *The Works of Charlotte Elizabeth* (1848 ed.), vol. 2, p. 391 ff.
[31] *Ibid.*, p. 391.
[32] *Ibid.*, p. 392.

5. IN LAST HOUR OF THE NIGHT WATCH.—The "general expectation, prevailing more and more throughout the church of our Lord's promised coming," gives added assurance.[33] But this is being countered by such extremes as the tongues manifestations in Irvingism, and the subversive teachings of the Oxford Movement.[34]

Even now popery is "heaping up its stately piles of architecture," filling in its "secret recesses" with a "vast machinery" for carrying on her great objectives.[35] But soon "the mother of harlots is hurled from her proud seat, where she sits a queen, and now boasts that she is no widow." Not till her "utter burning with fire, all coming upon her in one day, then, and not till then, shall the night watch of the Church give place to the glories of a day that knows no going down of the sun."

"That this time is not now far off, we have abundant proofs in the signs that thicken around us. The period that remains is but as an hour, and surely we may watch with the Lord that one hour." [36]

Such is the story of a talented laywoman who was won to the advent doctrine and wove its truths into her lifework.

II. Mueller's Orphanages—Inspired by Faith in Advent

One of the interesting by-products of the flaming hope of the second advent was the fire kindled in the heart of GEORGE MUELLER, Müller, or Muller (1805-1898), German-English philanthropist, of Bristol Orphanages fame. Born at Kroppenstaedt, near Halberstadt, Prussia, Mueller was converted by a Pietist family named Wagner. He offered himself to the Continental Society for service at Bucharest. But in 1829 he went to London to labor for the Jews under the Society for Promoting Christianity Amongst the Jews.[37] He was in Teignmouth, near Plymouth, recovering from an illness when he heard Henry Craik,[38] leader of the advent band of Plymouth, whose heart had

---

[33] *Ibid.*, p. 393.   [34] *Ibid.*, p. 394.   [35] *Ibid.*, p. 396.   [36] *Ibid.*, p. 457.
[37] A. T. Pierson, *George Muller of Bristol*, p. 52 ff.; George Mueller, *A Narrative of Some of the Lord's Dealings with George Muller*, First Part, pp. 44-46; George Muller, *The Life of Trust*, pp. 95-108.
[38] HENRY CRAIK (1805-1866) was author of numerous works on Scripture and the Hebrew language, such as *Popery of Protestantism* (1852), *Principia Hebraica* (1863), *Hebrew Language* (1860).

for some time been fired by the blessed hope.[39] Mueller spent
ten days with him, and received more Bible truth than he had
obtained in a long time previous. He saw clearly that there was
no warrant for the popular concept of the world's conversion,
and that the second advent is the sole hope of the world.[40]

Gripped by the conviction of the Lord's soon appearing, he
united with the Plymouth Brethren. In 1832 he founded
the Scriptural Knowledge Institution for Home and Abroad,
where thousands were trained. But his chief interest lay in his
orphan homes, which were supported by faith—and so conspicuously as to demonstrate the power of prevailing prayer. He had
been moved to ask, "What may I do for the Lord before He
returns, as He may come soon." So, beginning in 1836, he
erected five large buildings, at Ashley Downs, sufficient to care
for 2,000 orphans. He also distributed 2,000,000 copies of the
Scriptures and aided in foreign mission work. And the motivating power in it all was the compelling love of the second
advent, received in 1830. Such was one of the significant by-
products of the nineteenth-century Advent Awakening.

III. Protestant Association Calls "Out of Babylon"

The Protestant Association was still another organization
in which the prophetic emphasis was pronounced. It was
"constituted" in Exeter Hall in 1835 with searching messages
by Croly, Melville, M'Neile, and others. The call was sounded
in "Come Out of Babylon" (1839)[41] and in "Protestantism and
Popery," by Henry Melville, and the anniversary sermon by
Hugh M'Neile.

IV. Ashe—Irish Reflector of Standard Prophetic Exposition

Isaac Ashe (b.1802) Irish Protestant, who graduated from
the University of Dublin in 1825,[42] presents an epitome of the

---

[39] George Mueller, "Introduction," in W. Elfe Tayler, *Passages from the Diary and Letters of Henry Craik of Bristol*, p. xii.
[40] George Mueller, *The Life of Trust*, p. 110; Pierson, *op. cit.*, pp. 386-389.
[41] A tract prepared in same form and style as reports of the Continental Society.
[42] *Alumni Dublinenses* (1593-1860), p. 23.

"generally received" Protestant exposition in *The Book of Revelation* (1835). Ashe is obviously one of the hundred clergymen in Ireland mentioned by Leslie[43] as proclaiming the advent message there in its prophetic setting. His exposition reflects scores of published views of the time. These are:

1. EARLY TRUMPETS ARE BARBARIAN IRRUPTIONS.—The first four trumpets signify the irruptions of the northern barbarians, which "ended in the dismemberment of the Western Empire." [44] The first referred to Alaric and his Goths, impelled by a preternatural impulse to march on Rome.[45] The second was Genseric, tyrant of the sea, and his Vandals.[46] The third was Attila and the Huns, falling like a blazing torch upon the empire.[47] The fourth brought the extinction of the Western Empire by Odoacer and the Heruli.[48]

2. SARACENS AND TURKS FOR ALLOTTED PERIODS.—The fifth trumpet Ashe applies to the Arabian locusts, for the 150 years, from 612 to 762.[49] The sixth is the Mohammedan Turks for the 396 years (365 + 30 + 1), from 1057, the investiture of Togrul, to the capture of Constantinople, in 1453.[50]

3. SEVEN VIALS BEGAN UNDER FRENCH REVOLUTION.—The two beasts of Revelation 13 are secular and spiritual Rome.[51] The seven vials began to be poured out under the French Revolution in 1789, when "the authority of the pope was *judicially* disannulled," with the sixth plague involving the partition of the Ottoman Empire.[52] The Babylonian woman of Revelation 17 denotes popery; and her cup, the inflaming and seducing potion to inflame and allure her lovers, with her name labeled on her forehead, in harmony with the ancient practice.[53]

V. Bickersteth—Shifts Focal Point by Double Dating

EDWARD BICKERSTETH (1786-1850), evangelical rector of Watton, Herts, and from 1816 to 1830 secretary of the Church

---

[43] See p. 592 in this volume of *Prophetic Faith*.
[44] Isaac Ashe, *The Book of Revelation With Compendius Notes*, p. 67.
[45] *Ibid.*, p. 69.   [48] *Ibid.*, pp. 77, 78.   [51] *Ibid.*, p. 139.
[46] *Ibid.*, pp. 72, 73.   [49] *Ibid.*, pp. 79-88.   [52] *Ibid.*, pp. 164-183.
[47] *Ibid.*, pp. 74, 75.   [50] *Ibid.*, pp. 88-110   [53] *Ibid.*, pp. 194, 195.

Missionary Society, was another of the most popular writers on prophecy of his day. His works fill sixteen volumes, some having from eight to twenty-five editions. Back in 1800 he received an appointment in the general post office, and began the study of law in 1806. In the meantime he came under strong religious impressions, laying down strict rules for his conduct. His interest now lay largely in spiritual matters, though he was diligent in his daily duties and active in religious and charitable organizations. In 1812 he entered into partnership in his brother-in-law's law office at Norwich.[54] During this three-year period he wrote *Help to the Study of the Scriptures* (1815), which was enlarged as *A Scripture Help* (1816), passing through twenty-one editions.

In 1815 he abandoned the practice of law and studied for the ministry. Upon ordination he served for a short time as assistant minister of the Episcopal Chapel at Spitalfields, but soon arranged to go to Africa in the service of the Church Missionary Society, to inspect and report on the society's work. Although Bickersteth resigned his secretaryship on accepting the rectorship of Watton in 1830, he continued to travel for the Church Missionary Society. He also served as a deputy for a Society for the Conversion of the Jews. In 1832 he edited the Christian's Family Library—republications of various works. About this time Bickersteth was awakened concerning the soon coming of Christ and underwent a change of view on the prophecies, upon which he now began to preach and to write.[55]

Bickersteth was a strong Protestant and an ardent premillennialist. He wrote on the Mystery of Iniquity, the Man of Sin, the Antichrist, and the Apocalyptic Babylon.[56] He was active in opposing the Oxford Tractarian Movement[57] and unitarian activities. He was also one of the founders of the Parker Society in 1840, for reprinting the chief works of the English Reformers,[58] and he encouraged the Irish Church Missions. His writings, in their various editions, occupy ten columns in the British

---

[54] T. R. Birks, *Memoir of the Rev. Edward Bickersteth.*
[55] *Ibid.*, vol. 2, pp. 38-42.　　[56] *Ibid.*, pp. 69, 70.
[57] *Ibid.*, p. 186.
[58] *Ibid.*, p. 143.

Museum catalogue. His *Practical Guide to the Prophecies,* which was issued as *Remarks on the Prophecies* in 1824, ran through nine editions—the fourth edition in 1835 taking on new stature. In 1833, having read a copy of Cuninghame's *Dissertations,* he had the author spend several days with him, and his mind was directed more than ever to the imminent second coming of Christ.[59]

The titles of some of Bickersteth's other writings reveal his emphasis: *Remarks on the Progress of Popery* (1836), *Tracts for the Times* (1836), *Come Out of Rome* (a sermon, 1840), *The Divine Warning to the Church* (1842), the preface to and one of the sermons, "The Kingdom of Christ," in *The Second Coming, the Judgment and the Kingdom of Christ* (one of the collections of Bloomsbury[60] lectures, 1843), *The Signs of the Times in the East* (1845), "The Kingly Power of Our Lord Jesus Christ," in *Good Things to Come* (Bloomsbury lectures, 1847), "The Destruction of Babylon" in *Lectures on Subjects Connected With the Second Coming* (Bloomsbury lectures, 1848). Such writings, with others of a more general character, comprise the sixteen volumes of his *Works,* issued in 1853.

1. COMPREHENSIVE SURVEY FROM PREMILLENNIAL VIEW-POINT.—Dealing comprehensively with the principles of literal interpretation of prophecy and their application, Bickersteth discusses the first advent as the foundation, and from this leads to the period of Christ's second coming. Holding firmly to the return of the Jews, he deals in detail with the Christian church and the opposing Antichrist.[61] In considering the several "chronological prophecies" and the varied interpretations current, Bickersteth comes to the judgments connected with the coming of Christ, the harvest of the church, the millennium and first resurrection, and finally the kingdom of Christ. He is a firm premillennialist.[62]

---

[59] *Ibid.,* pp. 40, 41; see also *Dictionary of National Biography,* vol. 2, pp. 465, 466.
[60] The Society for the Investigation of Prophecy for several years published its series of Lenten prophetic lectures at Bloomsbury.
[61] Edward Bickersteth, *A Practical Guide to the Prophecies* (5th ed., 1836), pp. 1-178.
[62] *Ibid.,* pp. 179-359.

2. ROME: MAN OF SIN AND BABYLON.—Bickersteth holds
consistently that "Rome is the Man of Sin and Babylon of Revelation," basing his opinion upon the common consent of a great
galaxy of English and Continental Reformation writers, and
their successors—naming some thirty well-known churchmen.[63]
Reaching back into the Middle Ages, he cites the strong earlier
declarations of Arnulph, Bernard of Clairvaux, Joachim, Dante,
and Petrarch.[64]   He then adds the supporting witness of the historic Protestant creeds, confessions, homilies, and articles.[65]

3. SEVENTY WEEKS CUT OFF OF 2300.—Stressing the "common principle" of year-day application to all time prophecy,
Bickersteth, in his early editions, dates the seventy weeks from
458 B.C. to A.D. 33, and the seventy weeks cut off of the 2300 years:

"Of the whole period of 2300 years, 70 weeks of years were determined
or cut off, from the restoration of the daily sacrifice to the completing of the
perfect sacrifice of Christ, when the spiritual temple was raised up, (John
ii, 19-21,) and the most Holy was anointed. Heb. i.9, ix.24. We have here
then the ecclesiastical period of 70 weeks or 490 years distinct and perfect." [66]

He takes passing note of De Chéseaux's astronomical cycles
of 1260 and 2300 years, and the difference between them of 1040,
as the most perfect cycle known,[67] and bearing upon the year-day
question.

4. TIME PROPHECY DATES TABULATED.—A bird's-eye view
of Bickersteth's concept of the outline prophecies is afforded by
several pages of Scripture chronology date tables, tabulating the
various events from the centuries before Christ up to A.D. 1822.
Thus the names of the four prophetic empires appear at the date
of their respective beginnings, in 606, 536, 331, 168 B.C.; the
joint beginning of the seventy weeks and the 2300 years is here
placed at 457 B.C., and the crucifixion and the close of the seventy
weeks appear opposite A.D. 34.[68]   The "10 days' tribulation" in
the Smyrna church period is placed at 303-13.   The dating of the

---

        [63] *Ibid.*, pp. 168, 169.   [66] *Ibid.*, p. 191.   [67] *Ibid.*, p. 205.
        [64] *Ibid.*, pp. 170, 171.   For comprehensive discussion of these characters see volumes
1 and 2 of *Prophetic Faith.*
        [65] *Ibid.*, p. 171.
        [68] *Ibid.*, pp. 356, 357.   Note that the dating in the table, strangely enough, differs from
'he 458 B.C. to A.D. 33 dating on p. 191 of the text.

seals and the trumpets appears scattered over the centuries—
the 150 years of the Saracenic woe ending in 786, and the 390
years of the Turkish woe terminating in 1453, at the fall of
Constantinople.[69]

The fall of the tenth part of the city (France) is dated 1789,
with the seven vials beginning in 1792, along with the close of
the 1260 years. The end of the 1290 years—which Bickersteth
begins synchronously with the 1260—is placed at 1822, and the
preaching of the second advent for the new era is noted for this
date, along with the wasting away of the Turkish Empire.[70]

5. REGRETTABLE EFFECT OF FUTURIST IMPACT.—The impact of Futurism was not without some effect upon Bickersteth, as appears in the suggestion of an "additional week" at
the close of the "times of the Gentiles," when the "people of
Israel are again taken into covenant." The first half is for the
Jews, for "rebuilding the temple," with the second half "under
the terror of the infidel Antichrist," and at the close the "destruction of that Antichrist." [71]   However, the "seven times," or 2520
years, are set as from 677 B.C. to A.D. 1843.[72] And while Bickersteth chooses 533 to 1792 for the 1260 years, he notes Brown's
proposal of 584-1844 and other suggestions.[73]

6. DOUBLE DATING CONFUSES 2300 YEARS.—A second regrettable departure from the Historical School of interpretation
is the introduction of second starting and ending points for
the 2300 years, as part of the progressive or "continuationist"
scheme. The year 1843 is spoken of as "the *beginning* of the sacrifice restored." [74]   Here is Bickersteth's complete statement:

"There is a *second commencement* of this period from Nehemiah's
decree. His commission was in 446, B.C., which effected a complete
cleansing in 433. This would bring us to 1867-8 for the completed restoration of Israel. If this 2,300 years be taken from Ezra's decree, 457 years
before Christ, it will bring us to 1843, the beginning of the cleansing of the
sanctuary, and of the restoration of the Jews, and of the approach of the

[69] *Ibid.*, pp. 358, 359. He notes Habershon's placing of the 391 years from 1453 to 1843-4
on p. 190.   [72] *Ibid.*, p. 194.
    [70] *Ibid.*, p. 359.   [73] *Ibid.*, pp. 200-203.
    [71] *Ibid.*, pp. 192, 193.   [74] *Ibid.* (1853 ed., vol. 8 of his *Works*), p. 181.

great tribulation. If taken from Nehemiah's completed cleansing in 433-4, it will bring us to 1867-8, the completed Jewish restoration." [75]

7. 1867-68 BECOMES NEW FOCAL POINT.—Similarly, the 1260 years are terminated about 1793, the 1290 end thirty years later, or in 1822-23, and the 1335 come to a close forty-five years beyond that, in 1868—the year 1793 marking "when popery *began* to fall"; and 1868, its *"final* fall." [76] Thus the way was being prepared for the passing by of 1843-44 as of minor interest or consequence, and for 1867-68 as the real focal point.

8. COMPREHENSIVE LIST OF PROPHETIC WRITERS.—Bickersteth's *Practical Guide* closes with about thirty pages of "Principal Books on Prophecy." This comprehensive list runs all the way from the early church Fathers, Jewish writers, and Reformers, to his own day. Page after page of authors, titles, and dates, with often an evaluating note, evidences his familiarity with the field. General works are followed by those clustered under special topics, as Second Coming of Christ, Antichrist, Millennium, Kingdom of God, Daniel, Revelation. [77]

VI. Bishop Caulfeild—Papal 1260 Years from 533 to 1792

CHARLES CAULFEILD, or Caulfield (1804-1862), Irish vicar of Kilcock and rector of Downings, was educated at Trinity College, Dublin, with a B.A. in 1826 and an M.A., B.D., and D.D. in 1858. Caulfeild was ordained a deacon in 1827, and an Anglican priest the year following. He was made perpetual curate of Clamantagh in 1832, was rector of Kilcock 1832-43, and rector of Creagh 1843-58. He became archdeacon of the Bahamas in 1858 and bishop of Nassau 1861-62. [78]

1. BABYLON IS ROME; SEVENTY WEEKS BEGIN 458 B.C.—In the field of prophetic interpretation Caulfeild wrote *The Fall of Babylon, as Exhibited in Prophecy* (1839). Establishing Rome as the seven-hilled city of the Apocalypse, he applies the proph-

---

[75] *Ibid.*
[76] *Ibid.*, p. 180.
[77] Bickersteth was one of the checkers of Brooks' *Dictionary of Writers on Prophecy.*
[78] *Alumni Dublinenses 1593-1860*, p. 143; Frederic Boase, Modern English Biography. vol. 1, col. 572.

ecy of Revelation 17 specifically to papal Rome,[79] after the breakup of the empire and the establishment of Christianity.[80] The 1260 years, in the several presentations, are always the period of this power,[81] and the seventy weeks begin in 458 B.C., on the year-day principle.[82]

2. 1260 YEARS DATED 533-1792.—The ten horns of Daniel 7 and Revelation 13 are plainly the ten divisions of Rome.[83] And the blood of the saints was shed by the terrible Inquisition.[84] The timing of the 1260 years Caulfeild places from 533 to 1792 —from Justinian to the French Revolution, the great "earthquake" that fixes one of the great eras in the history of earth.[85] Bishop Caulfeild simply held the standard positions.

VII. Scott—Solemn Appeal to a Drowsy, Dreaming Church

The urgency that gripped men as they came to the year 1844 is illustrated by the Scottish minister JAMES SCOTT,[86] in *A Compendious View of the Scriptural System of Prophecy* (1844). After noting the slight disparity among chronologers, he cites the calculations of Cuninghame of Lainshaw, and Bickersteth, who date the 2300 years from 457 B.C. to A.D. 1843, or at most from 433 B.C. to A.D. 1867.[87] Scott notes some who prefer the terminals 453 B.C. and A.D. 1847. But in any case 1847 is only three years distant, and 1867 only twenty-three years hence. Scott also notes the 391 years, dated by Whitaker and others from 1453 to 1844, and observes that "a few short months" will test the accuracy of that.[88]

1. UNANIMOUS CONVICTION PERIODS NEARING CLOSE.— Scott makes this sweeping statement:

"Almost all writers on prophecy agree that the prophetical dates given us, terminate between this present time and the year 1868, beyond which period there is no date extends, if we make the deduction of a hundred

---

[79] Charles Caulfeild, *The Fall of Babylon as Exhibited in Prophecy*, pp. 50-52.
[80] *Ibid.*, p. 53.   [83] *Ibid.*, pp. 68, 69, 208, 209.
[81] *Ibid.*, pp. 54, 55.   [84] *Ibid.*, p. 127.
[82] *Ibid.*, pp. 56, 57.   [85] *Ibid.*, pp. 189, 190.   [86] Biographical data unavailable.
[87] James Scott, *A Compendious View of the Scriptural System of Prophecy*, pp. 384, 385.
[88] *Ibid.*, pp. 385-387.

and fifty-one, or a hundred and thirty-two years, the uncounted period during the time of the Judges.

"From whatsoever date we may reckon, or whatever interpreter of these dates we may consult, after making the necessary additions according to established facts and times which have by many been taken no account of, we cannot but conclude, that it is almost the unanimous opinion of those who have most closely investigated, and who best understand these periods, that we are drawing very near to the conclusion of the mystery of God, and the end of the world, and the glorious rest which remains for Christ's people." [89]

2. POPULAR CHURCHES NOT EXPECTING ADVENT.—Scott then turns to the general abandonment by popular Christendom of belief in the premillennial advent of Christ, and observes, "The visible churches of Christendom are at this time apparently as little expecting any coming of the Lord, as the antediluvians were expecting the deluge." [90]

3. CHALLENGE TO POSTMILLENNIAL DREAMS.—But the signs of the times intensify, and the revival of the papal Antichrist is marked. Soon there will be a universal combination of antagonists against Christ and His people—and then will come Armageddon and the advent of the Lord.[91] No prophetic periods extend beyond those whose end is awaited. Inasmuch as the Lord's advent will be sudden and unexpected, as a thief in the night, Scott observes appealingly:

"What a solemn and awful call is this to a drowsy church, dreaming of millennial days of prosperity, and to a world lying in wickedness, to awake and flee to Christ." [92]

[89] Ibid., p. 387.　　[90] Ibid., p. 392.　　[91] Ibid., pp. 392, 393.
[92] Ibid., p. 393.

CHAPTER THIRTY-FOUR

The Futurist Foundation
of the Oxford Movement

I. Protestants Revive Futurism to Neutralize Historicism

As became apparent in Volume 2 of *Prophetic Faith*, the Reformation of the sixteenth century, which gave birth to Protestantism, was not only based on the Bible but guided and motivated by the prophecies. Indeed, it was the virile interpretation of prophecy that added strength to the Reformation, leading the Reformers to separate from the established church of Antichrist. On the other hand, the Preterist and Futurist counterinterpretations of the Jesuits sought to undo the damage by parrying the prophetic application to Rome, and by splitting the essential unity of Protestantism. The vague concepts of the Preterists conceived the Apocalyptic predictions as having been fulfilled in the early centuries. This, as we have seen, was gradually accepted by the rationalistic wing of Protestants on the Continent.

But now, for the first time, Catholic Futurism, initially projected by Ribera about 1585, began to obtain a foothold and then gain momentum among Protestants in Britain. Thus the same concept that sought to break the force of the Reformation view of the papal Antichrist, by assuming a future infidel antichrist, was again invoked to weaken the force of the great evangelical advent and prophetic awakening. Protestant expositors, some leaning toward Rome and some prompted by rationalistic concepts, joined hands in the attempt—perhaps unwittingly—to promote the Jesuit position. This, moreover, came to be tied inseparably with the Oxford Tractarian Movement of the Anglican Church, wherein ninety tracts were scattered by the hundreds of thousands to favor Rome and to disprove the Protestant concept of Antichrist, as will be noted shortly.

The Rome of the sixteenth century had felt the force of these prophecies and had sought to evade them in Counter Reformation days. There was no way out but to deny their application to Rome. Their inescapable existence in Scripture could not be gainsaid, as they were assuredly there. So the Jesuit champions of Rome denied that the prophecies referred to the Roman Catholic Church and its head. They pushed them aside—one group thrusting them forward and the other backward—shifting them out of the entire field of the Middle Ages. As to Babylon, they evaded application by interpreting it to mean pagan Rome, not papal. They also denied the year-day principle.

But now, in the nineteenth century in Britain, the Futurist concept was again revived, by Samuel Maitland, James Todd, William Burgh, John Darby of the Plymouth Brethren, and the renowned John Henry Newman.[1] It was espoused by opposite parties—by those who, though Protestants, disavowed the Reformation and referred to it as an "unwarrantable schism." These leaned strongly toward Rome. But it was also espoused by others, who, though likewise Protestant, held that the Reformation stopped short of its mark, with much of Babylon still in the Reformed churches. Such refused to believe their brethren had come altogether out of Babylon.

However, both parties appealed alike to the authority and tradition of the primitive church that had expected the Antichrist to be an individual, atheistic blasphemer, whose tyranny would last three and a half years, and be exercised just prior to the advent. They chose to go back to the undeveloped concept

---

[1] Reliable and comprehensive discussions of this Futurist issue appear in H. Grattan Guinness, *History Unveiling Prophecy* (1905 ed., pp. 284-295), and in E. B. Elliott, *Horæ Apocalypticæ* (5th ed., vol. 4, pp. 554-563), which have aided in this presentation.

of the nature and length of the Christian dispensation held by the early church. They denied the progressive interpretation that had added fact to fact and principle to principle, and perspective, as history fulfilled, clarified, and confirmed the great positions held in common by the growing body of Historical School interpreters through the centuries.

It all started in 1826, the same year that Irving's English translation of Lacunza appeared, with its Futurist elements. Maitland's *Enquiry* into the generally received year-day view of the 1260 days of Daniel and the Apocalypse was then released, followed by later *Enquiries*. In these Maitland had militantly assailed the whole Protestant application to the Roman Papacy of the symbols of the little horn, Daniel's fourth beast, the Apocalyptic Beast, and Babylon—holding that a personal and avowedly infidel antichrist was meant, and asserting that the prophetic days of its dominance were simply literal days. And nearly contemporaneously with Maitland's first book, Burgh, of Ireland, likewise published his pamphlet on the Antichrist. Then came Todd's large treatise, re-enforcing the others and laying the foundation for Newman's major positions. (Title pages of Maitland, Todd, and Newman treatises reproduced on page 540.)

The contrast between Lacunza and Lambert on the one hand, and Maitland, Burgh, and Todd on the other is impressive. The three Protestants were now excusing the Papacy from any connection with the predicted Christian apostasy, the Beast, or Babylon; while the two Catholic writers, on the contrary, had declared that its resemblance to that apostasy had been so marked for centuries that the application was manifestly to papal Rome.[2]

One major point in the attack by the English recruits to the Futurist School was the marked discrepancy among the Historicists, or expositors of the Historical School, on various points of prophetic interpretation, such as the seals and the Two Witnesses, and the manifestly unsatisfactory nature of their explanations on some of these points. This was seized upon by

---

[2] Elliott, *op. cit.* (5th ed.), vol. 4, p. 554.

42

both Maitland and Todd, and the novelty of the year-day principle asserted, as if it had never been applied before the time of
Wyclif and Brute. This Historical School view, nevertheless,
made gradual but steady advance.

The Futurist scheme had now received the support of prominent Church of England clergymen. But while these Protestant Futurists had borrowed from Lacunza, they rejected that
which cost him most in taking his stand on the prophecies—
the admission that the Roman church is Babylon. In preference
to this, the Protestants joined Cardinal Bellarmine in the expectation that Rome will fall away from her present faith before the
days of Antichrist.

The inroads of the Futurist theory also served to divert attention and understanding from the relationship of the seventy
weeks to the terminus of the 2300 years. If the seventieth week
is separated from the sixty-nine weeks, then the inseparable relationship of the remaining 1810 years of the 2300 is hidden, and
the divine harmony and understanding of the whole is ruptured.
By fixing the eyes upon a transcendent future, one obscures the
epochal events of the present. And when the 2300 days are conceived of as but literal time, any consideration of a nineteenth-
century terminus is obviously puerile. Confusion of the Historical School of interpretation, and its final breakdown, is now
definitely under way. Let us note the new developments under
Todd, after a brief glance at Burgh.

II. Futurist Burgh—Contends Antichrist Still Future

WILLIAM BURGH, afterward De Burgh (1800-1866), Irish
Futurist, was educated at Trinity College, in the University of
Dublin. He was Donnellan lecturer at Trinity College in 1853
and 1862. As a writer on prophecy he produced a treatise on
Antichrist (1829), then *The Apocalypse Unfulfilled* (1832), and
Lectures on the Second Advent (1832). This last work was an
answer to Hugh M'Neile. Burgh states that about 1820 he
espoused the premillennial view of the advent, and the Histori-

cal view of interpretation, when as yet practically no publications had appeared on it in Ireland. So in 1821 he published a tract titled *A Discourse on the Coming of the Day of God, in connexion with the First Resurrection.*[3] But soon afterward he became persuaded of the Futurist concept of a personal antichrist that would be revealed before the Lord's coming. He also expressed "unfeigned gratification" over Maitland's Futurist *Attempt to Elucidate the Prophecies Concerning Antichrist* (1830).[4]

1. CONTENDS POPE IS NOT MAN OF SIN.—Burgh's basic contention was that the antichrist is an individual, not a system. He expressly states:

"First that 'THE MAN OF SIN' is not popery appears from the necessity that this chapter be understood of an *individual,* and not of a power or office vested in numbers or held by succession."[5]

"I would say that an *individual* is intended—one person *whose pretensions live and die with himself.*"[6] . . .

"Secondly, *the nature* of these same acts and pretensions prove that the 'man of sin' is not the Pope."[7]

Burgh holds that it is clear that the Man of Sin is "yet to be revealed."[8]

2. HOLDS SEALS ARE YET FUTURE.—At the very outset of his treatise on the Apocalypse, Burgh declares that "the Book of the Revelation consists of two great parts," the things which *are* and the things which *shall be hereafter.*[9] He asserts "these seals are yet unopened" and "these prophecies are yet unfulfilled."[10] The full implications of Futurism run all through his *Apocalypse Unfulfilled.*

III. Todd—Denies Protestant Interpretation; Clears Rome

JAMES H. TODD (1805-1869), Irish scholar and professor of Hebrew in the University of Dublin, was born in Dublin. After graduating from Trinity College with a B.A. in 1825, he con-

---

[3] William Burgh, *Lectures on the Second Advent* (2d ed.), p. iv.
[4] *Ibid.,* p. v.   [6] *Ibid.,* pp. 64, 65.   [8] *Ibid.,* p. 63.
[5] *Ibid.,* p. 63.   [7] *Ibid.,* p. 65.
[9] William Burgh, *The Apocalypse Unfulfilled,* p. 2.
[10] *Ibid.* pp, 44, 45.

tinued as a tutor at Trinity, and edited the *Christian Examiner*, a journal on the controversy between the Established Church and Rome. In 1832 Todd took Anglican priest's orders, and in 1833 made the acquaintance of S. R. Maitland and began writing papers on church history for the *British Magazine*.

In 1838 and 1839 Todd was Donnellan lecturer in Trinity College, and chose as his subject the prophecies relating to Antichrist. Openly proclaiming himself Maitland's follower, he boldly attacked the Reformers' Historical School view—still commonly held by the Protestant clergy in Ireland—that the Pope was Antichrist. He stoutly maintained that the fourth empire is not Rome, that the Church of Rome is not the Man of Sin, and that Protestantism was in gross error in applying these prophecies to the papal church. The lectures for 1838 were afterward published as *Discourses on the Prophecies Relating to Antichrist in the Writings of Daniel and St. Paul* (1840). (Title page reproduced on page 540.)

The dedication was to Maitland, "as an acknowledgment of the assistance derived" from his writings in the formulation of his lectures. In 1837 Todd was installed as treasurer of St. Patrick's Cathedral, in 1849 was made regius professor of Hebrew, and in 1852 was appointed librarian of Trinity. This library he built up until it ranked with the chief libraries of Europe.

1. PAPAL ANTICHRIST THEORY OF "LATE ORIGIN."—In his *Discourses* Todd stresses the early concept of Antichrist as an individual, to appear at the end of the world, immediately before the second coming of Christ, and connected with the Jewish rather than the Gentile church.[11] Ponderously documented, and displaying exhaustive research to prove his positions, his large work is in reality but a series of negations. Every major position of the Historical School of interpretation is challenged and denied, with no constructive alternative presented, no philosophy of exposition.

---

[11] James H. Todd, *Discourses on the Prophecies Relating to Antichrist in the Writings of Daniel and St. Paul*, p. 18.

Todd insists that the theory of interpretation held by Mede and most modern Protestants was given voice by the Waldenses and other heretical groups in the twelfth century—such as the Catharists and Albigenses, who applied the Scriptural symbols (born of Manichaeism) of beast, harlot, and synagogue of Satan, to the Papacy.[12]   The third supporting group for this school of interpretation was from within the bosom of the Church of Rome itself—the spiritual Franciscans, the Fratricelli, and Joachimites, who applied the same terms to their own church.[13]

2. FOURTH KINGDOM NOT ROME, YET FUTURE.—In the only counterinterpretation help offered, Todd plainly declares that "the fourth kingdom of Nebuchadnezzar's vision is even yet to come," and is not Rome.[14]   And again, the fourth kingdom of Daniel 7 is not the Roman Empire,[15] and the horns are not fulfilled in the Roman Empire.[16]   Furthermore, he maintains that the first, second, and third beasts are not identical with the gold, silver, and brass.[17]   He reiterates that the fourth kingdom "will at some future period be established upon the earth." [18] Moreover, Daniel 11 is "not a chronological prediction of the events of modern history." [19]

3. PROPHETIC DAYS ARE NOT YEARS.—The "days" of the prophecies do not stand for years, Todd insists, with specific denial of application to the 1260, 1290, 1335, and 2300 days.[20] And the controversy over 2400 versus 2300, in Daniel 8:14, is exploited as to the difficulties and impossibilities.[21]

4. INDIVIDUAL MAN OF SIN IN JERUSALEM TEMPLE.—Turning to the 2 Thessalonians 2 argument, Todd maintains that the Man of Sin must be a single individual,[22] and the temple in which he sits must be the literal temple at Jerusalem.[23]   The Roman Empire is now extinct, and no potentate possessing the character and marks of Antichrist has as yet been manifested in the earth.[24]   One other argument is advanced: that the Roman

---

[12] *Ibid.*, pp. 27-31.
[13] *Ibid.*, pp. 31-33.
[14] *Ibid.*, pp. xii, 61, 62.
[15] *Ibid.*, pp. xii, 67.
[16] *Ibid.*, pp. xii, 13-75.
[17] *Ibid.*, pp. xii, 75-78.
[18] *Ibid.*, pp. xii, 84.
[19] *Ibid.*, pp. xiv, 180-182.
[20] *Ibid.*, pp. 116-119, 169.
[21] *Ibid.*, p. 118.
[22] *Ibid.*, pp. xv, 233.
[23] *Ibid.*, pp. 217, 218, 221.
[24] *Ibid.*, p. 238.

Empire was not the power that "withholdeth," but that the reference is rather to the coming of the Lord." [25]

5. ROME'S ERRORS DO NOT CONSTITUTE APOSTASY.—Moreover, Todd maintains that "Romanism [is] not properly an apostacy from the faith." [26] And, "the Errors of Romanism do not amount to Apostasy." [27] He plainly says, "The Church of Rome [is] a true Christian Church." [28] He adds that the supposed criteria of the apostasy are "not peculiar to the Church of Rome," as the Greek and Oriental churches hold the same positions on many matters. [29] So, he continues, Rome "with all her deep corruptions, still maintains and inculcates the great essential truths of our religion." [30]

6. CAPITALIZES PROTESTANT DIVERSITY IN APPLICATION.—The latter third of this large treatise comprises extensive notes—from page 357 to page 526—which challenge the year-day principle among Christians and Jews. [31] And the disparity among certain Protestant writers on the chronological placing of the various periods is employed as major evidence. [32]

7. PRESS PRIMITIVE VIEWPOINT ON INDIVIDUAL.—Todd capitalizes on the constricted viewpoint of early-century writers who had not yet seen the application of the year-day principle to any other than the seventy weeks of years, and to whom Antichrist was naturally only an individual rather than a succession of individuals forming a system. He stresses the unwarranted expectations of the appearance of Antichrist at different periods, such as around A.D. 1000. [33]

8. ATTACKS CHARACTER OF THE WITNESSES.—The antiquity of the Waldenses teaching on Antichrist is attacked, and the authenticity and reliability of their *Treatise on Antichrist* is challenged. [34] The same is true of the Albigenses. [35] And finally, the character and credibility of Joachim and the Joachimites is

[25] *Ibid.*, pp. xv, 256-259.
[26] *Ibid.*, pp. xv, 259-267.
[27] *Ibid.*, pp. 320, 321.
[28] *Ibid.*, pp. 322, 323; running title at top of page.
[29] *Ibid.*, pp. 340-342.
[30] *Ibid.*, p. 347.
[31] *Ibid.*, pp. 358-361.
[32] *Ibid.*, pp. 362-365.
[33] *Ibid.*, pp. 366-390.
[34] *Ibid.*, p. 27; note A, pp. 399-417.
[35] *Ibid.*, p. 428 ff.

disparaged,[36] and that of the Franciscans,[37] particularly John d'Olivi.[38]

Frequently Roman Catholic authorities are cited by Futurists to counter the Waldensian witness, together with the witness of certain Protestants who have questioned the application to Rome—such as Maitland, who is lauded, and Burton, and Burgh. There is omission of the clearest and most prominent expositors, such as Cuninghame, Croly, Bickersteth, and Reformers and later writers by the score.

IV. Oxford Movement Adopts Futurist Antichrist

The Oxford Movement is the name applied to the early nineteenth-century Romeward movement in the Anglican Church. It covered a period of twelve years, beginning with Keble's noted sermon on "National Apostacy," at Oxford in 1833, and ending with the defection of Newman to the Roman church in 1845. It is also called the Tractarian Movement, because it produced a series of ninety *Tracts for the Times*, issued at Oxford between 1833 and 1841.

The chief objective of these tracts was to "unprotestantize the Church of England," [39] and the principal writers were Newman, Pusey, Keble, Froude, and Williams. These men readily seized upon the position of the Futurist writers Maitland and Todd, whose views removed the Roman Papacy from the application of the fearful prophecies concerning Antichrist, and consequently left Protestantism open to the charge of "unjustifiable schism." It likewise left the Papacy open to the Catholic desire of the Tractators for reunion. These tracts were scattered everywhere, as edition after edition came from the presses, to discredit the historic Protestant view of the papal Antichrist. And they succeeded to a tragic degree. By those tracts Newman and his party proceeded to demolish the doctrinal barriers that

---

[36] *Ibid.*, p. 453 ff.
[37] *Ibid.*, p. 476 ff.
[38] *Ibid.*, p. 467 ff. These are all discussed in detail in Volumes 1 and 2 of *Prophetic Faith*.
[39] Elliott, *op. cit.* (5th ed.), vol. 4, p. 555.

separated the Anglican Church from Rome, and so let down the bars for the re-entry of many in 1845-46.

At first the Oxford Tractarian Movement had apparently set out to stay the infidel revolutionary spirit. And at the outset it was looked upon as the ally of conservatism. But while professing to go back to the primitive church for its model, it actually drew its pattern from the fourth and fifth centuries, when the church was already corrupted, increasingly stressing the dogma of church sacraments as the means of communicating divine life to man, together with a priesthood of apostolic succession, and the mediation of living priests.[40] It came to deny the sufficiency of the Scriptures, and to teach that tradition and the commandments of men are necessary. It sought to inculcate reverence for the Bishop of Rome, and deplored the schism at the Reformation, lauding the Roman ritual and missal.

1. HOLDS ANTICHRIST IS NOT YET COME.—Various of these tracts stress the value and providential superintendence of the liturgies of the church.[41] Others deal with Antichrist; for example, in No. 83, *Advent Sermons on Antichrist,* there are four sermons devoted to the times, the religion, the city, and the persecutions of Antichrist. On the "time" of Antichrist the author says: "If, then, Antichrist is to come immediately before CHRIST, and to be the sign of His coming, it is manifest that he is not come yet, but is still to be expected," and couples with this the literal time-period feature: "Further, it appears that the time of Antichrist's tyranny will be three years and a half, which is an additional reason for believing he is not come." [42]

2. MAINTAINS ROMAN EMPIRE STILL EXISTS.—Moreover, the accompanying "time of unexampled trouble" has not yet come, neither had the restraining of Roman power been as yet taken out of the way, "for I do not grant that the Roman Empire is gone. Far from it: the Roman empire remains even to this

---

[40] See *Tracts for the Times,* by Members of the University of Oxford, nos. 10, 71, 80, 87; also Tract Number Ninety, *Remarks on Certain Passages in the Thirty-nine Articles,* by John Henry Newman.
[41] Such as nos. 83, 84, 87, 88.
[42] *Tracts for the Times,* vol. 5, no. 83, *Advent Sermons on Antichrist,* p. 4.

day." [43] "As the horns, or kingdoms still exist, as a matter of fact, consequently we have *not* yet seen the end of the Roman empire." [44]

3. CONTENDS ANTICHRIST TO BE SINGLE INDIVIDUAL.—The next proposition was that Antichrist is "one man, an individual, not a power or a kingdom." [45] Finally, "Antichrist will be an open blasphemer, opposing himself to every existing worship, true and false." [46]

V. Newman—Pope Not Antichrist but Spokesman for God

JOHN HENRY NEWMAN (1801-1890), famous High Church Anglican convert to Roman Catholicism, and one of the prime movers in the Oxford Tractarian Movement, was born in London. He experienced "conversion" when fifteen years of age, and in the same year entered Trinity College, Oxford. After finishing in 1821 he tutored for a while, was ordained in 1824, and became curate of St. Clements, Oxford. He was appointed to St. Mary's in 1827, and was preacher to the university in 1831-32. But he resigned and went on a tour of the Mediterranean with R. H. Froude—still leaning toward Protestantism, as indicated by comments while in Rome. It was while on a voyage in the Mediterranean during this tour that he wrote "Lead, Kindly Light," in the midst of conflict and groping.

Newman returned home in 1833, in time to hear John Keble's[47] famous sermon of July 14 on "National Apostasy," which later came to be regarded as the inauguration of the Oxford Movement. Newman picked up the work from there and gave it momentum. Before the close of the month a meeting of High-Churchmen was held at Newman's rectory, during which it was resolved to fight for "the apostolical succession and the integrity of the Prayer-Book." [48]

---

[43] *Ibid.*, pp. 4, 5.
[44] *Ibid.*, p. 6.
[45] *Ibid.*, p. 7.
[46] *Ibid.*, p. 26.
[47] JOHN KEBLE (1792-1866), Anglican clergyman and poet, was born in Gloucester. Ordained deacon in 1815 and priest in 1816, he became professor of poetry at Oxford, 1831-1841. He was the actual author of the Oxford Movement, to which he gave the initial impulse by this sermon of 1833.
[48] *Encyclopædia Britannica* (14th ed.), vol. 16, pp. 314, 315.

A few weeks later Newman started the *Tracts for the Times* series—begun independently but called "Oxford Tracts"—from which the movement subsequently derived the name Tractarianism. He composed twenty-nine of the ninety tracts, all intended to revive the Catholic spirit in Anglicanism and to secure a satisfying basis of doctrine and discipline. These tracts were supplemented by Newman's Sunday afternoon sermons at St. Mary's, which exerted much influence. In 1835 Edward B. Pusey[49] joined the movement as an ally. Thus some called the group "Puseyites."

Newman now became editor of *The British Critic* and gave a course of lectures in a side-chapel in defense of Anglicanism as a "middle way" between Romanism and Protestantism. By 1839 he began to question the soundness of the Anglican position, and finally in 1841 published Tract Number Ninety, on the Thirty-Nine Articles of the Church of England—which were the stumbling block—to show they were not against the authorized creed of the Roman church, but only against popular errors and exaggerations. It was an attempt to reconcile the Roman and Anglican faiths. There was talk everywhere, and excitement reached a high pitch. Violent opposition was matched by ardent support, as Newman was denounced by some as a traitor and defended by others as a savior of the day. But Tract Number Ninety ended the series, which was never condemned by the university as a whole. (Title page and Newman portrait reproduced on page 540.)

He resigned his vicarage and his editorship of *The British Critic*, and withdrew to Littlemore to study, living there under rigorous monastic conditions, seeking to reconcile himself with the Roman Catholic system. In 1843 Newman published a retraction of all the hard things he had formerly said against Rome. Finally, in 1845, he was received into the Roman communion, leaving Oxford for Rome, where, in 1846, he was

---

[49] EDWARD BOUVERIE PUSEY (1800-1882), English Hebrew scholar, was appointed regius professor of Hebrew at Oxford in 1828, holding the position until death. His avowed aim was to prevent the spread of German rationalism in England. In 1833 he joined Newman and Keble in the issuance of the *Tracts* series, and in 1836 began the translation of the writings of the ancient church Fathers. In 1843 he was suspended for three years from preaching at Oxford.

ordained a priest and later given a D.D. degree by the pope. In 1847 he returned to England, where he continued to reside. In 1854 Newman was called to Dublin as rector of the newly established Catholic University, and in 1879 he was given the cardinal's hat.

1. NEWMAN AGREES WITH TODD'S FUTURIST VIEWS.—Newman, in "The Protestant Idea of Antichrist," [50] written five years before he joined the Church of Rome, begins with this laudatory statement concerning the Todd lectures:

"The Discourses which Dr. Todd has recently given to the world, are, perhaps, the first attempt for a long course of years in this part of Christendom [Protestant England] to fix a dispassionate attention and a scientific interpretation upon the momentous 'Prophecies relating to Antichrist in the writings of Daniel and St. Paul.' " [51]

In this treatise Newman quotes from Todd, and builds his arguments upon Todd from beginning to end, declaring, "We have pleasure in believing that in matters of doctrine we entirely agree with Dr. Todd." [52] Todd's main position, be it particularly noted, is "that the prophecies concerning Antichrist are as yet unfulfilled, and that the predicted enemy of the Church is yet to come." [53]

2. ROME EITHER HOUSE OF GOD OR SATAN.—Newman plainly says, "We take up Dr. Todd's position." [54] And he goes to the heart of the question with these two propositions:

"The question really lies, be it observed, between those two alternatives, *either* the Church of Rome is the house of God *or* the house of Satan; there is no middle ground between them." [55]

"The question is, whether, as he [Todd] maintains, its fulfilment is yet to come, or whether it has taken place in the person of the Bishop of Rome, as Protestants have very commonly supposed." [56]

3. CHARGE SPRINGS FROM MEDIEVAL GROUPS.—Still following Todd, he charges that the concept of the papal Antichrist sprang from "three heretical bodies" between the eleventh and

---

[50] John Henry Newman, "The Protestant Idea of Antichrist" (first published in *The British Critic, and Quarterly Theological Review*, October, 1840, vol. 28, no. 56, pp. 391-440, as a review of Todd's *Discourses*, referred to above, pp. 660-663), in his *Essays Critical and Historical*, vol. 2, pp. 112-185.

[51] *Ibid.*, p. 112. [53] *Ibid.* [55] *Ibid.*, p. 116.
[52] *Ibid.*, p. 113. [54] *Ibid.*, p. 114. [56] *Ibid.*, p. 117.

sixteenth centuries—the Albigenses, Waldenses, and the Spiritual Franciscans, the third of which arose in the bosom of the Church of Rome itself, as well as the Fratricelli, and the Joachimites, including Olivi—and then the Hussites, Lutherans, Calvinists, and English Reformers.[57] Lauding the Futurist Maitland's earlier research,[58] Newman scores the position of Bishops Newton and Hurd in the past, and M'Neile and Irving in contemporary times.[59]

4. IS EITHER VICE-CHRIST OR ANTICHRIST.—Dealing with the claims of the Roman church—that of speaking for Christ, developing His words, suspending His appointments, granting dispensations, and absolving from sin—Newman sets forth the alternatives with a penetrating clarity that reveals his whole concept of what constitutes Antichrist:

"He who speaks for Christ must either be His true ambassador or Antichrist; and nothing but Antichrist can he be, if appointed ambassador there is none. Let his acts be the same in both cases, according as he has authority or not, so is he most holy or most guilty. It is not the *acts* that make the difference, it is the *authority* for those acts. The very same acts are Christ's acts or Antichrist's, according to the doer: they are Christ's, if Christ does them; they are Antichrist's if Christ does them not. There is no medium between a Vice-Christ and Antichrist." [60]

Thus he leads to the amazing conclusion that Christ left a visible church with invisible privileges, divinely endowed with authority to act for Him, irrespective of personal character or conduct.

5. APPLIES MOUNTAIN AND KINGDOM PROPHECIES TO CHURCH.—Newman comes finally to the specifications of Daniel's prophecy of the "stone cut out" of the mountain "without hands," which "broke in pieces and consumed" all former kingdoms and became a great mountain filling the earth; and of the saints of the Most High taking the kingdom and possessing it forever. This he applies to the reign of the church, as through her as His "vicar and representative, . . . He has truly and literally judged among the nations, and rebuked many people,

---

57 *Ibid.*, pp. 117-123.
58 *Ibid.*, pp. 118, 125.
59 *Ibid.*, p. 126.
60 *Ibid.*, pp. 171, 172.

reigned in righteousness, promoted peace, taught the nations, repressed the wicked." [61]

6. CHOOSES AGAINST PAUL'S ANTICHRISTIAN CORRUPTION.— Despite all the church's defects this is "but a literal accomplishment of the sure word of prophecy concerning the reign of Christ upon earth." [62] His concluding item is:

"If we must go to prophecy, *which set of prophecies* is more exactly fulfilled in the Church of the middle ages, those of Isaiah which speak of the evangelical kingdom, or those of St. Paul and St. John which speak of the antichristian corruption?" [63]

Having denied application of the prophecies to the Papacy, Newman undertakes to level the doctrinal barriers separating the Church of England from the Church of Rome. In Tract Number Ninety he boldly declares that "Scripture is not, on Anglican principles, the Rule of Faith." [64] Then he deals adroitly with pardons, the mass, purgatory, images and relics, invocation of saints, maintaining that the Articles do not condemn the doctrines of Rome but only her absurd excesses. Clever in concept, subtle and persuasive in reasoning, it gave the pro-Catholic slant to every one of the Articles and paved the way for the acceptance of Roman teaching.

Upon becoming a Catholic, in 1845, Newman accepted those "additional Articles which are not found in the Anglican creed"—including transubstantiation. Of this he said, "I had no difficulty in believing it as soon as I believed that the Catholic Roman Church was the oracle of God." It was this new conception of an infallible church that changed all things for Newman—that and the dismissal of the pope from the charge of being Antichrist.

Such were the beginnings and the basis of that Romeward movement in the church of England that attained such large proportions and materially weakened the force of the great advent and prophetic awakening. The new concept of prophecy was at the heart of it.

---

[61] *Ibid.*, pp. 174, 175.   [62] *Ibid.*, p. 176.   [63] *Ibid.*
[64] John Henry Newman, *Remarks on Certain Passages in the Thirty-nine Articles* (Tract Number Ninety), p. 20.

SWEDISH CHILD PREACHERS HERALD JUDGMENT HOUR

Royal Decree of 1726 Prohibiting Religious Meetings in Private Homes (Upper Left); Report of Dr. Sköldberg on Physical Condition of Preaching Children (Upper Right); Contemporary Press Articles Describe the Preaching Phenomenon (Lower Pair); and Typical Preaching Scene of the Time (Center)

CHAPTER THIRTY-FIVE

Child Preachers of Sweden
Warn of Judgment

I. Setting and Occasion of Their Remarkable Witness

The nineteenth-century Advent Awakening penetrated Scandinavia in the early forties, but by a means markedly different from that employed in any other country of the Old World or the New. In Sweden, preaching contrary to that of the established church was forbidden. The clergy of the state church opposed emphasis upon the soon coming of Christ. Their refusal to speak was met by the amazing spectacle of children and youth in the homes of humble cottagers—some of whom had not yet learned to read—proclaiming the impending judgment hour and imminent advent, and giving expositions of prophecy. This movement took place chiefly in southern Sweden, where many of the people were Pietists. A remarkable work was accomplished, the populace being profoundly stirred.

These were normal children, just like others, except when moved upon by a power outside themselves. Then their tone and manner changed, and they were impelled to proclaim a message calling for repentance and reformation of life. They condemned sin and apostasy, lifted up the standard of righteousness, and urged all to flee from the wrath to come. Men trembled and forsook their evil ways, searching the Scriptures anew. The

---

Note.—Due to postwar conditions, some of the Swedish accent marks for use with certain names of persons and places appearing in this chapter could not be secured for the linotype machine in time for this first edition. Their omission will not interfere in any way with the reading. For technical accuracy, they will, if possible, be added in future editions.

671

intemperate and godless were transformed, and even a bishop and a physician were constrained to admit that it was not Satan but God who impelled these child preachers.

1. Use of Children Not Without Precedent.—This use of children was not without precedent. At the first advent God put His Spirit upon little children, moving them to proclaim Jesus as the promised Son of David, as they waved their palm branches in the temple courts. Jesus had entered Jerusalem accompanied by the happy shouts of the multitudes. When the jealous Pharisees demanded that He silence them, Christ declared that their acclamations were in fulfillment of prophecy, and that if they should hold their peace, the very stones would cry out. The message must be given. So, when through fear of priests and rulers the adults became silent, these children caught up the refrain that had been dropped, waving their palm branches and crying, "Hosanna to the Son of David." When the angered Pharisees called Christ's attention to their testimony, He answered by saying, "Yea; and have ye never read, Out of the mouth of babes and sucklings Thou hast perfected praise?" [1] Just "as God wrought through children at the time of Christ's first advent, so He wrought through them in giving the message of His second advent." [2]

2. Historical Background Clarifies the Situation.—A retrospective glance over Swedish history will illuminate the picture. The Protestant Reformation had long before penetrated Sweden. Two brothers, Olaus (Olof or Olaf) and Laurentius (often given as Lars, or Lawrence) Petri (Latinized; sometimes spelled Petersen or Peterson), were educated at the University of Wittenberg under Luther and Melanchthon and embraced the doctrines of the Reformation. Returning to Sweden, they became its powerful advocates. On several occasions mobs inspired by the priests assailed them. But they were aided by the king, Gustavus Vasa I, who determined upon a reformation in both church and state.

---

[1] Matthew 21:8-16.
[2] Ellen G. White, *The Great Controversy*, pp. 367, 368.

Olaus became the professor of theology of Upsala, while Laurentius was appointed preacher in the cathedral at Stockholm, later becoming Archbishop of Sweden, in 1531. The two brothers translated the Bible into Swedish, and illustrated the prophetic symbols of Daniel and the Apocalypse by the classic woodcuts of Luther's Bible[3]—the four beasts of Daniel labeled with their respective names, the beast of Revelation surmounted by a triple crown, and the like. The Bible alone was their platform of faith. A monument in Orebro, now to be the scene of some of these later manifestations, commemorates the memory of these two eminent men.[4]

As Protestantism became the state religion, the clergy grew intolerant and oppressive. Preaching that was considered dangerous to the state church was forbidden. Thus on January 12, 1726, a royal decree from Stockholm prohibited the gathering of people in private homes for religious purposes, with penalties for disobedience.[5] This mandate remained in effect for a century and a quarter, until modified by Royal Regulation No. 90, on October 26, 1858, and completely removed a decade later.[6] It was therefore during the period of this enforcement that these child-preaching episodes took place.

3. INTENSE OPPOSITION TO CHILD WITNESSES.—In the 1840's the advent message began to be preached by several laymen, called *ropare,* or "criers," who proclaimed the impending hour of God's judgment.[7] Large numbers gathered to hear them, often in private homes or out in the woods. A real revival and reformation began. But frenzied attempts were made to stop them. They were declared insane or afflicted with some dread disease, and some were severely punished. Two young preachers —Ole Boqvist and Erik Walbom—still in their teens were arrested and accused in the parish of Karlskoga, in Orebro prov-

---

[3] See illustration in *Prophetic Faith,* vol. 2.
[4] Lars Anton Anjou, *Svenska kyrkoreformationens historia* (English ed., *The History of the Reformation in Sweden,* pp. 61-65, 277-291); J. A. Wylie, *The History of Protestantism,* vol. 2, pp. 14-33; Clement M. Butler, *The Reformation in Sweden,* pp. 116-118; see also the several works of Daniel Gerdes.
[5] *Förnyade Placat Och Förbud,* Stockholm, 1726. (Title page reproduced on page 670.)
[6] *Swensk Författnings-Samling,* nr. 76, 1868.
[7] Ellen G. White, "Notes of Travel," in *Historical Sketches,* p. 202.

ince. When tried, they defended their faith and conduct from the Scriptures. In later life Boqvist stated:

"When we were brought before the governor for examination, he demanded by what authority we were sent to preach. We referred him to Joel 2 and Rev. 14:6-8, and told him further that the Spirit of God came upon us with such power that we could not resist it." [8]

After being beaten they were taken to the hospital for mental examination by physicians. Their heads were shaved, with the exception of two strips of hair left in the form of a cross. Then they were imprisoned and tortured by powerful streams of cold water. Finally they were released, only to keep on preaching until 1844.

When in Sweden in 1885, Ellen G. White, who inquired into these episodes, declared that the children thus affected were unconscious of what was going on around them. They had all the characteristics of those in vision from God and spoke with convincing power that carried great influence. They lost their childish demeanor and spoke with all the force and power of full-grown men and women. Many who saw and heard them firmly believed God was using them to utter prophetically the message then due. An eyewitness account of one assembly in a cottager's house, addressed by a girl preacher, is cited:

"When the last [of the people] had arrived, her manner changed entirely, both in boldness and movements, clearly indicating that she was moved by an invisible power, and not by her own natural gifts. When she commenced speaking, her voice also changed. She said, 'Fear God, and give glory to him; for the hour of His judgment is come.' She reproved sins, such as drinking, theft, adultery, swearing, and backbiting, and also reproved churchgoers for attending church with worldly business in view, instead of listening to God's word and conforming their lives to it. Her voice and words were impressive. Many were weeping and sighing. They were told that time was given them to repent, but they must do it immediately, and not put it off." [9]

---

[8] *Ibid.*, p. 204. (The story, as recorded in their own words, was reprinted in the *Review and Herald*, Oct. 7, 1890 [vol. 67, no. 39], p. 612; while not a contemporary record, this constitutes valuable supplemental testimony from a personal participant.)

[9] *Ibid.*, pp. 205, 206. Mrs. White adds the significant comment: "Years ago, the work of the first message in these countries was presented before me, and I was shown circumstances similar to those related above. It was God's will that the tidings of the Saviour's coming should be given in Sweden, and when the voices of His servants were silenced, He put His Spirit upon the children, that the work might be accomplished."

Let us now examine contemporary Swedish newspaper accounts, which constitute our primary sources.

II. Contemporary Witness of the Swedish Press

1. RECOURSE TO THE PROPHECIES CONDEMNED.—Discussions of the strange "preaching sickness," afflicting some of the children of southern Sweden, permeated the Swedish press for two or three years—particularly in 1842 and 1843. Descriptions, denunciations, and defenses were intermingled. These youthful "preachers" were bitterly opposed by the state clergy, and their exact words come to us only through their enemies. Their testimony was condemned by the religious leaders for three reasons— first, because the people were not spiritually needy, then because children and women should be silent in church, and finally because the resultant reforms allegedly dealt with outward things. One writer, however, in a Stockholm paper, challenges the propriety of the commonly employed terms "preaching sickness," or "preaching fanaticism," for, he says, these terms do not fit the accepted concept of preaching, for it "presupposes education, official call, and ordination." [10]

Among the arguments he then employs for declaring that "this work is not of God" are these: First, the religious "condition in Smaland" [11] is not in such a state that something so extraordinary is necessary. God provides for the extension of the kingdom of Christ "by ordinary means, namely through the Word, the Sacraments, and the ministry." There are still worshipers in uprightness and truth; there is still spiritual food for those who hunger and thirst. But if a revival were due, then it would be needed more in other near-by provinces than in Smaland; second, the phenomenon is repudiated by the "spiritually enlightened teachers and other faithful"; third, it does not bear the "fruit of repentance"; and fourth, those who speak or prophesy are mostly children or unmarried girls. But, the

---

[10] *Nordisk Kyrkotidning* (Stockholm), argangen 3, sid. 268-271.
[11] Pronounced Smöland.

writer insisted, God said that the woman should be quiet in the church. God is the God of order. If He has commanded that women be quiet, they must be quiet. If He has commanded, aroused, and impelled the girls in Smaland to speak, then He must take back His former word.[12]

Apart from these criticisms the chief condemnation seems to center, significantly enough, on their "interpretation, or rather misinterpretation, of the Apocalyptic" messages. The writer sarcastically describes their alleged need for something sensational:

"One must see into the future! One must confound with new discoveries! One must prophesy! On what? On the imminent end of the world. To support their claims, they must make use of the holy and glorious revelation of Jesus to John. O, ye self conceited, do ye really believe that ye by all your prophecies can take one single nail out of the joints of the world-building? Do ye know the interpretation of a single one of the symbols in Revelation? Have ye really found the golden cord that helps one through the labyrinth of the apocalyptic time prophecies? Do ye possess the knowledge, or in the absence of it, the grace, the enlightenment of the Spirit, necessary to a sound, pure, and clear Biblical exegesis?" [13]

He then concludes that "it is easy to recognize which spirit is working through these diviners." This ecclesiastical writer confidently asserts that "these workings" come "from the devil." These very charges, however, are answered by others.

Knowledge of the phenomenon spreads to Germany. Adverse comments appear in the Berlin *Evangelische Kirchen-Zeitung* (Evangelical Church Journal) from Dr. C. W. Hengstenberg, professor in the University of Berlin, who criticizes it because it is not conducted by the "authorized ministry." Reason and education, he says, as well as piety, are needed, and in all religious services *who* is leading is to be definitely considered.[14] In support, under notes concerning Sweden, Hengstenberg quotes copiously from a hostile letter from the clergy in the Swedish *Aftonbladet* (Stockholm) of May 29, 1842,[15] to be cited later.

---

[12] *Ibid.* [13] *Ibid.*
[14] *Evangelische Kirchen-Zeitung* (Berlin), 30 Juli, 1842 (Band 30, Nr. 61), Spalte 486.
[15] *Ibid.*, 27 Juli, 1842 (Band 30, Nr. 60), Spalte 478 ff.

2. TELL CROWDS OF APPROACHING WORLD'S END.—In December, 1841, perhaps the earliest word of the innovation was received at the parish church of Hjelmseryd. Four young peasant girls had begun to speak strangely on the approaching end of the world. Then came word of "a large number" of "prophetesses of ten to twelve years of age" having similarly arisen in adjoining parishes. Because of this "preaching sickness," an attempt was made to isolate those "afflicted" from the other children, lest the contagion spread. The record in the Stockholm press, unfriendly to the phenomenon, continues:

"They claim to have received their revelations directly through the Holy Spirit and claim to have visited heaven and hell and seen the condition and state of the dead. They prophesy the soon-coming destruction of the world, etc., and preach repentance and conversion. A general superstition has taken hold of the people, who refute the warnings and instructions of the priests, and in multitudes ranging from 2,000 to 3,000 go to listen to those who claim to be the chosen messengers of heaven." [16]

Children of six, eight, and ten years of age caught the "disease."

3. HUNDREDS BELIEVE PREACHING IS FROM GOD.—Large numbers of people came to hear these child preachers, ranging from hundreds to actual thousands. The popular belief as to the divine origin of these messages is revealed in another contemporary paper.

"From far and near hundreds of persons come daily to listen to these girls. The girl from Swenarum, daughter of a poor peasant, preached twice a day, and had always two or three hundred listeners daily. The 6th and 7th of this February, which days she declared to be the last when she would preach publicly, she was visited by about 3,000 to 4,000 people. . . .

"The common people either believe the girls to be God's [messengers], as they themselves claim, or they do not know what to think. Few are they who do not see in this something marvelous, or feel this to be the voice of God to man. Almost everyone believes or trembles." [17]

4. SING AND PREACH CONCERNING JUDGMENT.—The specific case of Lisa Andersdotter of Hjelmseryd—a girl of sixteen, of good health and buoyant spirits—is noted. The press record states:

---

[16] *Aftonbladet* (Stockholm), 23 febr., 1842.   [17] *Wexiö-Bladet*, 4 mars, 1842.

"On September 29 [1841], the reporter [Dr. Carlsson, provincial health officer], says she began involuntarily to sing, and this kept on day after day, so that, as she herself says, she hardly had time to eat. The sound broke forth, although her lips were closed, and the melodies were usually unknown to her. . . . Two weeks later she was impressed to give a spiritual talk, and after an interval of a week and a half she began preaching. She never preached when she was alone. . . . Many people came to hear her wonderful sermons and admire her songs, which were impelled by a power entirely beyond her control. She often fell into a trance, like a magnetic [hypnotic] sleep, when she supposedly had revelations. . . . She preached mainly on repentance and some wonderful things, and the last judgment, for which she, however, did not fix any definite time." [18]

5. THE JUDGMENT AND PROPHECIES BLENDED.—In a lengthy circular letter from the Wexiö Consistory to the clergy, concerning the religious movements in Smaland, a hostile report nevertheless stresses marked characteristics in the content of their messages. The critical allusion to their exposition of prophecy will be noted, though there seems to be no record preserved of precisely what they expounded. This careful summarization of the circular discloses its spirit and content:

In addition to confused prophecies concerning the last events and the impending judgment of the world, coarse chiliastic dreams and miscellaneous figures from the book of Revelation are presented, to which a sensuous interpretation is given. The important doctrine of the work of grace particularly appears to be wrongly comprehended and applied. In common with all zealots these misguided ones believe that the Holy Spirit will communicate directly and perceptibly with man. This is particularly the case with the "sick ones."

The principal aim in their preaching consisted in depicting the agony of hell and appealing to people to repent, and instructing them as to how this should be done; viz., by casting away certain ornaments, by abstaining from the dance and other worldly pleasures, and above all by avoiding intoxicating beverages, as pertains to both the manufacturing and the consumption of the same. [19]

---

[18] *Aftonbladet*, 3 maj, 1842.
[19] *Ibid.*, 29 maj, 1842. (This is the item cited by Hengstenberg.)

This, be it remembered, is the testimony of a hostile witness appearing in the daily press in Stockholm.

6. GOD-SENT WARNING CONCERNING JUDGMENT.—After singing a psalm, a girl in Linhult, by the name of Carolina, began with an introductory text "after the fashion of the priests," according to another eyewitness. Then her alleged words are quoted—though there is room to question their accuracy. At least it is a contemporary press report:

"My beloved, blessed friends! I wish also to speak a few words of admonition tonight. Oh, that I could make you repent! But are not your hearts still as obstinate as before? The sun has just set. Who knows over whose heads it will rise again? Oh, the great and terrifying day of doom! Repent, repent, my beloved friends! Oh, that you would believe your teachers! But you have never done as they have told you. Therefore God must send this message of repentance." [20]

Then the eyewitness reporter adds:

"The whole meeting was a good example of proper worship of God, and the whole atmosphere was so quiet and peaceful, that if someone else besides the girl 'crier' had had anything to say from the Word of God, the little congregation would just as surely have listened thereto." [21]

7. REFORMATIONS SPRING FROM "REPENTANCE CRIERS."— Another eyewitness reports a group of "Repentance Criers," as they were often called, in Rada Parish, Varmland. After stating that "nearly the whole parish believed in the criers and their preaching as a great miracle from God," the writer tells of reformations of life wrought, stating—

"That the manner of life and state of mind during the six weeks that the calls to repentance lasted, changed perceptibly; that dancing, card playing, drunkenness, pomp and vanity, the flagrant desecration of Sunday, etc., have peculiarly decreased; that Sunday is now spent in attending meetings or in the reading and singing of God's word at home; that all women have removed combs and puffed sleeves; that because the criers have not mentioned the matter of taking God's name in vain this has not ceased, but the use of the Devil's name and the words *bra* and *vars,* which the criers have mentioned as gross sins, has ceased; that none among the peasantry scoff at the preaching mania [or malady]; that the use of medicine for physical ills is regarded as sin; that the word of Scripture, 'And it shall

---

[20] *Svenska Biet* (Stockholm), 4 okt., 1843.
[21] *Ibid.*

come to pass in the last days, saith God, I will pour out of my Spirit upon all flesh; and your sons and your daughters shall prophesy, and your young men shall see visions, and your old men shall dream dreams,' is considered to have met its fulfilment in this phenomenon." [22]

8. PLAYING CARDS THROWN AWAY AS RESULT.—Another writer, asserting that no adults and no married women had been "subject to this malady," tells of the effect of the preaching upon the populace: "Decks of cards are either thrown in the lake or burned. In the whole Parish of Rada, as well as in near-by places or adjoining parishes, it is doubtful that a single deck of cards could be found among the peasants." [23]

9. JOEL 2:28 QUOTED AS AUTHORIZATION.—Again and again in the contemporary press, Joel 2:28 is cited as the authorization claimed for their violations of the custom of silence for children in all religious services. Incidentally, this report appears in *The Pietist,* many in Smaland being Pietists:

"The editor has received a letter written by a man among the peasants of Smaland, regarding the rare phenomenon of some girls who began holding public meetings of a spiritual nature. They quoted Joel 2:28 as the reason for their public meetings, and gave powerful testimonies, admonishing the people to repentance. They also teach, that if the people do not believe their words, the children in the cradle shall begin to speak; they also believe that the Spirit tells them just when to speak." [24]

10. EYES OPEN; UNCONSCIOUS OF SURROUNDINGS.—Perhaps the most significant aspect of the entire record of the child-preaching phenomenon was the declaration that, in the province of Skaraborg, some preached with eyes closed and were unconscious of surrounding circumstances, according to a witness who had "seen and heard them." Thus:

"In the Province of Elfsborg I heard it told that they preached with the eyes open and standing. Here (in the Province of Skaraborg) I have seen and heard them preach, lying down, with closed eyes, and, as far as I could ascertain, entirely insensible and unconscious." [25]

An antagonistic pastor in the Broddetorps parish, near Skövde, in the Province of Vestergötland, reports that there those "affected by the epidemic" are boys. He adds:

[22] *Ibid.,* 9 aug., 1843.   [23] *Ibid.,* 12 okt., 1843.
[24] *Pietisten* (Stockholm), mars, 1842, sid. 45. (Title page reproduced on page 670.)
[25] *Svenska Biet,* 29 juli, 1843.

"Especially in Hornborga village has the epidemic furiously broken out, and six boys aged from 8 to 18 years are possessed with a dominant desire to preach, joined with fainting spells, when they seem to lie unconscious and with some strong shakings in the arms and the whole body." [26]

11. GOVERNOR THREATENS PENALTIES FOR VIOLATORS.—Because the "preaching sickness" has not disappeared from his district, Governor Carl Morner, of Växjö (Wexiö), complains that the peasants had not obeyed the decrees, warnings, and admonitions to keep away from those children afflicted with the "preaching sickness." He repeats the threat of fines for any "who open their houses to such meetings and the preaching of the sick one," and warns that violators will be prosecuted. [27]

III. Bishop Butsch Discusses Character, Content, and Claims

Fortunately, a remarkable testimony from Bishop J. A. Butsch, of Skara, has been left on record concerning the sanity, orthodoxy, humility, and wholesome character of these child preachers who had brought perplexity to his diocese. Their stress on the coming doom of the corrupted world, the rebuke of sin, and the fact that these children claimed to have received their messages through visions should not be overlooked. Clearly, as he says, the phenomenon is not to be passed off as mere "religious enthusiasm." He and others refer to certain accompanying bodily manifestations.

1. VISIONS ATTRIBUTED TO CHILD PREACHERS.—Writing in behalf of the Consistory of the Diocese of Skara, the bishop says:

"As far as I [the bishop] can see, this phenomenon is the result of combined mental and physical causes and cannot sufficiently be explained as being wrought by religious fanaticism. Many of the sick ones who were questioned, stated that the abnormal condition in which they now were, began with a strong impulse to repent and reform, accompanied by a feeling of weakness, fatigue in the head or in the body generally, sweat, or aching chest, etc. Asked whether the physical ailments and the spiritual promptings occurred altogether simultaneously, . . . many, or most of them, answered that the spiritual urge came first. . . . After the sick ones had

---

[26] *Aftonbladet*, 16 dec., 1842.
[27] *Wexiö-Bladet*, 3 juni, 1842.

begun shaking, they improved and felt better, and declared unanimously
that they felt physically better than ever. Even those in whom the malady
had advanced so far that they had visions and started preaching, said they
were in the same joyful condition. In spite of the fact that the sick ones
generally . . . had a happy, friendly, and affable look, I seemed to find,
nevertheless, . . . that the shining gladness in their eyes and faces was
something very peculiar and clearly suggested a condition of sickness. . . .
It was generally conceded that the shakings in no wise were an integral
part of Christian living, . . . but it was nevertheless commonly agreed that
they were the manifestations of the Holy Spirit and a sign of grace given
to the [allegedly] diseased . . . whereby . . . all who saw them should be
reminded and convinced of the awfulness and iniquity of sin. . . . The
preaching children stand in a peculiar, close relationship to each other.
They are drawn to one another, and always, when together, they continually give each other new tokens of the most hearty affection." [28]

2. FORETELL COMING DESTRUCTION OF THE WORLD.—The
bishop continues:

"The content of the talks or sermons of these sick ones . . . is almost
always the same. They consist of simple admonitions to reform and to
separate from sin. Sins especially pointed out are card playing, drunkenness, dancing, and frivolity. Often were added predictions of the imminent overthrow of the world, combined with warnings, admonitions, and
messages of comfort on the basis of the visions which had been granted the
speaker. All recognized, in the first place, their own need of God's grace
and mercy, and declared they left the judging of others to God.

"The people in this district generally are distinguished by an altogether
sufficient and often admirable understanding of Christianity, . . . and
the sick ones were no exception to this general rule. Rather, I ought to
admit that some among them expressed themselves on important religious
questions with unusual understanding and clarity. Orthodox and not adhering to any heretical concepts, the sick ones nevertheless retained their
conviction that not only their good impulses toward spiritual improvement
. . . but also the physical symptoms of their [alleged] disease were from the
Holy Ghost. In this they included their predictions of the imminent
destruction of the world.

"The spiritual pride, which usually follows fanatics and reveals itself
in judging others and having no patience with different thinking, was not
seen in one of these sick." [29]

---

[28] *Aftonbladet*, 6 sept., 1842. The high standing of Bishop Butsch is attested by these
biographical facts: JOHAN ALBERT BUTSCH (d. 1800) was appointed bishop of Skara in 1837, and
received an honorary degree of D.D. in 1844. He served several terms as a member of the
Swedish parliament, officiated at the royal coronation in 1844, and on other royal family
occasions. He was a member of various official and ecclesiastical commissions and boards, was
twice nominated for archbishop of the Swedish State Lutheran Church (in 1851 and 1856),
but declined on both occasions. He was honorary director of the Swedish Bible Society and
other organizations. (*Svenskt Biografiskt Lexikon*, Ny Följd, 2 bd., sid. 335, 336.)
[29] *Ibid.*, 7 sept., 1842.

IV. Doctor Skoldberg Offers Expert Medical Opinion

Vital testimony upon these cases is offered in *Something on the Crying Voices*,[30] *or the So-called Preaching Sickness in Smaland in the Years 1842 and 1843*, by an Eyewitness. This book, translated from the Swedish, was issued in German in 1843.[31] The translator's preface quotes a report from Dr. S. E. Sköldberg, medical officer of the province of Jönköping, Sweden;[32] the appendix is a translation of the statement already quoted from Bishop J. A. Butsch of Skara. The translator's foreword refers to this as "dependable information," based upon actual observation, and alludes to the difficulty of securing an "objective view." [33]

Dr. Sköldberg at first was hostile, but this attitude changed through examination of the evidence. He cites the case of Lisa Andersdotter, aged sixteen—already noted on p. 677—who engaged in this preaching and singing. Then he refers to Mary Swensdotter, thirteen, who, he says, contracted the "malady" from Lisa. He declares it "absolutely impossible" to stop her witness, even by compressing her nostrils and lips. She would not cease till she had finished her song. Next he refers to her alleged declaration that "the world would come to an end in five years, although, at another time, she declared that the thousand years would begin," [34] there being no conflict, however, between the two concepts. Other girls soon began to "preach and prophesy." Then still other cases of the "preaching sickness" are cited from the diary of another eyewitness.[35] This, be it remembered, is a physician's declaration.

---

[30] Like John 1:23: "I am the voice of one crying [*ropande*] in the wilderness."
[31] *Einiges über die rufenden Stimmen oder die sogenannte Predigtkrankheit in Smaland in den Jahren 1842 und 1843*. Von einem Augenzeugen.
[32] The caliber and competency of this eminent medical witness is attested by his biographical record: SVEN ERIK SKÖLDBERG (1806-1884), government medical officer of the Jönköping Province, from 1834 to 1864, and for a time medical director of the famous Serafimer-Hospital in Stockholm, was knighted in 1858. Member of the Swedish Medical Association board, 1843-1884, and contributor to medical journals, he was the official Swedish representative to several international medical congresses. Dr. Sköldberg was a leader in the field of medicine, having done extensive research work in medical science in general, particularly in public health service in the leading countries of Europe. In 1843 he published a scientific report on the religious movement in the province of Jönköping, from which these excerpts are taken. (*Svenskt Biografiskt Lexikon*, Ny Földj, 10 bd., sid. 25, 26.)
[33] *Einiges über die rufenden Stimmen*, S. v, vi.
[34] *Ibid.*, S. vii-xi.
[35] *Ibid.*, S. xii-xiv.

1. CLAIM DIVINE COMMISSION TO URGE REPENTANCE.—
Declaring that these calling "voices" sometimes continued "for
hours," Dr. Sköldberg adds that they cautioned the people
against believing that these calls had come from Satan. They
claimed that the Lord had sent them to turn the attention of
the people to the Bible, to the faith of Jesus, and to conversion.
They declared, "He who says that these admonitions come from
Satan is condemned." Whisky they called the "wine of wrath."
They opposed all immoral life, drunkenness, dancing, and all
kinds of vices, and asked the people to judge themselves in the
light of the Ten Commandments. The voices claimed that they
were not preachers, but that they were sent by the Lord to call
people to repentance, and that no one, not even the angels,
knows the exact time of the day of judgment.[36]

2. SIMPLY AGENTS OF "HIGHER INFLUENCE."—Their utterances called for the renunciation of sin and for receiving the
Saviour into the heart. Otherwise, "when the Lord will come,
these fruitless trees will be cut down." [37] Noting that the voices
were not confined to "any special sect," this further remarkable
conclusion is drawn:

"The language is simple and none of them tries to do as the preachers—
take a Bible verse and expound their text; but they have gotten truths
from God's Word to strengthen their calls to repentance, and lovely verses
of song were effectively used. Nearly all genuine voices speak without
understanding what they say, sometimes continuing for four consecutive
hours. Consequently the people look upon these appeals as signs and
wonders of God. The calls to repentance which I heard were so pure
that no one, . . . Bible in hand, could criticize them, much less say they
were heresy.

"I had a prejudice, an abhorrence for all these voices, and considered
them heretical and fanatical spirits. If an accidental circumstance had not
directed that I hear one of them, I would still have been of the same opinion. I had believed it depended on their free will to speak when they
wished. . . . But because I have become convinced that not a single
word that must be spoken when the inner compulsion comes, is dependent
on their own choosing—for then the message gushes from their breast like
a bubbling spring—I repent of all my harsh opinions and stand in amazement of them." [38]

---

[36] Ibid., S. 27.   [37] Ibid., S. 28.   [38] Ibid., S. 30, 31.

3. SEVENTY DISTILLERIES CLOSED IN FORTNIGHT.—The radical reformation of life resulting is next attested by the doctor:

"Very many listeners were prompted to denounce sin. Drinking, dancing, and card playing practically vanished. . . . When Stina Carlsdotter in Rydaholm began the call to repentance, within a fortnight seventy distillers declared themselves unwilling to distill further, which fact was publicly mentioned in the pulpit by Pastor Bexell." [39]

4. IS THE INTERVENTION OF THE ALMIGHTY.—Taking issue with the clergy, Dr. Sköldberg makes this amazing statement as to the origin of these manifestations:

"As to the voices, as already mentioned they have no free will, but are impelled by an inexplainable urge, which greatest theologians and doctors could with difficulty explain by natural means. Lo, it must be recognized as a sign by everyone who looks above and believes that God rules the world. To the wise men of the earth all this may appear merely as a natural phenomenon, yes, without exception as an illusionary illness combined with illusions; but He who created the world has also sent this so-called sickness as a sign of the times. It is the all-wise God and no one else who has instigated this call to repentance of the true and the just, so that these callers [Rufer] were no more responsible for what they had to speak than was the son of the widow of Nain when he again received life.

"The voices did not pose as teachers but as awakening voices, and certainly said nothing from which confusion might be feared. The voices directed to God's Word, to the ordained ministers, to the house of God, and pricked their consciences to search. . . .

"Certainly it is amazing that shepherds of the flock who devote themselves to the things of the spirit as leaders of others, have not considered it worthwhile to investigate for themselves what the real situation of these voices is, who bring a real awakening to the people, but listen only to the tales of other people.

"The spiritual leaders say: If this were of God's Spirit, these voices would be able to interpret the Bible." [40]

5. MEDICAL TESTIMONY ON PHYSICAL PHENOMENA.—Concerning the physical phenomena connected with this supernatural preaching, Dr. Sköldberg gives his objective witness as a physician who has personally examined them, in these words:

"As to the outward appearances, the true voices lie in a stunned condition, sometimes for an hour, before the urge to call opens the mouth. It is remarkable to see what happens to them, as soon as they fall asleep, how

---

[39] *Ibid.*, S. 32.
[40] *Ibid.*, S. 32, 33.

the convulsive motion begins in the fingertips and the feet, advances through the limbs to the chest, which begins to heave, and continues toward the lips. Some lie still, pale as a corpse, wholly motionless, only the chest heaving, until the call begins, a circumstance which takes place in all cases. Breath cannot be observed, although they doubtless must breathe. Of all these happenings the voices know absolutely nothing as long as the weakness and convulsion continue. I have endeavored to see and examine as much as I possibly could, but still can comprehend nothing, but only see and hear what transpires." [41]

"I have not brought this forth in order to sing the praises of the voices; no, I only wish to recount what I have seen and heard insofar as it can be useful in clarifying the facts. . . . Besides, what they stress from beginning to end of their speeches is the quintessence of Christianity—Jesus Christ, prayer, conversion, repentance, and renunciation. No one of objective judgment can say this is Satan's work (Kleiner von gesundem Urtheile kann sagen, dies sei Satans Werk). . . . The visions of these voices [concerning heaven and hell] may be interpreted by each as he is inclined. I have here stated my views, and what may be deficient in them, the more learned may correct. The persons whom I interrogated are still alive, so that further research might be undertaken at will." [42]

6. Declared a Fulfillment of Joel 2.—The doctor closes his "observations" concerning his investigations with this conclusion:

"What conclusions may we draw concerning this matter? The voices themselves believe they are continuing the words of the prophet Joel (second chapter), and that therefore the Holy Spirit of God has not ceased to show Himself in marvelous ways, because at one time at Pentecost He revealed Himself mightily through the apostles and diciples, and they themselves point out that the book of Acts does not mention that 'sons and daughters, menservants and maidservants,' received the Holy Ghost at that time. The voices believe that the prophecy of Joel reaches till the end of the world [time]." [43]

NOTE: For the translations from Swedish and German appearing in this chapter, indebtedness is here expressed to G. A. Lindsay, Leif Kr. Tobiassen, Dyre Dyresen, O. Granlund, J. F. Huenergardt, and Clara Witzke.

---

[41] *Ibid.*, S. 36.
[42] *Ibid.*, S. 36, 37.
[43] *Ibid.*, S. 38. In an Appendix to this work appears the report of Bishop Butsch on the so-called preaching sickness, issued August 10, 1842, from Skara Domkapitel, "In behalf of the Consistory in Skara," which has already been noted. (See pp. 39-50; quoted also in the Stockholm *Aftonbladet*, 6, 7 sept., 1842.)

CHAPTER THIRTY-SIX

Effective Expositors in Switzerland, France, and Germany

I. Gaussen—Uplifts Prophetic Torch in Geneva

The world character of the Advent Awakening is strikingly revealed in FRANCOIS SAMUEL ROBERT LOUIS GAUSSEN (1790-1863), French-Swiss Evangelical professor. Born of Protestant refugee parents at Geneva—city of Calvin, Beza, Farel, and of Knox during his exile from Scotland, also the city in which the French Huguenots found an asylum following the Revocation of the Edict of Nantes—Gaussen graduated from the University of Geneva in 1814, was licensed to preach in 1815, and was ordained the next year. From 1816 to 1828 he served as pastor at the rural town of Satigny, near Geneva. Here he succeeded Cellerier, who had retained his Christian fidelity and simple faith amid the general falling away from the ancestral beliefs on the part of the Swiss clergy.

The spirit of rationalism pervaded all Europe, and Socinianism had made heavy inroads at Geneva.[1] The liberalism of Rousseau was lauded, and D'Alembert and Voltaire gained a hearing. Edward Gibbon had chosen near-by Lausanne as his residence. The renewal of the evangelical faith in Switzerland about this time was largely due, as previously noted, to the arrival of Robert Haldane, in 1817, who soon became odious to the majority of the Geneva clergy—the Vénérable Compagnie

[1] See James I. Good, *History of the Swiss Reformed Church Since the Reformation,* pp. 278-282, 353, 354.

GAUSSEN LEADS PROPHETIC EXPOSITION IN SWITZERLAND

Clustered Around Gaussen's Portrait Are His Lessons on Daniel in French (Upper Left) and the Printed English Translation Up to Chapter 7, verse 25, With a Page From the Remaining Portion of Daniel in Lithographed Manuscript Only (Upper Right). Illustrations of the Fourth Beast of Daniel 7 and the Dragon and Beasts of Revelation 13 and 17 Impress the Lessons

des Pasteurs having passed four resolutions on May 3, 1817, prohibiting preaching upon certain important Christian doctrines.

Gaussen was profoundly influenced by Haldane, and later by Henry Drummond, who helped the ejected ministers to form an independent church—Malan, Mejanel, and Pyt being among them. In 1819 Gaussen and Cellerier upheld the Evangelical

faith, protested the action of the Company, and published the
Second Helvetic Confession, and so came under discipline. The
Company ordered Gaussen to use the emasculated and rationalistic catechism which had been substituted for Calvin's original.
Because he refused, he was regarded as heterodox and later
suspended. His aim, however, was not to divide but to reinspire
the church. Because of the clash, Gaussen, with Merle
d'Aubigné[2] and Galland, formed the Evangelical Society to dis-
tribute Bibles and tracts, and to foster missionary work for the
heathen.

The Consistory deposed Gaussen and suspended the others
in 1831, because of their activities as founders of the Geneva
Evangelical Society's School of Theology.[3] Gaussen accepted a
call to the chair of theology in 1834. Following this, he traveled
in England and in Italy, where he came in contact with many
evangelical leaders and students of prophecy, who used to meet
for "mutual improvement and edification."[4] Gaussen was a
zealous advocate of the doctrine of the second advent. And his
belief in the prophecies of Daniel was an anchor that held him
through many a storm. Gaussen's visit to Rome impressed him
more than ever that Antichrist was indeed reigning there.

During his teaching at the newly opened Theological Seminary at Geneva he gave particular attention to the exposition of
prophecy, and this resulted in his lessons on the prophet Daniel.
He pointed out the absurdity of explaining prophetic days as
natural days. Gaussen continued to teach for twenty-five years,
becoming one of the foremost representatives of orthodox
Protestantism on the Continent, his influence being felt through
the professor's chair, the pulpit, and the press. Gaussen is of
special interest because he was cited by Ellen G. White in *The
Great Controversy* as one of the conspicuous heralds of the
advent in the Old World second advent awakening.[5]

[2] JEAN HENRI MERLE D'AUBIGNE (1794-1872), celebrated Swiss church historian, was born
near Geneva. His *Histoire de la réformation au seizième siècle* gave him a wide reputation,
and has been translated into many languages. Afterward, in 1831 he was professor of historical
theology at the Ecole de Théologie Evangélique at Geneva.
[3] Alexander Haldane, *The Lives of Robert Haldane . . . and James Alexander Haldane*,
pp. 430, 431.   [4] Samuel Gobat, *Life and Work*, p. 43.
[5] Ellen G. White, *The Great Controversy*, pp. 364-366.

Of his writings, some of which had wide circulation, Gaussen is best known for his *Théopneustie, ou Pleine inspiration des saintes Ecritures* (1840, translated as *Théopneustia, or Plenary Inspiration of the Bible*, 1841). His *Daniel le prophète, exposé* (Daniel the Prophet Explained) (1839-1849),[6] *Geneva and Rome* (1844), and *Geneva and Jerusalem* (1844) are of special interest in our quest. His *Canon des Ecritures Saintes* (Canon of Holy Scripture) was not issued till 1860. This latter title, however, did not touch upon prophecy.

II. Address on Popery Reveals Penetrating Exposition

Gaussen's keen exposition can best be glimpsed through this recital. On October 3, 1843, just back from a trip to Rome, Gaussen delivered a remarkable address[7] to his students in Geneva, *Le Souverain pontife et l'Eglise de Rome, soutiens de la vérité, par l'accomplissement des Ecritures* (The Sovereign Pontiff and the Church of Rome, Upholders of the Truth Through the Fulfillment of the Scriptures). It sets forth fourteen marks for identification of the Little Horn, forming an inescapable composite picture. Translated into English for the *New York Observer*, it was reprinted by J. V. Himes in *The Midnight Cry!*[8] and published by him in tract form, with notes and illustrations of the four beasts of Daniel 7, under the title *The German Rebuke of American Neology*.

To the prophetic faith of their Geneva forefathers, Gaussen now adds "many new reasons which our fathers did not possess." His basic proposition is that "Rome is the Babylon of which John speaks; the pope, the Man of Sin, the son of perdition of whom Paul speaks; popery, the little horn of which Daniel speaks." This, he holds, has been the teaching of the church for centuries.

"This doctrine, constantly held in the church of God for more than twelve hundred years has been lightly esteemed" in

---

[6] English edition: *The Prophet Daniel Explained*, translated by Margaret Blackstone, 2 vols., 1873-1874.

[7] Extracts from this lecture are available in *Source Book for Bible Students*, pp. 308-310.

[8] "Popery, an Argument for the Truth, by Its Fulfilment of Scripture Prophecies," *The Midnight Cry*, July 11, 1844 (vol. 6, no. 26), pp. 409-411.

later times of laxity. Then mention is made of Waldo, Wyclif, Huss, Jerome, and the later Reformers in Switzerland and France.[9]

After their French forefathers had made their Confession of Faith at La Rochelle, says Gaussen, they added, at the Synod of Gap in 1603, Article 31 declaring that the bishop of Rome, having reared up for himself a monarchy in Christendom by claiming dominion over all churches and pastors, had lifted himself up to the extent that he called himself God, insisted on being worshiped, decided articles of faith, interpreted Scripture at will, released from vows and oaths, ordained new services of God, and trod underfoot the legitimate authority of magistrates. Gaussen adds that Protestant ministers were persecuted thereafter for fifty years because of this article. But they still retained their characterization of Antichrist in the Synod of Loudun, in 1659, with the declaration:

"We are resolved, after their example, never to abandon them [their positions regarding Antichrist] by the grace of God, but to preserve them inviolably to the last moment of our lives." [10]

In Daniel 2, Gaussen continues, the history of the nations is portrayed under the figure of the image, up to the second coming of our Lord Jesus Christ. In Daniel 7 "the same succession of four great monarchies" brings us to the time and place of "a most frightful apostasy," which would afflict the church for centuries, which would take "its rise in the empire of the Latins, soon after its division into ten distinct kingdoms," and which *should not be destroyed till the second coming of our Lord Jesus Christ.*"

Four great beast-kingdoms, symbolizing the four monarchies, equally cruel and tyrannical, will oppress the people of God—Babylon, Medo-Persia, Macedonia, and the Latin kingdom, which becomes divided in the ten horn-kingdoms of Gothic origin. These are the Visigoths, Heruli, Ostrogoths, Franks, Burgundians, Vandals, Alans, Suevi, Gepidi, and Lom-

---

[9] *Ibid.*, p. 409.
[10] *Le Souverain pontife et l'Eglise de Rome*, pp. 9, 10.

bards. Thus the time and place of the predicted apostasy is disclosed. It is the "Roman apostacy, it is the whole territory of the Latin monarchy; its time is the ages which shall follow the invasion of this empire by the ten barbarian kings." Popery is here found "completely described" by fourteen identification marks, which Gaussen now unfolds and integrates:

1. Its *nature*—a priest-king, among the ten but different from the others, having a "political and a religious character."

2. Its *geography*—the "lands of the church" are found in Italy, and the theater of its power is the "vast empire of the ten Latin kingdoms." It is the "city of seven hills." It has a Roman Pontiff, and its territory extends "between the Rhine, the Danube, the Greek Empire, the Adriatic, Mount Atlas, and the great ocean"—or throughout the territory of the fourth beast.

3. Its *origin*—slowly, imperceptibly, as a horn grows, appearing among the ten.

4. The *chronology*—"immediately after the division of the Latin empire into its ten Gothic kingdoms," in the sixth or seventh century.

5. Its *territorial acquisitions*—supplanting "the Herules, the Ostrogoths, and the Lombards," the pope's Babylonish tiara bearing the three crowns of the horns plucked up before him.

6. Its *extraordinary sagacity*—exercising consummate skill, policy, vigilance, and power, ruling the whole Catholic empire, and agitating the world. Its eyes are the "secret of its power," exercising constant oversight over every part of the earth by her religious orders, Jesuits, apostolical prelates, and confessionals. Its penetrating eye "never sleeps." It has the cumulative knowledge of centuries.

7. Its *deceivableness*—by false legends, books, relics, medals, cures, and especially its "false decretals" that deceived all Europe for 500 years, ministering to its success.

8. Its *pomp*—greater than the greatest kings, with pictures in the Vatican of kings like Henry IV and Frederick Barbarossa in penitence, and the Pontiff borne on the shoulders of men, as his subjects kneel and kiss his feet.

9. Its *language*—great swelling words, threatening words, words of pride and command, sending nations on remote expeditions and wars of extermination. For centuries its thunders and anathemas have resounded.

10. Its *duration*—until the coming of Christ, surviving the centuries with impunity.

11. Its *blasphemies*—called the pope Holy Father, Most Holy Father, His Holiness, declaring him infallible, releasing man from the commands of his Creator, creating priests who in turn create God in a bit of bread.

12. Its homicidal *hatred*—its persecution of true Christians through the dungeons and auto-da-fés of the Inquisition. Other governments kill men, but the Pontiff has put to death the saints, the duty of putting heretics to death being binding through the irrevocable decrees of councils.

13. Its audacious *heresies*—pretending to change the law of God, putting its decrees and traditions above Scripture, pretending to pardon sins and to dispense with duties which the law commands, forbidding the reading of the Scriptures in the vernaculars.

14. Its exact *duration*—for 1260 years, which period is repeated, specified, and exactly fulfilled. Such was Gaussen's penetrating identification of Antichrist in 1843, summarized under fourteen divisions.

III. Expositions for Children Reach Adults

1. DANIEL 2 IS KEY TO WORLD'S HISTORY.—Gaussen's Sunday school lessons on *Daniel the Prophet* were first given about 1837 as a series of Sunday school lectures, ostensibly for the children, but really in order to reach their parents. The plan succeeded, and older persons came to his lectures, filling the galleries. These included strangers visiting Geneva from other lands. Thus his message was carried to other parts. Then he published his lessons to foster the study of prophecy among the French-speaking people. At the very outset Gaussen cites Christ's admonition to read and understand the prophet Daniel, declaring

that Daniel 2 affords the "key to the world's history." [11] Gaussen's exposition in these lessons is not smooth flowing, but is repetitious because in weekly lesson form, repeating and reviewing the fundamental points and principles. But by that very process the teachings were driven home. Nevertheless it must have been rather deep for the children.

Portraying the history of the successive states of Babylon, Persia, Grecia, Rome, and then the ten Gothic nations, Gaussen comes to the last days and the "time of the end." [12] Moreover, he declares, the papal power is portrayed[13] in the paralleling prophecy of Daniel 7. And Daniel's "seventy weeks of years" stretch "between the decree of the King of Persia and the death of Jesus Christ." [14] Such are the rapid brush strokes used to paint in the background. Then he digresses, to note that Ptolemy, in his list of eclipses, divides the periods the same as Daniel, tabulating the eclipses occurring under the four successive empires of prophecy.[15] The breast and arms, he adds, involve two elements, representing Media and Persia.[16]

2. TEN DIVISIONS OF ROME ENUMERATED.—Toward the end of Rome's existence the empire was to be "divided by ten barbarous nations." Coming in from the north, they invaded the whole of it and continued under a new form, soon adopting Rome's laws, religion, and language.[17] The ten kingdom-divisions are listed by Gaussen as the Visigoths, Ostrogoths, Heruli, Lombards, Franks, Burgundians, Alani, Suevi, Gepidi, and Vandals.[18] The Huns, he says, are not to be counted.[19]

3. MINGLING OF CLAY AND IRON: CHURCHCRAFT AND STATECRAFT.—The four fierce beasts, or persecuting empires, of Daniel 7 Gaussen stresses as the same four powers of Daniel 2—with Rome the fourth.[20] The three horns plucked up in Italy, to make way for papal sway, were the Heruli, Ostrogoths, and Lombards.[21] The Persian ram and the Grecian he-goat are duly noted. Then

---

[11] Louis Gaussen, *The Prophet Daniel Explained* (Blackstone translation), vol. 1, pp. 41, 42.

[12] *Ibid.*, pp. 54-65; 149. [15] *Ibid.*, p. 49. [18] *Ibid.*, pp. 66, 67, 183.

[13] *Ibid.*, pp. 43-45, 48. [16] *Ibid.*, pp. 56-58. [19] *Ibid.*, pp. 67, 203.

[14] *Ibid.*, p. 48. [17] *Ibid.*, pp. 66, 69.

[20] *Ibid.*, pp. 162-165, 199-203, 219, 222. [21] *Ibid.*, pp. 211-213.

the mingling of the iron and the clay, in Daniel 2, is declared to be the union of statecraft and churchcraft.[22]

4. CARTOONS OF PROPHETIC SYMBOLS.—The third volume of *Daniel le prophète* strikingly cartoons the ten horns, with the three in process of uprooting[23] and the papal Little Horn in the act of emerging.   There is also the great dragon, the two beasts of Revelation 13, and the woman with the cup on the beast of Revelation 17.   A table of dates,[24] listing the leading events of the centuries, places the beginning of the 1260 years in 529, when Justinian made the Christians of the West amenable to the court of the Bishop of Rome.   It ends them with the cataclysmic French Revolution of 1789, which abolished the laws making the Christians of the West amenable to the Bishop of Rome.

5. LITTLE HORN, CAREER OF KINGLY BISHOP.—Volume 3 continues the explanation of Daniel.   Gaussen had published only up to Daniel 7:25 at the time of his death, though another volume was left in manuscript.   The chief burden of this third treatise is the "Little Horn . . . the chief enemy of God in the West," and "persecutor of the faithful."   The judgment is the grand climax, and the end—the slaying of the beast.[25]

This Little Horn power is a monstrosity, a "temporal prince" in Roman territory, wearing a crown like the other horns, and having "territorial and political power"—an "eleventh king in the midst of the ten others."   This amazing horn follows the ten, sprouting from the imperial head of the fourth beast.   While his territory is small, he becomes stouter, growing up in the foaming sea of nations, and uprooting three horns.   He has penetration.   He is a "see-er"—a king, prophet, and bishop with eyes, claiming to be a universal bishop.[26]

6. STONE SMITES IRON-CLAY AT ADVENT.—Then comes the judgment scene, with the judgment of the Man of Sin at the

---

[22] *Ibid.*, p. 246.
[23] The Heruli, Ostrogoths, and Lombards. See Lesson XXX on Daniel 7:19, 20, in Blackstone's translation, vol. 1, pp. 208, 211.
[24] *Daniel le prophète, exposé*, vol. 1 (2d ed.), p. [15].
[25] *Ibid.*, vol. 3, pp. 1-16.   [26] *Ibid.*, pp. 5-18.

second advent, as Christ comes in the clouds of heaven.[27] This will take place after the 1260 days are accomplished, and is portrayed by the Apocalypse as burning with fire.[28] This destruction also comes when the stone smites the image, and the iron and clay, or commingled state and church, are crushed and annihilated.[29]

7. LIFE SPAN IS 1260 YEARS.—The life of the Little Horn is three and a half times, or 1260 years, as cited in the various places—each recorded "time" being "360 prophetic days, each representing a year." [30] This horn, Gaussen says, is Paul's Man of Sin, sitting in the temple of God, but held back at first by the Roman Empire.[31] Antichrist is declared a vicarious functionary, a rival, a vice-Christ.[32]

8. MOHAMMEDANISM INVOLVED IN 2300 YEARS.—Gaussen's lesson on the Medo-Persian ram of Daniel 8 and the Macedonian he-goat—which vivid symbol was displayed on Grecia's Standards—is preserved in full, but is found only in plated manuscript form.[33] The little horn of chapter 8, Gaussen holds, represents Mohammedanism, and not Antiochus Epiphanes.[34] Mohammedanism, he feels, had been raised up as a fit punishment for the departures of the churches in Occident and Orient.[35] But Mohammedanism would perish through divine "intervention" at the end of the 2300 years. Others had studied diligently into the chronology of this period, and he leaves this research to them.[36]

9. SEVENTY WEEKS END WITH CHRIST'S DEATH.—The seventy weeks, or 490 years, of chapter 9, are dated by Gaussen from the seventh year of Artaxerxes, or from 458 B.C. to A.D. 33—that is, to Christ's death.[37] Six things happen in that seventieth week: the iniquity and revolt of the Jews reach their climax, the typical sin offerings end in the true Sin Offering, propitiation for

---

[27] *Ibid.*, pp. 32-42, 80.
[28] *Ibid.*, p. 45.
[29] *Ibid.*, vol. 1, pp. 174-187.
[33] Lithographed manuscript, pp. 339-343. These lessons reaching to Daniel 12, in February, 1838, were plated and duplicated.
[34] *Ibid.*, pp. 344, 352, 353.
[35] *Ibid.*, p. 356.
[37] *Ibid.*, pp. 394, 395. (Later, 457 B.C. to A.D. 34. See p. 700.)

[30] *Ibid.*, vol. 3, pp. 73-75.
[31] *Ibid.*, pp. 45, 46, 95, 132.
[32] *Ibid.*, p. 111.
[36] *Ibid.*, pp. 357, 358.

iniquity is accomplished through Christ's shed blood, everlasting righteousness is brought in, every prophecy thereon is fulfilled, and finally Christ is anointed.[38]

10. DANIEL 11 RETRACES COURSE OF EMPIRES.—Gaussen admits that Daniel 11 is difficult to present to such a class. However, he parallels the specifications of prophecy with the fulfillments of history, having one of the children read from the historians Millot and Royou.[39] Here for the fourth time Daniel outlines the four kingdoms of prophecy. The chapter is, in fact, "the prophetic calendar of the centuries." [40] Daniel 7 pertains to the Roman Empire, spread between the Rhine, the Danube, the ocean, and the Mediterranean Sea. It discusses the subsequent Papacy. As Daniel 8 pertains, he believes, to the Persian and Greek monarchies and the Mohammedan power, which begins simultaneously with the Papacy,[41] so Daniel 11 passes through Persia, Grecia, and Rome.[42]

11. LATTER PART PRESENTS THINGS TO COME.—The latter part of Daniel 11, Gaussen avers, deals with "events yet to come," [43] and leads to the "day of Jesus Christ" and the second advent.[44] This is the climax of all the prophecies. The Antichrist will have a new revival. And after the final struggle Christ will appear.[45] Verses 31-35 deal with the Romans,[46] introduced under the expression the "ships of Kittim," of verse 30. And verse 36 concerns Antichrist.[47] The "north," he feels, means Russia.[48] But here he treads rather lightly.

12. 1335 YEARS REACH TO RESURRECTION.—In introducing Daniel 12 Gaussen reiterates the year-day principle for the seventy weeks, and the 1260-, 1290-, and 1335-years periods.[49] The 1335 years extend seventy-five years beyond the 1260, he holds, and lead directly to the resurrection of the just.[50] This latter period is called the "time of the end." Here is to be found the running to and fro concerning the prophecies and the coming

---

[38] *Ibid.*, pp. 393, 394.
[39] *Ibid.*, no. 49, p. 116 (pagination not consecutive).
[40] *Ibid.*, p. 117.
[41] *Ibid.*
[42] *Ibid.*, no. 49, pp. 118-124; nos. 1 and 2, 1838, pp. 3-18.
[43] *Ibid.*, no. 2, p. 18.
[44] *Ibid.*, no. 3, p. 19.
[45] *Ibid.*, p. 21.
[46] *Ibid.*, no. 11, p. 28.
[47] *Ibid.*, pp. 26-29.
[48] *Ibid.*, p. 31.
[49] *Ibid.*, p. 32.
[50] *Ibid.*, no. 12, p. 34.

reign of God. A "science of prophecy" was being developed.[51] Gaussen closes the book of Daniel with an earnest appeal to be ever ready for the day of judgment, with our wedding garments on.[52]

13. IDENTIFIED WITH SYMBOLS OF APOCALYPSE.—Continuing lesson after lesson, repeating first from one approach, then from another, Gaussen builds an invulnerable case to show the children—and thus the parents—the prophesied character and identity of the little horn. He identifies the horn with the companion symbols of Paul and John.[53] He also identifies it with the second beast of Revelation 13,[54] the false prophet. It is likewise the unchaste, drunken woman of Revelation 17, sitting on the beast, astride the Latin Empire and dominating the great city of Rome.[55]

14. SEVEN CHURCHES REACH TO LAST TIMES.—Tracing the seven churches of Revelation 2 and 3 from the early church of desire, in primitive purity, the church of the pagan persecution —with the special tribulation for ten years—Gaussen comes to the church of the elevation, from Constantine onward, and then the consummation of the apostasy, under Thyatira, the Philadelphia church of the Reformation, and finally the lukewarm church of the last time—the church of the judgment of peoples.[56]

15. SEVEN SEALS EXTEND TO CONSUMMATION.—The seven seals similarly represent the "successive destinies of the Roman Empire from the days of St. John, until the consummation of all things." These are distinct epochs,[57] and in these the great apostasy is also portrayed.[58]

16. FIRST FOUR TRUMPETS IN THE WEST.—Like others, Gaussen holds that the seventh seal embraces the seven trumpets, from about A.D. 400 onward. The first four trumpets symbolize Alaric and the Goths, Genseric and the Vandals, Attila and his Huns, and Odoacer and the Heruli.[59]

---

[51] Ibid., p. 36.
[52] Ibid., p. 37.
[53] Louis Gaussen, Daniel le prophète, exposé, vol. 3, p. 131.
[54] Ibid., p. 133.
[57] Ibid., pp. 216, 217.
[55] Ibid.
[58] Ibid., p. 220.
[56] Ibid., pp. 209-212.
[59] Ibid., pp. 224-226.

17. SARACENS (612-762); TURKS (1057-1453).—The fifth
and sixth trumpets pertain to the East, the fifth referring to the
Saracens of Arabia, whose fierce horsemen spread like locusts,
with the national turban-diadems on their heads. The continuance of their invasion was 150 years—from 612 to 672, with the
building of Baghdad, the city of peace, on the Tigris.[60] The
sixth trumpet is the Turkish woe, beginning to sound on the
Euphrates and Tigris with Thorgrul Beg in 1057, and continuing the hour, day, month, and year—or 396 years—to 1453, at
the overthrow of Constantinople.[61] With this Gaussen connects
Russia, in Ezekiel 37-39, as the Magog of the North, of the seventh trumpet.[62] This sounding, he adds, is near.

18. LATIN HORN WARS 1260 YEARS.—Then in Revelation
10 and 11, John is commanded to measure the temple—the true,
invisible church of God—during which time the "Little Horn
of the Latins" makes war against the true church which worships
in the invisible sanctuary,[63] while the Witnesses prophesy in
sackcloth. Then the beast from the abyss—"the Latin Empire"
—kills the Witnesses at the end of the 1260 years, and they are
resurrected again.[64] Finally, the ruin of popery in the West is
paralleled by the ruin of the Turkish Empire in the East.[65]

19. EARTHQUAKE: REVOLUTION IN TENTH KINGDOM.—The
great earthquake is a "great political and social revolution,"
involving the fall of "one of the ten states of the Latin Empire." [66]

20. NOW LIVING IN THE LAST TIMES.—Finally comes the
fifth monarchy of Daniel, and the reign of the Son of man. We
have now reached the time of the anger of the nations, Gaussen
asserts, the time of God's wrath and the judging of the dead,
the reward of the saints and the destruction of the earth destroy-
ers. "Thus then, you see, we have at last reached those blessed
times" of Daniel 7:27, when the kingdom is soon to be given
to the saints.[67]

---

[60] *Ibid.*, pp. 226, 227.
[61] *Ibid.*, pp. 227, 228. (365 + 30 + 1 = 396.)
[62] *Ibid.*, p. 229.
[63] *Ibid.*, p. 230.
[64] *Ibid.*, pp. 232, 233.
[65] *Ibid.*
[66] *Ibid.*, p. 233.
[67] *Ibid.*, pp. 233, 234.

21. TRUE CHURCH: VAUDOIS, LOLLARDS, HUGUENOTS.—In Revelation 12 the beast is Rome, imperial and pagan, and in Revelation 13 in religious guise it persecutes the saints, while in Revelation 17 it goes into perdition.[68] The true church of Revelation 12, Gaussen avers, includes the Vaudois of Piedmont, the Paulicians of the East, the Lollards of England, the Moravians of Germany, the Huguenots of France, and even the Jansenists of the Catholic Church—and many Armenians, Nestorians, and others in modern times.[69]

22. ROME'S SEVEN HEADS AND TEN HORNS.—Expanding upon the dragon of Revelation 12, with the seven heads and ten horns, existing during the same period of 1260 years' war on the saints,[70] the first six of the seven heads are kings, consuls, dictators, decemvirs, military tribunes, and emperors. But in Revelation 13 the diadems are no longer on their heads but are now on the ten reigning horns that divided Rome.[71]

23. YEAR-DAY PRINCIPLE FOR ALL PERIODS.—Gaussen comes to his final lesson. All the characteristics of Antichrist are marshaled, as centering in the Little Horn. Such, he says, is "the box in which prophecy places the Antichrist." [72] The 1260 years is its allotted time, and its warfare is followed by its doom.[73] The false apostle of the East is noted, arising about the same time, but he is not the Antichrist who thinks to change times and laws.[74]

The 1260, 1290, 1335, and 2300, Gaussen insists, are "not natural days, but symbolical ones." [75] A prophetic day stands for a natural year; a month, thirty years; and forty-two months, 1260 years. He cites Ezekiel 4 and Numbers 14 for proof.[76] Thus also with the seventy weeks of Daniel 9. They are weeks of years, or 490 years, to Messiah's coming. These he places from 457 B.C. to A.D. 34, in which year Christ died, according to Isaac Newton.[77] Again we observe that this was "strong meat" for children, but it affords a faithful record of his exposition.

68 *Ibid.*, pp. 234, 235.
69 *Ibid.*, p. 241.
70 *Ibid.*, p. 235.
71 *Ibid.*, pp. 247-251.
72 *Ibid.*, pp. 332, 333.
73 *Ibid.*, p. 345.
74 *Ibid.*, p. 348.
75 *Ibid.*, pp. 332-335.
76 *Ibid.*, pp. 338-340.
77 *Ibid.*, p. 340.

IV. Richter—Terminates 2300 Years in 1847

Not only in France and Switzerland, but in Germany, the emphasis resounded on the 2300 years as ending about 1847. One important witness was JOHANN HEINRICH RICHTER (1799-1847), secretary of the Rhenish Missionary Society, who was born in Belleben, Germany. The death of his father brought a sudden change to the plans for him to become a forest ranger, as he followed the wish of his mother and studied theology at Halle. There his diligence was recognized by the ministry of culture. After completing his training he served as teacher in several seminaries and other educational institutions. In 1827 Richter was called from the Seminary at Haberstadt to take the leadership of the new Missionary Seminary at Barmen. Here he remained until his untimely death at the age of forty-eight.

Plans for a large mission work were laid, and in 1828 the first missionary ministers were sent out from Barmen Seminary to South Africa. Others were soon sent to Borneo, and even to labor for the Indians in North America. This latter plan was soon discontinued, however, and the candidates took up work among German-speaking settlers in the United States and Canada. In Richter's seminary, missionaries, preachers, and pastors for churches studied side by side for their lifework. Richter was also burdened for the Jews, and organized the Rhenish-Westphalian Society for the Conversion of Israel, with headquarters at Cologne.

Richter likewise edited and published several pedagogical and theological journals. Then he turned to his greatest work— the editing and publishing, with the help of William Richter, of his popular six volume *Erklärte Haus-bibel* (The Family Bible Explained) (1834-1840), which was an exposition of the Old and New Testaments. For the production of this valuable work he was awarded the title of Doctor of Theology by the University of Bonn. Through his extensive travels as well as by his literary activities, his name became well known throughout the Rhineland and Westphalia. He was esteemed by his students, who always regarded him as their spiritual father and friend. His brilliant career was cut short by a sudden attack of pneumonia.[78]

1. DANIEL OUTLINES THE CENTURIES.—The Old Testament section of Richter's popular commentary, *Erklärte Haus-bibel,* shows that he was influenced by Petri's earlier calculation of the 2300 years.[79] In his "Introduction to the Book of Daniel," Richter declares that Daniel not only proclaimed the destruction of Babylon but "also pointed forward to the rise and the development of other great worldly powers until the time when the Messiah would appear and found His kingdom."[80] Daniel received information "concerning the rebuilding of Jerusalem and also the duration of iniquity until the time of the coming of Christ and the cleansing of a true sanctuary."[81]

2. PROPHETIC SPAN OF 2300 YEARS.—Richter held that Daniel's prophecies were aimed at the last days, just as was Jesus' prophecy of Matthew 24.[82] Daniel, as the "Seer of History," gives a history of the people of God comprising about 2300 years.[83]

3. THE PANORAMA OF DANIEL 2 AND 7.—Of Daniel 2, Richter says, the stone is the kingdom of Christ. The golden head of the image is the Babylonian kingdom. Medo-Persia is symbolized by the breast and arms of silver. Alexander the Great follows. The feet and the legs symbolize the fourth world empire, Rome. The ten toes of the image are the ten divisions of the Roman Empire—England, Portugal, Spain, France, Belgium, Sardinia, Austria, Naples, Greece, Turkey—but this order is subject to change.[84]

4. 2300 YEARS REACH TO 1847.—Richter contended that the 2300 days designate "the duration of the desecration of the sanctuary."[85] Referring to some who see this only as literal days in the time of Antiochus Epiphanes, he refers to others who see these prophetic days as so many years, which would come to an

[78] *Allgemeine deutsche Biographie,* Band 28, S. 486, 487.
[79] See Volume 2 of *Prophetic Faith.*
[80] Heinrich Richter, *Erklärte Haus-bibel,* Band IV, S. 738.
[81] *Ibid.,* S. 743.   [83] *Ibid.,* S. 749, 750.
[82] *Ibid.,* S. 747.   [84] *Ibid.,* S. 763, 764.   [85] *Ibid.,* S. 797.

end in 1847[86]—1817 years after the thirtieth year of Christ. And this involves the great Roman Antichrist, for this vision belongs to the time of the end.[87]

5. DATES ANTICHRIST'S PERIOD: 587-1847.—In his comments on Revelation 11:2, Richter dates the forty-two months from 587, when the treading under foot sets in severely. And in Revelation 12:6 he also puts 1847 as the terminus of the 1260 years. Of the two beasts of Revelation 13, he applies the first to the secular dominion of Antichrist, and the second to his ecclesiastical phase.[88] A little later he ends the 666 in 1843.[89]

6. EARTHLY SANCTUARY TYPE OF HEAVENLY.—In this New Testament section Richter discusses the sanctuary further under the seven churches of the Apocalypse. Commenting on Hebrews 9, he recognizes the earthly sanctuary as a type of the heavenly sanctuary, the house or temple which God established, also mentioned in the Revelation, of which Christ is the minister.[90] (Richter's title page reproduced on page 378.)

So, whether heard in Germany, Switzerland, or England, essentially the same witness is borne of prophetic exposition by these earnest heralds of the soon-coming second advent.

NOTE.—The translators who aided in the preparation of this chapter were Jean Vuilleumier, Erna Borm, Alfred Richli, and Elvire Roth.

---

[86] *Ibid.*, S. 801.
[87] *Ibid.*, S. 802.
[88] *Ibid.*, Band 6, S. 1081.
[89] *Ibid.*, S. 1089.
[90] *Ibid.*, S. 738, 739.

CHAPTER THIRTY-SEVEN

Passing Over the Time
of Expectation

Strange to record, as the years of historical expectation—1843, 1844, and 1847—drew near, the eyes of Old World expositors came to be fixed more and more upon a later date for the time of consummation. The years 1867 or 1868 were stressed as the probable close of the 1335 years, and the expected end. There was still talk of an approaching climax. There were still voices in the Old World ardently advocating the soon coming of Christ. But they were on the wane, and the notes of the specific trumpet of alarm were fading out. Most prophetic interpreters now injected a period of time before the advent, and those who still noted 1843 or 1844 made it but a milepost on the way to the ultimate climax. So, in the period from 1843 to 1847 there were relatively few in the Old World looking for the advent or the establishment of the millennium in those years. That was left to the New World Adventists, who will be traced in Volume 4.

Many of the strong voices of these earlier prophetic and advent heralds—who preceded the witnesses in America—were now stilled. And among their successors specific expectation had given way to generalities. Strong expositors, such as Birks and Elliott, appeared; strong isolated defenses were made of the Historical School of interpretation and of the year-day principle; the Futurist School and its arguments were ably met. Nevertheless the inroads of Futurism continued, as did those of Preterism and postmillennialism. The force of prophetic emphasis for 1843-47 as the terminus of the 2300 years was on the way out in the Old World. Let us scan the leading features.

I. Brock—Reports Hundreds Heralding Midnight Cry

MOURANT BROCK (1802-1856), Church of England chaplain to the Bath Penitentiary and perpetual curate of Christ Church, Clifton, graduated from St. Mary Hall, Oxford, with a B.A. in 1825 and an M.A. in 1828.[1] He was ordained in 1826. He was a voluminous writer, his works occupying an entire column in the British Museum catalogue. In 1883 he published a searching history of *Rome: Pagan and Papal*. Earlier works are "The Assurance of Believers in the Prospect of the Second Advent," [2] *The Lord's Coming* (1845), and *Glorification* (1845). The last had several American reprints by the American Millennial Association, and by J. V. Himes for the Millerites. In addition he issued *The City Which Hath Foundations* (1849) and *Babylon and Her Fall* (1854).

1. SECOND ADVENT MUST PRECEDE MILLENNIUM.—Brock sharply rejected postmillennialism, and was a conspicuous advocate of premillennialism, as these trenchant words indicate:

"Where, then, are we to introduce the Millennium? It clearly has not been manifested; it is not now being manifested; whilst, the chronological prophecies plainly show, that, with the greatest latitude of interpretation, there is no space for it to be interposed between the present time and the coming of Christ. If, then, this reign of righteousness has not been, is not now, and cannot be before the Second Advent of Christ, it is evident that it must take place after he comes: hence, we look for a Premillennial Advent of our Lord." [3]

2. MIDNIGHT DARKNESS AND SLUMBER.—Regarding the proximity of the advent, he cites the parable of the virgins and the cry at midnight; holding the present to be the time predicted:

"It is at midnight that the cry is made. Look at Christendom; consider the gross darkness of the Papacy, the profound ignorance of the

---

[1] *Alumni Oxonienses*, 1715-1886, vol. 1, p. 163.
[2] In *The Hope of the Apostolic Church* (Bloomsbury lectures, 1845).
[3] Mourant Brock, *Glorification* (American Millennial Association reprint), p. 134.

Greek, Coptic, and Oriental churches, the deep slumber of the Protestant and other churches abroad; mark the unwillingness too generally displayed at home to hear this warning voice, which is now, blessed be God, from watchman to watchman taken up. Slumber is upon the eyelids, though the cry is being raised. What, then, hinders but that the Bridegroom should be at hand, even at the doors?" [4]

3. 700 ANGLICANS RAISING THE CRY.—The world-wide character of that cry that had been ringing in America, India, Continental Europe, is set forth in an important note:

"It is not merely in Great Britain that the expectation of the near return of the Redeemer is entertained, and the voice of warning raised, but also in America, India, and on the continent of Europe. I was lately told by one of our German missionaries that in Wirtemburgh there is a Christian colony of several hundreds, one of the chief features of which is the looking for the Second Advent. And a Christian minister from near the shores of the Caspian Sea has told me, that there is the same daily expectation among his nation. They constantly speak of it as 'the day of consolation.' In a little publication, entitled 'The Millennium,' the writer says that he understands in America about 300 ministers of the Word are thus preaching 'the Gospel of the kingdom;' whilst in this country, he adds, about 700 of the Church of England are raising the same cry." [5]

II. Birks—Makes Overwhelming Answer to Futurism

THOMAS R. BIRKS (1810-1883), theologian, controversialist, and champion of the year-day principle, was born in Derbyshire. At first a nonconformist, he was educated at the dissenting college of Mill Hill, and then at Trinity College, Cambridge. He joined the Church of England and settled at Watton, as curate to Edward Bickersteth. During this profitable stay he devoted much time to the study of prophecy, taking a strong affirmative in the growing conflict over the premillennial advent. In 1843-44 he engaged in numerous religious controversies, opposing Futurists, Universalists, and annihilationists alike. In 1844 he married Bickersteth's daughter. By 1866 he had charge of Trinity Church, Cambridge, and in 1871 he was canon of Ely Cathedral. In 1872 he became professor of moral philosophy at Cambridge.

---

[4] *Ibid.*, pp. 134, 135.
[5] *Ibid.*, p. 135.

Birks wrote much and widely, his most important literary contribution being *First Elements of Sacred Prophecy* (1843). Designed to sustain the year-day theory, it was "a powerful blow against the reveries of the Futurists." As he dealt with Maitland, Todd, and Burgh, his was an overwhelming answer to the Futurist theory. Then followed *The Four Prophetic Empires* (1844) and *The Two Later Visions of Daniel* (1846). Near the close of his life he wrote *Thoughts on the Times and Seasons of Sacred Prophecy* (1880). Birks was a painstaking investigator, fair in statement and sound in judgment. His grasp of the larger issue of prophetic interpretation was unsurpassed in his day. Indeed, for clarity of statement and cogency of argument in the discussion of prophecy, few men equaled him. He profoundly believed that the era of the impending destruction of the fourth empire had been reached, that the seven vials had begun with the French Revolution, and that human history was rapidly approaching the time of the second advent. (Title page of *First Elements* reproduced on page 540.)

It is generally conceded that Birks produced the most exhaustive and masterly treatise on the year-day principle of the entire nineteenth-century Advent Awakening. He held that the prophecies began with the time of their respective writing, and along with their gradual fulfillment there developed a prophetic understanding during the Christian Era, that was to reach its zenith at the end of the age.

1. THE "RECEIVED MAXIMS" OF THE HISTORICAL SCHOOL.— In his initial treatise, *First Elements of Sacred Prophecy* (1843), issued when the early nineteenth-century world study of prophecy was at its height, Birks divides the Bible into three parts— the law, the Gospels, and the prophecies—the latter being chiefly those of Daniel, John, and Paul, and Christ.[6] He writes as an avowed defender of the Historical view, as against the recently espoused Futurist concept. At the very outset he lays down a series of "received maxims of prophecy,"[7] held by

---

[6] Thomas R. Birks, *First Elements of Sacred Prophecy*, pp. iii, iv.
[7] *Ibid.*, pp. vi, 1.

Protestants since Reformation times. The visions of Daniel begin with the time of Daniel, and those of the Apocalypse with John. The fourth beast is Rome, as also is Babylon. The little horn is the Papacy, and so is the Man of Sin.[8] To these maxims he adds that the two woe trumpets are the Saracens and Turks, and the two beasts of Revelation 13 denote the civil and ecclesiastical principles of Rome. Many of these maxims were held by the early church as well as by various Romanist commentators.[9]

The post-Reformation breakdown of the prophetic concept, along with the resultant resurgence of Romanism, is discussed, and the specious arguments and false maxims of Maitland, Burgh, and Todd are painstakingly analyzed and answered. The Futurist argument of the conflicting views of the Historical interpreters is fully met by the fact that similar disparities obtain among the Futurists,[10] with glaring examples cited. Their disharmony is exploited with devastating effectiveness.[11]

2. STANDARD LISTING OF FOUR EMPIRES.—Birks stoutly maintains the historic four empires of prophecy—Babylon, Medo-Persia, Grecia, and Rome[12]—as against the conflicting and self-destructive views projected by the Futurists.[13] He is similarly explicit on the Persian ram and the Grecian he-goat,[14] as well as the literal prophecy of Daniel 11, extending from apostolic days on to the end of time.[15]

3. SEVENTY WEEKS CUT OFF FROM 2300 DAYS.—The parallelism of the Apocalypse to the Book of Daniel, and the common 1260-year time period are stressed.[16] But the main burden of the treatise is to deal with the year-day principle for all prophetic time periods.[17] Birk's proposition specifies the prophetic day as ever standing for a literal year, a prophetic month for thirty year-days, and a prophetic time, or year, as of 360 year-days.[18] This he applies to the 1260-, 1290-, 1335-, and 2300-day periods and the 70 weeks, as well as the 150 and 391 years.[19] That the 2300

---

8 *Ibid.*, p. 1.
9 *Ibid.*
10 *Ibid.*, pp. 8-13.
11 *Ibid.*, pp. 47-57.

12 *Ibid.*, pp. 61-66.
13 *Ibid.*, pp. 81-95.
14 *Ibid.*, pp. viii, 96-117.
15 *Ibid.*, pp. viii, 135-162.

16 *Ibid.*, pp. 293-307.
17 *Ibid.*, p. 308 ff.
18 *Ibid.*, p. 311.
19 *Ibid.*, pp. 312-337.

evening-mornings are years and not literal days, Birks explicitly declares with this argument:

"It is plain at once that this is not the usual and literal expression for a space of between six and seven years. There are only three instances in all Scripture history where a period of above forty days is expressed in days only (Gen. vii.3; Neh. vi.15; Est. i.4). And it is without any precedent in Scripture, or in common usage, that periods of more than one year should be thus described." [20]

While the "seven times" are noted as from 606 to 1843,[21] the 2300 years are stressed with the seventy weeks as cut off therefrom,[22] and the lesser period is "only a part of the numeral period 2300," with the ending of the latter placed either at 1843 or 1880.[23]

4. SACRED TIME PERIODS ARE CELESTIAL CYCLES.—The cyclical character of the prophetic periods, as suggested by De Chéseaux, is similarly noted.[24] Birks believed the 1260 and 2300 years were such celestial cycles. His comments are worth scrutinizing:

"We are raised out of the contracted range of human reckonings to a lofty elevation of thought, and catch some glimpses of that mysterious wisdom by which the Almighty blends all the works of nature and of providence into subservience to the deep counsels of His redeeming love." [25]

"When we reflect, also, that the celestial periods by which these cycles are determined, are themselves fixed by that law of attraction which gives the minutest atom an influence on the planetary motions, what a combination appears in these sacred times of the most contrasted elements of Omniscient wisdom! Human science sinks exhausted at the very threshold of this temple of divine truth. It has strained its utmost efforts in calculating the actual motions of the Moon and the Earth; but the determining causes which fixed at first the proportion of their monthly and yearly revolutions have altogether eluded its research. Yet these elements of the natural universe are linked in, by these sacred times and celestial cycles, with the deepest wonders of Providence, and the whole range of Divine prophecy." [26]

The ten days of Smyrna are applied to the ten years of Diocletian's persecution.[27] And the various attempts to locate the chronological position of the 1260 years are noted, from Brute

[20] *Ibid.*, p. 357.
[21] *Ibid.*, p. 254.
[22] *Ibid.*, p. 359.
[23] *Ibid.*, p. 360.
[24] *Ibid.*, p. 368.
[25] *Ibid.*, p. 371.
[26] *Ibid.*, p. 372.
[27] *Ibid.*, p. 373.

in the fourteenth century,[28] on to Cressener in the seventeenth, who looked for the terminus of the period about 1800,[29] as well as Fleming's expectation for 1794.[30]

5. YEAR-DAY PRINCIPLE ESTABLISHED BY SEVENTY WEEKS.—On the application of the year-day principle to the seventy weeks Birks makes this illuminating statement:

"THE PROPHECY OF THE SEVENTY WEEKS has always held the foremost place in the direct arguments for the year-day system. The reasoning is very simple in its nature. The word *week*, or *shabua*, is used elsewhere in Scripture to denote seven days; but in this prophecy it denotes *seven years*. Hence the words of time are enlarged beyond their.literal or usual sense, in the proportion of a *year* to a *day*. And since all these predictions of time bear one common character, occur in the same prophets, and have the same general object, they ought to be explained by one common rule. In the one instance, which is decisively fulfilled, the proportion holds of a year to a day; and therefore it must be applied, in consistency, to all the rest." [31]

"Firm and solid" evidence is shown for the Historical view of the year-day principle.[32] And the relationship of these prophetic times to symbolic prophecy is stated in these impressive words:

"The prophetic times, indeed, when separated from the context, and viewed in themselves only, are a dry and worthless skeleton: but when taken in connexion with the related events, clothed with historical facts, and joined with those spiritual affections which should attend the study of God's Providence; like the bones in the human frame, they give strength to what was feeble, and union to what was disjointed, and form, and beauty, and order, to the whole outline and substance of these sacred and divine prophecies." [33]

6. FOUR PROPHETIC EMPIRES AFFIRMED.—Birks' second volume, *The Four Prophetic Empires,* likewise gives the classic Protestant historical interpretation to Daniel 2, 7, 8, and 9.[34] Strong, convincing chapters are devoted to each of the kingdoms, the division of the fourth, the ten kingdoms, the Little Horn, and the grand finale. Much historical detail of a very depend-

[28] *Ibid.*, p. 412.   [29] *Ibid.*, p. 413.
[30] *Ibid.*, p. 414.   (Brute, Cressener, and Fleming, all discussed in *Prophetic Faith*, Volume 2.)
[31] *Ibid.*, p. 333.   [32] *Ibid.*, p. 420.   [33] *Ibid.*, p. 416.
[34] Thomas R. Birks, *The Four Prophetic Empires*, 1845 ed., pp. 11, 12.

able character is given. The parallelism of the several kingdoms appearing in the different chapters, and under various symbols, is developed—such as the bear and leopard being the same as the ram and he-goat.[35]

7. MACHIAVELLI'S LIST OF KINGDOMS FAVORED.—In tracing the division,[36] and then the later countries of divided Western Europe, Birks follows the kingdom list of Machiavelli—the "Herulo-Thuringi, Ostrogoths, Lombards, Franks, Burgundians, Visigoths, Sueves and Alans, Vandals, Huns, and Saxons." [37] The persistence of the divisions is illustrated by lists of the existent European powers in each succeeding century.[38]

The "ten horns" admit of change, some falling or being replaced by others. But the "tenfold character" is dominant throughout the whole, and appears distinctly both at the beginning and at the close of their history. The kings are more ruling powers than local divisions. Thus in Daniel 2 they mingle themselves with the seed of men but do not cleave. And, despite the uprooting of the three, the number still is ten—so the uprooted three are replaced.[39]

8. PAPACY ONLY IS LITTLE HORN.—Then follows the clear identification of the papal Little Horn:

"This unknown and mysterious Power was to arise amid the ten kingdoms of the west, soon after they appeared. It was to have a distinct seat and place in the body of the fourth empire. At the same time it was to claim a prophetic character, and to exert a direct or indirect sovereignty over all the surrounding kings. These features can be found in no power, whether past or future, but the Papacy of Rome." [40]

The statement is then amplified and placed as an inescapable identification. The presumptuous character of the Little Horn and his persecutions follow, with considerable documentation. The indictment ends with the impressive words:

"Thus every feature of the prophecy finds its full counterpart in the constitution, decrees, and history of the Roman popedom. And hence we may gather, with a firm and assured conviction, that this is the true

[35] *Ibid.*, p. 48.   [37] *Ibid.*, p. 146.   [39] *Ibid.*, pp. 143, 144, 152.
[36] *Ibid.*, p. 92 ff.   [38] *Ibid.*, pp. 150, 151.   [40] *Ibid.*, p. 173.

meaning of the vision, designed from the very first by the all-seeing Spirit of God." [41]

9. MILLENNIUM BOUNDED BY TWO RESURRECTIONS.—Chapter 15 deals with the millennium—the early true position, then the Augustinian Catholic perversion, and finally the Whitbyan Protestant distortion.[42] Birks held that there will be two literal resurrections of the dead—the first at the beginning and the second at the close of the thousand years.[43] The premillennial character of the second advent and the events surrounding the advent are clearly portrayed and urged.[44]

10. HORN OF DANIEL 8 IS ROMAN.—Birks' third volume, *The Two Later Visions of Daniel,* is a continuation of his historical exposition of Daniel, this time in chapters 8 and 11. In the preface Birks states that he no longer holds the horn of Daniel 8 to be Mohammedanism.[45] Of its identity he says, "The Little Horn [of chapter 8] was to cast down the sanctuary, and take away the daily sacrifice. Both of these characters met in the Romans." Again, "The Little Horn must denote the Roman, not the Mahometan empire." [46]

11. DANIEL'S "WILFUL KING" IS MAN OF SIN.—Another important division is the "Wilful King" of Daniel 11:36, which he holds is the same as the predicted "Man of Sin." [47] In finally discussing the events of the latter part of Daniel 11, Birks says, "Popery in the West, and the Turkish power in the East, have been the two grand adversaries of the truth, and oppressors of Israel, in the latter days." [48]

III. Cumming—Shifts Focal Point to 1867

JOHN CUMMING (1807-1881), Scottish expositor of prophecy and pastor of Scotch Church, Crown Point, received an M.A. from the Aberdeen University in 1827. After engaging in private tutoring he received a license to preach in 1832. He was

---

[41] *Ibid.,* p. 259.
[42] *Ibid.,* p. 292 ff.
[43] *Ibid.,* appendix, p. 432 ff.
[44] *Ibid.,* p. 297 ff.
[45] Thomas R. Birks, *The Two Later Visions of Daniel,* p. vi.

[46] *Ibid.,* pp. 178, 179.
[47] *Ibid.,* p. 283.
[48] *Ibid.,* p. 315.

particularly active in Romanist controversies and was widely known for his exposition of prophecy. He held that the last of the seven vials was to be poured out by 1867, and made 1867 the great focal point of prophetic expectation. In 1868 he sought to attend the Vatican council, but was refused. A glance at the titles of his books gives the scope of his study and his emphasis.[49]

Altogether Cumming produced more than twenty volumes, some of which were translated. *Apocalyptic Sketches* (1849), first delivered as lectures in Exeter and in London, passed through several printed editions. His leading works were: *The Sixth Vial* (1843); *Lectures for the Times; or an Exposition of Tridentine and Tractarian Popery* (1844); *Apocalyptic Sketches* (1849); *Prophetic Studies, or Lectures on the Book of Daniel* (1850); *Lecture . . . on Romanism Idolatrous* (1851); *Lecture on Romanism Persecuting* (1851); *The Signs of the Times* (1854); *The End* (1855); *The Great Tribulation* (1859); *The Great Preparation* (1860); *The Millennial Rest* (1862); *Behold, the Bridegroom Cometh* (1865); *The Sounding of the Last Trumpet* (1867); *The Last Warning Cry* (1867); *The Seventh Vial, or the Time of Trouble Begun* (1870); and *The Fall of Babylon* (1870).

1. WORLD'S TWILIGHT FOLLOWED BY ETERNAL DAY.—In an address on *The Sixth Vial: A Sermon for the Times* (1843), delivered in his church in April, 1843, Cumming couples the drying up of the Turkish power (the Euphrates) with the restoration of the kings of the East (the Jews), the latter being "the chief sign of the times in which we live." The marvel of their persistence through the years is noted,[50] along with the resurgence of Catholicism and the waning of Protestantism. On this he remarks:

"The very name of Protestant, which once was the rallying cry of this mighty land, and the secret of the eloquence of our senate and of the effects of our pulpit, is dying away like distant music; and the majestic truths of which it has been venerated as the symbol, are falling like the too

[49] *Dictionary of National Biography*, vol. 5, p. 297.
[50] John Cumming, *The Sixth Vial: A Sermon for the Times*, p. 10.

ripe ears of harvest before the sickle of the Papacy—like the verdure and the blossoms of earth before the blast of the siroc, or the breath of the simoom of the desert." [51]

The tragic inroads of the Oxford Tractarians are deplored —"The Church is made the substitute of Christianity—the priest, for the Holy Spirit." [52] The three unclean spirits are declared abroad "croaking like an unclean frog from behind decorated altars and gaudy rites." [53] The great day is at hand. Armageddon impends, and the world's ruin. He adds:

"We feel and hear creation groaning and travailing, waiting for the manifestation of the sons of God. Behind the lowering cloud, however, there is a glorious apocalypse. The twilight that closes in darkness shall be followed by a twilight that will be merged in eternal day. It is at the close of this Vial that Christ adds (ver. 15), 'Behold I come as a thief. Blessed is he that watcheth and keepeth his garments.' " [54]

2. 1260 YEARS DATED FROM 532 TO 1792.—In another address on *The Signs of the Times* (1854), before the Y.M.C.A., Cumming discusses the prophetic numbers of Daniel and Revelation. The 1260 years are there assigned to the Roman apostasy. "This is almost universally accepted," [55] the "witnesses in sackcloth" being the "saints worn out." This period he dates from Justinian's authorization of papal power in 532 and ending in 1792 when "great convulsions took . . . initial active operation." Now the scourging of the Papacy is under way, and in the final act it will be destroyed "by the brightness of His coming." [56]

3. 2300 YEARS PLACED FROM 430 B.C. TO A.D. 1820.—The 2300 year-days include "the duration of the Mahometan power." This Cumming dates from 430 B.C., the "era of the noon-tide glory of the Persian Empire." [57] From that date Daniel "looks along the centuries" and "predicts that 2300 years from that date its decay would begin." This "lands us on the year 1820," from which date the wasting away of the Mohammedan power had been progressing. In support, Cumming lists the

---

[51] *Ibid.*, p. 30.   [52] *Ibid.*
[53] *Ibid.*, p. 31.   [54] *Ibid.*, p. 32.
[55] John Cumming, *The Signs of the Times*, p. 160.
[56] *Ibid.*, pp. 160, 161.
[57] *Ibid.*, p. 161. (Later, 431 B.C. to A.D. 1821. See next page.)

Greek insurrections, revolts of provinces, destruction of Turco-Egyptian fleets, etc. This he refers to as the "progressive evap-oration of Mahometanism, beginning in 1820, and expected by every student of prophecy to end in a very short time." [58] This dying out, or "gradual decay," Cumming asserts, is assuredly under way, in proof of which he cites Habershon and others.[59] The same contention is set forth in his *Apocalyptic Sketches*.

4. 1867 MADE THE GREAT FOCAL POINT.—In his *Great Tribulation,* Cumming places stress upon 1867 as the great focal point, to which "the best, the wisest, and the most thoughtful" expositors were looking, on the basis of the 1260 years from A.D. 607, by some and the 1335 years by others.[60] By a different reckoning, the 1260 years of the "great Western apostasy" were from 532 to 1792.[61] The thirty additional years of the 1290 years would lead to 1822, when one commentator would also end the 2300 years, with the beginning of the exhaustion of Turkey. And the forty-five years more of the 1335 would lead to 1867.[62] Then he observes that "according to both theories," 1867 "evolves as the year of stupendous changes." [63]

In support he cites Lady Hester Stanhope, Irving, Major Denham, Cuninghame, Bickersteth, and Scott. So he maintains that "1867 is an era fraught with gigantic issues." Some think it is "the commencement of the millennial rest; others think it is the destruction of all the errors whose roots are struck deep into our world, and the universal spread of the empire of the Prince of Peace." [64]

5. SARACENIC WOES: 612-762; TURKISH WOE; 1057-1453.—Later treatises, such as *The Great Preparation* (1860), simply reiterate and amplify these positions, going into other details—the 2300 years from 481 B.C. to A.D. 1821, and the "waning of the Mahometan Crescent," or drying up of the Turco-Moslem power.[65] The 150 years of the Saracenic woe he places between 612 and 762,[66] and the 396 years (365 + 30 + 1) of the Turco-

---

[58] *Ibid.*, pp. 161, 162.
[59] *Ibid.*, p. 163.
[60] John Cumming, *The Great Tribulation,* pp. 240-243.
[61] *Ibid.*, p. 242.
[64] *Ibid.*, pp. 245, 246, 249
[62] *Ibid.*, p. 244.
[63] *Ibid.*, p. 245.
[65] John Cumming, *The Great Preparation*, pp. 168-173.
[66] *Ibid.*, pp. 188, 189.

Moslem woe he extends from the loosing of these forces in 1057, under the lead of Togrul Beg, to the possession of Constantinople in 1453;[67] thus also in his *Behold, the Bridegroom Cometh* (1865), in which he asserts that "the great chronological epochs of prophecy all expire in 1867," [68] and in *The Sounding of the Last Trumpet* (1867), Cumming's various tables[69] for the various time periods all stress the 1867 focal date. He even titled one prediction *The End of the World in 1867* (1866).

So again we see that the whole emphasis has been shifted, by means of the 1335-year interpretation, away from 1843-47, on to 1867, as the new great focal point.

IV. Elliott—Contributes History of Apocalyptic Interpretation

EDWARD BISHOP ELLIOTT (1793-1875), scholarly prophetic expositor, received his education at Trinity College, Cambridge, graduating in 1816. After traveling in Italy and Greece he was given the vicarage of Tuxford, Nottingham, in 1824, and later was made prebendary of Heytesbury, Wiltshire. In 1849 he became incumbent of St. Mark's Church, Brighton. A member of the Evangelical school, he was an earnest promoter of missionary enterprise and an ardent advocate of premillennialism. Elliott was thoroughly equipped as a scholar and was deeply interested in prophecy, spending a lifetime in investigation and seeking to understand God's mind thereon.

His *Horæ Apocalypticæ* (Hours with the Apocalypse) is doubtless the most elaborate work ever produced on the Apocalypse. Without an equal in exhaustive research in its field, it was occasioned by the Futurist attack on the Historical School of interpretation launched by Maitland, Burgh, and Todd. Begun in 1837,[70] its 2,500 pages of often involved and overloaded text are buttressed by some 10,000 invaluable references to ancient and modern works bearing on the topics under discus-

---

[67] *Ibid.*, pp. 190, 191.
[68] John Cumming, *Behold the Bridegroom Cometh*, p. 91.
[69] John Cumming, *The Sounding of the Last Trumpet*, pp. 399-403.
[70] Edward Bishop Elliott, *Horæ Apocalypticæ* (5th ed.), vol. 1, p. v.

sion. It ran through five editions (1844, 1846, 1847, 1851, and 1862).

Elliott stressed the evidence of the illustrative coins and medallions of the centuries as an original contribution in the field of prophetico-historical evidence.[71] He engaged in controversies with Candlish, Keith, and others, and exposed the fallacies of false interpretations which involved abandonment of the Protestant position on popedom as the intended Antichristian power of Scripture prophecy. He also wrote *The Question "What is the Image of the Beast?" Answered* (1838), and *The Delusion of the Tractarian Clergy*. His last contribution on the subject of prophecy was the Warburton Lectures for 1849-53 on *The Christian Church's Institution and Declension into Apostasy; the Apostate Church's Heading by the Romish Antichrist* (1856).

Doubtless his greatest contribution was a 288-page "History of Apocalyptic Interpretation." A most complete and scholarly work, it appears as Appendix I in volume 4 of the fifth edition of his *Horæ Apocalypticæ*.[72] This truly monumental treatise is invaluable for grasping the background and development of prophetic interpretation of the Apocalypse. Expositions on Daniel are touched only incidentally. Divided into seven parts, it covers the leading interpreters from John's to Constantine's day, from Constantine to Rome's division, from the fall of Rome to the twelfth century, from the twelfth century to the Reformation, the era of the Reformation, from 1600 to the French Revolution, and from 1790 to his own time.[73] In addition to its methodical and dependable nature, abundant documentation makes it of exceptional service to the investigator.

Perhaps its most unique feature is the concluding sketch of the rise and spread of the Jesuit countersystems of interpretation that had made such inroads upon Protestantism. Holding unswervingly to the Historical School of interpretation, Elliott gives the most complete exposure of these counterinterpretations

---

[71] *Ibid.*, Preface, pp. x, xi. Examples are scattered throughout the four volumes.
[72] *Ibid.*, vol. 4, pp. 275-563.
[73] *Ibid.*, p. 275.

to be found.[74] A clear grasp of eighteenth-century German rationalism's espousal of Preterism, that has become the characteristic of Modernism, and the nineteenth-century acceptance of Futurism, that is now the almost universal belief of Fundamentalism, places a key in the hand of the student that unlocks the mystery of the otherwise baffling conflict of opposing positions in present-day Protestant exposition.

Elliott's familiarity with the witness of the centuries was phenomenal, as shown by the fullness of his discussion concerning the Vaudois teaching, in the twelfth and thirteenth centuries, that the Roman church is the very Babylon and harlot of the Apocalypse, and that the Romish system was of Antichrist;[75] similarly concerning Luther's great discovery of Christ and Antichrist, his reviving the cry of Wyclif and Huss that had almost died away, and his burning of the papal bull as the bull of Antichrist;[76] or concerning the presumptuous claims of the developing Papacy,[77] and the recognition by the old writers—such as Brightman, Cressener, and Mann, prior to the French Revolution—of Justinian as the first to recognize the primacy of the Papacy.[78] It was his masterful grasp of the whole historical development of prophetic interpretation that gave weight to his own expositions—which were not, however, without certain serious defects.

1. PRECEDES TRUMPETS WITH SEVEN SEALS.—Elliott makes the seven seals precede the seven trumpets, the two together covering the Christian Era.[79] In this he differs from Campbell, Bickersteth, Birks, and others. However, his views on the trumpets were sharp, clear, and standard. The first four effected the Western Empire's downfall, starting with Alaric and his Goths,[80] then Genseric and his Vandals,[81] next Attila and his Huns,[82] and finally the extinction of the West by Odoacer and his Heruli.[83] The fifth and sixth trumpets cover the destruction of the East-

---

[74] *Ibid.*, p. 481 ff.
[75] *Ibid.*, vol. 2, p. 390.
[76] *Ibid.*, pp. 115, 118-120.
[77] *Ibid.*, pp. 132-134.
[78] *Ibid.*, vol. 3, p. 135. (These are all discussed in *Prophetic Faith*, Volume 2.)
[79] *Ibid.*, vol. 1, pp. xi, 119.
[80] *Ibid.*, pp. 375-377.
[81] *Ibid.*, pp. 378-380.
[82] *Ibid.*, pp. 380-382.
[83] *Ibid.*, pp. 383-385.

ern Empire—the fifth, or first woe, trumpet indicating the Islamic Saracens,[84] and the sixth the Osmanli Turks.[85]

2. A PROPHETIC PERIOD NOT A POINT OF TIME.—Elliott's exposition of the time element of the "hour day month and year" of the second woe of Revelation 9:15, is important technically. He declares that these time nouns are all to be "aggregated together." [86] That is, they indicate a *period* of prophetic time, and not a *point* of literal time. The latter construction he considers "inadmissible: I mean that which, taking them each separately, would render the clause thus; that *at the destined hour, and destined day, and destined month, and destined year, they should slay the third part of men.*" [87] A footnote refers to those holding such an exposition as "Vitringa, Daubuz, Heinrichs, M. Stuart, & c." [88]—expositors who had abandoned the Historical School of prophetic interpretation, along with the year-day principle for all prophetic time periods.

Elliott refutes such a view by saying:

"The *article* prefix, standing at its head, may be understood not only to govern all the accusatives that follow, so as we find done elsewhere, but also to be a means for the better uniting of them, *as it were under a bracket,* as an hour day month and year, all added together; at the same time that it may mark them also as making up *the* period; i.e. the period fore-ordained and fore-shown in the divine councils." [89]

This time prophecy of the Turks he takes to be a period of 396 years, from 1057 to 1453, on the basis of a 365-day year, a month of thirty days, and the one day—or 396 year-days.[90]

3. THE BEAST, HIS HEADS, AND HIS NUMBER.—Elliott proves convincingly that the Papacy answers the symbolic descriptions given in Revelation 13 and 17. He also holds that by the organization of the secular and regular clergy it had become the two-horned beast. He stresses the fact that along with the discovery of the Antichrist of prophecy and the conviction of its predestined final destruction, the establishment of Christ's

---

[84] *Ibid.*, pp. 443-446, 453-463.
[85] *Ibid.*, pp. 487-505.
[86] *Ibid.*, p. 517.
[87] *Ibid.*

[88] *Ibid.*
[89] *Ibid.*, p. 518.
[90] *Ibid.*, pp. 521, 522, 527.

kingdom at His second advent had been revived by students of prophecy as the climax of God's great prophetic mystery.[91]

The dragon of Revelation 12 is clearly pagan Rome, and the woman clothed with the sun is the church.[92] Constantine's concept of his own casting down of paganism is noted.[93] The common identity of Daniel's little horn, John's beasts, and Paul's Man of Sin, as Rome, is clearly established,[94] as well as their identical prophesied time period. The beast's seven heads are listed as kings, consuls, dictators, decemvirs, military tribunes, the Caesars, and the popes[95]—the seventh the one to be wounded.[96]

The beast's development as Antichrist, his legalization following, and then his suppression, are all depicted and thoroughly documented.[97] The various attempts to decipher the 666 are noted, with a strong leaning toward *Lateinos*.[98]

4. THE TEN KINGDOMS AND THE UPROOTED THREE.—Elliott lists the ten kingdoms of Western Rome, found between A.D. 486 and 490, as the Anglo-Saxons, Franks, Alemanni, Burgundians, Visigoths, Suevi, Vandals, Bavarians, and Ostrogoths, and Lombards.[99] This and other listings he discusses at length.[100]

5. HOLDS TWO WITNESSES NOT TWO TESTAMENTS.—The Two Witnesses were held to be the Eastern and Western human witnesses rather than the two Testaments,[101] and the "earthquake" of Revelation 11 is referred to as the Protestant Reformation, and not the French Revolution.[102]

6. APPLIED YEAR-DAY PRINCIPLE TO 1260 YEARS.—Elliott makes a masterful argument for the year-day principle that leaves little to be said.[103] Having demonstrated its soundness and logic, he immediately applies it to the 1260 year-days of the Apocalyptic beast, with primary application from the time of Justinian to the French Revolution.[104] Elliott recognized the stroke of the sword at Rome in 1798, and the "spoliation of the

---

91 *Ibid.*, vol. 2, pp. 145-147.
92 *Ibid.*, vol. 3, p. 6 ff.
93 *Ibid.*, pp. 39-45.
94 *Ibid.*, p. 87 ff.
95 *Ibid.*, pp. 116, 117.
96 *Ibid.*, p. 127.
97 *Ibid.*, pp. 147-162.
98 *Ibid.*, pp. 247-255.
99 *Ibid.*, pp. 140-143.
100 *Ibid.*, pp. 132-147.
101 *Ibid.*, vol. 2, pp. 201-408.
102 *Ibid.*, pp. 472-475.
103 *Ibid.*, vol. 3, pp. 260-298.
104 *Ibid.*, pp. 298-305, 408, 409.

harlot-Church," as the aged Pius VI was apprehended in the Sistine Chapel and carried captive into France.[105]

7. HAZY ON DATING OF THE 2300 YEARS.—In one of his brief discussions of the 2300 years Elliott applies the little horn of Daniel 8 to the Turk and the king of the north of Daniel 11.[106] But on the location of this long time period Elliott is hazy, dating it as possibly from 480 B.C. to A.D. 1820.[107] However, to Elliott the 2300 prophetic days are "years distant from that which marked its beginning, probably the successful pushing of the Persian ram." [108] He then observes that "Antiochus' death occurred between 300 and 400 years after it," and no satisfactory explanation is to be found on a "day-day basis." He believed the ending of the 2300 years from the date of the vision had some connection with papal Rome.[109] The sixth vial involves the drying up of the Euphrates, or Turks, with the plagues falling in the French Revolution.[110]

8. BECOMES "CONTINUATIONIST," SHIFTING TO SECONDARY DATES.—Elliott later became a "continuationist" on the prophetic time periods. He began to reconstruct the prophetic dates, referring to "primary" and "secondary" fulfillments. As 1793-98 and 1843-44 had only realized the beginning of what had been expected at the end of the 391, 1260, and 2300 years, he assigned later dates. He mentions the fact that since the days of Cellarius (1555) some had counted the 1260 years from the decree of Phocas in 606, and ended the time period in 1866.[111] This terminal year Elliott began to stress.

When 1866 had passed, Elliott wrote a "Counter-Retrospect" in *The Christian Observer,* calling attention to the fact that as there were several decrees from Cyrus to Artaxerxes to mark the beginning of the seventy weeks, and several events marking the beginning of the captivity, so also several events marked the beginnings and endings of the 1260 years. This

---

[105] *Ibid.,* pp. 395-401.
[106] *Ibid.,* p. 441 ff; vol. 4, p. 238.
[107] *Ibid.,* vol. 3, pp. 446-448.
[108] *Ibid.,* pp. 434-444.

[109] *Ibid.,* pp. 434, 435.
[110] *Ibid.,* p. 438 ff.
[111] *Ibid.,* vol. 1, p. xxiii.

he said, was given added emphasis because of the difference of seventy-five years between the 1260 and the 1335 years.[112]

As the interval between the decrees of Cyrus and Artaxerxes served to excite and keep up the lively expectation of the first advent as near at hand, so do the seventy-five years between the decrees of Justinian and Phocas concerning the nearness of the second advent. Elliott concludes that the final end of the Papacy and Mohammedanism, designed by the 1260, 1290, and 1335 years, "would 'end,' about 1866, 1896, and 1941 A.D. respectively." [113] So continuationism was increasingly stressed by voice and pen "to keep up the lively expectation" of Christ's second advent in glory.

Such is the testimony of one of the last of the leading Old World prophetic expositors of the first half of the nineteenth century, as he shifted from the primary to the secondary dates of continuationism.

V. Lawyer Appeals to Bishops to Discern Times

Not only did the appeals of clergymen mark the tractates of the times, but we find the unique situation of lawyers appealing to clergymen. For example, JOHN HALCOMBE (1790-1852), English barrister and "Serjeant at Law," magistrate of Middlesex and member of Parliament for Dover from 1831 to 1835, printed for private circulation a series of letters to the bishops of Great Britain and Ireland, under the title *The Evidence of Unfulfilled Prophecy, Arranged and Examined* (1845). Here he contrasts the common expectation of a "gradual diffusion of Christianity," and the advent as a "distant" event, with the repeated warnings of "sacred prophecy" as to Christ's soon coming.[114]

Since the popular "confident security" is "positively contradicted by the distinct revelations of Scripture," Halcombe admonishes the bishops to take heed to the "sure word of proph-

[112] *The Christian Observer*, December, 1868 (vol. 67, no. 372), pp. 945-949.
[113] E. B. Elliott, *Horæ Apocalypticæ* (5th ed.), vol. 4, p. 112.
[114] John Halcombe, *The Evidence of Unfulfilled Prophecy, Arranged and Examined*, p 6.

ecy." He warns that the age is speedily coming to its end, when the "time allotted" shall pass. Thus he appeals to the men of the cloth to discern the signs of the times and prepare for the "approaching time of our trial." [115]

VI. American Reprints of British Expositions

Note should be taken, in passing, of the extensive and systematic American reprinting of the recent leading British works on prophecy. Orrin Rogers of Philadelphia conducted an unusual semimonthly magazine called *The Literalist*,[116] at Philadelphia from 1840 to 1842. It was simply composed of reprints of British books by Way (Basilicus), Cuninghame, Anderson, Habershon, Brooks, M'Neile, Noel, Bickersteth, Cox, Thorp, Sirr, and others. A number of these were publicized in the early issues of the Millerite *Signs of the Times* before a distinctive American advent literature had been developed in the New World. And apart from these two, *The American Millenarian and Prophetic Review*, of New York, edited by I. P. Labagh, publicized Begg, Pym, Anderson, and Irving, and offered their works for sale.[117]

---

[115] *Ibid.*, pp. 6, 7.
[116] Because of the separate title pages and paging, *The Literalist* appears to be a collection of separately published works bound together, but it was issued as a true periodical, semimonthly. Its numbers contained an arbitrary number of pages, disregarding the beginning and ending of the individual works, as is shown by the continuous signature numbering. Volume 1 was published in 18 numbers, totaling 864 pages. (See "Notice to Subscribers" announcing volume 2.)
[117] *The American Millenarian and Prophetic Review*, vol. 2, nos. 3-6, 1843.

CHAPTER THIRTY-EIGHT

Old World Advent Awakening Collapses

Disintegration of the strong witness of former years is now far advanced. Confusion, conflict, and loss of interest become increasingly marked. Only occasionally are clear, strong voices heard—and they are submerged in the din of increasing differences. Or they are like isolated voices crying in the wilderness of growing silence. And certainty on the prophetic time periods had gone from most of these.

The Futurist School continues to counter the Historical School of interpretation, capitalizing to the full on variances in interpretation and conflict in the allocation of the time periods. Preterism was spreading among the rationalistic-minded. Catholicism continues its bid, with some success, for recognition by those who had abandoned the position of the Papacy as the historical Antichrist.

The nineteenth-century Old World Advent Awakening, based on prophecy, had broken down, just as did the Protestant Reformation witness on prophecy in the eighteenth century. Only in the New World was there left a strong Historical School of prophetic faith.

Before taking leave of the Old World, let us turn once more to the troubled scene. The familiar Historical position, reiterated by Baylee, is now blurred by the overtones of the Protestant Futurists, Maitland and Tyso. And into these is injected, like a premonition, the challenging voice of Catholic Cardinal Manning. Such is the parting glimpse of growing conflict, compromise, and confusion that marks the fading out of the Historical School witness in Britain in the middle of the nineteenth century.

I. *Prophetic Herald*—Prophetic Interpretation Increasingly Blurred

Still another journal on prophecy, *The Prophetic Herald and Churchman's Witness for Christ,* was edited by Principal Joseph Baylee, of the St. Aidan Theological College at Birkenhead, beginning in 1845. It was launched at a difficult time in exposition. In an introductory statement Baylee discloses how in 1829 he became convinced of premillennialism,[1] about which the church knew little. The contrasting views on the Revelation are set forth as in conflict—one that the prophecies have "all but received" their full accomplishment, the other that they are as yet largely "unfulfilled." In other words, the conflict between the Historical and Futurist schools is on in earnest.

Baylee holds to the "protestant interpretation of prophecy" —"that the apostate Popes of Rome are the man of sin and Antichrist, and that the city of Rome is the Babylon foredoomed of God, and the Roman diocese the mother of harlots; also that a day stands for a year in prophetical chronology." [2] But the new Futurist emphasis has already made its impress, for even Baylee says that certain predictions of "awful personages" will require an additional application.[3]

1. 2400-YEAR TERMINUS AND CONTINUATIONISM.—J. H. Frere contributes heavily to the pages of the *Prophetic Herald,*[4] furnishing a whole series of articles which stress his characteristic 2400-year argument for Daniel 8:14, in a letter to Joseph Wolff citing the manuscripts in which they are allegedly found.[5] The dating of the 2400 is placed, as usual, from 553 B.C. to A.D. 1847. But Frere has now become involved in a kind of cabalistic calculation of prophetic numbers, multiplying, dividing, and sub-

---

[1] *The Prophetic Herald and Churchman's Witness for Christ,* vol. 1, p. 2.
[2] *Ibid.,* p. 3.
[3] *Ibid.*
[4] *Ibid.,* p. 33 ff.
[5] *Ibid.,* p. 132 ff.

tracting, finding the square root, etc.[6] He stresses Mohammedan
epochs and Gentile periods, placing emphasis upon the Hegira,
in A.D. 622, and the Mohammedan feature. The return of the
Jews has its characteristic place.[7] The "continuationist idea" is
strongly in the forefront—the 1260 years ending in 1792, the
1290 in 1822-23, and the 1335 in 1867-68.[8]

2. SOCIETIES FULFILLING DEMANDS OF REVELATION 14.—
The formation of the Society for the Investigation of Prophecy,
back in 1826, is rehearsed,[9] supported by such men as Edward
Irving, James Stratton, Thomas White, and others. Then the
story of the Reformation Society in 1827 is told, with such men
as C. S. Hawtrey, Lewis Way, and Edward Irving. These were
formed with the express thought of helping to fulfill Revelation
14:8 and Revelation 14:9, 11 respectively.[10] The first heralded
the approaching fall of papal Babylon, and the second announced the fearful punishments to be inflicted upon those
remaining in her communion, and urged the people to come
out of her.[11]

3. HURRICANE WHEN WINDS RELEASED.—William Cuninghame contributes an article on the "order of events connected
with the second advent, and the war of Armageddon," declaring,
"The key to the present state of the world, and the position of
the Church of God appears to be the vision of the holding of
the four winds in the sixth seal."[12] The convictions of secular
writers are quoted from *Edinburgh Review*,[13] for example,
"There is a greater and more momentous contest impending
than ever before agitated human society." And from *Blackwood's Edinburgh Magazine,* after a comparison of the times
with the days of Rome's decay, the statement appears, "Great
changes are in prospect everywhere." "A HURRICANE IS SWEEP-
ING ONWARDS OF POLITICAL REVOLUTION."[14]

4. IN PERIOD OF AWFUL EXPECTATION.—The repetition of
the days of Noah and of Sodom is stressed by Baylee, with a

6 *Ibid.*, pp. 135-140.   9 *Ibid.*, p. 380.   12 *Ibid.*, p. 426.
7 *Ibid.*, p. 140.   10 *Ibid.*, pp. 380, 381.   13 *Ibid.*, p. 427.
3 *Ibid.*, pp. 473, 474.   11 *Ibid.*, p. 381.   14 *Ibid.*

"torrent of calamity" to break forth, and "universal dismay." [15]
He tells of the "never-ending Protocols" for the "ostensible and
avowed purpose of preserving the peace of Europe, while their
armies continuing strained to the highest pitch of a war establishment in the midst of their professions of peace, proclaimed
their deep forebodings of slaughter." [16] It is in the midst of such
scenes that Christ shall descend to raise the dead and translate
the living.[17] Said Baylee, "As it seems to me, we have entered
into that last period of awful expectation during which the
Church is likened to the ten virgins." [18]

5. SECOND ADVENT GOAL OF CONVERGING LINES.—Disappointed because of unfulfilled promises of articles from "eminent writers on prophecy," the editor plans to do more of the
writing himself. In this connection he says:

> "In examining unfulfilled prophecy, our great central point should be
> our blessed Lord's personal advent. It is that upon which all the rays of
> prophetic light converge, or from which they diverge. This is especially
> true of chronological investigations. We shall never attain to a true ar-
> rangement of unfulfilled prophecy until we have a clear view of the con-
> nection of predicted events with the Lord's advent." [19]

This principle he illustrates by certain "prophetic synchro-
nisms." Thus in Daniel 2, 7, and 11 the "destruction by the
stone," the "coming of the Son of Man in the clouds of heaven,"
and the "standing up" of the great Prince is stressed.[20] In the
book of Revelation the great heart is "the termination of our
present dispensation in judgment, . . . and the subsequent restoration of the world." [21] In Revelation 11 the measuring of the
temple and the slaying of the Witnesses is followed by the sounding of the seventh trump, when the kingdoms of the world become the kingdoms of Christ, and the anger of the nations, God's
wrath and judgment, the resurrection of the dead, and the deliverance of the earth all converge.[22] The history of Babylon yields
the same climax—Babylon's awful and sudden ruin, ushering in
the coming of the Lord, the overthrow of the assembled nations

---

[15] *Ibid.*, pp. 428, 429.
[16] *Ibid.*, p. 430.
[17] *Ibid.*, pp. 429, 431.
[18] *Ibid.*, p. 431.

[19] *Ibid.*, pp. 504, 505.
[20] *Ibid.*, vol. 2, pp. 230, 231.
[21] *Ibid.*, p. 233.
[22] *Ibid.*

—but with the restoration of the Jews.[23] There the journal terminates. We shall take a further glance, however, at Principal Baylee.

II. Baylee—Prophetic Lectures Before Youth's Society

JOSEPH BAYLEE (1808-1883), Irish theological writer and principal of St. Aidan's College, was a graduate of Trinity College, Dublin, receiving the degrees of B.A. in 1834, M.A. in 1848, and B.D. and D.D. in 1852. He was the founder and first principal of St. Aidan's Theological College, Birkenhead, and prepared many students for the ministry. He was an ardent champion of the Evangelical faith, and was fond of discussion with Roman Catholics.[24] Accounts were published of his controversies with Dr. Thomas J. Brown, bishop of Apollonia, on *The Infallibility of the Church of Rome* (1851), with Mr. Matthew Bridges on *Protestantism vs. Roman Catholicism* (1856), with Edward Miall, M.P., on *Church Establishments* (1864), and with Charles Bradlaugh on *God, Man, and the Bible* (1867). He also wrote *Principles of Scripture Interpretation* (1844), "The Kingdoms of Europe" in *The Signs of the Times: . . . Six Lectures* (1854), and *The Times of the Gentiles* (1871). Two columns in the British Museum catalogue are devoted to his works. His oral lectures on the prophecies were frequent and impressive.

1. KINGDOM OF GOD SUPERSEDES EARTHLY KINGDOMS.— Under the general title *The Signs of the Times*, Baylee joined five other clergymen of the Established Church in a series of "Six Lectures" before the Church of England's Young Men's Society in Southwark. His topic was "The Kingdoms of Europe Viewed in the Light of Scripture." Holding that as striking an analogy prevailed "in the present times," as with "the close of previous dispensations," Baylee said, "We are coming towards the close of God's dealings with the Gentile nations." [25] Declar-

---

[23] *Ibid.*
[24] *Dictionary of National Biography*, vol. 1, p. 1361; Frederic Boase, *Modern English Biography*, vol. 1, col. 199.
[25] Joseph Baylee, "The Kingdoms of Europe," in *The Signs of the Times: . . . Six Lectures*, part 1, p. 96.

ing that prophecy is the unfolding of the mind of God, including predictions of the future, he rehearses in sweeping survey the leading prophecies of Daniel and of Revelation.

The four empires of Daniel 2 are portrayed as succeeded by the "kingdom of Christ," His kingdom "breaking to pieces in a violent manner those kingdoms of the world." The wildness and ferocity of those same nations is portrayed in the symbols of the beasts of Daniel 7 "rising out of the stormy winds of human passions," until the Ancient of days comes, and the everlasting kingdom is established. The little horn of the fourth empire is "the Pope, and his usurped dominion and his tyranny against the saints of the Most High." [26]

2. DAYS OF TRAMPLING NUMBERED BY WONDERFUL NUMBERER.—In Daniel 8, Christ, the wonderful Numberer of the Secrets, is revealed as responding to the inquiry about the 2300 years and how long the trampling of the daily sacrifice and the transgression of desolation would continue, giving assurance that "every day is numbered in the Divine Councils." It shall come and not tarry. That end "will not be one moment after the right time." He "has numbered the days of the kingdoms of the world." [27]

3. HOUR OF JUDGMENT SOUNDING BEFORE BABYLON'S FALL.—As the Papacy is portrayed for the West, so, according to Baylee, in Revelation 9 the Mohammedan power is pictured in the East under the fifth and sixth trumpets. Then the seventh trumpet marks the resurrection of the dead in connection with the establishment of the kingdom of God. [28] And in Revelation 14:6, "we have a reference to our own time," as the angel flying with the everlasting gospel couples with it the warning, "The hour of His judgment is come." This is to be followed by the fall of Babylon and the harvest, and the judgments of Revelation 16 on Western Europe—the sixth vial, involving the drying up of the Euphrates, as "province after province has been torn from the Mohammedan power." [29] Then comes the grand climax as the

---

[26] *Ibid.*, pp. 104-106.
[27] *Ibid.*, p. 107.

[28] *Ibid.*, pp. 118, 119.
[29] *Ibid.*, pp. 119, 120.

"great earthquake" is accompanied by the declaration, "It is done," and Babylon falls. Then, at last, the King of kings and Lord of lords is seen "coming out of heaven with his returning saints to establish his glorious kingdom." [30]

III. Charles Maitland—Futurist Historian of Early Interpretation

CHARLES MAITLAND (1815-1866), the son of Captain Charles David Maitland, previously noted,[31] was also an expositor, but of the Futurist School. Born at Woolwich, Kent, he was educated at Brighton, and chose medicine as a profession. After graduating from Edinburgh University with an M.D., in 1838, he visited Malta, Italy, Greece, and Egypt, then returned to England. After receiving his license from the London College of Physicians, in 1842, he practiced medicine successfully at Windsor for a few years. But as his tastes ran toward theology, he entered Magdalen Hall, Oxford, in 1848, at thirty-three, graduating with a B.A. in 1852.[32] He was ordained a deacon in 1852 and an Anglican priest in 1853.[33]

Maitland served as curate at All Saints, Southampton, then at Lyndhurst, Hampshire, and Forest of Dean, Gloucestershire. While at Rome he had been impressed by the catacombs, and so wrote *The Church in the Catacombs* (1846), illustrating it with his own drawings. In 1849, in the first year of his theological course, he wrote *The Apostles' School of Prophetic Interpretation* (1849)—an attack on the Historical School of interpretation, particularly as represented by E. B. Elliott's *Horæ Apocalypticæ*.

1. STRESSES VARIANT POSITIONS OF DIFFERING SCHOOLS.— In *The Apostles' School of Prophetic Interpretation* Maitland gives a rather full history of the unfolding of prophetic interpretation from the Jewish writers before Christ[34] on through the early centuries, and into the Middle Ages.[35] But he avoids the

---

[30] *Ibid.*, pp. 120, 121.
[31] See p. 360.
[32] *Alumni Oxonienses: 1715-1886*, vol. 3, p. 903.
[33] *Dictionary of National Biography*, vol. 12, pp. 797, 798.
[34] Charles Maitland, *The Apostles' School of Prophetic Interpretation*, chap. 1.
[35] *Ibid.*, chaps. 2-4.

Reformation school of writers and, picking up Ribera's Futurism and Bellarmine's attack on the year-day principle, stresses Lacunza, and then the Futurists William Burgh and S. R. Maitland.[36]

Maitland stresses heavily the conflict among Protestant sponsors of the Historical, Preterist, and Futurist Schools of exposition.[37] He capitalizes on the marked variation on the dating of the 1260 years and other prophetic periods,[38] as well as on the identity of the little horn[39] and the two beasts of Revelation 13.[40]

2. TRACES VARIANT POSITIONS TO ORIGINATORS.—Fairly well documented, and the result of extensive investigation, Maitland's book has much of value to one who is aware of its thesis. It is quite full in the Middle Ages, especially with Joachim and the Joachimite school,[41] and the pre-Reformation Catholic writers. But Maitland holds that the "Remains of the Primitive Interpretation" were picked up by the Jesuits and Lacunza,[42] and in modern times by Maitland and Burgh, though not generally received. But he fails to note why the early writers held to literal time for the prophetic periods, and why they fixed upon an individual Antichrist, and also why many of those primitive positions were abandoned by Catholic and Protestant alike.

Maitland sketches the history of Porphyry's Antiochus Epiphanes theory of the little horn[43] and traces the idea of Mohammed, or the Turks, back to Joachim and the crusades,[44] and the "papal-antichrist and the year-day scheme" to the Cathari of the twelfth century,[45] to Eberhard and Brute. This work is helpful for reference.

IV. Futurist Tyso—Literal Time Periods Tied to Future Antichrist

A final glimpse at Futurism's demoralizing grip on one growing wing of Protestantism is afforded by JOSEPH TYSO,[46] whose *Elucidation of the Prophecies* (of Daniel and the Revelation) (1838), bears this revealing declaration on the title page:

[36] *Ibid.*, chap. 5.
[37] *Ibid.*, pp. 1-15.
[38] *Ibid.*, pp. 431-447.
[39] *Ibid.*, pp. 427-431.
[40] *Ibid.*, pp. 438, 439.
[41] *Ibid.*, p. 320.
[42] *Ibid.*, chap. 5.
[46] Biographical data lacking.
[43] *Ibid.*, pp. 427-430.
[44] *Ibid.*, pp. 430, 431.
[45] *Ibid.*, pp. 431-433.

"Shewing that the 70 weeks, the 1260 days, and the events predicted under the seven trumpets and seven vials, have not yet taken place, but that they will be accomplished within the space of about three years and a half from their commencement, and probably at no very distant period."

A frontispiece chart pictures the four empires of Daniel 2, their parallels in Daniel 7, and Medo-Persia and Greece in Daniel 8. But Tyso's scheme of dating begins the stone kingdom of Christ back at the first advent. The little horn of the fourth beast is declared to be neither the pope nor Mohammed. It is made "the Antichrist of the last days," and involves a "long interval of time" between those early events and the brief period of consummation.[47]

1. 2300 MADE LITERAL DAYS YET FUTURE.—Tyso holds that the Jews will be reinstated and will "rebuild the temple and restore the daily sacrifice." Then the Little Horn will wax great and "will take away the daily sacrifice and set up the predicted abomination, profane the sanctuary and the host and tread them under foot in contempt for 2300 literal days." [48] This will all take place in the approaching time of the end.

2. DISPARITY OF PERIOD DATINGS CAPITALIZED.—In his discussion of the seventy weeks Tyso capitalizes heavily upon the variant beginning and ending dates projected by Mede, Beverley, More, Newton, Prideau, Habershon, and others. He denies that the period had been fulfilled on the year-day principle at the first advent.[49] The three and a half "times" he makes literal years, and all the paralleling prophetic periods are likewise made literal time.[50] Again, the divergent dates of Historical School interpreters for the terminus of the 1260 year-days are paraded— ranging between 1789 and 1847.[51] And, stretching back to the proposals of Reformation expositors, they do make a diversified list, as men were but gradually beginning to perceive the appropriate beginning and ending of the period. This was inevitable.

The same procedure is followed with the different applications of the seven seals,[52] trumpets, and vials citing Bede, Bul-

[47] Joseph Tyso, *An Elucidation of the Prophecies,* p. 24.
[48] *Ibid.,* p. 24.
[49] *Ibid.,* pp. 38, 44, 45.
[50] *Ibid.,* pp. 56-65.
[51] *Ibid.,* pp. 67, 68, 78, 79.
[52] *Ibid.,* pp. 86, 87.

linger, Napier, Brightman, Mede, Poole, Godwin, Beverley, Jurieu, Fleming, Whiston, Daubuz, Faber, Frere, Fry, Scott, Cooper, Cuninghame, Keith, Habershon—and their naturally conflicting Historicist, Preterist, and Futurist expositions.[53] Likewise with the dissimilarities of the ten-horn tabulations, giving the different listings of Machiavelli, Napier, Eberhard, Brightman, Pareus, Mede, Daubuz, Newton, Whiston, Bishop Newton, Lloyd, Frere, Faber, Thorp, Cuninghame, Jurieu, Hale, Brooks—twenty-eight in all,[54] scattered over centuries. This variance is made the occasion for discarding all.

Thus the principles of Historical interpretation, built up by the cumulation of reverent scholarship of the centuries, are brushed aside by an all-comprehensive application of literalism, and by thrusting virtually all events into that brief, congested period of Antichrist's ascendancy just before the end.

V. Cardinal Manning—Issues Challenge of Inescapable Alternatives

Before taking leave of the Old World Interpreters of prophecy in this central span of the nineteenth century, we turn for a final word from Catholicism's contemporary expositor—her noted prelate, Cardinal Manning, of England. It is well to take this last fleeting look, "lest we forget"; for the basic conflict between Catholic Futurist and the Protestant Historical schools is here forcefully and inescapably portrayed. The utterly irreconcilable conflict of opposites still stands—with Catholicism consistently the same, and Protestantism seriously shorn of its testimony, confused, capitulating, and helpless when surrendering its historic ground. The battle lines are clearly drawn. And the conflict presented is fundamental. Here is Manning.

HENRY EDWARD MANNING (1808-1892), Church of England clergyman and leader of the High Church party, became a priest of the Roman Catholic Church in 1851, and a cardinal priest in 1875. He was born at Totteridge in Hertfordshire. He became

---

[53] *Ibid.*, pp. 86-100.　　　　　[54] *Ibid.*, pp. 100-113.

archdeacon of Chichester in 1840, but joined the Church of Rome a decade later. After studying at Rome Manning was made provost of Westminster in 1857, and in 1865 became archbishop of Westminster. Writing in the early sixties, Manning maintained that the independence of the Roman church dates from the time Rome was abandoned by the emperors, as they moved to the East.[55]   Later he wrote *Christ and Antichrist*.

1. ANTICHRIST HELD BACK BY ROME, PAGAN AND PAPAL.— Manning held that Antichristianism had been at work under various contradictory forms ever since apostolic times. And he added, pointedly, that "in the present array of the popular opinion of Europe against the Holy See and the Vicar of Jesus Christ, may be discerned the Antichristian instinct." [56]   According to Manning, paganism is to be restored briefly before the end of the world. And the hindering influences, which have held back the full revelation of Antichrist, he declared to be the secular power of heathen Rome and the spiritual power of the Church of Rome.[57]   Manning then makes the climactic statement that Antichrist is—

"the direct and mortal enemy of the One Holy Catholic and Roman church —the unity from which all schism is made; the sole organ of the Divine voice of the Spirit of God; the shrine and sanctuary of the Incarnation and of the continual sacrifice." [58]

2. PROTESTANT INTERPRETATION "MASTER-STROKE OF DECEIT."—In discussing the prophecy of 2 Thessalonians 2, Manning deals with its "four great facts"—the revolt, the manifestation, the hindrance, and the period of its power and persecution.[59]   After considering the first part at length, Manning asserts that Antichrist's manifestation is still future, and adds:

"Such, then, is the Revolt, which has been gathering strength these 1800 years, and ripening for the hour when it shall receive its leader and head." [60]

---

[55] Henry Edward Manning, *The Temporal Power of the Vicar of Jesus Christ* (2d ed.), pp. xxvii-xxxi, 14-16.
[56] *Ibid.*, p. 101.
[57] *Ibid.*, pp. 120-128.
[58] *Ibid.*, pp. 166, 167.
[59] *Ibid.*, pp. 82, 83.
[60] *Ibid.*, p. 103.

Then immediately he recognizes, but denies, the "universally received" historic Protestant position, completely reversing the Protestant argument:

"The interpretation universally received by Anti-catholic controversialists, whereby, first, Antichrist is held to be a spirit or system, and not a person, and next, to be the Catholic or Roman Church, or the Vicar of the Incarnate Word, is the master-stroke of deceit. It allays all fear, and inspires presumption and confidence, and fixes the attention of men to watch for the signs of his appearing any where except where they are to be seen; and draws it off from the quarter where they are already visible." [61]

3. HOLDS ANTICHRIST TO BE INDIVIDUAL JEW.—Manning identifies his future Antichrist by this description:

"That the man of sin, the son of perdition—the wicked one—is a person, in all probability, of the Jewish race; that he is to be a supplanter of the true Messias, and therefore an Antichrist in the sense of substituting himself in the place of the true." [62]

4. MOHAMMEDANISM FORERUNNER OF ANTICHRIST'S DEPREDATION.—Replying further to the question, "What is the taking away of the continual sacrifice?" of Daniel 8:11-14, Manning refers first to the morning-and-evening Jewish sacrifices in the temple, abolished by the destruction of Jerusalem. This he first applies "in type," to "the sacrifice of the Holy Eucharist, the true Paschal Lamb, which came in the place of the type—namely, the sacrifice of Jesus Himself on Calvary, renewed perpetually and continued for ever in the sacrifice on the altar." [63] Then follows a vital setting forth of the Catholic contention of relationship to the depredations of a future Antichrist for the brief period just before the world's end. But first of all he applies it initially to Mohammedanism in the East, and then to Protestantism's rejection of the mass in the West. These are described as "instalments" or "forerunners" of the actual Antichrist. Note the first application:

"Now has that continual sacrifice been taken away? That which was typical of it in old days has been already taken away. But has the reality been taken away? The Holy Fathers who have written upon the subject of Antichrist, and have interpreted these prophecies of Daniel, say that about the end of the world, during the reign of Antichrist, the public offering of

---

[61] *Ibid.*   [62] *Ibid.*, p. 117.   [63] *Ibid.*, p. 158.

the Holy Sacrifice for a little time will cease. Has there ever come to pass any thing which may be called an instalment or a forerunner of such an event as this? Look into the East. The Mahometan superstition, which arose in Arabia, and swept over Palestine and Asia Minor, the region of the Seven Churches, and Egypt, the north of Africa—the home of St. Augustine, St. Cyprian, St. Optatus—and finally penetrated into Constantinople, where soon it became dominant, has in every place persecuted and suppressed the worship and sacrifice of Jesus Christ." [64]

5. PROTESTANT ABOMINATION DESOLATES CATHOLIC SANCTUARY.—Turning to the later Protestant desecration, Manning continues his argument:

"Now let us look into the Western world: has the continual sacrifice been taken away in any other land?—for instance, in all those churches of Protestant Germany which were once Catholic, where the holy sacrifice of the Mass was daily offered?—throughout Norway, and Sweden, and Denmark, and one half of Switzerland, where there are a multitude of ancient Catholic churches—throughout England, in the cathedrals and the parish churches of this land, which were built simply as shrines of Jesus incarnate in the Holy Eucharist, as sanctuaries raised for the offering of the Holy Sacrifice? What is the characteristic mark of the Reformation, but the rejection of the Mass, and all that belongs to it, as declared in the Thirty-nine Articles of the Church of England to be blasphemous fables and dangerous deceits? The suppression of the continual sacrifice is, above all, the mark and characteristic of the Protestant Reformation." [65]

And now comes the remarkable conclusion:

"Nevertheless, this prophecy of Daniel has already its fulfillment both in the East and West,—in the two wings, as it were; while in the heart of Christendom the Holy Sacrifice is offered still. What is the great flood of infidelity, revolution, and anarchy, which is now sapping the foundations of Christian society, not only in France, but in Italy, and encompassing Rome the centre and sanctuary of the Catholic Church, but the abomination which desolates the sanctuary, and takes away the continual sacrifice?" [66]

6. EITHER MASTERPIECE OF SATAN OR KINGDOM OF GOD.—Nine years later Manning wrote *The Fourfold Sovereignty of God* (1871), in which he states that—

"the first great French Revolution was the inauguration of the reign of Antichrist, of the denial of Christian faith, of the ruin of the Christian order, of the subversion of the authority of the Church of God, both in

---

[64] *Ibid.*, pp. 158, 159.   [65] *Ibid.*, pp. 159, 160.   [66] *Ibid.*, pp. 160, 161.

public and private life; and from that day to this, the principles of turbulence and apostasy have scourged and tormented kingdoms." [67]

The point should not be lost that Manning puts the "inauguration of the reign of Antichrist" at the French Revolution, whereas the bulk of the Protestant commentators had put the end of his reign of 1260 years in this same French Revolution— the complete reversal.

Manning boasts of Romanism's universality, unity, and "1800 years of traditionary history," and then makes a challenging statement, doubtless filled with greater implication than designed, in which this issue is clearly and inescapably drawn:

"Now, a system like this [Catholicism] is so unlike anything human, it has upon it notes, tokens, marks so altogether supernatural, that men now acknowledge it to be either Christ or Antichrist. There is nothing between these extremes. Most true is this alternative. The Catholic Church is either the masterpiece of Satan or the kingdom of the Son of God." [68]

Such is the parting glimpse and alternative afforded by this noted Catholic champion in battle test with the increasingly decadent Protestant positions on prophecy.

---

[67] Henry Edward Manning, *The Fourfold Sovereignty of God*, p. 110.
[68] *Ibid.*, pp. 170, 171.

CHAPTER THIRTY-NINE

A Summary of the Evidence

I. Third Period of Pre-eminence of Prophetic Interpretation

A quick summary of the vicissitudes of prophetic interpretation through the centuries will give the setting of the nineteenth-century situation. The dawning of the nineteenth century marked the beginning of the third and final era, or period, characterized by general interest and emphasis upon prophecy. The first era of the dominance of prophecy spanned the first three or four centuries of the Christian Era. But it was submerged under the impact of direct attack upon the integrity of the actual books of Daniel and the Apocalypse, and of a flanking attack by the Latin Apostasy upon the five great determining factors in the exposition of prophecy.[1]

Those five factors were: (1) the literal resurrection of the righteous at the second advent; (2) the millennium, bounded by the two resurrections and introduced by the second advent; (3) the outline prophecies, reaching their climax at the second advent; (4) the Antichrist, emerging from the ruins of Rome, dominant during its own allotted era and destroyed at the second advent; and (5) the kingdom of God, established by divine interposition through the second advent.

Following the collapse of the initial epoch of prophetic interpretation, brought about during the fourth and fifth centuries, came the dreary Dark Ages, when men stumbled blindly in darkness without the guiding light of prophecy. Under the

---

[1] These are presented in detail in Volumes 1 and 2 of *The Prophetic Faith of Our Fathers.*

play of false concepts all five factors were distorted into a *spiritual* resurrection, a *present* millennium with Satan already bound, a *mysticized* view of the prophecies, an *individual* Jewish Antichrist in the future, and a *carnalized* kingdom of God in the form of the reigning Catholic Church.   This was effected by the great Latin apostasy.

The second era of the ascendancy, or dominance, of prophecy was during the Protestant Reformation—the sixteenth and early seventeenth centuries—introduced by pre-Reformation repudiators of the Dark Age misconceptions.   Again, the exposition of the great outline prophecies of Daniel and the Apocalypse, as reaching their climax at the second advent, came into ascendancy, marked with far greater understanding.   The Antichrist was almost universally recognized as the great papal apostasy, and the time of its doom believed to be drawing on, for the 1260 years were recognized as well advanced.   The kingdom of God, to be established by divine interposition at the advent, was again declared.   And finally, the millennium was once more properly placed in the future, to be introduced by the second advent and the literal resurrection of the dead.

But no sooner were these truths re-established than the great Catholic Counter Reformation, with its shrewd counter-systems of interpretation, struck at the militant prophetic exposition of the Reformation.   One scheme pushed the prophecies of Antichrist back into the early centuries, with the little horn as some despotic Roman emperor, and its allotted period only literal time.   The kingdom was nought but Roman Catholic Christendom, and the millennium the medieval church concept introduced by Augustine.

Tragically enough, through Protestant acceptance, these concepts began to undermine the Reformation platform.   There came a weakening and then, in the eighteenth century, a second collapse, this time of the strong Protestant stand on prophetic exposition.   And along with it appeared a captivating post-millennialism, introduced by the Protestant Whitby.   This blighting theory swept ruthlessly over Protestantism, premised on a spiritual resurrection and world conversion concept that introduced the millennium without divine intervention and put the second advent a thousand years into the future.

Such was the situation when the 1260-year era of the papal Little Horn ended in the time of the French Revolution. Then began the "time of the end," and with it the third great emphasis upon prophecy, and upon the now imminent second advent. Previously Daniel 7 had been the line of advancing study and emphasis—the four empires, with Rome the fourth; next, Rome's divisions; then the identification of the Little Horn as Antichrist; and finally the ending of its time period in the French Revolution.

Now the spotlight of interest and concern passes to that last judgment-scene phase of Daniel 7 and to the particular study of Daniel 8. Emphasis shifts from the ending of the 1260 years to the approaching close of the 2300-year period of Daniel 8:14, and its synchronous beginning with the seventy weeks of years of Daniel 9. With this was coupled the heralding of God's judgment-hour message of Revelation 14. And both of these were centered in the approaching second advent, which would raise the dead, bind the devil for the millennial period, end the great outline and time prophecies, destroy both the Papacy and Mohammedanism, and establish God's everlasting kingdom. All five factors were again ascendant. Prophetic interpretation was once more pre-eminent to a degree heretofore unknown.

Simultaneously in the different countries of the Old World, though at first centering most prominently in Great Britain— the advent message was given, the judgment hour stressed, the ending of the longest prophetic time period heralded, along with the approaching cleansing of the sanctuary. A voluminous body of literature was produced; organizations were formed for the study and proclamation of the particular message of prophecy then due. Periodicals were established, and important conferences held. Missionary travelers like Wolff hastened afar with the urgent message. There was even a stir within the ranks of Catholicism.

But alas, certain inherent weaknesses and differences developed that intensified with the years. There was tragic failure to secure unity of view and of testimony. And along with the odium brought upon the advent cause by the outbreak of the "tongues" manifestation in Irving's church, came the accentuation of differences in prophetic interpretation, the infiltration of the Catholic-born Futurist and Preterist theories, and the postponing effect of "continuationism." The proclamation of the fair and lovely advent message in the Old World began to wane, to lapse into generalities, and then into silence.

Meantime the torch that was now bedimmed in the Old World was uplifted in the New, and the message that was dying out in Britain began to swell into a mighty cry in far-off America. But that climactic development is left for the next volume of *The Prophetic Faith of Our Fathers* to portray. Such is the over-all picture of the transitions of the centuries.

II. The Prophetic Truth Whose Time Had Come

Nothing in this old earth is more powerful than a prophetic truth whose time has come. When Rome was ruling the Western world, a large group of contemporary students of prophecy recognized and proclaimed the identity and fate of the fourth prophetic world empire. When Rome was in process of tenfold division, another cluster of expositors left the written record of their perception, and their fears, of the coming Antichrist. When the papal Little Horn had unveiled its real character and identity, a great host of Reformers in many lands gave their witness to this advancing and then-present fulfillment of prophecy—so powerfully that it brought on the Counter Reformation with its clever countersystems of interpretation. When the 1260 years were ending, this solemn fact was also proclaimed on both sides of the Atlantic as then in process of fulfillment, while men awaited the next great event.

And now when the judgment hour was approaching, with the ending of prophetic time, and the time of the cleansing of the sanctuary and the imminence of the advent had come, suddenly the witness was heard in different continents and many lands, giving startlingly similar testimony and exposition of prophecy thereon—so much so that William Miller, in America, wrote in his first book, in 1836, that "one or two on every quarter of the globe have proclaimed the news, and agree in the time." [2] And yet that was two years before other ministers had definitely associated with Miller in that proclamation in America! He had definite knowledge of these men and their dominant message—more fully than we have today, for many never left a written record of their preaching or exposition that was well known then. But the attesting witness of over fifty men has been found.

To visualize the really amazing extent of the emphasis and application of the 2300 year-days in relation to the other prophecies, the accompanying tabular listing is here presented, with an explanatory note. It will repay careful scrutiny, as it portrays the powerful world character of the enunciation of the 2300-year prophecy when due. God never leaves a fundamental truth to a single witness. The table shows conclusively that this exposition was no one-man hobby or obsession, no localized emphasis. Instead, it was a world awakening upon a prophetic truth whose time had fully come.

With the coming of that hour the heralding witnesses appeared in different lands—just as they had done in the past for each truth for the time then present. And when adults refused to give it, as in Scandinavia, God placed His Spirit upon the children, that the message of the impending judgment might be given to men.

But the tabulation reveals something else—grave divergencies as well as similarities of exposition of the 2300-year prophecy. And therein is revealed the occasion of the ultimate breakdown of the great Advent Awakening in Great Britain and the Old World. The causes are not difficult to determine. But providentially, as the concepts became blurred and the voices

---

[2] William Miller, *Evidence from Scirpture* [sic] *and History of the Second Coming of Christ About the Year 1843*, p. 193.

waned in Europe, they came to the forefront in America with growing clarity, unity, and power, for the message must be heralded, as the hour of proclamation had come.

Nevertheless, the advent heralds first arose in the Old World, provided the initial literature from there, and afforded a great inspiration to other lands. Regrettably, they failed to "go on to perfection." So others caught up the strain, and the center of study and proclamation shifted to the New World, as will be seen in the concluding volume.

III. Causes of Old World Witness Breakdown

Five major factors made for the ultimate collapse of the Old World witness. These were:

1. The growing diversity of view over the integrity of the number 2300, of Daniel 8:14—whether 2300 or 2400. While the majority advocated the 2300 years and began the period synchronously with the seventy weeks of years, usually from the time of Artaxerxes, the militant adherents of the 2400-year position dated their longer span from the giving of the vision itself, without regard to, or certification from, the seventy weeks as the first segment—though they ended them approximately with the 2300-year advocates, namely, in 1847. This diversity led to increasing friction and variance.

2. The increasing division of view as to whether the last prophetic time period ended in 1844, or whether the 1335 year-days extended seventy-five years beyond the close of the 1260 years, or to about 1867. This was on the premise that the three related periods (the 1260, 1290, and 1335) began simultaneously in 533. With such proponents of the ending of the 1335 years about 1867, the 2300 years was not the grand terminal point, but only a waymark midway between the ending of the 1260 and the 1335 years, and came to lose its former significance under this emphasis of an accommodating "continuationism."

3. The wide diversity of view as to the nature of the cleansing of the sanctuary. To many, the cleansing of Jerusalem from

No.	Name	Page	Date	Dan. 2	Clay-Iron	Stone	Dan. 7	10 Horns	3 Horns	Little Horn	1260 Days	Dan. 8	2300 Days	70 Wks.	Dan. 11	1290 Days	1335 Days	2 Thes.
1	Lacunza, Man.	317	1799	4 Kgdms.	Divided Europe	Christ's Kgdm.	4 Religions	Mentioned			Years					(A Mystery)		Apostasy
2	Hales, Wm.	332	1803	B.-P.-G.-R		Christ's Kgdm.	B.-P.-G.-R	Listed	H-O-L	Papacy	620-1880		B.C. 420-1880	(27-31-34)	Papacy	70-1360	70-1405	
3	Faber, G. S.	340	1804	Standard	10 Divisions		Standard	Listed	H-O-L	Papacy	606-1866		-1866	B.C. 45B-	Papacy	622-1873	622-1917	
4	Scott, Thos.	347	1805	Standard	Secular-Eccl.	God's Kgdm.	Standard	10 Kgdms.	Ex-L-Rome	Papacy			Yrs. Are Closing	7th of Artax.	Turkey			
5	Fuller, And.	351	1810				Standard			Papacy								Papacy
6	Clarke, Adam	355	1810	Standard	Divisions	God's Kgdm.	Standard	Divisions		Popedom	Yrs.-Ending		B.C. 334-1966	7th of Artax.	Turks			
7	Toovey, Saml.	356	1813	Standard		God's Kgdm.	Standard	Listed	Ex-L-R		533-1792	P-G-R	B.C. 515-		Moham.	1260 + 30	1290 + 45	
8	Maitland, Capt.	360	1813	Standard		10 Divisions	Standard	Listed	H-O-L		533-1792	P-G-R	B.C. 515-		Moham.	1260 + 30	1290 + 45	
9	Cun.nghame, Wm.	366	1813	Standard		10 Divisions	Standard	Listed		Papacy	533-1792	P-G-R	B.C. 457-1843			533-1822	533-1867	
10	Frere, Jas. H	387	1815	Standard		Standard	Standard	10 Divisions		Papacy	533-1792	P-G-M	(B.C. 553-1847)		(In Judea)	533-1822	533-1867	Papacy
11	(Davis, W. C.)	392	1818				Standard			Papacy	588-1848	P-G-M	B.C. 453-1847	B.C. 453-37				Papacy
12	Mason, Arch.	397	1820	Standard		God's Kgdm.	Standard	10 Divisions		Papacy	533-1792	P-G-M	B.C. 457-1843	B.C. 457-33		533-1822	533-1867	Papacy
13	Brown, Jno A.	405	1823				Standard			Papacy	584-1844	P-G-M	B.C. 457-1844	B.C. 457-34				
14	Bayford, Jno.	409	1820	Standard	Divided Europe	Messiah's Kgdm.	Standard	Listed		Bp. Rome	529-1789	P-G-M	B.C. 481-1819	Years	Papacy	1260 + 30	1290 + 45	
15	Way, Lewis	418	1818	Standard	Divided Kgdms.	Christ's Kgdm.	Standard	Divisions		Papacy	531-1791		B.C. 509-1791	Years		531-1821	531-1866	
16	Gauntlett, Hen.	430	1821				Standard			Papacy	606-1866					1260 + 30	1260 + 75	
17	Drummond, Hen.	437	1830	Standard			Standard			Papacy			B.C. 453-1847			1260 + 30	1260 + 75	Papacy
18	Wolff, Jos.	471	1822	Standard		Christ's Kgdm.				Papacy	1260 Yrs.	P-G-R	B.C. 453-1847	To 1st Adv.				Papacy
19	Agier, Pierre J.	483	1823				Standard	10 Kgdms.		Chr. Rome								
20	Nicole, Alphonse	487	1829									P-G	B.C. 453-1847					
21	Fry, John	490	1822	Standard	Divisions		Standard	Listed	H-O-L	Papacy	537-1797	P-G-M	B.C. 457-1844	B.C. 457-33	Rome	537-1827	537-1872	
22	White, Thos.	500	1828								554-1814		B.C. 457-1844	B.C. 457-33		554-1844		
23	Homan, Ph.	502	1829										B.C. 457-1843					
24	Jones, Wm.	510	1830	Standard	Divisions		Standard	10 Kgdms.		Papacy	Years							Papacy
25	Irving, Edw.	520	1826	Standard		God's Kgdm.	Standard	Papal Eur.		Papacy	533-1792	P-G-R	(B.C. 553-1847)			533-1823	533-1867	Papacy
26	Stewart, J. H	528	1825							Papal Period								Papacy
27	Noel, Ger T	530	1828	Standard	10 Divisions	God's Kgdm.	Standard	10 Divisions		Papacy	533-1792							
28	Park, Jno. R.	534	1825				Standard				606-1866							
29	Cooper, Edw.	537	1825	Standard		God's Kgdm.	Standard			Papacy	533-1792	P-G-M	Years	B.C. 457-33	Rome	533-1822	533-1867	
30	Maitland, S. R.	542	1826	Future	Future	Future	Future	Not Div.	Future	Future	Days Only	Not Moh.	Literal Days			Future		Future
31	Croly, Geo	545	1827				Standard	Listed		Papacy	533-1793							
32	Vaughan, Ed. T.	548	1828	Standard		Christ's Kgdm.	Standard	10 Kgdms.		Papacy	537-1797	P-G-M	-1843					
33	Keyworth, Thos.	551	1828	Standard	10 Kgdms.		Standard	10 Kgdms.	3 Kgdms.	Papacy	606-1866	P-G-M	B.C. 457-1843	B.C. 457-33		1260 + 30	1260 + 75	
34	Addis, Alfred	557	1829	Standard	Divided Eur.	God's Kgdm.	Standard	Listed		Papacy	553-1813	P-G	B.C. 457-1843/4	B.C. 457-33	Rome	553-1843/4	1843-	Papacy
35	Begg, Jas. A.	562	1831	Standard	Intermarriages	God's Kgdm.	Standard	10 Nations		Papacy			Years		Turkey			Papacy
36	Hooper, Jno.	564	1829	Standard	Western Kgdms.	God's Kgdm.	Standard			Pope	533-1792-3		B.C. 453-1847	490 Yrs.		533-1823	533-1868	
37	Pym, Wm. W.	571	1829	Standard		God's Kgdm.	Standard			Papacy	533-1793		B.C. 453-1847	B.C. 453-37		533-1823	533-1867	
38	Allwood, Phil.	577	1829				Standard	West. Nations		Papacy	606-							
39	Hoare, Ed. N.	579	1830	Standard	10 Kgdms.	2d Advent	Standard	10 Divisions	Ex-L-R	Papacy	533-1793	P-G-M	B.C. 457-1843	B.C. 457-33				
40	Digby, Wm.	587	1831	Standard			Standard	Listed	H-O-L	Papacy	533-1793		B.C. 457-1843	B.C. 457-33				
41	Leslie, J. (Amici)	591	1831				Standard			Papacy	532-1792							
42	Lee, Saml.	596	1830		(Preterist)		(Preterist)				3½ Years			Indefinite				
43	Anderson, Wm.	597	1830			Christ's Kgdm.	Standard						B.C. 457-1843					Papacy
44	Brooks, Josh. W.	604	1831				Standard			Papacy	533-1793	P-G-M	B.C. 457-1843			1793 + 30	1793 + 75	Papacy
45	Thorp, Wm.	611	1831	Standard			Standard			Papacy	Nearly Out							Papacy
46	Wood, Lt. G. H.	615	1829				Standard			Papacy	533-1793	Moham.	, Years			533-1823	533-1868	
47	Wilson, Bp. Dan.	619	1836	Standard		God's Kgdm.	Standard			Papacy		P-G-M	B.C. 453-1847	B.C. 453-37	Papacy			Papacy
48	Keith, Alex.	623	1828	Standard			Standard			Papacy	533-1793	P-G-M	B.C. 480-1820	7th Art.-Cross	Turkey	1260 + 30		Papacy
49	Cox, John	627	1832	Standard		Christ's Kgdm.	Standard	10 Divisions		Papacy		P-G-M	Years	Turkey				Papacy
50	Sirr, Jos. d'A.	630	1833	Standard	Divisions	God's Kgdm.	Standard			Papacy								Papacy
51	Habershon, Matt.	633	1834	Standard		Christ's Kgdm.	Standard	10 Divisions		Papacy	533-1793	P-G-M	B.C. 457-1843/4	B.C. 457-33/4		1793 + 30		Papacy
52	Charlotte, Eliz.	642	1840				Standard			Papacy	(Years)							Papacy
53	Ashe, Isaac	647	1835								(-1789)							
54	Bickersteth, 'Ed.	649	1836	Standard			Standard				533-1792		B.C. 457-1844	B.C. 457-34		533-1822/3	533-1868	
55	Todd, Jas. H.	660	1840	(4th-Future)		(Futurist)	(4th-Not R.)	(Not Roman)		(Future)	(Not Yrs.)		(Days)			(Days)	(Days)	(Individual)
56	Newman, J. H.	667	1841	(Futurist)		(Cath. Ch.)				(Future)	(Days)					(Future)		(Future)
57	Gaussen, Louis	690	1837	Standard	Church-State	Christ's Kgdm.	Standard	Listed	H-O-L	Papacy	529-1789	P-G-M	Years	B.C. 457-34	Rome	529-1819	1260 + 75	Papacy
58	Richter, J. H.	702	1839	Standard	Listed	Christ's Kgdm.	Standard			Papacy	587-1847		B.C. 453-1847					Papacy
59	Birks, Th. R.	707	1843	Standard	Mingle		Standard	Listed	3 Kgdms.	Papacy	Papacy	P-G-R	B.C. 457-1843	(Years)	Rome	(Years)	(Years)	Papacy
60	Cumming, Jno.	713	1843	Standard			Standard			Papacy	532-1792	P-G	B.C. 481-1821			532-1822	532-1867	Papacy
61	Elliott, E. B.	718	1844	Standard		Christ's Kgdm.	Standard	Listed		Papacy	Just.-1798	P-G-M	B.C. 480-1820		Turkey	(Continuationist)		Papacy
62	Baylee, Jos.	728	1845	Standard	Divided Eur.	Christ's Kgdm.	Standard			Papacy	532-1792	P-G-M	B.C. 480-1820		(Years)	532-1822	532-1867/8	Papacy

Like the tabulation of "Leading Views of Principal American Writers on Prophecy" at the close of Part I, this summary of Old World Exposition epitomizes the principal positions of the nineteenth-century systematic interpreters covered in Part II. Read *horizontally,* and the teaching of each interpreter tabulated can be followed through, first on the prophecies of Daniel and then on Revelation. Read *vertically,* in the various columns, and a comprehensive view is afforded of their unity or variation of view upon each major point. The cumulative evidence is at once apparent. A study of this table, which is based on the text—with initial page noted, following each name—reveals the over-all exposition of the times.

Many minor expositors, not listed here, dealt with a few features only. Their testimony merely augments the sum total of evidence and strengthens recognized principles of interpretation—the four empires followed by the division of Rome, and these by the papal Antichrist, as Little Horn, Beast, Babylon, and Harlot, the year-day principle for all symbolic time periods, France the tenth part of the city, the 391 (or 396) years for the Turkish woe, the 2300 year-days as ending in 1843, 1844, or 1847, and the like. The angelic messengers of Revelation 14 is an added

Prophecy in 19th Century Advent Awakening

Churches	10 Days	7 Seals	4 Trumpets	5th Trump.	6th Trump.	2 Witnesses	3½ Days	1/10 of City	Rev. 12	Rev. 13 (1st B.)	Rev. 13 (2d B.)	666	Rev. 14	Rev. 16	Rev. 17	7 Heads	10 Horns	Rev. 20	7 Times (2520 Days)
			Barbarians	Saracens-150	1301-1697	Living Wit.		Christendom		Apostasy Papacy	Rom. Priests Gr. Church	Moham. Latinus			Chr. Rome			Pre-M	
			Barbarians	Saracens	1281-1672			France		Papacy	Papacy			6-Turkey	Papacy	Listed	Listed	Pre-M	
		Fall of Rome	Barbarians	612-762	1281-1672			France	Spiritual Ch.	Papacy	Hierarchy				Papacy			Pre-M	
							True Ch.	France		Papacy	Papacy			6-Turkey	Roman Ch.			Pre-M	
						2 Tests.		France	France	Papacy	France	Bonaparte		6-Turkey	Papacy	Listed	Listed	Pre-M	
		To Advent W. Rome	Barbarians	612-762 (East. Rome)	1302-1697	In Sackcloth 2 Tests.		Fr. Rev.	True Ch.	Papacy	Papacy	Lateinos	Flying	Falling	Papacy	Forms-Govt.	Listed	Pre-M	
									True Ch.	Papacy			Flying	Falling	Roman Ch.	Papacy		Pre-M	
7 Periods					1453-1844				True Ch.	Papacy	Papacy	B.C. 133-533	Flying	Falling 6-Turkey	Papacy		10 Kings	Pre-M	B.C. 604-1917
				612-762	1281-1672				Pagan R.	Papacy	Papacy	Latinus	Flying		Papacy	Listed		Pre-M	
									True Ch.				Flying		Papacy			Pre-M	
ex.-Jesuits		Early Cent. 1st-2d Adv.	Barbarians Barbarians	612-762 Saracens	1281-1672 Turks	Living Wit.			Pagan R. True Ch.	Papacy Rome	Hierarchy		Flying	Falling Falling	Papacy Papacy	Forms-Govt.		Pre-M	7 Times
		Chr. Era		Jesuits						Chr. Rome				5-Rome	Chr. Rome			Pre-M	
																		Pre-M	
			Barbarians	612-762	1453-1844 1453-1844			France		Papacy			Flying	6-Turkey	Roman Ch.			Pre-M	B.C. 677-1844
rhya.-R.C.			Barbarians Barbarians	Clergy Saracens	1453-1844 Turks Turks	2 Tests.		France	True Ch. True Ch.	Papacy Imp. R.	Hierarchy Papal R.		Flying	Falling	Papacy Papacy	Forms-Govt.	10 Kgdms. 10 Kgdms.	Pre-M Pre-M	B.C. 677-1843
		Ch. Apostasy			Turks 1453-1844	2 Tests.				Papacy Papacy	Papacy Papacy			Falling Falling	Latin Ch.	Listed	(Listed)	Pre-M Pre-M	
		Chr. Era	Barbarians	612-762 Saracens	1327-1718 Not Turk.	In Sackcloth		Not France	True Ch. Days	Papacy	Eccl. R.		Flying					Pre-M	
303-313		Chr. Era	(Papal Affliction of Church)			2 Tests.	1793-1797	France	True Ch.	Papacy	Dominicans	533-1198	Flying	Falling	Papacy	7 Hills	10 Kgdms.	Pre-M	
303-313			Barbarians	612-762 786-936	1281-1672	Living Wit.		France	Pagan R. True Ch.	Papacy	Papacy		Past	6-Turkey Ready Falling	Papacy		10 Kgdms.	Pre-M Pre-M	B.C. 680-1840
						2 Tests.		France					Flying	6-Turkey Papacy Falling	Papacy Papacy		Listed 10 Kgdms.	Pre-M Pre-M	B.C. 673-1847
										Papacy	Hierarchy		Flying	6-Turkey	Papacy			Pre-M	
		6-Fr. Rev. Early Perse. 6-Fr. Rev.	(Fall of Jews)	=3½ Times				France	True Ch. (Church)	Papacy Pagan R.			Flying	Falling	Papacy			Pre-M August.	B.C. 723-1793
								France		Papacy	Name		Flying Flying Flying	Falling Falling 6-Turkey	Papacy Papacy			Pre-M Pre-M	B.C. 677-1843
		Apostasy	Barbarians	Saracens Saracens	1057-1453 Turks	Living Wit.		France	True Ch.	Imperial Civil	Papal Papal		Warning	Falling 6-Turkey	Papacy Papacy		10 Kgdms.	Pre-M Pre-M	
rhya.-R.C.		Cover Era	Barbarians	612-762	1453-1844			France		Papacy Secular	Spiritual			6-Turkey Falling	Papacy Papacy			Pre-M	B.C. 677-1843
303-313			Barbarians	612-762 636-786	1057-1453 1053-1453			France						Falling	Papacy			Pre-M	B.C. 677-1843
hr. Era	10 Yrs.	7 Epochs	Barbarians	612-762	1057-1453			1/10 Europe	Pagan R.	Rome Civil	Papacy Eccl.				Papacy	Listed	10 Kgdms.	August Pre-M	
hr. Era	303-313			Saracens 612-762	Turks 1057-1453					Civil	Eccl.	-1843		6-Turkey	Papacy			Pre-M	B.C. 606-1843
		To Advent	Barbarians	Saracens (Mohammedanism)	1057-1453 1453-1844	Living Wit. Slain			Pagan R.	Papacy	Papacy	Lateinos	Flying	6-Turkey 6-Turkey	Papacy Papacy			Pre-M Pre-M	

feature. And the "7 Times," in the last column is likewise a new feature in prophetic exposition. Here is a key to the abbreviations employed: "B-P-G-R" indicates *Babylon, Persia, Grecia, Rome*; "Standard" means *these same four powers are taught*; "Kgdm." equals *kingdom*; "H-O-L" means *Heruli, Ostrogoths, Lombards*, and "EX-L-R" indicates *Exarchate of Ravenna, Lombardy*, and the *Principality of Rome*; "Listed" means the author *names the ten kingdoms*; "P-G-R" or "P-G-M" under Daniel 8, indicates *Persia, Grecia, Rome*, or *Persia, Grecia, Mohammedanism*—the last letter indicating the power symbolized by the exceeding Great Horn. Where period figures occur, under "Fifth Trumpet" and "Sixth Trumpet," these are always for *Saracenic* and *Turkish* Periods; "Tests." means *Testaments*, and "Wit." stands for *Witnesses*; "Ch." indicates *Church*, under Revelation 12; and "Chr." indicates *Christian*; "Pre-M" or "Post-M" stands for premillennialist or postmillennialist. The term Papacy is here used as a general equivalent for the Roman Catholic Church, or papal system, and not in the strict historical sense of the government of the church. Minor detail had, of course, to be omitted. Similar tabulations can easily be developed for these features.

Mohammedanism's pollutions seemed involved, as well as the restoration of the Jews. One of the most pronounced characteristics of the Old World Advent Awakening was belief in the restoration and conversion of the Jews. In this they differed sharply from their fellow heralds of the advent in America. This belief was tied inextricably into their prophetic concepts and expositions. Palestine must be reclaimed from Mohammedan rule, and that opposing power was regarded as variously portrayed by the horn of Daniel 8, the latter power of Daniel 11, the sixth trumpet of Revelation 9, and the vanishing Euphrates of Revelation 16. The eyes of such were increasingly fixed upon this Mohammedan concept.

4. The view of some that the threatened "judgments" of God upon the Papacy and Mohammedanism are the intent of the "judgment" to be heralded. Consequently their expectations now centered more upon the material transactions on earth than upon the second advent, with its attendant or preceding transcendent scenes.

5. The Catholic Futurist and Preterist counterinterpretations which broke the unity of Protestantism's interpretation that had existed upon the basic identification of Antichrist and the year-day principle. They effectively blunted her witness, as numerous Protestants of influence began to deny the very principles that made the Reformation possible and powerful.

These divisive factors, which prevented the essential unification, paved the way for growing misconceptions and disastrous variance. They proved the undoing of prophetic interpretation in the Old World Advent Awakening by the close of the first half of the nineteenth century. For centuries the Papacy and Mohammedanism had held sway, but with the awaited ending of the 1260-, 391-, and 2300-year prophecies past, their power diminished to the point where their former dominance was no longer possible. Mighty movements, motivated by the advent hope and based upon the prophecies, appeared and gave the warning message.

Then, when the earlier expectations did not materialize,

rationalistic theologians waxed bold and again denied that these had been inspired prophecies. They repeated the ancient argument of Porphyry that the book of Daniel had been written by some Jew in the time of the exile—with the little horn as Antiochus Epiphanes—and the quibble that the Apocalypse was produced by some presbyter named John. Thus the baleful effects of rationalistic higher criticism were added to the apathy and reaction following upon the breakdown of the Historical School of interpretation in the Old World.

IV. Judgment Message Heralded According to Schedule

The final portion of the great outline prophecies of Daniel, sealed until the specified time of the end,[3] had been opened to the understanding of men in the Old World. The wise were to understand, and now the students of prophecy had seen much of their import and declared in part the advent and judgment-hour message. No movement of this kind is to be found prior to 1798. Now the obscuring veil covering Daniel 8:14 had been lifted, and men saw the intent of the words of Daniel 8 and of Revelation 14:6, 7. Verily, the hour for understanding and proclamation had come.

This was all involved in the final verses of Daniel 7, beyond the close of the 1260 year-days of the Little Horn when "the Ancient of days did sit," and "thousand thousands ministered unto Him, and ten thousand times ten thousand stood before Him: the judgment was set, and the books were opened."[4] This portrays the judgment scene in heaven while error and evil are still at work here on earth. While the unbelieving knew not that the end is near and that the judgment is scheduled in heaven, to be followed by the second advent in glory, pious men all over the world were led to study the judgment-hour message then due, and to proclaim it with varying clarity and force, and to appeal to mankind to prepare against that day. Such was the divine purpose and plan.

---

[3] Cf. Ellen G. White, *The Acts of the Apostles*, p. 585.   [4] Dan. 7:9, 10.

This matter of the judgment hour is dealt with in three successive chapters—in Daniel 7, 8, and 9. In chapter 7 the assurance is given that the great apostasy against truth, the grievous falling away that was to follow apostolic times, and the domination of the Little Horn will at last be dealt with in the judgment review above, and Christ will be adjudged the rightful possessor of the everlasting kingdom, while the usurper will be condemned to destruction.

Next, in chapter 8, the prophet again saw in vision the historic apostasy—how it "cast down the truth to the ground; and it practised, and prospered." Truth seemed always to be trampled underfoot by error. But to the prophet's inquiry, "How long shall be the vision?" the answer was, "Unto 2300 days; then shall the sanctuary be cleansed." [5] This period, like all symbolic time periods, was of year-days, indicating when God's judgment hour would come, and when the opening of the great antitypical service of the cleansing of the sanctuary would begin. And while the verdict against sin and error was being prepared in the judgment court in heaven, the synchronous message on earth began to lift up again the truths so long trodden underfoot by tradition. Only this would answer the question, How long shall error trample upon truth without being challenged and answered from the Word? This cleansing of the sanctuary was to come in the latter day, for the angel declared, "Understand, O son of man: for at the time of the end shall be the vision." [6]

In chapter 9 the angel returns to Daniel to complete the explanation. The beginning of the 2300-year-day period has not been explained or identified. The angel begins with the time prophecy. A lesser period was "determined," or cut off, [7] from the full 2300 years and allotted to the Jewish state and people, the shorter period to lead to the times of the Messiah, when Jerusalem would fill up the cup of transgression. When this first portion of the prophetic period begins, the longer period of the 2300 years must also begin. And that would be

---

[5] Dan. 8:14.   [6] Dan. 8:12-17.   [7] Dan. 9:24.

from the command "to restore and to build Jerusalem" [8] which fell in 457 B.C.

It was this grand clue—of the seventy weeks as the first segment of the 2300 years, cut off for the Jews and climaxing with the Messiah—that burst simultaneously upon the minds of men in Europe and America, and even in Asia and Africa. This was the great advance truth that led to the emphasis upon the 2300 years from 457 B.C. to A.D. 1843 or 1844 which we have surveyed. Clearer and clearer became the perception in the first four decades of the nineteenth century, until it reached its peak in America in the summer and autumn of 1844, contemporaneously with the predicted time of the prophecy.

V. The Support of Reverent Scholarship

Attention is again drawn, in closing, to the fact that the scholastic attainments of the various expositors cited in the sketches scattered throughout these chapters, and the responsible preaching and teaching positions that they held, have been presented for this primary purpose: To indicate that the great majority of these interpreters of prophecy were graduates of various institutions of higher learning and held posts of recognized leadership in different denominational organizations; they therefore had highly trained minds and maintained well-balanced viewpoints; they were neither ignorant nor gullible; they were not given to fancy or vagary, but were sound, sensible, and stable; they were men of accomplishment, the intellectual peers of any in their day.

They ministered, moreover, to sober and sensible congregations. And they customarily continued that ministry, including the public exposition of prophecy, without serious censure or challenge. They were regarded as reputable, respectable, and representative men. And they were not confined to any one sect or denomination but were scattered through all, established churches as well as nonconformist. They were clergymen for

---

[8] Dan. 9:22 ff.

the most part, but included many laymen of conspicuous talent
and achievement. And they banded together in group study and
joint proclamation of the prophetic message.

These men were accomplished in Biblical languages, Latin,
and history, and were well acquainted with the principles of
sound exegesis. They were not inclined to catch up some fanciful or irrational theory. On the contrary, they were rather matter of fact and exacting in their scholarship. They had come
to their conclusions on the basis of substantial evidence, after
painstaking study consuming years and sometimes decades. Such
was the caliber and character of the nineteenth-century Old
World expositors of prophecy.[9]

The expressed convictions of the champions of the Historical School of prophetic interpretation are therefore entitled to
due weight, and respectful consideration. Moreover, the international character and geographical spread of its exponents is
evidence that the principles propounded must have been reasonably sensible or they would not have had such general appeal
and acceptance. (To this may be added the converse fact that
their opponents had adopted the distinctly Catholic systems
of Futurist and Preterist counterinterpretation specifically designed to thwart the Historical School of genuine prophetic
exposition. Or, they had accepted the popular postmillennial
theory of world conversion. So the issue was sharply defined.)

Bringing this impressive background to bear upon the problem of the extraordinary interest in the 2300 years which appeared for the first time in the nineteenth-century study of
prophecy, we are led to make this observation: The very fact
that the year-day principle was applied by the Historicists to all
prophetic time periods, and likewise that the 2300 days were
recognized as years by many scores of the ablest scholars, entitles
such a postulate to a respectful hearing. And, further, the

---

9 Of fifty-two leading Old World expositors whose full educational records are available,
forty-six had received the B.A. degree, and twenty-six the M.A. as well, while six had obtained
the B.D. degree, and ten had had the D.D. degree conferred on them. Five were graduates
in law, and two in medicine. Among them were three bishops, and at least five were professors
in universities or seminaries. Biographical data on others would doubtless increase the grand
total.

recognition by some fifty of these representative, trained, and often individualistic minds of the seventy weeks of years as the key to the chronological placing of the 2300 years, cannot be brushed aside as trivial and unworthy exegesis. They held firmly to the proposition that the seventy weeks of years was the first segment of time cut off from the beginning of the longer period for the Jews, and that it led to the crucifixion of the promised Messiah at His first advent.

Therefore, we may well bend our efforts to ascertaining what this remarkable prophecy really called for, and to discovering whether its impressive demands were actually met in events that may not have been recognized in the Old World at the time. This, among other features, will be pursued in the fourth volume of *The Prophetic Faith of Our Fathers*.

ACKNOWLEDGMENTS

TRIBUTE is due, first of all to the farsighted vision and generous provision of the officers and executive committee of the General Conference of Seventh-day Adventists, which made possible this extensive investigation. Faith in this project, and a sufficient annual budget, enabled the investigation to go forward with continuity for more than thirteen years. The quest not only involved intensive search throughout the great American historical archives, but included two extensive research trips abroad, in 1935 and 1938, to the great literary institutions and historical archives scattered over Continental Europe and Great Britain.

The hundreds of original source documents secured, and the thousands of supplemental photostats and microfilms obtained in these research tours, covering both Old World and New, now comprise what is known as the Advent Source Collection. Here is to be found the bulk of the documentation for all four volumes of *The Prophetic Faith of Our Fathers*. This unique library—the largest assemblage in its field ever to be brought together in one place—is housed in a special vault in the Seventh-day Adventist Theological Seminary, at Takoma Park, Washington, D.C. The value of the Collection has been enhanced, it should be added, by the fact that many of the priceless European originals, from which the photostat copies were made, have been destroyed by the desolating ravages of World War II.

Deep indebtedness is next expressed to those great American and European repositories of the book and periodical writings of men from which the majority of the sources have been obtained for this volume. While important individual items were secured from various smaller institutions and private libraries too numerous to list, the great majority of the treatises cited were consulted in, and photostatic copies obtained for study and verification from, the great libraries, historical societies, and universities hereafter listed. The uniform helpfulness of the directors, librarians, and curators of these great archives, which made this quest possible and successful, will ever be held in grateful memory. Extraordinary courtesies were so often extended as to make the investigation a joyous venture. Especial thanks is here tendered the following institutions for most of the sources for this volume:

Andover Theological Seminary, Cambridge, Mass.
American Antiquarian Society, Worcester, Mass.
Aurora College, Aurora, Ill.
Bibliothèque Nationale, Paris, France.
Bibliothèque Publique et Universitaire, Geneva, Switzerland.
Boston Athenaeum, Boston, Mass.

Boston Public Library, Boston, Mass.
British Museum, London, England.
Cambridge University, Cambridge, England.
Columbia University, New York City.
Congregational Library, Boston, Mass.
General Theological Library, New York City.
Harvard University, and its Houghton Library, Cambridge, Mass.
Huntington Library, San Marino, Calif.
John Carter Brown Library, Providence, R. I.
Kungliga Biblioteket, Stockholm, Sweden.
Library of Congress, and its Rare Book Division, Washington, D.C.
Massachusetts Historical Society, Boston, Mass.
Nationalbibliothek, Vienna, Austria.
New York Public Library, and its Reserve Division, New York City.
Oxford University, Oxford, England.
Preussische Staatsbibliothek, Berlin, Germany.
Review and Herald Library, Takoma Park, D.C.
S.D.A. Theological Seminary, Washington, D.C.
Union Catalogue and Inter-Library Loan Divisions of Library of Congress (through which single volumes have been borrowed for photostating or microfilming from libraries all over the United States and Canada).
Union Theological Seminary, New York City.
University of Glasgow, Glasgow, Scotland.

Special acknowledgment is here recorded for efficient collaboration in the quest for non-English sources. The following joined in the investigation in the respective European libraries: F. A. Dörner, in the libraries of Berlin and Vienna; Jean Vuilleumier, in the libraries of Paris; Alfred Vaucher, in the libraries of Geneva, Rome, and Torre Pellice; G. A. Lindsay, in the Royal Library at Stockholm. W. E. Read aided materially through extensive search for elusive English items in the libraries of Great Britain. Others aided in these and other libraries.

Lasting obligation is likewise recorded here for the generous time and thought given by readers of this Volume 3 in manuscript form. Their constructive suggestions have materially aided in improving the product. The importance of this venture, and its pioneering character in a relatively untouched field, as well as its contemplated use as a text and reference work, called for unusually thorough scrutiny. Indebtedness is here expressed to the following readers:

R. A. Anderson, Department of Theology, S.D.A. Theological Seminary.
H. M. Blunden, secretary Publishing Department, General Conference.
L. L. Caviness, professor of Biblical languages, Pacific Union College.
A. W. Cormack, associate secretary, General Conference.
C. B. Haynes, secretary, War Service Commission.
F. D. Nichol, editor, *Review and Herald*, Washington, D.C.
A. W. Peterson, secretary, Missionary Volunteer Department.

W. E. Read, former president, Northern European Division.

D. E. Rebok, president, S.D.A. Theological Seminary.

D. E. Robinson, E. G. White Publications staff.

A. W. Spalding, director of Social Service, Madison College.

W. H. Teesdale, former professor of history, Pacific Union College.

M. R. Thurber, book editor, Review & Herald Publishing Association.

H. A. Washburn, former professor of history, Pacific Union College.

Appreciation is also expressed to these special readers of technical sections: To A. Vaucher, principal, Séminaire Adventiste, Collonges, Haute-Savoie, France, on Lacunza; to G. A. Lindsay, president of the East Nordic Union; L. K. Tobiassen, former editor, *Tidens Tale*, Oslo, Norway; O. C. Granlund, editor, *Sions Vaktare*, Brookfield, Illinois; G. E. Nord, secretary of the Scandinavian Department of Bureau of Home Missions, and R. W. Engström, Swedish minister, Greater New York Conference, on the child preachers of Sweden; and to A. V. Olson, former president, and W. R. Beach, president of the Southern European Division, Bern, Switzerland, on Louis Gaussen.

Because of the technical nature of the work, extraordinary measures have been taken by the publishers not only to verify all direct quotations and indirect references, but to check the context as well as all pertinent facts and dates cited. This task, extending over many months, has been most competently done by M. R. Thurber, book editor of the Review and Herald Publishing Association, and his efficient assistants.

Finally, to those faithful "ground forces," so often unsung because usually unseen—secretaries, copy editors, proofreaders, artists, and printers who have all contributed to the mechanical excellence of the finished product—this acknowledgment is gratefully extended.

Bibliography

This list does not include hundreds of works alluded to, and often named in the text, but not specifically cited. It is virtually confined to those works for which specific credit appears in the footnotes.

1. Check List on Early American Prophetic Works.—The greatest single help to checking the works published in America prior to the nineteenth century is Charles Evans' twelve-volume *American Bibliography.* (Chicago: The Author, 1903-1934.) Listing 35,854 titles between 1639 and 1799, this giant bibliographical monument of exacting scholarship provides a faithful reflector of colonial times, as well as the early national period following.

Giving full name of author and full title of each book, then place, publisher, date, size, and edition, Evans' work provides an invaluable tabulation of most volumes in the field of our special quest. Chronological in arrangement, and with topical, title, author, and publisher indexes and cross references, it is unique for tracing literature in special categories. Since it is based on the holdings of all the leading American libraries and historical societies, few titles escaped inclusion.

The earliest American titles were, of course, published in the Old World. The early American presses, when they began to operate, were limited in number and capacity, and many works by colonial authors still continued to be printed in old England. There were but 648 American imprints in the seventeenth century. In fact, there were but 3,244 printed titles between 1639 and 1729. (Lawrence C. Wroth, "Evans' American Bibliography a Matrix of Histories," in Charles Evans, *American Bibliography, 1639-1729*, 4th preliminary leaf, recto Boston: C. E. Goodspeed and Co., 1943. A special edition of Evans' first volume in the Rare Book Collection of the Library of Congress.) The proportionate number, therefore, that bear upon prophecy is truly remarkable. And as ministers led in much of the literature of the day, their books, and printed convention, election, fast day, thanksgiving, and regular sermons, provide a faithful portrayal of the times. Their interpretations of prophecy are the more conspicuous because of the authoritative place occupied by the preacher. The American Antiquarian Society of Worcester, Mass., has the largest single collection of all Americana prior to 1820, comprising some 70 per cent of all titles.

It may pertinently be added that the history of the colonial American town was in large measure that of its churches; and in turn, the history of the churches was essentially that of their clergy. Ministers were usually the leaders not only in theology, but in education, law, medicine, and often in politics. Their training may be judged by the fact that nine tenths of the colonial clergy of Massachusetts were college graduates, and the others were privately tutored by college-trained men. It is also interesting to note that in New England three quarters of the ministry were Congregational. So says Dr. Weis, whose two volumes on colonial clergy are mines of biographical information for this period. (Frederick L. Weis, *The Colonial Clergy and the Colonial Churches of New England* [1620-1776]. Lancaster, Mass.: [Society of the Descendants of the Colonial Clergy], 1936. *The Colonial Churches and the Colonial Clergy of the Middle and Southern Colonies.* Lancaster, Mass.: [Society of the Descendants of the Colonial Clergy], 1938.)

2. Check Lists on Old World Prophetic Works.—Copies of the majority of the prophetic works of the Old World Advent Awakening are to be found in the British Museum and the university libraries of Oxford, Cambridge, Glasgow and Dublin. Some, however, were found only in the Staatsbibliothek of Berlin the Bibliothèque Nationale of Paris, the Bibliothèque Publique et Universitaire of Geneva, and the great libraries of America. The most complete and helpful single check list of Old World expositions was compiled in 1835 by Joshua W. Brooks, editor of *The Investigator*, in his *Dictionary of Writers on the Prophecies, With the Titles and Occasional Descriptions of Their Works*. (London: Simpkin, Marshall and Co., 1835.) The next best is doubtless the briefer list of Edward Bickersteth in *A Practical Guide to the Prophecies*, pp. 364-391. (London: R. B. Seeley and W. Burnside, 1836.)

3. Page Citations Listed in Bibliography.—Because of the extraordinarily large number of sources and authorities cited in the Bibliography, book and periodical titles, with accompanying references, are not repeated in the Index. The page references for the works cited therefore appear *only in the Bibliography*. As sources predominate in this list, the relatively few authorities have not been segregated—the publishing dates serving to distinguish them. Periodicals and manuscripts are listed separately.

BOOKS

Adams, Charles Francis. *Three Episodes of Massachusetts History*. Boston and New York: Houghton, Mifflin and Company, 1893. 2 vols. See p. 115.

Adams, James Truslow. *Provincial Society, 1690-1763*. New York: The Macmillan Company, 1938. (*A History of American Life*, vol. 3.) See pp. 29, 31, 32, 135, 141, 142, 159, 165, 166.

Addis, Alfred. *Heaven Opened, or, The Word of God: Being the Twelve Visions of Nebuchadnezzar, Daniel, and St. John*. London: Joseph Robins, 1829. See pp. 550, 556-560.

Advent Sermons on Antichrist. In *Tracts for the Times*, vol. 5, no. 83. See pp. 664, 665.

[Agier, Pierre-Jean]. *Commentaire sur l'Apocalypse, par l'auteur des explications des psaumes et des prophètes*. Paris: J.-M. Eberhart, 1823. 2 tomes. [Author identified in Paris Bibliothèque Nationale catalogue.] See pp. 483-485.

Allen, Joseph Henry, and Richard Eddy. *A History of the Unitarians and the Universalists in the United States*. New York: The Christian Literature Company, 1894. (*The American Church History Series*, vol. 10.) See p. 191.

Allgemeine deutsche Biographie. Leipzig: Verlag von Duncker & Humblot, 1875-1912. 56 vols. See p. 702.

Allibone, Samuel Austin. *A Critical Dictionary of English Literature and British and American Authors*. Philadelphia: J. B. Lippincott Company, 1902. 3 vols. See pp. 337, 339.

Allwood, Philip. *A Key to the Revelation of St. John, the Divine*. London: C. J. G. & F. Rivington, 1829. 2 vols. See pp. 577, 578.

Alumni Cantabrigienses. See Cambridge University.

Alumni Dublinenses. See Dublin University.

Alumni Oxonienses. See Oxford University.

Ambrose, Isaac. *Christ in the Clouds Coming to Judgment*. Boston: John Boyle, [1786]. See p. 194.

The American Church History Series. Edited by Philip Schaff, and others. New York: The Christian Literature Company, 1893-1897. 13 vols. See pp. 23, 191.

Anderson, William. *An Apology for Millennial Doctrine; in the Form in Which It Was Entertained by the Primitive Church*. 2 parts. Glasgow: Maurice Ogle, 1830-1831. See pp. 561, 592, 597, 598.

Anjou, Lars Anton. *The History of the Reformation in Sweden.* Translated from the Swedish by Henry M. Mason, D.D. New York: General Protestant Episcopal Sunday School Union and Church Book Society, 1859. **See p. 673.**

Armitage, Thomas. *A History of the Baptists.* New York: Bryan, Taylor & Co., 1887. **See p. 48.**

Ashe, Isaac. *The Book of Revelation With Compendious Notes.* Dublin: William Curry Jun. and Company, 1835. **See p. 647.**

Aspinwall, William. *A Brief Description of the Fifth Monarchy, or Kingdome, That Shortly Is to Come Into the World. . . . And in the Conclusion There Is Added a Prognostick of the Time When This Fifth Kingdome Shall Begin.* London: Printed by M. Simmons, . . . sold by Livewell Chap man, 1653. **See p. 88.**

Austin, David. *The Downfall of Mystical Babylon; or, A Key to the Providence of God, in the Political Operations of 1793-4. . . . A discourse.* [N.p., 1798.] **See p. 241.**

————. *The Millennium, or Thousand Years of Prosperity, Promised to the Church of God.* Elizabeth Town, [N.J.]: Printed by Shepard Kollock, 1794. **See pp. 240, 241.**

[————]. *A Prophetic Leaf . . . by a Friend to the Truth.* New Haven: Printed for the Author, 1798. [Author identified in Evans, *op. cit.,* vol. 12, no. 33341.] **See p. 242.**

Backus, Isaac. *A History of New England With Particular Reference to . . . Baptists.* 2d ed., with notes. Newton, Mass.: The Backus Historical Society, 1871. 2 vols. **See pp. 79, 81-83, 213.**

————. *The Infinite Importance of the Obedience of Faith, and of Separation From the World.* 2d ed. Boston: Samuel Hall, 1791. **See pp. 213, 214.**

————. *The Testimony of the Two Witnesses, Explained and Improved* Providence: Printed by Bennett Wheeler, and sold by James Arnold, Esq. and the Printer, 1786. **See pp. 214, 215.**

Baird, Robert. Biographical sketch in Samuel Gobat, *Journal of Three Years' Residence in Abyssinia,* pp. vii-xviii. New York: M. W. Dodd, 1850. **See p. 486.**

Baptist Confession or Declaration of Faith. See *A Brief Confession.*

Barber, John Warner. *Connecticut Historical Collections.* New Haven: Durrie & Peck, and J. W. Barber, [1846]. **See p. 215.**

Bateman, Josiah. *The Life of Daniel Wilson, D.D.* Boston: Gould and Lincoln, 1860. **See p. 617.**

Bates, M. Searle. *Religious Liberty: An Inquiry.* New York and London: International Missionary Council, 1945. **See pp. 203-205.**

Baxter, Robert. *Irvingism, in Its Rise, Progress, and Present State.* 2d ed. London: James Nisbet and Co., 1836. **See pp. 409, 437, 515, 525, 526.**

Bayford, John. *Messiah's Kingdom, or, a Brief Inquiry Concerning What Is Revealed in Scripture, Relative to the Fact, the Time, the Signs, and the Circumstances of the Second Advent of the Lord Jesus Christ.* London: Printed for the Author by F. Marshall, 1820. **See pp. 409-413.**

Baylee, Joseph. "The Kingdoms of Europe Viewed in the Light of Scripture," in *The Signs of the Times: . . . Six Lectures.* Part 1, pp. 96-124. London: Wertheim and Macintosh, 1854. **See pp. 728-730.**

Bayly, Thomas. See Thomas Parker, *The Visions and Prophecies of Daniel.*

Beard, Charles A. and Mary R. *The Rise of American Civilization.* New ed., rev. and enl. New York: The Macmillan Company, 1936. 2 vols. in 1. **See pp. 21, 28, 30, 135, 141, 148, 181, 182.**

[Begg, James A.]. *A Connected View of Some of the Scriptural Evidence of the Redeemer's Speedy and Personal Return.* 2d ed. London: James Nisbet, 1830. [Author identified in Wm. Fulton, "A Memorial Discourse," part 1, *The Sabbath Recorder*, May 13, 1869, p. 77.] See pp. 560, 562-564.

————. *An Examination of the Authority for a Change of the Weekly Sabbath at the Resurrection of Christ; Proving That the Practice of the Church in Substituting the First Day of the Week, for the Appointed Seventh Day, Is Unsanctioned by the New Testament Scriptures.* Glasgow: The Author, 1850. See p. 561.

Bellamy, Joseph. "The Millennium." See his *Sermons Upon the Following Subjects*. See pp. 145, 196, 197.

————. *Sermons Upon the Following Subjects, viz. The Divinity of Jesus Christ, the Millennium, the Wisdom of God, in the Permission of Sin.* Boston: Edes and Gill, and S. Kneeland, 1758. See pp. 145, 196, 197.

Ben-Ezra, Juan Josafat. See Lacunza.

Bicheno, James. *The Signs of the Times, in Three Parts.* A New Edition; With . . . An Appendix. London: Johnson [etc.], 1799. See p. 272.

Bickersteth, Edward. *A Practical Guide to the Prophecies.* 5th ed., enlarged. London: R. B. Seeley and W. Burnside, 1836.

————. Same, in *The Works of the Rev. Edward Bickersteth,* vol. 8; London Seeleys, 1853. See pp. 649-652.

Birks, T[homas] R. *First Elements of Sacred Prophecy.* London: William Edward Painter, 1843. See pp. 385, 540, 707-710.

————. *The Four Prophetic Empires.* London: Seeley, Burnside, and Seeley, 1845. See pp. 707, 710-712.

————. *Memoir of the Rev. Edward Bickersteth.* New York: Harper & Brothers, 1851. 2 vols. See pp. 648, 649.

————. *The Two Later Visions of Daniel.* London: Seeley, Burnside, and Seeley, 1846. See pp. 707, 712.

Boase, Frederic. *Modern English Biography.* Truro, [England]: Netherton and Worth, 1892-1921. 6 vols. Cited *passim.*

The Book of the General Lavves [or *Lauues*] *and Libertyes.* See Massachusetts.

[Bradstreet, Anne]. *The Tenth Muse . . . By a Gentlewoman.* London: Stephen Bowtell, 1650. See pp. 56-59.

————. *The Works of Anne Bradstreet.* Ed. by John H. Ellis. New York: Peter Smith, 1932. See pp. 55, 57, 59.

A Brief Confession or Declaration of Faith: Set forth by many of us who are (falsely) called Ana-Baptists. London: F. Smith, 1660. Also in broadside form, with "(Lately Presented to King Charles the Second)" included in the title. See pp. 83, 84.

Brigham, Clarence S. "Bibliography of American Newspapers, 1690-1820," part 3, in *Proceedings of the American Antiquarian Society,* New Series, April, 1915 (vol. 25, part 1), pp. 128-293. Worcester, Massachusetts: The Society, 1915. See p. 117.

Brock, Mourant. *Glorification.* London: J. Nisbet & Co., 1845.

————. Same. Boston: American Millennial Association, [1845].

————. Same. Boston: Joshua V. Himes, 1847. (Second Advent Library, New Series, No. 3.) See pp. 705, 706.

[Brooks, Joshua W.] compiler. *A Dictionary of Writers on the Prophecies,* compiled by the Editor of *The Investigator.* London: Simpkin, Marshall and Co., 1835. [Author identified by the British Museum catalogue.] See pp. **63, 378, 501, 600, 603, 604, 607.**

————. *Elements of Prophetical Interpretation.* London: R. B. Seeley and W. Burnside, 1836. See pp. **604-606.**

———— *Essays on the Advent and Kingdom of Christ and the Events Connected Therewith* (Originally Published in *The Investigator of Prophecy* Under the Signature of Abdiel). Reprint in *The Literalist,* vols. **1, 4** (i.e. [1], 2). Philadelphia: Orrin Rogers, 1840-1841. See p. **604.**

————. Same. 4th ed., enlarged. London: Simpkin, Marshall and **Co.,** 1843. See p. **605.**

————. *First Series of Lectures on Subjects Connected With Prophecy.* See Edinburgh Association for Promoting the Study of Prophecy.

[Brough, J. C. S.]. *The Centenary of Regent Square, 1827-1927. One Hundred Years of a. Presbyterian Congregation.* [London: Regent Square Presbyterian Church? 1927.] See p. **516.**

Brown, John Aq[uila]. *The Even-Tide; or, Last Triumph of the Blessed and Only Potentate, The King of Kings, and Lord of Lords; Being a Development of the Mysteries of Daniel and St. John.* London: J. Offor, 1823. 2 vols. See pp. **276, 290, 404-407.**

————. *The Jew, The Master-Key of the Apocalypse; in Answer to Mr. Frere's "General Structure," and the Dissertations of the Rev. Edw. Irving, and Other Commentators.* London: Hatchard and Son, 1827. See pp. **276, 404, 405, 407, 408.**

Buck, Charles. *A Theological Dictionary.* 3d ed. London: The Author, 1811. 2 vols. See pp. **337, 338, 638.**

Budington, William I. *The History of the First Church, Charlestown,* [Mass.], in nine lectures, with notes. Boston: Charles Tappan, 1845. See p. **188.**

Bulkeley, Peter. *The Gospel-Covenant; or The Covenant of Grace Opened.* London: M.S. for Benjamin Allen, 1646. See p. **67.**

Burgh, William. *The Apocalypse Unfulfilled.* 2d ed. Dublin: Richard M. Tims, 1833. See pp. **658, 659.**

————. *Lectures on the Second Advent of Our Lord Jesus Christ.* 2d ed., enlarged. Dublin: William Curry, Jun. and Company, 1835. See pp. **658, 659.**

[Burnet, William]. *An Essay on Scripture-Prophecy; Wherein It Is Endeavoured to Explain the Three Periods Contain'd in the XIIth Chapter of the Prophet Daniel. With Some Arguments to Make It Probable, That the First of the Periods Did Expire in the Year 1715.* [New York]: Printed [by W. Bradford] in the year 1724. See pp. **152, 169-171.**

Burr, Aaron. *The Watchman's Answer to the Question, What of the Night.* 2d ed. Boston: S. Kneeland, 1757. See pp. **198-200, 206.**

Butler, Clement Moore. *The Reformation in Sweden.* New York: Anson D. F. Randolph and Company, 1883. See p. **673.**

Butsch, Bishop J. A. Circular letter from the Consistory in Skara, on the so-called preaching sickness (German version), appendix to *Einiges über die rufenden Stimmen, . . . von einem Augenzeugen,* pp. 39-50. Leipzig: Leopold Michelsen, 1843. See pp. **683, 686.** See also same entry in the periodical section, p. 786.

The Cambridge History of American Literature. Edited by William Peterfield Trent, and others. New York: G. P. Putnam's Sons, 1917-1921. 4 vols. See p. **126.**

Cambridge University. *Alumni Cantabrigienses; . . . From the Earliest Times to 1900.* Compiled by John Venn . . . and J. A. Venn. Cambridge: The University Press, 1922. **See p. 577.**

—————. Trinity College. *Admissions to Trinity College, Cambridge.* Edited by W. W. Rouse Ball and J. A. Venn. London: Macmillan and Co., Limited, 1911-1916. 5 vols. **See 548, 556.**

Campbell, Helen. *Anne Bradstreet and Her Time.* Boston: D. Lothrop Company, [1891]. **See p. 55.**

Campbell, J[ohn] M['Leod]. *The Everlasting Gospel; Notes of a Sermon* (taken in shorthand). Greenock, [Scotland]: R. B. Lusk, 1830. **See p. 595.**

Cannon, Carl L. *American Book Collectors and Collecting From Colonial Times to the Present.* New York: The H. W. Wilson Company, 1941. **See p. 172.**

Carlyle, Thomas. "The Death of the Rev. Edward Irving," *Critical and Miscellaneous Essays,* vol. 4, pp. 79-83. Boston: James Munroe and Company, 1839. 4 vols. [First published anonymously in *Fraser's Magazine,* January, 1835, pp. 101-103.] **See p. 517.**

The Catholic Encyclopedia. New York: Robert Appleton Company, 1907-1914. 15 vols. and Index. **See pp. 311, 313.**

Caulfeild, Charles A. *The Fall of Babylon, as Exhibited in Prophecy.* Dublin: John Robertson, 1839. **See pp. 652, 653.**

The Century Cyclopedia of Names. New York: The Century Company, 1906. (*The Century Dictionary and Encyclopedia,* vol. 9.) **See p. 36.**

Charlotte Elizabeth. See [Tonna] Charlotte Elizabeth.

Chatterton, Bishop Eyre. *History of the Church of England in India Since the Early Days of the East India Company.* London: Society for Promoting Christian Knowledge, 1924. **See p. 619.**

Chauncy, Charles. *The Late Religious Commotions in New-England Considered.* Boston: Green and Russell, 1757. **See pp. 152, 160, 161.**

[—————]. *The Mystery Hid From Ages . . . or, The Salvation of All Men.* London: Charles Dilly, 1784. [Identified as Charles Chauncy in Joseph H. Allen and Richard Eddy, *op. cit.,* pp. 382, 383.] **See pp. 191, 192.**

—————. *A Sermon Occasioned by the Late Earthquakes in Spain and Portugal.* Boston: Edes & Gill, 1756. **See p. 191.**

Cheever, Ezekiel. *Scripture Prophecies Explained, in Three Short Essays.* Boston: Green and Russell, 1757. **See pp. 152, 160, 161.**

Chéseaux, Jean Philippe Loys de. "Remarques historiques, chronologiques, et astronomiques, sur quelques endroits du Livre de Daniel," in *Memoires posthumes de Monsieur Jean Philippe Loys de Cheseaux . . . sur divers sujets, d'astronomie et de mathematiques avec de nouvelles tables très exactes des moyens mouvemens du soleil & de la lune.* Lausanne: Antoine Chapuis, 1754. **See pp. 382-384.**

Clarke, Adam. *The Holy Bible, Containing the Old and New Testaments . . . With a Commentary and Critical Notes.* New edition, with the author's final corrections. New York: Lane & Scott, 1850-1851. 6 vols. **See pp. 355, 356.**

Clark[e], John. *Ill Newes From New-England: or A Narative of New-Englands Persecution.* London: Henry Hills, 1652. **See pp. 79-82.**

Clarke, Richard. *The Prophetic Numbers of Daniel and John Calculated; In Order to Shew the Time, When the Day of Judgment . . . Is to Be Expected.* Charles-town, (South-Carolina), Printed. Boston: Edes and Gill, and Green and Russell, . . . 1759. **See pp. 201, 202.**

Cobb, Sanford H. *The Rise of Religious Liberty in America.* New York: The Macmillan Company, 1902. **See p. 141.**

Confession of Faith Owned and Consented Unto by the Elders and Messengers of the Churches Assembled at Boston in New-England, May 12, 1680. Being the Second Session of That Synod. Boston: John Foster, 1680. **See pp. 111, 125, 152.**

Congressional Globe (25th Cong., 2d sess.), Dec. 18, 1837, proceedings of the House of Representatives, Dec. 15, 1837, pp. 29, 30. Washington: Globe Office, 1838. **See p. 479.**

Continental Society for the Diffusion of Religious Knowledge. *First Report,* 1819. London: J. Haddon, [1819]. **See pp. 440, 441.**

————. *Second Report,* [1820]. **See p. 441.**

————. *Proceedings,* Fourth Year, 1821-1822. **See pp. 441-443.**

———— *Proceedings,* Eighth Year, 1825-1826. London: A. Macintosh, 1826. **See pp. 440, 443, 445, 446.**

————. *Proceedings* . . . Eleventh Anniversary, [1829]. **See p. 446.**

————. *Proceedings* . . . Twelfth Year, 1829-30. **See pp. 446, 447.**

———— *Proceedings of the European Missionary Society, Formerly Designated "The Continental Society."* Eighteenth Year, 1835-6. **See pp. 447-449.**

Cooper, Edward. *The Crisis.* 1st American from the 3d London ed. Cincinnati: Morgan, Fisher, and L'Hommedieu, 1827. **See pp. 537-539.**

Cooper, Samuel. *A Discourse on the Man of Sin.* Boston: Greenleaf, 1774. (Dudleian Lecture, 1773.) **See pp. 174, 179, 180.**

Cotton, John. *The Bloudy Tenent, Washed, and Made White in the Bloud of the Lambe.* London: Matthew Symmons for Hannah Allen, 1647. **See pp. 36, 38, 42, 50, 53.**

[————] compiler. *An Abstract or [sic] the Lawes of New England as They Are Novv Established.* London: F. Coules and W. Ley, 1641. **See p. 35.**

————. *The Churches Ressurrection, or the Opening of the Fift and Sixt Verses of the 20th Chap. of the Revelation.* London: R. O. and G. D. for Henry Overton, 1642. **See pp. 36, 39, 40.**

————. *An Exposition Upon the Thirteenth Chapter of the Revelation.* . . . *Taken from his mouth in Short-writing.* London: Printed for Livewel Chapman, 1655. **See pp. 36-39, 56.**

————. *The Powring Ovt of the Seven Vials: or an Exposition, of the 16. Chapter of the Revelation.* London: Printed for R. S. . . . sold at Henry Overton's shop, 1642. **See pp. 36, 40-42.**

Cox, John. *A Millenarian's Answer of the Hope That Is in Him.* Reprint in *The Literalist,* vol. 2 (i.e. 1). Philadelphia: Orrin Rogers, 1840. **See pp. 626, 628, 629.**

————. *Thoughts on the Coming and Kingdom of Our Lord Jesus Christ.* Reprint in *The Literalist,* vol. 5 (i.e., 3). Philadelphia: Orrin Rogers, 1842. **See pp. 626-628.**

Croly, George. *The Apocalypse of St. John.* London: C. & J. Rivington, 1827. **See pp. 544-548.**

————. *Popery The Antichrist. A Sermon.* London: John Kendrick, 1848. **See p. 544.**

Crowe, William. *An Exact* . . . *Catalogue of Our English Writers on the Old and New Testament.* London: R. Davenport for John Williams, 1668. **See p. 61.**

Cumming, John. *Apocalyptic Sketches.* New ed. London: Arthur Hall, Virtue, and Co., 1858. 3 vols. See pp. 713, 715.

————. *Behold, the Bridegroom Cometh. The Last Warning Cry.* London: James Nisbet & Co., 1865. See pp. 713, 716.

————. *The Great Preparation; or, Redemption Draweth Nigh.* First Series. New York: Rudd & Carleton, 1860. See pp. 713, 715, 716.

————. *The Great Tribulation; or, The Things Coming on the Earth.* Third thousand. London: Richard Bentley, 1859. See pp. 713, 715.

————. *The Signs of the Times. A Lecture . . . Delivered Before the Young Men's Christian Association.* London: Arthur Hall, Virtue & Co., 1854. See pp. 713-715.

————. *The Sixth Vial: A Sermon for the Times.* London: Thomas Brooks, 1843. See pp. 713, 714.

————. *The Sounding of the Last Trumpet.* London: James Nisbet & Co., 1867. See pp. 713, 716.

Cuningham, Charles E. *Timothy Dwight, 1752-1817, A Biography.* New York: The Macmillan Company, 1942. See pp. 243, 244.

Cuninghame, William. *The Apostasy of the Church of Rome, and the Identity of the Papal Power With the Man of Sin and Son of Perdition of St. Paul's Prophecy.* Glasgow: M. Ogle, 1818. [For 2d ed., see next title.] See pp. 365, 368, 373.

————. *The Church of Rome the Apostasy, and the Pope the Man of Sin and Son of Perdition of St. Paul's Prophecy.* With an appendix containing an examination of the Rev. W. Burgh's attempt to vindicate the Papacy from these charges. 2d ed. Glasgow: J. Smith & Son, [1833]. [2d ed. of the preceding title.] See p. 373.

————. *A Critical Examination of Some of the Fundamental Principles of the Rev. George Stanley Faber's Sacred Calendar of Prophecy.* London: T. Cadell, 1829. See p. 366.

————. *A Dissertation on the Seals and Trumpets of the Apocalypse; and the Prophetical Period of Twelve Hundred and Sixty Years.* London: J. Hatchard, 1813. See pp. 274, 278, 365-372.

————. *The Fulness of the Times: Being an Analysis of the Chronology of the Greek Text of the Seventy.* London: James Nisbet & Co., 1836. See p. 373.

————. *On the Jubilean Chronology of the Seventh Trumpet of the Apocalypse and the Judgment of the Ancient of Days, Daniel VII. 9.* Glasgow: John Smith & Son, 1834. See pp. 381, 385.

————. *The Political Destiny of the Earth, as Revealed in the Bible.* Reprint in *The Literalist,* vol. 2 (i.e. 1), Philadelphia: Orrin Rogers, 1840.

————. Same. 3d ed. London: J. Nisbet & Co., 1842. See pp. 373-376.

————. *The Pre-Millennial Advent of Messiah Demonstrated From the Scriptures,* 3d ed. London: James Nisbet & Co., 1836. See pp. 373, 375.

————. *The Scheme of Prophetic Arrangement of the Rev. Edward Irving and Mr. Frere Critically Examined.* London: Thomas Cadell, 1826. See pp. 275, 278, 376, 377, 379-381, 404.

Currier, John J. *History of Newbury, Mass. 1635-1902.* Boston: Damrell & Upham, 1902. See p. 67.

Cushing, William. *Initials and Pseudonyms. A Dictionary of Literary Disguises.* New York: Thomas Y. Crowell & Co., 1885. See p. 365.

Dalton, Hermann. *Johannes Gossner.* Berlin: Verlag des Gossnerischen Missionsvereins, 1878. **See p. 298.**

Daly, Robert, Personal Recollections of. See Madden, Mrs. Hamilton.

Davenport, John. "An Epistle to the Reader," in *The Mystery of Israel's Salvation, Explained and Applyed,* by Increase Mather, sigs. A₂r-A₇r. [London: Allen], 1669. **See pp. 25, 87.**

————. *The Knowledge of Christ Indispensably Required of All Men That Would Be Saved . . . in Sundry Sermons on Acts 2:36.* London: L. Chapman, 1653. **See pp. 86-88.**

————. *The Saints Anchor-Hold in All Storms and Tempests.* London: Benj. Harris, 1701. [Signed D. J.; author identified in Sabin's *Dictionary,* vol. 5, p. 238.] **See pp. 25, 86.**

Davis, William C. *The Millennium, or a Short Sketch of the Rise and Fall of Antichrist.* Workington, [England]: William Bell, 1818. **See pp. 290, 391-396.**

Davis, W[illiam] C. *A Treatise on the Millennium.* Yorkville, S.C.: Printed at the Advocate Office, 1827. **See p. 392.**

Dexter, Franklin B. *Biographical Sketches of the Graduates of Yale College.* New York: Henry Holt and Company, 1885-1912. 6 vols. **See pp. 182, 236.**

Dialogues on Prophecy. See Drummond, Henry.

Dictionary of American Biography. New York: Charles Scribner's Sons, 1943. 20 vols. and index. Cited *passim.*

The Dictionary of National Biography. London: Oxford University Press, 1921-1922. 22 vols.

Same. London: Smith, Elder, & Co., 1885-1900. 63 vols. **See p. 423.**

Dictionnaire Historique & Biographique de la Suisse. Neuchatel, [Switzerland]: Administration du Dictionnaire Historique et Biographique de la Suisse, 1921-1933. 7 vols. **See pp. 486, 487.**

Digby, William. *A Treatise on the 1260 Days of Daniel and Saint John: Being an Attempt to Establish the Conclusion That They Are Years; and Also to Fix the Date of Their Commencement and Termination.* Dublin: R. M. Tims, 1831. **See pp. 587-590.**

Doane, George Washington. *The Apostolical Commission, the Missionary Charter of the Church: The Sermon at the Ordination of Mr. Joseph Wolff.* Burlington, N.J.: J. L. Powell, Missionary Press, 1837. **See p. 463.**

Drummond, Henry. *Introduction to the Study of the Apocalypse.* London: L. B. Seeley, 1830. **See pp. 436-438.**

[Drummond, Henry, Edward Irving, and others]. *Dialogues on Prophecy.* London: James Nisbet, 1828-1829. 3 vols. [Authors identified in British Museum catalogue; also Brooks, *Dictionary,* p. lxxi, xcvi.] **See pp. 277, 379, 407, 409, 437, 450, 452, 455-460.**

Dublin University. Trinity College. *Alumni Dublinenses* (Trinity College, 1593-1860). Edited by George Dames Burtchaell and Thomas Ulick Sadleir. New edition (with supplement). Dublin: Alex. Thom & Co., Ltd., 1935. **See pp. 408, 587, 630, 646, 652.**

[Dudley, Paul]. *An Essay on the Merchandize of Slaves & Souls of Men, Revel. XVIII. #13. With an Application Thereof to the Church of Rome.* Boston: B. Green (vol. 2). [Author identified in *Dictionary of American Biography,* vol. 5, p. 483.] **See pp. 172, 173-175, 177, 178.**

Duniway, Clyde A. *The Development of Freedom of the Press in Massachusetts.* New York: Longmans, Green and Company, 1906. (Harvard Historical Studies, vol. 12.) **See pp. 31, 207.**

Dwight, Timothy. *A Discourse in Two Parts.* New Haven: Howe and Deforest, 1812. **See pp. 247-249.**

————. *A Discourse on Some Events of the Last Century.* New Haven: Ezra Read, 1801. **See pp. 206, 245-247.**

[————]. *A Sermon, Preached at Northampton* (Nov. 28, 1781). Hartford: Nathaniel Patten, [1781]. [Author and date given in Evans, *op. cit.,* vol. 6, no. 17144.] **See pp. 244, 245.**

Edinburgh Association for Promoting the Study of Prophecy. *Lectures on Subjects Connected With Prophecy* (first series by J. W. Brooks). Edinburgh: John Johnstone, [1841]. **See pp. 444, 604.**

Edwards, Jonathan. *A History of the Work of Redemption.* Boston: Draper & Folsom, 1782. **See pp. 145, 182-185.**

————. *An Humble Attempt to Promote Explicit Agreement and Visible Union of God's People in Extraordinary Prayer.* Boston: Printed for D. Henchman in Cornhil, 1747. (Waterman Pamphlets, vol. 52, no. 2.) **See p. 183.**

Einiges über die rufenden Stimmen oder die sogenannte Predigtkrankheit in Smaland in den Jahren 1842 und 1843, von einem Augenzeugen (translated from the Swedish). Leipzig: Leopold Michelsen, 1843. **See pp. 670, 683-686.**

[Eliot, John]. *New Englands First Fruits.* London: R. O. and G. D., 1643. **See p. 126.**

————. *Tears of Repentance: or, a Further Narrative of the Progress of the Gospel Amongst the Indians in New-England.* London: P[eter] Cole, 1653. **See pp. 85, 86.**

Elliott, E[dward] B[ishop]. *Horae Apocalypticae; or, A Commentary on the Apocalypse.* 5th ed. London: Seeley, Jackson, and Halliday, 1862. **See pp. 280, 281, 317, 323, 325, 326, 596, 656, 657, 663, 716-722, 730.**

Ellis, John H., ed. *The Works of Anne Bradstreet, in Prose and Verse.* New York: Peter Smith, 1932. **See pp. 55, 57.**

Encyclopaedia Britannica. [14th ed.] Chicago: Encyclopaedia Britannica, Inc., 1945. **See p. 665.**

The End of All Things Is at Hand. Plymouth, [England]: Rowe, Printer, [c.1830-1833?]. **See pp. 607, 608.**

Ernst, James. *Roger Williams, New England Firebrand.* New York: The Macmillan Company, 1932. **See p. 48.**

European Missionary Society. See Continental Society for the Diffusion of Religious Knowledge (eighteenth year).

Evans, Charles. *American Bibliography. A Chronological Dictionary of All Books, Pamphlets and Periodical Publications Printed in the United States of America* (1639-1799). Chicago: The Author, 1903-1934. 12 vols. **See pp. 89, 135, 154, 202, 213, 221, 241.**

Faber, George Stanley. *A Dissertation on the Prophecies, That Have Been Fulfilled, Are Now Fulfilling, or Will Hereafter Be Fulfilled, Relative to the Great Period of 1260 Years; the Papal and Mohammedan Apostasies; the Tyrannical Reign of Antichrist, or the Infidel Power; and the Restoration of the Jews.* 2d ed., rev. London: F. C. and J. Rivington, 1807. 2 vols. **See pp. 273, 339-343.**

————. *A Dissertation on the Prophecy Contained in Daniel IX. 24-27; Generally Denominated The Prophecy of the Seventy Weeks.* London: F. C. and J. Rivington, 1811. **See pp. 340, 343-345.**

————. *A General and Connected View of the Prophecies, Relative to the Conversion, Restoration, Union, and Future Glory of the Houses of Judah and Israel; the Progress, and Final Overthrow, of the Antichristian Con-*

federacy in the Land of Palestine; and the Ultimate General Diffusion of Christianity. London: F. C. and J. Rivington, 1808. 2 vols. **See pp. 339, 340.**

————. *The Predicted Downfall of the Turkish Power. The Preparation for the Return of the Ten Tribes.* 1st and 2d eds. London: Thomas Bosworth, 1853. **See pp. 345, 346.**

————. *The Sacred Calendar of Prophecy: or a Dissertation on the Prophecies, Which Treat of the Grand Period of Seven Times, and Especially of Its Second Moiety or the Latter Three Times and a Half.* London: C. & J. Rivington, 1828. 3 vols. **See p. 340.**

————. *A Supplement to the Dissertation on the 1260 Years: Containing a Full Reply to the Objections and Misrepresentations of the Rev. E. W. Whitaker.* London: F. C. and J. Rivington, 1806. **See pp. 339, 343.**

Flint, Henry. *The Doctrine of the Last Judgment, Asserted and Explained.* (With a preface by Increase Mather.) Boston: B. Green, for Benj. Eliot, 1714. **See pp. 168, 169.**

Ford, Paul Leicester. *The New-England Primer. A History—Its Origin and Development.* With a reprint of the unique copy of the earliest known edition, [1727]. New York: Dodd, Mead and Company, 1897. **See pp. 115, 118-122.**

Förnyade Placat Och Förbud. Stockholm: Joh. Henr. Werner, Official Printer, 1726. **See pp. 670, 673.**

Frere, James Hatley. *A Combined View of the Prophecies of Daniel, Esdras, and St. John.* London: J. Hatchard, 1815. **See pp. 273, 278, 386-388.**

————. *Eight Letters on the Prophecies Relating to the Last Times.* London: Hatchard and Son, 1831. **See pp. 386, 389, 390.**

————. *The Great Continental Revolution Marking the Expiration of the Times of the Gentiles, A. D. 1847-8.* London: J. Hatchard and Son, 1848.

————. Same. 2d ed., 1849. **See pp. 386, 390, 499, 500.**

————. *The Harvest of the Earth.* London: James Nisbet and Co., 1846. **See pp. 386, 391.**

————. *Three Letters on the Prophecies.* London: Hatchard and Son, 1833. **See p. 389.**

Fry, John. *Observations on the Unfulfilled Prophecies of Scripture, Which Are Yet to Have Their Accomplishment, Before the Coming of the Lord in Glory, or at the Establishment of His Everlasting Kingdom.* London: James Duncan, 1835. **See pp. 490, 492-497.**

————. *The Second Advent; or The Glorious Epiphany of Our Lord Jesus Christ.* London: Ogle, Duncan, and Co., 1822. 2 vols. **See pp. 490-492.**

Fuller, Andrew Gunton. *The Complete Works of the Rev. Andrew Fuller, With a Memoir of His Life.* New ed. London: William Ball, 1837. 5 vols. **See pp. 350-354.**

Gale, Benjamin. *A Brief Essay, or an Attempt to Prove, From the Prophetick Writings of the Old and New Testament, What Period of Prophecy the Church of God Is Now Under.* New-Haven: Thomas & Samuel Green, [1788]. **See pp. 215-217.**

Gatchel, Samuel. *A Contrast to the Reverend Nathaniel Whitaker, D. D., His Confutation of the Reverend John Wise, A. M.* Danvers, [Mass.]: E. Russell, 1778. **See p. 212.**

————. *The Signs of the Times; or Some Expositions and Remarks on Sundry Texts of Scripture, Relative to the Remarkable Phenomenon, or Dark-Day,*

Which Appeared in New-England on the Nineteenth of May, 1780. Danvers, [Mass.]: E. Russell, 1781. See pp. 211, 232.

Gauntlett, Henry. *An Exposition of the Book of Revelation.* 2d ed. London: L. B. Seeley, 1821. See pp. 430-432.

[Gaussen, Louis]. *Daniel le prophète, exposé dans une suite de leçons pour une école du dimanche.* Paris: Librairie protestante, 1850 [vol. 1, 2d ed.]; Paris: M. Ducloux, 1848-1849. 3 vols. [Author identified in Paris Bibliothèque Nationale catalogue.] See pp. 688, 690, 695, 696, 698-700.

————. *The Prophet Daniel Explained.* Translated [from the French] by Margaret Blackstone. London: J. & C. Mozley, 1873-1874. 2 vols. See pp. 688, 690, 694, 695.

————. *Le Souverain Pontife et l'Eglise de Rome, soutiens de la vérité, par l'accomplissement des Ecritures . . . Discours prononcé dans l'Ecole de théologie de Genève, a sa rentrée le 30 octobre 1843.* Toulouse: Imprimerie de K. Cadaux, 1843. See pp. 690, 693.

[————]. Sunday school lessons on Daniel, lithographed from the manuscript, 1837. [Original in Bibliothèque des pasteurs de la ville de Neuchatel. Switzerland.] See pp. 688, 696-698.

Girdlestone, William. *Notes on the Apocalypse.* London: Painter, 1847. See p. 433.

————. *Observations on the Visions of Daniel, and on Part of the Book of the Revelation of St. John.* With an appendix. Oxford: J. Parker, 1820. See p. 433.

Glasgow University. *A Roll of the Graduates of the University of Glasgow (1727-1897),* compiled by William Innes Addison. Glasgow: J. MacLehose & Sons, 1898. See p. 597.

Gobat, Samuel. *Journal of Three Years' Residence in Abyssinia.* New York: M. W. Dodd, 1850. See p. 486.

————. *Samuel Gobat, Bishop of Jerusalem. His Life and Work.* With preface by the Right Hon. the Earl of Shaftesbury. London: James Nisbet & Co., 1884. See pp. 300, 486, 487.

Good, James I. *History of the Swiss Reformed Church Since the Reformation.* Philadelphia: Publication & Sunday School Board of the Reformed Church in the United States, 1913. See p. 687.

Gray, F. C. "Remarks on the Early Laws of Massachusetts Bay; With the Code Adopted in 1641, and Called The Body of Liberties, Now First Printed," in *Collections of the Massachusetts Historical Society,* 3d series, vol. 8, pp. 191-237. See pp. 35, 88.

Green, Samuel Abbott. *Ten Fac-Simile Reproductions Relating to Old Boston and Neighborhood.* Boston: [University Press], 1901. See pp. 117, 118.

Greene, Evarts B. and Virginia D. Harrington. *American Population Before the Federal Census of 1790.* New York: Columbia University Press, 1932. See p. 28.

Guinness, H. Grattan. *The Approaching End of the Age.* 4th ed. London: Hodder and Stoughton, 1880. See pp. 384, 385.

————. *History Unveiling Prophecy.* New York: Fleming H. Revell, 1905. See pp. 385, 656.

————. *Romanism and the Reformation.* Toronto: S. R. Briggs, [n.d.]. See p. 384.

Habershon, Matthew. *A Dissertation on the Prophetic Scriptures, Chiefly Those of a Chronological Character; Shewing Their Aspect on the Present Times, and on the Destinies of the Jewish Nation.* London, 1834. **See pp. 550, 633-635.**

————. "An Epitome of Prophetic Truth." introductory essay in *Pre millennial Hymns,* pp. 1-47. 2d ed. London: J. Nisbet & Co., 1841. **See pp. 638, 639.**

————. *An Historical Dissertation on the Prophetic Scriptures of the Old Testament.* London: James Nisbet and Co., 1840. [2d ed. of his *A Dissertation.*] **See p. 635.**

————. *An Historical Exposition of the Prophecies of the Revelation of St. John.* London: James Nisbet and Co., 1841. **See pp. 635-638.**

Hair, John. *Regent Square. Eighty Years of a London Congregation.* London: James Nisbet & Co., Limited, 1898. **See p. 516.**

Halcombe, John. *The Evidence of Unfulfilled Prophecy, Arranged and Examined* London: Printed for private circulation only, 1845. **See pp. 722, 723.**

Haldane, Alexander. *The Lives of Robert Haldane of Airthrey, and His Brother James Alexander Haldane.* 9th ed. Edinburgh: Andrew Elliott. **See pp. 436, 439, 440, 689.**

[Hales, William]. *The Inspector, or Select Literary Intelligence.* London: J. White, 1799. [Author identified in his *New Analysis of Sacred Chronology,* vol. 2, pp. 564, 565. For a review of *The Inspector,* see *The Gentleman's Magazine.*] **See pp. 334, 335.**

————. *A New Analysis of Chronology.* London: Printed for the Author, 1809-1812. **See pp. 273, 332-334.**

Halkett, Samuel, and John Laing. *Dictionary of Anonymous and Pseudonymous English Literature.* New and enlarged edition. Edinburgh: Oliver and Boyd, 1926-34. 7 vols. Cited *passim.*

[Harris, Benjamin]. *The Protestant Tutor.* London: Benjamin Harris, 1679. [A bound photostat from British Museum, London.] **See pp. 117-121.**

Harvard University Library. *Bibliographical Contributions.* (No. 38, 1890, no. 44, 1892.) Edited by Justin Winsor. Cambridge, Mass.: The College Press, 1896. **See p. 176.**

Harvard University Library *Harvard College Records,* Corporation Records, 1636-1750 (College Books 1, 3, 4), in *Publications of the Colonial Society of Massachusetts,* vols. 15, 16. Boston: The Society, 1925. **See p. 175.**

————. *Harvard University Bulletin* (vol. 6, nos. 45-52, 1890-1892). Edited by Justin Winsor. Cambridge: The Library, 1892. **See p. 177.**

[Hawtrey, C. S.]. *The Nature of the First Resurrection . . . A Sermon . . . by a Spiritual Watchman.* 2d ed. London: James Nisbet, 1828 **See p. 429.**

————. *A Summary Account of the Origin, Proceedings, and Success of the London Society for Promoting Christianity Amongst the Jews.* 4th ed. London: A. MacIntosh, 1826. **See p. 428, 444.**

Heartman, Charles Frederick. *The New-England Primer Issued Prior to 1830.* Rev. ed. New York: R. R. Bowker Company, 1934. **See pp. 119, 121, 122.**

Heintzpeter, H. *De Groote Wereldgebeurtinissen.* [n.p.], 1842. **See p. 300.**

Higginson, John. "Epistle Dedicatory," in Nicholas Noyes, *New-Englands Duty and Interest, to Be an Habitation of Justice, and Mountain of Holiness,* preliminary leaves 2-6. Boston: Bartholomew Green and John Allen, 1698. **See p 157**

Hoar, John Emory "Elhanan Winchester, Preacher and Traveler," in *Publications of the Brookline Historical Society.* Brookline, Mass., 1903. **See p 224**

Holmes, Thomas J. *Cotton Mather: A Bibliography of His Works.* Cambridge: Harvard University Press, 1910. 3 vols. **See pp. 148, 154, 157.**

————— *Increase Mather: A Bibliography of His Works.* Cleveland, Ohio: Harvard University Press, 1931. 2 vols. **See pp. 106, 126, 127.**

Holmes, W. A. *The Time of the End: Being a Series of Lectures on Prophetical Chronology.* London: R. B. Seeley and W. Burnside, 1833. **See pp. 299, 601, 602.**

Holyoke, Edward. *The Doctrine of Life, or of Mans Redemtion, by the Seed of Eve, the Seed of Abraham, the Seed of David, &c.* London: Printed by T. R. for Nath. Elkins, 1658. **See pp. 95-97.**

H[ooke], W[illiam]. "Preface to the Christian Reader" [Signed "W. H." and "J. C."], in John Davenport, *The Saints Anchor-Hold in All Storms and Tempests.* London: Benj. Harris, 1701. **See pp. 25, 105.**

Hooke, William. *The Priviledge of the Saints on Earth Beyond Those in Heaven. . . . To which is added, A Short Discourse of the Nature and Extent of the Gospel-Day.* London: John Wilkins, 1673. **See pp. 105-107.**

H[ooke], W[illiam]. "To the Reader," preface to Increase Mather, *The Mystery of Israel's Salvation, Explained and Applyed,* sig. b2r-b5v. [London: Allen], 1669. [Author identified in Thomas J. Holmes, *Increase Mather,* vol. 2, p. 354; publisher identified by Sabin & Holmes.] **See p. 106.**

Hooper, John. *The Advent; or, The Revelation, Appearance, and Coming of the Lord.* London: Seeley, Burnside, and Seeley, 1847. **See pp. 564, 569, 570.**

—————. *(Apocalypsis); or, The Revelation of Jesus Christ Minutely Interpreted and Considered. . . .* London: William Edward Painter, 1846. **See pp. 564, 569.**

—————. *The Doctrine of the Second Advent.* London: James Nisbet, 1829. **See pp. 564-566.**

—————. *The Present Crisis, Considered in Relation to the Blessed Hope of the Glorious Appearing of the Great God, and Our Saviour Jesus Christ.* London: James Nisbet, 1830. **See pp. 564, 566-569, 592.**

Hopkins, Samuel. *A Dialogue Concerning the Slavery of the Africans.* Norwich: Judah P. Spooner, 1776. **See p. 218.**

—————. *A Treatise on the Millennium.* Boston: Isaiah Thomas and Ebenezer T. Andrews, 1793. **See pp. 145, 218-221.**

Howard, Daniel. *Glimpses of Ancient Windsor from 1633 to 1933.* [Windsor, Conn.]: Windsor Tercentenary Committee, 1933. **See p. 60.**

Huit, Ephraim. *The Whole Prophecie of Daniel Explained, by a Paraphrase, Analysis and Briefe Comment: Wherein the Severall Visions Shewed to the Prophet, Are Clearly Interpreted, and the Application Thereof Vindicated Against Dissenting Opinions.* [London]· Henry Overton, 1644. **See pp. 56, 61-66.**

The Humble Advice. **See Westminster Assembly.**

H[utchinson], S[amuel]. *A Declaration of a Future Glorious Estate of a Church to Be Here Upon Earth, at Christ's Personal Appearance for the Restitution of All Things, a Thousand Years Before the Ultimate Day of the General Judgement . . . Together With the Testimony of Many Godly Divines, Both Ancient and Modern.* London: [n.n.], 1667. **See pp. 99-104.**

Imrie, David. *A Letter . . . Predicting the Speedy Accomplishment of the Great, Awful and Glorious Events Which the Scriptures Say Are to Be Brought to Pass in the Latter Times.* Edinburgh: Printed 1755. Boston: Reprinted by S. Kneeland, 1756. **See pp. 146, 193, 194.**

Independent Presbyterian Church in the United States of America. *The Constitution and Form of Government of the Independent Presbyterian Church in the United States of America, as Adopted by the Churches in Convention, Held at Salem Church, in Union District, So. Ca., A. D. 1838: Together With Mr. Davis's Solemn Appeal to an Impartial Public.* Columbia: South-Carolinian Print., 1839. See p. 392.

Index Librorum Prohibitorum. (SSMI D. N. Leonis XIII Iussu et Auctoritate.) Editio Altera. Romae: Typis Vaticanis, 1901. See pp. 304, 306, 309, 312, 313.

Irving, Edward *Babylon and Infidelity Foredoomed of God: A Discourse on the Prophecies of Daniel and the Apocalypse.* Glasgow: Chalmers and Collins, 1826. 2 vols. See pp. 275, 378, 387, 389, 516, 520-523.

————. *Exposition of the Book of Revelation, in a Series of Lectures.* London: Baldwin and Cradock, 1831. 4 vols., paged continuously. See pp. 523, 524.

————. *The Last Days; A Discourse on the Evil Character of These Our Times.* London: R. B. Seeley and W. Burnside, 1828. See p. 523.

————. "Preliminary Discourse by the Translator," in *The Coming of Messiah in Glory and Majesty,* by Juan Josafat Ben-Ezra (Manuel Lacunza), vol. 1, pp. iii-cxciv. London: L. B. Seeley and Son, 1827. 2 vols. See pp. 277, 313, 450-454, 519, 520, 591.

————, translator. See Lacunza, Manuel, *The Coming of Messiah in Glory and Majesty*

————, Trial of See *The Trial of Edward Irving.*

Irving, Joseph *The Book of Scotsmen.* Paisley, [Scotland]: Alexander Gardner, 1881. See pp. 365, 366.

The Jewish Encyclopedia. New York and London: Funk and Wagnalls Company, 1901-1906. 12 vols. See pp. 415, 417.

[Johnson, Edward]. *A History of New-England 1628-1652.* [Commonly known as reprint under running title: *Wonder-working Providence of Sions Saviour, in New England.*] London: N[ath]. Brooke, 1654. [Author identified in Halkett and Laing, *op. cit.,* vol. 3, p. 72.] See pp. 56, 92, 93.

Jones, William. *Biographical Sketch of the Rev. Edward Irving.* London: John Bennett, 1841. See p. 435.

———— *The Biblical Cyclopedia; or Dictionary of the Holy Scriptures* New ed., rev. London: T. Harjette, 1824. 2 vols. See pp. 510, 511.

————. *The History of the Christian Church, . . . Including the Very Interesting Account of the Waldenses and the Albigenses.* 1st American from the 4th London ed. New York: Gray & Bunce, 1824. 2 vols. See p. 510.

————. *Lectures on the Apocalypse.* London: Harjette and Savill, 1830 See pp 510-513.

Keith, Alexander. *Evidence of the Truth of the Christian Religion, Derived From the Literal Fulfilment of Prophecy.* From the 6th Edinburgh ed New York: J. & J. Harper, 1832. See pp. 486, 622, 623.

————. *The Harmony of Prophecy; or, Scriptural Illustrations of the Apocalypse.* Edinburgh: William Whyte, 1851. See pp. 623, 625.

————. *The History and Destiny of the World and of the Church.* London: T. Nelson and Sons, 1861. See pp. 623, 625, 626.

————. *The Signs of the Times, as Denoted by the Fulfilment of Historical Predictions* Edinburgh: William Whyte & Co., 1832. 2 vols., paged continuously. See pp. 623-625.

Kelber, L[eonhard] H[einrich]. *Der Antichrist, wer er ist.* Dritte Auflage Weimar. Bernh. Friedr. Voigt, 1839. **See p 299.**

————. *Das Ende kommt.* Stuttgart. J Scheible's Buchhandlung, 1842. [The first work under this title was *Das Ende kommt, es kommt das Ende* (Nürnberg: Verlag der Raw'schen Buchhandlung, 1824), subtitled "Part 3, a continuation of the first and second parts of my" *Vernünftige und Schriftmasige Gedanken über die Schöpfung und Dauer der Welt.* Then followed *Das Ende kommt* (Stuttgart: Friedrich Henne, 1835), "a continuation of" the 1824 book (see his *Der Antichrist,* page 20, and 1835 foreword in the 1842 edition of *Das Ende kommt).*] **See pp. 299, 378.**

————. *Vernünftige und Schriftmasige Gedanken über die Schöpfung und Dauer der Welt.* Nürnberg: Verlag der Raw'schen Buchhandlung, 1805-1817. 2 parts. **See p. 299.**

Keyworth, Thomas. *A Practical Exposition of the Revelation of Saint John, to Which Are Appended Tabular Views of the Revelations, Together With Those Parts of Daniel Which Correspond Thereto.* London: The Author, 1828. **See pp. 550-554.**

Kittredge, George Lyman. *Witchcraft in Old and New England.* Cambridge, Mass.: Harvard University Press, 1929 **See p. 135.**

Knowles, James D. *Memoir of Roger Williams.* Boston: Lincoln, Edmands and Co., 1834. **See pp. 79-82.**

Kohler, Max J. *Jewish Rights at the Congresses of Vienna (1814-1815) and Aix-la-Chapelle (1818).* New York: The American Jewish Committee, 1918. **See p. 417.**

Kunitz, Stanley J., and Howard Haycraft. *American Authors. 1660-1900.* New York: The H. W. Wilson Co., 1938. **See p. 126.**

[Lacunza, Manuel]. *The Coming of Messiah in Glory and Majesty,* by Juan Josafat Ben-Ezra, . . . translated from the Spanish [*La Venida del Mesias*], with a preliminary discourse, by Edward Irving. London: L. B. Seeley and Son, 1827. 2 vols. **See pp. 313-315, 317-324, 425, 450-454, 518-520.**

[————]. *A New Antichrist.* Extracts from *The Coming of the Messiah in Glory and Majesty,* by J. J. Benezra, (*1744-1801*). Translated by William D. Smart. Los Angeles, California: William D. Smart, 1929. **See pp. 317, 319.**

[————]. *Venida del Mesias en Gloria y Magestad.* Conpuesto por Juan Josafat Ben-Ezra. 2d (?) ed. [Valencia (?), Spain.] Por Felipe Tolosa, Impresor de la Ciudad, [1812]. 3 vols. [Slightly abr.] [Author identified in Vaucher, *op. cit.*] **See pp. 310, 313, 314, 316.**

[————]. *La Venida del Mesias en Gloria y Magestad. Observacionnes de Juan Josaphat Ben-Ezra.* Londres: Imprenta de Carlos Wood, 1816. 4 vols. **See pp. 311, 316.**

[————]. *La Venida del Mesias en Gloria y Magestad.* Por Juan Josafat Ben Ezra. Edicion enmendad . . . por P. de Chambrobert. Paris: Libreria de Parmantier, 1825. 5 vols. **See pp. 313, 316.**

[————]. *La Venida del Mesias en Gloria y Magestad. Observaciones de Juan Josafat Ben-Ezra.* Londres: R. Ackermann, 1826. 3 vols. **See pp. 313, 316.**

[For reference to *La Venida,* all editions, **see pp. 309-324, 425, 450-454, 478, 518-520.**]

Lambert, Le P[ère] Bernard. *Exposition des prédictions et des promesses faites a l'Eglise pour les derniers temps de la gentilité.* Paris: A. Clo, 1806. **See pp. 324-326.**

Lambert, Edward R. *History of the Colony of New Haven Before and After the Union With Connecticut.* New Haven: Printed and Published by Hitchcock & Stafford, 1838. See p. 21.

Langdon, Samuel. *Observations on the Revelation of Jesus Christ to St. John.* Worcester, Mass.: Isaiah Thomas, 1791. See pp. 206, 210, 211.

——————. *A Rational Explication of St. John's Vision of the Two Beasts, in the XIIIth Chapter of the Revelation.* Portsmouth: Daniel Fowle, 1774. See pp. 209, 210.

Lathrop, Joseph. *The Angel Preaching the Everlasting Gospel.* Springfield, Mass.: Thomas Dickman, [1812]. See pp. 236, 239.

——————. *The Prophecy of Daniel, Relating to the Time of the End.* Springfield, [Mass.]: Thomas Dickman, 1811. See pp. 236-239.

——————. *A Sermon on the Dangers of the Times.* Springfield: Francis Stebbins, 1798. See p. 237.

[Lee, Samuel, 1625-1691]. *Antichristi Excidium.* Londini: J. Streater, 1664. [1st ed. *De Exicidio Antichristi,* 1659. Author identified in Vincent Placcius, *Theatrum Anonymorum et Pseudonymorum* (1700), p. 72.] See pp. 112, 113.

——————. *A Summons or Warning to the Great Day of Judgment* [also known as *The Great Day of Judgment*]. Boston: B. Green, 1692. See pp. 112-114, 151.

Lee, Samuel [1783-1852]. *Events and Times of the Visions of Daniel and St. John.* London: Seeleys, 1851. See p. 596.

[Leslie, James]. *A Circular Letter on the Revolutions in Europe; With an Appendix on the Present Crisis in Church and State.* 3d ed. Edinburgh: John Ogle, [1832]. [Signed "Amici," dated Edinburgh, June 1, 1831, on page 11. Identified by signature in his letter to the Rev. Edward Irving, pp. (1), 15, and *A Circular Letter,* p. 1.] See pp. 590-592.

[——————]. *Letter to the Rev. Edward Irving.* Edinburgh: J. Lindsay & Co., 1832. See p. 592.

——————. *The Shaking of the Nations; or, An Essay on the Causes of Divine Judgments.* Edinburgh: Published by the Author, 1833. See pp. 592-595.

Lewis, Alonzo, and James R. Newhall, *History of Lynn, Essex County, Massachusetts. (1629-1864).* Boston: John L. Shorey, 1865. See pp. 94, 95.

Lindl, Ignaz. *Leitfaden zur einfachen Erklarung der Apokalypse.* Berlin: 1826. See p. 298.

Linn, William. *Discourses on the Signs of the Times.* New York: Thomas Greenleaf, 1794. See pp. 206, 228.

Littlefield, George E. *Early Boston Booksellers, 1642-1711.* Boston: The Club of Odd Volumes, 1900. See pp. 117-119, 135.

——————. *The Early Massachusetts Press, 1638-1711.* Boston: The Club of Odd Volumes, 1907. 2 vols. See pp. 135, 162.

Luther, Martin. *The Signs of Christ's Coming, and of the Last Day; Being Extracts From a Very Choice and Excellent Sermon . . . Upon Luke xxi. 25—34.* Edinburgh: Reprinted for John Lindsay and Company, 1832. See p. 608.

Macaulay, Thomas B. *Critical and Miscellaneous Essays.* Philadelphia: Cary and Hart, 1844. 5 vols. See p. 268.

M'Clintock, John, and James Strong. *Cyclopedia of Biblical, Theological, and Ecclesiastical Literature.* New York: Harper & Brothers, 1890-94. 12 vols. See pp. 392, 482.

M'Neile, Hugh. *The Abominations of Babylon.* London: Sherwood, Gilbert, & Piper, 1826. **See pp. 454, 455.**

————. *The Character of the Church of Rome.* Liverpool: George Smith, 1836. **See p. 455.**

[Madden, Mrs. Hamilton]. *Personal Recollections of the Right Rev. Robert Daly, D. D., Late Bishop of Cashel, by an Old Parishioner.* Dublin: George Herbert, 1872. [Author identified in Halkett and Laing, *op. cit.,* vol. 4, p. 327.] **See p. 585.**

Maitland, Charles [1815-1866]. *The Apostles' School of Prophetic Interpretation.* London: Longman, Brown, Green, and Longmans, 1849. **See pp. 360, 730, 731.**

Maitland, Captain [Charles David] [1785-1865]. *A Brief and Connected View of Prophecy: Being an Exposition of the Second, Seventh, and Eighth Chapters of the Prophecy of Daniel; Together With the Sixteenth Chapter of Revelation to Which Are Added Some Observations Respecting the Period and Manner of the Restoration of the Jews.* London: J. Hatchard, 1814. [Identified as Charles David in Brooks' *Dictionary,* p. lvi. See *Dictionary of American Biography,* vol. 35, p. 351.] **See pp. 360, 362, 363.**

————. *The History of the Beast of the Apocalypse; Being a Paraphrase of the Thirteenth and Seventeenth Chapters of the Revelation. Also, A View of the Twelfth, Fourteenth, Fifthteenth, and Sixteenth Chapters of the Same.* London: G. Dale, [1813]. [For a review of this book, see *The Eclectic Review,* February, 1814 (new series, vol. 1), pp. 127-140. Author and date identified in Brook's *Dictionary,* p. lvi.] **See pp. 360-362.**

Maitland, S[amuel] R[offey]. *An Attempt to Elucidate the Prophecies Concerning Anti-Christ: With Remarks on Some Works of J. H. Frere, Esq.* London: Francis & John Rivington, 1853. **See pp. 541, 543, 659.**

————. *An Enquiry Into the Grounds on Which the Prophetic Period of Daniel and St. John, Has Been Supposed to Consist of 1260 Years.* London: Hatchard and Son, 1826. **See pp. 540-542, 657.**

————. *Essays on Subjects Connected With the Reformation in England.* London and New York: John Lane, 1899. **See p. 542.**

————. *A Second Enquiry Into the Grounds on Which the Prophetic Period of Daniel and St. John, Has Been Supposed to Consist of 1260 Years.* London: C. and J. Rivington, 1829. **See pp. 541, 543.**

[Manning], Henry Edward [Cardinal]. *The Fourfold Sovereignty of God.* London: Burns, Oates, and Company, 1871. [Author identified in British Museum catalogue.] **See pp. 736, 737.**

Manning, Henry Edward [later Cardinal]. *The Temporal Power of the Vicar of Jesus Christ.* 2d ed. London: Burns & Lambert, 1862. **See pp. 734-736.**

[March, Edmund]. *Divine Providence . . . Visibly Engaged in Fulfilling Scripture-Prophecies . . . of the Church of God in the Latter Days.* Boston: Z. Fowle and S. Draper, 1762. [Author identified in Evans, *op. cit.,* vol. 3, p. 321.] See p. 202.

Marvin, Abijah P. *The Life and Times of Cotton Mather.* Boston and Chicago: Congregational Sunday-School and Publishing Society, 1892. **See p. 147.**

Mason, Archibald. *Appendix to an Inquiry Into the Prophetic Numbers Contained in the 1335 Days.* Glasgow: M. Ogle, 1818. [Also in the following title.] **See pp. 397, 400.**

————. *The Church's Happy Prospect, and the Christian's Present Duty: Containing an Inquiry . . . in Five Discourses: With an Appendix to the Discourse on the Prophetic Numbers. Also Two Essays on Daniel's Pro-*

phetic Number of 2300 Days, and on the Christian's Duty to Inquire Into the Church's Deliverance. New ed. Glasgow: Maurice Ogle, 1821. **See pp. 397-400, 403.**

————. *An Inquiry Into the Times That Shall Be Fulfilled at Antichrist's Fall; The Church's Blessedness in Her Millennial Rest; The Signs That This Happy Season Is at Hand; The Prophetic Numbers Contained in the 1335 Days; and The Christian's Duty, at This Interesting Crisis: in Five Discourses.* Glasgow: M. Ogle, 1818. [Also in *The Church's Happy Prospect.*] **See pp. 397-400.**

————. *Remarks on the Sixth Vial, Symbolizing the Fall of the Turkish Empire.* Glasgow: Maurice Ogle, 1827. **See pp. 403, 404.**

————. *Two Essays on Daniel's Prophetic Number of Two Thousand Three Hundred Days; and on the Christian's Duty to Inquire Into the Church's Deliverance.* Newburgh: Ward M. Gazlay, 1820 (printed from the Glasgow ed.). [Also in *The Church's Happy Prospect.*] **See pp. 274, 290, 381, 397, 400-404.**

Massachusetts Colony. *The Book of the General Lauues and Libertyes Concerning the Inhabitants of the Massachusets.* Cambridge, 1648. [Facsimile from original in Henry E. Huntington Library, Dec., 1927.] **See p. 80.**

————. *The Book of the General Lawes and Libertyes Concerning the Inhabitants of the Massachusets.* Cambridge: Printed According to Order of the General Court, 1660. **See p. 80.**

Mather, Cotton. "The Fall of Babylon." Essay I, in *The Way of Truth Laid Out, a Catechism . . . in Seven Essays.* Boston: S. Kneeland, 1721. **See pp. 153, 154.**

————. *Magnalia Christi Americana: or, The Ecclesiastical History of New-England.* (1620-1698.) London: Thomas Parkhurst, 1702. **See pp. 19, 25, 35, 36, 43, 61, 67, 68, 84-87, 93, 94, 109, 111, 113, 148.**

————. "Preparatory Meditations," in Samuel Lee, *A Summons or Warning to the Great Day of Judgment.* Boston: Printed by B. Green, for N. Buttolph, 1692. **See p. 151.**

————. *Things for a Distres'd People to Think Upon.* Boston: Printed by B. Green and J. Allen, for Duncan Campbel, 1696. **See pp. 151, 153.**

————. *Things to Be Look'd For.* Cambridge: Printed by Samuel Green, and Barth. Green, for Nicholas Buttolph . . . in Boston, 1691. **See pp. 148-150, 152.**

————. *The Wonders of the Invisible World: Being an Account of the Tryals of Several VVitches.* London: John Dunton, 1693. **See pp. 147, 150, 151.**

Mather, Increase. *A Discourse Concerning Earthquakes.* Boston: Printed by Timothy Green, for Benjamin Eliot, 1706. **See pp. 129, 130.**

Mather, I[ncrease]. *A Discourse Concerning Faith and Fervency in Prayer.* Boston: Printed by B. Green, for Benj. Eliot, 1710. **See pp. 132-134.**

————. *A Dissertation, Wherein the Strange Doctrine . . . Is Examined and Confuted.* Boston: Printed by B. Green, for Benj. Eliot, 1708. **See pp. 127, 130-132.**

————. *The Greatest Sinners Exhorted and Encouraged to Come to Christ . . . Together With a Discourse About the Day of Judgment. And on Several Other Subjects.* Boston: R. P. for Joseph Brunning, 1686. **See pp. 128, 129.**

————. *Heaven's Alarm to the World . . . Preached at the Lecture of Boston in New-England.* 2d impression. Boston: Printed for Samuel Sewall, 1682. **See pp. 128, 142, 206.**

————. *Ichabod or . . . the Glory of the Lord, Is Departing From New-England.* Boston: Timothy Green, 1702. **See p. 129.**

————. *The Mystery of Israel's Salvation, Explained and Applyed; or A Discourse Concerning the General Conversion of the Israelitish Nation . . . Being the Substance of Several Sermons Preached.* [London: Allen], 1669. [Publisher identified by Sabin and Holmes; see Library of Congress card.] **See pp. 25, 87, 106, 126-128.**

[Mather, Samuel, 1626-1671]. *A Defence of the Protestant Christian Religion Against Popery, Wherein the Manifold Apostasies, Heresies, and Schisms of the Church of Rome . . . Are Briefly Laid Open.* By an English Protestant. [Dublin?], 1672. [Author identified in British Museum catalogue.] **See p. 109.**

Mather, Samuel [1706-1785]. *The Life of the Very Reverend and Learned Cotton Mather.* Boston: Samuel Gerrish, 1729. **See pp. 148, 171.**

Mayhew, Jonathan. *A Discourse . . . Occasioned by the Earthquakes in November, 1755.* Boston: Edes & Gill, 1755. **See pp. 186, 192, 193.**

————. *Popish Idolatry.* Boston: R. & S. Draper, 1765. (Dudleian Lecture for 1765.) **See pp. 174, 176, 193.**

Mémoires sur l'état des Israélites, dédiés et présentés a leurs majestés impériales et royales, réunies au Congrès d'Aix-la-Chapelle. Paris: Imprimerie de Firmin Didot, 1918. [Attributed to L. Lavigne and also to Lewis Way.] **See p. 417.**

Miller, Edward. *The History and Doctrines of Irvingism.* London: C. Kegan Paul & Company, 1878. 2 vols. **See pp. 264, 409, 435, 436, 449, 450, 456, 506, 515, 526, 619.**

Miller, William. *Evidence From Scirpture [sic] and History of the Second Coming of Christ, About the Year 1843: Exhibited in a Course of Lectures.* Troy, [N.Y.]: Kemble & Hooper, 1836. **See pp. 392, 618, 742.**

Morison, Samuel E. *The Founding of Harvard College.* Cambridge, [Mass.]: Harvard University Press, 1935. **See p. 175.**

Müller, George. "Introduction," in Henry Craik, *Passages From the Diary and Letters of Henry Craik of Bristol.* London: J. F. Shaw & Co., [1866]. **See p. 646.**

————. *The Life of Trust: Being a Narrative of the Lord's Dealings With George Müller.* New ed. rev. [of the next title]. New York: Sheldon and Company, 1878. **See pp. 645, 646.**

————. *A Narrative of Some of the Lord's Dealings With George Müller.* Written by Himself. First Part. Seventh ed. London: J. Nisbet & Company, 1869. **See p. 645.**

National Covenant. See Scotland, Church of.

New England Primer (facsimile). See Ford, Paul Leicester.

The New England Primer, Twentieth Century Reprint. [Boston]: Ginn and Company, [1937]. **See pp. 118, 119, 123.**

New Englands First Fruits. See Eliot, John.

The New English Tutor Inlarged. [London: Harris? 1702-1714. Bound photostat from British Museum.] **See pp. 119-122.**

Newman, John Henry. "The Protestant Idea of Antichrist," in *Essays Critical and Historical,* vol. 2, pp. 112-185. London: Basil Montagu Pickering, 1871. 2 vols. **See pp. 667-669.**

————. Tract Number Ninety. *Remarks on Certain Passages in the Thirty-nine Articles.* American reprint from the 2d English ed. New York: H. B. Durand, 1865. **See pp. 540, 664, 666, 669.**

Noel, Baptist W. *Remarks on the Revival of Miraculous Powers in the Church*. London: James Nisbet, 1831. **See pp. 526-528.**

Noel, Gerard T. *A Brief Enquiry Into the Prospects of the Church of Christ, in Connexion With the Second Advent of Our Lord Jesus Christ*. Reprint in *The Literalist*, vol. 1. Philadelphia: Orrin Rogers, 1840. **See pp. 530-532.**

Nolan, Frederick. *The Chronological Prophecies*. London: William Pickering, 1837. **See pp. 609, 610.**

————. "On the Antiquity and Connexion of the Early Cycles, and Their Utility in Settling the Differences of Chronologists," in *Transactions of the Royal Society of Literature of the United Kingdom*, vol. 3, pp. 1-70. London: John Murray, 1839. **See p. 609.**

————. *The Time of the Millennium Investigated; and Its Nature Determined on Scriptural Grounds*. London: T. and W. Boone, 1831. **See pp. 609, 610.**

Norton, John. *The Orthodox Evangelist. Or A Treatise Wherein Many Great Evangelical Truths . . . Are Briefly Discussed, Cleared, and Confirmed*. London: Printed by John Macock, for Henry Cripps, and Lodowick Lloyd, 1654. **See p. 94.**

Norton, John N[icholas]. *Life of Bishop [Daniel] Wilson, of Calcutta*. New York: General Protestant Episcopal Sunday School Union and Church Book Society, 1863. **See p. 617.**

Notestein, Wallace. *A History of Witchcraft in England From 1558 to 1718*. Washington: The American Historical Association, 1911. **See pp. 142, 143.**

Noyes, Nicholas. *New-Englands Duty and Interest, to Be an Habitation of Justice, and Mountain of Holiness*. Boston: Bartholomew Green, and John Allen, 1698. **See pp. 157, 158.**

Oakes, Urian. *The Unconquerable, All-Conquering, & More-Then-Conquering Souldier: or, The Successful Warre Which a Believer Wageth With the Enemies of His Soul*. Cambridge, [Mass.]: Samuel Green, 1674. **See p. 110.**

Osgood, Charles S., and Henry M. Batchelder. *Historical Sketch of Salem, 1626-1879*. Salem, [Mass.]: Essex Institute, 1879. **See p. 49.**

Osgood, Herbert L. *The American Colonies in the Seventeenth Century*. New York: The Macmillan Company, 1926-1930. 3 vols. **See p. 49.**

[Osgood, Samuel]. *Remarks on the Book of Daniel and on the Revelations*. New York: Greenleaf's Press, 1794. [Author identified in Evans, *op. cit.* vol. 9, no. 26663.] **See pp. 221-224.**

Oxford University. *Alumni Oxonienses*, 1715-1886. Edited by Joseph Foster. Oxford and London: Parker and Co., 1888. 4 vols. Cited *passim*.

Palmer, H[urley] P. *Joseph Wolff, His Romantic Life and Travels*. London: Heath, Cranston, Limited, 1935. **See p. 463.**

Park, J[ohn] R. *A Concise Exposition of the Apocalypse, So Far as the Prophecies Are Fulfilled. To Which Are Prefixed the History of Christianity Epitomised: and A Vocabulary of Symbols*. 2d ed., much enlarged. London: James Duncan, 1825. **See pp. 533-536.**

————. *The History of Christianity Epitomised*. See his *A Concise Exposition*.

Parker, Thomas. *The Visions and Prophecies of Daniel Expounded: Wherein the Mistakes of Former Interpreters Are Modestly Discovered*. London: Edmund Paxton, 1646. **See pp. 68-77.**

Parrington, Vernon L. *The Colonial Mind 1620-1800*. New York: Harcourt, Brace and Company, [1927]. (*Main Currents of American Thought*, vol.

1.) See pp. 27, 28, 35, 36, 46, 84, 124, 125, 135, 142, 143, 147, 182, 183, 236, 243.

Parton, James. *Life and Times of Benjamin Franklin.* New York: Mason Brothers, 1864. 2 vols. See p. 195.

Paterson, James. *History of the County of Ayr: With a Genealogical Account of the Families of Ayrshire.* Edinburgh: T. G. Stevenson, 1847-52. 2 vols. See p. 366.

Perry, William Stevens, Editor. *Historical Collections Relating to the American Colonial Church.* Hartford: The Church Press, 1873. 5 vols. in 4. See p. 126.

Pierson, Arthur T. *George Müller of Bristol.* New York: Fleming H. Revell Company, 1899. See pp. 645, 646.

Pilling, James Constantine. *Bibliography of the Algonquian Languages.* Washington: Government Printing Office, 1891. See p. 85.

Powerscourt, Theodosia A. *Letters and Papers by the late Theodosia A., Viscountess Powerscourt.* Edited by the Rev. Robert Daly. London: Hatchard and Son, 1838. See p. 585.

Prentice, Thomas. *Observations . . . on the Late Terrible Night of the Earthquake. . . . A Sermon.* Boston: Printed by S. Kneeland, for D. Henchman, 1756. See pp. 186, 188-190.

Prince, Thomas. Preface, in Samuel Mather, *The Life of . . . Cotton Mather,* pp. 1-6. Boston: Samuel Gerrish, 1729. See p. 172.

————. *Six Sermons.* Edinburgh: David Paterson, 1785. See p. 172.

Prophecy Investigation Society, [Bloomsbury, London]. Brochure notifying members of the spring course of lectures and semi-annual three-day meeting of 1849. [London]: Printed for private distribution, [1848]. See also Society for the Investigation of Prophecy. See p. 499.

Protestant Tutor. See Harris, Benjamin.

Pym, William W. *Thoughts on Millenarianism.* Hitchin, [England]: T. Paternoster, 1829. See pp. 570, 571.

————. *A Word of Warning in the Last Days.* London: James Nisbet, 1836. Philadelphia: E. G. Dorsey, 1837. Philadelphia: J. Dobson and J. Whetham, 1839. See pp. 570-577.

Ramsay, David. *The History of South-Carolina* (1670-1808). Charleston: David Longworth, 1809. 2 vols. See p. 201.

Ranke, Leopold. *The History of the Popes.* London: Henry G. Bohn, 1853. 3 vols. See p. 327.

(Ray), Sister Mary Augustina. *American Opinion of Roman Catholicism in the Eighteenth Century.* New York: Columbia University Press, 1936. See pp. 122, 176, 177, 181, 195, 198.

Rhode Island Historical Tracts. See Williams, Roger, *Christenings Make Not Christians.*

Rich, Wesley Everett. *The History of the United States Post Office to the Year 1829.* Cambridge: Harvard University Press, 1924. (Harvard Economic Studies, vol. 27.) See p. 32.

Richards, George. *The Divine Origin of Prophecy Illustrated and Defended.* Oxford: University Press, 1800. See pp. 327, 328.

Richter, Heinrich. *Erklärte Haus-Bibel.* Barmen, Bochum, und Schwelm: Falkenberg'schen Verlagshandlung, 1834-1840. 6 vols. See pp. 299, 378, 701-703.

Rickaby, Joseph, S. J. *The Modern Papacy,* in *Lectures on the History of Religions,* vol. 3, [lecture 24]. London: Catholic Truth Society; St. Louis, Mo.: B. Herder, 1910-11. 5 vols. See p. 327.

Roads, Samuel. *The History and Traditions of Marblehead.* Boston: Houghton, Osgood and Company, 1880. See pp. 211, 212.

Robbins, Chandler. *A History of the Second Church, or Old North, in Boston.* Boston: John Wilson & Son, 1852. See p. 125.

Roberts, Peter. *A Manual of Prophecy.* London: Ogles, Duncan, and Cochran, 1818. See pp. 408, 409.

Rohrborn, C. T. *Höchst wichtige Weissagungen.* Stuttgart, 1832. See p. 293.

Roos, Magnus Friedr[ich]. *Auslegung der Weissagungen Daniels, die in die Zeit des Neuen Testaments hineinreichen, nebst ihrer Vergleichung mit der Offenbarung Johannis, nach der Bengelischen Erklarung derselben.* Leipzig: Ulrich Christian Saalbach, 1771. See p. 401.

Root, Jean Christie. *Edward Irving: Man, Preacher, Prophet.* Boston: Sherman, French & Company, 1912. See p. 517.

Sabin, Joseph (continued by Wilberforce Eames, completed by R. W. G. Vail). *A Dictionary of Books Relating to America, From Its Discovery to the Present Time* (Bibliotheca Americana). New-York: [Imprint varies] 1868-1936. 29 vols. See pp. 48, 49, 86.

Sanborn, Franklin Benjamin. *President Langdon; A Biographical Tribute.* Boston: C. E. Goodspeed, 1904. See p. 209.

Sander, [J.] Friedrich [E.]. *Versuch einer Erklarung der Offenbarung Johannis.* Stuttgart, 1829. See pp. 298, 299.

Savage, James. *A Genealogical Dictionary of the First Settlers of New England.* Boston: Little, Brown and Company, 1860-1862. 4 vols. See p. 95.

Scotland, Church of. "The National Covenant, or The Confession of Faith of the Kirk of Scotland, Subscribed at first . . . 1580 . . ." [See also a reprint in Philip Schaff, *The Creeds of Christendom,* vol. 3, pp. 480-485.] See p. 27.

Scott, James. *A Compendious View of the Scriptural System of Prophecy.* Edinburgh: W. P. Kennedy, [1844?]. See pp. 653, 654.

Scott, Thomas, editor. *The Holy Bible . . . With Original Notes, Practical Observations.* New York: Whiting and Watson, 1812. See pp. 348-350.

————. *Theological Works.* Buckingham: J. Seeley, 1806. 2 vols. See p. 348.

The Scriptural Doctrine of the Second Advent. An Essay: Read Before One of the Associations of the Edinburgh Young Men's Society. By a Member of the Society. Edinburgh: J. T. Smith & Co., 1833. See p. 608.

Sewall, Samuel. "Commonplace Book," in *Sewall Papers,* vol. 2, *Collections of the Massachusetts Historical Society,* 5th series, vol. 6, pp. 12-23. Boston: The Society, 1897. See p. 135.

————. *Proposals Touching the Accomplishment of Prophesies Humbly Offered.* Boston: Bartholomew Green, 1713. See pp. 136, 137.

————. *Phaenomena Quaedam Apocalyptica . . . A Description of the New Heaven as It Makes to Those Who Stand Upon the New Earth.* Boston: Bartholomew Green, and John Allen, 1697. See pp. 135, 136.

Shepard, Thomas. *The Parable of the Ten Virgins Opened & Applied: Being the Substance of Divers Sermons on Matth. 25.1,—13.* London: Printed by J. H. for John Rothwell . . . and Samuel Thomson . . . 1660. See pp. 43, 45, 46.

————. *The Sincere Convert, Discovering the Pavcity of True Beleevers and the Great Difficulty of Saving Conversion.* By Tho. Shepheard. London: T. Paine, for Humfrey Blunden, 1640. **See pp. 43-45.**

Sherwood, Samuel. *The Church's Flight Into the Wilderness: An Address on the Times.* New-York: S. Loudon, 1776. **See p. 203.**

Shipton, Clifford K. *Biographical Sketches of Those Who Attended Harvard College in the Classes of 1690-1700.* Cambridge, Massachusetts: Harvard University Press, 1933. (Sibley's Harvard Graduates, vol. 4.) 4 vols. **See p. 168.**

The Signs of the Times: Containing the First Six Lectures Delivered on Behalf of the Church of England's Young Men's Society. Part I. London: Wertheim and Macintosh, 1854. **See pp. 728, 729.**

Sirr, Joseph D'Arcy. *The First Resurrection Considered in a Series of Letters.* Reprint in *The Literalist,* vol. 5 (i.e. 3). Philadelphia: Orrin Rogers, 1841. **See pp. 630-632.**

Sköldberg, S. E., M.D. Extracts in German from a report to the Royal Board of Health *(Kungl. Sundhetskollegium,* rendered *Gesundheitscollegium),* in the translator's preface to *Einiges über die rufenden Stimmen, . . . von einem Augenzeugen,* pp. vii-xi. Leipzig: Leopold Michelsen, 1843. **See pp. 683-686.**

Smart, William David, translator. See [Lacunza, Manuel], *A New Antichrist.*

Society for the Investigation of Prophecy, [London]. *Papers Read Before the Society for the Investigation of Prophecy.* London: Andrew Panton, 1828. [See also Prophecy Investigation Society.] **See pp. 444, 500, 501, 506-509.**

Source Book for Bible Students, rev. ed. Washington: Review and Herald Publishing Association, 1940. **See p. 690.**

Spalding, Charles Warren. *The Spalding Memorial.* Chicago: American Publishers' Association, 1897. **See p. 231.**

Spalding, Joshua. *Sentiments, Concerning the Coming and Kingdom of Christ, . . . in Nine Lectures; With an Appendix.* Salem, [Mass.]: Thomas C. Cushing, 1796.

————. Same. 2d ed. With preface and appendices by the editors, J. V. Himes and Josiah Litch. Boston: Joshua V. Himes, 1841. **See pp. 172, 231-235.**

Sprague, William B. *Annals of the American Pulpit.* New York: Robert Carter and Brothers, 1857-[69]. 9 vols. **See pp. 68, 191, 201, 202, 392.**

S[teere], R[ichard]. *The Daniel Catcher. The Life of the Prophet Daniel: in a Poem.* [Boston: John Allen for Nicholas Boone?], 1713. [For identification of author and publisher, also for a facsimile reproduction, see George E. Littlefield, *The Early Massachusetts Press 1638-1711,* vol. 1, pp. 4, 5; vol. 2, pp. 61, 62, and appended facsimile.] **See pp. 162-164, 232.**

Sterling, A. M. W. *The Ways of Yesterday.* London: Thornton Butterworth, 1930. **See pp. 416-418, 436.**

Stewart, Rev. James Haldane. *A Practical View of the Redeemer's Advent in a Series of Discourses.* London: L. B. Seeley and Son, 1825. **See pp. 528, 529.**

Stiles, Ezra. *Extracts From the Itineraries and Other Miscellanies of Ezra Stiles.* Edited by F. B. Dexter. New Haven: Yale University Press, 1916. **See p. 205.**

Stiles, Henry R. *The History and Genealogies of Ancient Windsor, Connecticut, 1635-1891.* Hartford, Conn.: Case, Lockwood & Brainard Company, 1891. 2 vols. **See p. 61.**

Stoughton, W[illiam]. *New-Englands True Interest; Not to Lie: . . . a Sermon.* Cambridge: Printed by S. G. and M. F., 1670. **See p. 108.**

Styles, John. *Memoirs and Remains of the Late Rev. Charles Buck.* 1st American ed. Philadelphia: Anthony Finley, 1817. **See p. 337.**

Summers, Montague. *The History of Witchcraft and Demonology.* New York: Alfred A. Knopf, 1926. **See p. 135.**

Svenskt Biografiskt Lexikon (Ny Földj). Orebro, [Sweden]: N. M. Lindhs Boktryckeri, 1857-1907. Bd. 10. **See pp. 682, 683.**

Sweet, William Warren. *Religion in Colonial America.* New York: Charles Scribner's Sons, 1942. **See pp. 123, 165-167, 204, 205.**

Swensk Författnings-Samling. Stockholm, 1868, No. 76. **See p. 673.**

Symington, Andrew. *The Dismission, Rest, and Future Glory of the Good and Faithful Servant: Two Discourses, Preached . . . After the Funeral of the Rev. Archibald Mason, D.D.* Paisley, [Scotland]: Alex. Gardner, 1832. **See pp. 396, 397.**

Taylor, Daniel T. *The Reign of Christ on Earth.* Revised and edited by H. L. Hastings. Boston: Scriptural Tract Repository, H. L. Hastings, 1882. **See p. 69.**

Thomas, Isaiah. *The History of Printing in America.* Worcester, [Mass.]: Isaiah Thomas, 1810. 2 vols. **See pp. 31, 207.**

Thompson, Warren S., and P. K. Whelpton. *Population Trends in the United States.* New York: McGraw-Hill Book Company, Inc., 1933. **See p. 28.**

Thornton, John Wingate. *The Pulpit of the American Revolution.* Boston: Gould and Lincoln, 1860. **See pp. 29, 31, 192.**

Thorp, William. *The Destinies of the British Empire, and the Duties of British Christians at the Present Crisis.* London: Fauntleroy and Burton, Jun., 1831. **See pp. 611-615.**

Thube, Christian Gottlob. *Anleitung zum richtigen Verstande der Offenbarung Johannis.* Zwote Auflage. Schwerin und Wismar: Bödnerschen Buchhandlung, 1799. **See p. 328.**

————. *Das Buch des Propheten Daniels neu übersetzt und erklart.* Schwerin und Wismar: Bödnerschen Buchhandlung, 1797. **See p. 327.**

Todd, James Henthorn. *Discourses on the Prophecies Relating to Antichrist in the Writings of Daniel and St. Paul.* Dublin: The University Press, 1840. (Donellan Lecture, 1838.) **See pp. 540, 660-663, 667.**

[Tonna], Charlotte Elizabeth. *Personal Recollections.* (From the London ed.) New York: John S. Taylor & Co., 1842. **See pp. 641, 642.**

————. *Principalities and Powers in Heavenly Places,* in *The Works of Charlotte Elizabeth,* vol. 2, pp. 391 ff. New York: M. W. Dodd, 1848. 2 vols. **See pp. 644, 645.**

————. "War With the Saints," in *The Works of Charlotte Elizabeth,* vol 1. New York: M. W. Dodd, 1850. 2 vols. **See pp. 641, 643, 644.**

Tonna, Lewis H. J. *A Memoir of Charlotte Elizabeth.* New York: M. W. Dodd, 1847. **See p. 640.**

[Toovey, Samuel]. *An Essay on the Prophecies of Daniel, and the Revelation of St. John . . .* by Philo Britannicus. London: Hersee and Cooper, 1813. **See pp. 356-360.**

Tracts for the Times (for 1833-1840). By members of the University of Oxford. London: G. F. & J. Rivington, 1840-1842. 5 vols. (nos. 1-88). See also John Henry Newman, Tract Number Ninety. **See pp. 663-666.**

Tracy, Joseph. *The Great Awakening. A History of the Revival of Religion in the Time of Edwards and Whitefield.* Boston: Tappan & Dennet, 1842. **See pp. 165, 166.**

Tregelles, S[amuel] P. *Remarks on the Prophetic Visions in the Book of Daniel.* 6th ed. London: Samuel Bagster and Sons, 1883. **See p. 380.**

Trevor, G. *Rome: From the Fall of the Western Empire.* London: The Religious Tract Society, [1868]. **See p. 327.**

The Trial of the Rev. Edward Irving, M.A., Before the London Presbytery; Containing the Whole of the Evidence; . . . Taken in Short-Hand by W. Harding. London: W. Harding, 1832. **See p. 517.**

Trumbull, Benjamin. *A Complete History of Connecticut, Civil and Ecclesiastical.* (1630-1764.) New-Haven: Maltby, Goldsmith and Co., 1818. 2 vols. **See p. 166.**

Tudor, John. "On the Structure of the Apocalypse," in *Papers Read Before the Society for the Investigation of Prophecy,* pp. 1-22. London: Andrew Panton, 1828. **See pp. 506-509.**

Tyler, Moses Coit. *A History of American Literature During the Colonial Time.* New ed., rev. New York and London: G. P. Putnam's Sons, 1897. 2 vols. **See pp. 28-32, 36, 43, 57, 67, 89, 92, 107, 125, 135, 181, 191, 207, 208, 212.**

————. *The Literary History of the American Revolution, 1763-1783.* New York and London: G. P. Putnam's Sons, 1897. 2 vols. **See pp. 191, 192, 213.**

————. *Three Men of Letters.* New York and London: G. P. Putnam's Sons, 1895. **See p. 242.**

Tyso, Joseph. *An Elucidation of the Prophecies.* London: Jackson and Walford, 1838. **See pp. 731-733.**

Vaucher, Alfred-Felix. *Une célébrité oubliée, Le P. Manuel de Lacunza y Diaz (1731-1801) de la Société de Jésus, auteur de "La Venue du Messie en gloire et majesté."* Collonges-sous-Salève, [France]: Imprimerie Fides, 1941. **See pp. 308, 313.**

Vaughan, Edward Thomas. *The Church's Expectation: A Sermon on the Second Advent of the Lord Jesus Christ. Preached Before the Leicestershire District Committee of the SPCK, . . . 1827.* Leicester, [England]: T. Combe and Son, 1828. **See pp. 548-551.**

Vaughan, Robert. *The Nature and Duration of the Papal Apostacy.* London: Holdsworth and Ball, 1829. **See pp. 555, 556.**

Venn, John. *Biographical History of Gonville and Caius College, 1349-1897.* Cambridge: University Press, 1897-1912. 4 vols. **See p. 433.**

Vidler, William. *A Sketch of the Life of Elhanan Winchester, Preacher of Universal Restoration.* London: T. Gillett, 1797. **See p. 224.**

Vincent, Thomas. *An Explicatory Catechism.* Northampton: William Butler, 1805. **See p. 105.**

Walker, Francis A. "Growth and Distribution of Population." Theodore D. Woolsey, and others, *The First Century of the Republic,* pp. 211-237. New York: Harper and Brothers, 1876. **See p. 28.**

Walker, Williston. *The Creeds and Platforms of Congregationalism.* New York: Charles Scribner's Sons, 1893. **See p. 111.**

————. *A History of the Congregational Churches in the United States.* New York: The Christian Literature Co., 1894. (*The American Church History Series,* vol. 3.) **See p. 23.**

————. "The Services of the Mathers in New England Religious Development," in *Papers of the American Society of Church History* [1st series], vol. 5, pp. 61-85. New York and London: G. P. Putnam's Sons, 1893. See p. 126.

Way, Lewis. *The Household of Faith. A Sermon, Preached to the English Congregation, Assembled at Rome, Sunday, 6th April, 1823.* 2d ed., with appendix. London: J. Hatchard and Son, 1823. See p. 418.

————. *A Letter, Addressed to the Right Reverend the Lord Bishop of St. David's.* London: John Hatchard, 1818. See p. 417.

[————]. *Mémoires sur l'état des Israélites, dédiés et présentés a leurs majestés impériales et royales, réunies au Congrès d'Aix-la-Chapelle.* Paris: Imprimerie de Firmin Didot, 1918. [Also attributed to L. Lavigne. Way is identified as author in Max J. Kohler, *Jewish Rights at the Congresses of Vienna (1814-1815) and Aix-la-Chapelle (1818).*] See p. 417.

[————]. *Palingenesia. The World to Come.* Paris: Firmin Didot, 1824. See pp. 418, 420, 422-424.

[————]. *Thoughts on the Scriptural Expectations of the Christian Church,* by Basilicus. Gloucester, [England]: Hough & Pace, [1823]. [Reprinted from an intermittent series of articles in *The Jewish Expositor,* 1820-1822.] See pp. 299, 417, 419-422.

————. *Was hat die Christliche Kirche nach den Verheissungen der Heiligen Schrift zu erwarten?* [A translation of the 1828 edition of his *Thoughts on the Scriptural Expectations of the Christian Church.*] Hamburg: F. H. Nestler, 1830. See p. 299.

Webb, John. *Practical Discourses.* Boston: Printed by J. Draper for D. Henchman, 1726. See p. 171.

Weeks, Lyman Horace, and Edwin M. Bacon, compilers. *An Historical Digest of the Provincial Press.* Boston: The Society for Americana, Inc., 1911. See p. 118.

Weis, Frederick L. *The Colonial Clergy and the Colonial Churches of New England.* Lancaster, Mass.: [Society of the Descendants of the Colonial Clergy], 1936. See pp. 82, 107, 126.

Wendell, Barrett. *Cotton Mather, The Puritan Priest.* Cambridge: Harvard University Press, 1926. See p. 147.

Wertenbaker, Thomas Jefferson. *The First Americans, 1607-1690.* New York: The Macmillan Co., 1927. See pp. 24, 57, 89, 140-143, 159.

Westminster Assembly of Divines. *The Humble Advice of the Assembly of Divines . . . at Westminster, Concerning a Larger Catechisme* [The Westminster Larger Catechism]. London: A. M., [1647]. See p. 27.

Whitaker, Edward W. *A General and Connected View of the Prophecies Relating to the Times of the Gentiles.* Egham, [England]: C. Boult, 1795. See pp. 272, 293, 338.

White, Ellen G. *The Acts of the Apostles.* Mountain View, California: Pacific Press Publishing Association, 1911. See p. 747.

————. *The Great Controversy Between Christ and Satan.* Mountain View, California: Pacific Press Publishing Association, 1911. See pp. 672, 689.

————. "Notes of Travel," in *Historical Sketches . . . and a Narrative by Mrs. E. G. White of Her Visit and Labors in These Missions.* Basle: Imprimerie Polyglotte, 1886. See pp. 673, 674.

White, Thomas. "Diagram and Observations Intended to Illustrate the Arrangement and Assist the Exposition of the Apocalypse," in *Papers Read Before the Society for the Investigation of Prophecy,* pp. 109-125. London: Andrew Panton, 1828. See pp. 500, 501.

Wigglesworth, Michael. *The Day of Doom.* Newcastle upon Tyne: John White, 1711. **See pp. 89-91.**

Wilks, Washington. *Edward Irving: An Ecclesiastical and Literary Biography.* London: William Freeman, 1854. **See pp. 435, 516, 519, 525, 526.**

Willard, Samuel. *A Compleat Body of Divinity.* Boston: Printed by B. Green and S. Kneeland for B. Eliot, 1726. **See pp. 155, 156.**

————. *The Fountain Opened.* 2d ed. Boston: B. Green, 1722. **See pp. 155, 156.**

[Williams, Roger]. *The Bloudy Tenent, of Persecution, for Cause of Conscience, Discussed, in a Conference Between Truth and Peace.* [London], 1644. [Published anonymously, July 15. For authorship see Sabin's *Dictionary,* vol. 28, p. 438.] **See pp. 48-53.**

————. *The Bloody Tenent Yet More Bloody: By Mr. Cottons Endevour to Wash It White in the Blood of the Lambe . . . That Most Bloody Tenent of Persecution for Cause of Conscience, Upon a Second Tryal, Is Found Now More Apparently and More Notoriously Guilty.* London: Printed for Giles Calvert, 1652. **See pp. 50, 53.**

[————]. *Christenings Make Not Christians, or A Briefe Discourse Concerning That Name Heathen, Commonly Given to the Indians.* Henry Martyn Dexter, editor, *Rhode Island Historical Tracts,* no. 14. Providence: Sidney S. Rider, 1881. [A line-for-line and page-for-page reprint from 1st ed. (London: Iane Coe, 1645/46). See Sabin.] **See pp. 49, 53, 54.**

————. *The Hireling Ministry None of Christs, or A Discourse Touching the Propagating the Gospel of Christ Jesus.* London: [n.n.], 1652. **See pp. 49, 54.**

————. *A Key Into the Language of America: or, An Help to the Language of the Natives in That Part of America, Called New-England.* London: Gregory Dexter, 1643. **See p. 47.**

————. "A Letter . . . to Major Mason" in *Collections of the Massachusetts Historical Society,* [1st series], vol. 1, pp. 275-283. Boston: Belknap and Hall, 1792. **See p. 50.**

————. *Letters of Roger Williams.* Edited by John R. Bartlett. *Publications of the Narragansett Club,* 1st series, vol. 6. Providence: Narragansett Club, 1874. **See pp. 80, 82.**

[Wilson, Daniel], supposed author. *On the Numbers in Daniel.* Madras: The Church Mission Press, 1836. **See pp. 618-622.**

Winchester, Elhanan. *The Three Woe Trumpets.* 1st American ed. Boston: John W. Folsom, 1794. **See pp. 224-226.**

Windsor, Connecticut. *Some Early Records and Documents of and Relating to the Town of Windsor, Connecticut, 1639-1703.* Hartford: Connecticut Historical Society, 1930. **See p. 60.**

Winslow, Edw[ard]. "Briefe Narration." See his *Hypocrisie Unmasked.*

————. *Hypocrisie Unmasked: . . . Whereunto Is Added a Briefe Narration . . . of the True Grounds or Cause of the First Planting of New-England.* London: Printed by Rich. Cotes for John Bellamy, 1646. **See p. 20.**

Winslow, Ola E. *Jonathan Edwards, 1703-1758.* New York: The Macmillan Company, 1940. **See pp. 165, 181.**

Winsor, Justin, editor. *The Memorial History of Boston, 1630-1880.* Boston: James R. Osgood and Company, 1881-1883. 4 vols. **See p. 108.**

Winthrop, James. *A Systematic Arrangement of Several Scripture Prophecies Relating to Antichrist; With Their Application to the Course of History.* Boston: Thomas Hall, 1795. **See pp. 229, 230.**

Winthrop, John. *Journal, 1640-1649,* vol. 1. New York: Charles Scribner's Sons, 1908. (*Original Narratives of American History,* vol. 18.) See p. 47.

[Wolff, Joseph]. *Dr. Wolff's New Mission.* London: Saunders, Otley, and Co., 1860. See p. 471.

————. *Journal of the Rev. Joseph Wolff.* London: James Burns, 1839. See pp. 463, 471, 473, 477-479.

————. *Journal of the Rev. Joseph Wolff for the Year 1831.* London: James Fraser, 1832. See p. 470.

————. *Letter Addressed to the Citizens of Rome.* London: J. Hatchard and Son, 1849. See p. 478.

————. *Missionary Journal and Memoir, of the Rev. Joseph Wolff.* Revised and edited by John Bayford. New York: E. Bliss & E. White, 1824. See pp. 409, 463-465, 467-472, 478, 479.

————. *Narrative of a Mission to Bokhara,* 1843-1845. New York: Harper and Brothers, 1845. See pp. 471, 472, 481.

————. *Researches and Missionary Labours Among the Jews, Mohammedans, and Other Sects.* (*1831-1834.*) London: James Nisbet & Co., 1835. See pp. 470, 473-477, 603.

————. *Travels and Adventures of the Rev. Joseph Wolff.* London: Saunders, Otley, and Co., 1861. See pp. 408, 415, 417, 436, 450, 463-472, 477, 480, 481.

Wood, G. H. (Lieut.). *The Believer's Guide to the Study of Unfulfilled Prophecy.* With an Appendix. London: J. Nisbet, 1831. See pp. 615, 616.

[Wood, Hans]. *The Revelation of St. John.* London: Printed for the Author and sold by T. Payne & Son, 1787. [Author identified by Halkett & Laing, *op. cit.,* vol. 5, p. 106.] See p. 334.

Worcester, Samuel M. *A Memorial of the Old and New Tabernacle, Salem, Mass.* Boston: Crocker and Brewster, 1855. See p. 230.

Wroth, Lawrence C. *Roger Williams.* Providence: Brown University, 1937. See pp. 46, 47, 50.

Wurm, J. F. *Ueber die Beweisgründe.* Stuttgart: 1832. See p. 293.

Wylie, J. A. *The History of Protestantism.* London: Cassell and Company, Limited, 1899. 3 vols. See p. 673.

Ye Know Not When the Master of the House Cometh! London: R. B. Seeley and Burnside, 1832. See p. 608.

Young, Alexander. *Chronicles of the Pilgrim Fathers of the Colony of Plymouth, From 1602 to 1625.* Boston: Charles C. Little and James Brown, 1841. See p. 20.

MANUSCRIPTS

Cheever, Ezekiel. Last will and testament. (Also in Probate Court records, Liber 16, p. 466, no. 3119. Boston Court House.) See pp. 152, 160.

Concord Presbytery. See Presbyterian Church.

Dudley, Paul. Last will and testament, in Probate Court records (Boston), vol. 44, p. 476 (no. 9697); see also Harvard University, *Donations Book,* pp. 194-196 (Harvard Library); in *Dudleian Lectures, 1755-1770,* vol. 1 (Harvard Library). See pp. 174, 175.

Gates, O. H. *List and Dates of Dudleian Lectures, 1755-1918.* (Archives Division, Harvard University Library.) See p. 176.

[Lacunza, Manuel]. *La Venida del Mesias en Gloria, y Magestad. Observaciones de Dⁿ Juan Josaphat Ben-ezra.* Manuscript in Biblioteca Mariano Soler de Montevideo (diocesan library). **See p. 316.**

Mather, Cotton. "An Essay Concerning the Happy Estate Expected for the Church Upon Earth; Endeavoring to Demonstrate That the Second Coming of the Lord Jesus Christ Will Be at the Beginning of That Happy State. With Some Thoughts Upon the Characters and Approaches of It." See his *Problema Theologicum.*

————. *Problema Theologicum* (American Antiquarian Society, Worcester, Mass.) **See pp. 154, 155, 157, 159.**

Mather, Increase. *Triparadisus* (American Antiquarian Society, Worcester, Mass.) **See p. 126n.**

Mather, Samuel [1706-1785]. "Popery a Complexity of Falsehoods" (Dudleian Lecture, 1769). In *Dudleian Lectures,* Harvard University Library. **See pp. 174, 176, 178, 179.**

Presbyterian Church in the United States. *Records of Concord Presbytery,* Vol. I. Original in the archives of the Historical Foundation of the Presbyterian and Reformed Churches, Montreat, N.C. **See p. 392.**

Randolph, Corliss F. Letter to L. E. Froom, dated Feb. 11, 1935. **See p. 562.**

PERIODICALS AND NEWSPAPERS

Aftonbladet (Stockholm), 23 febr., 3, 29 mai, 6, 7 sept., 16 dec., 1842. **See pp. 677, 678, 681, 682, 686.**

The American Millenarian and Prophetic Review (New York). 2 vols., 1842-1844. **See p. 723.**

Begg, James A. Letter to [George B. Utter] editor, *The Sabbath Recorder* (New York), May 1, 1845 (vol 1, no. 45). **See p. 561.**

————. "The Original Sabbath Unchanged" (first of a continued series), *The Sabbath Recorder,* Nov. 13, 1845 (vol. 2, no. 21). **See p. 561.**

Boqvist, O. "The First Angel's Message in Sweden," *The Advent Review and Sabbath Herald* (Battle Creek, Mich.), Oct. 7, 1890 (vol. 67, no. 39), p. 612. **See p. 674.**

The Boston Gazette and Country Journal, April 4, 11, 1768. **See p. 195.**

Boston Weekly News-Letter (title varies), Jan. 9, 1756. **See pp. 186, 187, 207.**

B[rown], J[ohn] A[quila]. Articles in *The Christian Observer,* November, 1810, July, 1828 (vols. 9, 28). **See pp. 274, 276, 290-292, 295, 405.**

Butsch, Bishop J. A. Circular letter from the Consistory in Skara, on the so-called preaching sickness, published in *Aftonbladet* (Stockholm), 6, 7 sept., 1842. [See also same entry in book section.] **See pp. 681, 682, 686.**

The Christian Herald; A Monthly Magazine, Chiefly on Subjects Connected With Prophecy (Dublin). 5 vols., 1830-1835. **See pp. 414, 579-587.**

The Christian Instructor, June 29, 1830. **See pp. 298, 562.**

The Christian Observer (London; reprints Boston, New York), vols. 1-31, new series 5, 67, 1802-31, 1842, 1868. **See pp. 274, 276, 284-296, 405, 416, 456, 473, 478, 525, 721, 722.**

[Cuninghame, William]. Articles in *The Christian Observer,* November, December, 1807; April, June, 1808; January, April, October, 1810 (vols. 6, 7, 9). **See pp. 274, 285-289, 291.**

"Decease of the Fathers of New England," *The New England Historical and Genealogical Register,* January, 1847 (vol. 1, no. 1), p. 74. **See p. 61.**

Domestick Intelligence. See *Protestant (Domestick) Intelligence.*

[Dwight, Timothy]. "A Brief Account of the Revival of Religion Now Prevailing in Yale College," *The Connecticut Evangelical Magazine,* July, 1802 (vol. 3, no. 1), pp. 30-32. [Author identified in Charles E. Cuningham, *Timothy Dwight,* p. 393, note 10.] **See p. 244.**

————. "Lectures on the Evidences of Divine Revelation," *The Panoplist, and Missionary Magazine United* (Boston), various issues from June, 1810, through December, part 2, 1813 (vols. 6, 7, 9; or New Series, vols. 3, 4, 6). [Author identified in Charles E. Cuningham, *Timothy Dwight,* p. 393, note 13 ff.] **See pp. 243, 244.**

The Eclectic Review (London), February, 1814 (New Series vol. 1), pp. 127-140. **See pp. 353, 361, 362.**

Elliott, E. B. "Counter-Retrospect," *The Christian Observer,* December, 1868 (vol. 67, no. 372), pp. 945-949. **See pp. 721, 722.**

Evangelische Kirchen-Zeitung (Berlin), 27., 30. Juli 1842 (Band 30, Nrn. 60, 61), Spalten 478-486. **See p. 676.**

Faber, George Stanley. Article in answer to Talib and Philo, *The Christian Observer,* May, 1810 (vol. 9, no. 101), pp. 257-260. **See p. 291.**

Ferguson, Clement. "The New England Primer, 1690," *Magazine of American History,* August, 1888 (vol. 20, no. 2), pp. 148, 149. **See p. 115.**

Fraser's Magazine (London), January, 1835 (vol. 11, no. 61), pp. 99-103. **See p. 517.**

Fulton, William. "James A. Begg. A Memorial Discourse" (originally prefixed to *Summary of Doctrines Taught in Christian Meeting-House, 90 Norfolk Street, Laurieston, Glasgow, by the Late James A. Begg*), reprinted in *The Sabbath Recorder,* May 13 and 20, 1869 (vol. 25, nos. 20, 21), pp. 77, 85. **See p. 560.**

The Gallican Watchman. See *The Watchman* (Paris).

The Gentleman's Magazine (London), October, 1799 (vol. 69, part 2, no. 4), pp. 865-872 (book review). Also scattered obituaries in various volumes. **See p. 334** and *passim.*

[Gaussen, Louis]. "Popery, an Argument for the Truth, by Its Fulfillment of Scripture Prophecies," *The Midnight Cry!* (New York), July 11, 1844 (vol. 6, no. 26), pp. 409-411. **See pp. 690, 691.**

[Hales, William]. "Sacred Criticism. A Critique on Our Lord's Prophecies," a series (signed "Inspector") in *The Orthodox Churchman's Magazine and Review* (London), vols. 4-6, 1803, 1804. [Author identified in issue of March, 1803, pp. 140, 141, by reference to "my unpublished analysis of Sacred Chronology"; and in his *New Analysis of Sacred Chronology,* vol. 2, pp. 564, 565n (1809-12 ed.), or vol. 2, p. 518n (1830 ed.).] **See pp. 272, 273, 332, 334-337.**

The Investigator, or Monthly Expositor and Register, on Prophecy (London). 5 vols., 1831-1836. **See pp. 379, 380, 414, 463, 599-605.**

J. A. B. See Brown, John Aquila.

The Jewish Expositor, and Friend of Israel (London), vols. 1-13, New Series 1-3, 1816-28, 1831-33. **See pp. 414, 416-419, 426-428, 463, 469-471, 478, 479.**

Jewish Intelligence, and Monthly Account of the Proceedings of the London Society For Promoting Christianity Amongst the Jews, March, June, 1840 (vol. 6), pp. 55-61, 149-168. **See p. 415.**

Kelley, Lillian W. "Edward Irving Preaching in Britannia Fields, Summer, 1832. A Portrait by Faithful Christopher Pack, R.R.P.," *The Journal of the Presbyterian Historical Society of England* (Manchester), May, 1932 (vol. 5, no. 1), pp. 21-30. See p. 517.

The Literalist (Philadelphia: Orrin Rogers). 3 vols. in 5, 1840-1842. [A semi-monthly magazine, a republication of selected English works on prophecy, each with separate title page and paging.] [The separate works which are quoted from *Literalist* reprints are listed in this bibliography as books, since that was their original form.] See p. 723.

The London Magazine, December, 1755, p. 586, 587; February, 1756, p. 67. See pp. 187, 188.

London Society for Promoting Christianity Amongst the Jews. "Fourteenth Report," in *The Jewish Expositor*, June, 1822 (vol. 7), pp. 217-239. See p. 469.

——. *Seventeenth Report*, 1825, bound with *The Jewish Expositor*, vol. 10, paged separately. See p. 478.

——. *Eighteenth Report*, 1826, bound with *The Jewish Expositor*, vol. 11. See p. 478.

"Memoir of Governor Hutchinson," *The New England Historical and Genealogical Register*, October, 1847 (vol. 1, no. 4), pp. 297-310. See p. 99.

The Missionary (Burlington, N.J.), Sept. 23, 30, and Dec. 30, 1837. See p. 480.

Moorehouse, Clifford P. "Origins of the Episcopal Church Press From Colonial Days to 1840," *Historical Magazine of the Protestant Episcopal Church*, September, 1942 (vol. 11, no. 3), pp. 199-318. See p. 284.

The Morning Watch; or Quarterly Journal of Prophecy, and Theological Review (London). 7 vols., 1829-33. See pp. 300, 414, 436, 450, 479, 487-489, 498, 501-506, 516, 520, 525, 526.

The National Intelligencer (Washington, D.C.), Dec. 16, 21, 1837. See pp. 479, 480.

Nicole, Alphonse M. F. "Recherche sur Daniel viii. 13, 14," *The Morning Watch*, September, 1829 (vol. 1, no. 3), pp. 350-353. See pp. 487-489.

Nordisk Kyrkotidning (Stockholm), 3 argangen, 1842, sid. 268-272; Tolfte Supplementet, 14 dec., 1842, sid. 297. See pp. 670, 675, 676.

Pietisten (Stockholm), mars, 1842 (1 argangen, no. 3), sid. 45. See pp. 670, 680.

Price, Lucien. "Witchcraft: Then and Now," *The Nation* (New York), Oct. 4, 1922 (vol. 115, no. 2987), pp. 331-333. See p. 143.

The Prophetic Herald and Churchman's Witness for Christ (Birkenhead, England). 2 vols., 1845-47. See pp. 725-728.

Protestant (Domestick) Intelligence (London), February 27, 1679 (i.e. 1680, New Style). See p. 117.

The Protestant Magazine (London), June, 1840-December, 1841. (vols. 1, 2.) See pp. 642, 643.

The Pulpit (London), vol. 34, p. 146. See p. 472.

Sheppard, John H. "Commodore Samuel Tucker," *The New England Historical and Genealogical Register*, April, 1872 (vol. 26, no. 2), pp. 105-115. See p. 211.

Signs of the Times (Boston), December 15, 1840 (vol. 1, no. 18), pp. 145, 146. See pp. 571, 723.

Smith, Wilbur M. "Prophetic Literature of Colonial America," *Bibliotheca Sacra*, January-March, 1943 (vol. 100, no. 397), pp. 67-82. See p. 25.

Svenska Biet (Stockholm), 29 juli, 9 aug., 4, 12 okt., 1843. **See pp. 679, 680.**

The Watchman (Paris), May 7, 1831 (vol. 1, nos. 1 and 2 combined); (later *The Gallican Watchman*), October 8, 1831 (vol. 2, no. 1). **See pp. 418, 420, 425, 600.**

[Way, Lewis]. "Thoughts on the Scriptural Expectations of the Christian Church," by Basilicus, the first of a series in *The Jewish Expositor* (London), January, 1820 (vol. 5), pp. 24-30; continued in February, April, 1820; February, March, May, 1821; April, May, 1822 (vols. 5-7). See also same entry in the book section. **See pp. 417, 419.**

————. Extracts from letters to *The Jewish Expositor*, January, 1818 (vol. 3), pp. 75-79. **See pp. 418, 419.**

Wexiö-Bladet (Vaxjö, Sweden), 4 mars, 3 juni, 1842. **See pp. 677, 681.**

Whitmore, W. H. "A Brief Genealogy of the Hutchinson Family," *The New England Historical and Genealogical Register*, January, 1865 (vol. 19, no. 1), pp. 13-20. **See p. 99.**

Wolff, Joseph. Letters: in *The Jewish Expositor*, August, 1822, pp. 212-214; April, 1823, pp. 159-161; March, 1827, pp. 95-98 (vols. 7, 8, 12) **(see pp. 470, 471, 479)**; in *Monthly Intelligence of the Proceedings of the London Society*, December, 1830 (vol. 1), pp. 181-188 **(see p. 474)**; in the *Morning Herald* (London), Sept. 5, 1829 **(see p. 474)**; to Bishop [George W.] Doane, and to "American Friends," *The Missionary* (Burlington, N.J.), Dec. 30, 1837, p. 207 **(see p. 480)**; to the editor of *The Churchman* (in the New York *American*, Sept. 25, 1837), quoted in *The Churchman* (New York), Sept. 30, 1937 **(see p. 480)**; "To the public in general" (dated June 4, 1833), in the Calcutta *Journal*, reprinted in *The Churchman*, Sept. 30, 1837 **(see p. 481).**

NOTE: Because of strike conditions among type manufacturers at the time of publication, certain accent markings which should appear in citations from foreign-language sources were unobtainable in certain fonts of type. These will be supplied in any future editions.

Index

The names of expositors, the topics they discussed, and their prophetic terminology are thoroughly covered in this Index. The main discussion of the various commentators is indicated by the inclusive figures in italics, as *461-481*. A comprehensive analysis of their prophetic interpretations, with page references, is also set forth in the charts on pages 252, 253, 744, 745. Book, pamphlet, periodical, and manuscript titles are omitted. The page references to these items are included in the Bibliography, which begins on page 757.